Public Sector Reform and Modern Trends for Public Management

Vassilis Kefis
Panteion University, Greece

Ioannis Rossidis
Panteion University, Greece

Dimitrios Belias
University of Thessaly, Greece

IGI Global
Scientific Publishing
Publishing Tomorrow's Research Today

Published in the United States of America by
IGI Global Scientific Publishing
701 East Chocolate Avenue
Hershey, PA, 17033, USA
Tel: 717-533-8845 | Fax: 717-533-7115
Website: https://www.igi-global.com E-mail: cust@igi-global.com

Library of Congress Cataloging-in-Publication Data

LCCN: 2025035578 (CIP Data Pending)
ISBN13: 979-8-3373-3526-1
Isbn13Softcover: 979-8-3373-3527-8
EISBN13: 979-8-3373-3528-5

British Cataloguing in Publication Data
A Cataloguing in Publication record for this book is available from the British Library.

Table of Contents

Preface xiii

Chapter 1
Administrative Reforms and Transformation of Public Administration: Concept, Necessity, and Challenges 1
Fotini Vittou, Panteion University of Social and Political Sciences, Greece
Vasilis Kefis, Panteion University of Social and Political Sciences, Greece
Stavroula Ktistaki, Panteion University, Greece
Evangelia Balta, Panteion University, Greece

Chapter 2
The Evolution of Administrative Models in the Public Sector 47
Ioannis Rossidis, Department of Public Administration, Panteion University, Greece
Vassilis Kefis, Department of Public Administration, Panteion University, Greece
Stavroula Ktistaki, Panteion University, Greece
Evangelia Balta, Department of Public Administration, Panteion University, Greece

Chapter 3
Law and Public Administration 67
Subramanian Udayakumar, Vel Tech Rangarajan Dr. Sagunthala R&D Institute of Science and Technology, India
Pamarthi Satyanarayana, VEL TECH University, India
P. Selvakumar, Department of Science and Humanities, Nehru Institute of Technology, Coimbatore, India

Chapter 4
NPM Is Dead, Long Live NPM: Transformations of New Public Management in the Course of Administrative Reforms 93
Panagiotis Karkatsoulis, Institute for Regulatory Policy Research, Athens, Greece
Fotini Vittou, Panteion University of Social and Political Sciences, Greece

Chapter 5
Strategic Management in the Public Sector: Concepts, Challenges, and Evolving Practices 129
Foteini Vittou, Department of Public Administration, Panteion University, Greece
Labros Babalioutas, Panteion University, Greece
Vasiliadis Labros, National and Kapodistrian University of Athens, Greece

Chapter 6
Enhancing Public Sector Reform: The Impact of Change Management on Organizational Restructuring 169
Dimitrios Koumanakos, Hellenic Open University, Greece
Eleni Sfakianaki, Hellenic Open University, Greece

Chapter 7
The Dynamics of Public Sector Transformation: Key Change Management Variables, Measurement Tools, and the Institutional Context of Greek Reforms 197
Angelos Ntalakos, University of Thessaly, Greece
George Soklis, Panteion University, Greece

Chapter 8
Managing Public Enterprises in the Modern Administrative State: The Case of Greece 253
Ioannis Rossidis, Panteion University, Greece
Haralampos Chrysomallidis, University of the Peloponnese, Greece
George Kentas, University of Nicosia, Cyprus

Chapter 9
Judicial Reform, Performance, and Governance: Evidence From Norway 275
Anatoliy G. Goncharuk, NLA University College, Norway

Chapter 10
New Public Management in Morocco: Between the Quest for Performance and Challenges of Implementation 319
Zineb Loukili, Ibn Tofaîl University, Morocco
Azzouz Elhamma, Ibn Tofaîl University, Morocco

Chapter 11
Unlocking Hospital Performance: NPM Tool Appropriation as a Key Mediator in the Moroccan Context 343
Cherkaoui Dekkaki Achraf, Ibn Tofaîl University, Morocco
Azzouz Elhamma, Ibn Tofaîl University, Morocco

Chapter 12
Between National Discretion and Collective Norms: The Challenge of Revising the EU's Common Position on Arms Exports 367
Theofania Antoniou, Hellenic Open University, Greece

Chapter 13
Normative Gatekeepers: The Role of National Courts in Shaping EU Responses to the Gaza Crisis 387
Theofania Antoniou, Hellenic Open University, Greece
Maria-Daniella Marouda, Panteion University, Greece

Compilation of References 409

About the Contributors 469

Index 473

Detailed Table of Contents

Preface.. xiii

Chapter 1
Administrative Reforms and Transformation of Public Administration: Concept, Necessity, and Challenges 1
Fotini Vittou, Panteion University of Social and Political Sciences, Greece
Vasilis Kefis, Panteion University of Social and Political Sciences, Greece
Stavroula Ktistaki, Panteion University, Greece
Evangelia Balta, Panteion University, Greece

This chapter aims to explore the evolving role of administrative reforms within the broader context of modern public management and governance. Administrative reform is presented not as a singular or episodic action but as a strategic, continuous, and multi-level process aimed at improving structures, procedures, organizational cultures, and institutional responsiveness. The study focuses on the underlying causes that drive reform initiatives (e.g., polycrises, fiscal pressures, globalization, digital transformation), as well as the barriers to their implementation (e.g., political discontinuity, bureaucratic resistance, institutional inertia). It emphasizes the role of strategic planning, participatory models, and adaptive governance in achieving meaningful and sustainable change.

Chapter 2
The Evolution of Administrative Models in the Public Sector 47
Ioannis Rossidis, Department of Public Administration, Panteion University, Greece
Vassilis Kefis, Department of Public Administration, Panteion University, Greece
Stavroula Ktistaki, Panteion University, Greece
Evangelia Balta, Department of Public Administration, Panteion University, Greece

This chapter examines the evolution of administrative models in the public sector, from Weberian bureaucracy to modern hybrid schemes. Bureaucracy is defined as a model that provided stability and legitimacy, but its rigidity led to the gradual emergence of modern administrative approaches such as New Public Management (NPM), which introduced private economic criteria and emphasized efficiency and effectiveness. Despite its innovative perspective, NPM was criticized for limiting its social and democratic dimension. Public governance emerged as a response, emphasizing cooperation, multi-level policymaking and the participation of citizens and stakeholders. Following this evolution, hybrid models such as the Neo-Weberian State, New Public Governance, New Public Service and the theory of Public Value attempt to combine elements of legitimacy, efficiency and social legitimation. The analysis demonstrates that administrative reform is not a linear process of model replacement, but a perpetual process of overlaps and adaptations.

Chapter 3
Law and Public Administration 67
Subramanian Udayakumar, Vel Tech Rangarajan Dr. Sagunthala R&D Institute of Science and Technology, India
Pamarthi Satyanarayana, VEL TECH University, India
P. Selvakumar, Department of Science and Humanities, Nehru Institute of Technology, Coimbatore, India

Law serves as the bedrock of public administration, shaping the framework within which governments operate and ensuring the legitimacy, accountability, and fairness of administrative actions. In democratic societies, the rule of law governs the conduct of public officials, delineates the powers and responsibilities of administrative bodies, and safeguards the rights of citizens. Without a strong legal foundation, public administration would risk arbitrariness, corruption, and inefficiency. The role of law in public administration is thus multifaceted—acting both as an enabler and a constraint, guiding the formulation and execution of public policies while ensuring adherence to constitutional principles and ethical standards. At its core, law provides a structural foundation for the operation of the state and its various agencies. Administrative law, constitutional law, and statutory regulations form the legal scaffolding of public administration, outlining the authority of governmental institutions and defining the scope of their jurisdiction.

Chapter 4
NPM Is Dead, Long Live NPM: Transformations of New Public Management in the Course of Administrative Reforms 93
Panagiotis Karkatsoulis, Institute for Regulatory Policy Research, Athens, Greece
Fotini Vittou, Panteion University of Social and Political Sciences, Greece

Over the past decades, New Public Management (NPM) has been widely criticised for weakening the institutional role of the state and empowering economic elites and private actors, raising concerns about the erosion of cohesion and state capacity. Crises such as the pandemic, climate change, migration, and the rise of populism revealed that NPM reforms must either evolve or lose legitimacy. Reformers must respond by restoring the principles of the rule of law, democratic institutions, and sound public management practices. Technology, and especially Artificial Intelligence (AI), can support this renewal. This chapter reinterprets NPM as NPM 2.0, highlighting tools and techniques that integrate empirical and theoretical knowledge while adapting to the specific identities and needs of each administrative system. It concludes that the endurance of NPM's second generation depends on embedding technological innovation within constitutional safeguards, transforming digitalisation into a means of rebuilding state capacity.

Chapter 5
Strategic Management in the Public Sector: Concepts, Challenges, and Evolving Practices 129
Foteini Vittou, Department of Public Administration, Panteion University, Greece
Labros Babalioutas, Panteion University, Greece
Vasiliadis Labros, National and Kapodistrian University of Athens, Greece

In recent years, strategic management in the public sector has shifted from an optional tool to a perceived necessity in contexts of crisis, uncertainty and rising expectations. This chapter questions the uncritical transfer of private-sector strategic models to public organizations, arguing that they rest on linear and technocratic assumptions that conflict with the political and value-laden nature of public action. Drawing on a systemic review, public organizations are conceptualised as Complex Adaptive Systems, where interdependencies and competing norms generate non-linear outcomes, undermining claims of control through rational planning. The chapter therefore advances a Public Value perspective, exemplified by Moore's Strategic Triangle, which highlights the need to align value creation, operational capacity and the authorizing environment. Public strategy is thus understood as a dynamic, politically embedded practice aimed at sustaining public value under conditions of complexity.

Chapter 6
Enhancing Public Sector Reform: The Impact of Change Management on Organizational Restructuring 169
Dimitrios Koumanakos, Hellenic Open University, Greece
Eleni Sfakianaki, Hellenic Open University, Greece

Public organizations today face critical challenges, such as globalization, rapid technological developments, fiscal adjustments and increased expectations of citizens for efficiency, quality of services, transparency and accountability. A necessary condition for the public sector's effective response to these challenges, is the implementation of targeted administrative reforms through specific administrative adjustments. These administrative adjustments constitute changes that can be better analyzed in the light of the principles of change management. This analysis, examines in combination the basic theories of change management and organizational restructuring, exploring their interdependence within the framework of the public sector reform process. Emphasis is placed upon the importance of cultivating a strategically focused organizational culture, the role of leadership in coordinating change initiatives, and the integration of performance measurement and monitoring tools to assess progress and consolidate change.

Chapter 7
The Dynamics of Public Sector Transformation: Key Change Management Variables, Measurement Tools, and the Institutional Context of Greek Reforms 197
Angelos Ntalakos, University of Thessaly, Greece
George Soklis, Panteion University, Greece

This chapter aims to explore the multifaceted nature of change management in the public sector, focusing on six key dimensions: readiness for change, commitment to change, resistance to change, integration of change, successful implementation, and the content of change. The study examines how public institutions adapt to reform demands in diverse international contexts, with a dedicated section focusing on the Greek public administration. As a result of the related literature there is a successful change in the public sector requires a high level of readiness and commitment, supported by strategic leadership and clear communication. Internationally, resistance often stems from organizational culture and lack of engagement. In Greece, although reform agendas are frequent, change efforts are often undermined by bureaucratic rigidity, insufficient training, and lack of stakeholder alignment. However, recent digital and administrative initiatives suggest a growing capacity for structured change implementation.

Chapter 8
Managing Public Enterprises in the Modern Administrative State: The Case of Greece 253
Ioannis Rossidis, Panteion University, Greece
Haralampos Chrysomallidis, University of the Peloponnese, Greece
George Kentas, University of Nicosia, Cyprus

Public enterprises constitute a significant pillar of state administration, contributing both to the provision of basic services and to the formulation of strategic priorities. This analysis examines their adjustment in the light of modern administrative models such as New Public Management and Public Governance, including the adoption of modern administrative pursuits such as result oriented management, citizen-client satisfaction, integration of digital transformation, the development of learning structures, etc. This study analyses critically the privatization of public organizations as a means of improving competitiveness and efficiency along with the sharp criticism of undermining public value, transparency and the public interest. Special reference is made to the case of Greece, where public enterprises have historically served as tools of national development and employment policy, but have been characterized by inefficiency, political interference and negative economic results.

Chapter 9
Judicial Reform, Performance, and Governance: Evidence From Norway 275
Anatoliy G. Goncharuk, NLA University College, Norway

Judicial systems face growing pressure to improve efficiency while preserving fairness, quality, and access to justice. In 2021, Norway implemented a major judicial reform consolidating district courts to address delays and uneven workloads. This chapter evaluates the reform's early performance effects within a public sector governance framework. Using Data Envelopment Analysis (DEA) and the Malmquist Productivity Index, the study compares court efficiency, productivity, and quality before and after the reform, incorporating case timeliness as a quality indicator. The findings show mixed results. While the reform coincided with a positive technological shift linked to digitalization, overall technical efficiency and productivity declined in the short term. Many merged courts exhibited decreasing returns to scale, suggesting consolidation exceeded optimal size in several regions. Quality outcomes, measured by overdue cases, remained largely unchanged. The chapter emphasizes policy learning, benchmarking, and targeted adjustment rather than reform reversal.

Chapter 10
New Public Management in Morocco: Between the Quest for Performance and Challenges of Implementation 319
Zineb Loukili, Ibn Tofaîl University, Morocco
Azzouz Elhamma, Ibn Tofaîl University, Morocco

Public sector performance is the central objective of New Public Management (NPM), a model that emerged in the 1980s to modernize public sector organizations, making them more flexible and user-centered through private sector practices. In Morocco, this reform movement has inspired the implementation of major reforms such as program budgeting and Results-Based Management (RBM). These initiatives are based on three fundamental pillars: the definition of clear objectives, the efficient allocation of resources, and the rigorous evaluation of results. Although these principles reflect a desire for a profound transformation of public action, their implementation nevertheless encounters various structural and cultural constraints that can limit their impact.

Chapter 11
Unlocking Hospital Performance: NPM Tool Appropriation as a Key Mediator in the Moroccan Context 343
Cherkaoui Dekkaki Achraf, Ibn Tofaîl University, Morocco
Azzouz Elhamma, Ibn Tofaîl University, Morocco

In response to two decades of New Public Management (NPM) inspired reforms, the Moroccan public hospital sector is undergoing a profound transformation. This study analyzes the impact of NPM tool adoption on hospital performance, with a specific focus on the appropriation of these tools by local actors. Drawing on a quantitative survey of 240 hospital managers, our findings reveal that tool appropriation plays a crucial mediating role. This process, resulting in an organizational hybridization that merges managerial logics with public service values, is a critical determinant of effective performance improvement. Furthermore, the results confirm the influence of contingency factors, including hospital size, autonomy, and organizational culture. The study concludes that the simple transposition of NPM tools is insufficient. Instead, their effectiveness is contingent upon a contextual appropriation that promotes dynamics of hybridization.

Chapter 12
Between National Discretion and Collective Norms: The Challenge of Revising the EU's Common Position on Arms Exports 367
Theofania Antoniou, Hellenic Open University, Greece

The Common Position 2008/944/CFSP constitutes the principal legal instrument governing the European Union's regime for the control of military technology and arms exports. The escalation of hostilities in Gaza (2023–2025) has revealed significant structural deficiencies and implementation gaps within this framework, primarily stemming from the decentralised nature of enforcement and the divergent administrative and judicial practices of the Member States. These developments have raised criticism concerning the absence of a centralised supervisory authority, the limited enforceability of the Common Position's criteria, and the need for enhanced harmonisation and transparency. The Gaza crisis illustrates the enduring challenge of reconciling national discretion with collective EU norms, highlighting the necessity of further strengthening the legal coherence and practical effectiveness of the EU's export control regime in safeguarding compliance with international humanitarian law.

Chapter 13
Normative Gatekeepers: The Role of National Courts in Shaping EU Responses to the Gaza Crisis 387
Theofania Antoniou, Hellenic Open University, Greece
Maria-Daniella Marouda, Panteion University, Greece

EU's capacity to enforce International Humanitarian Law is constrained by national divergences. Increased political polarization, the prioritization of the humanitarian dimension, and the reinforcement of legal discourse on the unlawful nature of settlements have shaped the Union's external action. National judicial bodies have increasingly acted as normative gatekeepers by scrutinizing arms export authorizations for compliance with IHL. Recent landmark judgments in the Netherlands and Germany have annulled or suspended export licenses for military equipment destined for Israel, citing substantial risks of contributing to grave breaches of international law in Gaza.. By asserting the primacy of legal obligations over political choices, national courts thus function as a constraining and legitimizing force, shaping or even modifying the political discourse of a number of EU member states influencing indirectly EU's external affairs policies. This paper analyses the pivotal role of national courts in influencing the European Union's legal and policy responses to the Gaza crisis.

Compilation of References 409

About the Contributors 469

Index 473

Preface

INTRODUCTION

Public administration is currently at the center of a profound and multifaceted transformation. In a context characterized by continuous and overlapping crises—economic, health, environmental, social, and geopolitical—as well as rapid technological developments, growing social inequalities, and intense questioning of institutions, the public sector is called upon to redefine its role, functions, and fundamental values. The need for effective, transparent, democratic, and socially responsible public administration has never been more pressing. In this context, the edited volume *Public Sector Reform and Modern Trends for Public Management* aspires to make a substantive contribution to scholarly debate by offering a contemporary, interdisciplinary, and critical approach to administrative reforms and emerging trends in public management.

Administrative reforms cannot be understood as neutral or purely technical interventions limited to improving the administrative mechanics of the state. Rather, they constitute complex political, social, and institutional processes that reflect broader conceptions of the nature, function, and purpose of the state in each historical context. Every wave of reform embodies specific ideological assumptions regarding the state–market relationship, democratic participation, accountability, social justice, and the role of citizens in governance. From the traditional Weberian model of bureaucracy—which laid the foundations for institutional stability and formal equality—to New Public Management (NPM), Public Governance, and contemporary hybrid approaches, the evolution of administrative models reflects a continuous and dynamic search for balance among efficiency, democratic legitimacy, and social justice.

The shift from the Weberian model to the logic of NPM highlighted the need for greater flexibility, effectiveness, and accountability, but at the same time raised new questions concerning the social role of the state and the preservation of public value. The turn toward Public Governance underscored the importance of collaborative networks, multilevel governance, and the participation of citizens and stakeholders in public policymaking. Contemporary hybrid approaches seek to combine elements of efficiency, legitimacy, and social accountability, recognizing that administrative reform is not a linear process of model replacement but an ongoing process of overlap and adaptation.

In the twenty-first century, digital transformation has emerged as a decisive factor in reshaping the state and its administrative functions. The transition from e-government to broader forms of digital governance is not confined to the mere introduction of new technologies or the digitization of existing procedures. Instead, it entails deep organizational change, process redesign, the development of new administrative capacities, and a reconfiguration of the state–citizen relationship. Digital transformation raises new questions regarding transparency, data protection, citizen participation, and democratic accountability, making a critical approach to the use of technology in public administration essential.

At the same time, public sector reforms cannot be adequately understood without reference to change management and the organizational dynamics of public institutions. The success or failure of administrative reforms largely depends on the ability of public organizations to manage resistance to change, cultivate a culture of collaboration and learning, and strengthen their administrative capacity through strategic leadership and participatory processes. Human and managerial skills—including interpersonal, communicative, and emotional competencies—acquire particular significance in environments of intense organizational and technological change, where success depends not only on systems but also on the people who operate them.

The volume also examines the role of strategic management in the public sector, not as a narrowly technocratic process of planning and control, but as a dynamic capacity for adaptation under conditions of uncertainty, complexity, and rapid change. Contemporary public administration is required to address complex social problems that lack simple solutions, demand interdisciplinary approaches, and involve multiple actors. In this framework, the creation of public value, the strengthening of social trust, and the development of collaborative forms of governance constitute central challenges for public organizations.

Through a combination of theoretical perspectives, comparative analyses, and empirical studies, this collective volume seeks to offer a coherent and comprehensive framework for understanding contemporary trends in public administration. It does not merely describe reforms but aims to analyze their deeper causes, consequences, and contradictions. It addresses students, academics, researchers, public administration professionals, and policymakers who seek to understand not only the technical dimensions of reforms but also their political, social, and institutional implications.

Ultimately, the discussion of public sector reform is simultaneously a discussion about the future of democracy, social cohesion, and the state–citizen relationship. The quality of public administration directly affects the quality of democracy, the effectiveness of public policies, and citizens' trust in institutions. This volume may serve as a valuable resource for reflection, dialogue, and knowledge for all those interested in improving public administration and shaping a more just, effective, and democratic state in an ever-changing environment.

ORGANIZATION OF THE BOOK

Chapter 1: Administrative Reforms and Transformation of Public Administration: Concept, Necessity, and Challenges

The first chapter aims to explore the evolving role of administrative reforms within the broader context of modern public management and governance. Administrative reform is presented not as a singular or episodic action but as a strategic, continuous, and multi-level process aimed at improving structures, procedures, organizational cultures, and institutional responsiveness. The study focuses on the underlying causes that drive reform initiatives (e.g., polycrises, fiscal pressures, globalization, digital transformation), as well as the barriers to their implementation (e.g., political discontinuity, bureaucratic resistance, institutional inertia). It emphasizes the role of strategic planning, participatory models, and adaptive governance in achieving meaningful and sustainable change.

Chapter 2: The Evolution of Administrative Models in the Public Sector

This chapter examines the evolution of administrative models in the public sector, from Weberian bureaucracy to modern hybrid schemes. Bureaucracy is defined as a model that provided stability and legitimacy, but its rigidity led to the gradual emergence of modern administrative approaches such as New Public Management (NPM), which introduced private economic criteria and emphasized efficiency and effectiveness. Despite its innovative perspective, NPM was criticized for limiting its social and democratic dimension. Public governance emerged as a response, emphasizing cooperation, multi-level policymaking and the participation of citizens and stakeholders. Following this evolution, hybrid models such as the Neo-Weberian State, New Public Governance, New Public Service and the theory of Public Value attempt to combine elements of legitimacy, efficiency and social legitimation. The analysis demonstrates that administrative reform is not a linear process of model replacement, but a perpetual process of overlaps and adaptations.

Chapter 3: Law and Public Administration

Law serves as the bedrock of public administration, shaping the framework within which governments operate and ensuring the legitimacy, accountability, and fairness of administrative actions. In democratic societies, the rule of law governs the conduct of public officials, delineates the powers and responsibilities of administrative bodies, and safeguards the rights of citizens. Without a strong legal foundation, public administration would risk arbitrariness, corruption, and inefficiency. The role of law in public administration is thus multifaceted—acting both as an enabler and a constraint, guiding the formulation and execution of public policies while ensuring adherence to constitutional principles and ethical standards. At its core, law provides a structural foundation for the operation of the state and its various agencies. Administrative law, constitutional law, and statutory regulations form the legal scaffolding of public administration, outlining the authority of governmental institutions and defining the scope of their jurisdiction.

Chapter 4: NPM is Dead, Long Live NPM: Transformations of New Public Management in the Course of Administrative Reforms

This chapter reinterprets NPM as NPM 2.0, highlighting tools and techniques that integrate empirical and theoretical knowledge while adapting to the specific identities and needs of each administrative system. It concludes that the endurance of NPM's second generation depends on embedding technological innovation within constitutional safeguards, transforming digitalisation into a means of rebuilding state capacity.

Chapter 5: Strategic Management in the Public Sector. Concepts, Challenges, and Evolving Practices

This chapter questions the uncritical transfer of private-sector strategic models to public organizations, arguing that they rest on linear and technocratic assumptions that conflict with the political and value-laden nature of public action. Drawing on a systemic review, public organizations are conceptualised as Complex Adaptive Systems, where interdependencies and competing norms generate non-linear outcomes, undermining claims of control through rational planning. The chapter therefore advances a Public Value perspective, exemplified by Moore's Strategic

Triangle, which highlights the need to align value creation, operational capacity and the authorizing environment. Public strategy is thus understood as a dynamic, politically embedded practice aimed at sustaining public value under conditions of complexity.

Chapter 6: Enhancing Public Sector Reform: The Impact of Change Management on Organizational Restructuring

This chapter examines in combination the basic theories of change management and organizational restructuring, exploring their interdependence within the framework of the public sector reform process. Emphasis is placed upon the importance of cultivating a strategically focused organizational culture, the role of leadership in coordinating change initiatives, and the integration of performance measurement and monitoring tools to assess progress and consolidate change.

Chapter 7: The Dynamics of Public Sector Transformation: Key Change Management Variables, Measurement Tools, and the Institutional Context of Greek Reforms

This chapter aims to explore the multifaceted nature of change management in the public sector, focusing on six key dimensions: readiness for change, commitment to change, resistance to change, integration of change, successful implementation, and the content of change. The study examines how public institutions adapt to reform demands in diverse international contexts, with a dedicated section focusing on the Greek public administration. As a result of the related literature there is a successful change in the public sector requires a high level of readiness and commitment, supported by strategic leadership and clear communication. Internationally, resistance often stems from organizational culture and lack of engagement. In Greece, although reform agendas are frequent, change efforts are often undermined by bureaucratic rigidity, insufficient training, and lack of stakeholder alignment. However, recent digital and administrative initiatives suggest a growing capacity for structured change implementation.

Chapter 8: Managing Public Enterprises in the Modern Administrative State. The Case of Greece

This chapter examines their adjustment in the light of modern administrative models such as New Public Management and Public Governance, including the adoption of modern administrative pursuits such as result oriented management, citizen-client satisfaction, integration of digital transformation, the development of learning structures, etc. This study analyses critically the privatization of public organizations as a means of improving competitiveness and efficiency along with the sharp criticism of undermining public value, transparency and the public interest. Special reference is made to the case of Greece, where public enterprises have historically served as tools of national development and employment policy, but have been characterized by inefficiency, political interference and negative economic results.

Chapter 9: Judicial Reform, Performance, and Governance: Evidence from Norway

This chapter evaluates the reform's early performance effects within a public sector governance framework. Using Data Envelopment Analysis (DEA) and the Malmquist Productivity Index, the study compares court efficiency, productivity, and quality before and after the reform, incorporating case timeliness as a quality indicator. The findings show mixed results. While the reform coincided with a positive technological shift linked to digitalization, overall technical efficiency and productivity declined in the short term. Many merged courts exhibited decreasing returns to scale, suggesting consolidation exceeded optimal size in several regions. Quality outcomes, measured by overdue cases, remained largely unchanged. The chapter emphasizes policy learning, benchmarking, and targeted adjustment rather than reform reversal.

Chapter 10: New Public Management in Morocco: Between the Quest for Performance and Challenges of Implementation

Public sector performance is the central objective of New Public Management (NPM), a model that emerged in the 1980s to modernize public sector organizations, making them more flexible and user-centered through private sector practices. In Morocco, this reform movement has inspired the implementation of major reforms such as program budgeting and Results-Based Management (RBM). These initiatives are based on three fundamental pillars: the definition of clear objectives, the efficient allocation of resources, and the rigorous evaluation of results. Although these principles reflect a desire for a profound transformation of public action, their implementation nevertheless encounters various structural and cultural constraints that can limit their impact.

Chapter 11: Unlocking Hospital Performance: NPM Tool Appropriation as a Key Mediator in the Moroccan Context

This chapter analyzes the impact of NPM tool adoption on hospital performance, with a specific focus on the appropriation of these tools by local actors. Drawing on a quantitative survey of 240 hospital managers, our findings reveal that tool appropriation plays a crucial mediating role. This process, resulting in an organizational hybridization that merges managerial logics with public service values, is a critical determinant of effective performance improvement. Furthermore, the results confirm the influence of contingency factors, including hospital size, autonomy, and organizational culture. The study concludes that the simple transposition of NPM tools is insufficient. Instead, their effectiveness is contingent upon a contextual appropriation that promotes dynamics of hybridization.

Chapter 12: Between National Discretion and Collective Norms: The Challenge of Revising the EU's Common Position on Arms Exports

The Common Position 2008/944/CFSP constitutes the principal legal instrument governing the European Union's regime for the control of military technology and arms exports. The escalation of hostilities in Gaza (2023–2025) has revealed significant structural deficiencies and implementation gaps within this framework, primarily stemming from the decentralised nature of enforcement and the divergent administrative and judicial practices of the Member States. These developments have raised criticism concerning the absence of a centralised supervisory authority, the limited enforceability of the Common Position's criteria, and the need for enhanced harmonisation and transparency. The Gaza crisis illustrates the enduring challenge of reconciling national discretion with collective EU norms, highlighting the necessity of further strengthening the legal coherence and practical effectiveness of the EU's export control regime in safeguarding compliance with international humanitarian law.

Chapter 13: Normative Gatekeepers: The Role of National Courts in Shaping EU Responses to the Gaza Crisis

EU's capacity to enforce International Humanitarian Law is constrained by national divergences. Increased political polarization, the prioritization of the humanitarian dimension, and the reinforcement of legal discourse on the unlawful nature of settlements have shaped the Union's external action. National judicial bodies have increasingly acted as normative gatekeepers by scrutinizing arms export authorizations for compliance with IHL. Recent landmark judgments in the Netherlands and Germany have annulled or suspended export licenses for military equipment destined for Israel, citing substantial risks of contributing to grave breaches of international law in Gaza.. By asserting the primacy of legal obligations over political choices, national courts thus function as a constraining and legitimizing force, shaping or even modifying the political discourse of a number of EU member states influencing indirectly EU's external affairs policies. This paper analyses the pivotal role of national courts in influencing the European Union's legal and policy responses to the Gaza crisis.

Chapter 1
Administrative Reforms and Transformation of Public Administration:
Concept, Necessity, and Challenges

Fotini Vittou
http://orcid.org/0000-0001-5367-5042
Panteion University of Social and Political Sciences, Greece

Vasilis Kefis
Panteion University of Social and Political Sciences, Greece

Stavroula Ktistaki
Panteion University, Greece

Evangelia Balta
Panteion University, Greece

ABSTRACT

This chapter aims to explore the evolving role of administrative reforms within the broader context of modern public management and governance. Administrative reform is presented not as a singular or episodic action but as a strategic, continuous, and multi-level process aimed at improving structures, procedures, organizational cultures, and institutional responsiveness. The study focuses on the underlying causes that drive reform initiatives (e.g., polycrises, fiscal pressures, globalization, digital transformation), as well as the barriers to their implementation (e.g., political

DOI: 10.4018/979-8-3373-3526-1.ch001

discontinuity, bureaucratic resistance, institutional inertia). It emphasizes the role of strategic planning, participatory models, and adaptive governance in achieving meaningful and sustainable change.

1. INTRODUCTION

Administrative reforms constitute a fundamental instrument for the adaptation and improvement of public administration in response to contemporary social, economic, and technological challenges, with the aim of optimizing organizational structures, processes, and institutional culture. Globally, reforms respond to a wide range of triggers, such as polycrisis (health, environmental, geopolitical), fiscal pressures, globalization, and digital transformation, while simultaneously facing obstacles like political instability, bureaucratic resistance, and institutional inertia.

This chapter undertakes a comprehensive analysis of the concept, necessity, and challenges of administrative reforms, integrating theoretical perspectives, international comparisons, and empirical insights, with a particular focus on the Greek experience. It begins by exploring the definition of administrative reform, distinguishing it from mere change and examining its varied interpretations across different political and social contexts. Subsequently, it examines the factors rendering reforms necessary, such as polycrisis, digital governance, and international pressures, drawing on examples from countries like Estonia and Sweden. The chapter also analyzes implementation challenges, including the lack of political consensus and organizational dysfunctions, with specific reference to the Greek case. Finally, through qualitative research, this study examines the reasons behind the success or failure of reforms in Greece, emphasizing the need for a holistic approach that incorporates steadfast political will, participatory processes, and effective change management. Through this multidimensional analysis, the chapter seeks to contribute to an understanding of the dynamics shaping reform and to propose directions for a more efficient, resilient, and citizen-centric public sector.

2. THE CONCEPT OF ADMINISTRATIVE REFORM

"Reform" is one of those controversial concepts that can be interpreted in many different ways. Nevertheless, one thing is certain: regardless of its other meanings, "reform" always implies some change in the state (Cunha & Tsoukas, 2015).

The interpretation of the term "administrative reform" presents many challenges, as it varies depending on the political system of each country. In developed industrial countries, such as the US and European countries, the term mainly refers to changes in administrative structures and procedures to keep pace with social and political expectations. In Western European and North American countries, in particular, administrative reform is often linked to the introduction of New Public Management (NPM) principles, which promote efficiency, competitiveness, and customer focus in public services (Osborne & Gaebler, 1992).

In contrast, in developing countries, administrative reform is aimed more at strengthening the state and political stability and is often linked to efforts to modernize and change society, using administration as a tool for social and economic transformation (Farazmand, 2001; Farazmand, 1999). Global experience shows, however, that reforms in these countries are often dictated by international organizations such as the World Bank or the IMF, which raises questions about whether the reforms respond to internal needs or external pressures (Aphecetche, Canton, Garrone, & Hobza, 2022).

In other countries, such as Greece, administrative reform is a widely used and much-discussed concept and for this reason it is commonly equated with change. However, it is different from simple change, as well as from replacement, upgrading, modernization and evolution, progress or development, terms which it encompasses (Konstantinidou, 2020).

For Makrydimitris (2004), change is an essential and structural feature of social systems, and reform is a process of constantly seeking organizational and administrative changes that will bring about improvement and upgrading in organizational functioning and administrative behavior (at least at the level of reformers' announcements) in order to respond to the demands and conditions of its environment. This process is reinforced by the fact that modern societies are characterized by an inherent ability to provoke, promote, and absorb change.

Change, however, according to him, is a transformation that takes place and is accepted relatively easily, while reform is a change that provokes resistance, depending on its content, scope, and nature, but also on the upheaval or disruption it causes to established interests and the benefits of the old order. Therefore, addressing reactions and resistance to change must be part of the reform plan. This phenomenon is not unique to Greece, as in all countries reform encounters powerful interests and cultures that are difficult to change, even when there is international pressure for change(Brunsson, 2006; Cavatorto & La Spina, 2020).

Brunsson (2006) also highlights the fact that reform does not equate to change, as an organization may undergo several reforms, but the changes may be minor. In fact, after studying a plethora of reform arguments, he concluded that administrative reforms are more of a routine, a repetitive activity, rather than sudden, one-off changes. They may concern structures, in which case they may involve the reorganization of departments, the abolition or creation of new ones. They may also concern procedures, in which case they change the way a function is performed. In some cases, they aim to change organizational culture and ideology, introducing more democratic structures, values, or procedures. Often, their purpose is to improve the organization's results, i.e., to enhance its efficiency and effectiveness. However, it should be noted that while it is easy to initiate a reform process, it is equally difficult to achieve that reform and bring about the desired changes, and this ease is one of the factors contributing to its failure. Many countries experience the phenomenon of "reform recycling," where each new government announces reforms, but the structures remain unchanged (Farazmand, 1999; Brunsson, 2006).

Pollitt & Bouckaert (2017) give a deeper dimension to the concept and broadly define administrative reform as "*Deliberate efforts to change the structures, processes, and/or culture of public sector organizations with the aim of making them (in some sense) work* better" (2017, p. 2). The openness of the definition allows for different interpretations of its components depending on the context. This reflects the international complexity of administrative reforms, which may have different content and priorities between countries, even within the same continent, as shown by the comparison between the models of the Napoleonic states and the Scandinavian countries (Cole & Eymeri-Douzans, 2010; Ongardo, 2014).

The Encyclopedic Dictionary of Public Administration (Gow, 2012) also emphasizes the fact that administrative reform is a conscious and well-thought-out change and points out that its objectives include improving the quality of human resources, in addition to improving structures and functions.

The United Nations (UN) describes the concept in detail in its guide to administrative reform published in 2015 (UNDP, 2015): Administrative reform refers to processes of change in various areas of public administration, such as organizational structures, decentralization, personnel management, public finances, and regulatory reforms. It focuses on improving the efficiency, transparency, and accountability of public administration so that it can manage and implement government activities, enforce laws, regulatory provisions and government decisions, and provide public services.

As clarified in the report of the Dekleri Commission (1992, p. 13) the concept of administrative reform has evolved from a "*drastic and rather extensive intervention in the organization and functioning of public* administration," that is, from a "*periodic miracle* cure," to a "*methodically designed long-term strategy for improving administration*," which is now approached as a continuous organizational change, as recommended by contemporary organizational theory.

In conclusion, administrative reform is a process through which both structural and operational changes are attempted to improve the public sector so that, through a new mode of action, it can respond better and more efficiently to the needs of society, given the circumstances and environment at the time (Rossidis et al., 2023; Rossidis, 2014).

In this context, examining the causes that drive the need for administrative reforms constitutes the next step in understanding how and why these changes become necessary.

3. THE IMPORTANCE AND NECESSITY OF ADMINISTRATIVE REFORMS AND STATE TRANSFORMATION

The importance and necessity of administrative reforms stem from the need to adapt state structures to constantly changing social, economic, and technological conditions. Public administration is called upon to respond to new challenges, ensure effectiveness, efficiency, equality, and transparency, and strengthen the relationship of trust between the state and its citizens.

At the international level, the debate on the importance of administrative reforms is closely linked to the transformation of the state in the context of globalization, the economic crisis, and the technological revolution. The introduction of new technologies and the digitization of services, pressure to reduce public spending, and the need to address complex social problems (wicked problems)[1], such as climate change, are leading states to engage in a continuous process of reform (Pollitt & Bouckaert, 2017; Yankelovich, 2015).

Furthermore, in OECD countries, administrative reforms are now closely linked to sustainable development goals and the management of complex problems (wicked problems), such as climate change, demographic aging, and digital inequalities (OECD, 2020; Yankelovich, 2015).

Many researchers, such as Osborne & Gaebler (1992), point out that the traditional, bureaucratic model of administration is no longer sufficient to meet the demands of modern society. They favor the development of the "entrepreneurial state," which operates more flexibly, promotes innovation, and seeks to maximize the use of its resources. This idea has profoundly influenced many countries, with notable examples being New Zealand and Canada, which adopted extensive reforms emphasizing results-based management and the reduction of bureaucracy (Osborne & Gaebler, 1992; OECD, 2020). New Zealand, in particular, redefined the objectives of administrative reform, not only in terms of efficiency but also in terms of creating public value, by strengthening citizen participation in policy decisions and in shaping the services provided (Osborne & Gaebler, 1992). Similarly, the Scandinavian countries have included equal access to services and the reduction of social inequalities among their reform objectives (Pinheiro et al., 2019).

The reform momentum is also linked to the need to strengthen accountability and transparency. The crisis of confidence in institutions observed in many democracies makes it necessary to reform structures and processes so that citizens feel that the state is responding to their needs (Farazmand, 1999; Cavatorto & La Spina, 2020). The experience of countries such as Denmark and Sweden shows that continuous renewal and a focus on transparency contribute significantly to high levels of public trust in the state (Pinheiro, Geschwind, Hansen, & Pulkkinen, 2019).

Especially in the case of Greece, the importance of administrative reforms is historically linked to the need to modernize and streamline the state, especially after the economic crisis of the 2010s. However, despite repeated efforts, challenges remain, such as limited administrative capacity, a resistant bureaucratic culture, and political instability (Lampropoulou & Oikonomou, 2018; Rammata, 2018). The Greek case reflects the international phenomenon of "reform without substance" (reform as ritual), as described by Brunsson (2006), i.e. the proclamation of change to satisfy external pressures or expectations of legitimacy, without any real changes in practice.

The need for reform today is undeniable, as citizens demand high-quality services, financial resources are limited, and social inequalities are intensifying. Administrative reform is not a luxury, but a prerequisite for sustainable development, social cohesion, and democratic stability (Pollitt & Bouckaert, 2017).

To fully understand the importance and necessity of administrative reforms, it is necessary to examine the causes that lead to the need for structural changes, which are multifactorial and vary according to the historical, social and political context of each country.

Administrative reform is, after all, a global phenomenon and a common challenge for all national governments. At the international level, the literature converges on the view that administrative reform often arises not only from internal needs, but also from external pressures, geopolitical developments, technological advances, and social demands. The combination of these factors leads states with different institutional traditions to converge on similar reform patterns, although the specific manifestations vary considerably (Pollitt & Bouckaert, 2017; Farazmand, 1999).

In OECD countries, the main objectives of administrative reforms, which stem from the respective problems, are illustrated in the following diagram[2]:

Figure 1. Priorities for publica administration reform

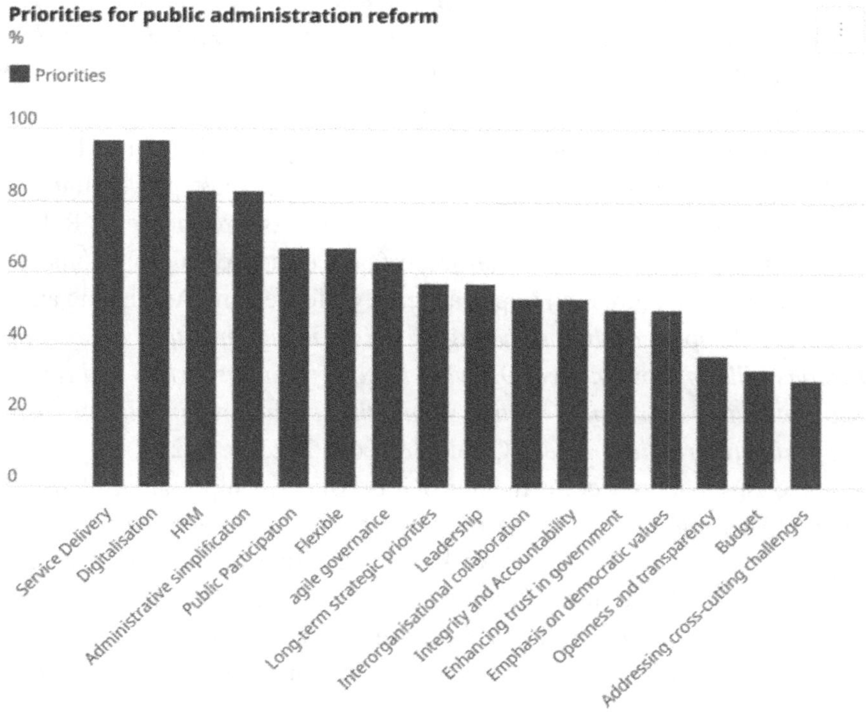

Diagram 1 : Priorities for administrative reform in OECD member countries

Furthermore, through analysis of the available literature, the main issues that necessitate the implementation of administrative reforms and the transformation of the state were identified, which can be considered as triggers, and were classified into the following categories.

3.2.1 Multiple Crises and Ongoing Crises

Contemporary societies are characterised by risk and uncertainty, plagued by a multitude of different and successive crises (health, environmental, energy, geopolitical instability, and wars), bringing back into our vocabulary the concepts of "multicrisis" and "permanent or ongoing crisis," which now seem to describe a normality rather than an unpredictable and exceptional situation (Beck, 1992; Kotarski, 2023).

This phenomenon is international. In Europe, the Covid-19 pandemic and the war in Ukraine have demonstrated the importance of the resilience of administrative systems. In countries such as Germany and Denmark, administrative reforms have focused on strengthening preventive crisis management and creating coordination networks between state and non-state structures (OECD, 2021; Cheung & Low, 2023). In the US, the Department of Homeland Security was established in part as a response to the need for coordination in times of crisis, demonstrating the link between administrative structures and multi-crisis response (Farazmand, 2001).

Multi-crises test governments, which in many cases have proven unprepared to deal with the magnitude, frequency, and flow of crisis phenomena. Reflecting on these failures and the fundamental importance of addressing phenomena in a timely manner in the future is an important catalyst for reform. As Cheung and Low aptly observe *"Coping with and managing crises now constitutes a key function and responsibility of governance. Drawing lessons from past crises and reforming public organization and administration should thus be factored into the mainstream administrative reform discourse"* (Cheung & Low, 2023, p. 182):

As polycrises tend to become the norm, it is critically important, as Schomaker & Bauer (2020) highlight in their study, for public administrations to focus on building and maintaining strong networks, documenting successful practices, and fostering a culture of learning — both from current and past crises. These strategies are essential for improving crisis response, ensuring resilience, and enhancing performance during unprecedented challenges, and they require holistic reform of structures, functions, processes, and culture.

3.2.2 Economic Crises and Fiscal Pressures

Economic crises are analyzed separately from multi-crises because of their particular impact on the global level. The recent fiscal crisis of 2010 led many governments to adopt austerity measures to address deficits and debts, affecting the functioning of public administration, especially in countries that received international financial assistance, such as Greece. In some cases, the reforms were considered inevitable, as the crisis revealed the weaknesses of existing systems and provided an "opportunity" for long-delayed changes (Randma- Liiv & Kickert, 2017).

On a global scale, the experience of the 2008-2010 economic crisis showed that countries with strong administrative systems, such as Germany or the Scandinavian countries, managed to push through long-term reforms. In contrast, in southern European countries, interventions were often limited to short-term austerity measures (OECD, 2010; European Commission, 2022). Similar experiences have been recorded in the past in Latin America, where fiscal pressures acted as a lever for externally imposed reforms, often without the necessary institutional adjustment (Farazmand, 1999). Consequently, the impact of the crisis on administrative reforms was not uniform, with the crisis intensifying pressure for reform in some cases, but limiting the possibility of substantive change in others, as the rush to address short-term problems limited the promotion of deeper reforms.

The findings of the study by Randma-Liiv & Kickert (2017) show that fiscal crises stimulate administrative reforms, or rather, create opportunities for reforms, as they necessitate a review of long-term policies and administrative practices. For Asatryan et al.(2017), the crisis proves to be a catalyst for pressure to promote administrative reforms, although they agree that the results are not always guaranteed. Their study shows that a strong bureaucracy can slow down the momentum for reform, as it reacts to changes that reduce control and transparency. Reforms are more likely when the power of the bureaucracy is limited and when there is motivation from the crisis, such as high unemployment or increased public debt.

3.2.3 International Influences and Globalization

During the fiscal crisis, there was a new series of direct interventions by EU institutions in the administrative reforms of national public administrations. Indicative of this are the recommendations issued by the "troika"[3] to countries such as Greece, Ireland, and Portugal, as well as the letters and reports full of detailed proposals for the redesign of the public sector sent by the European Central Bank to the Italian government in August 2011 (Ongardo, 2014).

This trend reflects the international phenomenon of "policy transfer," i.e., the transfer of administrative practices from one country to another (Dolowitz & Marsh, 2000). In South Korea, for example, reforms in public administration were strongly influenced by international management standards (Farazmand, 2001).

At the same time, increased market internationalization, participation in international organizations (e.g., EU, Council of Europe, IMF) and the need to comply with international standards (e.g., accounting) are powerful catalysts for administrative reforms. Through these, national public administrations, showing striking similarities despite their different backgrounds, comply with the obligations arising from their participation. At the same time, they are trying to adapt to the global environment and respond effectively to global changes in markets, organization, fiscal capacity, technology, politics, and public attitudes, creating a "new model of governance" with tactics based on the market and competition (Lynn, 2001; Killian & Eklund, 2008).

3.2.4 Bureaucracy, Inefficiency, and Public Management

Globalization is linked to an international movement of administrative reforms - with its most prominent manifestation being NPM - which has been attempted in many countries, but with unclear directions and impact in each. The NPM emerged in the 1970s in Australia and New Zealand, prompted a plethora of administrative reforms, and laid the foundations for changes focusing on the introduction of business practices, transparency, and accountability, improving internal processes, and making more efficient use of public resources, becoming a new global phenomenon (Dator, Pratt, & Seo, 2006; Lapuente & Van de Walle, 2020; Michalopoulos, 2003).

For several decades, it has been the approach through which it has been possible to overcome the inefficiency of the public sector, transcend the rigid bureaucratic model, and replace it with the methods and principles of administrative science. The main applications of NPM, which influenced administrative reforms, are presented in the table below[4]:

Table 1. Applications of NPM in public administration

Applications of NPM in public administration
Enhancement of programming
Human resource development
Results-based management
Enhancement of organizational flexibility
Decentralization of responsibilities and resources
Policy design based on competition logic
Performance-based employee remuneration
Benchmarking
Total quality management (TQM)
Utilization of information and communication technologies (ICT)
Monitoring and evaluation processes
E-government
Regulatory reform
Performance-based budgeting

However, at the international level, several scholars emphasize that NPM has not always been successfully adapted to the specific institutional and cultural characteristics of countries. In Japan, for example, the application of NPM practices has been limited due to strong traditions of collective management and hierarchy (Yamamoto, 2003). Similarly, in Eastern European countries, the adoption of NPM principles often remained at the level of rhetoric, without any substantial changes (Ongaro, 2010).

The introduction of NPM principles into national public administrations was initially marked by intense enthusiasm and rapid adoption, mainly due to the perception that the business practices it promotes would contribute to reducing public spending and fiscal consolidation of national economies (Lapuente & Van de Walle, 2020).

Many researchers have shown, however, that the number of countries that managed to resolve their governance issues by implementing the NPM model was remarkably insignificant, even though innovative and comprehensive changes in public policy were attempted almost everywhere (Inkina, 2022). The NPM was criticized for its negative effects, which, in short, are attributed to the economization and depopulation of the state, which ultimately led to the depopulation of democracy, with the degradation of the citizen to a customer and significant negative economic and social consequences (Karkatsoulis, 2004). The shortcomings, criticism, and reaction that followed the initial enthusiasm led to the development of new management approaches (post-NPM), such as Public Value, Public Governance, etc. (Tsagdi, 2024; Karkatsoulis, 2001).

3.2.5 Participation and Governance

A key element in new approaches to governance is the participation of citizens and, in general, of stakeholders, without, however, abandoning the principles of efficiency and flexibility of NPM (Rossidis, Belias, & Aspridis, 2023; Lindquist, 2022). Post-NPM models of administration, which succeeded NPM, emphasize cooperation between different levels of governance, as well as between state and non-state organizations. Networking, participation, and active engagement of citizens, not only for the purpose of receiving public services, but also as key shapers of public value. This leads to a more integrated and balanced approach to public administration (Tsagdi, 2024).

The new approach and the need for increased citizen participation in decision-making, i.e., active representation, expectations for greater transparency and accountability, demands for better services, justice, and equal treatment, are forcing administrations to adapt their structures and procedures and are strong incentives for reforms that develop and promote cooperation as a central mechanism of governance (Robinson, 2015).

International experience shows that participation strengthens the legitimacy of reforms. In Finland, for example, the "Open Government" approach uses digital platforms for the direct participation of citizens in policymaking (OECD, 2020). Similarly, in California, USA, referendums and consultation are used extensively, but with mixed results in terms of the quality of decisions (Osborne & Gaebler, 1992).

Through participatory governance, reforms gain greater legitimacy and acceptance because they strengthen the collective engagement and commitment of citizens and public officials. Thus, participation is not merely a tool for implementing NPM principles, but a means of enhancing transparency and accountability, while fostering a strong sense of responsibility and cooperation.

3.2.6 Technological Developments and Digital Governance

Digital governance appears to promote the goal of increasing participation and proximity to citizens. According to the OECD (2024), technology contributes to improving the efficiency of the public sector, the effectiveness of public policies, the openness of governments, innovation, participation, and credibility.

International practice shows that successful digital reforms require not only technological tools, but also strong institutional support and a culture of transparency. In Estonia, e-Estonia is considered an international benchmark, as it has dramatically reduced bureaucracy and enhanced transparency (OECD, 2020).

Digital governance has a catalytic effect on public administration reforms, reshaping both the way public services operate and their relationship with citizens. However, for digital transformation to be sustainable, a flexible regulatory framework and forward-looking governance are needed, among other things, so that it can incorporate developments in technology, in particular emerging artificial intelligence (OECD, 2024b). With this approach, public administrations around the world are reshaping their operations by adopting digital reforms that will enable them to improve their efficiency and fulfill their role more effectively (Rossidis & Belias, 2020) . However, in African countries such as Kenya, digitization is progressing more slowly due to lower administrative capacity and limited infrastructure (Farazmand, 2001).

3.2.7 Political Discontinuity and Political Competition

As noted by the OECD and many researchers[5], administrative reform has always been on the agenda of governments in order to solve problems, adapt public administrations to current conditions and requirements, and make them more efficient, effective, less wasteful, open, and ready to respond to contemporary challenges.

However, a change in political leadership, whether through elections or the replacement of a minister, can have a significant impact on administrative reforms, as it is accompanied by new goals, a different ideology, and the need to present work through legislative initiatives. This is because each politician brings their own agenda and priorities, which often leads to the discontinuation or redefinition of policies already in place. New ministers or governments may focus on different policy areas and thus significantly alter the direction, priorities, continuity, and speed of implementation of reform programs (Robinson, 2015).

It should also be considered that each time the government changes, the balance of power shifts, and administrative reforms, within the framework of public policies, serve as one of the techniques through which the new political leadership realigns formal and informal power alliances with stakeholders (Nissim, 2023)[6] . It thus becomes clear that different governments or government formations promote reforms that are aligned with their political motives, apart from the logic of problem solving (Maggeti & Trein, 2021).

The success of administrative reform depends on the commitment of key actors to effective policy implementation, with an emphasis on content, timing, and strategies (Cohen, 2023). As Post et al. (2010, cited in Cohen (2023) note, political will arises when several decision-makers, with a common understanding of a problem, commit to supporting a solution. Many scholars emphasize the importance of political will for public administration reform (Pollitt & Bouckaert, 2017; OECD, 2010). However, frequent changes in policy and senior personnel can undermine this commitment. In the UK, for example, constant changes in government have affected the progress of administrative reforms such as the Next Steps Agency Model (Pollitt & Bouckaert, 2017). In Italy, Cavatorto & La Spina (2020) show that frequent changes of government are associated with low institutional memory and difficulty in implementing long-term reforms. In contrast, in Sweden, broad consensus on fundamental administrative principles ensures institutional continuity despite political changes (Pinheiro et al., 2019).

4. THE CASE OF GREECE AND RELATED EXAMPLES OF ADMINISTRATIVE REFORMS

Reforms shape a country's direction and sustainability, contributing decisively to its development and progress (Papoulias, 2019). The need for administrative reforms presents different challenges and dynamics in each country. Greece, as a country that has experienced the fiscal crisis and the dictates of international organizations intensely, and also with a "weak public administration," is a typical example of a nation that has been forced to make significant administrative changes in recent years.

The starting point for the analysis is the period after the transition to democracy (1975-). It should be noted that the administrative laws passed during this fifty-year period are so numerous that they exceed the scope of this paper[7]. Thus, the specific examples mentioned in each category, as expressed through their legislation, are merely indicative of the effort to rationalize, modernize, and enhance the quality and effectiveness of the Greek public administration, based on their initial purpose and their declaration as "reforms", regardless of their outcome.

Regarding the reform outcomes, a systematic review of the abundant literature on the subject shows that very few of these efforts led to substantial changes. In terms of results, it appears that most of these reforms have turned into legislative measures with little significant impact, rather than constituting real transformations and breakthroughs at the core of the administrative problem.

The first post-dictatorship reform efforts[8] constitute a special category of reforms that were dictated by the need to democratize the state, organize the government and the public sector, the creation of new structures, the establishment of institutions for the consolidation of the rule of law and the development of the economy, following the country's exit from the seven-year period of dictatorship (Rammata, 2011; Sotiropoulos D. A., 2007; Gekas et al., 2022; Kalyvas et al., 2012)[9]. The 1975 Constitution laid the foundations for the restoration of the democratic system, strengthening individual rights and the separation of powers and defining the powers of the executive.

In the 1980s, the "democratization" and, shortly after, the "democratic modernization" of the state led to a wave of bold reform efforts (Spanou, 2012). At this time, there were measures that transferred responsibilities to local authorities (OTAs), strengthened decentralization and financial autonomy, and supported mergers, as well as the ratification of the Municipal and Community Code, which regulated the structure, functions, and powers of local government organizations. Additionally, there were regulations for public personnel, including the introduction of accountability and the establishment of disciplinary councils, changes to the recruitment system (e.g., laws 1235/82, 1558/85, 1622/86, 1320/83, 1735/87), and the founding of the National Center for Public Administration and the National School of Public Administration (law 1388/83) for the training and development of the public administration workforce. Meanwhile, efforts were made to regulate issues related to the functioning of public services, aiming to address organizational and operational problems that hindered their effective performance (law 865/79). During this period, many structures with specific responsibilities were also established, such as General Secretariats (e.g., for New Generation, Popular Education, etc.) and local government bodies, like public corporations (DEKO) and state organizations, as well as the foundations of the Independent Authorities, such as the Competition Commission and the National Radio and Television Council. The continuation of the reform process was enriched by the need for modernization and was clearly shaped by the country's entry into the EU and, later, into the EMU (Maistros, 2009).

Returning to the aforementioned categorization, it is evident that the reform momentum in Greece was not limited only to specifically mandated interventions but was manifested across all the categories mentioned.

The *multiple crises* that unfolded globally did not leave Greece unaffected. The economic crisis, the refugee crisis, climate change, and the COVID-19 pandemic tested the country's resilience and forced the state to undertake a series of reforms in order to manage the consequences and strengthen the sustainability of the state.

The crises related to the environment, climate change, natural disasters, and other risks highlighted the need for a rational and coordinated management of such phenomena under the supervision of civil protection, as a horizontal public policy. This approach only emerged in Greece in 2018, following the Mati wildfire (Karkatsoulis, 2023a), despite having been institutionalized since 1995[10]. This tragic event was the catalyst for significant changes, including the passing of Law 5023/13[11] on multi-level governance, which is a critical component for the successful management of crises and disasters, while various pieces of legislation reorganized existing structures and established new ones with a corresponding redistribution, upgrade, or replacement of responsibilities (Karamanou, 2021).

The coronavirus health crisis triggered rapid developments during the pandemic, particularly in terms of the relationship between citizens and public administration. Citizens were called upon to continue to interact with the state through an emerging digital environment, due to the physical distance imposed by health protection measures. In this context, many administrative procedures were digitized, new modes of (electronic) governance were established using modern information systems, such as tele-appointments and tele-services, and since then, the digital transformation of the state has been progressing at a faster pace than in the past[12] (Sotiropoulos, 2021).

Innovative practices for Greece, such as teleworking in the public sector, which was implemented exceptionally during the restrictive measures with the PNP and was subsequently established by Law 4807/21[13], also made their appearance during the crisis.

Digitalization was also reinforced in matters that arose due to the migration crisis. In particular, asylum and migration procedures were digitized, with electronic submission of applications and provision of information to applicants, reducing bureaucracy and speeding up procedures (European Commission, 2023 c). In addition, Law 4636/19[14] introduced significant changes to the asylum procedure, simplifying procedures and shortening deadlines, with the aim of reducing the workload and speeding up the examination of applications, in order to reduce delays, reduce the volume of work, and improve the efficiency of the system.

Overall, as Babalioutas comments (2022), with e-government, which was established and accelerated due to the crises faced by the Greek public administration, an attempt was made to address "modern formalism" and remedy inherent weaknesses in the Greek administrative system, such as centralization, complexity, and inadequate utilization of human resources, to strengthen controls and transparency, and to make it more effective and efficient.

In conclusion, crises can be a turning point in the functioning of public administration, leading to overall improvement (of processes, structures, culture, etc.).

The *digital transformation*[15] of the state and *digital governance* are obviously an ongoing challenge and one of the EU's top priorities, which includes among its digital objectives the 100% digitization of basic public services by 2030, providing significant funds to achieve this goal in our country (European Commission, 2024). In this context, various initiatives have been adopted or are underway to modernize public services, which have been incorporated into national objectives.

One such initiative is the "Greece 2.0" reform program, where the digital transformation of the state is the second pillar, with five axes: "2.2.1 Investment in improving cybersecurity in the public sector & creation of a National Cybersecurity Center, 2.2.2 Management and governance of public sector data and ensuring compliance with the GDPR, 2.2.22 Action plan for the provision of "customer-centric" digital services by the public administration, 2.2.23 Interconnection and Interoperability of Public Sector Registers & Systems, 2.2.24 Continuous integration of advanced technologies in public administration" (General Secretariat for Coordination, 2024).

"Improving the efficiency and digitization of public administration" is also a key, independent policy response to major economic, labor, and social developments and challenges and a key objective of the annual National Reform Programs from 2021 (General Secretariat for Coordination, 2024a). Key actions include upgrading system interoperability, data governance, the digital infrastructure of public administration, and improving processes.

In addition, the "National Digital Strategy 2020-2025" is being implemented, as outlined in the "Digital Transformation Bible 2020-2025"[16], which describes the strategy, action plan, and ways to implement the vision for "Digital Greece" (Rossidis et al, 2023).

The main tool for the digital transformation of Greece is the "Digital Transformation 2021-2027" program. The programme's interventions in the public sector focus on the following (EYDP PSIMET, 2024):

Figure 2. The "digital transformation" program 2021-2027 - public sector overview

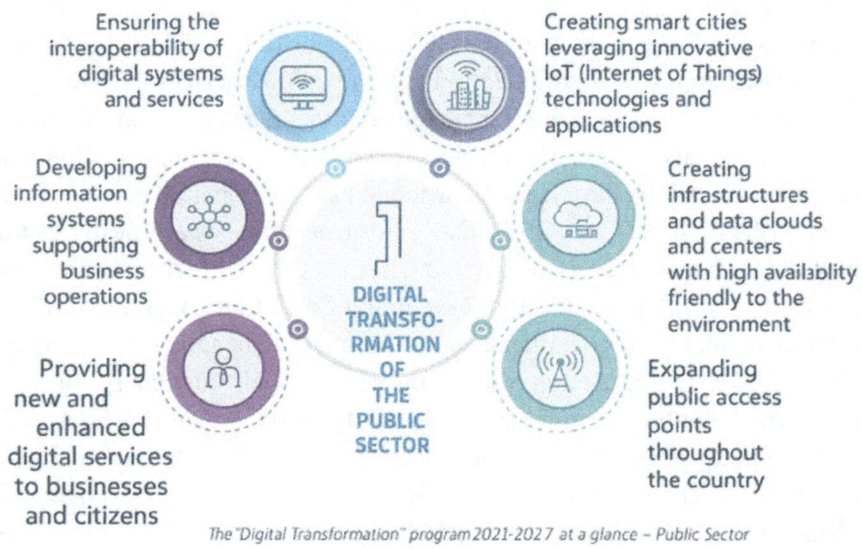

From the aforementioned points, it is evident that the digital transformation of the state, with the continuous advancement of technology and the introduction of artificial intelligence into the processes of the public and private sectors, is one of the most catalytic triggers for administrative reforms, in order to make public administration faster, better, more transparent, and more resource-efficient.

The coronavirus pandemic and artificial intelligence have acted as accelerators of digital transformation. Furthermore, as Rossidis & Belias (2021, p. 62) conclude, "*...the need to promote e-government systems* [during the pandemic] *helped to overcome difficulties in the recent past that had hindered the full implementation of digital reforms*." Thus, the health crisis evolved *into* "*... a unique opportunity to significantly develop e-government in Greece*."

The significant progress made in recent years continues unabated at all levels of government[17]. The complete transition to digital governance (e-governance) is gradually approaching, which refers not only to the integration of new technologies into governance, but also to its combination with organisational changes and new human resource skills, in order to support the entire cycle of public policy, strengthening democracy, and improving public administration (Rossidis & Belias, 2021).

The *fiscal crisis,* which peaked in 2010 with the risk of bankruptcy, led Greece to resort to the support mechanism of the International Monetary Fund, the European Commission, and the European Central Bank, and to the signing of the Memorandum of Economic and Financial Policy (Memorandum I). This is not just another catalyst for reform, but "*the largest and most serious, internationally supported, state intervention in the country's recent political and economic history since the 1950s*," as Papoulias (2019, p. 75) characteristically states. Memorandum II and Memorandum III followed, and the country theoretically emerged from the crisis with the completion of the latter in 2018. The terms of these memoranda of cooperation with the country's international lenders brought about a number of reforms that attempted to establish, in essence, a new framework of governance based on fiscal consolidation (Katsimardos & Bouas, 2013).

The aim was, through the radical restructuring of the Greek economy, to address, on the one hand, the fiscal problem (economic recession, deficits) and, on the other hand, to create the conditions for the Greek economy to break free from the mistakes of the past and to promote its entry into a growth trajectory (by restoring market confidence and strengthening competitiveness) (Katsimardos & Bouas, 2013) .

The administrative reforms and interventions of the fiscal consolidation programs mainly concerned the control of the size and cost of public administration (restrictions on hiring, a unified pay scale, National Payment Authority, reduction or complete abolition of bonuses and allowances), accountability ("DIAVGEIA"), human resource management (inventory, mobility, availability, digital organigrams and job descriptions, new evaluation system) and policy coordination ("MAZI" program, good lawmaking and codification of legislation). In fact, they have been catalysts for further reforms, particularly with regard to improving the performance of the Greek public administration (Nikitas & Vasilopoulou, 2022)[18]. Further reform of public administration is considered necessary because it could fuel a positive cycle of growth and prosperity (Karamouzis & Anastasatos, 2024) and because the reforms imposed by the memoranda have failed to achieve their original objectives, not only because they were simply transferred from abroad without being adapted to the Greek context, but also because of their strict adherence to the "correction" of economic indicators, without taking into account social needs and the changing environment.

More generally, most of the administrative reforms of recent years have been the result of the fiscal crisis on the one side, and *Greece's membership of the EU* and its Europeanization process on the other. As Graziano & Vink (2013) point out, it is now very rare for national public policies not to be linked in some way to EU policies. According to others, 80% of national legislation is produced by or linked to EU law and policies.

The EU, recognizing the importance of public administration for the success of its policies and its overall development, has made the reform of the public administrations of the Member States a key objective of its policies. This reform permeates almost all areas of EU action, with various initiatives and policies supporting the strengthening and modernization of national public administrations, considering the general strategic guidelines and the specific needs of each Member State.

EU interventions aim to coordinate and converge bureaucracies of a Weberian type, but which are essentially heterogeneous administrative systems. Greece is a country that had to try to bridge the gap between informal practices and formal rules in order to achieve administrative integration, but also because of its specific characteristics (Spanou, 2020), which we mentioned earlier.

In order to strengthen reform efforts, the EU uses various tools, mechanisms, and policies. These include European law, with directives and regulations setting standards for administrative procedures, public procurement[19] and the fight against corruption. The European Semester serves as an annual coordination cycle, during which national reform plans are submitted and recommendations for improvements in public administration are issued accordingly[20]. Cohesion Policy provides funding to support modernization and digitization projects in public administration, while the Technical Support Instrument (TSI) offers specialized assistance to reform efforts[21]. In addition, the EU encourages cooperation and exchange of practices between Member States in order to develop mutual learning and best administrative solutions (Vittou, 2023)[22] .

However, beyond the external pressures for reform, the need to restructure the Greek public administration also stemmed from internal challenges. Entrenched informal practices, weaknesses in resource and process management, and chronic pathologies that are endogenous features of the system, permeate all actions of public administration, rendering it ineffective. Under these circumstances, public administration was called upon to reform its bureaucratic dysfunctions in response to new challenges and demands and *to move from public bureaucracy to public management* (Mihalopoulos, 2003)[23] . The NPM trend, bringing practices from the private sector that focus on improving performance, transparency, and accountability, seemed to be the answer to these structural challenges.

The first reform effort to implement methods consistent with those of the NPM was the passing of Law 1943/91 on the "modernization of the organization and operation of public administration," the "upgrading of its personnel," and other related measures[24]. This law provided, among other things, for the promotion of transparency through the publication of administrative actions, a merit-based recruitment system through the reform of the existing system, and the education and training of civil servants with the aim of enhancing productivity, restructuring responsibilities and organizational structures in order to improve them, simplifying procedures for better and faster service to citizens, and establishing committees to monitor the implementation of the law (Rossidis, 2014) .

In the same spirit, Law 2389/00[25], with various provisions for improving the management of local authorities, combating corruption and maladministration through the Body of Inspectors-Auditors for Public Administration (SEEDD), establishing the National Council for Administrative Reform, etc. attempted to incorporate NPM practices and contribute to improving the efficiency of public administration.

One of the most important reform programs for the modernization of public administration, based on the principles of NPM, was the "Politeia" program (Law 2880/01)[26]. This program attempted to introduce the principles of Total Quality Management and Human Resource Management (motivation, evaluation, training, etc.), the use of ICT, the measurement and evaluation of results, the improvement of the quality of services provided, and the promotion of transparency and meritocracy, without, however, achieving the expected results (Rossidis, 2014).

This was followed by a series of administrative reforms reflecting the principles of NPM, which introduced institutions and mechanisms that strengthened meritocracy, transparency, and efficiency in public administration, such as the establishment of ASEP (Law 2190/94) for objective recruitment, the establishment of management by objectives and indicators (Law 3230/04), public-private partnerships (Law 3389/05), the restructuring of local government through the "Kallikratis" reform (Law 3852/10), the establishment of e-government (Law 3979/11), the implementation of new staff evaluation and mobility systems (Law 4369/16), target setting and linking evaluation to rewards (Law 4940/22), and the introduction of bonuses for achieving measurable results (Law 5149/24), marking the gradual transition of Greek public administration to standards of greater efficiency and accountability.

It is evident that attempts have been made from time to time to modernize Greek public administration. The application of the principles and methods of NPM has contributed to the achievement of specific administrative reform objectives (Karkatsoulis, 2004). Despite the positive prospects, the implementation of these principles has been delayed due to resistance to change and the long-standing influence of clientelistic practices, so the expected improvement has not been fully achieved, as reflected in the current quality of public administration and in numerous reports and studies.

Participatory or open governance is one of those issues that is still in progress, and there is a long way to go before it reaches a satisfactory level and a meaningful and intensive dialogue between the state and society is established. However, efforts are being made.

Since 2012, following the fulfilment of specific criteria[27], our country has been participating in the international Open Government Partnership (OGP) initiative, which aims to promote cooperation between governments, the information society, and citizens, to strengthen trust between them, and to ensure the meaningful involvement of all in the formulation of public policies. Based on the strategy it sets out and using various methods and techniques, it contributes to the implementation of the principles of open government, strengthening democracy and achieving better results.

As part of this participation, our country prepares annual Action Plans with specific government commitments, following collaborative formulation and consultation on the proposals. For example, the 5th National Open Government Action Plan 2023-2025, which places great emphasis on the use of ICT to facilitate and enhance openness and citizen engagement, includes commitments to create and make available open data, actions to activate citizen participation in decision-making, an upgraded presentation of the practices of the Parliament for better information, the creation of profiles of the legislative activity of Members of Parliament, etc. The website https://opengovmonitor.gr/5o_ethinko_sxedio_drashs/ presents the relevant information and monitors its implementation.

At the institutional level, citizen participation in decision-making and the exercise of power is primarily provided for in the Constitution, specifically in paragraph 2 of Article 44, which establishes the referendum. It is announced by the President of the Republic and may concern serious national issues or a bill regulating a serious social issue (excluding fiscal issues).

In addition, the possibility of holding referendums is also provided for by the legislature at the local level. Municipalities or regions may hold referendums on any issue, with some exceptions[28], pursuant to Article 133 of Law 4555/18 and in accordance with the procedure laid down in that law. It should be noted that a referendum may also be held at the request of at least 10% of the voters of the local authority.

In addition, citizens are free to participate indirectly in the regulatory process and in the drafting of bills submitted to Parliament through consultation. In Greece, consultation is provided for in Article 61 of Law 4622/19 and is treated as a principle of good lawmaking. According to the law, consultation must precede the passing of any bill, which must be published on the special platform opengov.gr and accept proposals and comments from citizens and interested parties for two weeks.

A very important function of consultation is to partially remedy the democratic deficit that arises from citizens' lack of involvement in decision-making, since the only opportunity they have to express their views is when they vote in elections held every four years. This single participation in public affairs is not sufficient to demonstrate their cooperation, nor does it legitimise the actions of the government, which in the interval between elections produces substantial legislative work—possibly even more than executive work (Rammata, 2021). It is a fact, however, that citizen participation is reduced and undermined by the supremacy of the executive power (Habermas, cited in Rammata, 2021), while the way consultation is currently conducted, as a formal rather than a substantive means, leads to its erosion and devaluation (Rammata, 2021).

The effective implementation of the above-mentioned means of promoting open government and citizen participation could enhance transparency, accountability, and, ultimately, trust in institutions and democracy. For this reason, further administrative reforms are needed to respond to the ever-changing needs of society.

In fact, administrative reform is constantly at the center of politics in Greece, and another reason for this is political succession and intense competition between political forces. As Spanou confirms (2012), *changes in government* have an undeniable impact on reform priorities and the continuity of change. In fact, they are a common way of approaching and understanding them, since the most critical turning points in reforms are largely linked to politics and political choices. He also argues that between 1974 and 2009, i.e. before the outbreak of the fiscal crisis, administrative reform efforts were shaped by the specific characteristics of the competition between the two major political parties, PASOK and New Democracy, which ultimately perpetuated the thorny issues of clientelism and unnecessary reforms that hindered reform (Spanou, 1996).

The crucial role of political culture and political motives in inspiring and driving administrative reforms, which are confrontational and polarizing in the Greek context, is also confirmed by the study by Sotiropoulos & Christopoulos (2017), in the light of polyphony and maladministration. As they point out, incessant legislation (including administrative measures) stems to a large extent from the need of governments and their members to prove that they are doing better and more work than their predecessors, but also to serve, in addition, their client networks by satisfying the demands of favored voters or voter groups, thereby intensifying the clientelistic nature of the state.

The above-mentioned framework for the inspiration and implementation of administrative reforms seems rather dystopian. In a comparative study by the Bertelsmann Stiftung on the "reform capacity"[29] of 31 OECD members, Greece ranked last in 2010 (Kalyvas et al., 2012). However, we must not overlook the fact that over the last fifty years, at least, Greece has undergone significant changes and improvements in various areas (Sotiropoulos D. A., 2021; OECD, 2023), even if these changes did not fully meet the expectations and objectives of the arguments initially put forward. Through many reform initiatives, it has made progress in areas such as transparency ("DIAVGEIA"), citizen services (KEP), meritocratic staffing of the public sector (ASEP), decentralization ("KALLIKRATIS"), combating chronic pathologies of public administration and arbitrariness of political power (Independent Authorities), digital and technological progress (gov.gr, myAADE.gr, interoperability, open data, remote operation and service), etc., without taking into account the fields of social and economic policy.

Moreover, almost in the early years of the transition to democracy, "*the country consolidated its democratic institutions and experienced rapid economic growth - which, after 1990, was higher than the European average - gained full partic-*

ipation in the European integration project and significantly improved its public infrastructure" (Kalyvas et al., 2012, p. 2).

It is clear, therefore, that failures and weaknesses in the reform of the state coexist with successes and progress, and that further improvement and continuous development of Greek public administration is not a utopia. In order to understand more fully the dynamics of this process and to gain a comprehensive understanding of the phenomenon, it is necessary to examine the root causes that led to both the successes and failures of administrative reforms.

5. THE CHALLENGES AND FACTORS INVOLVED IN IMPLEMENTING ADMINISTRATIVE REFORMS

For the reasons analysed in the previous section, administrative reforms have been an important political and mso claanagerial issue since at least the 1960s. Over time, national and global efforts to reform public services have aimed to improve their economy, efficiency, effectiveness, accountability, and responsiveness to citizens and users. Although there have been some successes, overall, these reform initiatives have failed to bring about meaningful change in the impact of public services on users, citizens, and society at large (Osborne S. P., 2020).

The challenges and the causes of success and failure of reforms are a function of the history, culture, values, administrative, regulatory, social, economic, and political environment in which they take place. According to various analysts, the Greek administrative system has particular characteristics, a unique self-referential code, and a turbulent historical background, all of which have shaped the culture and environment of reform efforts.

The organization and functioning of the Greek state and Greek public administration have long been a subject of interest to scholars from various disciplines. It is striking to note, as bibliographic research on the subject progressed, that the need for reform was based on roughly the same reasons as today. At the same time, the proposed changes remain relevant, despite the reform fever that periodically grips the country – to the point of "reform fatigue" – and in stark contrast to the number and frequency of changes attempted since the founding of the Greek state. Numerous studies, reports, analyses by international organizations, domestic committees, experts seem to have been left in some drawers, leading to the reasonable question of whether we ultimately want reform and whether the state is in a position to plan, organize, and implement it effectively.

This analysis provides a brief overview of the reasons for the successful or unsuccessful implementation of administrative reforms, focusing on the investigation of Greek drivers or inhibitors in the process of implementing administrative reforms, starting from their historical, political, and broader social context.

5.1. Historical, Political, and Sociological Approach

Greek public administration has been shaped, to a large extent, by its historical heritage. The Greek state, founded in 1830, was based on the Napoleonic model with an emphasis on legality and standardization. However, this system was not fully aligned with Greek social reality, leading to a combination of formal and informal practices and the maintenance of clientelistic relationships due to party conflicts. In the 20th century, political life was disrupted by monarchical interventions, parliamentary instability, the civil war (1946-49), and the military dictatorship of 1967-74, events that reinforced the state's lack of credibility. Later, the transition to democracy in 1974 brought polarized political confrontations, mainly between New Democracy and PASOK, with the result that any administrative reform was often undermined by political competition (Spanou & Sotiropoulos, 2011).

The historical development and political turmoil that shaped public administration in Greece largely explain the difficulties faced by contemporary administrative reforms, which encounter a multitude of obstacles stemming from institutional, political, economic, and social parameters, often leading to delays, failures, or fragmented implementation of changes. A comprehensive picture of these parameters is provided by the European Commission's report on the Quality of Public Administration (2019). The obstacles mentioned have been grouped and are presented below, based on their nature and impact on administrative reforms[30]:

Institutional and legal difficulties: The complexity of the legislative and regulatory framework is a key problem. Reforms are often limited to amendments to laws that are not accompanied by a substantive strategy, vision, or the appropriate tools for their implementation. Furthermore, the administration often lacks the flexibility or expertise to implement the changes, while the lack of coordination between the actors involved further complicates the situation.

Political will and competition: The absence of strong political will and vision that transcends narrow individual or party interests is a key obstacle. Politicians are often reluctant to support measures that may be considered unpopular, especially when they conflict with the interests of their electoral base and jeopardize their re-election. At the same time, political wrangling and poor competition between parties lead to procrastination and a lack of continuity in reforms.

Administrative and organizational weaknesses: The lack of administrative capacity and adequate resources is another major challenge. Public services often lack the appropriate staff, skills, or infrastructure to support change. Furthermore, complex bureaucratic procedures and resistance to accountability undermine the effectiveness of efforts. Aversion to risk and change reinforces the inability to introduce innovation and change.

Corruption and interest groups: Institutional and systemic corruption acts as an invisible barrier, making it difficult to implement changes that affect vested interests. Interest groups, which often benefit from the status quo, strongly resist any reform that threatens their privileges.

Lack of strategy and social trust: The absence of a clear and long-term vision for reforms limits the possibility of successful implementation. Furthermore, inadequate communication of changes to society, as well as the absence of shared ownership of both the change (in the planning and implementation phases) and its results, lead to mistrust, indifference, and resistance on the part of citizens and stakeholders. The persistent inability to promote change ultimately reinforces social apathy, tolerance of the status quo, and a lack of demand for progress.

External factors and constraints: Pressure from international organizations or other countries to adopt specific reforms can lead to adjustments that do not take local particularities into account. The application of models from other countries without the necessary adaptation to national conditions reinforces inefficiency and resistance.

Economic difficulties and costs: The cost of reforms is a critical parameter. The need for long-term investments, which may not yield immediate results, often discourages decision-making. In addition, fiscal constraints and insufficient resources prevent meaningful support for change.

Sotiropoulos (2007) studied reform developments in Southern European countries and identified eight "conditions" whose non-fulfillment leads to "closed windows of opportunity" for reforms. These conditions are: a) the existence of leaders within the government with a technocratic background and indifference to political costs, b) overcoming the "partisanization" of a reform and the consensus of all political forces in the country on its national value, c) stable political will, support from the entire government and the ruling party, and a reform team with knowledge and an action plan (knowledge, persistence, and vision), d) a clear plan with objectives, a timetable, and specific stakeholders, as well as the impact on them and others, e) gradual changes, to achieve smaller and more flexible reactions, f) the pursuit of consensus and alliances, consultation, and stakeholder participation, g) social support from those classes that benefit from the reform, and h) the appropriate political climate, avoiding contradictions between announcements and actions that undermine the credibility of the reforms. A ninth condition could be added to the above: the impetus for reform and better public administration provided by our country's participation in the EU.

In the context described so far in this chapter, reforms are undermined both by the inherent pathologies of public administration and by the broader environment in which they were attempted. The historical legacy of the Greek state and the political and social context in which reform initiatives are undertaken raise the legitimate question of whether reform of the state is really desirable or whether it is merely announcements made to serve clientelistic relationships or create the impression of productivity.

The answer to this question is, perhaps, the key to understanding the persistent and long-standing failure of administrative reforms. However, in order to provide a substantiated answer, a systematic investigation is required not only of the factors of failure, but also of those that determine success. So what distinguishes successful reforms from unsuccessful ones? In the context of writing this chapter, this question was posed to the participants in the qualitative research, with the results—analyzed in the next section—offering some preliminary insights into the issue.

The question also arises as to whether reforms are designed to manage the increasing complexity of the modern environment and whether they are implemented correctly and in a coordinated manner. The so-called "complex problems" – characterized by uncertainty, complexity, divergent values, and interdependent structures – require coordinated, adaptive, and well-managed solutions, rather than fragmented or superficial approaches (OECD, 2017).

Overall, administrative reforms in Greece are caught in a vicious circle of institutional, political, and social challenges. Overcoming these obstacles requires a holistic approach that includes political will, institutional restructuring, transparency, and strengthening administrative capacity in order to make implementation possible.

Another key factor for the success of administrative reforms is the technical-administrative dimension, i.e., the use of systematic and scientific methodologies for change management. A rational approach to change management can ensure the transition from planning to implementation by effectively addressing the obstacles that arise, as it offers the techniques and mechanisms necessary for the implementation and integration of changes.

5.2. Administrative and Organizational Dimension

The organization and management of reforms have not been seriously addressed to date by the state, the scientific community, or Greek public opinion, even though this is considered an essential dimension. The technical-administrative dimension is central to the transition from the theoretical formulation of policies to their practical implementation, which is usually overlooked in the implementation of Greek administrative reforms, which resemble "*ungoverned ships at sea, with many cap-*

tains, an unknown destination, and a crew that does not know its role" (Papoulias, 2019, p. 187).

Moreover, the implementation stage of administrative reforms is characterized by Caiden (1976) as "the Achilles heel" of the process. He identifies twelve points that lead to failure, including poor initial planning, incorrect diagnosis of the problem, unattainable goals, vague criteria for strategy selection, lack of impact assessment and feedback during implementation, as well as evaluation of individual results, etc.

Effective management of the change, that is the goal of administrative reform, requires the systematic application of scientific methodologies and modern management practices, including careful planning, clear goal setting, stakeholder engagement, and continuous evaluation of results. Change also requires organizational capacity to manage resistance, communication, and resources. When agencies lack a clear strategy or support for implementing these changes, reform often fails to achieve its objectives. Without this holistic approach to change management, reforms risk remaining fragmented, vague, and difficult to implement, while the risk of resistance from within the administration or society intensifies.

Public management is a "great art", a tool for organizing and managing change, but also a tool for improving the lives of employees and citizens. Provided that it is implemented in an appropriate – positive – atmosphere, with the right leadership, i.e. one that has culture, vision and experience, it has been proven to bear rich fruit (Papoulias, 2007). The lack of effective management and change management is a decisive factor in the failure of reforms, as failure to guide and monitor the implementation process renders the changes ineffective.

There is, of course, the view that administrative methods are of little importance and contribution when the reform does not respond to a social demand (Karkatsoulis, 2016) or when there is strong bureaucracy that hinders the momentum of change (Asatryan, Heinemann & Pitlik, 2017), but also when national political cultures, political will, and institutional history are not aligned with the need for state transformation (Pollitt & Bouckaert, 2017) or when the politicization of public administration and the clientelistic relationships that develop within it are ignored.

Effective management and change leadership alone do not constitute a sufficient condition for the success of reforms. It is a multi-dimensional and complex issue that requires a coalition of forces and a holistic approach for efforts to bear fruit. Any administrative reform must take into account the relationship between local and central governments, social, political, and economic pressures, as well as the interaction between theoretical ideas and practical needs that evolve over time Farazmand (1999).

In any case, the importance and necessity of administrative reforms make it essential to mobilize all means to promote their success and lead to the transformation and improvement of the state, including systematic and scientific management methods and, in particular, change management. Moreover, it should not be overlooked that management (must) combine the creativity of art, science, and practice based on empirical learning, rather than standardized and "one-size-fits-all" procedures or analytical methods. In this way, it learns, adapts, and specializes in the circumstances and needs of each case, offering, under certain conditions, the appropriate background, from diagnosis and planning to the implementation of reforms, for a successful transition to the new situation (Papoulias, 2007; Mintzberg, 2004).

5.3 Empirical Approach Through Primary Qualitative Research

The phenomenon of administrative reforms is approached empirically through qualitative research that seeks to bridge the gap between theory and practice in the field of administrative reforms and contributes to the understanding of the complex parameters that influence the implementation of changes in the public sector. Despite the fact that international literature recognizes the importance of context-specific factors in the success or failure of reforms (Pollitt & Bouckaert, 2017), in the Greek case, the relevant research documentation is limited and often fragmentary (Lampropoulou & Oikonomou, 2018).

Drawing on international methodological standards in qualitative research (Flick, 2014; Robson, 2010), the research project was grounded on gathering opinions from experts, executives, and scientists directly involved in the design, implementation, and/or evaluation of reform policies. This strategy is based on analytical generalization, as proposed by Yin (2014) and Flyvbjerg (2006), whereby an in-depth understanding of specific cases can provide interpretative models for broader phenomena. The selection of interviewees through purposive sampling allowed for the formation of an interdisciplinary sample with high empirical validity (Iosifidis, 2017), strengthening the theoretical validity of the research conclusions.

The empirical research component of this study was conducted through nine in-depth, semi-structured interviews with Greek public administration experts and practitioners, carried out between July and September 2024. Participants (N=9; 2 female, 7 male) were purposively selected based on their academic expertise and extensive professional experience in public administration, administrative reforms, and organizational change management. The interviews, each lasting more than 60 minutes and exceeding initial time estimates, employed 16 open-ended questions organized around three thematic areas: (1) the Greek administrative system and its characteristics, (2) change management dimensions and implementation strategies, and (3) human resources and employee receptiveness to reform. Seven interviews were recorded and subsequently transcribed in full; all interviews were accompanied by detailed researcher notes. Data analysis employed thematic coding and qualitative content analysis, identifying convergent patterns, key themes, and theoretical insights aligned with existing international literature on administrative reform implementation barriers and success factors. This methodological approach enables analytical generalization from the Greek case to broader phenomena in public administration reform, as the in-depth understanding of specific contextual factors provides interpretative models applicable to similar institutional settings internationally.

Main Empirical Findings

The findings of the interviews converge on the following main causes of failure of reform efforts, revealing patterns that align with international literature on reform implementation barriers (Brunsson, 2006; Pollitt & Bouckaert, 2017):

a) Lack of human resource involvement and preparation: As the responses show, change is often imposed as an external mandate rather than the result of consultation with stakeholders. Employees have no say in the planning and are rarely prepared for the new operating framework. Managing resistance to change, one of the key areas of change management (Kotter, 2012), is not common practice.
b) Policy discontinuity and lack of a stable administrative strategy: The majority of participants emphasized that the implementation of reforms is closely linked to the political situation and clientelistic interests, while it is rarely part of a long-term administrative plan. Changes in political leadership lead to the reversal, suspension, or partial implementation of interventions. The lack of institutional memory, due to the non-participation of the administration in the reform process and the increase in the number of senior executives with key responsibilities, exacerbates the problems of reform continuity and consistency.
c) Institutional and organizational obstacles: The Greek experience shows that phenomena such as institutional rigidities, centralization, lack of coordination, absence of management knowledge and practices, and meritocracy—characteristics of the Greek administrative system—are significant pathologies that hinder administrative reforms. Almost all participants described the Greek administrative system as clientelistic and excessively centralized. They also emphasized that political leaders maintain tight control over the administration, with the result that the latter is unable to take initiatives and operate strategically.
d) Dominance of informal culture and institutional inertia: As noted in the interviews, one of the most persistent features of Greek administration is the resilience of informal procedures and unofficial networks of influence. Even when institutions change formally, the internal functioning of organizations remains virtually untouched. Participants described several cases of reforms that remained "on paper" because they never managed to influence everyday practice. Instead, they were adapted in such a way as not to disrupt established

routines or upset existing balances. In such cases, institutional change is perceived more as a symbolic act of compliance and less as a real shift in the way the state operates, confirming Brunsson's (2006) analysis of ritualistic reforms.

The culture of public administration is described as introverted, oriented towards maintaining the status quo, with pronounced bureaucracy and fragmented actions. Interviewees refer to an organization that often operates on the basis of personal relationships, informal rules, and shadow procedures, which, although they sometimes facilitate day-to-day operations, also constitute an obstacle to broader change.

e) Multilevel resistance to change: The research documents the existence of multilevel resistance to change, which manifests itself at both the organizational and individual levels, from front-line employees to the administrative and political elites. It usually takes indirect forms, such as delays in implementation, pretextual or strictly linear interpretations of regulations, or even simple indifference. This resistance is not only due to fear or organizational inertia but is also an expression of deep mistrust regarding the real intentions and feasibility of the reforms. It is also fueled by the absence of positive incentives, the prevalence of clientelism, and the constant undermining of the sense of justice, meritocracy, and equality. This attitude is also linked to a broader administrative culture of minimal effort, in which employees wait for orders from political leaders instead of proceeding with the implementation of institutional changes. In such an environment, even willing executives quickly become disillusioned when they find that their actions are hampered by rigid administrative structures, entrenched practices, and powerful conflicting interests.
f) Lack of political will and instrumentalization of reforms: As the interviews show, political leaders approach administrative reform more as a communication management tool than as a necessary and strategic choice for modernizing the state. The relevant announcements are not accompanied by institutional commitments, operational plans, monitoring mechanisms, or adequate resources. On the contrary, they are used to signal a change of course or to gain political capital, without any intention of long-term implementation. The lack of political will to implement reforms and their use as tools for party or personal gain make it impossible for them to be effective and bring about real change.

The findings of the qualitative research, although drawn from the Greek experience, highlight patterns of failure in administrative reforms that are not exclusively domestic, but are part of a broader international debate on the nature, conditions, and limits of reform efforts in the public sector. As international studies show, the successful implementation of reforms depends not only on the quality of the design, but especially on the ability of institutions to integrate changes into existing structures of power, culture, and practice (Pollitt & Bouckaert, 2017).

Using the Greek example, the research documents the need for a model of administrative reform that takes into account the institutional complexity, informal practices, and social and political dynamics that shape the everyday life of public administration.

6. CONCLUSIONS

Administrative reform, as analyzed through the theoretical, comparative, and empirical analysis of this chapter, is a multifaceted and dynamic phenomenon shaped by the intersection of institutional, political, and social conditions. It is not a uniform or neutral undertaking, but a complex and constantly evolving process, influenced by both internal needs and external pressures. As analysed in this chapter, reform initiatives are often launched under pressure from exogenous factors – such as successive crises, international economic requirements, or the need for digital transformation—and are called upon to respond to a complex environment dominated by uncertainty, successive crises, constant technological change, and limited resources. Administrative reforms are a necessary and inevitable step towards modernising and strengthening the effectiveness of public administration and adapting it to this volatile and demanding environment. However, reform cannot be viewed in isolation from the social, institutional, and political conditions of each country, nor can it be based solely on models that are indiscriminately transferred from other administrative traditions.

International experience highlights the need for a new type of reform approach that takes into account institutional peculiarities, existing administrative cultures, management practices, and the limits of political and organizational capacity, continuity, and consistency. Greece is a typical example of a country with a long tradition of announcing reforms, but with limited implementation and effectiveness. Most reforms were adopted under the weight of external circumstances and fiscal pressures, without being accompanied by the necessary administrative capacity, social acceptance, or political continuity. The overall assessment shows that the lack of institutional memory, frequent changes in political leadership, and administrative complexity remain key obstacles to the implementation of stable and sustainable reform policies.

Although a picture of fragmented and incomplete interventions has prevailed over time, experience shows that there have also been moments of substantial institutional progress. Landmark interventions, such as the establishment of the ASEP, the operation of the KEP, the institution of "Diavgeia," or the acceleration of digital transformation over the last five years, demonstrate that systematic effort, when combined with political commitment, adequate tools, and acceptance by the public administration and citizens themselves, can yield measurable and sustainable results. Similarly, experience from health and natural crises has shown that, under pressure, public administration is able to mobilize and incorporate the necessary changes.

In summary, it is clear that administrative reform cannot be approached in a piecemeal or opportunistic manner. It requires institutional memory, consistent and coherent governance, administrative practices grounded in documentation, evaluation, and transparency, as well as a structured and strategic approach to change management within the public sector. Effective change management is not merely supportive but constitutes a core reform technique — essential for navigating resistance, aligning stakeholders, and ensuring the sustainability of transformation efforts. Only under these conditions can reform function as a truly effective tool for transforming the state and rebuilding citizens' trust in public administration.

In conclusion, administrative reform requires, beyond technical tools and regulatory arrangements, a stable political will, institutional consistency, and an administration capable of planning, implementing, and evaluating. Building on positive experiences, avoiding the mechanical transfer of foreign models, and actively involving society are critical factors for the transformation of the state. To be sustainable, reform must become an integral part of a state that responds to the needs of the present and the demands of the future.

REFERENCES

Aphecetche, T., Canton, E., Garrone, M., & Hobza, A. (2022). Understanding the Political Economy of Reforms: Lessons from the EU (Economic Brief 070). Luxembourg: European Commission, Directorate-General for Economic and Financial Affairs. Ανάκτηση 6 20, 2025, από https://economy-finance.ec.europa.eu/system/files/2022-01/eb070_en_political_economy_reforms_0.pdf

Asatryan, Z., Heinemann, F., & Pitlik, H. (2017). 6). Reforming the public administration: The role of crisis and the power of bureaucracy. *European Journal of Political Economy*, *48*, 128–143. DOI: 10.1016/j.ejpoleco.2016.08.004

Beck, U. (1992). *Risk Society Towards a New Modernity*. SAGE Publications.

Brunsson, N. (2006). 9). Administrative reforms as routines. *Scandinavian Journal of Management*, *22*(3), 243–252. DOI: 10.1016/j.scaman.2006.10.007

Caiden, G. (1976). Implementation - the Achilles Heel of Administrative Reform. In *The management of change in goverment* (pp. 142–164). MARTINUS NIJHOFF. DOI: 10.1007/978-94-010-1383-3_6

Cavatorto, S., & La Spina, A. (2020). The Politics of Public Administration Reform in Italy. Cham: The Politics of Public Administration Reform in Italy.

Cheung, A. B., & Low, D. (2023). Crisis management and administrative reforms: lessons from Hong Kong and Singapore. In S. F. Goldfinch (Ed.), Handbook of Public Administration Reform (pp. 182-206). Cheltenham·Northampton: Edward Elgar. DOI: 10.4337/9781800376748.00015

Chiu, M., & Salerno, H. (2019). *Change Change Management. An open-source approach*. Gartner.

Cohen, N. (2023). Public administration reform and political will in cases of political instability: Insights from the Israeli experience. *Public Policy and Administration*, *38*(4), 405–423. DOI: 10.1177/09520767221076059

Cole, A., & Eymeri-Douzans, J.-M. (2010). Introduction: Administrative reforms and mergers in Europe - research questions and empirical challenges. International Review of Administrative Sciences, 76(3), σσ. 395-406. DOI: 10.1177/0020852310373881

Cunha, M. P., & Tsoukas, H. (2015). Reforming the state: Understanding the vicious circles of reform. European Management Journal, 33(4), σσ. 225-229. DOI: 10.1016/j.emj.2015.05.001

Dalakou, V. (2022). Modern Legislation and Administrative Control Institutions: Complementarity with Respect to Ethics and Deontology Rules. In Proceedings of Two-Day Conference: Ethics and Deontology in Public Administration. Necessity and Prospects, 1-2 October, Association of Students PA-EAP (pp. 157-164). Athens: Association of Students PA-EAP.

Dalakou, V. (2022). Digital Transparency and Openness in the Contemporary Regulatory Framework for Digital Governance: Challenges and Opportunities for the Greek Public Administration. Public Administration and Digital Governance, 1, pp. 39-54. Athens: Association of Students of PA-EAP. Retrieved October 2, 2024, from https://heyzine.com/flip-book/ddfb84e80b.html

Dator, J., Pratt, D., & Seo, Y. (2006). *Fairness, Globalization, and Public Institutions. East Asia and Beyond*. University of Hawai'i Press. DOI: 10.2307/j.ctv3zp081

Dolowitz, D., & Marsh, D. (2000). Learning from Abroad: The Role of Policy Transfer in Contemporary Policy-Making. Governance, 13, σσ. 5-23. DOI: 10.1111/0952-1895.00121

European Commission. (2019). The Quality of Public Administration: A Toolbox for Public Administration Professionals (2nd ed.). (F. Hauser, Ed., & A. Karvounis, Trans.) Athens: Ministry of Interior. Retrieved November 26, 2024, from https://www.ypes.gr/wp-content/uploads/2019/12/Q_P_A_Final.pdf

European Commission. (2023c). *Report on Migration and Asylum 2022*. European Commision.

European Commission. (2024). The Digital Decade of Europe: Digital. *Targets, 2030*, •••. Retrieved October 23, 2024, from https://commission.europa.eu/strategy-and-policy/priorities-2019-2024/europe-fit-digital-age/europes-digital-decade-digital-targets-2030_el

European Parliament. (2024). Shaping Digital Transformation: Explaining the EU Strategy. Retrieved October 23, 2024, from https://www.europarl.europa.eu/topics/el/article/20210414STO02010/diamorfosi-psifiakou-metaschimatismou-epexigisi-tis-stratigikis-tis-ee

Farazmand, A. (1999). Administrative reform in global perspectives: A symposium. *International Journal of Public Administration*, *22*(6), 805–816. DOI: 10.1080/01900699908525405

Farazmand, A. (2001). *Administrative Reform in Developing Nations*. Bloomsbury Publishing.

Flick, U. (2014). *An Introduction to Qualitive Research* (5th ed.). SAGE Publications Ltd.

Flyvbjerg, B. (2006). Five misunderstandings about case-study research. Qualitative Inquiry, 12(2), σσ. 219-245. DOI: 10.1177/1077800405284363

Gekas, R., Goupios, G., & Koutsouri, D. (2022). The Reform Technique through the Historical Evolution of Administrative Reforms 1975-2020. Athens: ELIAMEP - E.E.T.A.A.

General Secretariat for Coordination. (2024). Greece 2.0 I National Recovery and Resilience Plan. Retrieved October 23, 2024, from https://gsco.gov.gr/rrp-reforms/

General Secretariat for Coordination. (2024a). National Reform Program. Retrieved October 23, 2024, from https://gsco.gov.gr/nrp/

Gow, J. I. (2012). "Administrative Reform". In L. Côté, & J.-F. Savard (Eds.), Encyclopedic Dictionary of Public Administration. Quebec City: École nationale d'administration publique. Retrieved 9 26, 2024, from https://dictionnaire.enap.ca/Dictionnaire/en/home.aspx

Graziano, P. R., & Vink, M. P. (2013). Europeanization: Concept, Theory, and Methods. In Bulmer, S., & Lequesne, C. (Eds.), *States of the European Union* (2nd ed., pp. 31–56). Oxford University Press.

Inkina, S. (2022). Comparative Administrative Reforms. In Farazman, A. (Ed.), *Global Encyclopedia of Public Administration, Public Policy, and Governance* (pp. 1942–1949). Springer., DOI: 10.1007/978-3-030-66252-3_1276

Kalyvas, S., Pagoulatos, G., & Tsoukas, H. (2012). Introduction. In Kalyvas, S., Pagoulatos, G., & Tsoukas, H. (Eds.), *From Stagnation to Forced Adjustment* (pp. 1–8). Columbia University Press.

Karamanou, A. (2021). Civil Protection and Risk Management: "The Greek Civil Protection System." Athens: EKDDA. Retrieved October 22, 2024, from https://eclass.ekdd.gr/esdda/modules/document/file.php/KZ_AEID_APP107/%CE%95%CE%9D%CE%9F%CE%A4%CE%97%CE%A4%CE%91%206%20%CF%83%CE%B7%CE%BC%CE%B5%CE%B9%CF%8E%CF%83%CE%B5%CE%B9%CF%82.pdf

Karamouzis, N., & Anastasatos, T. (2024, 3). Lessons from the Greek Crisis. Eurobank research. Economy and Markets, 14(1), pp. 1-38. Retrieved 10 25, 2024, from https://www.eurobank.gr/-/media/eurobank/omilos/oikonomikes-analuseis/oikonomiki-epitheorisi/2019/lessons-from-the-greek-crisis.pdf

Karkatsoulis, P. (2001). Governance as Content and as the Decision-Making Process for Public Affairs. Science and Society. *Review of Political and Ethical Theory*, (7), 205–224. DOI: 10.12681/sas.633

Karkatsoulis, P. (2004). *The State in Transition: From "Administrative Reform" and "New Public Management" to "Governance."*. I. Sideris.

Karkatsoulis, P. (2016). Administrative Reform in Greece: Public administration evolves through self-reflection – not borrowed identities. In Dimitropoulos, G., Gromitsaris, A., & Schulte, M. (Eds.), *State Reform for a Better Europe* (pp. 113–160). Duncker & Humblot.

Karkatsoulis, P. (2023a). *Crisis and Disaster Management in the Example of Civil Protection*. Ellinobooks.

Katsimardos, P., & Bouas, K. (2013). Strategic Analysis and Evaluation of Large-Scale Reform Programs: "The Memorandum as a Policy Tool." Athens: Institute for Regulatory Policy Research.

Killian, J., & Eklund, N. (2008). Handbook of administrative reform. An international perspective. Boca Rayton: CRC Press-Taylor & Francis Group. DOI: 10.1201/9780849380662

Konstantinidou, A. (2020). The Role of E-Governance and ICT in the Service of the Reform Framework of the Greek Public Administration. Public Administration. Athens: Panteion University of Social and Political Sciences. Retrieved September 26, 2024, from https://www.didaktorika.gr/eadd/bitstream/10442/48868/1/48868.pdf

Kotarski, K. (2023, 4 10). The New Era of Polycrisis and How to Tackle it. DOI: 10.53121/ELFFEUJ3

Lampropoulou, M., & Oikonomou, G. (2018). Theoretical models of public administration and patterns of state reform in Greece. International Review of Administrative Sciences, 84(1), σσ. 101-121. DOI: 10.1177/0020852315611219

Lapuente, V., & Van de Walle, S. (2020). The effects of new public management on the quality of public services. *Governance: An International Journal of Policy, Administration and Institutions, 33*(3), 461–475. DOI: 10.1111/gove.12502

Lindquist, E. A. (2022, 8 29). The digital era and public sector reforms: Transformation or new tools for competing values? Canadian Public Administration, 65(3), σσ. 547-568. DOI: 10.1111/capa.12493

Lynn, L. E. (2001). Globalization and Administrative Reform: What is Happening in Theory? Public Management Review, 3(2), σσ. 191-208. DOI: 10.1080/14616670010029584

Maggeti, M., & Trein, P. (2021). 3). More is less: Partisan ideology, changes of government, and policy integration reforms in the UK. *Policy and Society*, *40*(1), 79–98. DOI: 10.1080/14494035.2021.1908673

Maistros, P. G. (2009). *The Three Waves of Public Administration Reforms in Greece* [1975-2015+]. Papazisis Editions.

Makrydimitris, A. (2004). *Approaches to Organization Theory* (2nd ed.). Kastaniotis Editions.

Michalopoulos, N. (2003). *From Public Bureaucracy to Public Management*. Papazisis Editions.

Mintzberg, H. (2004). *Managers Not MBAs: A Hard Look at the Soft Practice of Managing and Management Development*. Berrett-Koehler Publishers.

Nikitas, V., & Vasilopoulou, V. (2022). Public Administration Reforms in Greece during the Economic Adjustment Programmes. Brussels: European Commission. Ανάκτηση 10 25, 2024, από https://economy-finance.ec.europa.eu/document/download/97fb3144-72fb-4ec6-aeef-f35edfdf4292_en?filename=dp167_en.pdf

Nissim, C. (2023). Public administration reform and political will in cases of political instability: Insights from the Israeli experience. *Public Policy and Administration*, *38*(4), 405–423. DOI: 10.1177/09520767221076059

OECD. (2010). *Making reform happen: Lessons from OECD countries*. OECD Publishing.

OECD. (2017). Systems Approaches to Public Sector Challenges-Working with Change. Observatory of Public Sector Innovation in the Public Sector Reform Division. Paris: OECD. Ανάκτηση 07 29, 2024, από https://oecd-opsi.org/wp-content/uploads/2018/07/Systems-Approaches-to-Public-Sector-Challenges_Working-with-Change.pdf

OECD. (2021). *Government at a Glance 2021*. OECD Publishing.

OECD. (2023). *Governance at a glance 2023*. OECD Publishing.

OECD. (2024). *2023 OECD Digital Government Index: Results and key findings*. OECD Publishing., DOI: 10.1787/1a89ed5e-

OECD. (2024a). OECD Survey on Drivers of Trust in Public Institutions 2024 Results - Country Notes: Greece. Paris: OECD. Retrieved 9 9, 2024, from https://www.oecd.org/en/publications/oecd-survey-on-drivers-of-trust-in-public-institutions-2024-results-country-notes_a8004759-en/greece_56edc018-en.html

OECD. (2024b). Public governance and administration reforms. Retrieved 10 5, 2024, from https://www.oecd.org/en/topics/sub-issues/public-governance-and-administration-modernisation.html

OGP. (2024). Joining OGP. Ανάκτηση 10 29, 2024, από https://www.opengovpartnership.org/process/joining-ogp/

Ongardo, E. (2014). The relationship between the new European governance emerging from the fiscal crisis and administrative reforms: Qualitatively different, quantitatively different, or nothing new? A plea for a research agenda. Administrative Culture, 15(1), σσ. 10-20. Ανάκτηση 10 6, 2024, από https://www.researchgate.net/publication/286111934_The_relationship_between_the_new_European_governance_emerging_from_the_fiscal_crisis_and_administrative_reforms_Qualitatively_different_quantitatively_different_or_nothing_new_A_plea_for_a_research_ag

Ongaro. (2010). The Napoleonic Administrative Tradition and Public Management Reform in France, Greece, Italy, Portugal and Spain. Στο M. Painter, & G. B. Peters (Επιμ.), Tradition and Public Administration (σσ. 174-190). London: Palgrave Macmillan. DOI: 10.1057/9780230289635_13

Osborne, D., & Gaebler, T. (1992). *Reinventing Government: How the Entrepreneurial Spirit is Transforming the Public Sector*. Addison-Wesley Publishing Inc., DOI: 10.2307/3381012

Osborne, S. P. (2020). *Public Service Logic: Creating Value for Public Service Users, Citizens, and Society Through Public Service Delivery*. Routledge. DOI: 10.4324/9781003009153

Papoulias, D. B. (2007). Gold Is the Public Sector: Rhetoric and Reality of Reforms. Athens: Bookstore "ESTIAS".

Papoulias, D. B. (2019). *How Reforms Are Accomplished*. Alexandria Editions.

Pinheiro, R., Geschwind, L., Hansen, H. F., & Pulkkinen, K. (2019). *Reforms, Organizational Change and Performance in Higher Education. A Comparative Account from the Nordic Countries*. Palgrave Macmillan. DOI: 10.1007/978-3-030-11738-2

Pollitt, C., & Bouckaert, G. (2017). *Public Management Reform: A Comparative Analysis – Into the Age of Austerity*. Oxford University Press.

Rammata, M. (2011). *Modern Greek Public Administration: Between Bureaucracy and Management.* Kritiki.

Rammata, M. (2018). Reform Attempts in the Greek Public Administration. Theory and Practice of Administrative Law(8-9), pp. 708-721. Retrieved October 8, 2024, from https://www.academia.edu/37631851

Rammata, M. (2021). *Public Policies: Citizens and Deliberation in Greece and Abroad.* Nomiki Bibliothiki.

Randma-Liiv, T., & Kickert, W. (2017, 3 15). The Impact of Fiscal Crisis on Public Administration Reforms in Europe. Journal of Comparative Policy Analysis: Research and Practice, 19(2), σσ. 1387-6988. DOI: 10.1080/13876988.2017.1286781

Robinson, M. (2015). From Old Public Administration to the New Public Service: Implications for Public Sector Reform in Developing Countries. Heng Mui Keng Terrace: UNDP.

Robson, C. (2010). Η έρευνα του πραγματικού κόσμου. Ένα μέσο για κοινωνικούς επιστήμονες και επαγγελματίες ερευνητές (2η εκδ.). Αθήνα: Gutemberg.

Rossidis, I. (2014). *Applications of Business Management in the Greek Public Administration* (1st ed.). A. Stamoulis.

Rossidis, I., & Belias, D. (2020). Combining Strategic Management with Knowledge Management: Trends and International Perspectives. International Review of Management and Marketing, 10(3), σσ. 39-45. DOI: 10.32479/irmm.9621

Rossidis, I., & Belias, D. (2021). Evolution of e-Governance in the Era of the Pandemic. Will the Crisis Become an Opportunity? The Cases of Cyprus and Greece. The Cyprus Review, 33(1), σσ. 37-66. Ανάκτηση 10 26, 2024, από https://cyprusreview.org/index.php/cr/article/view/775/627

Rossidis, I., Belias, D., & Aspridis, G. (2023). *Change Management and Leadership.* Tziola Publications.

Schomaker, R. M., & Bauer, M. W. (2020). What Drives Successful Administrative Performance during Crises? Lessons from Refugee Migration and the Covid-19 Pandemic. Public Administration Review, 80(5), σσ. 845-850. DOI: 10.1111/puar.13280

Sotiropoulos, D. A. (2007). *State and Reform in Contemporary Southern Europe: Greece-Spain-Italy-Portugal.* Potamos.

Sotiropoulos, D. A. (2021). Public Administration in the Post-Covid Era. Athens: diaNEOsis.

Sotiropoulos, D. A., & Christopoulos, L. (2017, November). Multiplicity, Maladministration and Bureaucracy in Greece: Analysis of Past Failures and Proposals for Remedial Interventions. Athens: diaNEOsis.

Spanou, C. (1996). 1). Penelope's suitors: Administrative modernisation and party competition in Greece. *West European Politics*, *19*(1), 97–124. DOI: 10.1080/01402389608425123

Spanou, C. (2012). The Quandary of Administrative Reform: Institutional and Performance Modernization. In Kalyvas, S., Pagoulatos, G., & Tsoukas, H. (Eds.), *From Stagnation to Forced Adjustment* (pp. 171–194). Columbia University Press.

Spanou, C. (2020). External influence on structural reform: Did policy conditionality strengthen reform capacity in Greece? *Public Policy and Administration*, *35*(2), 135–157. DOI: 10.1177/0952076718772008

Spanou, C., & Sotiropoulos, D. A. (2011). The Odyssey of Administrative Reforms in Greece, 1981–2009: A Tale of Two Reform Paths. *Public Administration*, *89*(3), 723–737. DOI: 10.1111/j.1467-9299.2011.01914.x

Tasiopoulos, S. (2021). General Presentation and Public's Sector Reforms in Greece. Ανάκτηση από https://site.imodev.org/nos-activites/europe/grece/general-presentation-and-publics-sector-reforms-in-greece

Tsagdi, G. (2024). Public Value: A New Governance perspective within the Parent Ministry-Agency context. Athens: Athens University of Economics and Business. Retrieved 10 7, 2024, from https://www.didaktorika.gr/eadd/bitstream/10442/56629/1/56629.pdf

Tsekos, Th. (2021). Introduction: From One Crisis to the Next. In Barouxis, Ch., Kakepaki, M., Saris, N., Tramontanis, A., & Tsekeris, K. (Eds.), *The Political Portrait of Greece II: Stakes and Challenges* (pp. 11–36). National Centre for Social Research., DOI: 10.17902/9789606834462

UNDP. (2015). *Public Administration Reform Practice Note*. UNDP.

UNDP/BDP/CDG. (2006). *Institutional Reform and Change Management*. UNDP.

Vittou, F. (2023, October 18). Ways of Strengthening and Reforming National Public Administrations by the European Union. Retrieved October 28, 2024, from https://odeth.eu/

Yamamoto, H. (2003). New Public Management - Japan's Practice. Tokyo: Institute for International Policy Studies. Retrieved 7 2, 2025, from https://npi.or.jp/en/research/data/bp293e.pdf

Yankelovich, D. (2015). *Wicked problems, workable solutions: lessons from a public life*. Rowman & Littlefield.

Yin, R. K. (2014). *Case Study Research: Design and Methods* (5th ed.). SAGE Publications, Inc.

ENDNOTES

1 As wicked problems, complex, complicated, or difficult to solve, as they have been translated into Greek, "*...they are characterized, according to Rittel and Webber (1973, pp. 155-169) as complex public problems with limited agreement on their meaning, with differences in the values and perceptions of those involved regarding their nature and how to deal with them, with many competing interests involved in their handling and their consequences, multiple causes that are not easily identified or understood, complex technical aspects that generate uncertainty in their handling, as well as institutional complexity and extensive inter-agency responsibilities. Intractable problems usually fall within several sectoral fields at the same time and require planners and decision-makers to set and achieve different objectives in parallel*" (Tsekos, 2021) . Such problems include corruption in public administration, asylum and immigration policy, the environmental crisis, etc.

2 Source:(OECD, 2024 b)

3 These are the International Monetary Fund, the European Commission, and the European Central Bank.

4 Source: (Rossidis, 2014, p. 71) [51] See, for example: (Chiu & Salerno, 2019; UNDP/BDP/CDG, 2006)

6 The accumulation of reforms occurs without previous regulations being easily abolished, intensifying the phenomenon of "policy accumulation" (Fernández-I-Marín et al., 2024).

7 For an extensive list, see, for example: (Maistros, 2009, pp. 152-160) . Specifically in the field of decentralization and local government, see (Gekas, Goupios, & Koutsouri, 2022) . According to Karkatsoulis (2012), between 1975 and 2005, 3,430 laws and a total of 171,500 regulations were produced (https://www.blod.gr/lectures/kratos-diafthora-thesmoi-apo-tin-ptosi-stin-anorthosi-stroggylo-trapezi-me-thema-dimosios-tomeas/).

8 That is, between 1975 and 1985, approximately.

9 It is rather discouraging that today we are returning to the same need for democratic and good governance, enriched, however, by the need for broader participation of the KtP in governance (OECD, 2024 a) .

10 Law 2344, "Organisation of civil protection and other provisions", Government Gazette A'212/11.10.1995.

11 Law 5013, "*Multilevel governance, risk management in the public sector and other* provisions," Government Gazette A 12/19.01.2023. See relevant section.

12 Part I of Law 4727/20 "*Digital Governance (Transposition into Greek Law of Directive (EU) 2016/2102 and Directive (EU) 2019/1024) Electronic Communications (Transposition into Greek Law of Directive (EU) 2018/1972) and other* provisions" (Government Gazette A 184/23-9-20) was the central law for digital governance in our country and the first to bring together in a single text provisions that were previously scattered across various sources of primary and secondary law, while also introducing new regulatory provisions (Dalakou, 2022) .

13 Law 4807, "*Institutional framework for teleworking, provisions for public sector human resources and other urgent* regulations," Government Gazette A 96/11.6.2021. Teleworking in the private sector has been institutionalized since 2010, with Law 3846, "*Guarantees for occupational safety and other* provisions," Government Gazette A' 66/11.05.2010.

14 Law 4636 "*On International Protection and other* provisions" (Government Gazette A' 169/01-11-2019 and Corrections of errors Government Gazette A' 173/05-11-2019), as replaced by Law 4939/22 "*Ratification of the Code of Legislation on the reception, international protection of third-country nationals and stateless persons and temporary protection in the event of a mass influx of displaced* foreigners," Government Gazette A 111/10.6.2022.

15 Defined by the EU as "*... the penetration of digital technologies in businesses and the impact of technologies on* society" (European Parliament, 2024) .

16 Ministerial Decision 120301 EX 2021 - Government Gazette 2894/B/5-7-2021 (AI Edited in English).

17 Despite efforts and significant progress, however, Greece continues to lag behind other EU Member States in terms of digital public services, ranking 24th in the DESI 2023 index and remaining below the European average in almost all public service digitization indicators, according to the DESI 2023 index (European Commission, 2023). As recommended in the relevant EU

reports, it must accelerate the implementation of its strategy and expand its successful applications.

18 With a view to improving efficiency, Laws 4325/2015 on combating bureaucracy and e-government measures, 4354/2015 on the new salary system for civil servants, 4369/2016 on the new evaluation system, and 4440/2016 on the mobility of civil servants (Tasiopoulos, 2021) .

19 Such as Directives 2014/24/EU and 2014/25/EU, 89/665/EEC & 29/13/EC, which were transposed into national law by Law 4412/16.

20 Detailed recommendations per country can be found here: https://ec.europa.eu/economy_finance/country-specific-recommendations-database/

21 For the period 2021-2027, more than €11 million will be allocated to fund actions to improve the digital services of businesses and 22,500 public bodies.

22 One such initiative is the technical support project "PACE – Public Administration Cooperation Exchange), under which meetings have already been held between officials from the Ministry of the Interior and their counterparts from other Member States (Vittou, 2023), as well as the European Commission's ComPAct initiative to create a common European administrative space (see https://reform-support.ec.europa.eu/public-administration-and-governance-coordination/enhancing-european-administrative-space-compact_en).

23 Their differences were summarized by Rossidis, Belias, & Aspridis(2023). See Appendix 2.

24 Law 1943/91 *"Modernization of the organization and operation of public administration, upgrading of its personnel, and other related* provisions," Government Gazette A' 50/11.4.1991

25 Law 2839/2000, *"Regulations on matters of the Ministry of the Interior, Public Administration and Decentralization and other* provisions," Government Gazette A'196/12.9.2000.

26 Law 2880, *"POLITEIA Program for the reform and modernization of public administration and other provisions,"* Government Gazette A' 9/30.01.2001.

27 To become a member, a country must meet specific criteria and then approve the OGP's "Open Government Declaration." Specifically, it must receive a satisfactory score in four areas: fiscal transparency, access to information, disclosure of public officials' assets, and citizen participation. In addition, it must be assessed as adequate in the Values Check, i.e., it must score at least three points in at least one of the indicators "Entry and exit of civil society

organizations" or "Repression of civil society organizations, as measured by the V-Dem Institute's "Dataset on Democracy" indicator (OGP, 2024).

28 Excluded are those relating to national security, foreign or immigration policy, the interpretation and application of international treaties, individual and social rights, freedom of religious conscience and worship, or the institutional organisation of all known religions, the financial management of local authorities, the imposition of fees, and the administrative division of the country (par. 1, Article 133, Law 4555/18, "Kleisthenes Program," Government Gazette A' 133/19.07.2018).

29 In other words, the ability to change, "*...the ability to successfully make significant deviations from the existing* situation" (Peters, 1996: 9, cited in (Spanou, 2020) . In the context of a fiscal consolidation program, it refers to the ability to comply and achieve objectives.

30 See the table with the parameters in Annex 4 for details.

Chapter 2
The Evolution of Administrative Models in the Public Sector

Ioannis Rossidis
http://orcid.org/0000-0003-0240-2241
Department of Public Administration, Panteion University, Greece

Vassilis Kefis
Department of Public Administration, Panteion University, Greece

Stavroula Ktistaki
Panteion University, Greece

Evangelia Balta
Department of Public Administration, Panteion University, Greece

ABSTRACT

This chapter examines the evolution of administrative models in the public sector, from Weberian bureaucracy to modern hybrid schemes. Bureaucracy is defined as a model that provided stability and legitimacy, but its rigidity led to the gradual emergence of modern administrative approaches such as New Public Management (NPM), which introduced private economic criteria and emphasized efficiency and effectiveness. Despite its innovative perspective, NPM was criticized for limiting its social and democratic dimension. Public governance emerged as a response, emphasizing cooperation, multi-level policymaking and the participation of citizens and stakeholders. Following this evolution, hybrid models such as the Neo-Weberian State, New Public Governance, New Public Service and the theory of Public Value

DOI: 10.4018/979-8-3373-3526-1.ch002

attempt to combine elements of legitimacy, efficiency and social legitimation. The analysis demonstrates that administrative reform is not a linear process of model replacement, but a perpetual process of overlaps and adaptations.

1. INTRODUCTION

The evolution of public sector management models - from bureaucracy to forms of governance - is one of the defining processes of transformation of public administration worldwide in recent decades (Rossidis, 2014). This transition, which is linked to the trends of New Public Management and Public Governance, has been significantly accelerated by the rise of digital public administration, public value creation and multi-level governance.

Contemporary studies on digital era governance (DEG) identify the initial importance of three components: reintegration, needs-based holism, and digitization, elements that now shape the framework of public action. Furthermore, a systematic review shows that digital governance is moving from simple service provision to active collaboration and citizen participation, promoting accountability, transparency and representation (collaborative governance) (Mihiotis et al., 2023).

Of particular importance was the contribution of e-governance to the creation of public value by contributing to the improvement of services provided, achieving high levels of efficiency and effectiveness, establishing trust on the part of citizens and generally promoting well-being (Twizeyimana & Andersson, 2019; Rossidis et al., 2020). Furthermore, it is noted that the use of digital tools, open data and participatory platforms strengthens citizen trust and promotes intergovernmental transparency (Manoharan et al., 2022).

The Greek experience is of particular interest: the institution of Citizen Service Centers (CSCs) and new initiatives for digital service evaluation highlight the trend towards more functional, accessible, efficient and transparent administrative practices (Ministry of Digital Governance, 2025). At the same time, administrative reforms such as the "Cleisthenes Program I" (Law 4555/2018) strengthened local self-government, representation and decision-making through consultation processes (2018–2019). Furthermore, the legislation on the Executive State (Law 4622/2019) introduced new frameworks for governance, transparency and organization of the central state.

Finally, studies on organizational culture in the Greek public administration point out that there are still difficulties in cultivating a modern, effective and consensual work environment, the adoption of characteristics of New Public Management and e-governance is necessary for the restructuring of administrative institutions (Aspridis & Pouliana 2021; Katsimardos et al., 2017).

2. HISTORICAL EVOLUTION OF ADMINISTRATIVE THEORIES IN THE PUBLIC SECTOR

2.1 Traditional Administrative Models

Public administration has historically developed with the Weberian bureaucratic model as its reference point. Weber (1978) defined bureaucracy as the most rational form of power, based on legal-rational legitimacy. Its main characteristics include strict hierarchy, clear distinction of duties, standardization of procedures and professional neutrality of civil servants. The aim of this model was to remove administrative functions from personal/client relationships and arbitrary practices, ensuring equal treatment of citizens and stability in the handling of public affairs. The Weberian approach was the theoretical starting point for the development of most administrative systems in Europe. In the northern and Anglo-Saxon countries, the model was translated into administrations that emphasized efficiency, professional training and institutional autonomy. In contrast, in the countries of southern Europe, such as France, Italy, Portugal and Greece, the Weberian model focused on legal formalism, centralization and ensuring equality through uniform rules (Ongaro, 2010; Lampropoulou & Oikonomou, 2021).

The Greek administration was formed with these characteristics, but it presents particularities that stem from its historical formation (Kefis et al., 2014). The establishment of an incomplete administrative system, the absence of a philosophy of technocratic professionalism in the early years of the Greek state, the delayed institutional maturation and the close intertwining of political and administrative personnel led to a particular type of "formally bureaucratic but essentially clientelist" system (Spanou, 2018). Institutional discontinuity and the lack of administrative capacity prevented the establishment of a stable organizational culture.

Criticism of the traditional model focused mainly on the rigidity, the difficulty of adapting to new social needs, the inability to promote innovation as well as the limited adaptability of bureaucratic administration in the context of dynamic, complex and uncertain administrative environments (Pollitt & Bouckaert, 2017; Peters, 2021; Belias et al., 2025). In the Greek case, these weaknesses were more pronounced due to the combination of institutional inadequacies and cultural factors, resulting in the public administration reproducing a vicious cycle of piecemeal reforms and institutional instability (Lampropoulou & Oikonomou, 2021).

2.2 Economic and Management Models

From the 1970s onwards, the traditional bureaucratic model began to be strongly challenged, as the expansion of the welfare state, budgetary pressures and generally increased demands from citizens highlighted the need for higher levels of efficiency. The analyses of New Institutional Economics (North, 1990) and Public Choice (Niskanen, 1971) provided new tools for investigating the scientific field of public administration. The Public Choice approach highlighted the phenomenon of the "budget-maximizing bureaucrat", that is, the bureaucrat who seeks the growth of his organization at the expense of efficiency. New Institutional Economics, on the other hand, emphasized the importance of institutions as constraints on the action of actors, influencing reform strategies at the international level.

In this context, the New Public Management (NPM) emerged, which promoted the introduction of principles and techniques of private management in the public sphere. The basic principles of NPM were: decentralization, the introduction of efficiency and effectiveness measurement systems, the improvement of the quality of services provided, the promotion of economy, the development of competitive conditions, the reduction of the citizen to a customer (Hood, 1991; Pollitt & Bouckaert, 2017). NPM has been a dominant example of reform at the international level for at least two decades, radically changing the organization and operation of many administrations.

The case of Greece presents different characteristics. As Lampropoulou and Oikonomou (2021) point out, the integration of NPM elements occurred late and mainly under the pressure of European integration. The initiatives focused on piecemeal measures, such as the establishment of new citizen service agencies, the attempt at decentralization and the introduction of personnel evaluation. However, the absence of a strategic plan, limited institutional capacity and the resilience of the clientelistic system did not allow the establishment of a stable reform perspective. Despite the significant benefits brought by the implementation of NPM, several points of strong criticism are also presented. O'Flynn (2021) underlines that the logic of business management undermined the social role of public administration, while studies at the European level show that the excessive focus on performance measurements and indicators led to a partial "transformation of the end into a means" (Pollitt & Bouckaert, 2017). In Greece, the partial adoption of NPM demonstrated the difficulties of adapting international standards to institutional environments with different traditions and limited administrative capacities (Kefis, 1998).

2.3 The Rise of Public Governance

The challenge to NPM and the search for new models led to the rise of the concept of public governance. The public governance model is not limited to the narrow public sector, but extends to networks of cooperation between the state, the private sector, civil society and international organizations (Rhodes, 2017; Klijn & Koppenjan, 2016). This specific administrative approach reflects the complexity and interdependence that characterize modern societies, emphasizing participation, transparency, multi-level governance and accountability.

Governance as a term has been associated with various versions: good governance (OECD, 2015), digital governance, network governance and interactive governance, with corporate governance as a starting point. All these approaches focus on the need to go beyond bureaucratic and hierarchical logic, recognizing that public policies can no longer be designed and implemented exclusively by the state but should be linked to a broader social consensus. The Greek experience reflects a partial uptake of these approaches. Since the 1990s, independent authorities have been established, transparency policies have been promoted and e-governance tools have been introduced (Spanou, 2018). Despite these initiatives, the lack of institutional capacity, the lack of strategic targeting and the limited participatory culture prevented the full consolidation of the governance logic, which was often limited to a formal level.

2.4 Hybrid Models

Recent literature focuses on hybrid models that attempt to synthesize elements of previous approaches. The New Public Governance (NPG) emphasizes collaboration and polycentricity, recognizing that public administration is a product of the interaction of many actors (Osborne, 2010). The New Public Service (NPS) emphasizes the value of serving the collective interest and the active participation of citizens, in contrast to technocratic or entrepreneurial logic (Denhardt & Denhardt, 2015). The Neo-Weberian State (NWS) seeks to combine the stability and legitimacy of bureaucracy with modern demands for efficiency, transparency and accountability (Pollitt & Bouckaert, 2017). Finally, public value theory focuses on legitimation through social deliberation and the production of value for society as a whole (Moore, 2014; O'Flynn, 2021).

In the Greek case, hybrid models have found some applications, mainly through the creation of institutions such as KEPs, the development of e-governance policies and the enhancement of transparency. However, these initiatives have remained fragmented, without constituting a comprehensive reform strategy. The result is an administrative system that can be considered an alloy of multiple models, without fully adopting any of them (Lampropoulou & Oikonomou, 2021).

3. FROM BUREAUCRACY TO NEW PUBLIC MANAGEMENT

Bureaucratic administration was the dominant administrative model for much of the 20th century, based on the principle of legality, the observance of a strict hierarchy and the application of a high level of standardization (Weber, 1978; Peters, 2021).

Despite its undeniable contribution to the formation of a climate of administrative discipline, from the 1980s onwards the increasing complexity of societies, budgetary pressures and the need for flexibility highlighted the multifaceted and significant weaknesses of the model (Pollitt & Bouckaert, 2017). The emphasis on following the process instead of focusing on the result, the centralized decision-making with obvious elements of time lags and the difficulty of adapting to dynamic environments were considered significant obstacles to the functionality of state administration.

The welfare state crises, the economic stagnation of the 1970s and the rise of neoliberal policies (such as those implemented by Thatcher) created the conditions for the search for new organizational models. Traditional bureaucracy began to appear inadequate not only in terms of efficiency, but also in relation to social demands for more transparency and accountability (Rhodes, 2017).

New Public Management (NPM) emerged in the 1980s as a response to the weaknesses of bureaucracy. This theory draws on Public Choice and New Institutional Economics, promoting the notion that administrative institutions should operate with private economic criteria of efficiency and competition similar to those of the market (Niskanen, 1971; North, 1990).

Hood (1991) described NPM through principles such as:

- decentralization of powers and responsibilities,
- separation of strategic and operational/executive functions
- cost control and evaluation of efficiency of services and policies introduction of principles of organization of private enterprises
- flexibility of management of public bodies
- introduction of conditions of competition
- strengthening of accountability of administrative units
- acknowledgement of the citizen as a "client"

The adoption of NPM at the international level was impressively extensive. Countries such as the United Kingdom, New Zealand, Australia and later the Scandinavian countries introduced radical reforms based on this logic (Pollitt & Bouckaert, 2017). Indicatively, the Thatcher government in the United Kingdom, promoted the extensive separation and reduction of public services, privatization and the emphasis on measuring the performance of organizations. In New Zealand, NPM led to one of the most radical reform programs, with the contracting out of almost all public services and institutional autonomy of the executive agencies, providing them with high levels of administrative freedom. Although NPM was introduced as a universal model, its implementation varied significantly depending on the national culture and existing administrative infrastructures. In the Anglo-Saxon countries, a more "clean" model prevailed with extensive use of privatization and the exploitation of outsourcing services. In Northern Europe, NPM was combined with the strong presence of policy networks and welfare systems, leading to more balanced practices (Christensen & Lægreid, 2020). In Continental Europe, reforms were more limited, with a dominant goal of modernization through efficiency and effectiveness tools (according to the private sector model), with less emphasis on privatization programs (Pollitt & Bouckaert, 2017). Of course, the adoption of NPM did not necessarily mean that the use of the bureaucratic system was discontinued. In most cases, it functioned as a process of "hybrid systems", where traditional administrative features coexist with new forms of management (O'Flynn, 2021). Thus, at the international level, NPM did not completely replace bureaucracy, but reshaped/evolved/supplemented it, creating new balances between legitimacy, efficiency and accountability.

The application of NPM principles contributed to the introduction of performance measurement and effectiveness control mechanisms (in combination with traditional legality controls), to the improvement of levels of efficiency, effectiveness and cost-effectiveness and to the strengthening of accountability (Christensen & Lægreid, 2020, Belias et al., 2025). On the other hand, it provoked criticism for the limitation of the democratic dimension of the administration, the possible destruction of values that the State should advocate, the overestimation of indicators at the expense of the real mission of the services and the strengthening of inequality in access to public goods (O'Flynn, 2021). This criticism has led to the search for new hybrid models, such as the Neo-Weberian State, New Public Governance and Public Value theory, which seek to synthesize the advantages of bureaucracy and NPM with more participatory and socially sensitive approaches (Osborne, 2010; Denhardt & Denhardt, 2015).

4. THE EMERGENCE OF PUBLIC GOVERNANCE

The gradual exhaustion of the potential of New Public Management (NPM) and the growing criticism that gradually developed, led to the emergence of a new theoretical and practical model: public governance. Public governance emerged as a response to the shortcomings of NPM, focusing not only on efficiency and performance measurement, but mainly on collaboration, participation and transparency (Pollitt & Bouckaert, 2017; O'Flynn, 2021).

This change reflected the increasing complexity of societies and the need to go beyond the central role of the state. In the new context, the state is not considered the sole policy-making and implementation agency, but an important (but no longer exclusive) actor in an environment of networks that include civil society organizations, private businesses, and international organizations (Rhodes, 2017; Klijn & Koppenjan, 2016).

The theory of public governance is not unified, but includes various approaches and versions. The main features of this model are:

- multi-level governance, where decisions are made at national, regional and international levels (Hooghe & Marks, 2016)
- collaborative management and development of policy networks (network governance), in which public and private actors participate (Klijn & Koppenjan, 2016)
- delegation of responsibilities to the private sector and civil society (Belias et al., 2025)
- emphasis on transparency, accountability and citizen participation, which are indicators of good governance (OECD, 2015)
- integration of new technologies, which facilitate e-governance and enhance accessibility and interaction (Manoharan et al., 2022; Twizeyimana & Andersson, 2019)
- the evaluation of services & policies based on their results (Rossidis, 2014)

In contrast to NPM, where the focus is on the "citizen-client" and cost-effectiveness, governance promotes the search for collective solutions through collaboration and participation, emphasizing the participation of citizens and actors in the design, implementation and evaluation of policies.

The concept of governance takes different forms and interpretations at the international level. In the European Union, multi-level governance refers to a complex process of shaping and implementing public policy at the local, regional, national and supranational levels in which individual actors coexist and interact in the decision-making process (Hooghe & Marks, 2016). In Northern Europe, governance is often identified with collaborative models of policy-making that incorporate strong participation of social partners through consultation processes. In Anglo-Saxon countries, governance has been associated with the effort to integrate market mechanisms and social networks into a more balanced system, taking into account economic dimensions and private economic criteria (Christensen & Lægreid, 2020).

Also important has been the emergence of "digital governance", which is based on the use of digital technologies in combination with organizational and administrative adjustments aimed at improving transparency, participation and efficiency (Manoharan et al., 2022, Rossidis et al., 2023). Correspondingly, the approach of "good governance" was considered important, adopted by international organizations (OECD, 2015; UNDP, 2019) and includes principles such as legitimacy, transparency, accountability and efficiency. An approach that, together with digital governance, complemented/framed the broader administrative model of public governance to a very large extent.

Despite its significant contribution to the evolution of administrative systems in the public sector, public governance has received considerable criticism. Polycentricity and the development of complex policy networks can lead to unclear responsibilities and difficulty in accountability (Rhodes, 2017). Excessive emphasis on cooperation can limit effectiveness, especially in crisis situations that require strong and rapid state action (Christensen & Lægreid, 2020). Furthermore, citizen participation, although desirable, often remains formal or uneven, leading to new forms of exclusion, while the lack of expertise may lead to erroneous decisions that do not represent the public interest. Despite these criticisms, governance can be considered one of the most important approaches to administrative analysis and practice for modern public administration. Its theoretical and practical dimension continues to evolve, especially with the integration of digital technologies and the exploration of the state-society relationship at a global level.

5. HYBRID MODELS OF PUBLIC ADMINISTRATION

5.1. The Search for New Compositions

The experience of the transition from bureaucracy to New Public Administration (NPM) and then to governance has highlighted the need for more complex and flexible administrative models that are able to adapt to the specificities of each country. The strict standardization of bureaucracy, the excessive managerial logic of NPM and the challenges of implementing governance in complex environments have led to the development of hybrid approaches (Christensen & Lægreid, 2020; Pollitt & Bouckaert, 2017). Hybrid models combine elements of different administrative approaches, seeking to exploit the advantages of each theory, while minimizing their weaknesses and ultimately aiming at their best possible application.

5.2. The Neo-Weberian State (NWS)

The Neo-Weberian State (NWS) was developed as an attempt to bridge the bureaucratic tradition with the demands of modern public management. The NWS maintains the central role of the state and the emphasis on legitimacy and stability, but incorporates principles of efficiency, strategic planning and citizen orientation (Pollitt & Bouckaert, 2017).

Characteristics of the NWS include:

- maintaining the bureaucratic view of focusing on legitimacy and administrative discipline,
- strengthening rational decision-making by utilizing modern tools and practices,
- incorporating basic principles of strategic management based on modern tools of private management,
- recognizing the citizen not only as a "customer", but also as a citizen with rights and obligations.

NWS found fertile ground in continental European countries, where administrative traditions were closely linked to a strong institutional background and legal-administrative culture.

5.3. New Public Governance (NPG)

New Public Governance (NPG) is a continuation of the logic of governance and focuses on the importance of networks, cooperation and the participation of multiple actors (civil society, businesses, international organizations, etc.). In contrast to NPM, which emphasized competition, NPG promotes trust, dialogue, two-way communication, openness and the joint production of public policies (Osborne, 2010; Klijn & Koppenjan, 2016). The core principles of NPG are:

- collaborative relationships between the state, private sector and civil society,
- the creation of "public value" through collective action,
- the flexibility and adaptability of institutions,
- the emphasis on long-term sustainability rather than short-term efficiency.

NPG tends to be more applicable in environments where social and institutional structures are pluralistic and require a high degree of coordination.

5.4. The New Public Service (NPS)

The New Public Service (NPS) was proposed by Denhardt & Denhardt (2015) and focuses on the dimension of democracy and participation. In contrast to NPM, which treats the citizen as a customer, NPS approaches him as an integral part of the decision-making process. The public sector does not "lead" or "provide services" in the sense of private management, but "serves" through processes that enhance trust and cooperation.

A basic principle of NPS according to Denhardt & Denhardt (2015) is that: "the role of public administration is to help citizens collectively express their interests and find common solutions".

5.5. Public Value Theory

The Public Value Theory, developed by Moore (2014), focuses on the creation of value for society through the collaboration of state, citizens and institutions. The concept of public value goes beyond economic efficiency and includes elements such as social trust, collective conscience, transparency, democratic legitimacy and equality. The creation of public value is now the central criterion for evaluating policies, especially in an era of digital transformation and increased social expectations (O'Flynn, 2021; Twizeyimana & Andersson, 2019).

5.6. Comparative assessment

Hybrid models do not fully replace bureaucracy, NPM or public governance. On the contrary, they draw elements from all administrative theories and shape and synthesize new forms that can be considered as an "alloy" of multiple approaches. International experience shows that their implementation depends on the institutional traditions, national and organizational culture and the functionality of each national administrative system (Christensen & Lægreid, 2020). However, in all cases a common component is the recognition of the need for a combination of legitimacy, efficiency, cooperation and social value as key parameters for modern public administration.

6. COMPARATIVE ANALYSIS OF ADMINISTRATIVE MODELS

The comparative mapping of administrative models highlights the transition from a normative and hierarchical administrative structure (bureaucracy) to more complex and multidimensional forms of administration. Bureaucracy was a foundation for institutional stability and equal treatment of citizens, but its rigidity and lack of adaptability led to the search for alternative models. New Public Management (NPM) was the first radical challenge, introducing market logic and management methods, but the excessive emphasis on principles such as effectiveness, efficiency and cost-effectiveness led to the possibility of challenging democratic legitimacy.

Governance came to cover this challenge, highlighting the need for cooperation, multi-level policymaking and citizen participation. However, polycentricity and the creation of complex policy networks created new issues of coordination and accountability and ultimately effectiveness. The existence of weaknesses for each administrative theory led to the formation of hybrid models that take characteristics from a wide range of theories.

The Neo-Weberian State (NWS) seeks to renew the bureaucratic tradition with elements of efficiency and strategic management, while the New Public Governance (NPG) and the New Public Service (NPS) emphasize the collaborative and participatory dimension of public action. The theory of Public Value adds a broader horizon, shifting the center of gravity from efficiency to social value and democratic legitimacy. Overall, this development does not reflect a linear replacement of models, but a continuous process of overlap and coexistence. In today's era, public administration is called upon to combine the stability of bureaucracy, the efficiency of NPM, the polycentricity of governance and the legitimizing power of hybrid approaches, in order to respond to the complex challenges of modern societies.

Table 1. Comparative analysis of administrative models

Model	Period of Emergence	Key Characteristics	Theoretical Basis	Citizen Conception	Advantages	Criticism / Limitations
Bureaucracy (Weberian)	Late 19th – early 20th century	Hierarchy, rules, standardization, neutrality, professionalism	Weber (1978), legal–rational legitimacy	Citizen as a subject enjoying equal treatment	Stability, predictability, equality before the law	Rigidity, slowness, resistance to innovation
New Public Management (NPM)	1980s – 2000s	Decentralization, goal-setting, performance measurement, competition, outsourcing	Public Choice (Niskanen, 1971), New Institutional Economics	Citizen as a client	Efficiency, adoption of management methods, improved services	Undermining of social dimension, overemphasis on indicators, erosion of accountability
Governance	1990s – present	Collaborative networks, multilevel policy-making, participation, transparency, e-governance	Network theory (Rhodes, 2017; Klijn & Koppenjan, 2016)	Citizen as participant and stakeholder	Collaboration, collective solutions, greater transparency	Accountability challenges, complexity, unequal participation

continued on following page

Table 1. Continued

Model	Period of Emergence	Key Characteristics	Theoretical Basis	Citizen Conception	Advantages	Criticism / Limitations
Neo-Weberian State (NWS)	2000s	Combination of bureaucratic legality with efficiency and strategic management	Pollitt & Bouckaert (2017)	Citizen as a rights-bearing and responsible individual	Strengthened institutional stability, modernization with professionalism	Limited transformation, risk of preserving rigidity
New Public Governance (NPG)	2000s – present	Networks, collaborative policymaking, trust, collective action	Osborne (2010), Klijn & Koppenjan (2016)	Citizen as partner/ participant	Enhanced collaboration, shared responsibilities	Slow processes, coordination difficulties among multiple actors
New Public Service (NPS)	2000s	Serving the public interest, participation, democratic dialogue	Denhardt & Denhardt (2015)	Citizen as participant in governance	Strengthened democratic legitimacy, trust-building	Limited practical application, difficult implementation in centralized systems
Public Value	2000s – present	Creation of social value, trust, legitimacy through consultation	Moore (2014), O'Flynn (2021)	Citizen as co-creator of value	Promotion of social value and legitimacy	Challenges in measurement and practical realization

7. PHASES OF ADMINISTRATIVE REFORM OF THE GREEK PUBLIC ADMINISTRATION

7.1. Post-War Period (1950–1980)

The Greek public administration in the post-war period was shaped in a context of strong state interventionism, centralization and limited institutional autonomy. Despite the formal adherence to the Weberian model, the operation of the administration presented strong phenomena of clientelism and strong politicization of institutions (Spanou, 2018). The lack of know-how, the absence of a professional administrative elite and institutional discontinuity prevented the establishment of a consolidated administrative model with significant dysfunctions, often referring to phenomena of mismanagement and corruption (Lampropoulou & Oikonomou, 2021).

This period highlighted the uniqueness of the Greek case, with characteristics such as the typical bureaucratic structure combined with informal networks serving party and social interests. The institutional weaknesses that were then established continued to influence subsequent administrative reform efforts (Peters, 2021; Rossidis, et al. 2016).

7.2. Modernization and European Orientation (1990–2009)

Accession to the European Union and the consolidation of European integration placed new pressures for administrative modernization in the context of the emerging need for administrative convergence. The 1990s were characterized by the introduction of reforms inspired by New Public Management, such as decentralization, evaluation, target setting and the establishment of new transparency institutions (Pollitt & Bouckaert, 2017). At the same time, the implementation of the reform establishing Citizen Service Centers (CSCs) was a typical example of improving state-citizen relations through the adoption of service tools and the reduction of bureaucracy (Spanou, 2018). However, the reforms were fragmented and often externally imposed. The lack of strategic planning and the institutional resistance of the clientelistic system limited the substantial impact of the changes (Rossidis, et al. 2020). As Lampropoulou and Oikonomou (2021) note, the Greek administrative system showed a high degree of adaptability in the integration of new tools, without however undergoing structural transformation.

7.3. Period of Economic Crisis (2010–2019)

The fiscal crisis and the imposition of the memoranda brought new pressures on public administration. The reforms of this period were strongly external in nature, determined by the terms of international organizations (Featherstone, 2015; Lampropoulou & Oikonomou, 2021). The emphasis was placed on cost reduction, fiscal discipline and rationalized human resource management, rather than on strategic transformation of the administrative function, often presenting a fragmented dimension without being based on strategically targeted long-term administrative improvements.

Despite the creation of new institutional mechanisms for transparency and accountability, the implementation of reforms encountered serious obstacles. The "implementation oxymoron" described by Lampropoulou and Oikonomou (2021) reflects the contradiction between the institutional overproduction of laws and policies and the inability to formulate the appropriate administrative mechanisms for their effective implementation. The result was an administration burdened with multiple, often contradictory, measures, but without a clear direction of reform strategy (Peters, 2021, Rossidis et al., 2020).

8. SEARCHING FOR THE RIGHT ADMINISTRATIVE SYSTEM

The transition from bureaucracy to New Public Management (NPM) and from there to public governance is often described as a "reasonable" succession of administrative theories (Pollitt & Bouckaert, 2017; O'Flynn, 2021). The development of the Greek administrative system, however, constitutes a rather differentiated case in relation to the broader international administrative environment. As Lampropoulou and Oikonomou (2021) point out, public administration in Greece is a system of "multiple characteristics" of different administrative models without a coherent regulatory and organizational basis. The coexistence of bureaucratic, clientelistic and piecemeal modern elements leads to what the authors describe as a "quasi-Weberian" or even "anti-paradigm".

The concept of "anti-paradigm" acquires particular importance as the Greek administration is not a variant of a general model, but an example of institutional discontinuity, hybridity and adaptability with the main problem being the lack of strategic orientation aiming at the consolidation of a strong and modern administrative system. This peculiarity explains why the country does not easily fit into either the NPM tradition or the later paradigm of public governance.

The discussion on the development of the Greek public administration is subject to a complex administrative and socio-political analysis. A particularly important element is the development of digital governance, which offers possibilities for overcoming chronic pathologies through the simplification of processes, the use of data, the improvement of the services provided and the enhancement of transparency (Manoharan et al., 2022; Twizeyimana & Andersson, 2019; Mihiotis et al., 2023). The experience of the creation of gov.gr and the unification of services shows that digital transformation can be a catalyst for change. At the same time, the cultivation of a new organizational culture and a strategically targeted organizational culture will strengthen professionalism, accountability and the removal of customer-oriented practices, which are a fundamental prerequisite for a stable administrative development (Aspridis & Pouliana, 2021; Belias et al., 2023). The institutional reforms of recent years, such as the establishment of the "Executive State" (Law 4622/2019), seek to establish a new mechanism for coordination and strategic planning, but their effectiveness depends on their sustainability and acceptance at the administrative and social levels.

At a theoretical level, the future of Greek administration will likely not be defined by the full adoption of an international model, but by the establishment of a hybrid scheme that will combine the stability of the Weberian state with elements of governance and public value creation (Lampropoulou & Oikonomou, 2021; O'Flynn, 2021). The challenge lies in whether the Greek state will manage to overcome the vicious circle of institutional discontinuity and shape a new administrative paradigm, capable of responding to the needs of a modern, democratic and digitally mature society.

9. CURRENT TRENDS AND CHALLENGES

9.1. Digital Transformation and E-Governance

The digital transformation of the public sector is one of the most defining trends of the last decade. E-governance and gov-tech services are transforming modern state-citizen relations based on enhancing: transparency, accountability and accessibility (Twizeyimana & Andersson, 2019; Manoharan et al., 2022). Digital transformation, beyond the provision of electronic services, focuses on deeper organizational changes, such as the use of big data, the inclusion of artificial intelligence and the utilization of accumulated knowledge capital for policy design. However, unequal access to technologies and the need to protect personal data raise critical administrative challenges.

9.2. Crisis Management and Resilience

The COVID-19 pandemic and the increase in natural disasters have highlighted the need for flexible and effective administrative systems. Public administrations in the modern volatile and dynamic administrative environment are called upon to respond simultaneously to unpredictable crises and long-term challenges, such as: climate change, health crises, rapid technological developments, international relations, etc. Addressing these challenges requires a combination of administrative efficiency (technocratic power and coordination) with collaborative forms of governance (Christensen & Lægreid, 2020). Crisis management now functions as a test of effectiveness, legitimacy and social trust.

9.3. Participation and Social Legitimation

Enhancing citizen participation in decision-making processes is a central element of modern administrative theories. The trend towards co-creation of public policies, participatory governance and accountability aims to create greater transparency and trust (Osborne, 2010; Denhardt & Denhardt, 2015). At the same time, the theory of public value emphasizes that policies are judged not only in terms of efficiency, but also based on the social benefit they produce (Moore, 2014; O'Flynn, 2021).

9.4. Globalization and Multi-Level Governance

The interdependence of national, regional and international institutions means that public administrations operate in an environment of multi-level governance (Hooghe & Marks, 2016). Issues such as economic policy, migration or climate change cannot be addressed exclusively at the national level. A contemporary necessity is the coordination of policies at different levels without compromising democratic legitimacy and effectiveness.

9.5. The Challenge of Equality and Social Cohesion

Despite progress in public administration, inequalities in access to services persist, both between social groups and between regions. The pursuit of efficiency often conflicts with the demand for equality and social justice. Sustainable administrative reform must balance efficiency, accountability and social cohesion (Christensen & Lægreid, 2020; Pollitt & Bouckaert, 2017).

10. CONCLUSION

The path from bureaucracy to NPM and from there to public governance and hybrid models does not follow a linear path of administrative evolution or a tendency to substitute theories. It evolves in a process of overlap and synthesis. Each model emerged as a response to the weaknesses of the previous one, enriching the arsenal of theoretical and practical tools of public administration. Bureaucracy offered stability and legitimacy, NPM brought efficiency, private economic criteria and modern (and tested) administrative tools, governance promoted cooperation and participation, while hybrid models seek to synthesize all of these.

In the modern administrative environment, public administrations around the world are faced with challenges that go well beyond the limits of traditional models such as: digital transformation and rapid technological developments, climate crisis, emergency management, multi-level governance, social inequalities, international interactions, etc. These conditions require an administration that combines rational stability with efficiency, flexibility, collaboration and the creation of public value.

The future course of public administration will depend on its ability to integrate digital technologies, foster participatory processes and ensure social legitimacy. The challenge is to overcome the contradictions of old models and establish a new balance, in which public value will be the main criterion for evaluation. In this way, public administration can effectively respond to the demands of the 21st century, combining efficiency, democracy and social justice.

REFERENCES

Aspridis, G., & Pouliana, E. (2021). Organizational culture in public administration: The case of Greece. *Academicus International Scientific Journal, 12*(23), 133–148.

Belias, D., & Rossidis, I. (2025). *Change Management. Organizational Change and elements of Organizational Behaviour.* Tziolas publications.

Belias, D., Rossidis, I., Papademetriou, C., Masouras, A., & Anastasiadou, S. (2023). *Managing Successful and Ethical Organizational Change.* IGI Global. DOI: 10.4018/979-8-3693-0235-4

Christensen, T., & Lægreid, P. (2020). The rise of the post-NPM regime. *Administration & Society, 52*(2), 247–271.

Denhardt, J., & Denhardt, R. (2015). *The new public service: Serving, not steering* (4th ed.). Routledge.

Featherstone, K. (2015). External conditionality and the debt crisis: The 'Troika' and public administration reform in Greece. *Journal of European Public Policy, 22*(3), 295–314. DOI: 10.1080/13501763.2014.955123

Hood, C. (1991). A public management for all seasons? *Public Administration, 69*(1), 3–19. DOI: 10.1111/j.1467-9299.1991.tb00779.x

Hooghe, L., & Marks, G. (2016). *Community, scale, and regional governance: A postfunctionalist theory of governance.* Oxford University Press. DOI: 10.1093/acprof:oso/9780198766971.001.0001

Katsimardos, P., Bouas, K., Rossidis, I., & Babalioutas, L. (2017). Greek crisis: It's not about growth. It's about governance. *International Journal of Current Research, 9*(3).

Kefis, V. (1998). *The Management of Public Enterprises and Organizations. Systematic Approach to its Impacts on the Development of the Greek Economy.* Interbooks Publications.

Kefis, V., & Aspridis, G. (2014). Management and development of the human resource of nongovernmental organizations (NGOs) in Greece. Utopia or reality? *International NGO Journal, 9*(4), 43–52. DOI: 10.5897/INGOJ2014.0289

Klijn, E.-H., & Koppenjan, J. (2016). *Governance networks in the public sector.* Routledge.

Lampropoulou, M., & Oikonomou, G. (2021). Theoretical models of public administration and patterns of state reform in Greece. *International Review of Administrative Sciences, 84*(1), 101–121. DOI: 10.1177/0020852315611219

Manoharan, A. P., Melitski, J., Holzer, M., Kim, S., & Song, M. (2022). E-governance and public trust: A global perspective. *Government Information Quarterly, 39*(1), 101663.

Mihiotis, A., Rossidis, I., & Koutsoukis, N. (2023). The effect of digital transformation in the development of Electronic Governance in Cyprus and Greece. A critical review through the analysis of the Digital Economy and Society Index. *The Cyprus Review, 35*(1).

Moore, M. (2014). *Public value: Theory and practice.* Palgrave Macmillan.

Niskanen, W. (1971). *Bureaucracy and representative government.* Aldine-Atherton.

North, D. (1990). *Institutions, institutional change and economic performance.* Cambridge University Press. DOI: 10.1017/CBO9780511808678

O'Flynn, J. (2021). From New Public Management to public value: Paradigmatic change and managerial implications. *Australian Journal of Public Administration, 80*(4), 741–755.

OECD. (2015). *Government at a glance 2015.* OECD Publishing.

Ongaro, E. (2010). The Napoleonic administrative tradition and public management reform in France, Greece, Italy, Portugal and Spain. In Painter, M., & Peters, B. G. (Eds.), *Tradition and Public Administration* (pp. 174–190). Palgrave Macmillan. DOI: 10.1057/9780230289635_13

Osborne, S. P. (2010). *The new public governance? Emerging perspectives on the theory and practice of public governance.* Routledge. DOI: 10.4324/9780203861684

Peters, B. G. (2021). *The politics of bureaucracy: An introduction to comparative public administration* (8th ed.). Routledge.

Pollitt, C., & Bouckaert, G. (2017). *Public management reform: A comparative analysis – Into the age of austerity* (4th ed.). Oxford University Press.

Rhodes, R. A. W. (2017). Understanding governance: Ten years on. *Organization Studies, 38*(10), 1243–1264.

Rossidis, I. (2014) *Applying Business Management in Greek Public Administration.* Athens: publ. Ath. Stamoulis.

Rossidis I., Aspridis, G., Katsimardos, P., Bouas, K., Blanas, N. (2016). Best practices for motivation and their implementation in the Greek public sector for increasing efficiency. *Academic Journal of Interdisciplinary Studies*. 5(3).

Rossidis, I., & Belias, D. (2021). Evolution of e-governance in the era of the pandemic. May the crisis become an opportunity? The cases of Cyprus and Greece. *The Cyprus Review*, *33*(1), 37–66.

Rossidis, I., Belias, D., & Papailias, S. (2020). *Strategic management in the Greek public sector. In search of best practices in the international environment*. Book of Proceedings International Conference on Business & Economics of the Hellenic Open University.

Rossidis, I., Mihiotis, A., & Ntalakos, A. (2023). The contribution of Change Management to the integration of E-Governance systems. Chapter 9 in "*Managing Successful and Ethical Organizational Change*", IGI Global.

Spanou, C. (2018). *Public administration and policy in Greece*. Routledge.

Twizeyimana, J. D., & Andersson, A. (2019). The public value of e-governance – A literature review. *Government Information Quarterly*, *36*(2), 167–178. DOI: 10.1016/j.giq.2019.01.001

UNDP. (2019). *Human Development Report 2019: Beyond income, beyond averages, beyond today*. UNDP.

Weber, M. (1978). *Economy and society: An outline of interpretive sociology*. University of California Press.

Chapter 3
Law and Public Administration

Subramanian Udayakumar
http://orcid.org/0009-0006-2239-7207
Vel Tech Rangarajan Dr. Sagunthala R&D Institute of Science and Technology, India

Pamarthi Satyanarayana
http://orcid.org/0009-0008-4041-3674
VEL TECH University, India

P. Selvakumar
http://orcid.org/0000-0002-3650-4548
Department of Science and Humanities, Nehru Institute of Technology, Coimbatore, India

ABSTRACT

Law serves as the bedrock of public administration, shaping the framework within which governments operate and ensuring the legitimacy, accountability, and fairness of administrative actions. In democratic societies, the rule of law governs the conduct of public officials, delineates the powers and responsibilities of administrative bodies, and safeguards the rights of citizens. Without a strong legal foundation, public administration would risk arbitrariness, corruption, and inefficiency. The role of law in public administration is thus multifaceted—acting both as an enabler and a constraint, guiding the formulation and execution of public policies while ensuring adherence to constitutional principles and ethical standards. At its core, law provides a structural foundation for the operation of the state and its various agencies. Administrative law, constitutional law, and statutory regulations form the legal scaffolding of public administration, outlining the authority of governmental institutions and defining the scope of their jurisdiction.

DOI: 10.4018/979-8-3373-3526-1.ch003

THE ROLE OF LAW IN PUBLIC ADMINISTRATION

Law serves as the bedrock of public administration, shaping the framework within which governments operate and ensuring the legitimacy, accountability, and fairness of administrative actions. In democratic societies, the rule of law governs the conduct of public officials, delineates the powers and responsibilities of administrative bodies, and safeguards the rights of citizens. Without a strong legal foundation, public administration would risk arbitrariness, corruption, and inefficiency. The role of law in public administration is thus multifaceted—acting both as an enabler and a constraint, guiding the formulation and execution of public policies while ensuring adherence to constitutional principles and ethical standards. At its core, law provides a structural foundation for the operation of the state and its various agencies. Administrative law, constitutional law, and statutory regulations form the legal scaffolding of public administration, outlining the authority of governmental institutions and defining the scope of their jurisdiction. For instance, administrative law governs the actions of regulatory agencies, public bodies, and civil servants, prescribing the procedures for making, enforcing, and reviewing decisions. It establishes the procedures for rulemaking, adjudication, and enforcement, thereby ensuring due process and transparency. Constitutional law, on the other hand, sets the overarching legal parameters within which all administrative action must occur, ensuring that government power is exercised in conformity with fundamental rights and democratic principles. Another critical role of law in public administration lies in facilitating the implementation of public policy. Once a policy is formulated, its success depends on its translation into law and the capacity of the administrative apparatus to enforce it. Legal instruments lend enforceability to policies, define the roles of various stakeholders, and specify penalties for non-compliance. For example, public health laws enable governments to respond effectively to epidemics by mandating quarantine measures or regulating the distribution of medicines.

In this way, law becomes the operational arm of policy implementation. Globalization and the increasing complexity of governance have expanded the scope and significance of law in public administration. In many countries, legal systems must now accommodate international obligations, such as human rights treaties, environmental agreements, and trade laws. These international legal instruments influence domestic administrative practices and require public administrators to operate in a more interconnected legal environment. For instance, the implementation of international environmental standards may demand new regulatory frameworks and compliance mechanisms at the national level. The rise of digital governance and e-administration further necessitates new legal regimes to protect data, ensure cybersecurity, and regulate artificial intelligence in public services. Additionally, law facilitates citizen engagement and participatory governance in public administration. Legal provisions mandating public consultations, stakeholder involvement, and community-based planning processes enable citizens to contribute to decision-making. Legal frameworks for civil society participation ensure that marginalized and minority groups have a voice in administrative affairs. In democratic societies, this participatory dimension of law not only enriches the quality of governance but also strengthens the legitimacy of administrative decisions. In conclusion, the role of law in public administration is foundational and far-reaching. It not only defines the structure and authority of administrative institutions but also ensures accountability, protects individual rights, supports policy implementation, and promotes professionalism in governance. By providing clarity, consistency, and legitimacy, law enables public administration to function effectively in service of the public good. As societies evolve and governance becomes more complex, the interplay between law and administration must remain dynamic, responsive, and grounded in democratic values. The future of effective public administration hinges on the continued strengthening of legal frameworks, the integrity of legal institutions, and the capacity of public servants to navigate the legal dimensions of their roles.

UNDERSTANDING THE INTERSECTION OF LAW AND PUBLIC POLICY

The intersection of law and public policy represents a critical nexus in the field of governance, wherein legal frameworks and public policy objectives work in tandem to shape societal outcomes. Law provides the formal, institutionalized rules that regulate behavior and enforce norms, while public policy reflects the strategic decisions and actions taken by governments to address public issues. Together, they serve as complementary tools for advancing social justice, economic development, national security, public welfare, and democratic governance (Bacong A M., et al, 2021). Understanding their intersection is essential for public administrators, lawmakers, legal scholars, and policymakers because it reveals how law operationalizes policy, how policy informs the evolution of legal norms, and how both shape the lived realities of citizens. Conversely, legal frameworks also shape and constrain the formulation and execution of public policy. All policy actions must conform to the constitution, adhere to statutory limits, and respect established legal doctrines such as due process, equality, and fundamental rights. The judiciary plays a crucial role in reviewing and potentially annulling policies that conflict with constitutional provisions. This ensures that policy-making remains within the bounds of legality and protects against arbitrary governance. For example, a public policy that mandates surveillance for national security must also balance individual privacy rights as guaranteed by the Constitution, creating a legal check on executive authority

(Maksimentseva N O., 2023). One of the most visible intersections of law and public policy occurs in the legislative process. Legislatures are responsible for crafting laws that reflect public policy goals, often based on research, expert input, stakeholder consultations, and political negotiations. The legislative process involves translating abstract policy ideas into precise legal language that outlines rights, obligations, enforcement mechanisms, and resource allocations. This transformation requires careful legal drafting to ensure clarity, enforceability, and constitutional validity. Poorly drafted laws can undermine policy objectives, lead to implementation challenges, and provoke legal disputes. Therefore, effective lawmaking necessitates a strong understanding of both legal principles and policy analysis.

Moreover, law and policy intersect in the regulation of markets and private behavior. Regulatory policy involves the use of legal tools to influence economic and social conduct—through licensing, taxation, subsidies, bans, mandates, and standards. Environmental policies are implemented through environmental laws that regulate pollution, conservation, and natural resource use. Health policies are supported by legal mandates around vaccination, drug safety, and hospital accreditation. Financial regulations reflect policy priorities in ensuring market stability and consumer protection. In each case, law provides the authority and structure for regulatory interventions, while policy defines the goals and outcomes of such regulation. International law and global policy issues offer another domain where law and public policy intersect (Berman E M., et al, 2021). In an increasingly interconnected world, states must align their domestic policies with international legal commitments. Treaties, conventions, and agreements in areas such as trade, climate change, human rights, and health (e.g., WHO regulations, Paris Agreement) require countries to design and implement domestic policies consistent with international obligations. This interplay influences national legislation and policy choices, requiring governments to balance local priorities with global responsibilities. For instance, a country's environmental law must integrate policy goals derived from international climate accords, influencing how it regulates carbon emissions, energy production, and conservation. In conclusion, the intersection of law and public policy is foundational to the functioning of modern democratic states (Zeraatkar S., et al, 2021). Law provides the legitimacy, structure, and enforceability that policies need to achieve their objectives, while policy offers the vision, direction, and responsiveness that law needs to remain relevant and effective. Together, they constitute the dual engines of governance, shaping how societies confront challenges, allocate resources, and uphold justice. A comprehensive understanding of their interplay enables more informed, equitable, and sustainable decisions in the public interest. As the global policy landscape grows more complex and interdependent, the capacity to harmonize legal frameworks with evolving policy goals will be crucial for promoting good governance, protecting rights, and advancing the public good.

PRINCIPLES OF ADMINISTRATIVE LAW

Administrative law is a fundamental branch of public law that governs the activities, organization, powers, procedures, and accountability of public administration and governmental agencies. It plays a vital role in ensuring that administrative authorities exercise their powers fairly, transparently, and within the boundaries established by law. At its heart, administrative law seeks to balance the need for effective governance with the protection of individual rights and the promotion of the rule of law. The principles of administrative law act as guiding norms that shape administrative action and safeguard the public interest. These principles include legality, rule of law, natural justice, fairness, reasonableness, proportionality, accountability, and transparency (Knies E., et al, 2021). Together, they form the cornerstone of good governance and democratic administration. Principle of Legality: The principle of legality asserts that all administrative actions must be based on legal authority. Public officials and administrative agencies cannot act arbitrarily or beyond the scope of their legally granted powers. This principle upholds the concept of "ultra vires," which means that any administrative action taken without legal sanction is invalid. The legality principle ensures that government agencies do not assume powers not granted to them by legislation, and it restrains abuse or misuse of authority. For example, if a licensing authority denies a permit without legal justification or outside the scope of statutory guidelines, such a decision can be challenged and quashed by the courts. Thus, the principle of legality reinforces the primacy of law over administrative discretion. Natural Justice (Procedural Fairness): The principle of natural justice, also referred to as procedural fairness, comprises two main rules: audi alteram partem (the right to be heard) and nemo judex in causa sua (no one should be a judge in their case). These rules ensure that individuals affected by administrative decisions are given a fair opportunity to present their case and that the decision-makers are impartial and free from bias. For instance, if a public employee is to be dismissed for misconduct, they must be informed of the charges, given a chance to respond, and have their case heard by an impartial authority. Violations of natural justice can render administrative decisions void or voidable. This principle strengthens public confidence in administrative processes and enhances the credibility of decision-making (Battaglio R P., 2021). Reasonableness (Wednesbury Principle): The reasonableness principle, developed in English administrative law under the landmark Wednesbury case, requires that administrative decisions be rational and within the range of acceptable options available to a decision-maker. A decision is deemed unreasonable if it is so irrational that no reasonable authority could have ever made it. Courts apply this principle to determine whether a decision is manifestly unjust or perverse. Reasonableness prevents arbitrary actions and ensures that decisions are not based on irrelevant considerations. It allows judicial oversight of discretionary powers without undermining administrative autonomy. However, courts generally exercise restraint and only intervene when the decision defies logic or basic moral standards.

Accountability: Administrative accountability means that public officials and agencies are answerable for their actions and decisions. Accountability can be legal, political, administrative, or ethical. Legal accountability is enforced through judicial review, where courts examine whether administrative actions comply with the law. Political accountability occurs through oversight by elected representatives, legislative committees, and public audits. Administrative accountability involves internal procedures such as performance evaluations, reporting requirements, and disciplinary mechanisms. Ethical accountability relates to the adherence to codes of conduct and moral standards (Riccucci N M., 2021). Together, these forms of accountability ensure that public power is exercised responsibly, transparently, and in the public interest. Equality and Non-Discrimination: The principle of equality mandates that administrative authorities treat all individuals equally before the law and refrain from discriminatory practices. Public policies and administrative decisions must not be based on irrelevant personal characteristics such as race, religion, gender, caste, or economic status. Equality in administrative law implies both formal equality (equal treatment under similar circumstances) and substantive equality (consideration of disadvantages to promote equity). For example, affirmative action programs may treat individuals differently to achieve fairness and inclusion. Administrative decisions must therefore be sensitive to the social context while ensuring compliance with constitutional guarantees of equality. Judicial Review: Judicial review is the mechanism through which courts supervise the legality of administrative actions. It is a cornerstone of administrative law and ensures that public authorities do not act beyond their powers, breach procedural rules, or violate constitutional rights. Judicial review does not question the merits of a decision but examines its legality, procedural propriety, and reasonableness. Grounds for judicial review include illegality, irrationality, procedural impropriety, and proportionality (Chib S., et al, 2025). Courts can quash unlawful decisions, compel administrative bodies to act, or provide remedies to aggrieved parties. Judicial review thus serves as a powerful check on administrative overreach. Public Interest: Administrative decisions must serve the public interest and not be driven by personal, political, or sectional interests. The public interest is a guiding concept in balancing individual rights with collective welfare. For instance, zoning laws that restrict construction in certain areas may inconvenience individuals but are justified in the broader interest of environmental protection or public safety. Administrative law provides a framework for ensuring that such decisions are reasoned, evidence-based, and aligned with societal needs. The concept of public interest also underlies exemptions in laws such as the RTI Act, where certain information may be withheld to protect national security or privacy.

RULEMAKING AND ADJUDICATION IN PUBLIC ADMINISTRATION

Rulemaking and adjudication are two fundamental functions of public administration that embody the exercise of delegated authority by administrative agencies. Together, they represent the quasi-legislative and quasi-judicial roles of public institutions, contributing significantly to the effective implementation and enforcement of public policy. These processes are essential in modern governance, especially in complex administrative systems where specialized bodies are entrusted with the responsibility of regulating economic, social, and environmental activities. Rulemaking involves the formulation of general norms and regulations, while adjudication deals with the resolution of disputes and the application of laws to specific cases. Understanding these twin pillars of administrative action is crucial for appreciating how government agencies exercise discretion, maintain order, ensure compliance, and deliver justice in administrative matters (Avalekar U A., et al, 2025). Rulemaking: Concept and Significance: Rulemaking refers to the process through which administrative agencies create rules, regulations, or standards that have the force of law. For instance, environmental protection agencies may be empowered to set pollution limits, while health authorities may establish standards for food safety and drug approval. These rules ensure uniformity, predictability, and coherence in administrative governance and enable agencies to fulfill their policy mandates efficiently. Legal Framework and Delegation of Authority: Rulemaking authority is derived from enabling legislation passed by the legislature. The statute provides the scope, limits, and objectives for rulemaking and delegates the power to a specific agency or regulatory body. The delegation must be accompanied by adequate guidelines to prevent excessive discretion and ensure accountability. Courts have established that delegation is constitutionally valid as long as the legislature provides an intelligible principle to guide the agency. In India, the doctrine of excessive delegation is used to check whether the delegation has crossed constitutional limits. In the United States, the Administrative Procedure Act (APA) governs the rulemaking process, ensuring due process, public participation, and judicial review (Vandy J F., 2023). Challenges in Rulemaking: Despite its importance, rulemaking faces several challenges: Complexity and Technicality: Regulations often involve complex technical issues that are difficult for the general public to understand or critique. Limited Participation: In practice, public participation may be dominated by well-resourced interest groups, marginalizing ordinary citizens and vulnerable populations. Regulatory Capture: Agencies may be influenced by the industries they regulate, resulting in biased or lenient rules. Overregulation and Bureaucratic Burden: Excessive rulemaking can stifle innovation, impose compliance costs, and lead to bureaucratic inertia. Addressing these challenges requires improving transparency, expanding stakeholder engagement, using impact assessments, and ensuring robust oversight by legislative and judicial bodies.

Types of Adjudication: Administrative adjudication can take various forms depending on the nature of the issue, the legal framework, and the authority involved. Formal Adjudication: Conducted under procedures similar to judicial trials, including evidence presentation, cross-examination, and a written decision. Often required where statutes mandate adjudication "on the record after an opportunity for hearing." Informal Adjudication: Involves more flexible procedures, such as interviews, document reviews, and written submissions. Suitable for routine matters like benefit determinations or licensing. Disciplinary Adjudication: Focuses on enforcing ethical and professional standards, often used in regulatory bodies overseeing medical, legal, or engineering professions (Haenraets & van Berkel, 2021). Penalty or Enforcement Adjudication: Deals with violations of regulations, imposing fines, suspensions, or other sanctions. Administrative Tribunals and Specialized Bodies: To handle the growing volume and complexity of administrative disputes, many countries have established specialized tribunals and adjudicatory bodies. These institutions are designed to offer accessible, efficient, and expert adjudication outside the formal court system. Examples include: Income Tax Tribunals, Central Administrative Tribunal (India), National Green Tribunal, Workers' Compensation Boards, Immigration and Refugee Boards. These bodies combine administrative expertise with quasi-judicial powers, often following simplified procedures and offering quicker resolution than traditional courts. Balancing Rulemaking and Adjudication: Rulemaking and adjudication are complementary processes. Rulemaking provides general norms, while adjudication applies those norms to individual cases. Together, they enable administrative agencies to function with both consistency and flexibility. Agencies must balance these roles to avoid rigidity or arbitrariness. For instance, too much reliance on adjudication without clear rules may result in inconsistent decisions, while rigid rules without room for individual circumstances may cause injustice (Tummers L., et al, 2021). A well-functioning administrative system requires coherence between rulemaking and adjudication, supported by transparent procedures, expert capacity, and effective oversight. Global Trends and Comparative Perspectives: Different countries approach rulemaking and adjudication in diverse ways, reflecting legal traditions, administrative structures, and governance models. In the U.S., the Administrative Procedure Act provides detailed guidelines for both rulemaking and adjudication. In the U.K., principles of common law and judicial precedent guide agency actions. In continental Europe, administrative courts play a larger role in supervising administrative decisions. International organizations such as the OECD and World Bank promote best practices in regulatory governance, emphasizing transparency, accountability, and stakeholder engagement. The global trend favors participatory rulemaking, specialized adjudication, and enhanced judicial oversight to strengthen administrative justice and public trust.

LEGAL FRAMEWORKS FOR PUBLIC POLICY IMPLEMENTATION

Legal frameworks are the cornerstone of effective public policy implementation. They provide the structure, authority, and procedural mechanisms through which government policies are operationalized, enforced, and sustained. Without a robust legal foundation, even the most well-intentioned policy initiatives risk failure due to lack of legitimacy, clarity, enforceability, and accountability. Legal frameworks not only define the rights and responsibilities of the various actors involved in policy implementation—such as public officials, private entities, and citizens—but also establish the institutional architecture, regulatory mechanisms, and enforcement tools necessary to translate policy objectives into practical outcomes. These frameworks ensure that public administration operates within the rule of law, upholds democratic principles, and adapts to changing social, economic, and technological conditions (Vermeeren B., 2021). Defining Legal Frameworks in Public Policy: A legal framework refers to the set of laws, regulations, statutes, constitutional provisions, administrative procedures, and judicial interpretations that collectively govern how public policies are implemented. It includes both substantive law (defining what is to be achieved) and procedural law (outlining how it is to be achieved). Legal frameworks form the bridge between abstract policy goals and concrete administrative action. They establish the authority under which policies are executed, delineate the roles of implementing agencies, provide procedural safeguards, and create avenues for public participation, oversight, and redress.

The Relationship Between Law and Implementation Agencies: Legal frameworks formally establish and empower administrative agencies that are responsible for implementing policies. These laws define the structure, jurisdiction, functions, and powers of agencies, as well as the procedures they must follow. For example, environmental protection agencies derive their authority from environmental legislation, which specifies their inspection powers, rulemaking authority, and enforcement mechanisms. Without legal clarity, agencies may act arbitrarily or face jurisdictional disputes, undermining the policy process. In federal systems, legal frameworks must also delineate responsibilities between national, regional, and local governments. This coordination is essential for policies that require intergovernmental collaboration, such as health, education, or infrastructure development (Thomann E., et al, 2024). A fragmented or overlapping legal authority can lead to inefficiencies, duplication, and gaps in service delivery. Judicial Oversight of Implementation:

Judicial institutions play a crucial role in interpreting legal frameworks and ensuring that policies are implemented within the bounds of legality and fairness. Courts may adjudicate disputes between citizens and the state, review administrative actions for legality, and provide redress in cases of rights violations. Through judicial review, courts can strike down unconstitutional or ultra vires actions, thereby maintaining the integrity of the implementation process. In many jurisdictions, public interest litigation has emerged as a powerful tool for judicial intervention in policy implementation. Courts have compelled governments to implement education, health, housing, and environmental policies by constitutional mandates. This judicial activism strengthens the rule of law and ensures that vulnerable populations are not excluded from policy benefits.

Best Practices for Effective Legal Frameworks: Effective legal frameworks for public policy implementation exhibit the following characteristics: Clarity: Laws should be precise, coherent, and accessible to all stakeholders. Flexibility: Legal provisions must allow room for adaptation, innovation, and responsiveness to changing realities (Overman S., et al, 2022). Inclusiveness: Legal processes should promote stakeholder participation, especially from marginalized groups. Accountability: Strong oversight, grievance redress mechanisms, and transparency must be embedded in the legal framework. Coordination: Integration with other laws and consistency across sectors and jurisdictions is essential for avoiding conflicts and redundancies. Evidence-Based Drafting: Laws should be based on data, impact assessments, and empirical research to ensure feasibility and effectiveness. Human Rights Orientation: Legal frameworks must align with constitutional rights and international obligations, protecting individuals from discrimination or harm. The Evolving Role of Legal Frameworks in the Digital Age: The rapid advancement of technology necessitates new legal frameworks to support emerging public policy domains such as data governance, cybersecurity, digital services, and artificial intelligence (Mehra J., et al, 2025). Traditional legal instruments may be ill-equipped to address issues like algorithmic bias, surveillance, and digital exclusion. Thus, governments must develop agile and forward-looking legal structures that balance innovation with ethical safeguards. Examples include data protection laws (e.g., India's Digital Personal Data Protection Act, 2023), digital signature laws, and e-governance regulations. These frameworks must be technologically neutral, rights-based, and adaptable to future developments.

ACCOUNTABILITY MECHANISMS IN PUBLIC ADMINISTRATION

Accountability in public administration refers to the obligation of public officials, institutions, and agencies to be answerable for their actions, decisions, and use of public resources. It is a cornerstone of good governance, ensuring that public power is exercised responsibly, transparently, and by the law and ethical standards. Accountability mechanisms are the tools, procedures, and institutions designed to hold public actors to account, prevent abuse of authority, foster trust in government, and promote efficiency and responsiveness. In an era of increased public scrutiny, complex governance networks, and growing demand for inclusive governance, robust accountability mechanisms are essential to ensure the integrity, effectiveness, and legitimacy of public administration (Limbore N V., et al, 2025). Types of Accountability in Public Administration: Political Accountability: This type ensures that elected representatives and top public officials are accountable to the public through democratic processes. Mechanisms include: Elections and voting, Parliamentary debates and questions, Party discipline, and public campaigns. Administrative Accountability: It focuses on internal controls within the bureaucracy to ensure efficiency, compliance with rules, and alignment with organizational goals. Tools include: Performance appraisal systems, Internal audits, and Civil service codes of conduct. Legal Accountability: Legal frameworks hold public servants accountable to constitutional and statutory laws. Mechanisms include: Judicial review, Tribunals and commissions, and Prosecutorial action for misconduct. Financial Accountability: This ensures that public funds are used lawfully, economically, and effectively. Institutions and processes include: Comptroller and Auditor General (CAG), Public Accounts Committees (PACs), and Independent financial audits (Shava E., et al, 2021). Social Accountability: Driven by citizen participation and civil society engagement, this involves non-institutional mechanisms like: Public hearings, Citizen charters, Social audits, and grievance redressal platforms. Digital and Technological Mechanisms for Accountability: The rise of e-governance and digital technologies has transformed accountability practices in public administration. Innovations include: Online RTI platforms allowing citizens to request information from public authorities. Digital grievance redressal systems track complaints and ensure timely responses. Real-time dashboards displaying key performance indicators for government schemes. Geo-tagging and biometric tracking in welfare programs to prevent leakages and monitor service delivery. These tools enhance transparency, reduce human discretion, and facilitate citizen monitoring of public services.

Performance-Based Accountability: Modern public administration emphasizes performance management to promote results-oriented governance. Key elements include: Key Performance Indicators (KPIs): Quantifiable metrics used to evaluate agency and individual performance. Results-Based Management (RBM): Frameworks linking resource inputs to outcomes and impacts. Performance Audits: Independent evaluations assessing the efficiency, effectiveness, and economy of public programs (Loi M., et al, 2021). This shift from input-based to outcome-based accountability enhances service quality and public satisfaction. Challenges in Implementing Accountability Mechanisms: Despite institutional arrangements, several challenges hinder effective accountability in public administration: Bureaucratic opacity and resistance to scrutiny, Weak enforcement of audit or ombudsman recommendations, Political interference in oversight bodies, Low awareness among citizens of their rights and entitlements, Inadequate legal protection for whistleblowers, Overlapping jurisdictions and lack of coordination. Addressing these requires legal reform, administrative training, digital integration, and citizen empowerment. Conclusion: Accountability mechanisms are the lifeblood of ethical and effective public administration. They transform abstract ideals like transparency, fairness, and rule of law into concrete practices that shape governance outcomes (Brummel L., 2021). From formal audits and legal review to participatory forums and digital platforms, the range and diversity of accountability tools underscore the need for a multifaceted approach. However, accountability is not merely a function of procedures—it depends on the political will to enforce norms, the capacity of institutions to act independently, and the engagement of citizens in monitoring governance. Strengthening accountability in public administration requires an integrated strategy involving legal reforms, institutional innovation, civic education, and the use of technology. In doing so, public institutions can become more responsive, equitable, and resilient—ultimately restoring public trust and advancing the goals of democratic governance and sustainable development.

TRANSPARENCY AND OPEN GOVERNMENT

Transparency and open government are essential principles of modern public administration, fostering trust, accountability, and participation in democratic governance. At its core, transparency refers to the openness and accessibility of government processes, decisions, and data to the public, enabling citizens to monitor, evaluate, and influence public affairs. Open government expands upon this notion by institutionalizing mechanisms that promote citizen engagement, collaborative policymaking, and the proactive disclosure of information (Wang Q., et al, 2023). Together, transparency and open government ensure that public power is exercised in the light of day, not behind closed doors, thereby deterring corruption, improving service delivery, and reinforcing democratic legitimacy. In an era defined by digital technology, globalization, and increasing demands for accountability, transparency, and open government have become indispensable for responsive, inclusive, and efficient governance. The Evolution of Open Government: The concept of open government emerged as a response to rising demands for participatory democracy, government accountability, and the democratization of information. It gained global prominence with the launch of the Open Government Partnership (OGP) in 2011, a multilateral initiative involving over 70 countries committed to promoting transparency, empowering citizens, fighting corruption, and harnessing new technologies to strengthen governance. Open government rests on three pillars: Transparency: Making government information freely available in accessible formats. Participation: Enabling citizens to influence policymaking and service delivery. Collaboration: Encouraging partnerships between government, civil society, and the private sector to co-create solutions. These principles redefine the relationship between the state and its citizens, promoting mutual trust, shared responsibility, and collective innovation. Digital Technologies and E-Governance in Transparency: Digital transformation has revolutionized transparency and open government (Baudet & Medina, 2023). Through e-governance, public administration leverages digital tools to streamline operations and improve citizen engagement. Examples include: Online Portals for Budget and Expenditure Tracking: Allowing real-time access to government financial data. E-Procurement Systems: Ensuring transparency and fairness in public contracts. Interactive Dashboards: Providing updates on service delivery indicators. Mobile Apps for Grievance Redressal: Enabling citizens to report issues and receive feedback. Open data platforms such as data.gov or India's Open Government Data (OGD) platform serve as repositories of information on diverse sectors, from health and education to transportation and environment, enhancing policy transparency and data-driven governance.

Citizen Engagement and Participatory Governance: Transparency alone is insufficient without meaningful citizen engagement. Open government promotes participatory mechanisms that allow citizens to contribute to policymaking and service delivery. These include: Public Consultations and Hearings: Allowing community input into legislative or administrative proposals. Participatory Budgeting: Involving citizens in decisions on how public funds are spent. Social Audits: Verifying the implementation of public programs through community oversight (Christofoletti R., 2021). Civic Technology Platforms: Tools like FixMyStreet or SeeClickFix facilitate citizen feedback and co-production of services. These participatory mechanisms deepen democracy by giving citizens a voice in decisions that affect their lives, leading to better policies and greater legitimacy. Challenges and Limitations of Transparency Initiatives: Despite its significance, implementing transparency and open government faces several obstacles: Information Asymmetry: Citizens may lack the capacity or tools to interpret and use complex government data. Bureaucratic Resistance: Public officials may be reluctant to disclose information due to institutional inertia or fear of exposure. Tokenism in Participation: Some participatory processes may be symbolic rather than substantive. Security and Privacy Concerns: Excessive openness may compromise national security or individual privacy if not properly managed. To overcome these challenges, transparency must be embedded in a broader culture of openness, integrity, and citizen empowerment, supported by capacity building and legal safeguards (Chowdhary S., et al, 2025). The Future of Transparency and Open Government: The future of transparency and open government is being shaped by emerging technologies, evolving citizen expectations, and global efforts to build resilient, inclusive institutions. Key trends include: Artificial Intelligence and Data Analytics: Improving data use for policymaking and fraud detection. Blockchain Technology: Enhancing the integrity and traceability of public transactions. Open Algorithms and Explainable AI: Ensuring transparency in automated decision-making. Digital Citizenship and Civic Education: Building informed and engaged communities that can hold power to account. As governments confront complex challenges—from climate change and pandemics to inequality and misinformation—transparent and participatory governance will be crucial for building public trust and legitimacy.

CHALLENGES IN APPLYING LAW IN PUBLIC ADMINISTRATION

The application of law in public administration plays a crucial role in ensuring legality, fairness, and accountability in government actions. However, despite its importance, integrating legal principles into the administrative process is fraught with a variety of challenges. These challenges arise due to the complexity of governance, evolving societal demands, legal ambiguities, institutional limitations, and the need to balance administrative efficiency with legal compliance. Public administrators are required to operate within legal frameworks while navigating political pressures, limited resources, public expectations, and often conflicting statutory directives. As governments expand their functions and interact with increasingly diverse populations and sectors, applying law consistently, fairly, and effectively becomes more difficult (Coates J M., et al, 2025). These challenges can affect service delivery, public trust, and the legitimacy of administrative actions. The following analysis explores the multifaceted nature of these challenges, highlighting key areas of concern for modern public administration. Balancing Legal Compliance and Administrative Efficiency: Public administrators often face the difficult task of balancing legal compliance with the need for efficient service delivery. Legal procedures, while necessary to protect rights and ensure accountability, can be time-consuming and resource-intensive. Administrators must walk a fine line between adhering to legal norms and maintaining organizational agility, which is particularly challenging in crises that demand rapid action. Judicial Overreach and Legal Uncertainty: The role of the judiciary in interpreting laws and reviewing administrative actions is vital for upholding the rule of law. However, there are instances where judicial intervention may be perceived as excessive or inconsistent. Judicial overreach, where courts intervene in matters traditionally within the executive domain, can blur the separation of powers and create uncertainty in administrative decision-making. Moreover, inconsistent judicial rulings can lead to unpredictability and legal confusion for public administrators (Scupola A., et al, 2022). Different courts may interpret the same statute in divergent ways, complicating policy implementation and regulatory enforcement. Unclear or contradictory precedents can erode confidence in legal frameworks and increase the likelihood of litigation. Political Interference and Lack of Autonomy: Legal application in public administration can be undermined by political interference. When public administrators are pressured to act in ways that violate legal norms or bypass due process, it undermines the rule of law and public confidence in institutions. Political patronage, favoritism, or retaliation can distort administrative decisions, leading to corruption and abuse of power. In some contexts, the legal apparatus itself may be manipulated to serve partisan interests, weakening institutional independence and fairness. Regulatory bodies, anti-corruption commissions, and law enforcement agencies may face political constraints that compromise their effectiveness and credibility.

Figure 1. Career in public administration

Conflicting Legal Mandates and Interagency Coordination: Public administration frequently involves multiple agencies, each governed by its laws, regulations, and procedures. In complex policy domains such as urban planning, healthcare, or education, conflicting legal mandates can lead to jurisdictional disputes, policy incoherence, and administrative paralysis. Lack of coordination among agencies complicates compliance and accountability. For instance, environmental protection may fall under several ministries with overlapping or contradictory legal responsibilities. Without harmonized legal frameworks and integrated governance mechanisms, the effectiveness of public administration is undermined. Corruption and Ethical Failures: Corruption poses a significant obstacle to the legal integrity of public administration (Neumann O., et al, 2024). When officials misuse legal authority for personal gain or selectively apply rules to benefit certain groups, the credibility of the entire legal system is eroded. Corruption undermines fair and impartial enforcement of laws, diverts public resources, and weakens trust in institutions. Ethical failures—such as ignoring due process, concealing information, or discriminating against certain populations—can occur even in the absence of overt corruption. These practices not only violate legal principles but also perpetuate inequality, inefficiency, and injustice in administrative processes. Technological Disruption and Legal Adaptation: The rise of digital technologies, artificial intelligence, and data governance presents new legal challenges for public administration. Issues such as data privacy, algorithmic bias, cybersecurity, and digital exclusion require updated legal frameworks and administrative practices. The law often lags behind technological innovation, creating regulatory vacuums or outdated rules. Public administrators must navigate legal uncertainty in deploying new technologies while ensuring compliance with constitutional rights, due process, and ethical standards. Moreover, digital transformation may necessitate rethinking traditional legal procedures and safeguards in areas such as service delivery, public procurement, and dispute resolution (Levin A T., et al, 2022). Conclusion: Applying law in public administration is a foundational requirement for good governance, but it is fraught with challenges. Legal complexity, institutional limitations, political interference, corruption, and evolving societal demands all contribute to the difficulties faced by public administrators in maintaining legal compliance and accountability. While legal frameworks are essential for guiding and restraining administrative action, their effectiveness depends on institutional capacity, leadership integrity, citizen participation, and continuous legal adaptation. To overcome these challenges, governments must invest in legal training, simplify legal procedures, strengthen oversight institutions, promote transparency, and foster a culture of legality and ethical conduct. Innovations in legal technology, participatory governance, and inter-agency coordination offer new opportunities to enhance the rule of law in public administration. Ultimately, a well-functioning legal system not only enables effective administration but also safeguards the rights, dignity, and trust of the people.

THE IMPACT OF TECHNOLOGY ON LAW AND PUBLIC ADMINISTRATION

The rapid advancement of technology has fundamentally transformed the way public administration and legal systems operate, reshaping the interaction between government, law, and society. From digitizing administrative processes to enabling smarter governance and legal analytics, technology has introduced new opportunities and challenges in public sector governance. These innovations have accelerated service delivery, increased transparency, and improved access to justice, while simultaneously raising complex legal, ethical, and administrative concerns related to privacy, algorithmic accountability, cybersecurity, and digital equity. Understanding the impact of technology on law and public administration requires an exploration of its multifaceted influence on institutional frameworks, policy implementation, legal reform, citizen engagement, and administrative ethics. Digitization of Administrative Processes: One of the most profound impacts of technology on public administration is the digitization of bureaucratic processes (Amelicheva L., et al, 2021). E-governance platforms now enable public agencies to provide services such as tax filing, license issuance, benefits disbursement, and legal document registration through digital portals. This transition from paper-based systems to electronic platforms increases efficiency, reduces corruption, and shortens service delivery timelines. Digital systems enable real-time data processing, automated workflows, and seamless inter-agency coordination. They reduce the administrative burden for both citizens and civil servants and improve responsiveness. For instance, the introduction of single-window clearance systems for business permits streamlines regulatory approvals and enhances ease of doing business. Legal implications of such digitization include the need to update administrative procedure laws, electronic signature regulations, and evidence standards to accommodate digital records, e-filing, and online hearings. Governments must ensure these systems are inclusive, accessible, and secure. AI and Algorithmic Decision-Making: Artificial intelligence (AI) and machine learning are increasingly being integrated into administrative decision-making processes, from fraud detection and welfare eligibility assessments to predictive policing and case management in courts. While AI promises to increase efficiency and objectivity, its use raises significant legal and ethical questions (Osborne S P., et al, 2021). The opacity of algorithmic models—commonly referred to as the "black box" problem—complicates efforts to ensure transparency and explainability in public decisions. Biased algorithms can lead to discrimination and reinforce existing social inequities if not properly audited and regulated. Legal systems must evolve to establish standards for algorithmic accountability, due process, and human oversight in automated decisions. There is a growing call for "algorithmic transparency laws" that mandate the disclosure of AI systems used by government agencies, their logic, data sources, and mechanisms for appeal or redress. Transparency and Open Government Initiatives: Technology has empowered open government initiatives by enabling greater transparency, civic participation, and government accountability. Open data platforms allow citizens, journalists, and civil society organizations to analyze government performance, monitor public spending, and detect irregularities. Many public institutions now publish datasets on budgets, procurement, education, health, and environmental indicators. Participatory technologies such as crowdsourcing, digital petitions, and consultation portals allow for more inclusive policymaking. Legal frameworks must support these initiatives by enacting freedom of information (FOI) laws, mandating proactive disclosure of information, and protecting whistleblowers and data users. Reforms are also needed to ensure the integrity, security, and usability of open data ecosystems.

Digital Inclusion and Equity in Service Delivery: The adoption of technology in public administration must be guided by the principles of equity and inclusion. Despite the benefits of digital services, not all citizens have equal access to digital tools, internet connectivity, or digital literacy. This digital divide can exacerbate social inequalities and lead to exclusion from essential public services. Legal frameworks can play a key role in promoting digital inclusion by mandating universal access to internet services, subsidizing digital devices for marginalized groups, and ensuring that public platforms are accessible to persons with disabilities and those with limited literacy. Administrative reforms must incorporate digital literacy campaigns and provide alternative channels (such as community service centers) to ensure no one is left behind in the digital governance revolution (Naimi-Sadigh A., et al, 2022). Smart Cities and Urban Governance: Smart city initiatives exemplify the convergence of technology, law, and public administration. These urban ecosystems leverage sensors, data analytics, and IoT (Internet of Things) devices to manage infrastructure, transportation, waste, energy, and public safety. The deployment of surveillance cameras, facial recognition, and location-tracking technologies raises privacy and civil liberties concerns. Legal reforms are needed to regulate data ownership, consent, and oversight in smart city projects. Additionally, administrative law must be adapted to accommodate rapid experimentation and technological deployment in urban governance, while ensuring legal safeguards against misuse. Blockchain and Legal Record-Keeping: Emerging technologies such as blockchain have the potential to revolutionize legal record-keeping and administrative integrity. Blockchain-based systems can provide immutable and transparent records for land titles, identity verification, contract registration, and financial transactions. By reducing fraud, enhancing auditability, and eliminating intermediaries, blockchain can improve trust in government processes. However, implementing such technologies requires legal reforms to recognize the validity of decentralized ledgers, smart contracts, and digital assets (Nisha Angeline M., et al, 2025). Legislatures must also address issues of interoperability, governance of blockchain platforms, and liability in case of system failure or misuse. Technology has become a central force in shaping the legal and administrative landscape of modern governance. Its transformative potential lies in improving efficiency, transparency, inclusiveness, and responsiveness in public administration. However, these gains are not automatic—they require deliberate legal reforms, ethical oversight, and robust regulatory frameworks to ensure that technology serves the public interest rather than undermines it. As governments embrace digital transformation, they must prioritize the development of laws that protect rights, build trust, and foster innovation. The legal system must evolve in tandem with technological advancements, ensuring that principles of accountability, due process, and equality remain at the heart of public administration. The future of governance will be defined not just by technological capability, but by the legal and ethical choices societies make in deploying those technologies.

THE FUTURE OF LAW AND GOVERNANCE IN THE DIGITAL AGE

The digital age marks a profound transformation in the foundations of law and governance. The exponential growth of information technologies—ranging from artificial intelligence (AI), big data, and blockchain to the Internet of Things (IoT), cloud computing, and quantum systems—is reshaping how laws are formulated, interpreted, enforced, and experienced by citizens. This technological evolution compels a revaluation of traditional legal principles and governance models, while simultaneously creating opportunities to build more responsive, inclusive, transparent, and efficient public institutions (Upadhyaya A N., et al, 2025). As societies become increasingly interconnected and digitalized, the future of law and governance hinges on their ability to adapt to this complex landscape while preserving democratic values, the rule of law, and human rights. Digital Transformation of Legal Frameworks: The legal system of the future must accommodate the realities of a digital society. Static, text-based statutes are giving way to dynamic, data-informed, and machine-readable legal instruments. Legislative bodies are exploring ways to codify digital rights, regulate digital markets, and provide a legal foundation for emerging technologies such as smart contracts, decentralized autonomous organizations (DAOs), digital currencies, and AI systems. The digitization of law also means that legal codes can be embedded into software systems, making compliance automatic and continuous—a concept known as "code as law." However, this transformation raises new questions about accountability, interpretation, and judicial oversight. The future legal order will need to harmonize human discretion with algorithmic governance, ensuring fairness, adaptability, and redressability. Cybersecurity and

Legal Resilience: As digital systems become integral to governance and legal operations, the risks associated with cyber threats, digital espionage, data breaches, and ransomware attacks escalate (Fernandez & Hui, 2022). The future of law must prioritize cybersecurity as a legal, administrative, and national security imperative. Laws will need to define liability for cyber incidents, set standards for digital hygiene and resilience, and establish international protocols for cooperation and response. Public institutions will require robust cyber-governance frameworks, data protection regimes, and cybercrime units equipped with legal authority and technical expertise. Simultaneously, legal systems must protect civil liberties in cyberspace, balancing security needs with freedom of expression, privacy, and due process. Cyber law will evolve as a hybrid domain intersecting constitutional rights, criminal law, international relations, and administrative governance.

Digital Rights and Legal Personhood: In the digital age, rights are no longer limited to physical space. The future of law will expand to protect digital personhood, including rights to digital identity, online anonymity, data sovereignty, algorithmic fairness, and freedom from surveillance. Legal systems will need to recognize digital identities and protect individuals' control over their data across platforms and borders. Concepts like the right to be forgotten, digital self-determination, and biometric privacy will become foundational pillars of law. There is also an emerging debate around the legal status of autonomous systems—whether advanced AI or robots should be granted limited legal personhood or liability (Yallop A C., et al, 2021). Courts and legislatures will need to grapple with unprecedented questions of intent, agency, and moral responsibility in digital contexts. Regulatory Innovation and Agile Lawmaking:/Traditional lawmaking processes are often too slow and rigid to keep pace with technological innovation. In response, governments are embracing more adaptive regulatory approaches, including regulatory sandboxes, living regulations, and outcome-based rulemaking. These methods allow experimentation with new technologies and policies in controlled settings, promoting innovation while managing risk. Digital technologies also support real-time monitoring, feedback loops, and iterative policy design based on data analytics and user behavior. The future of lawmaking will involve continuous, evidence-based refinement of rules, supported by digital tools and cross-sector collaboration. This transformation offers unprecedented opportunities to enhance justice, transparency, efficiency, and civic participation (Abernethy A., et al, 2022). Yet it also presents serious challenges related to equity, privacy, accountability, and the legitimacy of automated systems. The future of law and governance will depend on our ability to strike a balance between innovation and regulation, automation and human oversight, global integration and local autonomy. It will require bold leadership, inclusive dialogue, and adaptive legal frameworks that evolve with technological change while remaining rooted in democratic principles and the rule of law. In embracing the digital future, law and governance must not lose sight of their foundational purpose: to serve the public good, protect human dignity, and uphold justice in all its forms. With thoughtful reform, ethical innovation, and a commitment to inclusive governance, societies can build legal systems that are not only digitally empowered but also deeply humane and resilient in the face of change.

CONCLUSION

Law serves as the cornerstone of public administration, establishing the framework within which governmental functions are organized, policies are crafted, and public services are delivered. Its presence ensures that administrative power is exercised not arbitrarily but within the boundaries of legality, accountability, and fairness. As governments navigate an increasingly complex and dynamic socio-political landscape, the relevance and indispensability of law in public administration have grown exponentially. Law not only guides the structure and operation of administrative institutions but also functions as a vital safeguard for public interest, human rights, and democratic governance. At its core, public administration is an instrument of the state, charged with implementing laws and delivering services that meet public needs. The law empowers administrative agencies, defines their functions, and regulates their relationships with citizens and other branches of government. From the drafting of policies to their execution, and from regulation enforcement to dispute resolution, law ensures predictability, uniformity, and legitimacy in administrative processes. Without a firm legal foundation, public administration risks devolving into inefficiency, arbitrariness, and potential abuse of power. Law also plays a central role in legitimizing public policies. While policy is rooted in political will and administrative judgment, its legitimacy and sustainability depend heavily on legal validation and enforceability. Well-drafted laws translate policy objectives into actionable mandates, allocate responsibilities across institutions, and define standards for implementation and evaluation. This legal codification ensures continuity, transparency, and enforceability—three elements that are essential for policy success in complex, multi-level governance environments. In sectors like healthcare, education, environmental regulation, taxation, and social welfare, legal frameworks ensure that public administration adheres to established principles while adapting to emerging needs. Moreover, law serves as a critical instrument in advancing equity, justice, and inclusivity in public administration. It protects marginalized communities from discrimination, mandates affirmative action in service delivery, and ensures equal access to governmental programs. Administrative procedures grounded in law provide mechanisms through which grievances can be addressed and remedial measures enforced. By institutionalizing these protections, the legal framework empowers citizens to engage with and influence public administration, thereby fostering participatory governance and social justice. Legal literacy among public officials is thus crucial. Administrators must understand the statutory basis of their authority, the rights of the citizens they serve, and the legal consequences of their decisions. This requires continuous training, interdisciplinary collaboration, and institutional support. Legal capacity-building enhances the overall quality of governance by reducing bureaucratic errors, preventing litigation, and fostering trust between the state and its citizens. In conclusion, law is not an adjunct to public administration—it is its very foundation. It legitimizes authority, delineates responsibilities, guides decision-making, safeguards rights, and ensures accountability. As societies continue to evolve and face new challenges, the relationship between law and public administration must remain dynamic, principled, and citizen-centric. Ensuring that public administration remains grounded in law is essential for the continued health of democratic institutions, the promotion of social equity, and the realization of the public good. Only through a deep and enduring commitment to legal governance can public administration truly fulfill its mandate of serving the people with justice, integrity, and efficiency.

REFERENCES

Abernethy, A., Adams, L., Barrett, M., Bechtel, C., Bhatia, A., Brawley, O., Conway, P., & Gorman, P. (2022). The promise of digital health: Then, now, and the future. *NAM Perspectives*, *2022*(22), 1–25. DOI: 10.31478/202206e PMID: 36177208

Amelicheva, L., Martyniuk, O., Pyroha, I., Qaracayev, C., & Myroshnychenko, V. (2021). Implementation of constitutional human rights and social guarantees of security in the context of digitalization. *Amazonia Investiga*, *10*(43), 375–385. DOI: 10.34069/AI/2021.45.09.26

Avalekar, U. A., Mehta, V., Mishra, B. R., Prasanna, L., Rajlakshmi, P. V., & Manjunath, T. C. (2025). The current advances in AI-driven education. In Babulak, E. (Ed.), *Educational AI humanoid computing devices for cyber nomads* (pp. 173–196). IGI Global Scientific Publishing., DOI: 10.4018/979-8-3693-8985-0.ch008

Bacong, A. M., & Menjívar, C. (2021). Recasting the immigrant health paradox through intersections of legal status and race. *Journal of Immigrant and Minority Health*, *23*(5), 1092–1104. DOI: 10.1007/s10903-021-01162-2 PMID: 33656653

Battaglio, R. P. (2021). *Public human resource management: Strategies and practices in the 21st century* (2nd ed.). SAGE Publications., DOI: 10.4135/9781071809273

Baudet, C., & Medina, M. J. (2023). The paradoxes of trust and transparency of blockchain technologies. *Journal of Global Information Management*, *31*(12), 1–22. DOI: 10.4018/JGIM.321111

Berman, E. M., Bowman, J. S., West, J. P., & Van Wart, M. R. (2021). *Human resource management in public service: Paradoxes, processes, and problems* (7th ed.). CQ Press., DOI: 10.4135/9781071809266

Brummel, L. (2021). Social accountability between consensus and confrontation: Developing a theoretical framework for societal accountability relationships of public sector organizations. *Administration & Society*, *53*(9), 1437–1463. DOI: 10.1177/0095399720988529

Chib, S., Mehta, A. K., Saravanan, A., Mishra, B. R., & Manjunath, T. C. (2025). Mental health challenges and solutions in high-pressure work environments. In Harriott, S. (Ed.), *Innovative approaches to managing conflict and change in diverse work environments* (pp. 247–272). IGI Global Scientific Publishing., DOI: 10.4018/979-8-3693-9556-1.ch011

Chowdhary, S., Selvakumar, P., Sangeetha, B., Sarvaani, V. V., Anute, N., & Sharma, M. (2025). The role of social capital in entrepreneurial development. In Martínez-Falcó, J., Sánchez-García, E., & Marco-Lajara, B. (Eds.), *Support networks for entrepreneurs: Social capital and strategic collaborations* (pp. 311–338). IGI Global Scientific Publishing., DOI: 10.4018/979-8-3693-9836-4.ch013

Christofoletti, R. (2021). Transparency, innovation, and journalism. In Stahl, B. C., & Coeckelbergh, M. (Eds.), *Innovation reconsidered: Ethics and values in a digital world* (pp. 125–138). Wiley., DOI: 10.1002/9781119730767.ch6

Coates, J. M., Santhanalakshmi, K., Dinesh, N., Gandhimathi, S., Chandel, P. S., & Mohit. (2025). Assessment and evaluation in transnational staff development. In G. Morris & J. Ye (Eds.), *Training and development in transnational higher education* (pp. 387–406). IGI Global Scientific Publishing. DOI: 10.4018/979-8-3373-1897-4.ch019

Fernandez, C. B., & Hui, P. (2022). Life, the metaverse and everything: An overview of privacy, ethics, and governance in metaverse. In *2022 IEEE 42nd International Conference on Distributed Computing Systems (ICDCS)* (pp. 1515–1524). IEEE. https://doi.org/DOI: 10.1109/ICDCS54860.2022.00192

Haenraets, R., & van Berkel, R. (2021). Sustainable employability in public sector HRM: A comparative study. *Journal of Public Administration: Research and Theory*, *29*(2), 112–130. DOI: 10.1093/jopart/muaa032

Knies, E., Boselie, P., Gould-Williams, J., & Vandenabeele, W. (2021). Strategic human resource management and public sector performance: Context matters. *International Journal of Human Resource Management*, *32*(14), 2432–2444. DOI: 10.1080/09585192.2017.1407088

Levin, A. T., Owusu-Boaitey, N., Pugh, S., Fosdick, B. K., Zwi, A. B., Malani, A., Soman, S., Besançon, S., Kashnitsky, I., & Inddy, F. (2022). Assessing the burden of COVID-19 in developing countries: Systematic review, meta-analysis and public policy implications. *BMJ Global Health*, *7*(5), e008477. DOI: 10.1136/bmjgh-2022-008477 PMID: 35618305

Limbore, N. V., Anute, N., Ahluwalia, G. K., Chordiya, P. B., & Kalshetti, P. (2025). Ethical leadership and corporate responsibility. In Harriott, S. (Ed.), *Innovative approaches to managing conflict and change in diverse work environments* (pp. 193–218). IGI Global Scientific Publishing., DOI: 10.4018/979-8-3693-9556-1.ch009

Loi, M., & Spielkamp, M. (2021). Towards accountability in the use of artificial intelligence for public administrations. In *Proceedings of the 2021 AAAI/ACM Conference on AI, Ethics, and Society* (pp. 760–768). DOI: 10.1145/3461702.3462631

Maksimentseva, N. O. (2023). The principles of administrative law vs. the principles of public administration. *Formy Mediatsii ta Yikh Znachennia u Yurydychnii Praktytsi, 6*, 311–321. DOI: 10.32782/chern.v6.2023.18

Mehra, J., Madaan, S., & Balu, N. Mohit, & Manjunath, T. C. (2025). The ubiquitous internet and smart computation available 24/7 for anyone and anywhere. In E. Babulak (Ed.), *Educational AI humanoid computing devices for cyber nomads* (pp. 247–270). IGI Global Scientific Publishing. DOI: 10.4018/979-8-3693-8985-0.ch010

Naimi-Sadigh, A., Asgari, T., & Rabiei, M. (2022). Digital transformation in the value chain disruption of banking services. *Journal of the Knowledge Economy, 13*(2), 2915–2934. DOI: 10.1007/s13132-021-00759-0

Neumann, O., Guirguis, K., & Steiner, R. (2024). Exploring artificial intelligence adoption in public organizations: A comparative case study. *Public Management Review, 26*(8), 1234–1257. DOI: 10.1080/14719037.2022.2048685

Nisha Angeline, M., Selvakumar, P., Gupta, M. K., Nazar, N., Elumalai, D., & Bhattacharya, S. (2025). Emerging materials for energy storage and environmental applications. In K. Muduli, B. Moharana, S. Ales, & D. Biswal (Eds.), *Using computational intelligence for sustainable manufacturing of advanced materials* (pp. 53–72). IGI Global Scientific Publishing. DOI: 10.4018/979-8-3693-7974-5.ch003

Osborne, S. P., Nasi, G., & Powell, M. (2021). Beyond co-production: Value creation and public services. *Public Administration, 99*(4), 877–891. DOI: 10.1111/padm.12718

Overman, S., & Schillemans, T. (2022). Toward a public administration theory of felt accountability. *Public Administration Review, 82*(4), 763–776. DOI: 10.1111/puar.13417

Riccucci, N. M. (2021). *Public personnel management: Current concerns, future challenges* (6th ed.). Routledge., DOI: 10.4324/9781003124567

Scupola, A., & Mergel, I. (2022). Co-production in digital transformation of public administration and public value creation: The case of Denmark. *Government Information Quarterly, 39*(2), 101685. DOI: 10.1016/j.giq.2021.101650

Shava, E., & Mazenda, A. (2021). Ethics in South African public administration: A critical review. *International Journal of Management Practice, 14*(4), 526–544. DOI: 10.1504/IJMP.2021.115107

Thomann, E., & Lieberherr, E. (2024). Public policy implementation and accountability. In *Handbook of Public Policy Implementation* (pp. 53–66). Edward Elgar Publishing., DOI: 10.4337/9781800885905.00011

Tummers, L., & van Berkel, R. (2021). Employer engagement and inclusive HRM in public organizations. *Human Resource Management Journal, 31*(3), 456–472. DOI: 10.1111/1748-8583.12245

Upadhyaya, A. N., Debnath, P., Rani, P., Manjunath, T. C., & Bhattacharya, S. (2025). AI-based disaster prediction and early warning systems. In Mobo, F. (Ed.), *AI and emerging technologies for emergency response and smart cities* (pp. 55–74). IGI Global Scientific Publishing., DOI: 10.4018/979-8-3693-9770-1.ch003

Vandy, J. F. (2023). Bridging the gap for effective public sector management: Reviewing the critical role of strategic human resource management. *International Journal of Research Publication and Reviews, 4*(4), 347–360. DOI: 10.55248/gengpi.2023.4.4.34741

Vermeeren, B. (2021). HRM and performance in public sector organizations: A review of the evidence. *Public Management Review, 23*(5), 678–695. DOI: 10.1080/14719037.2020.1722213

Wang, Q., & Guan, Z. (2023). Can sunlight disperse mistrust? A meta-analysis of the effect of transparency on citizens' trust in government. *Journal of Public Administration: Research and Theory, 33*(1), 11–31. DOI: 10.1093/jopart/muac040

Yallop, A. C., Gică, O. A., Moisescu, O. I., & Coro , M. M. (2021). The digital traveller: Implications for data ethics and data governance in tourism and hospitality. *International Journal of Contemporary Hospitality Management, 33*(10), 293–308. DOI: 10.1108/IJCHM-10-2020-1207

Zeraatkar, S., & Rajabi Farjad, H. (2021). Exploration of the challenges of human resource management in the public sector and their effects on productivity. *Human Resource Management Journal, 15*(1), 35–54. DOI: 10.52547/hrmj.15.1.3

Chapter 4
NPM Is Dead, Long Live NPM:
Transformations of New Public Management in the Course of Administrative Reforms

Panagiotis Karkatsoulis
Institute for Regulatory Policy Research, Athens, Greece

Fotini Vittou
http://orcid.org/0000-0001-5367-5042
Panteion University of Social and Political Sciences, Greece

ABSTRACT

Over the past decades, New Public Management (NPM) has been widely criticised for weakening the institutional role of the state and empowering economic elites and private actors, raising concerns about the erosion of cohesion and state capacity. Crises such as the pandemic, climate change, migration, and the rise of populism revealed that NPM reforms must either evolve or lose legitimacy. Reformers must respond by restoring the principles of the rule of law, democratic institutions, and sound public management practices. Technology, and especially Artificial Intelligence (AI), can support this renewal. This chapter reinterprets NPM as NPM 2.0, highlighting tools and techniques that integrate empirical and theoretical knowledge while adapting to the specific identities and needs of each administrative system. It concludes that the endurance of NPM's second generation depends on embedding technological innovation within constitutional safeguards, transforming digitalisation into a means of rebuilding state capacity.

DOI: 10.4018/979-8-3373-3526-1.ch004

1. INTRODUCTION

For about thirty years now, criticism has been levelled at the theory and practice of public management and, in particular, at the New Public Management (NPM) variant. It is interesting to note that both the NPM concept and its criticism originate from the same womb, namely the United Kingdom, which spearheaded the development and promotion of NPM reforms, along with other Anglo-Saxon countries (the US, Canada, Australia, New Zealand).

Criticisms and objections to the theories and policy proposals of public management were always expressed and had to do, on the one hand, to the methodological clarity and adequacy of the evidence supporting its proposals and, on the other hand, to the dominance of market and economic rules over institutions and the rule of law. While the arguments have been repeated, more or less, over the last three decades, the cataclysmic developments of the last two decades, starting with the collapse of the Western financial system and continuing with the ongoing brutal wars in the Middle East and Ukraine, show that the state is in dramatic decline—at least in the form handed down to us by the French Revolution and thereafter. Its collapse is dragging down institutions, nullifying achievements relating to the organization of the core of power, and those at the forefront of its decline changes in the organization and functioning of the state that would make it more effective or efficient are considered a minor issue.

What is interesting and original in this case is not the repetition of the arguments and critical proposals of the NPM, but the paradox that is recorded with the emergence of major crises. While the state appears to have failed to control/prevent/avert the crises, it is precisely the same state that is called upon to restore society and the economy to normality and regularity.

In our study, we show that this phenomenon—the state accused of failure being called upon to restore the disrupted socio-political order—characterizes the new post-NPM period, which is referred to as the period of permanent and multiple crises. In other words, the state that was exhausted by its economization is making a comeback. Only this time, the savior state has, in many cases, the characteristics that it was supposed to have eliminated during its reform. The new state is authoritarian, demagogic, and populist. It is an unreformed state, a 19th-century state, as has been aptly said, resulting from an anti-reformist conservative ideology.

Hence, the question arises: Did the reforms that promised to reduce bureaucracy and curb political arbitrariness lead to the exact opposite result? And if so, how did this happen?

Could it be that, in the end, the public management reforms had so many flaws and weaknesses that they were unable to meet the challenges they faced? So, the dilemma in this case is: Either one sides with those who see the reforms as the cause of the problem, or with those who continue to believe in them, after the necessary adjustments and the incorporation of technological developments into the functioning of the state, in a way that overcomes the pathologies of the past.

The study revisits some of the views that have been put forward on this subject and proposes upgrading the NPM to the new environment, which can only be NPM 2.0.

2. METHODOLOGICAL APPROACH

The methodological approach of this study constitutes a coherent strategy aimed at reframing the debate on administrative reform and the NPM and includes a synthesis of multiple analytical tools: qualitative, interpretative, and dialectical. It adopts a qualitative methodological approach that combines critical literature review with comparative analysis of administrative reforms across different national contexts and applies a hermeneutic synthesis of theoretical models - NPM, Post-NPM, and Digital Era Governance - alongside empirical evidence from reform implementation over the past four decades.

This approach allows for the analysis of a multidimensional and evolving phenomenon such as administrative reform from different perspectives: historical, critical, theoretical, and propositional.

Its basic elements are as follows:

- Historical and Diachronic Analysis: It places NPM in an evolutionary context, examining the course of ideas and practices over time.
- Critical-Synthetic Review: It bases its argumentation on critical dialogue with existing academic knowledge, incorporating and transcending criticism.
- Conceptual Reconstruction: Clarifies existing concepts and proposes new terms (NPM 2.0) as tools for understanding contemporary reality.
- Pragmatic Focus: Emphasizes the results of implementation and evaluates reforms within their specific socio-political context, with an emphasis on the Greek paradigm of financial crisis and recovery.

Through an extensive literature review, our analysis is grounded in a wide range of existing academic literature, creating an ongoing dialogue with previous research. In addition, qualitative data from four decades of empirical examples are incorporated. This practice, on the one hand, provides the historical and conceptual framework, outlining the evolution, dominance, and adaptability of NPM, and on the other hand, maps the broader theoretical landscape, placing NPM in relation to later models that emerged in the "post-NPM" era, such as "digital governance" (Dunleavy, et al., 2006) and "new public governance" (Osborne, 2010).

The entire study is permeated by in-depth critical analysis and interdisciplinary analysis. Recognizing that NPM does not belong exclusively to one scientific discipline, the study synthesizes conceptual and analytical approaches from a range of social sciences: economic analysis (cost-effectiveness), organizational theory (structure, change, culture), psychology (motivation, behavior), legal theory (legislation, procedural guarantees), and political analysis (power, interests, ideology). This approach makes it possible to understand NPM not as a technical solution but as a political and social phenomenon that shapes the structure and functioning of the modern state.

Finally, the study moves from critical analysis to conceptual synthesis, on the basis of which we propose an evolved and revised version of NPM – instead of its complete rejection – NPM 2.0.

The aim of this multifaceted and synthetic methodology is to go beyond a simple description of the state of public debate and to intervene normatively in the debate, to shape the agenda and propose a specific path for its future, arguing that the solution lies not in rejecting the reformist logic, but in its mature and adapted development, according to each public administration's local, cultural, and socio-economic-political environment.

Finally, the study is explicit about its own analytical boundaries. Given that reform outcomes vary significantly depending on local and national contexts, specific historical moments, and the relative power of different stakeholders, the work avoids sweeping generalization. Instead, it pursues a dialectical synthesis: presenting the thesis of NPM as an existing system, acknowledging the antithesis through documented critiques and implementation failures, and proposing a synthesis through NPM 2.0 that incorporates hard-won lessons from four decades of experimentation and critical reflection.

3. NPM: ADMINISTRATIVE REFORM IN THE ERA OF GLOBALIZATION

A necessary introductory remark: There are substantial differences in the understanding and implementation of New Public Management in the USA and Europe. These must be borne in mind when discussing the scope and success/failure of NPM reforms.

In the USA, NPM transferred the basic values and management techniques of private enterprise to the public sector, while in Europe it was more closely associated with the concept of "governance." Governance is a broader term than management and differs from it in that it includes concepts such as civil society and social justice.

However, even in Europe, there is no uniform degree of absorption of NPM methods and techniques, just as there is no uniform degree of understanding and perception of the concepts and practices that comprise it. To give an example, there are countries, such as Germany, that lagged in the practical implementation of reforms in the 1980s, placing emphasis on their political and institutional consolidation, but developed them rapidly in the 1990s. The opposite happened in the Netherlands, where reforms were implemented en masse in the 1980s and were followed by their institutional consolidation in the following decade.

NPM is currently implemented in many countries, notably the USA, the UK, New Zealand, Canada, Australia, Finland, Norway, and the Netherlands. In these countries, NPM is the latest successor to older models, such as Public Administration, PPBS (a budget system based on planning and design), ZBBS (zero-based budgeting), etc., which these countries have implemented extensively, and less an innovation that requires a radical revision of principles and values.

In addition, these countries have experienced the greatest economic, technological, and social prosperity in recent years, which has created fertile ground for the development of experiments and new administrative models.

It should also not be overlooked that in the Anglo-Saxon tradition, where the logic of pragmatism prevails, there are more conditions for the development of organizational and management models, such as NPM, which are characterized by their commitment to implementation and the achievement of results and much less by their regulatory imprint and institutional consolidation.

The actions that comprise NPM do not constitute a strictly defined agenda. The NPM includes actions from classic business management, administrative science, and organizational theory, which, depending on the particularities of the countries where they are applied, give the total of reforms a corresponding tone—more programmatic, organizational, or supervisory tone.

The best-known applications of New Public Management are:

-Results-based management
-Total quality management
-E-government
-Benchmarking
-Controlling
-Performance based budgeting
-Employee payroll based on performance indicators
-Regulatory reform.

A characteristic of the NPM openness is its ability to assimilate ideas and proposals that give it greater legitimacy. Two of these are now an integral part of its reforms:

The first is the widespread use of referendums in local communities. At this level of government, direct democracy applications are much more feasible than at the level of central government. In an effort to convince citizens that the reforms concern them, local governments have held mass referendums on issues of local interest. However, it remains doubtful whether this form of governance can be considered an alternative to the representative system, which, at least in Europe, has a long tradition. There is probably more complementarity than rivalry between these two forms, and we believe that the same applies to the relationship between representative governance and civil society, a relationship that appears, at first glance, to be contradictory.

The second has to do with citizen participation in the decision-making process. More and more municipal councils are "opening up" more and more of their processes to citizens. Decisions are increasingly being made collectively. Interactive management, which transforms the municipality/community into a guarantor of a process of confrontation and/or dialogue between interested parties, is found in an increasing number of municipal affairs.

It goes without saying that the degree of acceptance and success of the above actions varies depending on the culture of dialogue and consensus that prevails in each local community.

Most of the above applications can be found in various administrative reform programs in all European countries, as well as in other developed countries around the world. These programs have, of course, different degrees of maturity and success in each country, but it is important to note that, today, it is difficult to find administrative reform programs that do not include some of the previous actions.

In this sense, we can say that NPM is a proposal for the organization and operation of globalized public administration. For the first time since the Weberian bureaucratic model, a completely different proposal for the organization and operation of public administration has emerged. This fact alone is enough to demonstrate the importance of the new paradigm and mark the beginning of a new era.

From its inception, public management has supported the possibility of osmosis between the public and private sectors, as well as the adoption of measures and benchmarks for the production of quality results by the public sector.

One could consider the two pillars of public management to be on the one hand, the knowledge and legacy of private management and, on the other hand, the contribution of the quality movement, as the greatest revolution in the administrative /organisational sciences.

NPM, which differs from traditional public management by the addition of the adjective "new," is part of a series of efforts by public organizations to maximize the benefits they can derive from adopting private management methods.

Public management—like all social sciences- changes, often, the titles of the scientific areas and research topics in order to give more emphasis to them without these investigations meaning necessarily implying new theoretical findings.

The bibliography refers extensively to the development of NPM and its dominance in the 1980s and 1990s (Lapsley, 2009; Funck & Karlsson, 2020). The scientific community welcomed the models that followed NPM with the same enthusiasm from 2000 onwards. Those that appeared in the "post-NPM" era emphasize governance as well as the digital era that took hold in the two decades after 2000 (Dunleavy, et al., 2006).

Among other noteworthy developments are the attempt to reestablish a new bureaucracy (e.g., the neo-Welfare State of C. Pollitt/G. Bouckaert, 2017), the establishment of a "new public governance" (Osborne, 2010), as well as multi-level governance understood as an articulated whole (Christensen & Lægreid, 2007; Hood, 2004).

However, none of these developments render NPM an outdated model and tool for administrative change. NPM continues to provoke discussion and, above all, to serve as a practical guide for action due to its plasticity and adaptability (Lapsley & Miller, 2024).

Of course, one should not overlook the fact that many of the NPM's flagship actions (goal setting, performance-based evaluation, etc.) are already established examples that were founded after much effort and hard work in many public administrations. For this reason, it is neither desirable nor feasible to abandon them in favor of other, rather vague, priorities.

Whatever the criticism, it is not enough to lead to the cancellation of implemented reforms, so NPM has gained a vital space and legitimacy despite the claims of its critics, who are mainly ideological and political in nature (Christensen & Lægreid, 2007).

An interesting, though not particularly developed, aspect of the NPM is its learning character. This refers to its capacity to provide stimuli and frameworks for action, rather than ready-made packages of solutions and actions, leaving ample room for adaptation to local/national specificities.

It is assumed that organizations learn and develop expertise as they implement reforms and have the capacity and know-how to use them to advance their strategies and objectives (Dan & Pollitt, 2015) . As an extremely flexible and adaptable set of ideas and practices, NPM serves multiple political and administrative purposes, such as controlling public spending, organizational performance, accountability for results, and competition.

Two of these, related to improving public sector productivity, have met with the strongest reactions from citizens, civil servants, and academics who study public administration and organizational theory.

3.1 Privatization as a Blow to the Hard Core of the State

Criticism focuses, in particular, on the "new" element of the NPM, namely the transfer of purely public projects to private individuals, as well as on privatization. The extent of the application of co-administration of purely state affairs with the private sector is not new. What is new, however, are the many ways in which concession contracts can be differentiated, depending on the nature of the goods/services and the general situation of the country in which they are applied, which have led to the sell-off of parts of the hard core of the state[1] .

The sale of public assets to private interests has had the obvious effect of worsening the quality of services provided, despite improving competition. Although in many countries, especially the most developed ones, strong competition authorities tried to achieve market balance and maintain a high level of service provision ("value for money"), the outcome has been (and remains) negative.

A key reason for the failure of the regulated market was and is the corruption of government officials and businesspeople, with the phenomenon of "revolving doors" having become widespread (Kotanidis, 2024).

In light of this, the need for institutional strengthening of states and improvement of control mechanisms is becoming urgent.

3.2 Program Based Budgeting

The NPM placed particular emphasis on cost-effectiveness relationship. The assessment of economic costs in relation to benefits, as well as the assessment of costs in relation to effectiveness, are the basic tools of the NPM, borrowed from the private sector and classical management. At the practical level, the cost-effectiveness of administrative action was reflected primarily in the drafting of public budgets, both for the central government and other public organizations.

Until the advent of PPBS (programming/planning/budgeting systems), the budget as a central tool of organization and administration was understood as a complex system of accounting entries with an incremental character (OECD, 2006).

Incremental budgets are, par excellence, deficit-oriented and highly anti-developmental. In fact, in countries with clientelist politics and public organizations, they serve as basic tools for promoting relevant practices.

The architecture of incremental budgets has the following specific characteristics:

- The wide dispersion of revenue and expenditure codes, so that the mazes formed between them are more complex than the Labyrinth. Who could, for example, keep track of the flow of money circulating in 6,500 codes when Greece entered the "memoranda" (Karkatsoulis, 2010) .

- The uneven, non-standardized accounting coding and the rejection of those international standards that facilitate the control not only of legality but also of feasibility.
- The resulting inability to allocate costs or evaluate the performance of structures, which is exacerbated by their constant mobility.
- The centralized management system: The Ministry of Finance acts as a controller and allocator of funds, rather than acting strategically.

The opposite of an incremental budget is a budget based on a program. Its main features are:

1. Its focus on strategy and the organization of operational activities (rather than on individual actions reflected in the codes).
2. Multi-year planning/estimation of ministry expenditures, their documentation and linkage to the long-term economic and fiscal framework as well as to government policy objectives.
3. Strengthening the autonomy and accountability of ministries and all those who manage public funds.

However, program budgeting is one of those reforms that are extremely difficult to implement and require many continuous and coordinated efforts in countries with a tradition of clientelism.

Program budgeting cannot be established and be effective with a government that not only lacks a program for rationalizing public spending but also continues to view public money as a means of satisfying the interests of its own people and those close to it. Otherwise, it would not be looking for ways to fill the "revenue" field that must balance the "expenses" field, but would assess whether it is worthwhile/necessary to use all possible means of revenue collection in order to balance the expenditure it currently covers. In other words, it would have to do what it disagrees with, what goes against the levelling effect of populism: evaluate expenditure. This would mean that we would have to examine from scratch whether the amounts allocated to the respective codes, both as remuneration and as operating expenses, correspond to the achievement of specific objectives and results. Not just any objectives, but those that meet the expressed or implied needs of the citizens whom the specific service is supposed to serve.

However, designing a budget based on the needs and expectations of citizens is not just a matter of top-down reform, but also the result of a different, non-egocentric approach to public affairs.

4. ECONOMY, EFFICIENCY, AND EFFECTIVENESS

The principle of economy also applies to other widely used economic management tools, such as agreements between employees and employers following negotiations (rather than based on predetermined rules of public law), the planning and monitoring of administrative action based on objectives and results, policy measurement and evaluation indicators, comparative evaluation and competition between public services, etc.

The problem with these tools is that the (Napoleonic) state, which is based on non-economic categories (e.g., competences, hierarchy of legal rules, strict procedural provisions) must translate and incorporate into its operational decision-making code concepts and practices that do not conflict with its constitutional and operational regulations and practices.

To give just one example of the different rationales and assumptions between reform and anti-reform policies: The measures and actions of the NPM for the management and development of human resources are the antithesis of bureaucratic organization and the traditional perception of human resource utilization, according to which civil servants are simply tools (an executive mechanism) for implementing the will of their political superiors. For this reason, there is, as a rule, no personal responsibility for acts or omissions of the service.

According to the NPM, however, there is personal responsibility on the part of the employee, based on the individual description of his duties. The individual performance of the employee is measured and evaluated in comparison with the performance of other employees. The organization's human resources are an integral part of it, and the characteristic expression that shows the new perception and importance attached to human resources is "internal customers."

The difficulty with implementing the NPM's human resources policy lies in the existence of entrenched cultural constructs that reflect the values and attitudes of a society. And it is precisely these that give a different meaning to the concepts of productivity and efficiency.

The same differences can be observed in the administrative structures of the administrative system. NPM rejects, for example, the concept of vertical hierarchy, i.e., the administrative pyramid, where each level of management acts as a conveyor belt for orders from the top to the bottom of the public organization.

The organizational structures favored by the NPM are either "network" organization between service units or the networking of public policies and the transfer of decision-making from the different levels of the bureaucratic model to a "single point" ("one stop").

Although technology facilitates networking and collaboration without eliminating roles and responsibilities, the transition from a traditional hierarchical structure to a flexible and multi-level one faces the same obstacles as those mentioned above for human resource management.

Despite the difficulties that arise, especially in European countries with a tradition of positive law, the logic of effectiveness and efficiency is constantly gaining ground. This is not unrelated to the primacy of economy, the basic principle on which public policy analysis and management were built.

5. METHODOLOGICAL LIMITATIONS OF NPM

Firstly, it should be noted that the debate on method as a necessary prerequisite for assessing the scientific nature of a discipline, a theory or even a practice remains absolutely crucial for supporters of rational discourse.

That said, we are strongly opposed to the position held by some contemporary scholars that reforms can be categorized as either NPM or "post-NPM." Indeed, in the absence of strict methodological principles that characterize our era, all the reforms are combined, like supermarket products that the interested party has only to choose and put in their basket those that suit them (Bel & Casula, 2024).

Complexity can only be reduced by corresponding complexity, not by simplistic logic, to paraphrase Ashby's principle of "requisite variety" (1968).

Before referring to the other differences between the bureaucratic model and NPM, we must point out that the supporters of methodological plurarism (Kelly & Hofbauer, 2023), reject the contradiction between new and traditional values of organization and management. The basic principles of NPM (quality, effectiveness, efficiency, economy) are considered complementary to the traditional principles of legality and equal opportunity. They therefore believe that it is possible to reconcile these principles and overcome any contradictions.

However, with regard to the refutation of many of the principles and priorities of NPM, such as, for example, the case of imposing decisions and interests through the power of one player at the expense of the network's priorities, it is a fact that this is due to the neglect or cancellation of important parameters of the NPM.

In the example of the criticism that the market imposes itself on the state, one could argue that this has been observed where there are no strong independent competition authorities and authorities to monitor corruption and economic crime.

When it comes to assessing the importance of each of the key stakeholders in governance, i.e., the state, the private sector, and civil society, one should not be misled by the current power of each of them in a particular country.

This raises a philosophical-methodological problem that the NPM must resolve or, in any case, take a position on. The problem concerns the relationship between theory and practice, one of the perennial questions of philosophy. In this case, the question is whether one will defend the NPM, maintaining the position/view of the continuous improvement of its measures and proposals, or whether one should take a definitive stance against it after assessing its impact on concrete examples of certain countries, at specific historical moments and under specific conditions.

A similar, but not equally important, issue is that of the scientific nature of the NPM. Criticism includes points such as, for example, that the NPM is a theory without inventors. It emerged as the sum of individual practices—which, however, have had a common reflection of principal values. They have further developed by international organizations, led by the OECD, and established due to their successes in organizational and administrative matters over the last three decades.

In addition, the UN, the World Bank, and the International Monetary Fund have contributed significantly to the development of NPM as a globalized model of public sector organization and management. These organizations did not function as mere conduits for information, but as policy designers and motivators of member countries in their implementation. At the same time, in addition to their traditional supervisory role, they also acted as precursors to the corresponding national policies. Their subsequent assistance to third countries wishing to implement policies similar to those of their member states resulted in a significant upgrade of their political role.

However, it should also be noted that states and administrations have attempted to exploit the recommendations of international organizations in order to cover up their own planning shortcomings and to overcome the resistance of citizen groups and interest groups that oppose them.

Today, at least for EU member states, it is an indisputable fact that the formulation and implementation of public policies for public sector reform passes through international organizations, and the transfer of good practices is as important as the policies designed at national and local level.

It is a fact, however, that NPM does not belong exclusively to a certain scientific discipline. There are proposals, ideas, and assumptions from various social sciences (economics, sociology, psychology, law, political science) that are incorporated into NPM, without, however, adhering to a single, clear methodology. It is also a fact that NPM itself has not shown particular interest in methodological purity. Of course, neither did its predecessor, "Administrative Science," distinguish itself in this regard.

The interdisciplinary formulation of NPM is still sought after, but interest in it is limited to specialists who delve into the philosophical and epistemological principles of science. The rapid development of technology has solved many of the problems raised in previous decades, such as whether it is a science of "being" (Sein) or a science of "ought" (Sollen). The development of theoretical models that transcended the division between theory and practice at a higher level of abstraction, such as the proposals of the theory of self-referential social systems, has attracted the interest of many researchers (Luhmann, 1984). In any case, the methodological documentation of NPM is necessary for its further development and adaptation to our globalized environment.

6. CRITICISM OF NPM IS MORE POLITICAL THAN ADMINISTRATIVE

The debate over whether NPM, one of the longest-lasting "brands" of public management, has run its course or is transforming itself to adapt to new conditions continues. And as is often the case with such discussions, which seek knowledge not in the «field» but in their academic boundaries, they are counterproductive (Bourdieu, 2007).

An easy answer is that the NPM reforms that did not have a common methodological or value assumption dissolved into the elements from which they were composed. Some are still in force, others are not. This is a realistic approach that emphasizes the catch-all nature of the NPM (Hood, 1991).

However, the evaluation of the application of the NPM is not and cannot be uniform, since different applications take place in different circumstances, without there being a blueprint for the different governments at different levels.

It is a natural consequence that responses vary. During the 1980s, led by the USA and Canada on the other side of the Atlantic and the Netherlands and the UK in Europe, the NPM's proposals were seen as a panacea, both theoretically and, above all, practically and politically. The problems that the NPM sought to solve at that time were problems of rational resource management. It is a fact that the rationalisation attempted through the measures and actions of the NPM, particularly in local governments (municipalities, communities), substantially improved their financial management. The widespread use of contracts/agreements between the central government and local government organizations, which described their cooperation with mutual commitments, resulted in the widespread expansion of the concept of "privatised public goods". The pace of public sector operations changed, employees became motivated and enthusiastic, and many public organisations rushed to follow the pioneers.

In the late 1990s, however (especially from 1996-1997 onwards), certain observations began to be made, such as that citizens are not simply customers and that the role of state services cannot be limited to the provision of services. Politics seemed to be making a comeback, along with society's demand for the state to play a guiding role.

However, there has been no discussion of what, specifically, the NPM did not foresee, and criticism has been limited to political criticism.

The central idea of the NPM was that reforms implemented in the private sector to improve the efficiency and effectiveness of businesses could, if transferred to the public sector, transform it into a productive sector by freeing it from bureaucratic burdens. However, when it was implemented in different countries, different rationales and practices prevailed, which had a negative impact. The prevalence of competition between principles and rules serving different aspects of governance resulted in either one-sidedness (see the insistence on the opposition between public and private and the inherent superiority of the private sector: "to run the state like a business") or oversimplification with the politicization of the objectives and implementation of reforms.

For example, in "better regulation" issues, there is not only cost-benefit analysis but also consultation throughout all stages of regulatory process as a critical element. Many of the reforms were altered or watered down when implemented. Some of them, as the quality control, while it is applied in the manufacturing industry, over the globe, it is very difficult to be implemented in the public sector due to the heterogeneity of its objectives.

The negative experience of Margaret Thatcher's privatizations and the experiment with neoliberalism in the Anglo-Saxon world was decisive in the generalization of criticism of NPM.

Among the most prominent critics of the NPM is that of Rod Rhodes. He argues that the British state was weakened by privatization policies, the existence of alternative service providers beyond the state, EU regulations, and NPM. According to him, their implementation has led to the fragmentation of state services and a decline in their quality, the dispersion and limitation of responsibility, and a reduction in the accountability that was ensured by the bureaucratic model of administration. Ultimately, the NPM, together with EU Law, is responsible for the general decline of the state into a "minimal" state (Rhodes, 2017).

Despite the temporary gains made by the private sector, which expanded into businesses that had previously been state monopolies, it became apparent that these solutions were not sustainable over time. In fact, some of them proved to be negative experiences. Many of the supporters of "weakening the state" attributed the failure of the NPM to the measures themselves (e.g., privatization, decentralization), when in fact what happened was that during their implementation, the safeguards that were theoretically in place were violated, and so the results were not as expected. The public procurement control sector, for example, did not operate on the basis of strict protocols for checking the borrowing capacity of many contractors, with the result that many of the projects awarded to private individuals failed, speculation developed, and state resources were squandered.

From the perspective of its critics, the NPM is said to have promoted reforms which, instead of strengthening the established functions of the state, with a view to "scientific management" and, in essence, the strengthening of the democratic exercise of power, led to their erosion. The main tool of the NPM that allowed it to slide into a - seemingly only - reformist function (hollowing out) was privatization. These were seen as allowing the state to relinquish its basic functions, especially with regard to the privatization of energy and water networks water supply networks, as well as the transfer of essential powers to supranational and sub-national institutions and governance structures.

The consequences of the weakening of the state, according to its advocates, are serious:

Loss of capacity: The state may retain its fundamental powers, but it loses the ability to exercise them effectively.

Fragmentation: Public services and responsibilities are fragmented across different levels of governance and between public and private actors.

Accountability issues: The shift towards networks and private actors can create challenges in terms of ensuring accountability and transparency.

Shift from government to governance: The focus is shifting from direct service delivery by the state to a broader concept of governance, where multiple actors are involved in managing collective public goods.

The question here, however, is whether the weaknesses in the implementation of many of the NPM reforms are due to this very fact or to an anti-reform agenda that does not consider the issues included in the NPM agenda to be particularly important.

Political criticism of the EU has also led to criticism of the administrative side of the reforms. Thus, under the NPM, many other issues have piled up, such as the accumulation of power among the elite.

What is interesting about this criticism, however, is the description of a situation that is found in many public administrations with different qualities of governance. It is a situation in which anti-reform forces do not openly reject reforms, but undermine them during their implementation, thereby creating negative impressions among citizens and causing them to be canceled.

In this sense, one could include criticism per se as part of a reform agenda. In fact, this would be even more useful if it could include practices from various such cases. The most common are:

A) The passing of provisions and regulations that are limited to announcing future results that never materialize. The literature that has been developed on symbolic legislation and symbolic laws is important here (van Klink, 2016) .

B) The amendment or supplementation of the regulatory framework before it is implemented, or its amendment following reactions from specific interest groups. The resistance of the bureaucracy, which seeks constant amendments on the grounds of specificity, is important here.

C) The nullification of the essence of reform policy through vague, inadequately defined, and uncertified procedures that follow a legislative regulation. The old—and convenient for governments—view that the work of politicians ends with the passing of a regulation, leaving its implementation for the administration serves as a basis for the autonomy of administrative procedures and bureaucracy. Even when administrative procedures are certified, they are undermined by an established administrative culture that seeks through them not to resolve a public problem but, first and foremost, to ensure the security of bureaucrats.

The resistance of the bureaucracy proved to be particularly significant. Initially underestimated, it was perceived more as a technical obstacle than as socially and organizationally embedded perceptions and attitudes. It took considerable effort to highlight the central role of administrative culture in promoting change.

In this context, the principle of the "learning organization" was also promoted, as it became clear that both the organization and its employees would have to "unlearn" what they knew and learn something different, something new. Undoubtedly, this effort requires a lot of time and money, and this is probably not unrelated to the objections raised against the effectiveness of NPM, since many of the countries that adopted the NPM had neither the means nor the capacity to support the reformed institutions and their staff with appropriate training programs.

Add to this the statist perception of citizens and politicians that the "state" is obliged to solve all kinds of problems and disputes, the corruption of public organizations and officials, the fragmented organizational structure, with the consequent dispersion and overlap of responsibilities, and the multiplicity of laws that turns the resolution of even a simple problem into a torturous process.

Furthermore, the promotion of NPM reforms is hampered by those factors that consistently act negatively on any administrative reform. Excessive legislation, confusion of competences between different levels of administration, and organizational fragmentation aimed at securing trade union interests have always been the main obstacles to administrative reforms and continue to be obstacles to the implementation of the NPM.

Of these obstacles, the one that appears particularly strong today is corruption, and the reason is to be found in the expansion of the economic subsystem into the sphere of politics and state activities and in the lack of rules setting clear boundaries between the two.

7. WHAT CAN THE NPM CONTRIBUTE TODAY?

Although the failures and shortcomings have been repeatedly pointed out, and although changes and additions have been proposed to put the reforms back on a positive track, subsequent developments have not vindicated those who believed in the self-regulating corrective capacity of the reforms, nor, however, those who generally dismiss the reformist project due to the prevalence of anti-reformist forces in many parts of the world.

The dramatic change in socio-political conditions brought about by the emergence of multiple crises and leaders who flirt with anti-democratic ideas and practices of governance has brought the NPM back into the spotlight. This time, however, adapted to the new environment and taking advantage of the possibilities offered by modern technology, it seems to have more chances of success than in previous decades when liberal views and policies prevailed.

Those attracted by the charm of administrative reforms may see the otherwise bleak social, economic, and political reality as fertile ground for a new NPM—an NPM 2.0.

7.1 Crises and Threats to Democracy and the Rule of Law

Contemporary crises share some common characteristics that should not be overlooked. Firstly, there is a temporal sequence to their manifestation that many consider to be permanent in nature (permacrisis). As aptly described, the term "Permacrisis" (permanent crisis) perfectly expresses the sense of dizziness caused by the transition from one unprecedented event to another, as we wonder pessimistically what new horrors may await us in the future" (The Conversation, 2022) .

Secondly, crises are of different natures (military, economic, energy, climate, migration, etc.) but have certain characteristics in common:

A) They test the limits of public organizations in terms of their ability to cope with them. All the basic principles of the administrative state, such as the principles of equality, impartiality, the rule of law, transparency, and accountability, are being challenged because they are considered responsible for the quality of governance.

B) Losses, mistakes, and omissions in different policy areas are blamed on the administrative state. Thus, for the first time, the questioning of a public policy (e.g., protection against natural disasters) is not limited to the confrontation between political parties but also affects the mechanisms for its implementation.

C) The basic principles of the administrative state that are severely affected are the rule of law, accountability, and judicial review.

The scope of decision-making powers granted to the civil service, transparency, and accountability, which ensure the consistency of public policies and procedural fairness in decision-making, are also undermined.

The ultimate goal of the administrative state (Waldo, 1948) is to support the constitutionally defined functions of the state (legislative, executive, and judicial) as well as governance in favor of the governed, in order to prevent arbitrary governance and ensure smooth and rational governance, is being dangerously undermined. The foundations of representative democracy, as handed down to us by the forefathers of the Enlightenment, are under threat.

The economic crisis, triggered by the collapse of Lehmann Brothers, was accompanied by a fiscal crisis in some EU Member States and had severe consequences due to the impact of the "remedial" measures chosen and implemented to restore their fiscal balance and their institutions. The principles of democratic governance were effectively nullified, constitutional principles were brutally violated, and citizens became convinced that the problematic state had not been corrected in their favor, but remained largely the same, serving the economic interests of specific elites.

Similarly, the emergence of the Covid-19 pandemic had an adverse impact on governance systems. According to recent literature, the pandemic can be seen as another step toward authoritarianism. Governance systems responded to the coronavirus with a series of decisions that showed significant weaknesses both in their decision-making process and in their substance. Most of these decisions violated the principle of legality and were issued under a "state of emergency" framework.

During the pandemic, there has been a systematic rollback of the Better Regulation Agenda. Recent studies show that the lower the quality of governance, the greater the negative impact of the coronavirus on regulatory policies. In Greece, the crisis intensified corporatist regulation and decision-making. Covid-19 served as an alibi: many agencies and public bodies bypassed legal procedures in areas such as staff recruitment and public procurement. What truly shifts in a crisis like the pandemic is public attitudes toward government, creating a window of opportunity for advancing reforms. However, if the governance system itself remains unchanged, these reforms are likely to fade once the crisis subsides (Karkatsoulis, 2020).

What is common to both crises is that in both cases the state was called upon to achieve a way out of them. In fact, at that time, there were supporters of "bringing the state back in" and "big governments" (Evans, et al., 1985; Spar, 2024). The major criticism of the public policies pursued both in the fiscal crisis and in the case of COVID-19 was mainly criticism of unbridled capitalism. This is said to be responsible for ghost banks and the sale of hot air to greedy investors. The truth is that the general withdrawal of the state from regulatory procedures never formally took place, but in practice, controls were relaxed, and these practices prevailed. The same thing happened, more or less, with the uncontrolled development of China and the destruction of the environment that led to the pandemic.

One of the greatest tests of the rule of law and its fundamental principles—the protection of individual rights and freedoms—is immigration. The challenges of migration have, in many cases, led to a weakening of the state's ability to control the security of its citizens and the sovereignty of the countries hosting migrants.

It is very important to emphasize here that migration has mutated into a particularly lucrative illegal market (Lambropoulou, 2013). In fact, research shows that the organization of these markets has developed clever ways to grow by circumventing rules and legal practices.

Of decisive importance in the transformation of illegal migration into a threat to the security and integrity of host states is the involvement of NGOs, which act as agents, deriving further profit in the process. In this case too, the common denominator is the absence of control and coordination policies among the structures involved. Most European countries did not even have a framework for organizing migration policy or structures for implementing it. The basic law on immigration is a transposition of a EC directive, and the implementing agency, the Ministry of Immigration in Greece—a country of particular importance and significance in stemming migration flows—remains a small and minor ministry. On the other hand, the European agency responsible for monitoring the EU's borders, Frontex, has not been able to act as a reliable mechanism for stemming the flows.

Climate change is another globalized problem that has emerged as a product of rampant capitalism. Indeed, the disregard and dismissal of warnings from climate experts has resulted in widespread (economic, environmental, social) destruction, much of which is irreparable.

The hasty reaction of governments to successive crises and disasters was accompanied by a domino effect of arbitrariness, illegal financing, and lack of transparency. Under the pretext of the urgent and unpredictable nature of environmental threats, a new generation of corrupt individuals was created with the help of state support. Direct assignments—as was the case with the pandemic—are the main tool for collusion and abuse of public funds. The concept that opened the door to corruption is that of "emergency and unforeseen needs"—a theoretical construct whose validity cannot be verified by conventional means of control.

Another issue of paramount importance in addressing climate change is long-term planning and cooperation between the public and private sectors, with the involvement of volunteers. Despite the emphasis placed by the NPM on consultation, subsequent developments have shown that we need much more: Stable consultation structures with strong links between them at all stages of the policy cycle, from planning to addressing their devastating effects and monitoring their implementation (Karkatsoulis, 2023).

Populism poses a particularly significant risk of a governance crisis with unpredictable scope and consequences. Its intense emergence in various parts of the world is undoubtedly due to mistrust of institutions and the rule of law, particularly their inability to avert risks and disasters.

Their successive defeats paved the way for the triumphant rise of populists and populism. One of the characteristic features of populists is their fierce attack on institutions and the administrative state. A typical example is the statement by Steve Bannon, Donald Trump's ideological guru, who declared that the destruction and abolition of the administrative state is one of the top priorities of the Trump administration (Rucker & Costa, 2017).

Observing this attack—especially in the USA, given the importance of its role—shows us not only the resilience of the so-called "deep state," which populists use to refer to the administrative state, but also its vulnerabilities.

8. FOR AN NPM 2.0

The "Good governance" concept which was conceived as a correction to the reforms, was unable to halt the decline of the state and democracy and the rise of populists.

Nevertheless, good governance brought back the political and social aspect to administrative reforms, which had largely been lost since the logic of an economized "one size fits all" prevailed. This was the result of the commodification of reforms on the one hand and the downgrading of the specific elements of organizational culture in each country, on the other.

Good governance, when it first appeared in the context of the NPM, provided the ethical foundation that was lacking in the reforms. The importance of consultation emerged as a practical application of what it proclaimed. We know of many successful examples of reforms that had a positive outcome because of the integration of their philosophy and intervention in the daily lives of citizens by the citizens themselves.

New variations, such as New Public Governance (NPG), seek similarities and differences with other models, such as NPM, and focus on the study of the internal mechanisms of governance, with their collaborative capacity and networked nature as the central objective and point of reference (Krogh & Triantafillou, 2024; Scott & Boyd, 2020).

The emergence of consultation as a key means of ensuring the acceptance and success of reforms is not limited to the formal channels of communication between the state and its citizens. This is a hugely important issue on which, until now, no satisfactory answers have been found that would allow the transformation of the media from, for the most part, propaganda tools into means of information and unhindered dialogue.

On the contrary, social media enjoy much greater degrees of freedom, albeit with different secondary problems.

Many argue that the digitalization of public administration will solve all the problems that previous models of intervention, including the NPM, have failed to solve.

The NPM faces a prime opportunity to expand its resources, personalize its interventions, and create a public administration for everyone. A plethora of digital applications attest to this.

NPM 2.0 incorporates critical observations, eliminates elements that functioned as categorical imperatives, and restores critical thinking and dialogue as the only tool for irrefutable legitimation.

However, there are no other guarantors over time outside and beyond the citizens of a society themselves -even a globalized one.

The personalization of NPM solutions can be achieved today with the help of modern technology, especially Artificial Intelligence (AI).

8.1 Defining NPM 2.0

Against this background, NPM 2.0 must be defined not as a loose reform agenda, but as a coherent administrative and institutional framework, derived from accumulated reform experience and documented implementation failures.

NPM 2.0 can be understood as the evolution of classic New Public Management, which retains the core principles of efficiency, economy, and effectiveness, but reinterprets them in today's environment of contemporary challenges and increasing authoritarianism. Unlike the classic NPM, which focused mainly on transferring private management techniques to the public sector, privatization, competition, and treating citizens as "customers," NPM 2.0 brings the democratic and social dimensions of administration back to the fore, explicitly incorporating openness, accountability, and democratic legitimacy as goals equal to efficiency, while it retains managerial discipline as a core organizing principle.

Therefore, NPM 2.0 is not simply a "second generation" of management techniques, but a synthetic framework in which the classic practices of NPM (program budgeting, results-based management, performance indicators, benchmarking, etc.) are re-examined in light of the risks highlighted in the first phase: weakening of institutional capacity, fragmentation of services, difficulties in accountability, and the primacy of "economic" logic over democratic logic. NPM 2.0 recognizes that the "economization" of public administration has, in many cases, led to the strengthening of private and market rationales at the expense of democratic accountability, and therefore seeks a synthesis: maintaining efficiency tools, but within an institutional framework that protects democracy, the rule of law, and social justice.

A central element of this development is the response to the critical juncture where contemporary challenges coexist with the rise of authoritarian practices. NPM 2.0 treats governance as a field where fundamental democratic goods are at stake and not as a neutral technical process. In this context, it incorporates the concept of "algorithmic democracy" and the requirement that algorithmic and data-driven decision-making be subject to democratic standards of transparency, explainability, verifiability and accountability. This means that citizens are not just recipients of services or "customers", but participants and judges of the rules by which public decisions are made. The goal is to re-establish a hybrid state - institutionally strong, capable, and democratically accountable - capable of exploiting the potential of modern governance for better services and preventive administration, without ceding its sovereignty to opaque structures or neo-authoritarian practices.

At the governance level, NPM 2.0 requires that openness, accountability, and democratic legitimacy be applied at every step of the policy cycle: from design and legislation to implementation, execution, and evaluation. At the design stage, this means meaningful consultation processes and open access to data and decision-making criteria. At the implementation stage, it means transparent operation of systems, the possibility of control and appeal by citizens, and a clear allocation of responsibilities – so that no decision is 'hidden' behind opaque procedures. At the evaluation stage, it means publication of results, open monitoring of impacts, and the possibility of revising policy regulations.

This paradigmatic shift has significant implications for contemporary reform strategies. While classic NPM viewed reforms primarily as a means of increasing efficiency, NPM 2.0 sees them as a source of opportunities for better governance, but also as a serious risk of concentration of power and authoritarian control if not institutionally framed. It offers a framework within which administrative changes are not disconnected from their political and institutional environment, but are part of a strategy to strengthen the state as a capable, reliable, and controlled mechanism of governance. At a time when crises serve as an excuse for the erosion of guarantees and the reinforcement of arbitrariness, NPM 2.0 attempts to restore the balance between administrative flexibility and democratic legitimacy, leveraging technology and accumulated experience without substituting political responsibility. The key difference, therefore, is that NPM 2.0 is structured as a framework of democratically framed management logic, where NPM tools (targets, indicators, programs, evaluation) intersect with the requirements of algorithmic democracy, institutional empowerment, and strengthening of the public sphere. It is a form of "upgraded" NPM which, instead of dismantling the state, seeks to reestablish it as a capable, transparent, and democratically accountable actor.

The era when public administration could function as a dry simulation of the market is definitively over. NPM 2.0 is not a simple administrative improvement, but rather a political necessity.

This development differentiates NPM 2.0 in terms of its stance on privatization and outsourcing. Whereas the original NPM often treated the market as an almost self-evident mechanism for improving quality and reducing costs, NPM 2.0 incorporates the experience of failures, corruption, and loss of state capacity and requires the existence of strong mechanisms for regulation, control, and institutional learning. The relationship between the state and the private sector is no longer seen as a simple transfer of functions, but as a complex administrative choice with political and social consequences that must be assessed both before and after.

In a world of increasing complexity and institutional upheaval, an obsession with efficiency without democratic ballast is no longer an advantage but a danger. The theoretical innovation of NPM 2.0 lies in the assumption that the state is not "modernized" when it simply reduces its costs, but when it shields its transparency, guarantees its accountability, and invests in its institutional credibility.

NPM 2.0 transforms the administrative arsenal into a shield of democracy. It reestablishes the state-citizen relationship on the basis of trust and inclusion, demonstrating that competent administration is, above all, democratically accountable administration. It is the answer to the need for a state that is not only "smaller" or "faster," but essentially fairer.

In concluding and based on the above, we could define NPM 2.0 as follows:

NPM 2.0 is a reformulated, sophisticated framework for public administration, management which maintains and upgrades the principles of efficiency, economy, and effectiveness within a democratically structured institutional framework where administration is a field of values, choices, and social relations that is subject to local conditions and democratic constraints. It places at the center an administratively capable, accountable, and democratically embedded state as the necessary infrastructure for managing systemic crises, delivering public goods in a reliable, effective and legitimate manner.

In terms of practice, NPM 2.0 seeks to establish a framework for reforms that strengthen legitimacy, institutional resilience, and sustainable democratic governance under conditions of permanent uncertainty, through the strategic use of digital technologies, the uncompromising reaffirmation of the rule of law, and sustained investment in organizational learning and public service professionalism.

NPM 2.0 does not seek global solutions but rather adaptable action plans that strengthen state capacity, legitimacy, and democratic governance in modern times.

In this sense, the increasing use of digital technologies and artificial intelligence does not constitute a separate reform agenda, but a critical test of whether NPM 2.0 can reconcile administrative capacity with democratic control.

9. ARTIFICIAL INTELLIGENCE AND THE REBUILDING OF ADMINISTRATIVE CAPACITY

The integration of information and communication technologies (ICT) into public administration was one of the central features of NPM. Digital-era governance (DEG) was the "technical" expression of a deeper promise: that technology can make the state more efficient, more transparent, and more flexible. Artificial intelligence, more user-friendly and easier to use, is more easily integrated, replacing human functions, contributing to decision-making, and offering immediate services. Behind this technical ease, however, lies a transformation, not only in the way administrative work is carried out, but also in the way power and administrative judgment are redefined.

9.1 Concept of AI and Its Applications in Governance

There are many definitions of AI in the literature, mainly depending on the approach and level of technological development. Combining the main ones (Simmons & Chappell, 1988; IBM, 2024; John McCarthy1955, as reported in Stanford Medicine Magazine, 2023), we could say that AI is the simulation of the *cognitive dimensions* of human intelligence through machines, with broad application in fields where decisions and processes are based on data, which is processed at tremendous speed. However, they lack moral judgment, emotional intelligence, and political discernment, elements that are at the core of democratic governance.

This distinction is crucial for governance, as AI revives the expectations that once accompanied the NPM and their subsequent refutation. This experience can serve as a reminder that neither AI nor technology in general can replace human judgment and administrative culture, nor can they function effectively outside the value-based and democratic framework that defines good governance.

Along with the increase in the use of AI, the scope of its application is also expanding. Today, thanks to its advanced capabilities, such as machine learning, image recognition, natural language processing, and speech recognition, it can be used in a wide range of fields, such as health, education, entertainment, industry, and more.

Public administrations are not immune to this development. Despite the limitations (social, technological, economic), governments around the world consider the use of AI to be useful and necessary in order to provide better services to citizens, solve complex problems, assess critical situations, and reduce their operating costs (MacCarthaigh, et al., 2024; Alvina, et al., 2024; Sheikh, et al., 2023; Valle-Cruz, et al., 2024). The growing and intense interest of governments is reflected in investments and national strategies developed for the use of AI. By 2023, more than 60 countries had developed relevant strategies—led by Canada, but with examples from countries such as Kenya and Mexico—in addition to the unified European strategy (Sheikh, et al., 2023) .

The chart below clearly illustrates this trend:

Figure 1. Artificial intelligence gains momentum outside the laboratory

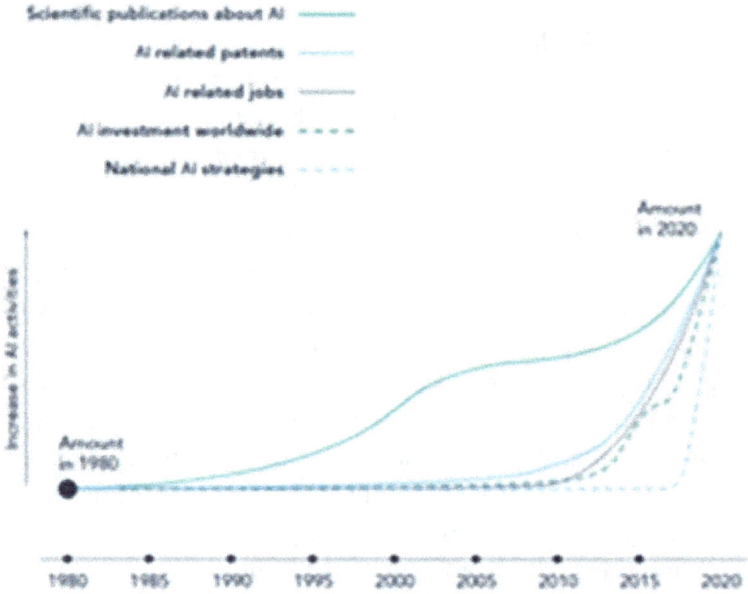

(Source: Sheikh, et al., 2023, p.48)

Artificial intelligence can offer significant benefits to public policy, such as enhancing transparency and collaboration in identifying and addressing public issues, improving the accuracy and efficiency of decision-making, and enabling real-time monitoring and evaluation of policies (Valle-Cruz, et al., 2019) .

In practice, AI is already being used in a wide range of functions, replacing traditional processes: digital assistants (chatbots) serve citizens and answer their daily questions; in the US, the police recognise faces in seconds and make predictions about crime; while in Austria, the use of AI and the automatic comparison of digital building models with regulatory standards is used to check building permits, speeding up and simplifying the approval process. Similar applications can be found in Greece, Estonia, Sweden, and Spain, where artificial intelligence is used to predict needs and improve administrative response, e.g. by automating the reading, categorisation and evaluation of supporting documents, and even professional profiles for more targeted employment programmes and resource allocation (OECD, 2025; Ubaldi, et al., 2019; Schnitzer & Betcherman, 2025). It also makes an important contribution to the field of civil protection, where it is used for the analysis and timely prevention of risks and crises, improving preparedness and response to disasters (Kohler & Scharte, 2020; Galliano, et al., 2024)

9.2 Risks and Challenges

The use of AI in public administration has created high expectations for increasing the capacity of the state and, at the same time, for the creation of a non-partisan, transparent, and accountable environment in which public administration can develop and, by extension, for the strengthening and stability of democracies (Gianluca & Giovanni, 2025).

The challenges and risks of using AI can be grouped into two basic categories: technological, concerning issues of reliability, security, and control of systems; and ethical or institutional, relating to transparency, accountability, bias, and respect for democratic principles in public decision-making and implementation.

Technological risks include deliberate alterations of input data (*adversarial attacks*) that mislead artificial intelligence models, hallucinations, i.e., the production of unfounded information, low availability and quality of training data, technological infrastructure limitations, as well as the gradual degradation of machine learning models (*model drift*), which reduces the accuracy and predictability of results.

Particularly important is the problem of *the* "*black* box"[2], i.e., the inability to supervise, understand and verify how systems make decisions, which limits their control, transparency, and reliability.

Additional problems relate to the lack of interoperability between information systems, the lack of digital skills and technical training among civil servants, difficulties in scaling applications, and the risk of public administration becoming addicted to a technology that is evolving rapidly and provides seemingly easy and quick solutions (Wirtz, al., 2019; Kalema, 2025).

The main ethical and institutional risks associated with the use of artificial intelligence include, among others, the violation of privacy and personal data, the inability to supervise[3] and allocate responsibility for autonomous decisions made by systems[4], as well as algorithmic bias, which causes discrimination and inequality in areas such as access to social services or treatment based on gender and ethnicity. Added to this are the macroeconomic risks from the creation of misleading content (*deepfakes*), the assignment to machines of the formulation or application of rules of human behavior without moral or emotional filters, and excessive dependence on private entities that collect huge amounts of personal data, weakening state sovereignty. These developments contribute to the creation of a democratic and legitimacy deficit, as decisions are made without sufficient transparency, justification, and the possibility of review (Wirtz, et al., 2019; Τσέκερης, et al., 2023; Council of Europe, 2025; Acemoglu, 2024; Kalema, 2025; Liu, 2024) .

9.3 Discussion

The risk of transitioning from multi-level to so-called algorithmic governance may seem remote at present, but it is real and requires institutional vigilance. And as experience shows, despite the undeniable benefits, the ambitions accompanying the use of AI are far from the desired results of administrative action, particularly in terms of the effectiveness and reliability of the relevant systems (Berman, et al., 2024) .

Artificial intelligence shifts judgment from humans to algorithms and concentrates cognitive power in technological systems that act without political accountability. The manner in which this transfer will take place and the democratic safeguards that will accompany it will determine what type of Leviathan we will end up with (Acemoglu & Robinson, 2019): the Absent Leviathan, where the state remains weak and technology operates unchecked, the Despotic Leviathan, where technology reinforces the authoritarian concentration of power; or the Slacked Leviathan, where innovation is embedded in institutions of accountability and political control. In practice, hybrid or changing forms of these are not ruled out, depending on how the relationship between the state, society, and technology is balanced.

This dynamic highlights the same tensions that characterized NPM, reviving the debate about its limits and failures. The criticism levelled at the NPM to date (hollowing of the state, biased administration, lack of citizen participation in decision-making, privatization, turning citizens into customers, etc.) and the search for new methods and models of governance could fuel arguments in favor of the complete digitization of the state and the integration of AI tools into every possible function.

However, AI does not in itself remove the pathologies that stem from the way the public sector is organized and operates, nor does it replace the need for institutional accountability, democratic control, and social sensitivity. On the contrary, technology is likely to reproduce, or even reinforce, existing inequalities and bureaucratic dysfunctions if it is not integrated into a framework of human-centered and ethically oriented governance (Roehl & Hansen, 2024), not based on the theoretical assumptions and good practices of NPM and not defined as a component of NPM 2.0.

Artificial Intelligence cannot assess social or ethical contexts or replace the values and operating rules of democracy and the rule of law. Technological progress must be integrated into a regulatory framework. Whereas in the Napoleonic state administrative tools had to be aligned with the fundamental principles of law and administrative order, in the case of AI it is considered imperative to ensure even stricter compliance with these principles. It must also be accompanied by institutional accountability and shaped by interdisciplinary approaches that combine technical solutions with political interventions and social awareness.

The effort to define the legal and ethical boundaries of artificial intelligence is in full swing, although it usually comes "late" because technology is advancing at a much faster pace. At the European level, the Regulation on Artificial Intelligence (EU AI Act, 2024) is the first comprehensive legal framework in the world that seeks to classify AI systems based on risk, establishing rules for transparency, accountability, and respect for fundamental rights. In Greece, Law 4961/2022 sets out the institutional framework for the development and use of AI, while the "National Strategy for the Development of Artificial Intelligence" and the establishment of a High-Level Advisory Committee on Artificial Intelligence seek to align public policy with the principles of responsible and trustworthy innovation.

At the same time, civil society is playing an active role in shaping this new digital culture. Organizations such as Homo Digitalis, EL/LAK, and internationally the Algorithmic Justice League and the Center for AI and Digital Policy (CAIDP) are developing initiatives for transparency, control of algorithmic systems, and public awareness of the ethical dilemmas of AI. These actions complement institutional measures, seeking to ensure that AI works for the benefit of society as a whole, serving people and the public interest rather than certain elites.

NPM 2.0 cannot exist outside these basic parameters. It will have succeeded if, ultimately, it leads to the strengthening of legitimacy and democratic institutions.

10. CONCLUSION

NPM 2.0 must acquire a robust identity of its own and not be dictated to by social systems. It can engage in dialogue with them in order to "understand" the needs and priorities of each administration, but it cannot and must not submit to the rationality of the system (economic, political, etc.) at any given time.

Based on this principle, the sum of administrative practices that define NPM reforms in each country should not be interpreted as an exclusive list of major or minor interventions, but as a way, as an equivalence of proposals that can give meaning and substance to the values of the NPM.

There is no "royal road" to administrative reform, nor will there ever be. Each country and each public organization will adapt reforms to its operational environment. Nor is administration merely a technical system, but a field of values, choices, and social relations. Thus, AI can enhance efficiency and transparency, but it does not replace human judgment, democratic accountability, and institutional control. The essence, therefore, is not to replace humans, but to use AI as a complement to achieve more participatory and equitable governance. And the administration of the future will not be judged by how "smart" its systems are, but by how wisely it sets their limits. Therefore, the future outcome will depend on the regulation and political framework that will be imposed. AI is a source of tension: it can contribute either to further decentralisation of the state or to the development of a new, more accountable and participatory public administration – depending on who sets the rules for its use.

The implementation of NPM reforms in a globalized context, incorporating local characteristics, needs, and peculiarities, can also lead to a theoretical reorientation of NPM, ultimately shaping a tool that could be useful for reforming public administration, especially in difficult times. The demand for institutional strengthening of states and improvement of control mechanisms remains relevant.

REFERENCES

Acemoglu, D. (2024). The simple macroeconomics of AI*. *Economic Policy, 40*(121), 13–58. DOI: 10.1093/epolic/eiae042

Acemoglu, D., & Robinson, J. (2019). *The Narrow Corridor: States, Societies, and the Fate of Liberty*. Penguin Press.

Alvina, L., Venky, S., & Ouh Eng, L. (2024). Enhancing citizen service management through AI-enabled systems – a proposed AI readiness framework for the public sector. In Charalabidis, Y., Medaglia, R., & van Noordt, C. (Eds.), *Research Handbook on Public Management and Artificial Intelligence* (pp. 79–96). Edward Elgar Publishing.

Ashby, W. R. (1968). Variety, constraint and the law of requisite variety. In Buckley, W. (Ed.), *Modern systems research for the behavioural scientist*. Aldine Publishing Co.

Bel, G., & Casula, M. (2024). *Re-organizing the service-delivery machine in a "post-NPM" era: a shopping-basket approach?* DOI: 10.1080/14719037.2024.2315569

Berman, A., de Fine Licht, K., & Carlsson, V. (2024). Trustworthy AI in the public sector: An empirical analysis of a Swedish labor market decision-support system. *Technology in Society, 76*, 102471. Advance online publication. DOI: 10.1016/j.techsoc.2024.102471

Bourdieu, P. (2007). *Science of Science and Reflexivity*. Patakis.

Christensen, T., & Lægreid, P. (2007). The Whole-of-Government Approach to Public Sector Reform. *Public Administration Review, 67*(6), 1059–1066. DOI: 10.1111/j.1540-6210.2007.00797.x

Dan, S., & Pollitt, C. (2015). NPM Can Work: An optimistic review. *Public Management Review, 17*(9), 1305–1332. DOI: 10.1080/14719037.2014.908662

Dunleavy, P., Margetts, H., Bastow, S., & Tinkler, J. (2006). New Public Management Is Dead—Long Live Digital-Era Governance. *Journal of Public Administration: Research and Theory, 16*(3), 467–494. DOI: 10.1093/jopart/mui057

Evans, P. B., Rueschemeyer, D., & Skocpol, T. (Eds.). (1985). *Bringing the state back in.* Cambridge: Cambridge University Press.

Gianluca, L., & Giovanni, C. (2025). The Process of 'Capacity Building' in the Public Administration: Artificial Intelligence, Transparency and New Models of the Administrative Decision. *Frontiers in Political Science, 7*, 1605729. Advance online publication. DOI: 10.3389/fpos.2025.1605729

Hood, C. (1991). A public management for all seasons? *Public Administration, 69*(1), 3–19. DOI: 10.1111/j.1467-9299.1991.tb00779.x

Hood, C. (2004). Controlling public services and government: towards a cross-national perspective. In Hood, C., James, O., Peters, B. G., & Scott, C. (Eds.), *Controlling Modern Government. Variety, Commonality and Change* (pp. 3–24). Edward Elgar. DOI: 10.4337/9781845423599.00009

IBM. (2024). *What is artificial intelligence (AI)?* Retrieved 8 20, 2025, from https://www.ibm.com/think/topics/artificial-intelligence

Johnson, D. (2015). Technology with No Human Responsibility? *Journal of Business Ethics, 127*(4), 707–715. DOI: 10.1007/s10551-014-2180-1

Kalema, N. L. (2025). *What DOGE Could Mean for the Future of Democracy. Notes from the New Frontier of Power [Blog Series].* Retrieved 10 10, 2025, from Carr Center for Human Rights Policy, Harvard Kennedy School: https://www.hks.harvard.edu/centers/carr-ryan/our-work/carr-ryan-commentary/what-doge-could-mean-future-democracy#:~:text=divesting%20critical%20capabilities%20and%20skills,%E2%80%9Cmanaged%20services%E2%80%9D%20of%20cloud%20empires

Karkatsoulis, P. (2010). The crisis effect on performance based budgeting. *Public Administration Quarterly, 34*(4), 449–469.

Karkatsoulis, P. (2020). The impact of Covid-19 on Better Regulation agenda. *HAPSc Policy Briefs Series, 1*(1), 100–106. DOI: 10.12681/hapscpbs.24954

Karkatsoulis, P. (2023). *Crisis and disaster management in the example of Civil Protection*. Ellinoekdotiki.

Kelly, P., & Hofbauer, S. (2023). Methodological Pluralism and the Pursuit. In Parker, L. (Ed.), *Education in the Age of Misnformation. Philosophical and Pedagogical Explorations* (pp. 33–54). Palgrave Macmillan. DOI: 10.1007/978-3-031-25871-8_3

Kohler, K., & Scharte, B. (2020). Integrating AI into Civil Protection. *CSS Analyses in Security Policy*(260). DOI: 10.3929/ethz-b-000408269

Kotanidis, S. (2024). *Rules on 'revolving doors' in the EU: Post-mandate restrictions on members of EU institutions and parliamentarians in Member States. In-depth analysis.* European Parliamentary Research Service. Brussels: European Union. Retrieved 9 20, 2025, from https://www.europarl.europa.eu/RegData/etudes/IDAN/2024/762290/EPRS_IDA(2024)762290_EN.pdf

Krogh, A. H., & Triantafillou, P. (2024). Developing New Public Governance as a public management reform model. *Public Management Review*, *26*(10), 3040–3056. DOI: 10.1080/14719037.2024.2313539

Lambropoulou, E. (2013). Illegal markets in a collapsing economy. In P. Saitta, J. Shapland, & A. Verhage (Eds.), *Getting by or Getting Rich? The Formal, Informal and Criminal Economy in a* (pp. 61-94). Haag: Eleven International Publishing. Retrieved from https://ierp.gr/ergo/erevnes/illegal-markets-in-a-collapsing-economy-el

Lapsley, I. (2009). New Public Management: The Cruellest Invention of the Human Spirit? *Abacus*, *45*(1), 1–21. DOI: 10.1111/j.1467-6281.2009.00275.x

Lapsley, I., & Miller, P. (Eds.). (2024). *The Resilience of New Public Management.* Oxford University Press. DOI: 10.1093/oso/9780198883814.001.0001

Liu, S. (2024). *Research on the Characteristics, Limitations, and Future Directions of Artificial Intelligence.* Applied and Computational Engineering., DOI: 10.54254/2755-2721/97/20241398

Luhmann, N. (1984). *Soziale Systeme: Grundriß einer allgemeinen Theorie.* Suhrkamp.

MacCarthaigh, M., Simoes, S., & Deepak, P. (2024). AI in the public sector: fundamental operational questions and how to address them. In Charalabidis, Y., Medaglia, R., & van Noordt, C. (Eds.), *Research Handbook on Public Management and Artificial Intelligence* (pp. 45–61). Edward Elgar Publishing. DOI: 10.4337/9781802207347.00012

OECD. (2006). *OECD Journal on Budgeting.* Public Governance and Territorial Development Directorate, OECD. Paris: OECD Publishing. Retrieved 9 20, 2025, from https://www.oecd.org/content/dam/oecd/en/publications/reports/2007/05/oecd-journal-on-budgeting-volume-2006-issue-4_g1gh7bf9/budget-v6-4-en.pdf

OECD. (2009). *Contracting Out Government Functions and Services: Emerging Lessons from Post-Conflict and Fragile Situations.* Partnership for Democratic Governance Series. Paris: OECD Publishing. Retrieved 9 20, 2025, from https://www.oecd.org/content/dam/oecd/en/publications/reports/2009/12/contracting-out-government-functions-and-services_g1ghb7b6/9789264066212-en.pdf

OECD. (2025). *Governing with Artificial Intelligence: The State of Play and Way Forward in Core Government Functions.* OECD Publishing., DOI: 10.1787/795de142-

Osborne, S. P. (2010). *The New Public Governance? Emerging Perspectives on the Theory and Practice of Public Governance.* Routledge., DOI: 10.4324/9780203861684

Pollitt, C., & Bouckaert, G. (2017). *Public Management Reform: A Comparative Analysis – Into the Age of Austerity*. Oxford University Press.

Rhodes. (2017). The Hollowing Out of the State. In *Network Governance and the Differentiated Polity: Selected Essays* (Vol. I). Oxford: Oxford University Press. DOI: 10.1093/oso/9780198786108.003.0008

Roehl, U. B., & Hansen, M. B. (2024). 3 26). Automated, administrative decision-making and good governance: Synergies, trade-offs, and limits. *Public Administration Review, 84*(6), 1–16. DOI: 10.1111/puar.13799

Rucker, P., & Costa, R. (2017). *The Washington Post*. Retrieved 10 5, 2025, from https://www.washingtonpost.com/politics/top-wh-strategist-vows-a-daily-fight-for-deconstruction-of-the-administrative-state/2017/02/23/03f6b8da-f9ea-11e6-bf01-d47f8cf9b643_story.html

Schnitzer, P., & Betcherman, G. (2025). *World Bank Blogs – Digital Development*. Retrieved 10 5, 2025, from https://blogs.worldbank.org/en/digital-development/ai-in-public-employment-services--unlocking-potential--avoiding-

Scott, R. J., & Boyd, R. (2020). Determined to succeed: Can goal commitment sustain interagency collaboration? *Public Policy and Administration, 38*(1), 3–33. Advance online publication. DOI: 10.1177/0952076720905002

Sheikh, H., Prins, C., & Schrijvers, E. (2023). *Mission AI: The New System Technology*. The Netherlands Scientific Council for Government Policy (WRR). Cham: Springer. Retrieved 8 25, 2025, from https://link.springer.com/content/pdf/10.1007/978-3-031-21448-6.pdf

Simmons, A., & Chappell, S. (1988). Artificial intelligence-definition and practice. *IEEE Journal of Oceanic Engineering, 13*(2), 14–42. DOI: 10.1109/48.551

Spar, D. L. (2024). *Has the 'battle over big government' era ended?* Retrieved 10 5, 2024, from Institute for Business in Global Society: https://www.hbs.edu/bigs/has-the-battle-over-government-ended

tenCouncil of Europe. (2025). *Common ethical challenges in AI*. Retrieved 10 10, 2025, from https://www.coe.int/el/web/human-rights-and-biomedicine/common-ethical-challenges-in-ai#%22123745781%22:[7]

The Conversation. (2022). *Permacrisis: what it means and why it's word of the year for 2022*. Retrieved 10 5, 2025, from https://theconversation.com/permacrisis-what-it-means-and-why-its-word-of-the-year-for-2022-194306

Ubaldi, B.-C., Van Ooijen, C., & Welby, B. (2019). *A data-driven public sector. Enabling the strategic use of data for productive, inclusive and trustworthy governance*. OECD Publishing., Retrieved from https://www.researchgate.net/publication/364119468_A_data-driven_public_sector_Enabling_the_strategic_use_of_data_for_productive_inclusive_and_trustworthy_governance

Valle-Cruz, D., Gil-Garcia, J. R., & Sandoval-Almazan, R. (2024). Artificial intelligence algorithms and applications in the public sector: a systematic literature review based on the PRISMA approach. In Charalabidis, Y., Medaglia, R., & van Noordt, C. (Eds.), *Research handbook on public management and artificial intelligence* (pp. 8–26). Edward Elgar Publishing., DOI: 10.4337/9781802207347.00010

Valle-Cruz, D., Ruvalcaba-Gomez, E. A., Sandoval-Almazan, R., & Criado, J. I. (2019). A review of artificial intelligence in government and its potential from a public policy perspective. In Chen, Y.-C., Salem, F., & Zuiderwijk, A. (Eds.), *A review of artificial intelligence in government and its potential from a public policy perspective-Dubai* (pp. 91–99). Association for Computing Machinery., DOI: 10.1145/3325112.3325242

van Klink, B. (2016). Symbolic Legislation: An Essentially Political Concept. In van Klink, B., van Beers, B., & Poort, L. (Eds.), *Symbolic Legislation Theory and New Developments in Biolaw* (pp. 19–36). Springer., DOI: 10.1007/978-3-319-33365-6_2

Waldo, D. (1948). *The administrative state; A Study of the Political Theory of American Public Administration*. Ronald Press Company.

Wirtz, B. W., Weyerer, J. C., & Geyer, C. (2019). Artificial Intelligence and the Public Sector—Applications and Challenges. *International Journal of Public Administration, 42*(7), 596–615. DOI: 10.1080/01900692.2018.1498103

ADDITIONAL READING

Aucoin, P. (1995). *The New Public Management: Canada in Comparative Perspective*. IRPP.

Barzelay, M. (1992). *Breaking through Bureaucracy: A New Vision for Managing in Government*. University of California Press.

DiIulio, J. J.Jr, Garvey, G., & Kettl, D. F. (1993). *Improving Government Performance: An Owner's Manual*. Brookings Institution.

Ferlie, E., Ashburner, L., Fitzgerald, L., & Pettigrew, A. (1996). *The New Public Management in Action*. Oxford University Press. DOI: 10.1093/acprof:oso/9780198289029.001.0001

Hood, C. (1991). A Public Management for All Seasons? *Public Administration, 69*(1), 3–19. DOI: 10.1111/j.1467-9299.1991.tb00779.x

Jones, L. R., & Thompson, F. (1999). *Public Management: Institutional Renewal for the 21st Century*. Stanford University Press.

Lynn, L. E. (1996). *Public Management as Art, Science and Profession*. Chatham House.

Osborne, D., & Gaebler, T. (1992). *Reinventing Government: How the Entrepreneurial Spirit is Transforming the Public Sector from Schoolhouse to Statehouse, City Hall to the Pentagon*. Addison-Wesley.

Pollitt, C. (1993). *Managerialism and the Public Services*. Blackwell.

ENDNOTES

1 See, for example, the development of a separate scope of application for concession contracts for countries undergoing post-war reconstruction (OECD, 2009) .

2 For an extensive analysis of the subject, see Bathaee's interesting study (2018). It points out that the main cause for concern about the black box, i.e., autonomous learning and decision-making by AI systems, is the failure of two central legal concepts, intention and causality, as they are based on human behavior and cannot be applied to algorithmic processes that lack transparency and predictability.

3 According to some analysts, this is a matter of human choices, political decisions, and social consensus, rather than technological complexity (Johnson, 2015).

4 Wirtz, et al. (2019), for example, ask who is responsible and accountable when an autonomous public transport vehicle causes damage to a pedestrian?

Chapter 5
Strategic Management in the Public Sector:
Concepts, Challenges, and Evolving Practices

Foteini Vittou
http://orcid.org/0000-0001-5367-5042
Department of Public Administration, Panteion University, Greece

Labros Babalioutas
Panteion University, Greece

Vasiliadis Labros
http://orcid.org/0000-0003-0272-4806
National and Kapodistrian University of Athens, Greece

ABSTRACT

In recent years, strategic management in the public sector has shifted from an optional tool to a perceived necessity in contexts of crisis, uncertainty and rising expectations. This chapter questions the uncritical transfer of private-sector strategic models to public organizations, arguing that they rest on linear and technocratic assumptions that conflict with the political and value-laden nature of public action. Drawing on a systemic review, public organizations are conceptualised as Complex Adaptive Systems, where interdependencies and competing norms generate non-linear outcomes, undermining claims of control through rational planning. The chapter therefore advances a Public Value perspective, exemplified by Moore's Strategic Triangle, which highlights the need to align value creation, operational

DOI: 10.4018/979-8-3373-3526-1.ch005

capacity and the authorizing environment. Public strategy is thus understood as a dynamic, politically embedded practice aimed at sustaining public value under conditions of complexity.

1. INTRODUCTION

1.1 Chapter Purpose and Significance

The basic claim in this chapter is simple but has far-reaching consequences: in today's conditions, public organizations cannot treat strategy as a luxury or an optional management fashion; it has become part of how governing actually works (Joyce, 2015). That statement already creates a problem for many of the standard models that circulate in textbooks, because those models usually assume organizations that look more like private firms than like ministries, municipalities or agencies answerable to politicians and citizens at the same time. Public bodies operate in a political space, with contested goals and legal constraints, and they also behave more like Complex Adaptive Systems than like well-oiled machines, constantly dealing with what Rittel and Webber (1973) called wicked problems – messy, value-laden issues that refuse to stay within neat boundaries (Kiel, 1995; Rittel and Webber, 1973). For that reason, the chapter proposes that public strategy has to be seen less as a single written plan and more as a capability that develops over time: the organizational habit of learning, working with others and moving carefully through political tensions in order to protect and create public value under demanding, often unstable conditions (Teece, 2007; Bryson and George, 2020).

The importance of the chapter lies in the way it brings together several strands that are often discussed separately. One strand is the insistence that strategy in the public sector is always tied up with politics and it is not a neutral technical recipe that managers can apply in a vacuum (Moore, 1995). Public managers stand between professional knowledge on the one hand and democratic control on the other, and they have to live with that tension instead of pretending it does not exist. Another strand is the focus on wicked problems. These are issues that are hard even to define in a way that everyone can accept, that pit different stakeholder values against one another and that rarely respond to simple technical fixes. In such situations, the idea that everything can be solved through better forecasting and more data-driven plans becomes very fragile (Rittel and Webber, 1973). A third strand comes from Moore's Strategic Triangle, which is used to show that public organizations only really succeed when three things line up: the value they produce for the public, the capacities and resources they can actually mobilize, and the political and legal authorization that allows them to act. If one of these corners is weak or missing, apparently efficient strategies can still fail badly (Moore, 1995).

Empirical studies show that many public managers say they believe strongly in formal strategic planning, yet when researchers look at performance indicators, the link between planning and outcomes is often weak or inconsistent (Johnsen, 2016). This gap between what managers think works and what the data suggest is not a minor detail, but it rather warns against treating planning processes as a kind of ritual that must be good simply because it looks rational. The chapter therefore stresses that public organizations function through non-linear interactions in which decisions, routines and external pressures combine in ways that are hard to predict and sometimes produce surprising, emergent effects (Stacey and Mowles, 2016). Under such conditions, the idea of complete strategic control becomes more illusion than reality.

Finally, the discussion takes resistance to change seriously. Instead of labelling all resistance as irrational or obstructive, it points out that staff often have understandable worries about job security, professional identity or the survival of their institution, and that these worries shape how they respond to new strategies (Baker, 2007). Seeing resistance in this more human way opens up the possibility of change management that listens, negotiates and adapts, rather than simply pushing harder (Belias et al., 2019). Together, these elements – awareness of politics, attention to complexity, caution about the evidence and a more respectful reading of resistance – form the backbone for the chapter's later arguments about how strategic management in the public sector should be understood and practiced.

1.2 Methodology and Analytical Approach: Systemic Narrative Review

The chapter adopts a methodological stance that deliberately resists treating strategic management in the public sector as a neat sequence of technical steps and instead assumes from the outset that strategy is woven into political, social and institutional contexts that shift over time and are only partially knowable (Joyce, 2015). To do justice to this complexity, it relies on a systemic narrative review rather than on a narrowly specified systematic review, bringing together empirical studies, case material and theoretical contributions in order to build an integrated picture of why strategic thinking is both necessary and difficult in public organizations (Bryson, 2004; Joyce, 2015). The narrative element signals an interest in interpretation and synthesis rather than exhaustive cataloguing: the review seeks to understand how different strands of literature speak to each other, where they converge and where they leave gaps instead of counting every available publication on the topic (Paré et al., 2015; Popay et al., 2006). At the same time, the "systemic" qualifier points to an explicit anchoring in complexity theory and Complex Adaptive Systems thinking, which treat public-sector challenges as the outcome of non-linear interactions within and between organizations, policy fields and wider societies and not as isolated problems that can be solved by applying the right tool (Kiel, 1995; Stacey and Mowles, 2016; Kooiman and van Vliet, 1993).

Within this broad orientation, the selection of literature followed a structured but flexible logic. We did not apply rigid inclusion and exclusion criteria that might be appropriate for a tightly bounded medical trial, but prioritized three considerations: relevance to core questions in public strategic management, scholarly robustness and diversity of perspective across disciplines and national contexts (Sukhera et al., 2022; van Wee and Banister, 2016). The corpus therefore brings together peer-reviewed articles in public administration and complexity science (identified through databases such as JSTOR, Google Scholar and Scopus), classic texts that established key ideas like Moore's Strategic Triangle and Bryson's strategy frameworks, empirical case studies that show how strategic management actually unfolds in organizations, and more critical contributions that highlight theory–practice gaps or emerging issues such as digital transformation, network governance and crisis resilience. The review opts for depth of engagement, on the premise that a carefully constructed synthesis can illuminate the field more effectively than a mechanically comprehensive list of sources.

The methodological rationale for this choice is closely tied to the nature of the phenomena under study. Wicked problems in the public sector, i.e. challenges which are inherently complex, multi-dimensional and resistant to neat technical fixes[1], cannot easily be captured by research designs that assume clear causal chains and stable contexts (Rittel and Webber, 1973). A systemic narrative review is better equipped to trace how ideas travel across contexts, how particular models fare when confronted with political realities and where their assumptions break down. It also supports the development of "transferable theory" – mid-range explanations and concepts that are grounded in specific organizational and institutional settings but that retain enough abstraction to inform practice elsewhere (Pawson, 2002; Moore, 1995; Williams and Lewis, 2008). Finally, this approach dovetails with the chapter's substantive argument about strategy as a dynamic capability: by treating strategic management as the evolving capacity of organizations to sense change, learn, reconfigure and adapt while maintaining some coherence of purpose, the review framework mirrors the very processes it seeks to analyze (Teece, 2007; George et al., 2019).

A further feature of the methodology is its explicitly critical orientation. The review does not simply line up private-sector concepts and assume their relevance, but asks which of them can be meaningfully adapted to public organizations and why others – such as unreflective uses of SWOT analysis, Porter's generic strategies or rigid rational-planning cycles – tend to run into trouble when confronted with political contestation and multi-stakeholder environments (Williams and Lewis, 2008). It also probes the recurring finding that public managers often express strong belief in the value of formal strategic planning even when empirical studies show modest or ambiguous links to actual performance, treating this as a signal to question taken-for-granted planning rituals rather than to celebrate them uncritically (Johnsen, 2016; Andrews et al., 2012). At the same time, it traces how more recent strands of the literature have moved away from static plans and forecast-driven models towards an emphasis on dynamic capabilities, adaptive learning and the deliberate pursuit of public value as a more realistic and normatively grounded way of thinking about strategy in complex public settings (Mintzberg, 1994; Bryson and George, 2020).

1.3 Strategic Management as Necessity

Seen against the background of the past few decades, it is difficult to maintain the idea that public organizations can simply "opt out" of strategy and still function effectively, because the environment in which they operate has become too volatile, too demanding and too tightly constrained for purely short-term, reactive management to cope (Poister, Pitts and Edwards, 2010). Governments and public agencies now face a rolling sequence of fiscal crises, environmental shocks and social disruptions, together with an almost permanent state of political and media scrutiny, and these pressures collectively push them towards more deliberate thinking about direction, priorities and trade-offs. At the same time, structural trends – fiscal austerity, demographic ageing or diversification, rapid technological change and the globalization of services – have made it harder for public organizations to rely on inherited routines, because the conditions that once made those routines viable are no longer in place (Baker, 2007). Unlike private firms, which can sometimes exit unprofitable markets or redefine their customer base, public bodies are tied to legally mandated service obligations and must respond to multiple constituencies whose expectations often clash, which means that some form of strategic thinking is not just useful but a basic condition for legitimacy and effectiveness.

This argument becomes clearer when one looks at how these pressures combine in practice. Across many advanced democracies, public organizations are asked to do more with less, to adopt new digital technologies, to respond to shifting social norms and to manage the fallout from crises, such as financial collapses or pandemics, often at the same time and with limited room for manoeuvre (Joyce, 2015). In such a setting, relying solely on ad hoc decisions or incremental adjustments is unlikely to be enough, because the scale and speed of change can quickly overwhelm fragmented responses. Strategic management, in the sense developed in this chapter, does not promise perfect foresight or control, but it does provide a way of imposing some order on competing demands, of clarifying which goals matter most, of aligning resources with those goals and of engaging with political and societal actors around explicit choices. In that sense, strategy has evolved from being a discretionary tool, used mainly by particularly ambitious or reform-minded managers, into a core element of how public organizations try to preserve and enhance public value under conditions that are both unstable and structurally constrained.

2. CORE CONCEPTS AND FRAMEWORK

2.1 Defining Strategic Management

Debates about strategic management in the public sector have moved a long way from the early, rather narrow focus on formal planning, but it is still useful to begin with those early definitions to see what they captured and what they missed. Berry and Wechsler (1995, p. 159) described strategic planning as a "systematic process for managing the organization and its future direction in relation to its environment and the demands of external stakeholders, including strategy formulation, analysis of strengths and weaknesses, identification of agency stakeholders, implementation of strategic actions, and issue management," a formulation that already brought together several important elements such as environmental awareness, stakeholder engagement and an eye on implementation. At the same time, this way of thinking tended to underplay two features that later work has shown to be crucial in public settings: the thoroughly political character of strategic choices, and the fact that strategies have to evolve over time instead of being fixed once and for all.

More recent authors therefore talk less about strategic planning as a one-off exercise and more about strategic management as an ongoing organizational practice. Moore (1995), for example, explicitly distinguishes between drawing up a plan and managing strategically, arguing that the latter involves a continuing cycle of formulating directions, implementing them, allocating and reallocating resources, and monitoring and evaluating results, all under conditions of political oversight and contestation. In this view, strategy is not a document that sits on a shelf but a capacity of the organization to connect decisions across time, to learn from what works and what fails, and to adjust its course in light of changing circumstances. In a similar vein, Poister, Pitts and Edwards (2010) emphasize that strategic management covers not only the initial design of strategies but also the routines of review, learning and adaptation that keep those strategies alive and relevant.

A useful way to bring these strands together is offered by Bryson and George (2020, p. 3), who describe strategy as "a concrete approach to aligning the aspirations and the capabilities of public organizations or other entities in order to achieve goals and create public value". This phrasing quietly shifts the center of gravity from plans and procedures to questions of purpose and value: what is the organization trying to achieve for the public, what can it realistically do given its resources and constraints, and how can it bring these two dimensions closer together. It also resonates with Mintzberg and colleagues' (2009) well-known suggestion that strategy can appear as plans, patterns, positions, perspectives and even plots – that is, as both deliberate intentions and observed regularities in behaviour. Rumelt's (2011) description of strategy as a "cohesive response to an important challenge," built around a clear diagnosis, a guiding policy and coherent action, fits well with this picture and is particularly relevant for public managers who must confront complex, politically sensitive problems rather than straightforward market opportunities.

For leaders in public organizations, then, strategic management involves more than producing a polished document for external audiences. It means looking ahead, using structured analysis and planning to shape change and innovation, steering and supporting those changes as they unfold, and trying to ensure that day-to-day decisions contribute to longer-term visions and goals (Joyce, 2015). It also means recognizing that, in the public sector, these visions and goals are rarely set unilaterally by managers, but that they emerge from interactions with elected officials, stakeholders and citizens, and they are continually renegotiated as circumstances and political priorities shift.

2.2 Public Value and the Strategic Triangle

Once strategic management is situated in the public sector, many of the assumptions that underpin standard strategy definitions begin to look fragile, because public organizations operate under conditions that are quite different from those of private firms. They do not normally enjoy the freedom to choose their mission or target market; instead, their basic goals, mandates and resource envelopes are largely the product of political decisions, legislation and wider constitutional arrangements (Rainey, 2009). This means that public managers cannot simply search for profitable niches or redesign their portfolios in pursuit of competitive advantage. They are expected to work with, and often reconcile, multiple and sometimes conflicting policy objectives that have been handed down through political processes, and to do so in ways that remain democratically legitimate.

A key step in rethinking strategy under these conditions is Moore's (1995) concept of the strategic triangle, which has become one of the most influential frameworks for understanding public value creation. The triangle identifies three interdependent elements that must be aligned if a public strategy is to be viable over time. The first is public value itself: the substantive benefits that policies, programmes or services generate for citizens and communities, in terms of outcomes such as safety, health, fairness, opportunity or trust. The second is operational capacity: the organizational, financial, human and inter-organizational resources and capabilities that allow those benefits to be produced in practice. The third is the authorizing environment: the web of legal mandates, political support and societal approval that gives public organizations the right and the space to act. Moore's argument is that these three corners of the triangle cannot be treated in isolation. A brilliant idea for improving public value will go nowhere if the necessary capacities are absent or if political and legal authorization is weak; conversely, strong capacity and firm authorization will not be enough if the activities being pursued do not actually generate value that citizens recognize and care about (Moore, 1995; Höglund at al., 2021).

Public organizations operate within dense ecosystems of stakeholders – elected officials, service users, employees, unions, civil society organizations, regulators and others – each of whom may hold a legitimate but different view of what public value looks like in a given context. A hospital, for instance, must constantly balance pressures to contain costs with professional commitments to high-quality care; a police service has to weigh crime-reduction targets against the protection of civil liberties; a school system must reconcile demands for academic rigour with expectations of broad, inclusive access. Strategic management cannot simply dissolve these tensions; it needs to navigate them, making choices transparent and subject to democratic debate rather than leaving them implicit.

These features help explain why strategy in the public sector differs in important ways from strategy in competitive markets. Whereas private-sector strategy typically assumes rivalry between firms and focuses on gaining and defending advantages over competitors, public-sector strategy is better understood as a means of improving organizational performance and service quality in a context where "success" is defined in terms of public outcomes rather than market share (Boyne and Walker, 2010). Joyce (2015) notes that the notion of priorities plays a much more central role in public organizations than in many private firms, because managers must constantly rank and re-rank objectives within fixed or shrinking resource envelopes, under the watchful eye of elected representatives and the public. Political accountability adds a further layer of tension. Democratic legitimacy requires that major strategic directions ultimately be sanctioned by elected representatives who are answerable to citizens, but professional expertise and long-term organizational considerations do not always align with short-term electoral incentives (Joyce, 2015; Niiranen and Joensuu, 2014). Effective strategic management in the public sector therefore does not aim to remove this tension – which would be neither realistic nor desirable – but to work within it, crafting strategies that are both democratically authorized and informed by evidence and professional judgement about how best to create and sustain public value.

2.3 Strategic Management Framework: Process and Dynamic Capability

If earlier debates tended to equate strategy with the production of a formal plan, more recent work – especially in public-sector contexts – has shifted attention towards strategy as something that organizations *do* continuously rather than something they *have* once and for all. Instead of picturing a tidy sequence in which managers analyze the environment, formulate strategies, implement them and then evaluate the results, newer approaches suggest that these activities overlap, loop back on one another and are frequently disrupted by political events, organizational learning and unforeseen developments (Mintzberg, 1994; Bryson and George, 2020). In this more process-oriented view, strategy is not a static blueprint but a stream of decisions, interpretations and adjustments through which an organization tries to keep its aspirations, its capabilities and its external circumstances in some kind of workable alignment.

The language of dynamic capabilities provides a helpful way of making this idea more concrete. Teece (2007) and later George et al. (2019) describe dynamic capabilities as the abilities that allow an organization to sense changes in its environment, to seize opportunities and to reconfigure its structures and resources in response, without losing coherence of purpose. Applied to public organizations, this means that strategic management is less about predicting the future in detail and more about being able to adapt intelligently as the future unfolds. It involves monitoring political, social and economic trends; listening to stakeholders and front-line staff; reflecting on past successes and failures; and being willing to adjust plans, priorities and partnerships when the evidence or the context demands it. Strategic learning – the capacity to draw lessons from experience and feed them back into future decisions – thus becomes a core strategic competence, encompassing both incremental improvements and more fundamental questioning of assumptions (Argyris and Schön, 1978; Bryson, 2004).

From this perspective, strategic management in the public sector is best understood as a dynamic capability and an ongoing process rather than a one-off planning event. Joyce (2015) suggests that it can be thought of as a continuous cycle of thinking, planning and delivering, while also noting that in real organizations these elements do not always appear in neat order and some may be neglected altogether. The dynamic view underlines that public organizations must be able to respond to evolving challenges and opportunities – new policy mandates, emerging crises, changing citizen expectations – without losing sight of their wider mission and values. It also helps to explain why so many public management reforms, which often arrive as top-down initiatives, place heavy demands on the adaptive capacities of organizations: unless managers and staff can learn, adjust and integrate reforms into their existing practices, even well-intentioned strategies are likely to remain symbolic rather than transformative (Joyce, 2015).

2.4 Relationship to Politics and Administration

In the public sector, strategy is never confined to the administrative sphere; it is always entangled with politics, because questions about what should be done, for whom and with what resources are inherently political questions. Over the past few decades, public management has moved closer to the center of political debate, as governments link administrative performance to economic competitiveness, social cohesion and trust in democratic institutions (Joyce, 2015). Strategic choices about priorities, resource allocation or organizational design therefore cannot be treated as neutral technical matters. They are shaped by electoral promises, party programmes, coalition bargains and public controversies, and they in turn shape how citizens experience the state.

The traditional textbook distinction between politics "setting the goals" and administration "implementing the goals" has long been criticized as misleading in practice (Wilson, 1989). Public managers are not passive executors of decisions taken elsewhere; they operate at the point where political intentions, legal rules, professional norms and practical constraints collide. Moore's strategic triangle offers a clear way of thinking about this. To create public value, managers must constantly adjust the match between their organization's operational capacity, a working definition of public value that has been negotiated with political and societal actors, and the authorizing environment that grants permission and resources for action (Moore, 1995). In everyday terms, this means that managers help to interpret and sometimes reshape political goals, advise elected representatives on what is feasible, and build support for particular directions among staff, stakeholders and the wider public. Their discretion is real but bounded: they can influence agendas and frame options, but they remain subject to oversight and answerability to elected officials.

The spread of newer governance arrangements adds more layers to this picture. Public policies are increasingly designed and delivered through networks of agencies, municipalities, private providers and civil-society organizations, rather than by a single hierarchical bureaucracy (Joyce, 2015). In such settings, strategic management involves not only navigating the classic political–administrative relationship inside government, but also working across organizational and sectoral boundaries. Managers must broker agreements in partnerships, align strategies in multi-level governance structures and participate in broader arenas of societal problem-solving, all while remaining accountable to parliaments, councils or ministers. Empirical studies suggest that where politicians and senior administrators manage to develop a shared strategic outlook and a degree of mutual trust, public organizations are better able to sustain coherent long-term directions; where this relationship is adversarial or fragmented, strategies are more likely to oscillate with electoral cycles or be undermined in implementation (Joyce, 2015).

2.5 Strategic Planning Models and Critical Evaluation

Strategic planning is the systematic process through which an organization or business formulates and implements its strategy, determining its overall course and making decisions about the effective allocation of available resources, such as financial capital and human resources. One of its components is vision, which, on the other hand, captures the desired future image of the organization or business. It is a long-term guiding concept, which often expresses not only how the organization itself aspires to be in the future, but also how it would like the environment in which it operates to be shaped (Rossidis & Belias, 2025).

The strategic vision expresses the ultimate strategic goal and long-term direction that the organization seeks to follow. This includes the necessary changes required for the company to be able to realize its vision. Consequently, a close and direct relationship is formed between vision and change management. Once the vision is understood and accepted within the organization, it becomes necessary to implement the corresponding organizational changes and effectively address the anxiety and resistance that these may cause. Indicative of this is the central role assigned to vision in the context of organizational change implementation, as described in Kotter's model (2012).

Many public organizations still use familiar strategic planning models that follow a fairly standard recipe: scan the environment, analyze stakeholders, clarify mission and vision, set goals and objectives, agree on actions, and then monitor what happens (Rossidis et al., 2020b). These frameworks can be helpful. They give people a shared language, force managers to step back from day-to-day pressures and make it harder to ignore important issues. However, they were mostly designed with private firms in mind, and that creates problems when they are applied too literally in public settings. Williams and Lewis, looking at seven public-sector consultancy projects in the UK, found that tools such as value-chain analysis and stakeholder mapping only became genuinely useful when they were adapted to local political and institutional realities; when used "out of the box", they produced neat diagrams but weak insights (Williams and Lewis, 2008).

Private-sector imports such as SWOT analysis and Porter's generic strategies show the same tension. SWOT – strengths, weaknesses, opportunities and threats – can be a useful way to structure a discussion, but it easily encourages a static, over-tidy picture of an organization and its environment, as if both were far more stable and predictable than they really are (Hill and Jones, 2013). Porter's ideas about cost leadership, differentiation and focus are grounded in competition for market share and profit (Porter, 1980). In the public sector there is rarely a "market" in that sense, and agencies are usually expected to cooperate rather than compete. When these models are used without adjustment, they can push thinking towards questions – such as "our competitors" – that simply do not fit the public context, and they tend to hide the political and value-laden nature of public choices behind a thin technical veneer.

Some scholars have tried to clarify when orthodox strategic management theories fit better or worse in public settings. Hansen and Ferlie (2016), for example, propose a typology based on three conditions: how much administrative autonomy an organization has; how far its funding depends on performance; and how much it faces market-like competition. Where autonomy is high, budgets are tied closely to results and rivals can win or lose contracts, Porter-style and resource-based models may travel more easily. In more traditional bureaucracies, where mandates are fixed in law, budgets are allocated politically and competition is limited or non-existent, those same models need substantial reworking. Overall, the chapter's argument is that while established strategic frameworks offer structure and useful prompts, their underlying logic often clashes with the political, multi-stakeholder and value-driven reality of the public sector – a clash that becomes sharper as new pressures and expectations build up around public organizations.

2.6 Limits of Rational Planning

Classical strategic planning assumes that, with enough data and analysis, organizations can forecast their environment, choose the best course of action and then follow it in a largely linear way. Experience from the public sector, such as the economic shocks in the 1970s which already revealed that even sophisticated forecasting models could not keep pace with rapid change, and later crises that have reinforced that lesson (Joyce, 2015; Mintzberg, 1994), prove how fragile is this assumption. Mintzberg's well-known critique of the "rise and fall of strategic planning" argued that when planning becomes too formal and technocratic, it can stifle creativity, detach strategy from what actually happens on the ground and encourage a false sense of certainty. Studies of Norwegian municipalities, for example, found that while managers often expressed strong faith in their formal planning systems, there was little clear evidence that these plans had a strong or consistent impact on performance indicators such as service quality or efficiency (Johnsen, 2016). Strategy in practice turned out to be a mix of deliberate intentions and responses that emerged over time (Belias et al., 2024).

Standard planning sequences – environmental analysis, identification of strategic issues, formulation of responses, implementation, monitoring and evaluation – look tidy in textbooks and can be reassuring because they suggest that nothing important will be forgotten (Joyce, 2015; Bryson, 2004). Many public managers report that they find value in this structure: it organizes discussions, surfaces assumptions and gives a framework for decision-making (Flynn and Talbot, 1996; Berry and Wechsler, 1995). But when these models are applied in genuinely complex and uncertain environments, several weaknesses appear. First, tools like SWOT rest on the idea that opportunities and threats "out there" can be identified with reasonable confidence. In reality, some developments are simply unknowable in advance, and a neat list of factors can give a misleading impression of control (Stacey and Griffin, 2005). Second, the assumption that strategic issues can be clearly defined and then resolved one by one breaks down in the face of wicked problems, where issues are intertwined, values clash and no final solution is available. Third, rational planning often sidelines politics, even though strategic choices always involve winners and losers and therefore provoke disagreement (Stoker, 2006; Joyce, 2015).

A related concern is the spread of template-driven planning. Rumelt criticizes the habit of filling in standard forms – vision statements, mission statements, lists of values and goals – without serious engagement with the tough choices and trade-offs that real strategy requires (Rumelt, 2011). In public organizations, this can lead to documents full of high-sounding but obvious statements, presented as if they were hard-won insights, while the real strategic problems remain unaddressed. In such cases, planning becomes more about meeting procedural requirements than about thinking honestly and creatively about the organization's situation. The chapter therefore argues for a move away from treating rational planning models as recipes to be followed, and towards using them, when helpful, as loose guides within a broader, more flexible and politically aware approach to strategy.

2.7 Performance Management and Strategy Implementation

There is a widespread belief that "good strategy" will automatically lead to "better performance" in public services. It sounds intuitive and is often taken for granted in policy debates and reform programmes, yet empirical research paints a more complicated picture and forces a more cautious reading of this assumption. Studies of Welsh local government by Andrews et al. (2012) show that strategic management can indeed influence service performance, but not in the simple, linear way that some models imply; instead, its effects depend on how the substance of the strategy (its content) and the way it is developed and carried out (its process) interact with organizational structures, local environmental conditions and existing patterns of administration and politics. In other words, there is no universal "best" strategy that guarantees success across contexts, and no straightforward one-to-one correspondence between the presence of formal strategic plans and improved outcomes; what matters is the fit between strategy, organization and environment, and that fit is often fragile and context-specific.

A particularly sensitive point in this chain is implementation, where broad ambitions meet the crowded realities of organizational life. Broadly supported strategies can falter when they encounter internal resistance, political pushback, funding cuts, skill shortages or simple overload, even when they are well-argued. Baker's analysis of failed change initiatives highlights a long list of recurring problems: leaders who do not provide consistent direction or visible commitment; staff who feel uninformed, threatened or simply exhausted; limited capacity to manage multiple projects at once; a tendency to repeat past mistakes; weak or overly optimistic planning; lack of clear ownership; poor measurement systems; little effort to communicate successes; unrealistic expectations about speed and impact; "manufactured" consensus that evaporates when hard decisions appear; self-centred attitudes among key actors; exclusive, top-down implementation styles; absence of a genuine sense of urgency; and, finally, a failure to acknowledge both past achievements and earlier disappointments (Baker, 2007). In such conditions, the content of a strategy on paper tells only part of the story; the way it is introduced, discussed, resourced and adjusted over time is just as important.

These complications led many authors to describe the strategic management process as a cycle in which formulation, implementation, coordination, monitoring and feedback are linked in an ongoing loop rather and not separated into once-off stages (Marr and Creelman, 2011). Within this broader cycle, performance management systems are often presented as the main instruments for turning strategic intent into day-to-day practice, by translating high-level goals into indicators, targets, reports and reviews. The Balanced Scorecard (BSC), originally developed for private firms, has been one of the most influential tools adapted for public use. Kaplan and Norton designed it to counterbalance an exclusive focus on financial metrics by adding perspectives on customers, internal processes and learning and growth, thereby encouraging organizations to see performance in a more rounded way (Kaplan and Norton, 1996; 2000). When public organizations take up the BSC, they typically have to modify it to reflect the absence of profit as a bottom line: some versions replace the "customer" box with a broader "stakeholder" perspective, while others insert public value more explicitly, asking whether activities genuinely advance the organisation's mission and produce benefits that citizens and communities actually experience (Bryson et al., 2014).

However, experience with public-sector scorecards shows that these adaptations are far from straightforward. Evaluations frequently find that BSC in government agencies and non-profit organizations end up dominated by operational measures – numbers of cases processed, average waiting times, cost per unit of service – while outcomes and wider public value receive much less systematic attention (Norman,

2007; Höglund et al., 2021). The situation can become even more problematic in politically charged environments. Höglund et al. (2021) point out that BSC-style systems are highly vulnerable to politically driven management control: targets and indicators may be chosen or adjusted to suit short-term political narratives rather than longer-term public value, and the presence of a sophisticated performance framework can give a misleading impression of rationality and objectivity even when underlying choices are primarily political. Knowles et al. (2013) describe how, in some organizations, the scorecard degenerates into a "tick-box" routine, where staff focus on feeding the system with data rather than using the information for reflection and learning, thereby reinforcing bureaucratic compliance rather than strategic thinking.

These observations suggest that the critical question is not simply whether the Balanced Scorecard – or any other performance tool – can be technically adapted to public settings, but whether its underlying logic can be re-oriented away from a narrow managerialist focus on internal perspectives and towards a more open, contested and political understanding of public value. One way forward, proposed in the literature, is to repurpose the scorecard from a control mechanism into a device for structured conversation, in which managers, politicians, staff and stakeholders jointly explore how everyday activities, processes and investments are connected (or not) to the outcomes they care about (Spano, 2009; Weinberg and Lewis, 2009). Used in this way, indicators become prompts for discussion rather than fixed judgements, and the risk of "goal displacement" – of chasing what is easiest to measure rather than what is most important – can at least be made visible and debated. Strategic leadership then involves resisting the temptation to equate what appears on dashboards with what truly matters, and instead using performance information as one input among others in an ongoing effort to keep organizational action aligned with both public aspirations and the shifting authorizing environment.

3. CONTEMPORARY CHALLENGES

Public organizations no longer operate within stable, national borders. Strategic management in the public sector operates within a context shaped by distinctive contemporary challenges that traditional planning models were not designed to address. These challenges extend beyond the operational difficulties of implementation to fundamental questions about whether classical strategic frameworks remain adequate for the world public organizations actually inhabit.

3.1 Macro-Environmental Forces

Due to the dense webs of interdependence created by globalization, economic, social, and environmental issues transcend national boundaries, affect multiple jurisdictions, and call for coordinated responses across states rather than just within them. Digitalization and the proliferation of information technologies are intensifying this increasing interconnectedness, shifting not only how people organize and communicate but also what they expect from public authorities in terms of transparency, responsiveness, and accessibility (Peters and Savoie, 2000). In many countries, citizens have grown accustomed to the seamless, on-demand services offered by large private-sector platforms, and they increasingly expect governments to match that standard, a shift that translates into strong pressure for ambitious e-government programmes, investments in interoperable systems and more sophisticated approaches to data governance and protection (Vittou, 2024).

The broader environment is further marked by a series of major shocks that have disrupted any lingering sense of stability. The 2008 global financial crisis, the COVID-19 pandemic and the accelerating climate emergency have each, in their own way, exposed structural vulnerabilities in existing institutional arrangements and highlighted the costs of strategic complacency and under-preparedness (Morris and Hodges, 2020). These widespread disruptions change the fiscal room for maneuver, reshape social risks and inequalities, and intensify political contestation over priorities and responsibilities; they cannot be viewed as transient operational issues that can be resolved with small adjustments. They consequently compel public organizations to increase their capacity for strategic resilience, which is the capacity to withstand shocks, adjust under extreme pressure, and reorganize services and policies in ways that maintain or restore public value in the face of ongoing instability. (Vittou, 2024).

3.2 Networked and Multi-Level Governance

As public problems have become more tangled and wide-ranging, it has become increasingly clear that no single organization has all the authority, resources or expertise needed to address them in isolation, which means that governance itself now takes place largely in an inter-organizational space characterised by shared steering and joint management among many different actors (Kooiman, 1993). Instead of a single center issuing commands, policy processes are populated by ministries, agencies, municipalities, non-profits, professional bodies, private firms and citizen groups, all of which hold pieces of the puzzle and must find ways of working together if they are to make progress on complex issues.

One visible result of this shift is the growth of networked forms of organization and cross-sector collaboration. Tackling challenges such as public health, regional economic development or environmental sustainability typically requires the alignment of funding streams, information systems and professional practices across public agencies, non-governmental organizations and private-sector partners (Agranoff and McGuire, 2001). In this setting, strategic management cannot be understood simply as directing a single hierarchical bureaucracy; it becomes a matter of convening, facilitating and orchestrating multi-actor networks in order to produce outcomes that no participant could achieve alone (Bryson et al. 2014).

At the same time, the rise of multi-level governance adds another layer of complexity. Public organizations are embedded in vertical chains that link local, regional, national and supranational institutions, while also participating in horizontal networks that include cross-sector partnerships, contracted service providers and quasi-governmental bodies. Strategic decisions taken at one level – for example, national austerity policies or supranational regulations – can significantly constrain what is possible at other levels, and implementation often depends on coordination among organizations whose interests overlap only partially. Under these conditions, traditional hierarchical models of strategic management, which assume clear lines of authority and a unified command structure, struggle to cope; strategy making and execution are dispersed across arenas and actors, and success depends less on control and more on the patient work of alignment and coordination.

3.3 Strategy Under Deep Uncertainty

When the various trends described so far are taken together – complexity, networked governance, recurrent crises and rapid technological and social change – they produce an environment better described as one of deep uncertainty than of ordinary risk. Insights from complexity and chaos theory are useful here: in systems marked by non-linear interactions and feedback loops, the future is not just hard to forecast in practice; it is, to a significant extent, unpredictable in principle, because small differences in initial conditions can lead to very different outcomes over time (Kiel, 1995; Stacey and Mowles, 2016). In such circumstances, linear projections that treat the future as a smooth extension of the past become unreliable, and the comforting assumption that careful analysis today will yield a single robust plan for tomorrow turns into a dangerous simplification.

This level of uncertainty undermines the appeal of universal, one-size-fits-all recipes for public management reform. The trajectory of New Public Management (NPM) illustrates the point (Rossidis et al., 2020c). For several decades, many governments imported private-sector tools and ideas – market mechanisms, performance contracts, internal competition – on the promise that they would automatically make public services more efficient and responsive, often with little attention to the political, cultural and institutional specificities of the public realm (McCabe, 2015; Karkatsoulis, 2004). Critics have shown that these reforms frequently rested on a rather negative image of public servants as lazy or self-interested bureaucrats who needed the "discipline" of the market to perform, an image that not only overlooked intrinsic motivation and professional ethics but also risked undermining commitment and trust inside organizations (Diefenbach, 2010). Where such models were applied mechanically, without adaptation to context, they often produced disappointing or perverse effects.

The lesson drawn in this chapter is that effective public strategy under deep uncertainty has to be context-sensitive and emergent rather than rigid and uniform. Instead of assuming that a single set of tools or structures will work everywhere, public managers need to craft strategies that are tailored to the specific problem, institutional setting and stakeholder constellation they face, and to remain willing to revise those strategies as they learn from experience. This does not mean abandoning all structure or analysis, but it does mean approaching models and "best practices" with a critical eye, treating them as starting points to be tested and adapted rather than as templates to be copied wholesale.

3.4 Complexity and Institutional Contexts

3.4.1 The Inherent Complexity of Public Organizations

Complexity, in this setting, needs to be kept distinct from what is simply complicated. A jet engine is complicated: it consists of many components, but their functions and interactions can be mapped, modelled and controlled with a high degree of precision. A rainforest, by contrast, is complex: its many agents – plants, animals, micro-organisms, weather systems – interact in non-linear ways that generate patterns no one designed and no one can fully predict. Public organizations, the chapter suggests, resemble rainforests far more than engines. They are shaped by dense interdependencies, feedback loops and non-linear interactions that produce outcomes which cannot be straightforwardly traced back to a single cause or controlled from a central point (Kiel, 1995; Yolles, 2006). They are made up of heterogeneous human actors – employees, politicians, service users, citizens – whose perceptions, interests and relationships combine to create collective behaviours that are not reducible to individual intentions and that routinely surprise senior decision-makers.

In such complex adaptive systems, strategy rarely emerges as the tidy end-product of a single, rational design process carried out at the top of the hierarchy. More often, what actually happens is that high-level directives interact with countless small adjustments, workarounds and negotiations made by people at different levels and in different parts of the system, so that the organisation's "real" strategy is co-created day by day through these interactions (Bovaird, 2008; Stacey and Mowles, 2016). Formal strategy documents may set out broad intentions and priorities, but front-line staff, middle managers, partner organizations and stakeholders constantly reinterpret and modify these intentions in light of local constraints, opportunities and values. As a result, the lived pattern of action – which projects move forward, which policies are enforced strictly or loosely, which innovations spread and which die out – can diverge markedly from the official plans recorded in reports and presentations.

The implications for strategic management are significant. Linear planning models rest on the assumption that clear causes will produce reasonably predictable effects, provided that analysis is sound and implementation is diligent. In complex systems, however, many important properties emerge from interactions across units, levels and organizations, so that strategic decisions can send ripples through networks in ways that are hard to foresee. Intended outcomes may be deflected, amplified or undermined as strategies encounter unanticipated coalitions, behavioural responses and constraints. The much-cited "butterfly effect" from chaos theory captures this intuition: tiny differences in information, timing or framing can, under certain conditions, lead to disproportionately large consequences for strategic trajectories (Stacey and Griffin, 2005). A policy shift that appears modest and manageable in the abstract can, once implemented, trigger knock-on effects – reconfigured alliances, changes in professional norms, cascades in resource use – that were not visible at the design stage, reminding public managers that strategy in complex adaptive systems is always, to some extent, an experiment whose full results only become clear over time.

3.4.2 Wicked Problems and Necessity for Collaborative Strategy

Wicked problems have become a key reference point for explaining why traditional strategic management approaches in the public sector so often fall short (Rittel and Webber, 1973; Conklin, 2006). Phenomena such as homelessness, chronic poverty, major public health emergencies, environmental degradation and criminal justice reform are commonly cited examples. They share several distinctive features. First, they are marked by ambiguity: there is no single, definitive way of formulating "the" problem, because different stakeholders describe and interpret it in different ways. Second, they are characterised by interconnectedness: what shows up as a problem in one domain is typically a symptom of issues elsewhere, so that interventions in one area have knock-on effects – sometimes helpful, sometimes harmful – in others. Third, they lack clear-cut solutions: there is no final right or wrong answer, only options that can be judged as relatively better or worse, and each attempted solution is a "one-shot operation" that changes the situation and creates new conditions that must in turn be addressed (Rittel and Webber, 1973; Conklin, 2006).

Conventional strategic management, drawing on private-sector traditions of competition and rational problem-solving, usually assumes that problems can be clearly defined, that experts can design technically optimised solutions, and that success can be determined against a stable set of criteria. Wicked problems disrupt these assumptions at every point. Stakeholders disagree fundamentally even about basic definitions: is homelessness mainly a shortage of affordable housing, a manifestation of untreated mental illness and addiction, a failure of labour markets to provide secure jobs, or a matter of individual responsibility and moral behaviour? Each framing leads towards different interventions and policy mixes, many of which are incompatible with each other. Focusing on housing supply while neglecting mental-health services or access to employment, for example, may reduce visible street homelessness in some locations but leave the underlying drivers largely untouched. Even assessing whether a given strategy has "worked" is difficult, because there is no objective benchmark: a reduction in recorded homelessness might stem from successful interventions, but it might just as well reflect changes in counting practices or the displacement of people to other jurisdictions, making causal attribution highly uncertain (Rittel and Webber, 1973; Conklin, 2006).

For these reasons, wicked problems demand collaborative and evolutionary strategies that move beyond the boundaries of single organizations. Multi-sector partnerships that bring together public agencies, non-profit organizations, private firms and community groups are often the only realistic way to assemble the diverse knowledge, authority and resources needed to make progress, yet such collaborations pose their own strategic difficulties (Crosby and Bryson, 2010). Authority is widely dispersed; organizational cultures and professional languages differ; incentives and accountability regimes only partly overlap; and underlying power relations remain contested. In this context, strategy cannot be reduced to a one-off plan imposed from the top. It becomes a continuing process of shared problem-framing, negotiation, trial-and-error experimentation and collective learning, in which participants repeatedly adjust both their understanding of the problem and the mix of actions they are willing and able to pursue (Crosby and Bryson, 2010).

As illustrated in Figure 1, these contemporary challenges—wicked problems, declining institutional trust, financial constraints, political fragmentation, and multi-level governance pressures-converge with the need to develop dynamic capabilities across the three corners of the public value strategic triangle.

Figure 1. Public value strategic triangle: Dynamic capabilities and contemporary challenges. This figure integrates the three corners of the strategic triangle, the key dynamic capabilities for each corner, and the contemporary challenges facing public sector organizations

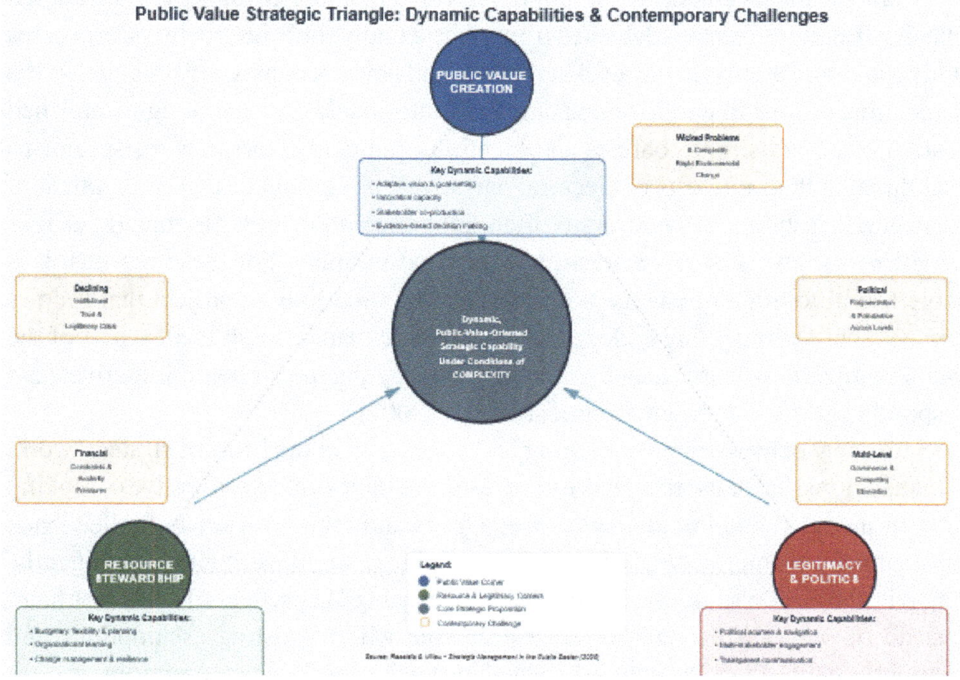

Systems theory and complexity science offer alternative analytical frameworks that are better aligned with the nature of wicked problems than classic rational-planning models. Instead of seeking an exhaustive understanding of all relevant variables in order to design a single optimal solution, systems approaches encourage practitioners to map relationships, identify feedback loops and explore how patterns and "system properties" emerge from multiple interactions, often in ways that no single actor controls (Rittel and Webber, 1973; Conklin, 2006). Rather than promising detailed prediction, complexity-informed approaches emphasize scenario thinking, adaptive management and the expectation that strategy will have to evolve as actors learn more about the system and about one another. This style of working departs sharply from the textbook image of rational-comprehensive strategy, but it corresponds more closely to the realities of public organizations and networks grappling with wicked problems, where the search for perfect solutions must give way to more modest aims of continual adjustment, improvement and the negotiated management of inevitable trade-offs.

4. MANAGING CHANGE IN COMPLEX ENVIRONMENTS

4.1 Change as Endogenous Element of Strategy

Strategic management in the public sector inevitably involves organizational change; if strategy remains detached from what actually shifts in structures, processes and behaviours, it stays at the level of rhetoric and never becomes real practice. At the same time, change in public organizations is notoriously difficult: long-established institutions carry strong routines and identities, political actors may resist reforms that threaten their interests or electoral narratives, professionals can be sceptical of managerial fashions, resources are often tight and authority is fragmented across departments, levels of government and external partners. For these reasons, it is more useful to think of change not as a separate, time-limited project that follows strategy, but as something endogenous to strategic management itself – part of the way organizations learn, adapt and evolve as they pursue strategic initiatives and respond to shifts in their environment (Baker, 2007).

This view places strategic learning and adaptation at the heart of strategy work. Organisations that pause to reflect on the results of their strategic initiatives – looking at both intended and unintended consequences and taking seriously the feedback emerging from implementation – are better placed to adjust course intelligently. Argyris and Schön's notion of "double-loop learning" is particularly relevant here: instead of only asking how to solve problems within existing assumptions and routines, double-loop learning asks whether those underlying assumptions are still valid and, if not, how they might need to change (Argyris and Schön, 1996). Public organizations that develop this deeper learning capacity tend to have fewer rigid hierarchies and more open channels for information to move upwards and sideways; they cultivate cultures in which experimentation is possible and failures can be discussed without automatic blame; they build systems and routines that encourage ongoing reflection and collective sense-making; and their leaders actively support questioning and challenge rather than insisting that existing approaches are beyond debate (Senge, 1990).

One practical attempt to embed such learning into the core of public-sector modernisation is the MATE model, which links Management, Training and Evaluation into a single, mutually reinforcing system (Sotirakou and Zeppou, 2004). Instead of treating these three functions as separate silos, MATE conceives them as elements in a continuous cycle: strategic management processes identify new priorities and capabilities, which in turn generate training needs; training builds the skills and understanding required for managers and staff to implement strategic choices; evaluation then assesses results, captures lessons and feeds insights back into the next round of strategic thinking. In this way, management, training and evaluation support each other rather than pulling in different directions. The underlying assumption is that moving from a rigid, rule-bound bureaucracy to a more adaptive, learning-oriented organization does not happen automatically as a side-effect of reforms; it requires deliberate investment in the capacity to learn at individual, team and institutional levels, so that change becomes part of how the organization routinely operates rather than an exceptional state reserved for occasional "restructuring" exercises.

4.2 Imperatives of Change and Sources of Resistance

Research on change management in the public sector consistently shows that change is pushed by powerful forces from outside the organization while, at the same time, being slowed or distorted by equally powerful forces from within, so that any realistic account of strategic change has to recognize both the necessity of adaptation and the reasons why implementation is so often difficult. External pressures stem from technological disruption, fiscal constraints, demographic trends, shifting social expectations and mounting environmental challenges, all of which reshape what citizens demand from government and what governments can realistically provide. Internally, however, public organizations tend to display strong institutional inertia: existing structures, procedures, cultures and relationships have accumulated over time and acquire their own momentum and legitimacy, making them resistant to alteration even when new strategies call for different ways of working. Resistance from employees, in this perspective, is usually not a matter of simple irrationality or stubbornness; it often reflects perfectly understandable worries about job security, role ambiguity, increased workload or the loss of familiar working patterns and relationships, as well as doubts about the credibility of yet another reform wave. Conflicts between political and administrative actors likewise express genuine disagreements over policy direction and implementation choices rather than mere misunderstanding (Vittou, 2024).

Institutional inertia and bureaucratic culture are central here. Public organizations are frequently marked by deeply embedded rules, routines and norms that place a premium on stability, predictability and rule adherence. Wilson's idea of a "bureaucratic personality" captures this tendency: an organizational character shaped by long-standing procedures and professional identities, which provides continuity and reliability but also acts as a powerful brake on efforts at reform (Wilson, 1989; Baker, 2007). In such settings, ambitious strategic plans can run aground on everyday habits and unwritten rules that quietly steer behaviour back towards the familiar. For employees, change can be personally unsettling. It can threaten professional identities built up over years, disrupt social ties within teams and erode feelings of psychological safety. The cynicism often reported in studies of organizational change is therefore better understood as a rational response to a history of top-down reforms that have ignored or overridden deep institutional cultures, rather than as an attitude problem to be corrected (Baker, 2007).

On top of this, change processes inevitably redistribute resources, authority and symbolic status, which means they create winners and losers. Reforms can trigger open or covert struggles between departments, professional groups and political factions over budgets, decision rights and the organisation's core purposes, making it difficult to maintain a coherent strategic direction (Joyce, 2015). Perhaps the most serious obstacle, however, is the failure to generate genuine ownership of change among public employees. When reforms are experienced as something imposed "from above" – driven by ministers, central agencies or external consultants – rather than as a process in which staff have a real voice and stake, commitment tends to be shallow and short-lived, and implementation is sustained only as long as formal pressure lasts. Strategic change in the public sector, as recent analyses underline, therefore depends not only on sound ideas and external necessity but also on the patient work of building shared purpose and ownership at multiple levels inside the organization (Vittou, 2024).

4.3 Managing Change Under Complexity

Traditional, linear models of change management – in which top-down directives cascade through clear hierarchies, comprehensive plans are drawn up before anything happens on the ground, and resistance is expected to give way once communication campaigns and incentive schemes are in place – fit poorly with the realities of complex public organizations. They rest on the assumption that decision-makers can specify the desired end-state in advance, gather sufficient information about the system and then identify an optimal path from "here" to "there." Complexity-informed perspectives challenge this logic: in genuinely complex systems, the information needed for optimization is often incomplete or unreliable; desired end-states cannot be fully described upfront because they are themselves evolving and contested; crucial learning arises only during implementation; and emergent properties, generated by countless interactions among actors and institutions, cannot be captured by pre-implementation analysis alone.

In response, adaptive management and other complexity-aware approaches to change emphasize iterative cycles of small-scale experimentation, learning and adjustment rather than a single, comprehensive analysis followed by full-scale rollout. Instead of treating implementation as the final stage of a long planning process, these approaches see it as a structured form of inquiry: organizations probe their environment with limited interventions, observe both expected and unexpected consequences, and then refine or redirect their efforts on the basis of what they have learned (Roberts & Timothy, 2024). This is particularly appropriate for public organizations dealing with wicked problems, where understanding deepens only through engagement with the system and where attempts to impose uniform, large-scale reforms in one stroke often generate overload, resistance or unintended effects that undermine their own goals.

Strategic leadership plays a decisive role in promoting and implementing strategic change. It contributes to formative visioning, strengthening cooperation, and developing modern knowledge management systems, among other functions (Rossidis et al., 2020a). Leaders take responsibility for transforming the existing system, must be open to innovative ideas, and must have the ability to anticipate and understand both immediate and long-term developments (Rossidis & Belias, 2025).

Strategic leaders under such conditions require a distinct set of capacities. They must be able to operate with ambiguity and incomplete information, recognizing that neither they nor their advisers can foresee all relevant developments. They need to frame goals in ways that allow for revision as insight grows, to tolerate experimentation and failure, and to treat setbacks as opportunities for learning rather than simply as occasions for blame. They must also engage a wide range of stakeholders so that multiple perspectives on complex problems are brought into the conversation, and they need to think in systemic terms, asking how actions in one part of the organization or governance network might create feedback loops and unintended consequences elsewhere. These capabilities differ markedly from older models of public-sector leadership that prioritised hierarchical authority, strict rule adherence and the disciplined execution of fixed plans.

A central idea in this context is what Heifetz and Linsky (2002) describe as adaptive leadership. For them, leadership under uncertainty is less about providing ready-made answers and more about mobilizing people to confront uncomfortable realities and to learn new ways of working. This involves creating spaces in which difficult questions can be raised without immediate sanction, managing conflict so that it becomes a source of insight rather than paralysis, and sustaining attention on the underlying adaptive work – changes in norms, roles, relationships and mindsets – that must accompany any formal restructuring of policies or organizations. Within this frame, communication and training cease to be mere tools for cascading information from the top. They become essential means of helping employees understand the reasons for change, deal with the stress and uncertainty it produces, and acquire the skills and confidence needed to function effectively in a new environment.

Ultimately, managing change in complex public systems returns us to the logic of wicked problems. Because there is no single, predefined "solution" waiting to be implemented, progress depends on iterative, experimental and participatory approaches rather than on one-off, top-down rollouts. Effective change processes often start with pilot projects or small-scale experiments, used to explore what works in particular contexts and what does not, and only then move towards broader adoption of practices that have proved robust. In this sense, change is not a discrete event that happens once and for all, but an ongoing, collective effort to navigate complexity while preserving and, where possible, enhancing public value in conditions that are inherently uncertain (Heifetz and Linsky, 2002).

5. CRITICAL REFLECTIONS AND LIMITATIONS

5.1 Limitations of Strategic Management

A closer and more skeptical look reveals that the use of strategy can bring with it several serious limitations and pathologies that should be addressed rather than ignored, despite the fact that discussing strategy has become almost synonymous with discussing improvement in the public sector and that strategic management is frequently described as essential for effectiveness. First, strategy runs the risk of devolving into a form of technocracy in which fundamental political decisions—such as which values should be prioritized, whose interests should be upheld or furthered, and what trade-offs society is willing to accept—are reframed as problems to be resolved by instruments and methods. Frameworks for strategic analysis can certainly help managers to structure choices and see options more clearly, but they cannot legitimately decide which goals public organizations ought to pursue or how competing claims should be balanced; Strategic management should be a support for democratic deliberation and not start to replace it, shifting key value judgements from open political arenas into expert or managerial ones where conflict is often managed away rather than confronted.

A second difficulty concerns how strategic management frameworks handle public value. Because outcomes are complex and multi-layered, there is a constant temptation – and often a formal requirement – to translate them into metrics that can be monitored and reported, and it is at this point that the vulnerability identified by Höglund et al. (2021) becomes visible: once indicators are in place, organizations come under intense pressure to show good performance against them, and the focus can gradually move from the broader, messy reality of public value to the narrower task of "doing well on the numbers." Some familiar examples: a hospital keen to improve its efficiency indicators shortens average length of stay through earlier discharge, which looks like progress on paper but may worsen patients' health once they leave; a police force under orders to reduce recorded crime cracks down aggressively in ways that bring figures down but damage relations with communities and undermine trust in the long term. In such cases, measurement does exactly what it is supposed to do at the level of indicators, yet something important is lost. The point is not that measurement should be abandoned – it is vital for accountability and learning – but that managers and politicians alike must remain constantly aware of the danger that metric fixation will push attention away from the deeper question of whether public value, in all its dimensions, is really being enhanced (Höglund et al., 2021).

A third problem appears when strategic management is rolled out mainly through hierarchical instructions: central authorities demand strategic plans in a standard format, impose common templates and timetables, and expect that this formal apparatus will by itself make organizations more strategic. In practice, these arrangements can narrow rather than widen strategic thinking, because they encourage compliance with prescribed procedures rather than careful adaptation to specific circumstances. Sotirakou and Zeppou (2004), studying organizations that tried to move from rigid, resistant bureaucracies towards learning organizations, found that such transitions often coincide with dips in performance, as staff time and energy are diverted into planning meetings, drafting documents and coping with organizational reshuffles; day-to-day work does not stop while all this happens, and the strain shows. Strategic management has real costs – in planning time, in disruption caused by reorganization, and in the risks that come with experimentation – and if it is not genuinely rooted in organizational capabilities and given enough room to mature, those costs may outweigh the intended benefits, leaving people more tired and cynical but not significantly better equipped to deal with their environment (Sotirakou and Zeppou, 2004).

Finally, there is the more subtle phenomenon that might be called the illusion of strategy. An organization can have thick strategic plans, glossy brochures, detailed performance scorecards and regular review meetings, and yet very little may change in how services are actually delivered or how stakeholders experience them. Implementation remains patchy or weak, engagement with citizens and partners is limited to consultation rituals, and lessons from success and failure do not travel far beyond the immediate team involved. On the surface, the presence of elaborate strategic artefacts suggests that the organization is forward-looking and well managed, but underneath, core patterns of behaviour and power remain much as before. In such situations, the main impact of strategic management may be to create a reassuring narrative that "we have a strategy," while the harder work of building capacity, sustaining leadership commitment and aligning key actors around difficult choices is left largely undone.

5.2 Gap Between Perceived and Objective Impact

One of the most awkward facts for advocates of strategic planning in the public sector is the stubborn gap that emerges, time and again, between what managers believe their strategies are achieving and what performance data actually show.

Studies of Norwegian municipalities, for instance, report that senior officials express strong confidence in the value of formal strategic planning, often describing it as central to improved governance and service delivery, yet this subjective assurance does not consistently line up with measurable gains in objective indicators such as efficiency or service quality (Johnsen, 2016). One plausible explanation is that strategic planning is doing a different kind of work from the one usually claimed for it: rather than reliably driving better outcomes, it may function primarily as a legitimizing ritual, signalling rational control, modernity and managerial competence, and offering participants a sense of order and purpose even when the concrete impact on results is modest or hard to discern.

This observation connects directly to a broader pattern in the history of public management reform, where importing management technologies from the private sector without sufficient critical adaptation has often produced disappointing and sometimes damaging effects. New Public Management reforms are a well-known example: while they did succeed in drawing attention to performance, efficiency and results, they also generated a series of unintended consequences, including an excessive focus on outputs that were easy to count at the expense of outcomes that were harder to measure but no less important, declines in morale and professional discretion as tightly specified targets and contracts proliferated, the fragmentation of previously integrated services into competing units, and a gradual erosion of a distinct public-service identity and ethos in some settings (Pollitt and Bouckaert, 2011; Rossidis, 2014). In many cases, the tools and logics of private-sector management were applied as if they were universally valid, with too little regard for the political, ethical and institutional specificities of the public realm.

If strategic management is to avoid repeating these mistakes, it has to acknowledge and work with, rather than wish away, the political character of public value. Stoker (2006) makes the point sharply: what counts as public value is not given in advance or defined by experts alone; it is constituted through political processes in which multiple stakeholders argue, negotiate and, at times, compromise over what public organizations should try to achieve. Democratic governance requires that final authority over public purposes rests with elected representatives and engaged citizens, even if those purposes are informed and shaped by managerial expertise. Public managers contribute crucial knowledge about feasibility, costs and implementation, but they do not have a mandate to settle value questions on their own. Strategic management frameworks that treat politics simply as "context" or, worse, as a set of obstacles to be neutralized risk drifting into technically sophisticated but democratically problematic territory: they may look impressive in methodological terms, yet they sideline precisely those deliberations and conflicts through which public value is supposed to be defined.

5.3 Toward Adaptive and Democratic Strategies

5.3.1 Emerging Paradigm Shifts

Across the strategic management literature there is a clear shift away from viewing strategy as a single, comprehensive plan that can be designed in advance and then rolled out, and towards approaches that foreground flexibility, adaptation and participation as core features rather than afterthoughts. In this newer paradigm, strategies are treated less as rigid blueprints and more as working hypotheses about how public value might be created under particular conditions: they give direction and coherence to action, but they are explicitly understood as provisional, to be tested in practice and revised when experience and new information show that assumptions were incomplete or mistaken. This stance is especially important in public settings marked by complexity and uncertainty, where insisting on sticking to an initial plan in the face of contrary evidence is more likely to undermine value than to protect it.

At the same time, participatory approaches have gained prominence as a way of making strategy more democratic and more grounded in lived realities. Rather than bringing stakeholders into the process only once decisions have been made – for example, to help with implementation or communication – these approaches involve them from the outset, in problem-framing and strategy formulation. The aim is twofold: to ensure that strategies reflect a wider range of perspectives and knowledge than those available within a single organization, and to build a stronger sense of shared ownership that can sustain implementation over time. In this spirit, Bryson, Crosby and Bloomberg's (2014) Public Value Governance Triangle extends Moore's original strategic triangle by explicitly recognizing that public value is often created through the interplay of multiple sectors (government, business and non-profit), multiple levels of governance (local, regional, national and beyond) and multiple stakeholder viewpoints. Instead of assuming that public agencies are the sole or even the primary creators of value, their framework treats cross-sector collaboration as a normal and necessary condition for tackling complex issues. Under these conditions, strategic management is reimagined less as the hierarchical direction of a single organisation's actions and more as the craft of bringing diverse actors together, aligning their efforts and sustaining collaborative arrangements through which substantive public value can emerge (Bryson, Crosby and Bloomberg, 2014).

5.3.2 Strategic Capabilities Rather Than Plans

A growing strand of research argues that what really matters for public organizations is not whether they possess impressive strategic plans, but whether they have developed robust strategic capabilities – that is, the organizational abilities to spot emerging issues, craft appropriate responses, implement them in practice and learn from the results over time. Studies suggest that agencies which treat strategic management as an evolving capability rather than as a one-off document are better able to navigate uncertainty and complexity, precisely because they can adjust and recombine their responses as conditions change instead of being locked into a fixed blueprint (Poister, Pitts and Edwards, 2010). In concrete terms, such capability shows up in several interrelated practices: systematic scanning of the environment and shared sense-making about what signals mean; the inclusive engagement of stakeholders so that different perspectives and forms of knowledge are brought into the discussion; analytical work that is rigorous but also modest about what can and cannot be predicted; a willingness to experiment and to treat failure as a source of learning; iterative adjustment of strategies as new experience accumulates; and leadership that is not confined to the top, but distributed across levels and units so that initiative and insight can surface where problems and opportunities actually arise (Poister, Pitts and Edwards, 2010).

Seen in this light, the emerging shift is as much about mindset as it is about methods. It asks public managers to move away from thinking of themselves primarily as master planners who design a complete strategy in advance and then oversee its execution, and to adopt instead the stance of facilitators, cultivators and navigators operating in dense social and political landscapes. Their task is not simply to choose a path and insist that others follow it, but to help people inside and outside the organization make sense of changing circumstances, to create conditions in which constructive experimentation is possible, and to keep strategy connected to lived realities by adjusting course when evidence and experience demand it. Strategy, under this conception, is less an event that happens every few years around a planning cycle and more a continuous process of learning, sense-making and adaptation that is woven into the everyday life of the organization.

6. SUMMARY OF MAIN ARGUMENTS

As explored throughout this chapter, public strategy is best understood as a dynamic, public-value-oriented capability that enables organizations to navigate profound complexity and political constraints

Strategic management has undeniably moved close to the center of contemporary debates about public-sector effectiveness, but this prominence has not brought with it a settled consensus on what "doing strategy" in government actually means or how far it delivers on its promises. The analysis developed in this chapter suggests that strategic management cannot be treated as a neutral set of tools borrowed wholesale from the private sector. Instead, it has to be understood as an adaptive practice that must be continually reinterpreted and reshaped in light of public-sector institutions, politics and values. Several, partly uncomfortable, conclusions follow from this.

To begin with, strategy *does* appear to matter. Comparative studies indicate that public organizations which have recognizable strategies and reasonably well-developed strategic management processes tend, on average, to perform better than those that lack them, especially when performance is examined over longer periods rather than in isolated snapshots (George, Walker and Monster, 2019). Yet these same studies also undermine any simplistic belief that "having a strategy" is enough: the effects of strategy are filtered and sometimes distorted by environmental constraints, organizational structures, leadership quality and the degree of stakeholder alignment. In some contexts, a well-designed strategy can be blunted by hostile politics, rigid rules or resource shortages; in others, strong leadership and supportive environments can compensate for weak or vague strategic documents. Strategy, in other words, is one important ingredient in a much more complex mix, and treating it as a silver bullet risks blinding decision-makers to other, equally crucial determinants of performance.

A second conclusion is that effective strategic management in the public sector is not about eliminating tensions but about living with and working through them. Public managers are constantly pulled between analytical rigour and appropriate modesty about what can be predicted; between providing clear direction and leaving room to adapt; between holding to core values and responding to shifting circumstances; between top-down leadership and the need for distributed initiative; between the claims of professional expertise and the requirements of democratic accountability. These are not dilemmas that can be "solved" once and for all by better frameworks. They represent enduring features of governing in complex, pluralist societies. The risk, if this is forgotten, is that strategic management lapses into overconfident planning cultures that promise more control than they can deliver, or into reactive pragmatism that abandons any attempt at coherent direction.

Third, the chapter underlines that public-sector strategy is normatively bounded: it must ultimately be judged by its contribution to public value in democratic societies, not merely by its internal coherence or its success in raising output metrics. When strategic management drifts away from democratic legitimacy, meaningful public engagement and sensitivity to questions of equity and justice, it easily collapses into a narrow project of efficiency improvement or becomes a vehicle for technocratic displacement of political argument. Conversely, where strategic practices remain connected to political processes, draw seriously on multiple stakeholder perspectives and keep their focus on public purposes rather than organizational convenience, they can support forms of governance that are both more effective and more legitimate. The critical point is that neither outcome is guaranteed by the mere presence of "strategy"; everything depends on how strategic management is framed and used.

Finally, the spread of complexity and the growing salience of wicked problems mean that traditional images of strategy as a linear cycle of planning and implementation are increasingly hard to defend. Challenges such as climate change, long-term social exclusion or systemic health inequalities are not going to yield to single, master plans. They require collaborative, adaptive and experimental approaches in which strategies evolve over time, in step with learning and changing conditions. For public organizations facing such issues, strategic management cannot remain a periodic, document-driven exercise; it has to be institutionalised as a set of capabilities for ongoing inquiry, cross-sector collaboration and evolutionary refinement of direction. The critical question, going forward, is whether public institutions and political systems are willing to invest in building and sustaining these capabilities, or whether strategy will remain, too often, a rhetorical commitment sitting uncomfortably alongside entrenched routines and short-term pressures.

6.1 Theoretical Proposals

On the basis of the preceding analysis, several directions for further theoretical development suggest themselves, each of which points away from universal recipes and towards more context-sensitive, politically aware and complexity-attuned understandings of strategy in the public sector.

First, a more explicitly contextualized contingency theory of strategic management is needed. Rather than searching for general principles that can be applied across all public organizations, future work should focus on clarifying the conditions under which different strategic approaches are likely to succeed or fail. This entails paying close attention to factors such as the degree of organizational autonomy (how much room managers actually have to manoeuvre), the stability or volatility of the environment, the clarity or ambiguity of the organization's mission, the level of stakeholder alignment or conflict, and the broader institutional setting in which the organization operates. Without such contingency-sensitive frameworks, prescriptions for "best practice" in strategy risk oscillating between over-generalization and hindsight bias.

Second, theory needs to move beyond the comfortable but misleading separation of "politics" and "management" that still lingers in much public administration thinking. In reality, political and managerial dimensions are tightly intertwined in public organizations: political processes define and legitimate strategic directions, but they do so through institutions and routines that managers help to design and operate; managerial capacity, in turn, shapes what is practically implementable and feeds back into political judgements about what is desirable or acceptable. A more sophisticated account of strategic management would therefore examine how these two dimensions interact in concrete settings, how political contests shape strategic options, and how managerial practices can either support or undermine democratic responsiveness and accountability.

Third, there is considerable scope for developing what might be called democratic strategic management. Most existing frameworks are largely silent on normative questions, yet in the public sector, strategy processes inevitably have democratic implications: they can either narrow or broaden who gets to participate in defining public purposes. Future research should therefore ask how strategic planning and management can be designed so that they strengthen, rather than displace, democratic deliberation. This could involve exploring ways in which strategy processes function as educative forums, helping citizens, politicians and staff to clarify values and trade-offs, and as vehicles for meaningful participation rather than as closed, technocratic exercises conducted by a small group of insiders.

Finally, the field would benefit from a more systematic incorporation of insights from complexity science into theories of public-sector strategy. While complexity has become a common rhetorical reference point, its implications for how strategies are conceived, tested and revised have not yet been fully worked through. There is a need for adaptive, experimental strategic frameworks that are explicitly designed for wicked problems and turbulent environments, and for studies that examine how organizations can hold on to a sense of strategic coherence – a recognisable direction and purpose – while remaining flexible enough to adjust as learning accumulates and conditions change. Such work would have to confront the tension between the political demand for clear, stable commitments and the practical necessity, under complexity, of revisiting and revising those commitments over time.

6.2 A Final Redefinition of Public Strategy

Strategic management in the public sector is best seen not as a tidy sequence of steps that capable managers "apply," but as a messy, ongoing and very human collective effort through which public organizations – and the networks they form with others – try to make sense of what they are for and how they might live up to that purpose in a world that rarely cooperates. In practice, this means repeatedly clarifying and contesting aspirations for public value, testing those aspirations against what organizations can actually do and against the political, fiscal and social constraints around them, working to secure enough legitimacy and support from authorizing environments to act at all, setting broad directions for change, attempting to turn those directions into coordinated action with and through stakeholders, and then reflecting – more or less honestly – on what these efforts have really produced. None of this unfolds in a straight line, and none of it is fully under managerial control; strategy is pulled about by elections, crises, internal politics and sheer contingency. Yet without some form of this continuous, collective work, public organizations are left drifting, reacting piecemeal to events rather than making any deliberate contribution to public purposes.

From this angle, the familiar ideal of a perfect strategic plan, flawlessly implemented, looks not only unrealistic but also faintly dangerous, because it invites a kind of managerial hubris that sits badly with complex, value-laden problems. What seems more helpful – and more honest – is a humbler standard: strategic management is doing its job when it helps organizations think a little more clearly about the difficult choices they face, when it keeps a reasonably coherent sense of purpose alive in the midst of pressure and distraction, and when it supports the capacity to adjust course without losing that sense of purpose altogether. It adds value when it creates real spaces for disagreement and dialogue among stakeholders rather than staging pre-scripted "consultations," when it forces technical analysis to answer to democratic argument and not the other way round, and when it protects time and room for professional judgement and moral reflection instead of squeezing them out in the name of procedural compliance or target-chasing.

Seen in this more critical light, public strategy is less about producing glossy documents and more about how people inside and around public organizations use whatever power, knowledge and legitimacy they have to make some headway on problems that cannot be solved once and for all. It is about mobilizing collective intelligence to navigate contested issues where reasonable people disagree, where evidence is incomplete and where every choice has winners and losers. Strategic management, accordingly, is not a neutral technique but a political practice: a continuous, sometimes uncomfortable process of learning and adaptation in which public organizations try to do better – and to be held to account for what "better" should mean – in a world that keeps moving the goalposts. If it forgets the politics and the limits, it turns into a technocratic ritual; if it acknowledges them and still tries to organize thoughtful, value-conscious action, it has a chance of becoming a genuinely useful part of democratic governance.

REFERENCES

Agranoff, R., & McGuire, M. (2001). Big questions in public network management. *Journal of Public Administration: Research and Theory, 11*(3), 295–326. DOI: 10.1093/oxfordjournals.jpart.a003504

Andrews, R., Boyne, G. A., Law, J., & Walker, R. M. (2012). Strategic management and public service performance: The way forward. *Public Administration Review, 72*(3), 405–413.

Argyris, C., & Schön, D. A. (1978). *Organizational learning: A theory of action perspective*. Addison-Wesley.

Argyris, C., & Schön, D. A. (1996). *Organizational learning II: Theory, method, and practice*. Addison-Wesley.

Baker, D. (2007). *Strategic change management in public sector organizations*. Chandos Publishing.

Belias, D., Rossidis, I., & Papademetriou, C. (2024). *Organizational Behavior and Human Resource Management for Complex Work Environments*. IGI Global. DOI: 10.4018/979-8-3693-3466-9

Belias, D., Velissariou, S., Papailias, S., Manta, F., & Rossidis, I. (2019). Change Management – Obstacles and Perspectives for the Integration of Changes in Greek Public Hospitals. *Advances in Management & Applied Economics., 9*(2), 37–50.

Berry, F. S., & Wechsler, B. (1995). State agencies' experience with strategic planning: Findings from a national survey. *Public Administration Review, 55*(2), 159–168. DOI: 10.2307/977181

Bovaird, T. (2008). Emergent strategic management and planning mechanisms in complex adaptive systems. *Public Management Review, 10*(3), 319–340. DOI: 10.1080/14719030802002741

Boyne, G. A., & Walker, R. M. (2010). Strategic management and public service performance: Moving beyond the rhetoric. *Public Administration Review, 70*(3), 415–423.

Bryson, J. M. (2004). *Strategic planning for public and nonprofit organizations: A guide to strengthening and sustaining organizational achievement* (3rd ed.). Jossey-Bass.

Bryson, J. M., Crosby, B. C., & Bloomberg, L. (2014). *Public value and public administration*. Georgetown University Press.

Bryson, J., & George, B. 2020. Strategic management in public administration. In Oxford research encyclopedia: politics (pp. 1–26). DOI: DOI: 10.1093/acrefore/9780190228637.013.139

Conklin, J. (2006). *Wicked problems and social complexity*. CogNexus Institute.

Crosby, B. C., & Bryson, J. M. (2010). Integrative leadership and the creation and focus of governing for networks. *The Leadership Quarterly*, *21*(2), 231–245.

Diefenbach, T. (2009). New public management in public sector organizations: The dark sides of managerialistic enlightenment. *Public Administration*, *87*(4), 892–909. DOI: 10.1111/j.1467-9299.2009.01766.x

Flynn, N., & Talbot, C. (1996). Strategy and strategists in UK local government. *Journal of Management Development*, *15*(2), 24–37. DOI: 10.1108/02621719610109186

George, B., Walker, R. M., & Monster, J. (2019). Does strategic planning improve organizational performance? A meta-analysis. *Public Administration Review*, *79*(6), 810–819. DOI: 10.1111/puar.13104

Hansen, J. R., & Ferlie, E. (2016). Applying strategic management theories in public sector organizations: The importance of context-specificity, ambiguity, and power relations. *Public Management Review*, *18*(1), 17–40.

Heifetz, R. A., & Linsky, M. (2002). *Leadership on the line: Staying alive through the dangers of leading*. Harvard Business School Press.

Hill, C. W. L., & Jones, G. R. (2013). *Strategic management: An integrated approach* (10th ed.). Cengage Learning.

Hoglund, L., Martensson, M., & Thomson, K. (2021). Strategic triangle and public value in Swedish public sector: A longitudinal case study on management control practices. *Accounting, Auditing & Accountability Journal*, *34*(7), 1608–1634. DOI: 10.1108/AAAJ-11-2019-4284

Höglund, L., Holmgren Caicedo, M., Mårtensson, M., & Svärdsten, F. (2021). Strategic management accounting in the public sector context: The case of the Swedish Transport Administration. *Journal of Public Budgeting, Accounting & Financial Management*, *33*(4), 468–486. DOI: 10.1108/JPBAFM-12-2019-0180

Johnsen, Å. (2016). Strategic management in a complex world: Perspectives on knowledge creation and strategy process in Norwegian municipalities. *International Review of Administrative Sciences*, *82*(3), 517–534.

Joyce, P. (2015). *Strategic management in the public sector* (2nd ed.). Routledge. DOI: 10.4324/9781315740355

Kaplan, R. S., & Norton, D. P. (1996). *The balanced scorecard: Translating strategy into action*. Harvard Business School Press.

Karkatsoulis, P. (2004). *The State in Transition. From "administrative reform" and "New Public Management" to "Governance."*. I. Sideris.

Kiel, L. D. (1995). *Managing chaos and complexity in government: A new paradigm for managing change, innovation, and organizational renewal*. Jossey-Bass.

Kooiman, J., & van Vliet, M. (1993). Governance and public management. In Eliassen, K. A., & Peters, B. G. (Eds.), *Modern governance: New government-society interactions* (pp. 58–72). SAGE Publications.

Knowles, B., Greatbanks, R., & Manville, G. (2013) Scorecards and strategy maps: top ten factors in performance management. In: Third Sector Performance: Management and Finance in Not-for-Profit and Social Enterprises. Gower, Farnham, GB, pp. 189-198.

Marr, B., & Creelman, J. (2011). *More than a pretty face: A holistic review of the balanced scorecard*. Cranfield School of Management.

McCabe, L. (2015). *Understanding and managing organizational change in the public sector*. Routledge.

Mintzberg, H. (1994). *The rise and fall of strategic planning: Reconceiving roles for planning, plans, planners*. The Free Press.

Mintzberg, H., Ahlstrand, B., & Lampel, J. (2009). *Strategy safari: A guided tour through the wilds of strategic management* (2nd ed.). Prentice Hall.

Moore, M. H. (1995). *Creating public value: Strategic management in government*. Harvard University Press.

Morris, B., & Hodges, J. (2020). Public sector resilience during crises: A comparative analysis. *International Review of Administrative Sciences, 86*(2), 234–251.

Niiranen, V., & Joensuu, S. (2014). Managerial decision-making in public administration: An empirical examination of administrative reform. *International Review of Administrative Sciences, 80*(1), 97–118.

Norman, L. (2007). Controlling financial management: The use of management control systems to manage agency costs. *Journal of Management Control, 18*(2), 125–149.

Paré, G., Trudel, M. C., Jaana, M., & Kitsiou, S. (2015). Synthesizing information systems knowledge: A typology of literature reviews. *Information & Management, 52*(2), 183–199. DOI: 10.1016/j.im.2014.08.008

Pawson, R. (2002). Evidence and policy and the realist perspective. In Tilley, N. (Ed.), *Analysis for policy: Evidence and every day practice* (pp. 14–32). Policy Press.

Peters, B. G., & Savoie, D. J. (Eds.). (2000). *Governance in the twenty-first century: Revitalizing the public service*. Canadian Centre for Management DevelopmentDOI: 10.1515/9780773568884

Poister, T. H., Pitts, D. W., & Edwards, L. H. (2010). Strategic management research in the public sector: A review and synthesis. *American Review of Public Administration, 40*(5), 522–545. DOI: 10.1177/0275074010370617

Pollitt, C., & Bouckaert, G. (2011). *Public management reform: A comparative analysis* (3rd ed.). Oxford University Press.

Popay, J., Roberts, H., Sowden, A., Petticrew, M., Britten, N., Arai, L., & Duffy, S. (2006). *Narrative synthesis in systematic reviews: A product from the ESRC methods programme*. University of Southampton.

Porter, M. E. (1980). *Competitive strategy: Techniques for analyzing industries and competitors*. The Free Press.

Rainey, H. G. (2009). *Understanding and managing public organizations* (4th ed.). Jossey-Bass.

Rittel, H. W. J., & Webber, M. M. (1973). Dilemmas in a general theory of planning. *Policy Sciences, 4*(2), 155–169. DOI: 10.1007/BF01405730

Rossidis, I. (2014) Applying Business Management in Greek Public Administration. Athens: publ. Ath. Stamoulis.

Rossidis, I., & Belias, D. (2020a). Combining Strategic Management with Knowledge Management. Trends and International perspectives. *International Review of Management and Marketing, 10*(3), 39–45. DOI: 10.32479/irmm.9621

Rossidis, I., & Belias, D. (2025). *Change Management. Organizational Change and Elements of Organizational Behavior.* Tziolas.

Rossidis, I., Belias, D., & Papailias, S. (2020b). Strategic management and performance in the international environment. Book of Proceedings International Conference on Cotemporary Marketing Issues.

Rossidis, I., Belias, D., & Papailias, S. (2020c). Strategic management in the Greek public sector. In search of best practices in the international environment. Book of Proceedings International Conference on Business & Economics of the Hellenic Open University.

Rumelt, R. P. (2011). *Good strategy, bad strategy: The difference and why it matters*. Crown Business.

Senge, P. M. (1990). *The fifth discipline: The art and practice of the learning organization*. Doubleday.

Sotirakou, T., & Zeppou, M. (2004). The "MATE" model: a strategic knowledge management technique on the chessboard of public-sector modernization. *Management Decision*, *42*(1), 69–88. DOI: 10.1108/00251740410504430

Spano, A. (2009). Public Value Creation and Management Control Systems. *International Journal of Public Administration*, *32*(3–4), 328–348. https://doi-org.proxy.eap.gr/10.1080/01900690902732848

Stacey, R. D., & Griffin, D. (Eds.). (2005). *A complexity perspective on researching organizations: Taking experience seriously*. Routledge.

Stacey, R. D., & Mowles, C. (2016). *Strategic management and organizational dynamics: The challenge of complexity* (7th ed.). Pearson Education.

Stoker, G. (2006). Public value management: A new narrative for networked governance? *American Review of Public Administration*, *36*(1), 41–57. DOI: 10.1177/0275074005282583

Sukhera, J. (2022). Narrative reviews: Flexible, rigorous, and practical. *Journal of Graduate Medical Education*, *14*(4), 414–417. DOI: 10.4300/JGME-D-22-00480.1 PMID: 35991099

Teece, D. J. (2007). Explicating dynamic capabilities: The nature and microfoundations of (sustainable) enterprise performance. *Strategic Management Journal*, *28*(13), 1319–1350. DOI: 10.1002/smj.640

Vittou, P. (2024). The contribution of change management during the implementation process of administrative reforms [Master's thesis]. Panteion University of Social and Political Sciences.

Weinberg, D. B., & Lewis, D. (2009). Strategic management: Combining human resources and information technology. *International Journal of Strategic Human Resource Management*, *9*(1), 21–37.

Williams, M. R., & Lewis, D. (2008). Strategic management tools and public sector management: The challenge of context specificity. *Public Management Review, 10*(5), 653–671. DOI: 10.1080/14719030802264382

Wilson, W. (1989). The study of administration. *Political Science Quarterly, 104*(3), 481–506.

Yolles, M. (2006). Organizations as complex systems. *Journal of Applied Systems and Cybernetics, 35*(2), 183–202.

ENDNOTES

1 According to Rittel and Webber (1973), wicked problems refer to public issues of particular complexity. These are problems for which there is no broad agreement on their meaning and definition, while the parties involved have different values, perceptions, and interpretations of both their nature and how to deal with them. They are characterized by the conflict of many and often competing interests, multiple and indistinct causes, and technical and institutional difficulties that create a high degree of uncertainty and administrative complexity. They usually span more than one policy area and require planners and decision-makers to pursue different and sometimes conflicting objectives simultaneously (Tsekos, 2021). Indicative examples of such problems include corruption in public administration, asylum and migration policy, and the environmental crisis.

Chapter 6
Enhancing Public Sector Reform:
The Impact of Change Management on Organizational Restructuring

Dimitrios Koumanakos
Hellenic Open University, Greece

Eleni Sfakianaki
Hellenic Open University, Greece

ABSTRACT

Public organizations today face critical challenges, such as globalization, rapid technological developments, fiscal adjustments and increased expectations of citizens for efficiency, quality of services, transparency and accountability. A necessary condition for the public sector's effective response to these challenges, is the implementation of targeted administrative reforms through specific administrative adjustments. These administrative adjustments constitute changes that can be better analyzed in the light of the principles of change management. This analysis, examines in combination the basic theories of change management and organizational restructuring, exploring their interdependence within the framework of the public sector reform process. Emphasis is placed upon the importance of cultivating a strategically focused organizational culture, the role of leadership in coordinating change initiatives, and the integration of performance measurement and monitoring tools to assess progress and consolidate change.

DOI: 10.4018/979-8-3373-3526-1.ch006

1. INTRODUCTION

Modern socio-economic perceptions increasingly emphasize the need for effective administrative restructuring. Changing social conditions, multiple technological developments and market liberalization, combined with the current state of public administration, create the conditions for the beginning of a new era; an era of reforms. In recent years, from the rise of New Public Management to the emergence of Public Governance and the corresponding hybrid models (Lampropoulou et al., 2021; Rossidis, 2014), administrative reforms have sought to improve the functioning of public organizations, enhance their efficiency and effectiveness, promote accountability and transparency, and contribute to adaptation to a particularly dynamic and volatile environment (Belias et al., 2025). The reform attempts to upgrade the functioning of the public sector by focusing on achieving high levels of effectiveness and efficiency. A characteristic feature of today's societies is their ability to incorporate improvements and modernizing transformations in their structure, organization and operation. The most modern administrative models are becoming more targeted by focusing on solving defined administrative dysfunctions, emphasizing organizational flexibility, resilience and the ability to adapt to complex challenges such as digital transformation, optimal use of available resources, focus on the human factor, budgetary constraints, flexibility in relation to imposed administrative changes, etc. (Christensen & Lægreid, 2020; Pollitt, 2019; Mihiotis et al., 2023; Peters, 2021).

Within this broader reform context, change management is emerging as a critical tool for public sector readjustment. Change management refers to the strategies, tools and practices through which organizations identify the need for change, formulate a change plan and proceed with its implementation and maintenance (By et al., 2023). Although it originates mainly from the private sector, its application in the public sector is increasingly expanding as a critical administrative tool for implementing reforms. Public administration now recognizes that structural reforms and organizational restructuring cannot succeed without careful management of the human, cultural and administrative parameters of change (Van der Voet & Steijn, 2021; Kuipers et al., 2018; Rossidis et al., 2016).

Effective public sector reform, in addition to institutional and organizational changes, is based on the systematic implementation of administrative practices where the integration of the attempted change holds the central role (Rossidis et al., 2020). Organizational restructuring not based on careful administrative planning according to the principles of change management, may lead to resistance, poor implementation or even failure – as shown by the problematic implementation of many reform projects. On the contrary, reforms that incorporate practices that are part of the theory of change management such as stakeholder participation, the use of leadership behaviors, targeted communication, the provision of incentives, etc.

are more likely to yield sustainable results in terms of efficiency and effectiveness (Fernandez & Rainey, 2017; Vogel & Masal, 2023).

Organizational restructuring (i.e. changing the structure or processes of a public organization) is one of the most common types of reforms and is a particularly important area of administrative adjustment, linked to the broader functioning of the organization (Katsimardos et al., 2017). Changes at the organizational design level may include: redesigning hierarchical levels, differentiating job descriptions, the level of decentralization, and the structure of an organization's processes and functions. Governments adopt restructuring models to achieve specific objectives such as: improving administrative functioning, fiscal consolidation, accelerating processes, increasing the level of efficiency, improving the services provided, and overall better responding to strategic objectives, socio-economic expectations and timely adaptation to technological developments (OECD, 2019; Andrews et al., 2017). However, restructuring in the public sector is by nature a particularly complex process. Unlike private enterprises, public organizations operate within complex legislative frameworks and political and social networks, where reform is not only an administrative but also a deeply political process (Peters, 2022; Kuhlmann & Wollmann, 2019).

The discipline of change management provides the framework through which leaders and managers acquire the assurances and management tools to address resistance, foster shared commitment, and strengthen organizational capacity to fulfill meaningful management goals (Kuipers & Van der Voet, 2020). In the case of the public sector, this means balancing efficiency demands with democratic values, ensuring transparency, and maintaining citizen trust throughout the reform process (Christensen & Lægreid, 2020; Vogel & Masal, 2023).

In recent years, new challenges have reinforced the importance of change management for public sector reform:

- Digital transformation requires an extensive review of organizational structures and processes since the digital transition implies that extensive organizational adjustments have been made, such as simplifying and reducing processes, reviewing the necessary resources that will be needed to carry out a process, etc. (Mergel, Edelmann & Haug, 2019).
- The COVID-19 pandemic has highlighted the importance of organizational resilience, adaptive leadership and rapid implementation of changes in public administration (Ansell & Trondal, 2022).
- Sustainability and environmental governance have introduced cross-sectoral coordination challenges that require flexible structures and collaborative capacity (Lodge & Wegrich, 2020).

Despite the growing literature linking change management to public administration, significant gaps remain. Many studies focus on individual countries or specific reform initiatives, while comparative and theoretically informed analyses remain limited (Kuipers et al., 2018). The present analysis contributes to how change management interacts with organizational restructuring in the public sector by offering a comprehensive approach, drawing on both theoretical insights and international empirical evidence.

2. ORGANIZATIONAL RESTRUCTURING AND CHANGE MANAGEMENT AS COMPONENTS OF ADMINISTRATIVE REFORMS

2.1. Overview of Organizational Restructuring

Public sector reform refers to the conscious and systematic efforts of governments to modify institutional structures, organizational processes and governance frameworks, with the aim of improving efficiency, accountability, legitimacy and quality of services provided (Pollitt, 2019; Christensen & Lægreid, 2020). Reform is not a one-dimensional process, it is shaped by factors such as political systems, administrative traditions, national culture, administrative infrastructure and socio-economic pressures (Kuhlmann & Wollmann, 2019).

Organizational restructuring is one of the most visible and frequently implemented reform strategies. It includes a series of changes at the organizational design level such as: the type of organizational structure, the degree of formality, the procedures and processes used, the structure of hierarchical levels, the span of control, the outline of jobs, the degree of centralization/decentralization, etc. The goal of organizational restructuring refers to better serving strategic objectives, the convergence of institutions with new priorities, and the improvement of the ability of organizations to respond to external challenges (Peters, 2022). Restructuring can take various forms: downsizing, mergers, decentralization, the creation of semi-autonomous organizations, or digital redesign of service delivery structures. Although the rationale for restructuring is often based on efficiency, its results depend largely on administrative capacity, political support and cultural alignment (Kuipers & Van der Voet, 2020).

2.2 Change Management in the Public Sector

Change management is broadly defined as the set of approaches, tools and processes that facilitate organizational adaptation to new strategies, environments and practices (By et al., 2023). According to Belias and Rossidis (2025): "Change management is a specialized field of management, encompassing a set of theories, principles, knowledge and practices, which enable an organization to recognize the need for change, plan its various dimensions, deal with potential resistance to the change process and ultimately integrate an organizational change in a timely and effective manner, thus ensuring its adaptation and survival in a constantly changing environment." Although the theoretical foundations of change management were developed with private enterprises in mind, the trend of their utilization by the public sector is becoming increasingly important, as state administrations face the challenge of shaping complex reforms that require not only technical adjustments, but also administrative and especially behavioral changes among employees and stakeholders (Van der Voet & Steijn, 2021).

The application of change management principles in the public sector draws on a wide range of models (Fernandez & Rainey, 2017; Vogel & Masal, 2023). Classic models such as Lewin's three-stage model (unfreeze-change-refreezing) and Kotter's 8-step model provided the first frameworks for planned transformation, emphasizing the development of a highly managerially analyzed change plan, the use of leadership behaviors, and the use of targeted communication policies (Rossidis et al., 2020; Christensen & Lægreid, 2020; Kotter, 1996). Although useful, these models have been criticized for oversimplifying the complexity of modern public organizations (Kuipers et al., 2018; Giannakos et al., 2024).

The New Public Management (NPM), which dominated from the 1980s onwards, introduced principles of efficiency, competition and market-oriented mechanisms (Pollitt, 2019; Rossidis, 2021). It promoted extensive restructuring, aiming to create more functional administrative systems, emphasizing decentralization, redesigning administrative processes, and generally shaping an organization capable of responding to the strategic objectives of public organizations (Klijn & Koppenjan, 2016; Rhodes, 2017; O'Flynn, 2021).

Finally, more recent hybrid models of governance, such as the Neo-Weberian State (NWS), New Public Governance (NPG), and Public Value Management, attempt to incorporate elements of legitimacy, efficiency, and collaboration. They argue that public administration should create and maintain public value by combining private economic criteria and modern administrative tools with democratic participation and legitimacy (Moore, 2014; O'Flynn, 2021). These paradigms provide the theoretical framework within which change management practices should be implemented.

2.3 Linking Change Management to Organizational Restructuring

The interaction between change management and restructuring is at the core of the success of public sector reforms (Belias et al., 2019). Structural adjustments such as modifying processes, changing responsibilities, adapting the organizational structure, introducing digital platforms, etc., are likely to cause strong resistance to the attempted change since they cause significant upheavals in the structure and functioning of organizations (Kuipers et al., 2018).

The implementation of change management practices can bring about notable improvements in the results of restructuring in several ways:

1. By reducing resistance, through the participation of employees and stakeholders in the design of reforms as well as through the development of targeted communication policies to better inform those affected by organizational change (Van der Voet & Steijn, 2021).
2. By aligning organizational culture with structure, ensuring that organizational values and behaviors support the new institutional arrangements (By et al., 2023).
3. By strengthening leadership capacity, so that reforms are consolidated and not susceptible to influence by changes in government (Vogel & Masal, 2023).
4. Maintaining citizens' trust, through transparent communication and accountability mechanisms (Christensen & Lægreid, 2020).

Consequently, change management does not function simply as a supporting tool, but as a critical tool for implementing reforms. Organizational restructuring is evolving into a multidimensional administrative change that requires separate analysis to enable the achievement of the objectives associated with its implementation (Fernandez & Rainey, 2017).

By synthesizing the above findings, a comprehensive analytical framework is identified, which places change management in the broader context of public sector reform and organizational restructuring. This framework is based on three analytical pillars:

- Institutional framework, which recognizes how administrative traditions and political systems shape reform processes.
- Administrative know-how, with an emphasis on leadership, communication and stakeholder participation as key drivers of change.
- Emphasis on reform outcomes to focus efforts on high levels of efficiency, effectiveness, transparency and quality.

3. PUBLIC SECTOR REFORM IN THE 21ST CENTURY

Administrative reforms in the modern era are characterized by increasing complexity, uncertainty and interdependence. Public administrations no longer face stable environments where gradual adjustments are sufficient, but instead are confronted with complex problems that include (often in combination): emerging technologies, socio-political changes, diversified strategic pursuits, caused by globalization, fiscal crises, digital transformation, climate change, demographic changes and pandemics (Ansell & Trondal, 2022; Lodge & Wegrich, 2020). These developments lead to the redefinition of the objectives, tools and scope of reforms, making the need for adaptability, efficiency, transparency and citizen orientation a modern requirement.

In contrast to recent past, where reform interest was limited to the transition from bureaucracy to New Public Management (NPM) and then to governance models, the 21st century reform agenda highlights flexibility, adaptation and public value creation as central objectives (O'Flynn, 2021; Christensen & Lægreid, 2020). This marks a radical repositioning, in which structural efficiency remains important, but must be combined with: focusing on meeting citizens' needs, strengthening multi-level governance, promoting stakeholder participation in policy design, implementation and evaluation, etc. International developments mark a new era of reforms that includes multifaceted features. The main ones are summarized as follows:

A. Digital Transformation and Data-Driven Governance

Digital transformation is perhaps the most important factor driving public sector reform in the 21st century, leading to a new administrative reality (Mihiotis et al., 2023). Digital technologies have not only changed the tools for service delivery, but have also reshaped the entire nature of public administration (Rossidis et al., 2023). The development of e-government and digital transformation systems allows state administrations to ensure multifaceted benefits (Mergel, Edelmann & Haug, 2019; Rossidis et al., 2021; Manoharan et al., 2022) such as:

- improving their internal administrative functioning,
- providing better, faster and more economical services to citizens and businesses,
- strengthening the competitiveness of their national economies
- promoting transparency and equality
- strengthening cooperation between domestic authorities and international European organizations,
- strengthening democratic institutions through equal information and participation of citizens in public affairs, promoting e-democracy

- eliminating elements of mismanagement and corruption.

At the same time, the rise of big data, artificial intelligence and algorithmic decision-making, combined with the use of knowledge management and organizational learning techniques, are shaping the conditions for both a rapid growth in administrative efficiency and a significant improvement in the process of designing public policies. It should of course be noted that the use of such technologies also poses significant risks with regard to the management of personal data, the security of information systems and the general assurance of ethical governance (Sun & Medaglia, 2019). Therefore, reform efforts must balance innovation and technological efficiency combined with democratic legitimacy and citizen trust.

B. Fiscal Consolidation and Austerity Pressures

The 2008 global financial crisis and the subsequent sovereign debt crises marked the beginning of a prolonged period of fiscal austerity in many countries. Even in the 2020s, fiscal consolidation and economic efficiency continue to be the dominant pursuit of most reform efforts (Pollitt, 2019). Governments have significantly modified their administrative functioning, emphasizing on spending cuts, staff reductions, privatizations and outsourcing, and in general strategies to reduce public spending.

However, austerity-driven reforms often produce mixed results. Although they may achieve short-term fiscal goals, they may undermine long-term institutional capacity and distort the strategic orientation of public organizations, adversely affecting the final administrative outcome and consequently socio-political aspirations (Peters, 2022). The challenge of the 21st century, therefore, is to design reforms that reconcile the principles of economy and fiscal responsibility with social justice and long-term administrative effectiveness.

C. Multilevel and Networked Governance

The increasing interdependence of national, regional and international institutions has brought multilevel governance to the center of reform efforts. Problems such as migration, climate change and pandemics transcend national borders and require coordination between different levels of government, as well as with non-state actors (Hooghe & Marks, 2016; Klijn & Koppenjan, 2016).

Reforms now include redistributing responsibilities between central and local governments, strengthening intergovernmental relations and promoting collaborative networks involving civil society and the private sector. This development reflects a shift from hierarchical models towards more polycentric governance structures, although issues of accountability and coordination remain urgent and need to be addressed (Rhodes, 2017).

D. Citizen-Centered Reforms and Co-Design of Services

One of the defining features of contemporary reforms is the emphasis on citizen participation and co-design of public services. In contrast to the introversion, centralization and authority that characterize traditional administrative systems, the need for extroversion, interdependence and the promotion of social cooperation is highlighted. Instead of treating citizens as passive recipients, governments increasingly seek to involve them as partners in policy-making and service delivery (Denhardt & Denhardt, 2015; Osborne, 2020). Governance-focused administrative reforms aim to establish horizontal, participatory, multi-stakeholder and consultative decision-making and choice-making processes in the public sphere, highlighting the coordinating and regulatory role of the State. Examples of such tools include participatory budgeting, e-consultation procedures and digital feedback platforms, which aim to improve participation and responsiveness.

Although these approaches are promising, they face obstacles such as uneven participation (inability of groups of citizens to use information and communication technologies, creating conditions for uneven service) and the risk of "tokenism", where citizen participation remains superficial rather than substantive (Fung, 2015; Van der Voet & Steijn, 2021). Effective reform requires institutional arrangements that ensure broad and meaningful participation.

Figure 1. Characteristics of modern reforms

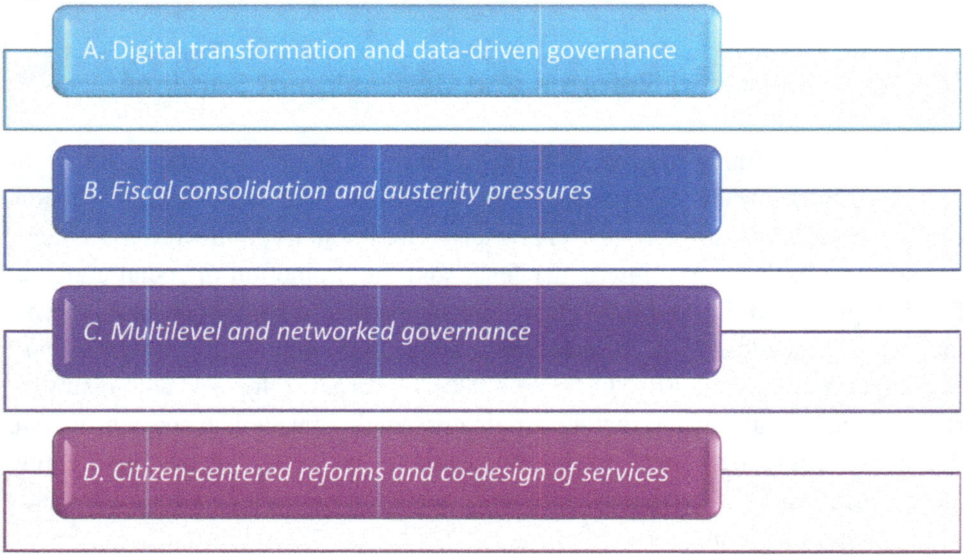

At the same time, the literature review highlights critical factors that determine the compositions of administrative reforms. The main groups of factors are listed below.

A. Economic and Fiscal Factors

Public sector reforms continue to be driven by economic imperatives such as: improving efficiency and effectiveness, controlling public finances, attracting investment and economic growth. In many cases, international organizations such as the OECD, the IMF and the World Bank act as external influencers, co-shaping domestic reform agendas (OECD, 2019).

B. Political Factors

Declining trust in governments has intensified the need for reforms that enhance transparency, accountability and responsiveness to citizens' needs (Vogel & Masal, 2023). Political legitimacy is increasingly linked not only to electoral processes, but also to the ability of administrations to deliver results and uphold ethical standards. Many administrative reforms moving in this direction incorporate the need for collaboration, consultation, two-way communication and social dialogue with citizens and civil society organizations.

C. Social and Demographic Factors

Demographic changes - such as population aging and increasing diversity - create pressures for reforms in the areas of health, pensions and social services. These challenges require innovative forms of restructuring to maintain the provision of quality services while ensuring social justice (Peters, 2021).

D.Crisis and Resilience Factors

The COVID-19 pandemic has highlighted the imperative need to build resilient public administrations, capable of adapting quickly to crisis conditions. Reforms focused on crisis management emphasize flexibility, international and cross-departmental cooperation, and the ability to rapidly reallocate resources, elements that require relevant care during organizational redesign in order to form flexible horizontal organizational structures, with a high span of control and an expanded level of responsibilities for each job position (Ansell & Trondal, 2022).

Figure 2. Administrative reform factors

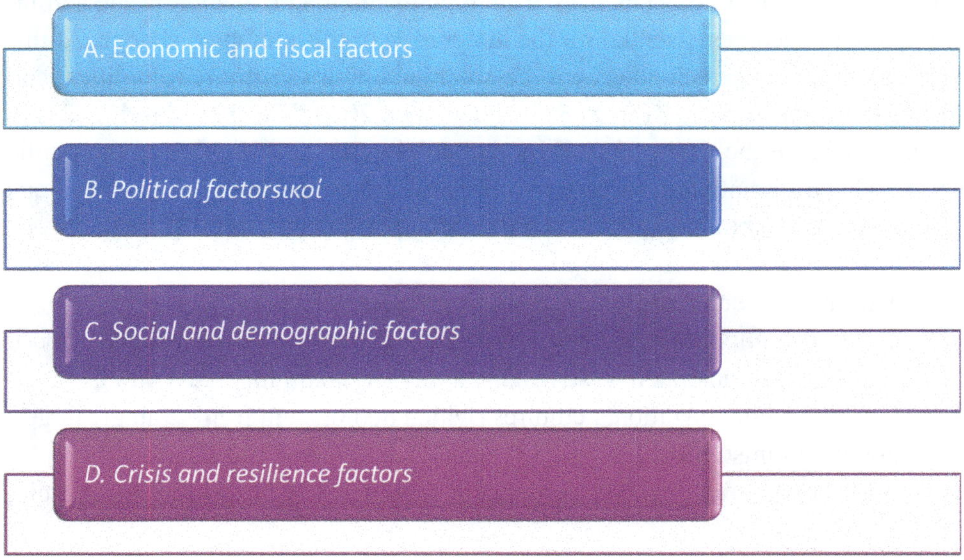

The path of reform varies according to administrative traditions, national culture and administrative infrastructure. Anglo-Saxon countries often pursue more market-oriented reforms, emphasizing performance measurement, outsourcing and administrative autonomy. In contrast, Nordic countries combine efficiency goals with strong social welfare commitments and collaborative governance models (Christensen & Lægreid, 2020). Central European administrative systems, influenced by legalistic traditions and strict application of administrative law, often follow gradual, evolutionary reforms (Kuhlmann & Wollmann, 2019). These variations show that, although reform factors are universal in nature, their institutional translation and administrative implementation depend on the respective context.

4. CHANGE MANAGEMENT APPROACHES IN PUBLIC ADMINISTRATION

While organizational restructuring is a distinct aspect found in most attempted administrative reforms (almost all reforms affect individual dimensions of organizational design), the practical dimension of implementation and ultimately the sustainability of such administrative actions depends largely on the way in which change is managed. Change management in public administration includes targeted strategies for guiding organizational members, stakeholders and institutions through adaptation processes. Changing the organizational structure of an organization constitutes a groundbreaking modification of the administrative reality, disrupting established administrative balances. The implementation of an appropriate administrative tool becomes essential for the integration of the attempted change. At this level, administrative techniques will be combined with sensitivity to political and institutional constraints (Kuipers & Van der Voet, 2020; Vogel & Masal, 2023) in order to achieve the desired result by recognizing the specificities of the public sector. This differentiation (between public and private sectors) lies in the unique challenges that public organizations are called upon to face, such as:

- Multiple, different and often conflicting objectives,
- The constraints imposed by the institutional framework (especially when it comes to administrative systems that apply strict administrative law),
- Established organizational cultures (which do not stem from strategic targeting of administrations),
- And the need to maintain democratic legitimacy (Christensen & Lægreid, 2020).

Effective change management in the public sector uses a wide range of tools to support the implementation of reforms, which are considered proven from years of application in the private sector. Some of the most important areas of change management practice are the following:

- Communication strategies. Clear, consistent and transparent communication reduces uncertainty and builds trust between employees and citizens. Communication plans in reforms often include multi-channel approaches, combining official announcements, digital platforms and participatory forums (Van der Voet & Steijn, 2021).
- Employee participation in decision-making and collaboration. Employee participation in decision-making shows people across the organization that their input is respected and valued (Van der Voet & Steijn, 2021). It makes employees feel less like "cogs in the wheel" and more like experts and consultants in the areas they work in. Job satisfaction and employee engagement naturally improve when employees have a sense of ownership associated with participation in corporate decision-making, and, of course, employees can be ready to accept any change (Fung, 2015). Public administration reforms are increasingly implemented through collaborative governance models, which include not only employees but also external actors, such as citizens, NGOs, businesses and international organizations (Klijn & Koppenjan, 2016; Osborne, 2020).
- Training and capacity building. Organizational change requires new skills and competencies. Capacity building programs – especially in digital transformation – are essential to equip staff with the tools to adapt to new roles and technologies (Mergel, Edelmann & Haug, 2019).
- Pilot projects and defined goals: Governments are increasingly adopting pilot projects to test reforms on a smaller scale before full implementation. This practice reduces risk and promotes learning through experience. At the same time, the development of carefully designed goals demonstrates a commitment to the outcome and forms a structured "pathway" for decoding the change into individual goals (Christensen & Lægreid, 2020).
- Communication. According to Kotter and Schlesinger (2008), among the most popular strategies for reducing resistance to change is communication. Choosing the appropriate communication policy, the appropriate communication channel, the written or oral form of communication, individual or group communication are critical issues for recognizing the importance and parameters of change and, by extension, for the successful implementation of a reform. Communicating the company's vision helps people see the necessity and logic of reform.
- Leadership is consistently recognized as a key factor in successful change management (Giannakos et al., 2023). Leaders who embody the values of reform enhance credibility and commitment (Vogel & Masal, 2023). In the public sector, leaders must balance administrative efficiency with the social values that the State must uphold (Christensen & Lægreid, 2020).

- Transformational leadership, which inspires and motivates employees through a shared vision and values, has been associated with higher rates of reform success (Vogel & Masal, 2023). At the same time, distributed leadership, which highlights the role of middle managers, is equally critical in large bureaucracies, where success depends on those who translate policies into action (Kuipers & Van der Voet, 2020).
- Reward management system. Individuals who embrace and encourage change should be recognized for it. Praise, recognition, feedback, development, and even financial incentives are examples of rewards (Rossidis et al., 2016). Recognizing employees for performing in the desired way is a successful way to promote change. Reward systems help organizations achieve specific change goals.
- Performance measurement and feedback mechanisms. Monitoring the results of reforms ensures accountability and allows for corrective interventions during implementation. However, performance indicators need to combine quantitative measures with qualitative assessments of legitimacy and trust (O'Flynn, 2021).

Resistance is a constant feature of public sector reforms. Employees may react due to fear and uncertainty about the unknown, lack of self-confidence, habituation to a particular way of working, lack of motivation, limited professional autonomy or lack of trust in the political motivations for changes, belief that interests are being harmed, etc. (Fernandez & Rainey, 2017; Giannakos et al., 2024). Furthermore, administrative inertia, rigid and rigid institutional frameworks and weak political will often hinder change (Peters, 2022). Change management is not an optional methodology or set of tools. It is a fundamental prerequisite for the success of restructuring. Structural reforms often fail when the way in which the attempted change is introduced is neglected (Fernandez & Rainey, 2017). Integrating change management into restructuring processes requires:

- Aligning new structures with organizational culture,
- Commitment of leadership at all hierarchical levels,
- Establishing continuous learning processes,
- Integrating accountability and transparency mechanisms.

At the level of administrative systems, hybrid approaches, combining planned planning with adaptive flexibility, appear to be the most effective in complex public sector environments (By et al., 2023). Change management approaches in public administration highlight the importance of a balance between structure and culture, planning and adaptation, authority and participation. Literature research shows that reforms are more successful when supported by appropriate communication policies, active stakeholder participation, strong leadership and capacity building mechanisms. At the same time, the specificity of the public sector requires tailored strategies that go beyond traditional administrative orthodoxy.

5. ORGANIZATIONAL RESTRUCTURING: MODELS AND PRACTICES

Organizational restructuring is one of the most tangible and frequent forms of public sector reform. Its tangible nature arises from the clear and unambiguous aspects of the modifications that need to be made at the organizational design level (e.g. changing a process or changing the outline of a job). Furthermore, its appearance is particularly frequent as it is included in most administrative reforms either as a central aspect of the reform or as a side effect. For example, a reform that falls within the scope of digital transformation must necessarily include some aspects of organizational design, as organizational changes must necessarily occur (as could happen in the change of a Workflow Management System carried out in the context of the digital transition).

Organizational restructuring refers to the deliberate redesign of structures, processes and power relations within public organizations, with the aim of better serving organizational goals, improving efficiency, strengthening accountability, improving quality, etc. (Pollitt, 2019; Peters, 2022). Although restructuring is often presented as a technical process of redesigning hierarchies or workflows, in practice it evolves into a deep administrative act that greatly affects human resources and the overall functioning of the organization (Christensen & Lægreid, 2020).

A common form of reform in the field of organizational design is the centralization and decentralization of powers. Each public organization must choose whether to have an orientation towards centralization of powers or decentralization. In the case of centralization, decision-making authority is taken from the upper levels of the hierarchical pyramid and diffused to the remaining hierarchical levels as orders or standardized procedures, seeking greater control, coordination and administrative discipline. Decentralization, on the other hand, transfers powers to lower hierarchical levels or to semi-autonomous bodies, with the aim of enhancing responsiveness, flexibility and innovation by transferring problem solving as close as possible to the point of decision implementation or, in the case of the public sector, to the citizen (Kuhlmann & Wollmann, 2019).

Historically, most reform projects have tended to emphasize decentralization, where responsibilities are selectively transferred, depending on the institutional capacity of individual actors, aiming to speed up procedures and better serve citizens. Scandinavian countries, for example, have transferred welfare responsibilities to municipalities, while maintaining central oversight mechanisms to ensure equality (Ladner et al., 2019). Administrative systems with weak institutional capacity, of course, often struggle to effectively implement decentralization, leading to fragmentation and accountability deficits (Peters, 2021). Although the general trend is towards decentralised systems, in recent years, due to the extensive digital transformation, there has been a reversal of the climate and a return to centralised models (since processes are digitalised, there is no longer any reason to decentralise powers). Change management plays a crucial role: successfully changing the centralisation/decentralisation model requires not only structural reforms, but also capacity building, stakeholder engagement and clear communication to avoid ambiguities and resistance (Kuipers & Van der Voet, 2020).

Another element that makes up the modern essence of organisational design is digital transformation, often described as "digital-era governance" (Mergel et al., 2019). Governments are reshaping public organizations in a digital-centric way (Belias et al., 2023). Estonia's e-government reforms and Denmark's digital-first strategies are examples of how organizational structures can be redesigned around digital ecosystems (Manoharan et al., 2022). However, digital restructuring presents many administrative challenges that require special attention, such as data security issues and resistance from staff who have not received the required digital skills and have not acquired a digital work culture (Ntalakos et al., 2023). Effective change management therefore requires strong investments in training, clear vision formulation, and participatory planning to ensure effectiveness (Sun & Medaglia, 2019). The applications of types of organizational restructuring vary from administrative system to administrative system as they adapt to the specificities of each country. A categorization according to different administrative traditions follows (Kuhlmann & Wollmann, 2019; Peters, 2021).

Table 1.

Administrative system	Form of organizational restructuring
Anglo-Saxon systems	Emphasis on administrative autonomy, performance measurement and contracting/outsourcing
Scandinavian systems	Emphasis on collaborative restructuring with strong welfare commitments and participatory cultures
Central European systems	Adapt more cautiously, constrained by legalistic traditions and a strong regulatory framework based on the strict application of administrative law

These differences highlight the importance of differentiating restructuring models, highlighting that reforms cannot be implemented as is, but must be adapted to the socio-political, administrative and institutional specificities of each country and each administrative system (Christensen & Lægreid, 2020).

Organizational restructuring remains a central axis of modern administrative reforms. Whether through strategic readjustment of organizational design aimed at better serving organizational objectives or redesign due to administrative and socio-political adjustments, the reorganization of the organization's functioning seeks to align organizations with evolving requirements. However, management analysis suggests that organizational restructuring alone cannot fulfill the expected goals as an organizational change requires a multifaceted analysis and implementation that goes beyond the simple formulation of a reform with implications for organizational design. Success depends on the partnership of formal structural/organizational changes with effective change management practices that address employee behavior, infrastructure and legitimacy.

6. EVALUATING THE IMPACT OF CHANGE MANAGEMENT ON REFORM OUTCOMES

Evaluating the success of public sector reforms has always been a complex task. Structural and organizational reforms are judged in relation to their contribution to the fulfillment of objectives. It should therefore be ensured that the integration of organizational changes is carried out in such a way as to produce the sustainable results that were budgeted (Fernandez & Rainey, 2017; Kuipers & Van der Voet, 2020). The results of public sector reform can be assessed on multiple dimensions, reflecting the complex nature of administrative objectives (Christensen & Lægreid, 2020; Peters, 2022):

- Efficiency. Efficiency mainly concerns the internal functioning of the organization and expresses the resources sacrificed to achieve an outcome. Efficiency benefits are often central to reforms with roots in NPM.
- Effectiveness. Efficiency can be characterized as the extent to which the public organization achieves its objectives. Effectiveness is the ratio of a specific outcome sought to the cost required to achieve that outcome.
- Transparency and accountability. Accountability determines the degree of responsibility of administrative and governmental bodies towards citizens and society. Overall, it determines the extent to which an administrative mechanism and its produced result can be subject to administrative and social control.

- Citizen trust and satisfaction. They refer to social indicators that highlight the acceptance of administrative mechanisms by society (Manoharan et al., 2022).
- Equality and social inclusion. Ensuring that reforms do not exacerbate inequalities in access to services (O'Flynn, 2021).
- Adaptability and flexibility. It refers to the timely and effective adaptation to the conditions of an uncertain and volatile environment, making the State capable of responding to its evolving role. (Ansell & Trondal, 2022).

These dimensions are not evaluated in isolation. The success of reforms depends on the balance between efficiency and legitimacy, effectiveness and integration, adaptability and stability (Rossidis, 2014). Several modern management tools contribute to the substantive evaluation of change management in public organizations, such as the following:

- Logic models & theory of change: They map inputs, processes, outputs and outcomes, linking administrative practices with the expected reform outcomes (Kuipers et al., 2018).
- Balanced scorecards: Balanced scorecards support the effort to integrate, measure and exploit knowledge management systems by integrating the perspective of their use into the strategic orientation of the organization. This specific technique evaluates performance in multiple dimensions (financial, "customer"/citizen, internal processes, learning). Public versions place particular emphasis on citizen satisfaction, efficient resource management and the prospective fulfillment of predetermined results.
- Public value frameworks. They are found in hybrid models aiming to evaluate reforms based on their contribution to collective goals, legitimacy and citizen trust, going beyond narrow efficiency indicators (Moore, 2014; O'Flynn, 2021).
- Benchmarking. The term Benchmarking refers to the technique or tool used to evaluate the performance of an organization and highlight advantages or shortcomings compared to a similar organization that is characterized as a model. Cross-national comparisons, such as OECD indicators, offer a picture of relative performance, although distinct national differences limit the possibilities for direct transfer (OECD, 2019; Rossidis et al., 2020).

Figure 3. Administrative tools for assessing change management outcomes

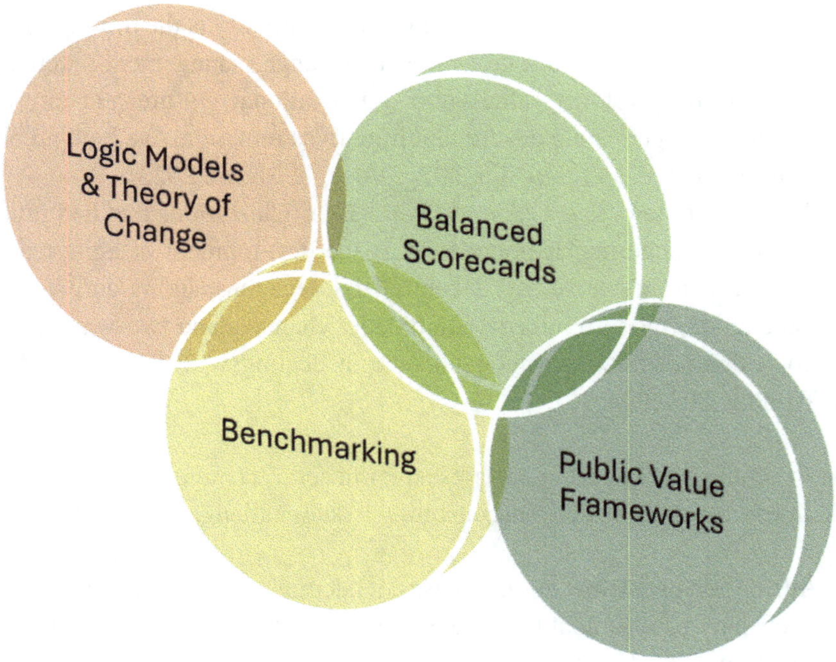

The contribution of Change Management to improving the results of reforms is extremely important. Whether through targeted practices stemming from the philosophy of change management or through supportive administrative practices that aim to strengthen the consolidation process, the reforms undertaken acquire the guarantees to fulfill their mission. Some characteristic approaches to strengthening results are listed below.

- Building legitimacy and trust. Change management strategies significantly strengthen the legitimacy of reforms by developing strong levels of commitment and an adapted culture through participation and communication tools. For example, digital transformation initiatives in Northern Europe achieved higher levels of citizen trust when state administrations activated tools for co-configuration of digital platforms with users (Mergel et al., 2019).
- Strengthening efficiency and effectiveness. Training and development programs ensure that staff are appropriately trained to integrate into a new organizational environment (e.g., implementing new processes, assigning new tasks, etc.). Studies of shared service reforms in the United Kingdom and

Canada show that employee engagement and training have been crucial in achieving high levels of efficiency (Dunleavy & Carrera, 2020).

- Sustaining reforms over time. Political discontinuity is the most common reason for the discontinuation of reforms. Change management practices, such as embedding reform values into organizational culture and empowering middle managers, help ensure that initiatives remain active beyond electoral terms (Van der Voet & Steijn, 2021; Vogel & Masal, 2023).
- Adaptability to crises. During COVID-19, organizations that had invested in adaptive change management such as the development of agile teams (e.g. through matrix structures), decentralized decision-making and strong communication (modern information transfer channels and two-way information flow) demonstrated greater resilience in dealing with the crisis (Ansell & Trondal, 2022).

In the context of the effort to assess the impact of change management, several difficulties are also identified that constitute critical challenges, such as the following:

- Attribution problems. In many cases, it becomes difficult to isolate the impact of change management from other factors, such as political will or budgetary resources (Peters, 2022).
- Time lags. The complexity of the change management process can often lead to the formulation of a long-term design and implementation plan. Therefore, the bulk of the results can be expected to appear a long time after the implementation of the reforms, making short-term evaluations significantly difficult.
- Measurement limitations. Although one of the most basic features of modern goal-setting is the production of measurable results, in practice this is not always easy. Many results cannot be easily quantified. Accordingly, quantitative indicators often do not capture intangible results, such as cultural adaptation or legitimacy.
- Comparability: Differences in administrative traditions, national culture and infrastructure limit the generalizability of findings. In practice, it is particularly difficult to compare methods and practices applied in different administrative systems (Kuhlmann & Wollmann, 2019).

To address these challenges, mixed-methods approaches are increasingly used, leveraging a combination of surveys, case studies and performance indicators (Kuipers et al., 2018). Summarizing the findings, the relationship between change management and reform outcomes could be summarized as follows:

- Structural reforms create potential space for efficiency and effectiveness.
- Strong change management enhances reform outcomes, while its absence undermines them.

From the above, it becomes clear that change management is not just a complementary factor, but a necessary condition for the success of reforms. Assessing its impact requires multidimensional and context-sensitive approaches. While efficiency and fiscal performance remain important, legitimacy, adaptability and public value are becoming increasingly important criteria. International empirical evidence shows that reforms supported by strong change management with an emphasis on communication, participation, leadership and education achieve more sustainable results.

7. CONTEMPORARY CHALLENGES AND EMERGING TRENDS

Public sector reform is a dynamic process that is a process of perpetual search for organizational and institutional changes with the aim of improving and upgrading the behavior and operation of the Public Sector. This process in the modern era, evolves in environments of complexity and uncertainty. While traditional administrative models focused on efficiency, accountability and fiscal consolidation, modern reforms must also address new global and societal challenges, such as digitalization, climate change, demographic pressures and crises of legitimacy. These new conditions lead to a synthesis of organizational structures and administrative implementation tools, shaping a new administrative reality (Christensen & Lægreid, 2020; Ansell & Trondal, 2022). Emerging trends include: digital transformation, crisis management, social equity and inclusion, and shifting boundaries between state, market, and civil society.

1. While digital transformation is a beneficial technological development, it is also a particularly complex and difficult public sector reform (Manoharan et al., 2022; Rossidis et al., 2023). Governments are increasingly modernizing their operations by integrating: digital platforms, decision-making information systems, artificial intelligence (AI) technologies, and purely digital processes to improve efficiency and service delivery (Mergel, Edelmann & Haug, 2019). The challenge for reformers is twofold:
    - to design organizational structures that will "take off" the effectiveness of digital tools while maintaining the social status of the state
    - to take into account factors that will complicate the process of implementing digital reforms due to the upheavals they will bring (Rossidis et al., 2021).

2. The COVID-19 pandemic, the energy crisis, war situations, economic crises, etc. have shown that upheavals of stability and transnational crises are not rare situations, but recurring realities that to a certain extent define the external environment of public administration. Public organizations have had to readjust their strategic orientation by forming organizational structures capable of managing dynamic changes in external conditions (Ansell & Trondal, 2022). In this context, the development of flexibility, understood as the ability to anticipate, absorb and recover from shocks, has emerged as a central reform objective (Lodge & Wegrich, 2020). Adaptable and resilient organizations are based on flexible structures, empowered leadership and cross-sectoral collaboration. However, building flexibility requires continuous investment in modern structures (organic instead of hierarchical), modern skills (broad training instead of high specialization), adapted job profiles (with an emphasis on rotation and task enrichment instead of limited and strictly defined responsibilities), effective communication (sophisticated channels and forms of communication instead of the traditional standard form of one-way communication), etc. (Vogel & Masal, 2023). Change management, in this context, involves building consensus among heterogeneous stakeholders, fostering innovation, and embedding sustainability values in the administrative culture. Without this cultural transformation, structural reforms risk remaining symbolic or inconsistent.
3. Modern reforms must also respond to growing social demands for equal treatment but also to reading differentiated needs in a context of diversity of social structure. Demographic changes, migration and extensive social needs highlight the requirement for administrations to provide not only efficient, but also fair services adapted to the diversified social fabric (O'Flynn, 2021). Public sector restructuring in this area includes redesigning welfare systems, introducing equity audits and implementing diversity policies in recruitment and leadership (Papapolychroniadis et al., 2017). However, changes at the organizational design level do not ensure the achievement of such aspirations. They need to be complemented by change management strategies that address biases, encourage participation and promote organizational learning (Van der Voet & Steijn, 2021). Analyses show that reforms that listen to social needs and utilize administrative tools that will promote their satisfaction (such as promoting participation, dialogue, two-way communication, engagement) are more likely to maintain citizens' trust and legitimacy (Christensen & Lægreid, 2020).
4. Another challenge concerns the evolving boundaries between state, market and civil society. Since the rise of NPM, governments have increasingly relied on external assignments, collaborations and public-private partnerships. The governance paradigm further emphasized policy networks, cross-sectoral collaboration, and multi-level arrangements (Klijn & Koppenjan, 2016). In the modern

era, hybrid governance models are gaining more ground serving similar goals. Governments now act as regulators, supporting processes of co-formulation of public policies. Such practices can lead to the prospect of high social acceptance but also innovation and efficiency since they will offer choices from complex multi-stakeholder institutions and not only from the sovereign political power or purely technocratic administration (Rhodes, 2017).

8. CONCLUSION

This study identified the neural link between public sector reform, organizational restructuring, and change management. A detailed examination of the aspects of applied change management as a tool for implementing public sector reforms highlights that organizational transformation is not explained only by structural or institutional adjustments, but requires attention to the behavioral and specific administrative structure of the organizations undergoing reform (By et al., 2023). From the preceding analysis, some key points emerge:

1. Contemporary reforms are increasingly complex and multidimensional. They are driven not only by elements of economic efficiency and budgetary imperatives, but also by elements of adaptability, flexibility and sustainability (Christensen & Lægreid, 2020; Peters, 2022). Traditional paradigms of bureaucracy, NPM, and governance provide useful foundations, but contemporary challenges require hybrid approaches that combine efficiency with public value and democratic legitimacy (O'Flynn, 2021).
2. Organizational restructuring is placed at the center of management reforms. However, changing organizational functioning alone rarely produces sustainable improvements. Evidence from different management models suggests that outcomes depend largely on the quality of change management, leveraging elements of leadership, communication, stakeholder engagement, and shaping a strategically focused organizational culture (Kuipers & Van der Voet, 2020; Vogel & Masal, 2023).
3. Various management analyses confirm that change management acts as a mediator between formal reforms and practical outcomes. It reduces resistance, builds trust, and enhances efficiency and effectiveness, while preserving legitimacy (Fernandez & Rainey, 2017; Van der Voet & Steijn, 2021). Without systematic application of change management principles, attempted organizational restructuring often leads to fragmentation, resistance or symbolic compliance.
4. Modern reform agendas are shaped by digitalization, crises, social equality and the development of a tripartite cooperation of state – market – civil society for

the co-formation of public policies. These developments reduce change management not as a supporting tool, but as a strategic necessity (Kriemadis et al., 2023).

Public sector reform in the 21st century is characterized by a process of transition from fixed, bureaucratic, centralized administrative systems, to multilateral, consultative, flexible and efficient ones. The preceding analysis argued that the decisive factor for the transition to this new administrative reality is the effective application of change management principles (Belias et al, 2025).

Reforms succeed when structural innovations are embedded within supportive cultural and behavioral processes that foster trust, participation, and adaptability. They fail when change management is neglected, leading to resistance, superficial compliance, or legitimacy deficits. The overall conclusion is that change management should no longer be viewed as an administrative technique imported from the private sector, but as an integral component of modern reforms, necessary for the fulfillment of the desired goals.

REFERENCES

Andrews, M., Pritchett, L., & Woolcock, M. (2017). *Building state capability: Evidence, analysis, action.* Oxford University Press. DOI: 10.1093/acprof:oso/9780198747482.001.0001

Ansell, C., & Trondal, J. (2022). Governing turbulence: Leadership and adaptation in public administration. *Public Administration Review*, *82*(5), 849–862.

Belias, D., & Rossidis, I. (2025). *Change Management. Organizational Change and elements of Organizational Behaviour.* Tziolas publications.

Belias, D., Rossidis, I., Papademetriou, C., Masouras, A., & Anastasiadou, S. (2023). *Managing Successful and Ethical Organizational Change.* IGI Global. DOI: 10.4018/979-8-3693-0235-4

Belias, D., Velissariou, S., Papailias, S., Manta, F., Rossidis, I. (2019). Change Management – Obstacles and Perspectives for the Integration of Changes in Greek Public Hospitals. *Advances in Management & Applied Economics.* 9(2).

By, R. T., Kuipers, B. S., & Proctor, S. (2023). Understanding change in public organizations: The role of leadership and culture. *Journal of Organizational Change Management*, *36*(2), 213–229.

Christensen, T., & Lægreid, P. (2020). The rise of the post-NPM regime: Lessons from international public sector reform. *Administration & Society*, *52*(2), 247–271.

Denhardt, J., & Denhardt, R. (2015). *The new public service: Serving, not steering* (4th ed.). Routledge.

Dunleavy, P., & Carrera, L. (2020). *Growing the productivity of government services.* Edward Elgar.

Dunleavy, P., Margetts, H., Bastow, S., & Tinkler, J. (2006). *Digital-era governance: IT corporations, the state, and e-government.* Oxford University Press. DOI: 10.1093/acprof:oso/9780199296194.001.0001

Fernandez, S., & Rainey, H. G. (2017). Managing successful organizational change in the public sector. *Public Administration Review*, *77*(6), 789–803.

Fung, A. (2015). Putting the public back into governance: The challenges of citizen participation and its future. *Public Administration Review*, *75*(4), 513–522. DOI: 10.1111/puar.12361

Giannakos, K., Belias, D., Ntalakos, A., & Rossidis, I. (2024). Change Management and Communication Satisfaction: Adopting Effective Change Management Strategies for Enhancing Communication Satisfaction, Chapter 12 in "*Organizational Behavior and Human Resource Management for Complex Work Environments*". Publisher: IGI Global, pp. 221-241.

Giannakos, K., Belias, D., Ntalakos, A., Rossidis, I., & Koustelios, A. (2024). Are Leadership Styles related to Change Integration and Commitment? The case of General Hospitals. *Archives of Hellenic Medicine, 41*(3).

Hooghe, L., & Marks, G. (2016). *Community, scale, and regional governance: A postfunctionalist theory of governance*. Oxford University Press. DOI: 10.1093/acprof:oso/9780198766971.001.0001

Katsimardos, P., Bouas, K., Rossidis, I., & Babalioutas, L. (2017). Greek crisis: It's not about growth. It's about governance. *International Journal of Current Research, 9*(3).

Klijn, E.-H., & Koppenjan, J. (2016). *Governance networks in the public sector*. Routledge.

Kotter, J. P. (1996). *Leading change*. Harvard Business School Press.

Kriemadis, A., Rossidis, I., & Belias, D. (2023). Strategic Human Resources Management as a key element in the implementation of organizational changes. An extensive literature review. Chapter 1 in "*Managing Successful and Ethical Organizational Change*", IGI Global. DOI: 10.4018/979-8-3693-0235-4.ch001

Kuhlmann, S., & Wollmann, H. (2019). *Introduction to comparative public administration: Administrative systems and reforms in Europe* (2nd ed.). Edward Elgar.

Kuipers, B. S., Higgs, M., Kickert, W., Tummers, L., Grandia, J., & Van der Voet, J. (2018). The management of change in public organizations: A literature review. *Public Administration, 96*(1), 144–171.

Kuipers, B. S., & Van der Voet, J. (2020). Change management in government: Balancing continuity and innovation. *Public Management Review, 22*(6), 838–856.

Ladner, A., Keuffer, N., & Baldersheim, H. (2019). *Self-rule index for local authorities (1990–2014)*. Routledge.

Lampropoulou, M., & Oikonomou, G. (2021). Theoretical models of public administration and patterns of state reform in Greece. *International Review of Administrative Sciences, 84*(1), 101–121. DOI: 10.1177/0020852315611219

Lodge, M., & Wegrich, K. (2020). *Executive politics in times of crisis*. Palgrave Macmillan.

Manoharan, A. P., Melitski, J., Holzer, M., Kim, S., & Song, M. (2022). E-government and public trust: A global perspective. *Government Information Quarterly*, *39*(1), 101663.

Mergel, I., Edelmann, N., & Haug, N. (2019). Defining digital transformation: Results from expert interviews. *Government Information Quarterly*, *36*(4), 101385. DOI: 10.1016/j.giq.2019.06.002

Mihiotis, A., Rossidis, I., & Koutsoukis, N. (2023). The effect of digital transformation in the development of Electronic Governance in Cyprus and Greece. A critical review through the analysis of the Digital Economy and Society Index. *The Cyprus Review*, *35*(1).

Moore, M. H. (2014). *Public value: Theory and practice*. Palgrave Macmillan.

Ntalakos, A., Belias, D., Rossidis, I., Koustelios, A., Tsigilis, N., & Vasiliadis, L. (2023). Communicating the Vision of the Change: The Linkage Between Organizational Communication, Organizational Culture, and Organizational Change. Chapter 4 in "*Managing Successful and Ethical Organizational Change*", IGI Global.

O'Flynn, J. (2021). From New Public Management to public value: Paradigmatic change and managerial implications. *Australian Journal of Public Administration*, *80*(4), 741–755.

OECD. (2019). *Government at a glance 2019*. OECD Publishing.

Osborne, S. P. (2020). *Public service logic: Creating value for public service users, citizens, and society through research and practice*. Routledge. DOI: 10.4324/9781003009153

Peters, B. G. (2021). *The politics of bureaucracy* (8th ed.). Routledge.

Peters, B. G. (2022). Institutional theory and public sector reform: Change, stability, and adaptation. *International Review of Administrative Sciences*, *88*(3), 469–487.

Pollitt, C. (2019). *Public management reform: A comparative analysis* (4th ed.). Oxford University Press.

Rhodes, R. A. W. (2017). Understanding governance: Ten years on. *Organization Studies*, *38*(10), 1243–1264.

Rossidis, I. (2014). *Applying Business Management in Greek Public Administration*. Athens: publ. Ath. Stamoulis.

Rossidis I., Aspridis, G., Katsimardos, P., Bouas, K., Blanas, N. (2016). Best practices for motivation and their implementation in the Greek public sector for increasing efficiency. *Academic Journal of Interdisciplinary Studies*. 5(3).

Rossidis, I., & Belias, D. (2021). Evolution of e-Government in the era of the pandemic. May the crisis become an opportunity? The cases of Cyprus and Greece. *The Cyprus Review*, *33*(1), 37–66.

Rossidis, I., Belias, D., & Aspridis, G. (2020). *Change Management and Leadership*. Tziolas Publishing.

Rossidis, I., Mihiotis, A., & Ntalakos, A. (2023). *The contribution of Change Management to the integration of E-Governance systems*. Chapter 9 in "Managing Successful and Ethical Organizational Change", IGI Global. DOI: 10.4018/979-8-3693-0235-4.ch009

Sun, T. Q., & Medaglia, R. (2019). Mapping the challenges of artificial intelligence in the public sector: Evidence from public health. *Government Information Quarterly*, *36*(2), 368–383. DOI: 10.1016/j.giq.2018.09.008

Van der Voet, J., & Steijn, B. (2021). Organizational change and public employees: The role of leadership and participation. *Review of Public Personnel Administration*, *41*(4), 589–608.

Vogel, R., & Masal, D. (2023). Leadership and change in public organizations: A systematic review. *Public Management Review*, *25*(1), 1–22.

Weber, M. (1978). *Economy and society: An outline of interpretive sociology*. University of California Press.

Chapter 7
The Dynamics of Public Sector Transformation:
Key Change Management Variables, Measurement Tools, and the Institutional Context of Greek Reforms

Angelos Ntalakos
http://orcid.org/0000-0003-2491-6606
University of Thessaly, Greece

George Soklis
http://orcid.org/0000-0001-8553-6530
Panteion University, Greece

ABSTRACT

This chapter aims to explore the multifaceted nature of change management in the public sector, focusing on six key dimensions: readiness for change, commitment to change, resistance to change, integration of change, successful implementation, and the content of change. The study examines how public institutions adapt to reform demands in diverse international contexts, with a dedicated section focusing on the Greek public administration. As a result of the related literature there is a successful change in the public sector requires a high level of readiness and commitment, supported by strategic leadership and clear communication. Internationally, resistance often stems from organizational culture and lack of engagement. In Greece, although reform agendas are frequent, change efforts are often undermined by bureaucratic

DOI: 10.4018/979-8-3373-3526-1.ch007

rigidity, insufficient training, and lack of stakeholder alignment. However, recent digital and administrative initiatives suggest a growing capacity for structured change implementation.

1. INTRODUCTION

The modern public sector is subjected to demands for change and adjustment to the societal needs that change rapidly, technological advances, and budget limitations (Pollitt & Bouckaert, 2017; Kuipers et al., 2014). Public organizations in different countries are making changes in their organizations that could be considered as structural reforms and digital transformation initiatives, as well as the adoption of New Public Management (NPM) principles and service delivery innovations (Osborne, 2006; Dunleavy et al., 2006). However, the rate of success of these changes in the public sector remains very low, with research indicating that in about 70% of cases, the results of such changes are far from what was expected (Fernandez & Rainey, 2006; Burnes et al., 2018).

Grasping and efficiently handling organizational change within the public sector has become an essential task that attracts the attention of public administrators, policymakers, and scholars (Van der Voet, 2014; Kickert, 2014). In contrast to private sector organizations, which can adjust rapidly to market changes, public sector organizations are subject to operating within intricate institutional systems that are characterized by a large number of stakeholders, political control, bureaucratic structures, and requirements for accountability which, altogether, have a great impact on the processes of change (Boyne, 2002; Rainey, 2014; Andrews et al., 2017). These specific contextual factors call for the implementation of specially designed change management methods that recognize the different characteristics of public organizations (Kuipers et al., 2014; By et al., 2016).

This chapter probes how key change management variables interact in the public sector, emphasizing concepts of measurement and empirical evidence from recent studies (Fernandez & Rainey, 2006; Shea et al., 2014). The investigation encompasses the general public sector environments and an analysis of change management in the Greek public administration, which has undergone significant reforms over the last fifteen years, particularly following the economic crisis (European Commission, 2021; Lampropoulou & Oikonomou, 2018; Makrydemetres et al., 2016). Incorporating theory, validated measurement instruments, and empirical findings from recent scholarly works, this chapter seeks to map the complex network of change management variables and their impact on public sector organizational transformation outcomes (Kuipers et al., 2014; Van der Voet et al., 2016).

2. DEFINING CHANGE MANAGEMENT VARIABLES IN THE PUBLIC SECTOR

2.1. Organizational Change: Conceptual Foundation

Organizational change is essentially any change in the organization's form, quality, or state, including changes to its structure, processes, culture, strategy, or technology (Armenakis & Bedeian, 1999; Burke, 2018; Daviotis et al., 2025; Belias & Rossidis, 2025; Rossidis et al., 2020). Within the public sector, organizational changes are mainly the developments that come from the introductor of new policies, programs, practices, administrative reforms, or service delivery models directed at achieving better organizational performance, higher organizational efficiency, or making the organization more responsive to the needs of the citizens (Pollitt & Bouckaert, 2017; Walker et al., 2011; Cepiku et al., 2016).

Changes in public organizations may be classified by various dimensions (Pettigrew et al., 2001; By, 2005; Kuipers et al., 2014). First-order change refers to incremental types of changes, which still fall within the existing organizational paradigms, whereas second-order change implies a complete revolution of organizational assumptions, values, and operating models (Levy & Merry, 1986; Bartunek & Moch, 1987). A planned change is a set of changes deliberately and step by step controlled and managed by management, whereas an emergent one is an evolution that happens naturally through continuous adaptations to environmental pressures (Bamford & Forrester, 2003; By, 2005). Episodic changes are those changes that happen in different periods that are separated by stability, whereas continuous changes are changes that occur as a result of ongoing adaptation, which is deeply rooted in the organizational routines (Weick & Quinn, 1999; Burnes, 2004).

2.2. Change Management: Core Construct

Change management refers to the deliberate use of knowledge, tools, and resources to adjust to changes resulting from external factors and the business environment by means of defining and implementing changes in strategies, structures, processes, and technologies of the organization (Hiatt & Creasey, 2012; Hayes, 2018; Cameron & Green, 2019; Belias et al., 2024; Belias et al., 2023b; Belias et al., 2023c). In the public sector, change management is about the organizational transformation processes, methods, and techniques that aim at managing the preparation and readiness of individuals and teams for change, as well as the provision of support during the transition from the current to the desired future state (Fernandez & Rainey, 2006; Van der Voet, 2014; Kuipers et al., 2014).

Managing change efficiently in public organizations involves dealing with both the technical and human sides of the issue (Kotter, 1996; Armenakis & Harris, 2009; Hughes, 2018). The technical side is about creating and rolling out new systems, structures, and processes, whereas the human side is about the psychological and behavioral aspects of the change, thus it includes employee readiness, resistance, commitment, and capacity to adapt to new ways of working (Holt et al., 2007; Oreg et al., 2011; Rafferty et al., 2013).

2.3. Key Variables in Public Sector Change Management

Organizational Readiness for Change

Organizational readiness for change is a key factor leading to the successful implementation of change, and it is considered the degree to which the members of the organization are mentally and behaviorally ready to carry out a change in the organization (Armenakis et al., 1993; Weiner, 2009; Shea et al., 2014). A complex concept like this one, involves on the one hand conditions at the organizational level such as resources, structures, and a climate conducive to change and, on the other hand, individual-level perceptions, such as commitment to change and confidence in one's ability to change (Holt et al., 2007; Weiner, 2009; Helfrich et al., 2009).

Change commitment is characterized by the determination to back change and the conviction that such change is necessary and advantageous (Herscovitch & Meyer, 2002; Weiner, 2009). Change efficacy is about the shared belief among organizational members that they, as a group, have the capability to bring change successfully (Bandura, 1997; Weiner, 2009; Shea et al., 2014). As a result, these factors chiefly decide whether the individuals targeted by change perceive the proposed change as helpful and feasible; hence, they strongly determine the level of their readiness to decide to put effort into the change implementation process (Armenakis et al., 2007; Rafferty et al., 2013; Choi & Ruona, 2011).

Leadership for Change

Leadership has been identified as the most significant element that determines the success of the change process in public organizations (Higgs & Rowland, 2005; Gill, 2003; Van der Voet et al., 2016; Belias et al., 2024; Belias et al., 2024b; Belias et al., 2023; Belias et al., 2025a; Belias et al., 2025b). Change leadership refers to the leaders' interventions and the habits through which they enable organizational change. Such interventions include, among others, presenting a persuasive vision of change, gaining support and commitment, explaining the reasons for change and its advantages, giving power to employees and helping them, showing the desired behavior, and checking up on the progress (Kotter, 1996; Battilana et al., 2010; Higgs & Rowland, 2011).

Transformational leadership, a style marked by the use of the leader as a role model, the leader's ability to motivate through shared vision, the leader's encouragement of creativity, and the leader's individual support, has been shown to be very effective in change situations (Bass, 1985; Judge & Piccolo, 2004; Gilley et al., 2008; Giannakos et al., 2024c). Public sector leaders of change have to deal with more complex situations than their counterparts in the private sector. These complexities include the management of political stakeholders, the balancing of different demands for accountability, and working within institutional constraints that limit the freedom of the manager (Fernandez & Rainey, 2006; Van der Voet et al., 2015; Hassan & Wright, 2020).

Communication for Change

One of the main tools used by organizational members to understand a change, figure out the change requirements, and carry out the implementation activities is a communication process (Klein, 1996; Lewis, 2000; Elving, 2005). Along with information dissemination, effective change communication also comprises dialogue, participation, and feedback mechanisms, which make it possible for a two-way contact to be established between change agents and recipients (Bordia et al., 2004; Allen et al., 2007; Men, 2014).

Some of the main aspects of change communication are how often and how quickly the communication is done, the quality and correctness of the information given, the means and methods used to deliver the messages, the chances for the recipients to take part in the communication processes, and the being addressed to the questions and concerns (Lewis, 2000; DiFonzo & Bordia, 1998; Elving, 2005). In public sector enterprises, communication becomes even more complicated due to the presence of numerous stakeholder groups having different information requirements and expectations (Graaf et al., 2019; Rainey, 2014).

Employee Participation and Involvement

Some of the main aspects of change communication are how often and how quickly the communication is done, the quality and correctness of the information given, the means and methods used to deliver the messages, the chances for the recipients to take part in the communication processes, and the being addressed to the questions and concerns (Lewis, 2000; DiFonzo & Bordia, 1998; Elving, 2005).

In public sector enterprises, communication becomes even more complicated due to the presence of numerous stakeholder groups having different information requirements and expectations (Graaf et al., 2019; Rainey, 2014).

One of the roles of participation in the process of change is to import a wealth of information from the environment about difficulties and opportunities of the implementation to the change agents. Also, it increases employee understanding and acceptance of change, while also improving the quality of change decisions through the involvement of frontline expertise. Moreover, it creates commitment owing to the psychological ownership of change outcomes (Coch & French, 1948; Bordia et al., 2004; Rafferty & Restubog, 2010). On the other hand, participation brings problems, such as the increase in the time required, the possibility of conflicts arising from the different viewpoints of stakeholders, and the necessity to deal with power dynamics (Lines, 2004; Van der Voet et al., 2016)

Organizational Culture and Climate

Organizational culture refers to those shared values, beliefs, assumptions, and norms that define the organization and determine the behavior of its members (Schein, 2010; Cameron & Quinn, 2011; Giannakos et al., 2024b; Ntalakos et al., 2022; Ntalakos et al., 2024a, 2024b). Climate is about the shared perceptions of the organizational members regarding the organizational policies, practices, and procedures (Schneider et al., 2013; Kuenzi & Schminke, 2009). Both culture and climate have a major impact on the willingness to change, as well as the degree of difficulty in carrying out the changes (Schein, 2010; Jones et al., 2005; Jacobs et al., 2013).

Cultures with these characteristics —innovation orientation, learning focus, flexibility, and trust —are likely to facilitate the change adoption process. On the other hand, cultures that mainly show features such as stability, hierarchy, risk aversion, and control are more likely to resist the change (Cameron & Quinn, 2011; Ahmed, 1998; Lok & Crawford, 2004). Bureaucratic cultures that are typical of public-sector organizations and are characterized by the emphasis on rules, procedures, and hierarchical authority have been the main factors that, according to literature, have constrained change in these organizations (Wilson, 1989; Scott & Davis, 2015). However, public sector reforms are increasingly focusing on changing organizational culture to be more performance-oriented, customer-focused, and innovative (Osborne, 2006; Walker et al., 2011).

Change Recipients' Beliefs and Attitudes

Individual-level factors, specifically the beliefs and attitudes of the members of the organization towards the change, are the chief determinants of the successful implementation of change (Armenakis et al., 2007; Oreg et al., 2011; Choi & Ruona, 2011; Belias and Trihas, 2023; Belias et al., 2023d; Belias and Trihas, 2023b; Belias and Trihas, 2023c; Belias et al., 2025c). The main concepts involved are, among others, change-related self-efficacy (change being the situation and one is capable of doing it), perceived appropriateness (identification of the change as a legitimate one and suitable for the situation), management support (feeling that the leadership is committed to change) and personal valence (recognition of the ways in which change will impact one's interests) (Holt et al., 2007; Rafferty et al., 2013; Bouckenooghe, 2010).

These psychological and emotional reactions to change have an impact on the behavioral intentions and the actual change-related behaviors (Ajzen, 1991; Piderit, 2000). Negative beliefs and attitudes become resistance to change, while positive orientations create a proactive change support and adoption behavior (Oreg, 2006; Ford et al., 2008). Employees in the public sector may have different kinds of beliefs that are influenced by their professional identities, public service motivation, and the experiences of the previous reform initiatives (Perry & Wise, 1990; Moynihan & Pandey, 2007).

Organizational Resources and Capacity

To carry out a change successfully, the organization must have sufficient resources and capabilities. These should comprise monetary resources to finance change activities, qualified and available staff, suitable technological infrastructure, and time for planning and implementing the change (Klarner et al., 2008; Huber et al., 2015). Limited capacities are often the reason for the failure of the public sector to implement changes, especially in situations where there is a reduction in government spending (Kickert & Randma-Liiv, 2017; Overmans & Noordegraaf, 2014).

Besides material resources, the organizational capacity also includes different intangible elements, among which are the knowledge and skills of the change management, the previous experience with similar changes, and the absorptive capacity to combine the new practices with the already existing operations (Cohen & Levinthal, 1990; Zahra & George, 2002). Generally, public organizations are deficient in specialized change management knowledge and thus continue depending on external consultants or learning by trial and error (Kuipers et al., 2014; Fernandez & Rainey, 2006)

External Environment and Institutional Context

One of the things that characterizes public organizations is their operation within complicated institutional environments, which, according to DiMaggio & Powell

(1983) and Scott (2014), have a significant influence on their change processes. The environment of an organization may be described as a set of factors made of political dynamics and stakeholder pressures, legal and regulatory frameworks, inter-organizational networks and dependencies, societal expectations and public opinion, and economic conditions (Rainey, 2014; Pollitt & Bouckaert, 2017). These external forces may be the facilitators that push the organization towards a necessary change, or they may be the roadblocks that restrict the options of change and the approaches to the implementation thereof (Meyer et al., 1990; Greenwood & Hinings, 1996).

The environment of public organizations, which is marked by numerous accountability relationships, political supervision, and conflicting stakeholder interests, is the source of a different kind of challenge for change management (Boyne, 2002; Bozeman, 1987; Bryson et al., 2009). Managers in the public sector are required to steer through political cycles, handle the expectations of different stakeholders, adhere to the law, and keep the trust of the public, at the same time as they are carrying out the necessary changes in the organization (Fernandez & Rainey, 2006; Van der Voet, 2014).

Table 1. Key variables in public sector change management

Variable	Definition	Key Dimensions	Relationship to Change Outcomes	Key References
Organizational Readiness for Change	Extent to which organizational members are psychologically and behaviorally prepared to implement change	• Change commitment • Change efficacy • Resource availability • Organizational climate	Strongly predicts implementation success, employee adoption behaviors, and change sustainability	Weiner (2009); Shea et al. (2014); Armenakis et al. (1993)
Leadership for Change	Behaviors and practices leaders employ to guide organizational transformation	• Vision communication • Coalition building • Employee empowerment • Modeling behaviors • Monitoring progress	Directly influences employee commitment, readiness, and active participation in change initiatives	Van der Voet et al. (2016); Higgs & Rowland (2011); Battilana et al. (2010)
Change Communication	Information sharing and dialogue processes that create understanding and coordination	• Communication frequency • Information quality • Two-way dialogue • Channel diversity • Responsiveness	Mediates relationship between leadership and employee outcomes; reduces uncertainty and resistance	Allen et al. (2007); Elving (2005); Klein (1996)

continued on following page

Table 1. Continued

Variable	Definition	Key Dimensions	Relationship to Change Outcomes	Key References
Employee Participation	Degree of employee involvement in planning, decision-making, and implementation	• Information sharing • Consultation • Joint decision-making • Employee-driven initiatives	Increases understanding, acceptance, commitment, and quality of change decisions	Lines (2004); Bordia et al. (2004); Rafferty & Restubog (2010)
Organizational Culture & Climate	Shared values, beliefs, and perceptions characterizing the organization	• Innovation orientation • Learning focus • Trust levels • Risk tolerance • Flexibility	Facilitates or constrains change receptivity; bureaucratic cultures may resist while adaptive cultures embrace change	Schein (2010); Cameron & Quinn (2011); Jones et al. (2005)
Change Recipients' Beliefs	Individual-level cognitive and affective responses to change	• Change self-efficacy • Perceived appropriateness • Management support • Personal valence	Directly predicts resistance, commitment, and adoption behaviors at individual level	Holt et al. (2007); Armenakis et al. (2007); Oreg et al. (2011)
Organizational Resources & Capacity	Tangible and intangible assets available for change implementation	• Financial resources • Human resources • Time availability • Knowledge/ expertise • Prior experience	Determines feasibility and pace of implementation; capacity constraints predict failure	Klarner et al. (2008); Judge & Douglas (2009); Ahmad et al. (2020)
External Environment & Institutional Context	Political, legal, and social forces shaping change processes	• Political dynamics • Stakeholder pressures • Legal frameworks • Public expectations • Economic conditions	Creates drivers and constraints unique to public sector; influences change approach and outcomes	Rainey (2014); Pollitt & Bouckaert (2017); Boyne (2002)

3. EMPIRICAL MEASUREMENT TOOLS AND VALIDATED INSTRUMENTS

3.1. Organizational Readiness Assessment Instruments

It is a fact that many verified tools are available to quantify an organization's readiness to undergo change, particularly in public sector contexts (Gagnon et al., 2014; Weiner et al., 2008). One instrument, the Organizational Readiness for Change Assessment (ORCA), which was designed following the Promoting Action on Research Implementation in Health Services (PARIHS) framework, comprises three main scales that measure the strength of the evidence, the quality of the organizational context, and the facilitation capacity (Helfrich et al., 2009). The ORCA has been through the process of validation in different public sector organizations, especially in healthcare settings, and it is found to have a good set of psychometric properties (Helfrich et al., 2009; Miake-Lye et al., 2020).

Based on Weiner's organizational readiness theory, the Organizational Readiness for Change (ORIC) unit mainly measures two aspects: change commitment and change efficacy (Shea et al., 2014). The short 12-item measure has been tested in various studies, and it provides a neat solution to the problem of determining the readiness of an organizational unit or a team to implement a particular change (Shea et al., 2014; Weiner et al., 2017). ORIC is very reliable (Cronbach's alpha > 0.90) and has good construct validity (Shea et al., 2014).

Cinite, Duxbury, and Higgins (2009) created a detailed scale measuring Organizational Readiness to Change that is tailored for public sector settings and comprises five dimensions: the commitment of senior managers to the change, the competence of change agents, the support of immediate managers, poor communication of change (negative dimension), and the adverse impact on work (negative dimension). The tool was tested with data from publicly-funded organizations in Canada and reflects strong psychometric characteristics appropriate for both research and practical use (Cinite et al., 2009).

3.2. Change Leadership Measurement

The Multifactor Leadership Questionnaire (MLQ) is an instrument that has been used most frequently to measure leadership behaviors that are transformational and transactional and are relevant to change situations (Bass & Avolio, 1997; Avolio et al., 1999). The MLQ measures the following: idealized influence (attributed and behavioral), inspirational motivation, intellectual stimulation, individualized consideration, contingent reward, management by exception (active and passive), and laissez-faire leadership (Bass & Avolio, 1997; Judge & Piccolo, 2004). Although the MLQ was initially created for the private sector, it has been widely used and confirmed to be reliable in public sector research (Wright & Pandey, 2010; Jensen et al., 2019).

Leadership scales specific to change situations have been created in order to identify those behaviors that are especially relevant to the implementation of changes (Herold et al., 2008; Higgs & Rowland, 2011). The authors Van der Voet, Kuipers, and Groeneveld (2016) have come up with various measures of change leadership in public organizations, pointing out the characteristics that include the communication of the vision, the creation of the coalition, the empowerment, and the short-term wins. When these instruments are applied to public sector change milieus, they attest to being of good reliability and validity (Van der Voet et al., 2016).

3.3. Communication and Participation Scales

The Involved Communication scale defines the degree of communication related to change as being two-way, hence, through dialogue and feedback mechanisms rather than just one-way information dissemination (Hameed et al., 2019). This concept has been translated into measurable elements through questions that evaluate communication frequency, information quality, channel effectiveness, participation opportunities, and responsiveness to feedback (Allen et al., 2007; Elving, 2005). Various studies have confirmed that there is a positive correlation between involved communication and change results in the public sector settings (Hameed et al., 2019; Van der Voet et al., 2016).

Frequently, employee participation is gauged via various scales that delineate the level of involvement in change planning, decision-making, and implementation activities (Lines, 2004; Sagie & Koslowsky, 2000). The items usually represent formal participation structures (e.g., task forces, committees) and informal involvement opportunities (e.g., suggestion systems, consultation processes) (Bordia et al., 2004; Wanberg & Banas, 2000). Participation scales relate to change-related outcomes such as commitment, acceptance, and implementation effectiveness (Lines, 2004; Rafferty & Restubog, 2010).

3.4. Organizational Change Questionnaire (OCQ-CPR)

Bouckenooghe et al. (2009) created a thorough 42-item Organizational Change Questionnaire that measures the Climate of Change, Processes, and Readiness (OCQ-CPR). The instrument, which was confirmed valid for more than 3,000 organizational members from the public and private sectors, measures five climate-of-change dimensions (trust in the leadership, sense of cohesion, commitment toward change, information about change, and trust in benefits), three process dimensions (support by supervisors, willingness of management to provide resources, and participation), and three readiness dimensions (appropriateness of change, management support, and change efficacy) (Bouckenooghe et al., 2009). The OCQ-CPR has very good psychometric properties and offers a comprehensive evaluation that can be used for both research and diagnostic purposes (Bouckenooghe et al., 2009; Rafferty et al., 2013).

3.5. Readiness for Organizational Change (ROC) Scale

Holt and colleagues operationally created the Readiness for Organizational Change scale, which measures individual-level readiness through four dimensions: appropriateness (beliefs regarding whether the change was needed and proper), management support (perceptions of the organization's commitment to change), change efficacy (beliefs about the ability to carry out the change), and personal valence (evaluation of personal impact) (Holt et al., 2007). The ROC scale has been confirmed in different situations, such as the public sector, and it indicates that it has good psychometric properties with Cronbach's alpha coefficients of more than 0.70 for all subscales (Holt et al., 2007; Rafferty et al., 2013).

3.6. ADKAR Model Assessment

Prosci's ADKAR model is a goal-centered change management framework that evaluates five successive milestones: Awareness of need for change, Desire to support and participate in change, Knowledge of how to change, Ability to implement change, and Reinforcement to sustain change (Hiatt, 2006). The ADKAR assessments were not initially created as a research tool, but have been modified for empirical research and organizational diagnosis, mainly in practitioner-oriented studies (Hiatt, 2006; Prosci, 2018). The easy-to-understand and user-friendly characteristics of the model have been cited as the main reasons for its widespread adoption in public sector change initiatives (Hussain et al., 2018).

3.7. Change Management Maturity Assessment

Several frameworks measure the organizational change management maturity of an organization. These frameworks reflect how sophisticated and effective the change management capabilities are (Prosci, 2018; CMI, 2019). The Prosci Change Management Maturity Model determines the five maturity levels from initial/ad-hoc to optimizing/organizational competency. The model assesses the dimensions of leadership sponsorship, change agent competency, change management integration, and change management methodology (Prosci, 2018). The Change Management

Institute has a different maturity model that focuses on the development of organizational change capability in various dimensions (CMI, 2019; Ahmad et al., 2020).

3.8. Performance and Outcome Measures

To measure the success of a change properly, it is necessary to have suitable outcome indicators that are in line with the change objectives (Armenakis & Bedeian, 1999; Burke, 2018). Typically, the categories are adoption measures (e.g., utilization rates, compliance with new procedures), individual performance indicators (e.g., proficiency with new systems, productivity metrics), organizational performance measures (e.g., efficiency gains, service quality improvements, cost reductions), and employee attitude measures (e.g., satisfaction with change, organizational commitment, turnover intentions) (Fernandez & Rainey, 2006; Walker et al., 2011). The first thing research points out is the necessity of assessing the effects at various levels - individual, group, and organizational - and also making a difference between the immediate implementation outcomes and the longer-term sustained impacts (By, 2005; Kuipers et al., 2014)

Table 2. Validated instruments for measuring change management variables

Instrument	Authors & Year	Variables Measured	Number of Items	Subscales/Dimensions	Reliability (Cronbach's α)	Validation Context	Key Strengths
Organizational Readiness to Change Assessment (ORCA)	Helfrich et al. (2009)	Evidence, Context, Facilitation	77 items	• Evidence strength (4 subscales) • Context quality (6 subscales) • Facilitation capacity (3 subscales)	α = 0.72-0.95 across subscales	Veterans Health Administration; healthcare settings	Comprehensive; theory-based (PARIHS framework); public sector validated
Organizational Readiness for Implementing Change (ORIC)	Shea et al. (2014)	Change commitment, Change efficacy	12 items	• Change commitment (6 items) • Change efficacy (6 items)	α = 0.93 (commitment) α = 0.91 (efficacy)	Healthcare organizations; cross-industry validation	Brief; strong psychometric properties; theory-driven (Weiner's theory)
Organizational Readiness to Change Scale (Public Sector)	Cinite et al. (2009)	Readiness dimensions specific to public sector	25 items	• Senior manager commitment • Change agent competence • Immediate manager support • Poor communication (negative) • Adverse work impact (negative)	α = 0.82-0.91 across subscales	Canadian public sector organizations	Specifically designed for public sector contexts
Organizational Change Questionnaire (OCQ-CPR)	Bouckenooghe et al. (2009)	Climate, Process, Readiness	42 items	• Climate (5 dimensions) • Process (3 dimensions) • Readiness (3 dimensions)	α = 0.75-0.94 across dimensions	3,000+ participants; public and private sectors	Comprehensive; validated across sectors; multi-dimensional

continued on following page

Table 2. Continued

Instrument	Authors & Year	Variables Measured	Number of Items	Subscales/Dimensions	Reliability (Cronbach's α)	Validation Context	Key Strengths
Readiness for Organizational Change (ROC) Scale	Holt et al. (2007)	Individual readiness dimensions	25 items	•Appropriateness (6 items) • Management support (6 items) • Change efficacy (7 items) • Personal valence (6 items)	α = 0.70-0.93 across dimensions	Multiple organizational contexts including public sector	Individual-level focus; systematic development; widely adopted
Multifactor Leadership Questionnaire (MLQ)	Bass & Avolio (1997)	Transformational and transactional leadership	45 items (full) 36 items (short)	•Transformational (5 subscales) • Transactional (2 subscales) • Laissez-faire • Outcomes (3 subscales)	α = 0.74-0.91 across factors	Extensive validation; public and private sectors	Most widely used leadership measure; validated in public sector contexts
Change Leadership Measures (Public Sector)	Van der Voet et al. (2016)	Change-specific leadership behaviors in public organizations	Variable	• Vision communication• Coalition building •Empowerment• Short-term wins	α = 0.78-0.88	Dutch public sector organizations	Public sector specific; change-focused behaviors
Involved Communication Scale	Hameed et al. (2019)	Quality of change communication	8 items	• Two-way dialogue • Participation opportunities • Feedback mechanisms	α = 0.86	Public sector R&D organizations (Pakistan)	Public sector validated; captures participatory communication
Employee Participation Scale	Lines (2004)	Degree of employee involvement in change	6 items	Single dimension measuring participation intensity	α = 0.82	Multiple organizational contexts	Brief; directly measures participation construct
Change Recipients' Beliefs Scale	Armenakis et al. (2007)	Beliefs about change	25 items	• Discrepancy • Appropriateness• Efficacy• Principal support• Valence	α = 0.75-0.92 across dimensions	Multiple organizational settings	Theory-based; comprehensive belief assessment
ADKAR Assessment	Hiatt (2006)	Individual change milestones	15 items (3 per dimension)	• Awareness • Desire • Knowledge• Ability• Reinforcement	Varies by implementation	Practitioner contexts; cross-industry	Practitioner-friendly; sequential milestone focus
Change Fatigue Scale	Bernerth et al. (2011)	Physical and psychological exhaustion from repeated changes	12 items	• Physical fatigue • Emotional fatigue	α = 0.93 (total scale)	Multiple organizational contexts	Addresses emerging concern; newly validated
Resistance to Change Scale	Oreg (2006)	Individual dispositional resistance	17 items	• Routine seeking • Emotional reaction • Short-term focus • Cognitive rigidity	α = 0.78-0.89 across dimensions	Cross-cultural validation	Dispositional focus; personality-based

Figure 1. Empirical measurement tools and validated instruments

4. LITERATURE REVIEW: CHANGE MANAGEMENT IN THE PUBLIC SECTOR

4.1. Comprehensive Reviews and Meta-Analyses

Kuipers and colleagues (2014) conducted a huge systematic literature review on change management in public organizations. They looked at 203 publications from 1990 to 2013. Their analysis brought up the key points about the state of research on change in the public sector (Kuipers et al., 2014). Firstly, the field is characterized by fragmentation, which means that there is very little knowledge that is being built up, and theoretical development is also at a very low level (Kuipers et al., 2014; Oreg et al., 2011). Secondly, the researchers mostly decide to put their focus on the 'what' and 'where' factors, thus 'what changes' and 'environmental factors', while less concentration is on process (how change unfolds) and leadership dimensions (Pettigrew et al., 2001; Kuipers et al., 2014). Third, methodological issues still remain, such as the heavy dependence on only one case study, the use of cross-sectional designs in studies, and the lack of longitudinal research that looks at the change process over time (Van de Ven & Poole, 2005; Kuipers et al., 2014).

The review found these factors to be the main causes of the successful implementation of changes in public organizations over and over again: commitment from the leadership to the cause and the active support thereof, communication strategies that effectively inform and engage stakeholders, having the right resources at disposal for the change initiatives, adopting a participatory approach whereby employees are engaged in planning and implementation, giving due attention to the organizational culture and climate, dealing with individual reactions and resistance to change, as well as managing relationships with external stakeholders and the political dynamics (Fernandez & Rainey, 2006; Kuipers et al., 2014; By et al., 2016). Nevertheless, the review also pointed out the shortage of rigorous empirical research that looks at causal relationships and tests theoretical propositions (Kuipers et al., 2014; Van der Voet, 2014).

4.2. Leadership and Change in Public Organizations

Van der Voet, Kuipers, and Groeneveld (2016) performed a quantitative investigation to unveil the interaction of leadership and affective commitment to change in the public sector in the Netherlands. Their empirical research, which is based on a survey of 1254 public employees, showed that transformational leadership behaviors of direct supervisors were the main significantly predictive variables of employee commitment to change (Van der Voet et al., 2016). Moreover, this link is facilitated through excellent change communication and employee involvement in the change process (Van der Voet et al., 2016; Allen et al., 2007). The results point to the indispensable role of middle managers and frontline supervisors in interpreting organizational change strategies into tangible work and ensuring employee endorsement (Huy, 2001; Balogun, 2003).

As a matter of fact, their study had also brought to light that the bureaucratic features that are typical of public organizations tend to influence the effectiveness of leadership (Van der Voet, 2014; Wright & Pandey, 2010). When the environment is highly bureaucratic, characterized by formalized procedures and decision-making based on hierarchy, the transformational leadership behaviors have less strong relationships with employee commitment as compared to the situations that are less bureaucratic (Van der Voet, 2014). Therefore, this indicates that the structural characteristics of public organizations may limit the leaders' capacity to excite and energize employees during a change process; thus, it becomes imperative not only to deal with leadership behaviors but also to address organizational structures when implementing change (Rainey, 2014; Fernandez & Rainey, 2006).

4.3. Employee Readiness and Commitment to Change

Hameed, Khan, and Sabharwal (2019) conducted a study to identify the main factors that influence the employees' readiness for change in public sector R&D organizations in Pakistan. The researchers, upon analyzing the data from a survey of 330 public servants, found that one of the most powerful drivers of employee readiness for change is involved communication—this being essentially a two-way dialogue, participation, and feedback—(Hameed et al., 2019). The effect of this variable on the outcome is indirect through organizational identification (employees' feeling of belonging and psychological attachment to the organization) and changes recipients' beliefs about the correctness and fairness of the change (Hameed et al., 2019; Armenakis et al., 2007).

The research shows that in such cases where public organizations use a participatory communication approach for the change process which implies that employees are involved in the dialogue and decision-making, employees as a result get stronger organizational identification and develop more positive beliefs about the change, thus they become more willing to support and implement the change (Hameed et al., 2019; Rafferty & Restubog, 2010). Such results indicate that the change process in the public sector strongly depends on the quality of communication and the use of employee involvement mechanisms since the traditional top-down communication approach may not be enough to gain employee support (Klein, 1996; Lewis, 2000).

4.4. Change Management Approaches: Planned Versus Emergent

One of the debates that research has looked into is whether public organizations should use deliberately planned and sequential methods when changing (e.g., following Kotter's eight-step model) or rather adopt emergent, adaptable methods that develop naturally (Bamford & Forrester, 2003; By, 2005). Van der Voet and Vermeeren (2017) conducted a study to compare the effectiveness of planned and emergent change approaches in Dutch public organizations that were undergoing significant organizational restructuring. Their results showed that bureaucratic public organizations are capable of bringing about change through either method and thus, their finding goes against the idea that public sector rigidity would necessitate exclusively planned approaches (Van der Voet & Vermeeren, 2017).

Nevertheless, the study found significant contingencies that affect the effectiveness of changes (Van der Voet & Vermeeren, 2017; Burnes, 2004). Planned approaches show more effectiveness when changes are clearly defined, the interests of the stakeholders are relatively aligned, and the implementation timelines are clear (Kotter, 1996; By, 2005). On the other hand, emergent approaches become more appropriate when changes are characterized by a high level of uncertainty, continuous adaptation is required based on the feedback, and the different perspectives of the stakeholders need to be taken into account (Weick & Quinn, 1999; Burnes, 2004). The research indicates that public managers should deliberately decide on change methods in accordance with the features of the change and the organizational environment instead of simply using planned approaches by default (Van der Voet & Vermeeren, 2017).

4.5. Change Capacity and Organizational Performance

One of the main factors that influences the public sector performance, according to the latest research, is the change capacity of the organization—the ability to start, carry through, and maintain a change in the organization (Judge & Douglas, 2009; Klarner et al., 2008). Such organizations react more effectively to the demands of their environment, implement innovations, and achieve their strategic goals (Ahmad et al., 2020; Walker et al., 2011). The concept of change capacity is, in fact, quite broad and includes leadership commitment, employees' skills, knowledge, a corporate culture that supports change, availability of resources, and previous change experience (Judge & Douglas, 2009; Heckman et al., 2021).

Empirical research has shown that public organizations differ significantly in their ability to change, which in turn affects the success of the change and the overall effectiveness of the organization (Walker et al., 2011; Andrews et al., 2017). Those organizations that purposely build change capacity through leadership development, employee training, cultural interventions, and knowledge management experience better change outcomes as compared to the organizations that lack such investments (Ahmad et al., 2020; Heckman et al., 2021). This is evidence that developing organizational capabilities in handling change should constitute part of the strategic agenda of public sector leaders (Walker et al., 2011).

4.6. Digital Transformation and Change Management

Recently, research has focused on change management as a major issue of digital transformation narratives, which in turn have been gaining considerable attention in the public sectors all over the world (Mergel et al., 2019; Vial, 2019). The digital transformation change management problems are different; among them, there is the technical side of the issue, the need for new skills and competences, the resistance of employees who are used to the traditional way of work, and the problem of coordination not only across different units of the organization but also with the external partners (Mergel et al., 2019; Layne & Lee, 2001; Lindgren & Van Veenstra, 2018).

Research on the digital transformation in public organizations reveals the key factors that contribute to the successful implementation of such changes. These factors are: the securing of the executive sponsorship and sustaining the political support, giving the employees the adequate training and support, managing the communication of stakeholders and their expectations, addressing of the issues of cybersecurity and privacy, ensuring the technical infrastructure adequacy and keeping the focus on the citizen/user needs during the whole implementation process (Mergel et al., 2019; Goldfinch, 2007). The studies also emphasize the importance of digital transformation as a change in the organization, rather than just a technology implementation, which consequently requires attention to process redesign, cultural adaptation, and new ways of working (Fountain, 2001; Mergel et al., 2019).

4.7. Change Fatigue and Multiple Change Initiatives

Public sector organizations are often subject to many change initiatives at the same time, which leads to the phenomenon of change fatigue - the employees' physical and psychological exhaustion caused by their repeated exposure to changes in the organization (Bernerth et al., 2011; McMillan & Perron, 2013). Studies indicate that change fatigue significantly obstructs the achievement of implementation goals. It is reflected in the negative attitude towards change, reluctance to respond to new initiatives, and decreased motivation to put the effort into change adoption (Bernerth et al., 2011; Bordia et al., 2011).

Research focused on change fatigue in public organizations lists a large number of factors contributing to such fatigue, as noted by the authors. These include: the changes made too often and too intensively, the absence of time for recovery between initiatives, bad management of change (lack of communication, insufficient involvement), the feeling that the previous changes were a failure, and the accumulation of stress caused by the intensification of work (McMillan & Perron, 2013; Rafferty & Griffin, 2006). Studies show that public organizations need to implement portfolio strategies for change management, which involve coordinating the initiatives in such a way that employees are not overwhelmed, making sure that there is enough time between the major changes, and checking change capacity as well as employee well-being through indicators (Burnes, 2004; Rafferty & Griffin, 2006).

4.8. Change Communication and Stakeholder Management

Communication is at the core of the very mechanism that brings about change in public organizations, and research has been emphasizing this for quite a long time (Klein, 1996; Lewis, 2000; Elving, 2005). Effective change communication goes even further than just giving out information as it calls for inventing shared understanding, creating commitment, treating concerns and resistance, as well as coordinating the implementation activities (Armenakis & Harris, 2002; Lewis, 2000; Giannakos et al., 2024a; Ntalakos et al., 2023). Several studies have confirmed that there are various aspects of communication that relate to the success of change i.e. message quality (clarity, consistency, accuracy), communication frequency and timeliness, channel diversity (using multiple communication methods), dialogue and feedback opportunities, and communication by trustworthy sources including top leaders and immediate supervisors (Allen et al., 2007; Elving, 2005; Men, 2014).

One of the key requirements of a public sector change initiative is to effectively communicate with a diverse range of stakeholders. These groups comprise employees, elected officials, citizen groups, media, unions, and partner organizations (Rainey, 2014; Bryson et al., 2009). The research shows that the strategies used to communicate with stakeholders should be adjusted according to the characteristics of the audience, their needs for information, and their influence on change outcomes (Bryson et al., 2002; Fernandez & Rainey, 2006). Not enough communication with the key stakeholders is a reason for change initiatives that have been unsuccessful in public organizations most frequently (Kuipers et al., 2014; Graaf et al., 2019).

4.9. Resistance to Change

Resistance to change is still a major hurdle for public sector organizations that can be traced back to various origins: among those causes are definitely the condition of not knowing what the change will bring, the fright of being sacked or losing the autonomy, the lack of agreement with the reason or the way of changing, the mistrust of the leader, the change of habits and relations, and the lack of money (Piderit, 2000; Oreg, 2006; Ford et al., 2008). The scholars have stopped considering resistance an unreasonable antagonism to be defeated; instead, they acknowledge that resistance may be a signal of concern that needs to be addressed through dialogue and the finding of a solution (Ford et al., 2008; Piderit, 2000).

Research studies have shown that the intensity of resistance and types of resistance change depending on the change contexts and stakeholder groups (Oreg, 2006; Bordia et al., 2011). Those employed in the public sector might resist changes that they see as a threat to their professional values or loss of autonomy (Noordegraaf, 2007; Thomas & Davies, 2005). The frontline staff may resist changes that increase their workload or make their job more difficult without providing clear benefits (Hupe & Hill, 2007). Middle managers can also be found to resist changes that limit their authority or span of control (Huy, 2001). Successful change management entails having a plan for where the resistance will come from; therefore, it is good practice to have the first conversations with potential resistors, to deal with their concerns by listening to them and talking with them, thus engaging the stakeholders in solving the problem together (Ford et al., 2008; Lines, 2004).

4.10. Sustainability of Change

Research on the whole is turning to that question of what factors in the end determine whether the changes introduced become the usual practices of the organization or simply fade after the initial implementation (Buchanan et al., 2005; Jacobs et al., 2015). There are studies which show that very often the organizations, even on purpose, behave like they did not receive the change message, so Stirman et al. (2012) and Buchanan et al. (2005) in their works report the rates of such behavior backed up by the reversion of the companies to the prior ways when change management attention and resources abate. Factors linked to change continuation include, among others, support and reinforcement through organization systems (e.g. regulations, routines, performance management), leadership's ongoing care and encouragement, making changes a part of the organization's cultural values and standard practices, providing clear and visible benefits that motivate further use, continuous training and assistance of new employees, as well as the presence of monitoring instruments for checking the degree of implementation (Jacobs et al., 2015; Stirman et al., 2012; Wiltsey Stirman et al., 2013).

Political cycles that can change priorities, a change of political appointees and senior executives, a budget being stretched limiting the further support of a change, and a public administration system that, due to its nature, is more likely to conserve than to allow innovations are among the reasons why public sector organizations have difficulties in sustaining changes (Pollitt & Bouckaert, 2017; Fernandez & Rainey, 2006). Literature on the subject indicates that the continuation of change should be deliberately planned and handled continuously, and changes should not be simply left to their own devices after the implementation phase (Buchanan et al., 2005; Jacobs et al., 2015).

5. CHANGE MANAGEMENT IN GREEK PUBLIC ADMINISTRATION

5.1. Context of Greek Public Sector Reform

The Greek public sector has been undergoing various reform measures for the past fifteen years; these reforms have become more rigorous after the economic crisis in 2010 and the following International Monetary Fund (IMF) and European Union institutions' intervention (European Commission, 2021; Lampropoulou & Oikonomou, 2018). The restructuring of the administration, the consolidation of public finances, the modernization of personnel management, the digitalization of services, and the introduction of performance management systems have been the major areas covered by these reform initiatives, which in effect, have amounted to one of the deepest public sector transformations in Europe (European Commission, 2021; Makrydemetres et al., 2016).

The historical context clearly indicates that features inherent to Greek public administration have been the main factors creating distinctive challenges for the implementation of change management strategies for a long time (Sotiropoulos, 2004; Spanou, 2008). Among these are highly bureaucratic structures that put great emphasis on formal rules and procedures, politicization of administrative appointments and decisions, clientelism and patronage relationships, as well as weak horizontal coordination among ministries and agencies, limited managerial autonomy and flexibility, resistance to performance accountability mechanisms, and tension between administrative law traditions and managerial reform principles (Sotiropoulos, 2004; Lampropoulou & Oikonomou, 2018; Spanou, 2008). The occurrence of these contextual factors has a great impact on the manner in which change initiatives are crafted, carried out, and the extent to which they are accepted by public servants (Makrydemetres et al., 2016; European Commission, 2021).

Table 3. Major reform initiatives in Greek public administration (2010-2021)

Reform Initiative	Period	Key Objectives	Change Management Approach	Implementation Challenges	Outcomes	References
Kallikratis Reform	2010-2011	Restructure local and regional administration; reduce number of municipalities from 1,034 to 325	Top-down, planned approach; limited stakeholder consultation	Strong resistance from affected municipalities; inadequate communication; insufficient employee support	Partial success: structural changes implemented but limited cultural transformation	Akrivos et al. (2013); European Commission (2021)
Administrative Reform 2013 (AR2013)	2013-2015	Restructure central government ministries; reduce organizational units and staff; establish administrative secretaries	Centralized, rapid implementation mandated by Troika; minimal employee involvement	Low employee morale; perception of punitive reform; political instability; lack of change management practices	Mixed: structural downsizing achieved but limited capacity building; employee skepticism increased	Makrydemetres et al. (2016); Akrivos et al. (2013)
Diavgeia (Transparency Program)	2010-present	Mandate online publication of all government decisions; enhance transparency and accountability	Technology-focused implementation; gradual rollout with training support	Initial technical issues; resistance from civil servants; concerns about workload	Moderate success: high compliance rates; recognized internationally; changed administrative culture toward transparency	Charalabidis et al. (2015); European Commission (2021)

continued on following page

Table 3. Continued

Reform Initiative	Period	Key Objectives	Change Management Approach	Implementation Challenges	Outcomes	References
Human Resource Management Reforms	2013-2018	Implement mobility schemes; establish performance appraisal systems; introduce competitive selection for managers	Mixed approach: some participatory elements but overall top-down under crisis pressure	Union resistance; lack of trust in merit-based systems; political interference; insufficient training	Limited success: systems formally established but implementation inconsistent; limited behavioral change	Spanou (2008); European Commission (2021)
Digital Transformation Initiatives	2015-2021	Digitalize public services; establish interoperability frameworks; develop integrated platforms	Technology-led with gradual process redesign; uneven change management across agencies	Inadequate training; resistance from employees; technical integration challenges; resource constraints	Partial success: progress in specific domains (tax, social security) but uneven across government	European Commission (2021); Charalabidis et al. (2015)
Fiscal Consolidation Measures	2010-2018	Reduce public sector wage bill through salary cuts (up to 40%) and workforce reduction (25% decrease)	Crisis-driven, emergency approach; limited consultation; focus on speed over acceptance	Severe employee morale decline; increased turnover intentions; loss of experienced staff; change fatigue	Fiscal targets met but significant costs: reduced capacity, low morale, reform skepticism, brain drain	European Commission (2021); Lampropoulou & Oikonomou (2018)
Institutional Memory Initiative	2016-present	Establish administrative secretaries in ministries to ensure continuity and institutional knowledge	Planned approach recognizing prior change management failures	Slow implementation; role ambiguity; resistance from political appointees; limited resources	Very limited success: few positions filled; unclear impact on institutional memory	European Commission (2021); Makrydemetres et al. (2016)
EU Technical Assistance Programs	2011-2021	Provide expertise and support for administrative modernization through EU Structural Reform Support Programme	Collaborative approach involving Greek officials and EU experts	Adaptation challenges; knowledge transfer limitations; coordination issues among multiple providers; sustainability concerns	Mixed: valuable expertise provided but limited sustainable capacity building; reliance on external support	European Commission (2021); Featherstone (2015)

5.2. Administrative Reform 2013: Strategic Change Implementation

Akrivos, Reklitis, and Prifti (2013) conducted a seminal study that examined the implementation of strategic change during the reforms of local and regional administration in Greece in 2012-2013. Their work used Kotter's eight-step change model as a lens for evaluating the level of strategic change implementation in the Greek public administration (Akrivos et al., 2013; Kotter, 1996). The study involved a survey of 180 public employees who were directly impacted by the reforms and asked them to report their impressions of the implementation of Kotter's steps based on their experience: establishing urgency, creating a guiding coalition, developing a vision and strategy, communicating the change vision, empowering broad-based action, generating short-term wins, consolidating gains and producing more change, and anchoring new approaches in culture (Akrivos et al., 2013).

The research has shown that there were severe shortcomings in the way change management was handled during these structural changes (Akrivos et al., 2013). The Greek public administration failed to effectively integrate core management principles, remaining a highly bureaucratic organization with limited vertical upward communication (Akrivos et al., 2013; Sotiropoulos, 2004). The reforms were regarded as forced measures imposed from above with the lack of involvement of stakeholders, indistinct communication about the reasons for change and the benefits expected, insufficient training and provision of support for employees affected, and absence of the so-called 'quick wins' showing benefits of change (Akrivos et al., 2013). As a result, the study found that civil servants were demotivated, distrustful of reform intentions and outcomes, and unwilling to go beyond the minimum requirements to actively support the changes (Akrivos et al., 2013).

These findings demonstrate that Greek public administration still largely reflects the characteristics of traditional bureaucratic systems despite the reform rhetoric over the last few decades. These traditional systems continue to pose obstacles to the implementation of changes in public administration (Sotiropoulos, 2004; Lampropoulou & Oikonomou, 2018). The study highlighted a significant gap between reform designers, who focused on structural and fiscal objectives, and employees who were affected by the reforms, experiencing them as threatening and feeling that they were poorly managed (Akrivos et al., 2013; European Commission, 2021). Such a disconnect leads to the inefficiency of change and thus to the continuation of the resistance to reforms, which has been a recurrent feature of the Greek public administration (Spanou, 2008; Sotiropoulos, 2004)

5.3. New Public Management Implementation Challenges

Using the lens of theoretical public administration models, Lampropoulou and Oikonomou (2018) analyzed the extent to which NPM principles were implemented in a restructuring of the Greek public administration system. According to their research, the reform rhetoric appeared to be heavily influenced by NPM language, which stressed efficiency, performance management, and market-oriented approaches, but the execution was selective and superficial most of the time (Lampropoulou & Oikonomou, 2018; Hood, 1991; Osborne, 2006).

Research indicates that reforms in Greek public administration were largely centered on fiscal consolidation through measures such as salary cuts and reductions in the number of employees in public administration, while less attention was paid to building up the administrative capacity and changing the culture of the public sector (Lampropoulou & Oikonomou, 2018; European Commission, 2021). In order to achieve the objective of reducing the size of the state, various structural reforms were put in place, such as the consolidation of ministries and the abolition of public entities (Makrydemetres et al., 2016). Nevertheless, changes in the areas of human resource management, implementation of performance management systems, innovation in service delivery, and managerial autonomy have been only sporadically realized (Lampropoulou & Oikonomou, 2018; Spanou, 2008).

The research highlighted several reasons for the limited effectiveness of the reforms. Among them, it was mentioned that there was a strong resistance from public sector unions, which were protecting the traditional employment conditions and job security, political instability and frequent changes of government which were interrupting the continuity of the reforms, lack of administrative capacity for designing and implementing complex reforms, less than necessary attention to change management and staff engagement, a conflict between austerity measures and reform investments that required resources, and the continuation of clientelistic political culture that was getting in the way of merit-based management (Lampropoulou & Oikonomou, 2018; Sotiropoulos, 2004). The results of the research indicate that managing change in the Greek public sector should not only involve the technical aspects of reform design but also the deeper institutional and cultural factors that influence the implementation process (Spanou, 2008; European Commission, 2021).

5.4. Digital Transformation and E-Government Initiatives

Greek public administration has implemented various digital transformation initiatives over the years, but the results have been mixed (European Commission, 2021; Charalabidis et al., 2015). Some of the most important initiatives are Diavgeia (a transparency program that makes it mandatory to publish government decisions online), the building of integrated digital service platforms, the setting up of interoperability frameworks that link different public sector systems, and the digitization of administrative procedures (Charalabidis et al., 2015; Kalampokis et al., 2013). These changes amount to a major restructuring of the organizations, which, besides the technological aspect, involve process revision, employee skill upgrading, and an ideological change towards the provision of services via the digital channel (Mergel et al., 2019).

Various studies on digital transformation in the Greek public administration disclose a mixed picture of advancement and obstacles that still exist (Charalabidis et al., 2015; European Commission, 2021). As a result of the availability of robust political support, sufficient funding, and the continuation of the implementation, a successful digitalization has been achieved in some specific areas such as the tax administration, social security, and business licensing (European Commission, 2021). On the other hand, a considerable number of digital initiatives have been delayed, have experienced only a partial implementation, and have been limited in the adoption by citizens and public servants (Charalabidis et al., 2015).

The change management issues related to digital transformation include, among others, the inadequate training and support of employees who are transitioning to digital systems, resistance of employees who are used to paper-based procedures, technical problems, and difficulties in system integration, neglect of user experience and citizen needs, and lack of process changes accompanying the implementation of technology (Charalabidis et al., 2015; Mergel et al., 2019). Research works point out that the successful digital transformation means that technology should be considered as a facilitator of organizational change, not as a solution, and therefore, enough attention should be given to change management practices, which prepare and support employees and redesign work processes (Fountain, 2001; European Commission, 2021).

5.5. Leadership and Organizational Identification

Trivellas and co-workers (2013) conducted an investigation into the relationship between leadership and employee satisfaction in Greek local government, revealing the integral connection between leadership and employee satisfaction in the context of change. Their research revealed that employees in the Greek public sector show weak organizational identification and low job satisfaction, which is part of the reason that a hostile discourse against public servants during the economic crisis and a series of changes in the organizations without the support and the consultation have been blamed for those phenomena (Trivellas et al., 2013; Papadopoulos et al., 2013).

The study found that the transformational leadership behavior of direct supervisors towards employees positively influenced employee attitudes and organizational identification (Trivellas et al., 2013; Bass, 1985). Nevertheless, the research acknowledged that there were limitations to the effectiveness of leadership in the Greek public administration arising from lack of managerial autonomy because of centrally controlled decision-making, staff rules that are rigid and thus, restrict the issuing of rewards and recognition, political interference in administrative matters and absence of leadership development programs which prepare managers to be leaders of change in the organization (Trivellas et al., 2013; Sotiropoulos, 2004). Therefore, the results suggest that fostering change leadership capability in the Greek public sector requires both individual leader development and the implementation of structural reforms to enhance managerial discretion (Lampropoulou & Oikonomou, 2018; Spanou, 2008).

5.6. Human Resource Management Reforms

The reforms in the Greek public sector have been deep and wide-ranging, with changes in the human resources management system as a major component. Some of these changes are the introduction of mobility programs that enable employees to transfer laterally between different organizations, the establishment of performance appraisal systems, the appointment of administrative secretaries (professional managers) in ministries, and the adoption of competitive selection processes for managerial positions (European Commission, 2021; Makrydemetres et al., 2016; Spanou, 2008). These HRM reforms signal the Greek public sector as an organization whose employees are the main target of these changes in their roles, career expectations, and working conditions (European Commission, 2021).

Research shows a variety of mixed effects regarding the actual implementation of HRM reforms (Makrydemetres et al., 2016; European Commission, 2021). Performance appraisal systems have been put in place at least on paper, but in most cases, they are void of any real consequences for career progression or remuneration; thus, their motivational effect is very limited (Spanou, 2008). Mobility schemes have primarily served the purpose of workforce reduction through forced transfers rather than talent development (European Commission, 2021). The competition to be selected for managerial positions is confronted with a number of challenges in its execution, among which are the political intervention and the lack of transparent criteria (Sotiropoulos, 2004; Lampropoulou & Oikonomou, 2018).

Resistance from employees who view reforms as a threat to their job security and career prospects is a significant challenge in change management during HRM reforms. Other difficulties include the lack of trust in the intentions of the reforms due to the history of politically motivated personnel decisions, the insufficient training of managers in the implementation of new HRM practices, and the absence of a supporting organizational culture that promotes performance and merit (Spanou, 2008; Sotiropoulos, 2004). Studies indicate that a successful HRM reform needs to be led by a sustained commitment, implemented transparently, show fairness, and have patience as trust is built through the consistent application over time (European Commission, 2021; Makrydemetres et al., 2016).

5.7. Fiscal Consolidation and Cutback Management

The Greek public administration had to go through a major fiscal consolidation that was achieved by cutting salaries significantly, reducing the number of employees in the public sector through hiring freezes and early retirement programs, making budget cuts that affected the supply of operational resources, and abolishing or merging public entities (European Commission, 2021; Kickert & Randma-Liiv,

2017). The management of these cutbacks is a special kind of organizational change that has some unique features, such as the loss of resources instead of resource growth, the negative impact on employees due to the reduction of their compensation and the increase of their workload, and the limited possibility to provide positive incentives for the cooperation (Overmans & Noordegraaf, 2014; Van der Voet & Vermeeren, 2017).

Research into cutback management in the Greek public administration reveals substantial challenges (European Commission, 2021; Lampropoulou & Oikonomou, 2018). Those who serve the public reported that the reforms and cutbacks were experienced as punishments imposed on them without proper explanation of the need and without consideration for fairness (Papadopoulos et al., 2013). The combination of salary cuts, reduced hiring, resulting in staff shortages, and increased workloads for existing staff led to low morale, stress, and burnout (Trivellas et al., 2013; European Commission, 2021). Publications show that during the austerity periods, the motivation of the public servants deteriorated and the intention to leave their jobs increased among the Greek civil servants (Papadopoulos et al., 2013; Sotiropoulos, 2004).

Implementing change management strategies during a period of cutbacks necessitates that one closely monitors the fairness of interactions with staff, communicates the reasons and criteria for the cutdowns in a very transparent way, ensures the core organizational capabilities are not compromised, provides support to the employees who are affected and, at the same time, tries to keep the organizational commitment despite the losses of resources (Van der Voet & Vermeeren, 2017; Overmans & Noordegraaf, 2014). The findings show that the Greek public administration has been managing the budget-cut-related issues in such a way that has neglected these considerations most of the time, thus resulting in negative effects on organizational capacity and employee attitudes over the longer term, which, in turn, may be still there even after the crisis has ended (European Commission, 2021; Lampropoulou & Oikonomou, 2018).

5.8. Institutional Memory and Capacity Building

The Administrative Reform 2013 brought about changes that included the provisions for the development of institutional memory through the setting up of Administrative Secretaries—professional managers who were given permanent appointments and were expected to be the ones providing continuity in the case of political turnover (Makrydemetres et al., 2016; European Commission, 2021). This reform highlighted that frequent changes in political appointees and senior executives result in the loss of knowledge, leading to the problem of reform discontinuity (Spanou, 2008). Nevertheless, the enactment of the law has been slow, as many ministries still lack fully established Administrative Secretaries, and there is some ambiguity regarding the functions and authority of their roles (European Commission, 2021; Lampropoulou & Oikonomou, 2018).

Studies show that the Greek public administration is plagued by a lack of deep organizational learning and knowledge management capabilities (Sotiropoulos, 2004; Spanou, 2008). As a result, change initiatives are frequently carried out without the systematic evaluation of previous reform experiences, thus causing the same errors to be repeated and the inability to move forward with the successful approaches (Lampropoulou & Oikonomou, 2018). The recording of reform processes and results remains at a low level, making it difficult to transfer knowledge (European Commission, 2021). The availability of professional development programs for public servants remains limited, which in turn restricts the skill enhancement necessary for addressing current administrative challenges, such as change management (Makrydemetres et al., 2016).

In order to create a change management system that works well with the public administration in Greece, it is necessary to make planned investments in knowledge management systems that keep track of reform experiences, professional development programs for civil servants of all levels, the establishment of centers of expertise in change management and organizational development, mechanisms that help learning from international best practices adapted to Greek context, and evaluation systems that produce evidence about the effectiveness of reforms (European Commission, 2021; Spanou, 2008). These capacity-building measures are the long-term investments that will pave the way for the more efficient handling of the current and future change initiatives (Makrydemetres et al., 2016).

5.9. Change Fatigue and Reform Skepticism

Reforms in the Greek public administration have been intense and frequent since 2010. These factors have made the public servants of the Greek administration quite indifferent to change, as evidenced by the numerous studies quoted by the authors (European Commission, 2021; Bernerth et al., 2011). The public sector employees' tiredness has been caused by the existence of various simultaneous reform initiatives without adequate coordination, insufficient time for consolidating changes before introducing new ones, and frequent policy reversals. As a result of these factors, employees have become more exhausted, cynical, and disengaged (Lampropoulou & Oikonomou, 2018; McMillan & Perron, 2013). Studies show that a large number of civil servants in Greece have become so skeptical of the reform intentions and their effectiveness that they consider reforms as a political tool used to gain advantage rather than real efforts to increase administrative capacity and improve service delivery (Akrivos et al., 2013; Papadopoulos et al., 2013).

This skepticism about reform constitutes a main obstacle to any future changes that require the employees' consent. The latter, according to the research, usually show some kind of passive resistance or minimal compliance with the so-called dark side of the organization, namely, lack of engagement and support (Akrivos et al., 2013; Ford et al., 2008). Greek civil servants are reported in numerous studies to be characterized by a wait-and-see attitude toward new reforms, and they consider that such initiatives will either disappear with the next government change or that they are superficial exercises that are detached from the operational realities (Sotiropoulos, 2004; Lampropoulou & Oikonomou, 2018). To get rid of such a mood, it is necessary first of all to show the real commitment to reform sustainability, and also to involve employees in reform design and implementation, demonstrate the benefits of the changes, and re-establish trust by a consistent and reliable implementation (European Commission, 2021; Fernandez & Rainey, 2006)

Figure 2. Skepticism about organizational change

5.10. European Union Influence and Technical Assistance

Reforms to the Greek public sector have been largely driven by the influence of the European Union institutions and technical assistance programs (European Commission, 2021; Featherstone, 2015). One of the main instruments of the European Commission, the Structural Reform Support Programme, has been the main source of both the expertise and the resources needed to carry out the administrative modernization objectives (European Commission, 2021). Further, technical assistance from different EU member states has thus enabled international expertise and provided Greece with a broad range of comparative perspectives to its reform efforts (Featherstone, 2015). These external interventions have been a double-edged sword in that they have facilitated the reform process by offering technical knowledge and resources, on the one hand, and complicated change management by bringing in more stakeholder perspectives and accountability relations, on the other (European Commission, 2021; Lampropoulou & Oikonomou, 2018).

Research on the impact of the EU's technical support to the Greek public administration indicates that the results are not clear-cut (Featherstone, 2015; European Commission, 2021). The external experts have been a source of knowledge on the best practices and the design of the reforms (European Commission, 2021). Nevertheless, among the obstacles listed are such as the difficulty of converting international examples into the Greek institutional framework, the problem of ensuring that knowledge is transferred to Greek civil servants beyond the duration of the project, the coordination of various technical assistance providers, and the management of the conflict between the external reform prescriptions and domestic political and administrative preferences (Featherstone, 2015; Lampropoulou & Oikonomou, 2018). Successful change management in situations with international technical assistance should focus on issues like local ownership, capacity building, cultural sensitivity, and long-term institutional development instead of simply bringing in external models without any adaptation (European Commission, 2021)

6. DISCUSSION

6.1. Key Findings From the Literature

The literature review has identified consistent findings regarding change management in publicly-funded organizations (Kuipers et al., 2014; Fernandez & Rainey, 2006). It was emphasized in the first place that carefully considering a multitude of interdependent factors is what ultimately leads to the success of change implementation, rather than a blind focus on technical or structural aspects (Kotter, 1996; Burke, 2018). These factors could be exemplified as leadership commitment, communication, employee involvement, provision of resources, a culture of support, and also the management of stakeholders from outside the organization, all of which have been found to influence the outcomes of change (Armenakis & Harris, 2009; Van der Voet et al., 2016). If change management practices ignore this or these aspects of a person or factor, then the failure of the implementation stage is inevitable (Kuipers et al., 2014).

Secondly, changes and results in the public sector are very much influenced by the government sector environment (Boyne, 2002; Rainey, 2014). Features such as politics, various accounts of management, a bureaucratic system, the professional characters, and the public's close watching give the public sector a different kind of both limitations and advantages to those of the private sector (Bozeman, 1987; Perry & Wise, 1990). Innovations in management and the use of such practices that have been worked out in the private sector need to be adjusted to the public sector's standards instead of being directly applied there (Kickert, 2014; Van der Voet, 2014).

Thirdly, factors at the personal level, particularly the employee's readiness, commitment, and belief in change, are the major determinants of the success of the implementation (Holt et al., 2007; Armenakis et al., 2007). A change in the organization whose employees are not supported due to bad communication, lack of participation, or employees' indifference has a very low chance of success, even if it is technically sound (Hameed et al., 2019; Rafferty & Restubog, 2010). An effective change in a company must involve the human aspect in the situation through the processes of preparing, equipping, and supporting employees in their changes (Weiner, 2009; Shea et al., 2014).

Fourth, leadership is a decisive but intricate factor that influences changes in the public sector (Van der Voet et al., 2016; Higgs & Rowland, 2005). Leadership commitment and an active role of the leader as a sponsor are, indeed, necessary for the success of the change; however, leadership behaviors have to be changed in accordance with public sector contexts, which are characterized by shared power, political oversight, and limited managerial discretion (Fernandez & Rainey, 2006; Hassan & Wright, 2020). Leading change effectively in public organizations entails, besides the usual change leadership skills, also the ability to manage political stakeholders, to deal with the institutional constraints, and to form coalitions crossing the organizational boundaries (Battilana et al., 2010; Van der Voet, 2014).

Fifth, change sustainability continues to be a major problem that needs thoughtful planning and continuous handling (Buchanan et al., 2005; Jacobs et al., 2015). A large number of change initiatives show success at the stage of the first implementation and then their results gradually vanish as the attention and resources are allocated to other places (Stirman et al., 2012). The process of sustaining change involves several key steps: firmly associating it with organizational systems, structures, and culture; demonstrating ongoing benefits; providing additional support; and, through effective leadership, maintaining the board's attention beyond the initial implementation stage (Jacobs et al., 2015; Buchanan et al., 2005).

Table 4. Critical success factors and barriers to change management in public sector organizations

Dimension	Critical Success Factors	Common Barriers	Evidence from Literature	Recommendations for Practice
Leadership	• Strong executive sponsorship • Active middle manager engagement • Transformational leadership behaviors • Visible commitment and role modeling • Coalition building across stakeholders	• Weak or inconsistent leadership support • Political interference • Frequent leadership turnover • Limited managerial authority • Conflicting priorities among leaders	Van der Voet et al. (2016); Fernandez & Rainey (2006); Battilana et al. (2010); Higgs & Rowland (2011)	Develop change leadership capabilities; secure multi-level sponsorship; establish governance structures; protect reforms from political cycles
Communication	• Early, frequent, and honest communication • Two-way dialogue and feedback • Multiple communication channels • Tailored messages for stakeholders • Addressing concerns transparently	• Inadequate or delayed communication • One-way information dissemination • Inconsistent messages • Failure to address employee concerns • Communication overload	Allen et al. (2007); Elving (2005); Klein (1996); Hameed et al. (2019); Graaf et al. (2019)	Develop comprehensive communication plans; establish feedback mechanisms; train managers in change communication; use diverse channels
Employee Participation	• Involvement in planning and decisions • Employee input genuinely considered • Participatory implementation approach • Empowerment and ownership • Recognition of contributions	• Top-down impositions • Token consultation without influence • Exclusion of affected employees • Limited opportunities for input • Perception of predetermined decisions	Lines (2004); Bordia et al. (2004); Rafferty & Restubog (2010); Hameed et al. (2019)	Create meaningful participation structures; involve employees early; ensure input influences decisions; balance participation with timely action

continued on following page

Table 4. Continued

Dimension	Critical Success Factors	Common Barriers	Evidence from Literature	Recommendations for Practice
Organizational Readiness	• Adequate resources allocated • Supportive organizational culture • Prior change experience • Capability and capacity present • Realistic expectations	• Resource constraints • Bureaucratic, resistant culture • Change fatigue from prior initiatives • Insufficient capacity • Unrealistic timelines	Weiner (2009); Shea et al. (2014); Helfrich et al. (2009); Klarner et al. (2008)	Assess readiness before launch; build capacity through training; address cultural barriers; secure adequate resources; sequence changes strategically
Individual Beliefs & Attitudes	• Positive beliefs about change necessity • Confidence in ability to change • Trust in management intentions • Perceived personal benefits • Low resistance	• Skepticism about change rationale • Low self-efficacy • Distrust of leadership • Fear of negative impacts • Active resistance	Holt et al. (2007); Armenakis et al. (2007); Oreg (2006); Piderit (2000)	Build compelling case for change; provide training to build efficacy; demonstrate management commitment; address resistance constructively; show early wins
Organizational Culture	• Innovation-oriented culture • Learning and adaptation valued • Trust and psychological safety • Flexibility and openness • Customer/citizen focus	• Bureaucratic rigidity • Risk aversion • Status quo bias • Punishment of mistakes • Inward focus	Schein (2010); Cameron & Quinn (2011); Jones et al. (2005); Lok & Crawford (2004)	Develop change-supportive culture long-term; model desired values; reward innovation; tolerate learning failures; align incentives with change
External Environment	• Political support and stability • Stakeholder alignment • Favorable public opinion • Adequate time for implementation • Learning from other contexts	• Political instability and opposition • Conflicting stakeholder demands • Negative media coverage • Crisis-driven urgency • Institutional constraints	Rainey (2014); Pollitt & Bouckaert (2017); Fernandez & Rainey (2006); Kickert & Randma-Liiv (2017)	Build stakeholder coalitions; manage political relationships; engage media strategically; balance urgency with thoroughness; adapt proven practices

continued on following page

Table 4. Continued

Dimension	Critical Success Factors	Common Barriers	Evidence from Literature	Recommendations for Practice
Change Process Management	• Clear vision and objectives • Structured but flexible approach • Adequate planning and preparation • Pilot testing and learning • Monitoring and adjustment	• Unclear goals • Rigid or chaotic process • Insufficient planning • No pilots or testing • Lack of progress monitoring	Kotter (1996); Van der Voet & Vermeeren (2017); Burnes (2004); Fernandez & Rainey (2006)	Articulate clear vision; balance planning with emergence; test and learn through pilots; establish metrics; adjust based on feedback
Sustainability Mechanisms	•Institutionalization in systems • Ongoing training and support • Performance measurement • Continued leadership attention • Knowledge management	• Lack of reinforcement • Decay after initial push • Loss of momentum • Staff turnover • Return to old practices	Buchanan et al. (2005); Jacobs et al. (2015); Stirman et al. (2012); Wiltsey Stirman et al. (2013)	Embed changes in policies/ procedures; provide continuous support; measure and reinforce; plan for transitions; document lessons learned
Context-Specific Factors (Greek Public Administration)	• EU technical support • Digital transformation successes • Crisis creating urgency • Some capacity building efforts • Learning from failures	• Change fatigue and skepticism • Clientelistic culture • Political instability • Austerity constraints • Limited institutional memory	Akrivos et al. (2013); Lampropoulou & Oikonomou (2018); European Commission (2021); Sotiropoulos (2004); Spanou (2008)	Address accumulated skepticism; build trust through consistent action; develop local capacity; ensure reform sustainability; learn systematically from experience

6.2. Implications for Greek Public Administration

A detailed study of Greek public administration indicates that difficulties in managing change in the public sector are a mix of common features of the public sector in general and also certain local aspects that are related to the Greek institutional traditions and the recent reform history (Lampropoulou & Oikonomou, 2018; Sotiropoulos, 2004). There are several implications for Greek public organizations to change management effectively (European Commission, 2021).

Initially, reform efforts should not only be concerned with the structural and financial aspects but also have a comprehensive change management component dealing with communication, participation, employee support, and cultural transformation (Akrivos et al., 2013; European Commission, 2021). The main focus of changes in structures from above has been inadequate to bring about the desired and lasting changes, which can be inferred from the cases of the failed implementation and the resistance of employees cited in the studies (Lampropoulou & Oikonomou, 2018; Sotiropoulos, 2004).

Secondly, according to the cited studies, one of the prerequisites for public sector reform to regain the level of trust from the society is building the trust and credibility of the political figures by continuing to implement them fairly, and being transparent over a period of time (Spanou, 2008; European Commission, 2021). The inheritance of reforms which were politically motivated, the frequent reversals of the policies, and the lack of sufficient attention to the employees' concerns have led to the creation of such a deep skepticism that it is impossible to overcome it only by the rhetorical statements of the officials (Akrivos et al., 2013; Papadopoulos et al., 2013). It will certainly be necessary to regain trust and ensure cooperation by demonstrating genuine commitment through actions, involving employees in reform processes, and showing them tangible benefits (Fernandez & Rainey, 2006; Hameed et al., 2019).

Thirdly, a Greek public administration strategic priority is to equip itself with change management capacity to be able to carry out lasting reforms (Makrydemetres et al., 2016; European Commission, 2021). As such it features the development of leadership change skills among managers at all levels, the creation of competence centers for organizational development and change management, the establishment of knowledge management systems recording reform experiences and getting ready for future challenges in the public sector, and the implementation of professional development programs provision civil servants with the necessary skills to handle the administrative challenges of today (Spanou, 2008; Ahmad et al., 2020).

Fourth, handling change fatigue necessitates additional strategic and synchronized methods for management of reform portfolios (Bernerth et al., 2011; McMillan & Perron, 2013). Instead of continuing several parallel projects without sufficient coordination, the Greek public administration ought to focus first on the essential reforms, plan the initiatives in such a way that there are periods for consolidation, coordinate the activities among the different departments so that the citizens are not misled with double information and to reduce the confusion and also keep track of the organizational capacity and employee well-being in order to be able to avert that the system gets too loaded (Rafferty & Griffin, 2006; European Commission, 2021).

Deleting political culture based on clientelism, focusing on rigid rules rather than results, aversion to risk, and limited horizontal coordination are all manifestations of deep institutional patterns that cannot be changed just by structural reforms (Spanou, 2008). According to recent research, cultural management is a long-term issue that must be at the top of the leadership's priorities list (Sotiropoulos, 2004; Lampropoulou & Oikonomou, 2018). Changing culture requires leadership's attention over a long period of time, a different incentive system, new employees getting used to reformed work cultures, and the fact that new ways of working produce better results (Schein, 2010; Cameron & Quinn, 2011).

6.3. Directions for Future Research

A number of significant gaps in the existing literature highlight the need for further research on change management in public sector organizations. These gaps are especially relevant to the context of the Greek public administration (Kuipers et al., 2014; Van der Voet, 2014).

Firstly, there are still very few longitudinal studies that follow change processes over time (Pettigrew et al., 2001; Van de Ven & Poole, 2005). The majority of research has been conducted using cross-sectional designs, which capture snapshots at single time points. Consequently, the process of change unfolding through phases, the impact of early implementation experiences on later outcomes, and the factors distinguishing sustained from temporary changes remain largely unknown (Kuipers et al., 2014). The panel studies following organizations and employees through complete change cycles would be instrumental in revealing the temporal dynamics and factors of sustainability (Buchanan et al., 2005; Jacobs et al., 2015).

Secondly, comparative research on change management across various public sector contexts, different types of organizations, and countries might pinpoint those results that generalize across settings and those that are due to specific factors of the context (Pollitt & Bouckaert, 2017; Andrews et al., 2017). Comparative research comprising Greek public administration and other European countries in the process of reform would make it clear whether the Greek difficulties are a reflection of the general dynamics of the public sector or of the specific features of the institution (Lampropoulou & Oikonomou, 2018; Featherstone, 2015).

Thirdly, more rigorous causal research using experimental or quasi-experimental designs may provide more solid evidence regarding which change management practices lead to improved outcomes (Shadish et al., 2002). Most of the research to date has been correlational, thereby causal inference is not made with a high degree of confidence (Kuipers et al., 2014). The use of field experiments that test different change management strategies, natural experiments that take advantage of variation in implementation timing or approaches, and advanced statistical techniques that deal with selection bias and confounding would, indeed, be a great step forward in the effectiveness determination process (Fernandez & Rainey, 2006; Van der Voet, 2014).

Fourth, studies on the mechanisms that show how change management practices affect the results would help to understand the theory more deeply (Armenakis & Harris, 2009; Rafferty et al., 2013). It is acknowledged by the research that these factors, e.g., leadership, communication, and participation, lead to change success; however, the psychological, social, and organizational processes involved in these factors are still not extensively understood (Hameed et al., 2019; Van der Voet et al., 2016). Mediation analyses and process-tracing studies can create a picture of the causal mechanisms (Oreg et al., 2011).

Fifth, studies on change management in emerging areas such as digital transformation, artificial intelligence adoption, collaborative governance, and public sector innovation would help address the modern challenges that the public sectors are facing (Mergel et al., 2019; Vial, 2019). As the public sector progressively implements these sophisticated changes, it is essential to determine how the fundamental principles of change management remain relevant in these new contexts (European Commission, 2021).

Finally, studies on the ways to surmount accumulated change fatigue and reform skepticism would be very instrumental in solving the problem of Greek public administration, which is not only suffering from such situations but also other contexts that are experiencing intense periods of reforms (Bernerth et al., 2011; McMillan & Perron, 2013). Knowing which measures can re-establish trust, bring back employee engagement, and foster receptivity to change after the times of reform overload would be an excellent resource for practitioners (Akrivos et al., 2013; European Commission, 2021).

7. CONCLUSIONS

This report conceptualizes and empirically measures change management in public sector organizations. They have also reviewed and synthesized recent research on public sector change management worldwide, while they have analyzed in detail the case of change management challenges and experiences in Greek public administration (Kuipers et al., 2014; Fernandez & Rainey, 2006; European Commission, 2021). From this discussion, a number of main conclusions can be derived.

Firstly, change management in public sector organizations is a complicated, multilayered issue that involves handling different aspects like technical, human, political, and institutional (Burke, 2018; Rainey, 2014). The success of the change depends on how well the various interrelated factors, such as leadership, communication, participation, resources, culture, individual attitudes, and external stakeholder relationships, are managed simultaneously (Armenakis & Harris, 2009; Van der Voet et al., 2016). Simple, narrowly targeted strategies that only bring structural or technical changes while ignoring the human and political aspects are quite unsuccessful in achieving the desired results (Kuipers et al., 2014; Kotter, 1996).

Secondly, the situation of the public sector is a very important factor that influences the manner in which processes of change unfold, as well as what management practices result in being effective (Boyne, 2002; Kickert, 2014). Public institutions function in highly unique and specialized surroundings with certain features like political dynamics, multiple accountability relationships, bureaucratic stances, and public scrutiny that, on one hand, pose challenges for change management and, on the other hand, provide opportunities for it (Bozeman, 1987; Pollitt & Bouckaert, 2017). Change management models and interventions that have been formulated in private sector settings have to be greatly altered to accommodate the realities of the public sector, and scholarly work should keep up with developing knowledge that is specific to the public sector instead of assuming that there can be a direct transfer of the private sector findings (Van der Voet, 2014).

Thirdly, to a large extent, valid measurement instruments represent the necessary tools to evaluate change management variables, to identify the organization's readiness, to keep track of the implementation, and to assess the results (Holt et al., 2007; Shea et al., 2014; Bouckenooghe et al., 2009). The instruments examined in this chapter have been found to possess not only strong psychometric qualities but also considerable applicability to the public sector (Helfrich et al., 2009; Cinite et al., 2009). Nevertheless, the decision of which instruments to use rests with practitioners and researchers who should determine the appropriateness of the instruments based on their specific objectives, organizational contexts, and change initiatives. They should not, however, make the mistake of any single instrument being suitable for all situations (Rafferty et al., 2013).

Fourth, the combined research evidence has the potential to guide public sector change management very effectively. However, it also indicates that there are quite a few gaps in our knowledge that call for more research to be done (Kuipers et al., 2014; Oreg et al., 2011). While the studies have identified the major points, such as leadership, communication, and involvement being the most crucial factors, there are still many questions about the causal mechanisms, contextual contingencies, implementation processes, and sustainability factors (Fernandez & Rainey, 2006; Buchanan et al., 2005). More stringent research designs, longitudinal studies, comparative analyses, and studies on the impact of the latest change issues would be advantageous to the field (Van der Voet, 2014; Pollitt & Bouckaert, 2017).

Finally, the Greek public administration example not only reveals the common management challenges that occur in the public sector during a change process but also shows the factors that are specific to the context and are influenced by the institutional traditions and the reform history, which has been recently changed (Lampropoulou & Oikonomou, 2018; Sotiropoulos, 2004). The Greek situations of the public sector reforms that have been carried out in reaction to the economic crisis teach how to lead changes during times of fiscal constraint and political pressure, the necessity of the change management to deal with employees' concerns and to ensure their engagement, the long-term effects of the reforms that are not properly managed including the change fatigue and the skepticism as well as the need for sustainable capacity building instead of the reform efforts that are only short-term (Akrivos et al., 2013; European Commission, 2021). Although the Greek public sector is encountering some issues which are a reflection of its institutional setting, the core ideas of the successful change management - leadership commitment, stakeholder engagement, communication, participation, resource adequacy, and sustained attention to implementation - are valid in any environment (Fernandez & Rainey, 2006; Kuipers et al., 2014).

As public sectors all over the world keep facing challenges that demand changes, such as budget cuts, technological progress, citizens' expectations, and complicated policy issues, the ability to manage changes effectively will be the main factor that determines the performance of the organization and the creation of public value (Pollitt & Bouckaert, 2017; Osborne, 2006). The present chapter has integrated the existing theoretical and empirical evidence to enhance both scholarly understanding and practical application of change management principles in public sector contexts (Kuipers et al., 2014). Further research, sharing of knowledge, and upgrading change management skills will be the main factors that will allow public organizations to be in a position to navigate the on-going transformations as well as those in the future and still be able to maintain the trust of the public and the effectiveness of the organization (Fernandez & Rainey, 2006; Van der Voet, 2014; European Commission, 2021).

REFERENCES

Ahmad, A., Faisal, F., Akhtar, R., & Abdul Wahab, S. (2020). Change management capability: The contribution of organizational structure and leadership. *Journal of Organizational Change Management, 33*(7), 1503–1519.

Ahmed, P. K. (1998). Culture and climate for innovation. *European Journal of Innovation Management, 1*(1), 30–43. DOI: 10.1108/14601069810199131

Ajzen, I. (1991). The theory of planned behavior. *Organizational Behavior and Human Decision Processes, 50*(2), 179–211. DOI: 10.1016/0749-5978(91)90020-T

Akrivos, D., Reklitis, P., & Prifti, E. (2013). Greek public administration reform: How to improve the effectiveness of strategic changes. *Procedia: Social and Behavioral Sciences, 73*, 710–717. DOI: 10.1016/j.sbspro.2013.02.109

Allen, J., Jimmieson, N. L., Bordia, P., & Irmer, B. E. (2007). Uncertainty during organizational change: Managing perceptions through communication. *Journal of Change Management, 7*(2), 187–210. DOI: 10.1080/14697010701563379

Andrews, R., Beynon, M. J., & McDermott, A. M. (2017). Organizational capability in the public sector: A configurational approach. *Journal of Public Administration: Research and Theory, 26*(2), 239–258. DOI: 10.1093/jopart/muv005

Armenakis, A. A., & Bedeian, A. G. (1999). Organizational change: A review of theory and research in the 1990s. *Journal of Management, 25*(3), 293–315. DOI: 10.1177/014920639902500303

Armenakis, A. A., Bernerth, J. B., Pitts, J. P., & Walker, H. J. (2007). Organizational change recipients' beliefs scale: Development of an assessment instrument. *The Journal of Applied Behavioral Science, 43*(4), 481–505. DOI: 10.1177/0021886307303654

Armenakis, A. A., & Harris, S. G. (2002). Crafting a change message to create transformational readiness. *Journal of Organizational Change Management, 15*(2), 169–183. DOI: 10.1108/09534810210423080

Armenakis, A. A., & Harris, S. G. (2009). Reflections: Our journey in organizational change research and practice. *Journal of Change Management, 9*(2), 127–142. DOI: 10.1080/14697010902879079

Armenakis, A. A., Harris, S. G., & Mossholder, K. W. (1993). Creating readiness for organizational change. *Human Relations, 46*(6), 681–703. DOI: 10.1177/001872679304600601

Avolio, B. J., Bass, B. M., & Jung, D. I. (1999). Re-examining the components of transformational and transactional leadership using the Multifactor Leadership Questionnaire. *Journal of Occupational and Organizational Psychology, 72*(4), 441–462. DOI: 10.1348/096317999166789

Balogun, J. (2003). From blaming the middle to harnessing its potential: Creating change intermediaries. *British Journal of Management, 14*(1), 69–83. DOI: 10.1111/1467-8551.00266

Bamford, D. R., & Forrester, P. L. (2003). Managing planned and emergent change within an operations management environment. *International Journal of Operations & Production Management, 23*(5), 546–564. DOI: 10.1108/01443570310471857

Bandura, A. (1997). *Self-efficacy: The exercise of control.* W.H. Freeman.

Bartunek, J. M., & Moch, M. K. (1987). First-order, second-order, and third-order change and organization development interventions: A cognitive approach. *The Journal of Applied Behavioral Science, 23*(4), 483–500. DOI: 10.1177/002188638702300404

Bass, B. M. (1985). *Leadership and performance beyond expectations.* Free Press.

Bass, B. M., & Avolio, B. J. (1997). *Full range leadership development: Manual for the Multifactor Leadership Questionnaire.* Mind Garden.

Battilana, J., Gilmartin, M., Sengul, M., Pache, A. C., & Alexander, J. A. (2010). Leadership competencies for implementing planned organizational change. *The Leadership Quarterly, 21*(3), 422–438. DOI: 10.1016/j.leaqua.2010.03.007

Belias, D., Ntalakos, A., Rossidis, I., Giannakos, K., & Koustelios, A. (2025). Can Leadership Styles Affect the Integration to Change and the Commitment to Change? A Case Study on Employees of Greek Four and Five-Star Hotels. In Pivac, T., Castanho, R. A. M. D., Martinelli, E., & Gonçalves, E. C. C. (Eds.), *The Innovative Pathway on Sustainable Culture Tourism. CST 2024. Advances in Science, Technology & Innovation.* Springer., DOI: 10.1007/978-3-031-86745-3_20

Belias, D., & Rossidis, I. (2025). *Change Management: Organizational Change and Organizational Behavior* [in Greek]. Tziolas Publications.

Belias, D., Rossidis, I., Mantas, C., & Ntalakos, A. (2024). Change Management and Emotional Intelligence Leadership: Strategies That the Emotional Intelligence Leadership Can Adopt During a Change Industry. In *Belias, D., Rossidis, I, Papademetriou, C. Organizational Behavior and Human Resource Management for Complex Work Environments* (pp. 186–203). IGI Global., DOI: 10.4018/979-8-3693-3466-9.ch010

Belias, D., Rossidis, I., Mantas, C., Ntalakos, A., Trihas, N., & Bakogiannis, D. (2023). The Effect of Strategic Leadership on the Integration and Success of Organizational Change. In *Managing Successful and Ethical Organizational Change* (pp. 54–74). IGI Global., DOI: 10.4018/979-8-3693-0235-4.ch003

Belias, D., Rossidis, I., Ntalakos, A., Trihas, N., Mantas, C., & Bakogiannis, D. (2023c). Ethics in Change Management: Current Issues and Directions for Future Research in the Post-COVID-19 Era. In *Managing Successful and Ethical Organizational Change* (pp. 279–300). IGI Global. DOI: 10.4018/979-8-3693-0235-4.ch012

Belias, D., Rossidis, I., Papademetriou, C., Masouras, A., & Anastasiadou, S. (2023b). *Managing Successful and Ethical Organizational Change*. IGI Global. DOI: 10.4018/979-8-3693-0235-4

Belias, D., Rossidis, I., Stavrinoudis, T., & Kakarougkas, C. (2024c). The Relationship between Change Management and Business Ethics: An Investigation on the Latest Developments - Key Issues on This Topic. In *Belias, D., Rossidis, I, Papademetriou, C. Organizational Behavior and Human Resource Management for Complex Work Environments* (pp. 148–165). IGI Global., DOI: 10.4018/979-8-3693-3466-9.ch008

Belias, D., & Trihas, N. (2023). How can we predict the integration and the success of organizational change in the hospitality sector? *Journal of Quality Assurance in Hospitality & Tourism*, *25*(6), 2011–2045. DOI: 10.1080/1528008X.2023.2216952

Belias, D., Trihas, N., Dimou, I., & Kourgiantakis, M. (2023d). The effect of goal motivation on the integration and the success of an organizational change in the hospitality sector. *In Proceedings on the 6th International Conference on Tourism Research*, 34-42. DOI: 10.34190/ictr.6.1.1083

Belias, D., Trihas, N., & Ntalakos, A. (2024b). Crisis Leadership, Group Dynamics, and Change Management: A Literature Review and Future Perspectives. In Katsoni, V., & Cassar, G. (Eds.), *Recent Advancements in Tourism Business, Technology and Social Sciences. IACuDiT 2023. Springer Proceedings in Business and Economics*. Springer., DOI: 10.1007/978-3-031-54342-5_13

Belias, D., Trihas, N., Ntalakos, A., Dimou, I., Rossidis, I., & Kourgiantakis, M. (2025b). Strategic Leadership and Its Effect on the Integration and the Success of Organizational Change on Four and Five Star Hotels. In Castanho, R. A., Pivac, T., & Mandić, A. (Eds.), *Legacy and Innovation. CST 2023. Advances in Science, Technology & Innovation*. Springer., DOI: 10.1007/978-3-031-59325-3_21

Belias, D., Trihas, N., Ntalakos, A., Dimou, I., Rossidis, I., & Kourgiantakis, M. (2025c). Can Human Resource Training Affect the Integration and Success of Organizational Change? A Case-Study on Employees of Greek Four and Five Star Hotels. In Castanho, R. A., Pivac, T., & Mandić, A. (Eds.), *Legacy and Innovation. CST 2023. Advances in Science, Technology & Innovation.* Springer., DOI: 10.1007/978-3-031-59325-3_19

Bernerth, J. B., Walker, H. J., & Harris, S. G. (2011). Change fatigue: Development and initial validation of a new measure. *Work and Stress, 25*(4), 321–337. DOI: 10.1080/02678373.2011.634280

Bordia, P., Hunt, E., Paulsen, N., Tourish, D., & DiFonzo, N. (2004). Uncertainty during organizational change: Is it all about control? *European Journal of Work and Organizational Psychology, 13*(3), 345–365. DOI: 10.1080/13594320444000128

Bordia, P., Restubog, S. L. D., Jimmieson, N. L., & Irmer, B. E. (2011). Haunted by the past: Effects of poor change management history on employee attitudes and turnover. *Group & Organization Management, 36*(2), 191–222. DOI: 10.1177/1059601110392990

Bouckenooghe, D. (2010). Positioning change recipients' attitudes toward change in the organizational change literature. *The Journal of Applied Behavioral Science, 46*(4), 500–531. DOI: 10.1177/0021886310367944

Bouckenooghe, D., Devos, G., & Van den Broeck, H. (2009). Organizational change questionnaire–climate of change, processes, and readiness: Development of a new instrument. *The Journal of Psychology, 143*(6), 559–599. DOI: 10.1080/00223980903218216 PMID: 19957876

Boyne, G. A. (2002). Public and private management: What's the difference? *Journal of Management Studies, 39*(1), 97–122. DOI: 10.1111/1467-6486.00284

Bozeman, B. (1987). *All organizations are public: Bridging public and private organizational theories.* Jossey-Bass.

Bryson, J. M., Crosby, B. C., & Bryson, J. K. (2009). Understanding strategic planning and the formulation and implementation of strategic plans as a way of knowing: The contributions of actor-network theory. *International Public Management Journal, 12*(2), 172–207. DOI: 10.1080/10967490902873473

Bryson, J. M., Cunningham, G. L., & Lokkesmoe, K. J. (2002). What to do when stakeholders matter: The case of problem formulation for the African American Men Project of Hennepin County, Minnesota. *Public Administration Review, 62*(5), 568–584. DOI: 10.1111/1540-6210.00238

Buchanan, D., Fitzgerald, L., Ketley, D., Gollop, R., Jones, J. L., Lamont, S. S., Neath, A., & Whitby, E. (2005). No going back: A review of the literature on sustaining organizational change. *International Journal of Management Reviews, 7*(3), 189–205. DOI: 10.1111/j.1468-2370.2005.00111.x

Burke, W. W. (2018). *Organization change: Theory and practice* (5th ed.). Sage Publications.

Burnes, B. (2004). Emergent change and planned change–competitors or allies? The case of XYZ construction. *International Journal of Operations & Production Management, 24*(9), 886–902. DOI: 10.1108/01443570410552108

Burnes, B., Hughes, M., & By, R. T. (2018). Reimagining organisational change leadership. *Leadership, 14*(2), 141–158.

By, R. T. (2005). Organisational change management: A critical review. *Journal of Change Management, 5*(4), 369–380. DOI: 10.1080/14697010500359250

By, R. T., Burnes, B., & Oswick, C. (2016). Change management: Leadership, values and ethics. *Journal of Change Management, 12*(1), 1–5. DOI: 10.1080/14697017.2011.652371

Cameron, E., & Green, M. (2019). *Making sense of change management: A complete guide to the models, tools and techniques of organizational change* (5th ed.). Kogan Page.

Cameron, K. S., & Quinn, R. E. (2011). *Diagnosing and changing organizational culture: Based on the competing values framework* (3rd ed.). Jossey-Bass.

Cepiku, D., Giordano, F., Boviatsou, A., & Tcherning, K. (2016). The second wave of performance management reforms in Southern Europe: Weberian bureaucracy and the Greek case. *Public Organization Review, 16*(1), 81–97.

Charalabidis, Y., Lampathaki, F., & Askounis, D. (2015). A comparative analysis of national interoperability frameworks. In Janssen, M., Scholl, H. J., Wimmer, M. A., & Tan, Y. (Eds.), *Electronic Government and Electronic Participation: Joint Proceedings of Ongoing Research and Projects of IFIP EGOV and EPart 2015* (pp. 91–98). IOS Press.

Choi, M., & Ruona, W. E. (2011). Individual readiness for organizational change and its implications for human resource and organization development. *Human Resource Development Review, 10*(1), 46–73. DOI: 10.1177/1534484310384957

Cinite, I., Duxbury, L. E., & Higgins, C. (2009). Measurement of perceived organizational readiness for change in the public sector. *British Journal of Management, 20*(2), 265–277. DOI: 10.1111/j.1467-8551.2008.00582.x

CMI (Change Management Institute). (2019). *The Organizational Change Maturity Model*. Change Management Institute.

Coch, L., & French, J. R. P.Jr. (1948). Overcoming resistance to change. *Human Relations, 1*(4), 512–532. DOI: 10.1177/001872674800100408

Cohen, W. M., & Levinthal, D. A. (1990). Absorptive capacity: A new perspective on learning and innovation. *Administrative Science Quarterly, 35*(1), 128–152. DOI: 10.2307/2393553

Daviotis, F., Belias, D., & Ntalakos, A. (2025). Organizational Commitment, Organizational Culture and Readiness for Change: Case study – Prevention Centers for Addiction and Promotion [in Greek]. *Epitheorisi Dimosias Dioikisis, 5*(1), 1–24.

DiFonzo, N., & Bordia, P. (1998). A tale of two corporations: Managing uncertainty during organizational change. *Human Resource Management, 37*(3-4), 295–303. DOI: 10.1002/(SICI)1099-050X(199823/24)37:3/4<295::AID-HRM10>3.0.CO;2-3

DiMaggio, P. J., & Powell, W. W. (1983). The iron cage revisited: Institutional isomorphism and collective rationality in organizational fields. *American Sociological Review, 48*(2), 147–160. DOI: 10.2307/2095101

Dunleavy, P., Margetts, H., Bastow, S., & Tinkler, J. (2006). New public management is dead—Long live digital-era governance. *Journal of Public Administration: Research and Theory, 16*(3), 467–494. DOI: 10.1093/jopart/mui057

Elving, W. J. (2005). The role of communication in organisational change. *Corporate Communications, 10*(2), 129–138. DOI: 10.1108/13563280510596943

European Commission. (2021). *Public administration reforms in Greece during the economic adjustment programmes: 2010-2018. Discussion Paper 167*. Publications Office of the European Union.

Featherstone, K. (2015). External conditionality and the debt crisis: The 'Troika' and public administration reform in Greece. *Journal of European Public Policy, 22*(3), 295–314. DOI: 10.1080/13501763.2014.955123

Fernandez, S., & Rainey, H. G. (2006). Managing successful organizational change in the public sector. *Public Administration Review, 66*(2), 168–176. DOI: 10.1111/j.1540-6210.2006.00570.x

Ford, J. D., Ford, L. W., & D'Amelio, A. (2008). Resistance to change: The rest of the story. *Academy of Management Review, 33*(2), 362–377. DOI: 10.5465/amr.2008.31193235

Fountain, J. E. (2001). *Building the virtual state: Information technology and institutional change*. Brookings Institution Press.

Gagnon, M. P., Attieh, R., Ghandour, E. K., Légaré, F., Ouimet, M., Estabrooks, C. A., & Roch, G. (2014). A systematic review of instruments to assess organizational readiness for knowledge translation in health care. *PLoS One, 9*(12), e114338. DOI: 10.1371/journal.pone.0114338 PMID: 25474622

Giannakos, K., Belias, D., Ntalakos, A., & Rossidis, I. (2024a). Change Management and Communication Satisfaction: Adopting Effective Change Management Strategies for Enhancing Communication Satisfaction. In *Belias, D., Rossidis, I, Papademetriou, C. Organizational Behavior and Human Resource Management for Complex Work Environments* (pp. 221–241). IGI Global., DOI: 10.4018/979-8-3693-3466-9.ch012

Giannakos, K., Belias, D., Ntalakos, A., & Rossidis, I. (2024b). Creating the Appropriate Organizational Culture for Change Management. In *Belias, D., Rossidis, I, Papademetriou, C. Organizational Behavior and Human Resource Management for Complex Work Environments* (pp. 166–185). IGI Global., DOI: 10.4018/979-8-3693-3466-9.ch009

Giannakos, K., Belias, D., Ntalakos, A., Rossidis, I., & Koustelios, A. (2024c). Are leadership styles related to change integration and commitment? The case of general hospitals in the area of Thessaly (Greece). *Archives of Hellenic Medicine/Arheia Ellenikes Iatrikes*, 41(3).

Gill, R. (2003). Change management—Or change leadership? *Journal of Change Management, 3*(4), 307–318. DOI: 10.1080/714023845

Gilley, A., Dixon, P., & Gilley, J. W. (2008). Characteristics of leadership effectiveness: Implementing change and driving innovation in organizations. *Human Resource Development Quarterly, 19*(2), 153–169. DOI: 10.1002/hrdq.1232

Goldfinch, S. (2007). Pessimism, computer failure, and information systems development in the public sector. *Public Administration Review, 67*(5), 917–929. DOI: 10.1111/j.1540-6210.2007.00778.x

Graaf, G., Hengeveld-Bidmon, E., Carnochan, S., Salomone, M., & Austin, M. J. (2019). Change communication in public sector cutback management. *Public Organization Review, 19*(4), 453–472. DOI: 10.1007/s11115-018-0408-8

Greenwood, R., & Hinings, C. R. (1996). Understanding radical organizational change: Bringing together the old and the new institutionalism. *Academy of Management Review*, *21*(4), 1022–1054. DOI: 10.2307/259163

Hameed, I., Waris, I., & Amin ul Haq, M. (2019). Predicting eco-conscious consumer behavior using theory of planned behavior in Pakistan. *Environmental Science and Pollution Research International*, *26*(15), 15535–15547. DOI: 10.1007/s11356-019-04967-9 PMID: 30945077

Hassan, S., & Wright, B. E. (2020). The public service motivation causal chain: Personality, socialization, public service motivation, and work outcomes. *International Public Management Journal*, *23*(3), 356–379.

Hayes, J. (2018). *The theory and practice of change management* (5th ed.). Palgrave Macmillan. DOI: 10.1057/978-1-352-00132-7

Heckman, R., Nimon, K., Chuang, A., & Kinney, T. B. (2021). The relationship between HR capability and business strategy, competitive strategy, and macro-environmental factors. *Personnel Review*, *50*(2), 589–603.

Helfrich, C. D., Li, Y. F., Sharp, N. D., & Sales, A. E. (2009). Organizational readiness to change assessment (ORCA): Development of an instrument based on the Promoting Action on Research in Health Services (PARIHS) framework. *Implementation Science : IS*, *4*(1), 38. DOI: 10.1186/1748-5908-4-38 PMID: 19594942

Herold, D. M., Fedor, D. B., Caldwell, S., & Liu, Y. (2008). The effects of transformational and change leadership on employees' commitment to a change: A multilevel study. *The Journal of Applied Psychology*, *93*(2), 346–357. DOI: 10.1037/0021-9010.93.2.346 PMID: 18361637

Herscovitch, L., & Meyer, J. P. (2002). Commitment to organizational change: Extension of a three-component model. *The Journal of Applied Psychology*, *87*(3), 474–487. DOI: 10.1037/0021-9010.87.3.474 PMID: 12090605

Hiatt, J., & Creasey, T. J. (2012). *Change management: The people side of change* (2nd ed.). Prosci.

Hiatt, J. M. (2006). *ADKAR: A model for change in business, government, and our community*. Prosci Learning Center Publications.

Higgs, M., & Rowland, D. (2005). All changes great and small: Exploring approaches to change and its leadership. *Journal of Change Management*, *5*(2), 121–151. DOI: 10.1080/14697010500082902

Higgs, M., & Rowland, D. (2011). What does it take to implement change successfully? A study of the behaviors of successful change leaders. *The Journal of Applied Behavioral Science*, *47*(3), 309–335. DOI: 10.1177/0021886311404556

Holt, D. T., Armenakis, A. A., Feild, H. S., & Harris, S. G. (2007). Readiness for organizational change: The systematic development of a scale. *The Journal of Applied Behavioral Science*, *43*(2), 232–255. DOI: 10.1177/0021886306295295

Hood, C. (1991). A public management for all seasons? *Public Administration*, *69*(1), 3–19. DOI: 10.1111/j.1467-9299.1991.tb00779.x

Huber, T., Swart, J., & Hecker, A. (2015). Initial impacts of organizational change: Emotions in a technology company. *Team Performance Management*, *21*(5/6), 303–318.

Hughes, M. (2018). *Managing and leading organizational change*. Routledge. DOI: 10.4324/9781351265966

Hupe, P., & Hill, M. (2007). Street-level bureaucracy and public accountability. *Public Administration*, *85*(2), 279–299. DOI: 10.1111/j.1467-9299.2007.00650.x

Hussain, S. T., Lei, S., Akram, T., Haider, M. J., Hussain, S. H., & Ali, M. (2018). Kurt Lewin's change model: A critical review of the role of leadership and employee involvement in organizational change. *Journal of Innovation & Knowledge*, *3*(3), 123–127. DOI: 10.1016/j.jik.2016.07.002

Huy, Q. N. (2001). In praise of middle managers. *Harvard Business Review*, *79*(8), 72–79. PMID: 11550632

Jacobs, G., van Witteloostuijn, A., & Christe-Zeyse, J. (2013). A theoretical framework of organizational change. *Journal of Organizational Change Management*, *26*(5), 772–792. DOI: 10.1108/JOCM-09-2012-0137

Jacobs, S. R., Weiner, B. J., Reeve, B. B., Hofmann, D. A., Christian, M., & Weinberger, M. (2015). Determining the predictors of innovation implementation in healthcare: A quantitative analysis of implementation effectiveness. *BMC Health Services Research*, *15*(1), 6. DOI: 10.1186/s12913-014-0657-3 PMID: 25608564

Jensen, U. T., Andersen, L. B., & Holten, A. L. (2019). Explaining a dark side: Public service motivation, presenteeism, and absenteeism. *Review of Public Personnel Administration*, *39*(4), 487–510. DOI: 10.1177/0734371X17744865

Jones, R. A., Jimmieson, N. L., & Griffiths, A. (2005). The impact of organizational culture and reshaping capabilities on change implementation success: The mediating role of readiness for change. *Journal of Management Studies*, *42*(2), 361–386. DOI: 10.1111/j.1467-6486.2005.00500.x

Judge, T. A., & Piccolo, R. F. (2004). Transformational and transactional leadership: A meta-analytic test of their relative validity. *The Journal of Applied Psychology*, *89*(5), 755–768. DOI: 10.1037/0021-9010.89.5.755 PMID: 15506858

Judge, W. Q., & Douglas, T. (2009). Organizational change capacity: The systematic development of a scale. *Journal of Organizational Change Management*, *22*(6), 635–649. DOI: 10.1108/09534810910997041

Kalampokis, E., Tambouris, E., & Tarabanis, K. (2013). Linked open government data analytics. In Wimmer, M., Janssen, M., & Scholl, H. J. (Eds.), *Electronic Government* (pp. 99–110). Springer. DOI: 10.1007/978-3-642-40358-3_9

Kickert, W. (2014). Specificity of change management in public organizations: Conditions for successful organizational change in Dutch ministerial departments. *American Review of Public Administration*, *44*(6), 693–717. DOI: 10.1177/0275074013483871

Kickert, W., & Randma-Liiv, T. (2017). *Europe Managing the Crisis: The Politics of Fiscal Consolidation*. Routledge.

Klarner, P., Probst, G., & Soparnot, R. (2008). Organizational change capacity in public services: The case of the World Health Organization. *Journal of Change Management*, *8*(1), 57–72. DOI: 10.1080/14697010801937523

Klein, S. M. (1996). A management communication strategy for change. *Journal of Organizational Change Management*, *9*(2), 32–46. DOI: 10.1108/09534819610113720

Kotter, J. P. (1996). *Leading change*. Harvard Business School Press.

Kuenzi, M., & Schminke, M. (2009). Assembling fragments into a lens: A review, critique, and proposed research agenda for the organizational work climate literature. *Journal of Management*, *35*(3), 634–717. DOI: 10.1177/0149206308330559

Kuipers, B. S., Higgs, M., Kickert, W., Tummers, L., Grandia, J., & Van der Voet, J. (2014). The management of change in public organizations: A literature review. *Public Administration*, *92*(1), 1–20. DOI: 10.1111/padm.12040

Lampropoulou, M., & Oikonomou, G. (2018). Theoretical models of public administration and patterns of state reform in Greece. *International Review of Administrative Sciences*, *84*(1), 101–121. DOI: 10.1177/0020852315611219

Layne, K., & Lee, J. (2001). Developing fully functional e-government: A four stage model. *Government Information Quarterly, 18*(2), 122–136. DOI: 10.1016/S0740-624X(01)00066-1

Levy, A., & Merry, U. (1986). *Organizational transformation: Approaches, strategies, theories*. Praeger Publishers. DOI: 10.5040/9798400693960

Lewis, L. K. (2000). Communicating change: Four cases of quality programs. *Journal of Business Communication, 37*(2), 128–155. DOI: 10.1177/002194360003700201

Lindgren, I., & Van Veenstra, A. F. (2018). Digital government transformation: A case illustrating public e-service development as part of public sector transformation. *In Proceedings of the 19th Annual International Conference on Digital Government Research: Governance in the Data Age* (pp. 1-6). DOI: 10.1145/3209281.3209302

Lines, R. (2004). Influence of participation in strategic change: Resistance, organizational commitment and change goal achievement. *Journal of Change Management, 4*(3), 193–215. DOI: 10.1080/1469701042000221696

Lok, P., & Crawford, J. (2004). The effect of organisational culture and leadership style on job satisfaction and organisational commitment: A cross-national comparison. *Journal of Management Development, 23*(4), 321–338. DOI: 10.1108/02621710410529785

Makrydemetres, A., Zervopoulos, P. D., & Pravita, M. E. (2016). Reform of public administration in Greece: Evaluating structural reform of central government departments in Greece. *GreeSE Paper* No. 97. Hellenic Observatory, London School of Economics.

McMillan, K., & Perron, A. (2013). Nurses amidst change: The concept of change fatigue offers an alternative perspective on organizational change. *Policy, Politics & Nursing Practice, 14*(1), 26–32. DOI: 10.1177/1527154413481811 PMID: 23549748

Men, L. R. (2014). Why leadership matters to internal communication: Linking transformational leadership, symmetrical communication, and employee outcomes. *Journal of Public Relations Research, 26*(3), 256–279. DOI: 10.1080/1062726X.2014.908719

Mergel, I., Edelmann, N., & Haug, N. (2019). Defining digital transformation: Results from expert interviews. *Government Information Quarterly, 36*(4), 101385. DOI: 10.1016/j.giq.2019.06.002

Meyer, A. D., Brooks, G. R., & Goes, J. B. (1990). Environmental jolts and industry revolutions: Organizational responses to discontinuous change. *Strategic Management Journal, 11*, 93–110.

Miake-Lye, I. M., Delevan, D. M., Ganz, D. A., Mittman, B. S., & Finley, E. P. (2020). Unpacking organizational readiness for change: An updated systematic review and content analysis of assessments. *BMC Health Services Research, 20*(1), 106. DOI: 10.1186/s12913-020-4926-z PMID: 32046708

Moynihan, D. P., & Pandey, S. K. (2007). The role of organizations in fostering public service motivation. *Public Administration Review, 67*(1), 40–53. DOI: 10.1111/j.1540-6210.2006.00695.x

Noordegraaf, M. (2007). From "pure" to "hybrid" professionalism: Present-day professionalism in ambiguous public domains. *Administration & Society, 39*(6), 761–785. DOI: 10.1177/0095399707304434

Ntalakos, A., Belias, D., & Koustelios, A. (2024b). The Relationship between Leadership Styles, Organizational Culture and Group Dynamics in the Hospitality Industry. In Katsoni, V., & Cassar, G. (Eds.), *Recent Advancements in Tourism Business, Technology and Social Sciences. IACuDiT 2023. Springer Proceedings in Business and Economics.* Springer., DOI: 10.1007/978-3-031-54342-5_19

Ntalakos, A., Belias, D., Koustelios, A., & Tsigilis, N. (2022). Organizational culture and group dynamics in the tourism industry. *In Silva, C., Oliveira, M., Silva, S., ICTR 2022 5th International Conference on Tourism Research, Porto, Portugal,* 19-20 May, 2022, 286-293.

Ntalakos, A., Belias, D., Rossidis, I., Koustelios, A., Tsigilis, N., & Vasiliadis, L. (2023). Communicating the Vision of the Change: The Linkage between Organizational Communication, Organizational Culture, and Organizational Change. In *Managing Successful and Ethical Organizational Change* (pp. 76–101). IGI Global., DOI: 10.4018/979-8-3693-0235-4.ch004

Ntalakos, A., Belias, D., & Tsigilis, N. (2024a). Analyzing the Organizational Factors that Influence Hotel Employees' Team Efficiency. In Katsoni, V., & Cassar, G. (Eds.), *Recent Advancements in Tourism Business, Technology and Social Sciences. IACuDiT 2023. Springer Proceedings in Business and Economics.* Springer., DOI: 10.1007/978-3-031-54342-5_11

Oreg, S. (2006). Personality, context, and resistance to organizational change. *European Journal of Work and Organizational Psychology, 15*(1), 73–101. DOI: 10.1080/13594320500451247

Oreg, S., Vakola, M., & Armenakis, A. (2011). Change recipients' reactions to organizational change: A 60-year review of quantitative studies. *The Journal of Applied Behavioral Science, 47*(4), 461–524. DOI: 10.1177/0021886310396550

Osborne, S. P. (2006). The new public governance? *Public Management Review*, *8*(3), 377–387. DOI: 10.1080/14719030600853022

Overmans, T., & Noordegraaf, M. (2014). Managing austerity: Rhetorical and real responses to fiscal stress in local government. *Public Money & Management*, *34*(2), 99–106. DOI: 10.1080/09540962.2014.887517

Papadopoulos, I., Ozbilgin, M., & Ozbilgin, N. F. (2013). Understanding changing patterns of migration behaviour during the Greek crisis. *International Migration (Geneva, Switzerland)*, *52*(3), 61–80.

Perry, J. L., & Wise, L. R. (1990). The motivational bases of public service. *Public Administration Review*, *50*(3), 367–373. DOI: 10.2307/976618

Pettigrew, A. M., Woodman, R. W., & Cameron, K. S. (2001). Studying organizational change and development: Challenges for future research. *Academy of Management Journal*, *44*(4), 697–713. DOI: 10.2307/3069411

Piderit, S. K. (2000). Rethinking resistance and recognizing ambivalence: A multidimensional view of attitudes toward an organizational change. *Academy of Management Review*, *25*(4), 783–794. DOI: 10.2307/259206

Pollitt, C., & Bouckaert, G. (2017). *Public management reform: A comparative analysis—Into the age of austerity* (4th ed.). Oxford University Press.

Prosci. (2018). *Best practices in change management (10th ed.)*. Prosci.

Rafferty, A. E., & Griffin, M. A. (2006). Perceptions of organizational change: A stress and coping perspective. *The Journal of Applied Psychology*, *91*(5), 1154–1162. DOI: 10.1037/0021-9010.91.5.1154 PMID: 16953776

Rafferty, A. E., Jimmieson, N. L., & Armenakis, A. A. (2013). Change readiness: A multilevel review. *Journal of Management*, *39*(1), 110–135. DOI: 10.1177/0149206312457417

Rafferty, A. E., & Restubog, S. L. D. (2010). The impact of change process and context on change reactions and turnover during a merger. *Journal of Management*, *36*(5), 1309–1338. DOI: 10.1177/0149206309341480

Rainey, H. G. (2014). *Understanding and managing public organizations* (5th ed.). Jossey-Bass.

Rossidis, I., Belias, D., & Aspridis, G. (2020). *Change management and leadership*. Tziolas Publications. (Original work published 2020). [in Greek]

Sagie, A., & Koslowsky, M. (2000). *Participation and empowerment in organizations: Modeling, effectiveness, and applications*. Sage Publications. DOI: 10.4135/9781452231341

Schein, E. H. (2010). *Organizational culture and leadership* (4th ed.). Jossey-Bass.

Schneider, B., Ehrhart, M. G., & Macey, W. H. (2013). Organizational climate and culture. *Annual Review of Psychology, 64*(1), 361–388. DOI: 10.1146/annurev-psych-113011-143809 PMID: 22856467

Scott, W. R. (2014). *Institutions and organizations: Ideas, interests, and identities* (4th ed.). Sage Publications.

Scott, W. R., & Davis, G. F. (2015). *Organizations and organizing: Rational, natural and open systems perspectives*. Routledge. DOI: 10.4324/9781315663371

Shadish, W. R., Cook, T. D., & Campbell, D. T. (2002). *Experimental and quasi-experimental designs for generalized causal inference*. Houghton Mifflin.

Shea, C. M., Jacobs, S. R., Esserman, D. A., Bruce, K., & Weiner, B. J. (2014). Organizational readiness for implementing change: A psychometric assessment of a new measure. *Implementation Science : IS, 9*(1), 7. DOI: 10.1186/1748-5908-9-7 PMID: 24410955

Sotiropoulos, D. A. (2004). Southern European public bureaucracies in comparative perspective. *West European Politics, 27*(3), 405–422. DOI: 10.1080/0140238042000228077

Spanou, C. (2008). State reform in Greece: Responding to old and new challenges. *International Journal of Public Sector Management, 21*(2), 150–173. DOI: 10.1108/09513550810855645

Stirman, S. W., Kimberly, J., Cook, N., Calloway, A., Castro, F., & Charns, M. (2012). The sustainability of new programs and innovations: A review of the empirical literature and recommendations for future research. *Implementation Science : IS, 7*(1), 17. DOI: 10.1186/1748-5908-7-17 PMID: 22417162

Thomas, R., & Davies, A. (2005). Theorizing the micro-politics of resistance: New public management and managerial identities in the UK public services. *Organization Studies, 26*(5), 683–706. DOI: 10.1177/0170840605051821

Trivellas, P., Reklitis, P., & Platis, C. (2013). The effect of job related stress on employees' satisfaction: A survey in health care. *Procedia: Social and Behavioral Sciences, 73*, 718–726. DOI: 10.1016/j.sbspro.2013.02.110

Van de Ven, A. H., & Poole, M. S. (2005). Alternative approaches for studying organizational change. *Organization Studies*, *26*(9), 1377–1404. DOI: 10.1177/0170840605056907

Van der Voet, J. (2014). The effectiveness and specificity of change management in a public organization: Transformational leadership and a bureaucratic organizational structure. *European Management Journal*, *32*(3), 373–382. DOI: 10.1016/j.emj.2013.10.001

Van der Voet, J., Groeneveld, S., & Kuipers, B. S. (2014). Talking the talk or walking the walk? The leadership of planned and emergent change in a public organization. *Journal of Change Management*, *14*(2), 171–191. DOI: 10.1080/14697017.2013.805160

Van der Voet, J., Kuipers, B. S., & Groeneveld, S. (2015). Held back and pushed forward: Leading change in a complex public sector environment. *Journal of Organizational Change Management*, *28*(2), 290–300. DOI: 10.1108/JOCM-09-2013-0182

Van der Voet, J., Kuipers, B. S., & Groeneveld, S. (2016). Implementing change in public organizations: The relationship between leadership and affective commitment to change in a public sector context. *Public Management Review*, *18*(6), 842–865. DOI: 10.1080/14719037.2015.1045020

Van der Voet, J., & Vermeeren, B. (2017). Change management in hard times: Can change management mitigate the negative relationship between cutbacks and the organizational commitment and work engagement of public sector employees? *American Review of Public Administration*, *47*(2), 230–252. DOI: 10.1177/0275074015625828

Vial, G. (2019). Understanding digital transformation: A review and a research agenda. *The Journal of Strategic Information Systems*, *28*(2), 118–144. DOI: 10.1016/j.jsis.2019.01.003

Walker, R. M., Brewer, G. A., Boyne, G. A., & Avellaneda, C. N. (2011). Market orientation and public service performance: New public management gone mad? *Public Administration Review*, *71*(5), 707–717. DOI: 10.1111/j.1540-6210.2011.02410.x

Wanberg, C. R., & Banas, J. T. (2000). Predictors and outcomes of openness to changes in a reorganizing workplace. *The Journal of Applied Psychology*, *85*(1), 132–142. DOI: 10.1037/0021-9010.85.1.132 PMID: 10740964

Weick, K. E., & Quinn, R. E. (1999). Organizational change and development. *Annual Review of Psychology*, *50*(1), 361–386. DOI: 10.1146/annurev.psych.50.1.361 PMID: 15012461

Weiner, B. J. (2009). A theory of organizational readiness for change. *Implementation Science : IS*, *4*(1), 67. DOI: 10.1186/1748-5908-4-67 PMID: 19840381

Weiner, B. J., Amick, H., & Lee, S. Y. D. (2008). Conceptualization and measurement of organizational readiness for change: A review of the literature in health services research and other fields. *Medical Care Research and Review : MCRR, 65*(4), 379–436. DOI: 10.1177/1077558708317802 PMID: 18511812

Weiner, B. J., Lewis, C. C., Stanick, C., Powell, B. J., Dorsey, C. N., Clary, A. S., Boynton, M. H., & Halko, H. (2017). Psychometric assessment of three newly developed implementation outcome measures. *Implementation Science : IS, 12*(1), 108. DOI: 10.1186/s13012-017-0635-3 PMID: 28851459

Wilson, J. Q. (1989). *Bureaucracy: What government agencies do and why they do it.* Basic Books.

Wiltsey Stirman, S., Calloway, A., Toder, K., Miller, C. J., DeVito, A. K., Meisel, S. N., & Crits-Christoph, P. (2013). Community mental health provider modifications to an evidence-based psychosocial treatment and implications for sustained implementation. *Psychiatric Services (Washington, D.C.), 64*(10), 1056–1059. DOI: 10.1176/appi.ps.201200456 PMID: 24081406

Wright, B. E., & Pandey, S. K. (2010). Transformational leadership in the public sector: Does structure matter? *Journal of Public Administration: Research and Theory, 20*(1), 75–89. DOI: 10.1093/jopart/mup003

Zahra, S. A., & George, G. (2002). Absorptive capacity: A review, reconceptualization, and extension. *Academy of Management Review, 27*(2), 185–203. DOI: 10.2307/4134351

Chapter 8
Managing Public Enterprises in the Modern Administrative State:
The Case of Greece

Ioannis Rossidis
http://orcid.org/0000-0003-0240-2241
Panteion University, Greece

Haralampos Chrysomallidis
http://orcid.org/0000-0003-3889-1868
University of the Peloponnese, Greece

George Kentas
University of Nicosia, Cyprus

ABSTRACT

Public enterprises constitute a significant pillar of state administration, contributing both to the provision of basic services and to the formulation of strategic priorities. This analysis examines their adjustment in the light of modern administrative models such as New Public Management and Public Governance, including the adoption of modern administrative pursuits such as result oriented management, citizen-client satisfaction, integration of digital transformation, the development of learning structures, etc. This study analyses critically the privatization of public organizations as a means of improving competitiveness and efficiency along with the sharp criticism of undermining public value, transparency and the public interest. Special reference is made to the case of Greece, where public enterprises have historically served as tools of national development and employment policy, but have been characterized by inefficiency, political interference and negative economic results.

DOI: 10.4018/979-8-3373-3526-1.ch008

1. INTRODUCTION

Public enterprises constitute a particularly important part of the public sector, serving defined missions. The multifaceted roles they assume are most often located between public governance and market dynamics, undertaking various tasks such as the provision of public utility services, the development of entrepreneurial activity and the protection of public interests. Their value orientation incorporates the principles of effectiveness, efficiency, cost-effectiveness and competitiveness (Christiansen and Kim, 2020; OECD, 2021). Public enterprises are administrative structures that present elements of a public organization and at the same time a commercial entity, making their work particularly complex as they are called upon to serve (directly or indirectly) specific public policies while at the same time having to ensure sustainability in highly competitive environments. Their mission is rendered even more difficult in the uncertain, dynamic and volatile contemporary environment governed by globalized conditions, rapid technological developments, intense budgetary constraints, increasing demands for transparency and accountability, etc. (Rossidis, 2014).

The importance of public enterprise management has been at the center of strategic analysis in recent years, since the role of the state as an economic actor is being reexamined after the Financial Crisis and the COVID-19 pandemic (Florio and Fecher, 2021; Musacchio and Lazzarini, 2022). Public enterprises have at times played key roles in dealing with crises, at multiple levels such as: energy, transport, telecommunications, banking, etc. (OECD, 2023). The readjustment of the economic and political aspirations of governments (focusing on the regulatory role of the State) has led to the reexamination of the governance frameworks of public enterprises in order to shape a new balance between business performance and broader public value (Cui and Jiang, 2019; Bruton et al., 2021). These developments have reignited the scientific debate and administrative analyses on the contribution of public enterprises to the evolving architecture of state administration.

In this context, the case of Greece is examined as a country with a historically multifaceted activity of public enterprises. The Greek state administration is undergoing a prolonged period of reforms attempting to reshape the structure and improve the overall efficiency of the public sector. In this spirit, public enterprises are undergoing a comprehensive redefinition of their role and mode of operation. Over the last four decades, public enterprises in Greece have faced intense phenomena of politicization, liberalization of their sectors of activity, privatization, administrative restructuring and the integration of a large part of them into the Hellenic Company for Holdings and Property (HCEPP) (Spanou and Sotiropoulos, 2021; Kalogeropoulou and Karkatsoulis, 2022). The Greek government debt crisis marked the beginning of a period of fiscal consolidation during which there were significant cuts in the operation of public enterprises in Greece such as extensive restructuring, external supervision by the European Commission and the International Monetary Fund and the transfer of many public utilities to the Greek State Enterprises and Public Sector Development Fund (Lalousis and Papalexopoulos, 2019; OECD, 2021).

These reforms have yielded mixed results (Katsimardos et al., 2017). The reform projects of public enterprises present significant cuts such as: the integration of private economic criteria, the integration of modern management tools, the utilization of advanced technologies, etc. However, significant structural problems remain such as: frequent political interventions, bureaucratic weaknesses, fragmented procedures, incomplete strategic planning, etc. (OECD, 2023; HCAP, 2023; Spanou and Sotiropoulos, 2021; Florio and Fecher, 2021). Furthermore, the emergence of new challenges such as the green transition, digital transformation, demographic pressures and the demand for resilient public services raises fundamental questions about the future role, purpose and governance of public enterprises in Greece.

This approach adopts an interdisciplinary perspective that combines insights from economics, public administration and political science to explore how public enterprises can be effectively governed and managed in a modern administrative system. The study focuses on the analysis of the institutional framework, administrative practices, performance improvement prospects and broader reform paths of Greek public enterprises, while utilizing comparative data from other European Union member states.

2. PUBLIC ENTERPRISES AND THEIR EVOLVING ROLE IN MODERN PUBLIC ADMINISTRATION

Public Legal Entities of Private Law that engage in purely business activity take a corporate form and are called public enterprises (OECD, 2021). The way in which the concept of the public sector is understood varies from person to person and from country to country. Often, the concept of central public administration, which undertakes the handling of all issues related to state action, is confused with the concept of public enterprises. The latter, known in the international economic environment as government-controlled enterprises or state-owned enterprises, undertake the business activities of the state, participating in a competitive environment and operating under market conditions (Rossidis, 2014). Public enterprises operate according to the standards of private enterprises, have a significant degree of autonomy, are managed by a board of directors and are controlled by the state. Public Enterprises are organizations that are owned or controlled by the state and engage in commercial or quasi-commercial activities (Christiansen and Kim, 2020). According to the official definition of the European Centre for Public Enterprises:

"*Public Enterprise is any enterprise in which the State, public authorities, foundations or other public enterprises are, collectively or individually, directly or indirectly, owners of part of the capital referred to as public capital and whose percentage either exceeds 50% of the share capital of the enterprise or is less than 50% but special rights exist that allow the public authority to have control over the enterprise*" (www.ceep.eu access date 31.10.2025). Based on the Greek institutional framework, a public enterprise is understood to be any public limited company in which the Greek public may exercise, directly or indirectly, decisive influence, by virtue of its participation in its share capital or its financial participation or the rules governing it (Law 3429/2005, article 1, paragraph 1). The legal status of public enterprises is governed by both public and private law (Akrivopoulou and Anthopoulos, 2015). Public enterprises under public law: a) are established, transformed and dissolved by formal or substantive law, b) their organization, the appointment of their bodies and their supervisory control are exercised by the State, c) the service status of their employees is assimilated to that of civil servants. On the other hand, the employment relations of public enterprises with their staff are governed by private law rules, while at the same time the financial management of public enterprises is governed by free market and competition rules (Bruton et al., 2021; Musacchio and Lazzarini, 2022). Public enterprises are called upon to implement a series of social, economic, administrative, national, developmental and political objectives (Bambanasis, 1999). In particular:

- Social objectives are linked to the development of the social character of the State, through: strengthening social justice (favoring fair income distribution), establishing the welfare state (by limiting social inequality), improving the distribution of productive resources (avoiding distortions in the smooth functioning of the economic system) and finally through the promotion of the public interest (implementation of social policy, protection of the environment, accessibility to public goods, etc.).
- Economic objectives are linked to the financial independence of public enterprises and the consequent obligation for sustainability and profitability. Public enterprises, like any other type of enterprise, owe their shareholders (whether the State and private individuals participate in them in percentage terms or whether they consist exclusively of the State) the obligation to record the highest possible economic surplus (profit) as a return on their capital investments (maximization of investment efficiency).
- Administrative objectives refer to achieving the highest possible efficiency, productivity and cost-effectiveness, respecting the principles of the competitive environment in which they operate and operating under the regime of private-economic criteria.

- National objectives are distinguished into those related to the nature of the object of public enterprises (infrastructure development enterprises, defense industry, public utilities, etc.) and those related to the contribution of public enterprises to the stabilization of the national economy (state monopolies, market intervention, strengthening of competition, etc.).
- Development objectives refer to the participation of public enterprises in the exercise of the State's fiscal policy through the implementation of public investments for the benefit of economic development and progress.
- Finally, political objectives refer to the implementation of public policies through public enterprises and their action.

The organization of public enterprises is carried out according to individual administrative principles that are related to the sector in which they operate, the functions of the economy, their object of activity, the geographical distribution, the political situation of the country in which they are incorporated, etc. (OECD, 2023; Grossi et al., 2022)

Public enterprises differ from traditional public administration units in several respects (Thynne, 2017; Florio and Fecher, 2021). They are often established under private corporate law, operate under commercial rules and enjoy greater managerial autonomy (Xanthopoulou and Kefis 2019). However, they remain under state supervision and must adhere to principles of accountability and transparency (Christiansen and Kim, 2020). This particular regulatory framework that governs them and their particular administrative status requires a specialized management style, defining an administrative structure that is significantly different from both classic bureaucracies and private companies (Bruton et al., 2021; Cuervo-Cazurra et al., 2020).

Public enterprises have been an important sector of state administration through which multifaceted administrative, economic, developmental and socio-political objectives were implemented (Ktistaki, 1991). During the post-war period, they were used to a very large extent to support individual government objectives such as: industrialization, the promotion of the public interest, the development of infrastructure, the provision of public services, especially in Europe and the USA, as well as in other advanced economies (Musacchio and Lazzarini, 2022; OECD, 2023). However, since the 1980s, multiple waves of privatizations, mainly influenced by the New Public Management (NPM) model, have sought to reduce the role of the state in the productive/business sectors – while maintaining a regulatory role – and provide more room for private enterprises to grow (Christensen and Lægreid, 2020; Florio and Fecher, 2021; Rossidis et al, 2020a). In recent years, however, there has been a trend towards reconsidering the business role of the state as expressed through the operation of public enterprises. The economic crisis and the COVID-19 pandemic have demonstrated the strategic importance of state ownership in protecting critical services and addressing systemic dysfunctions (Bruton et al., 2021; HCAP, 2023). Furthermore, global challenges such as the climate crisis, digital transformation and rising social inequalities are driving the need for increased state activity in specific sectors (Florio and Fecher, 2021; OECD, 2023). This emerging trend is largely in line with the Public Value Theory, according to which public enterprises should not be evaluated solely on the basis of economic performance but also on the basis of their broader contribution to social, environmental and development goals (Moore, 2019; Christensen and Lægreid, 2020). Therefore, public enterprises are expected to increasingly function as vehicles for implementing targeted strategies, balancing commercial demands with the fulfillment of public policies (OECD, 2021; Christiansen and Kim, 2020).

Over the years, several management models have been applied to analyze the behavior, governance, and performance of public enterprises, each highlighting different aspects of their unique hybrid nature.

- Public Choice Theory views public enterprises as inefficient due to their vulnerability to political intervention and the absence of meaningful competitive pressures in the market (Boycko et al., 1996; Christensen and Lægreid, 2020). This approach has advocated privatization as an administrative and economic remedy, emphasizing the need to limit state ownership.
- According to New Public Management, public enterprises that serve state interests are oriented towards the application of private management practices and theories, the use of private economic criteria, a focus on performance, the pursuit of high levels of competitiveness and the development of mechanisms that resemble the market (Christensen and Lægreid, 2020; Cuervo-Cazurra et al., 2020). While New Public Management contributed to achieving high levels of efficiency and effectiveness for public enterprises, it also moved largely towards privatization, removing the State, according to many critics, from the promotion of the public interest,
- According to the Public Value Theory, public enterprises are perceived as instruments for creating long-term social value by promoting the balancing of economic sustainability with multifaceted social, environmental and development objectives. The Public Value Theory aims to activate stakeholder participation in order to achieve a more democratic administration based on transparency, accountability and legitimacy (Moore, 2019; Florio and Fecher, 2021; Grossi et al., 2022).
- More recent approaches focus on developing an integrated governance perspective, recognizing public enterprises as complex hybrid organizations that require adaptive, networked and multi-level governance arrangements (Bruton et al., 2021; Musacchio and Lazzarini, 2022). This approach finds

application in a wide range of international policy frameworks, including the Organization for Economic Co-operation and Development (OECD) Guidelines on Corporate Governance of Public Enterprises (OECD, 2021).

3. PUBLIC ENTERPRISES AND THE MODERN ADMINISTRATIVE STATE

Public enterprises play critical roles in the functioning of the overall administrative system. The broad categories of roles of public enterprises are summarized as follows:

- as an owner of productive factors, setting strategic goals and overseeing governance structures
- as a regulator, ensuring competition, consumer protection and environmental compliance
- as a market actor, collaborating or competing with private enterprises in strategic sectors (Musacchio and Lazzarini, 2022; OECD, 2023).

This multiple role configuration creates inherent role conflicts, requiring institutional mechanisms to prevent distortions or dysfunctions. The evolution of the modern administrative state has radically reshaped the role of Public Enterprises. Governments have used public enterprises to a large extent as direct economic actors, pursuing multifaceted objectives such as: generating public revenues, influencing the market, directing individual sectors, promoting economic growth, etc. However, with the advent and consolidation of the New Public Management administrative model and the resulting redefinition of the role of the State, a clear transition from interventionism to supervision is noted (Christensen and Lægreid, 2020; OECD, 2021; Kefis, 1998). This shift reflected a broader reshaping of the state as a regulatory agent rather than as a direct producer of goods and services (Mazzucato and Kattel, 2020; Florio and Fecher, 2021).

Despite decades of market liberalization, public enterprises continue to play a central role in achieving strategic state objectives, especially in utilities and in the development of critical infrastructure (e.g., network configuration). They are widely used as policy instruments, in areas where the private sector has not typically shown any additional activity, either due to low expected profitability, high risk, or the requirement of particularly large investment capital (Cuervo-Cazurra et al., 2020; Bruton et al., 2021). Furthermore, public enterprises play an active role in promoting social cohesion by contributing to employment growth, supporting regional development and ensuring equal access to services (Florio and Fecher,

2021), although this aspect has been criticized due to the potential risk of over-sizing organizations and increasing operating costs (OECD, 2021). Within the European Union, the strategic use of public enterprises has been further strengthened by recent policies on green growth, digital transformation and economic resilience (European Commission, 2022; OECD, 2023).

A particular area of concern is the dual mission undertaken by public enterprises, having as their main objectives commercial viability combined with the promotion of the public interest. Objectives which in many cases may have significant differences or even become contradictory. This creates conflicts of strategic objectives and ambiguities in performance objectives (Christiansen and Kim, 2020; Grossi et al., 2022). The objective of economic sustainability may be affected by the obligation to support parallel state objectives such as employment protection, universal access, price regulation, infrastructure development, etc. On the contrary, focusing exclusively on economic efficiency may undermine equality, social justice and the quality of services (Cuervo-Cazurra et al., 2020; Bruton et al., 2021). Regarding the goal of supporting governance, mixed objectives complicate the design of performance indicators, incentive systems and accountability mechanisms (Florio and Fecher, 2021). The resulting confusion is common in network industries where public enterprises are often natural monopolies and must balance efficiency with social obligations (OECD, 2023). A burning issue regarding the governance of public enterprises is the intense political interference that affects strategic objectives, undermines the professionalism of management and limits the values of accountability and transparency (Christensen and Lægreid, 2020; OECD, 2021, Rossidis et al., 2018a). Legitimacy is another crucial dimension. As hybrid entities, public enterprises are under the control of the State and must meet economic objectives while promoting social values and policy goals (Moore, 2019; Grossi et al., 2022).

Internationally, many different approaches are identified under different governance models. In particular:

- France has adopted a central ownership model with strong state coordination through the Agence des Participations de l'État, emphasizing strategic control and meritocratic board appointments (OECD, 2023).
- Sweden implements a decentralized but performance-oriented model, providing operational autonomy while imposing strict disclosure and financial targets (Christiansen and Kim, 2020).
- Finland combines dual boards and transparent reporting, emphasizing long-term value creation and professional management (Grossi et al., 2022).
- Germany uses networked governance structures, with the federal and state governments jointly managing businesses, supported by corporate structures and co-decision arrangements (Bruton et al., 2021).

The analysis of the above governance models reflects differentiated forms of governance, concluding that there is no single governance plan capable of operating effectively in all possible situations.

4. EVOLUTION OF PUBLIC ENTERPRISES IN GREECE: HISTORICAL, POLITICAL AND ECONOMIC PERSPECTIVES

Public Enterprises in Greece have gone through various phases embedded in various reform frameworks that express administrative reforms, economic consolidation, digital transformation, political restructuring and privatization acts. In the post-war period (1950s–1970s), Greek governments followed a strategy of state industrialization and infrastructure development, establishing numerous public enterprises in sectors such as energy, transport, telecommunications, mining and banking (Kefis, 2010; Pitelis, 2018; Christodoulakis, 2018). This intensive establishment of public enterprises reflected, on the one hand, the limited interest of private investment and, on the other hand, the strategic need for focused development of specific critical sectors of the domestic economic system (Florio and Fecher, 2021). Public enterprises were often used as tools for economic development and infrastructure formation, operating under extensive government control with little managerial autonomy (Spanou and Sotiropoulos, 2021).

During the 1980s, under socialist governments, the public enterprise sector was further expanded through nationalization programs of troubled private enterprises, from which new public organizations were created (Lalousis and Papalexopoulos, 2019). The management of public enterprises exhibited strong political influences and often functioned as vote-buying vehicles for job creation, customer development and income redistribution (Featherstone and Papadimitriou, 2020). Board appointments were often politically motivated, while lax financial discipline and soft fiscal constraints undermined efficiency and effectiveness, with the adverse consequence of widespread losses (Pitelis, 2018). By the late 1980s, many private enterprises were facing accumulated losses, overstaffing, dysfunctional processes and intense bureaucracy, leading to macroeconomic imbalances and a ballooning public debt (Spanou and Sotiropoulos, 2021).

In the 1990s and early 2000s, successive governments initiated market-oriented reforms, influenced by the principles of New Public Management and based on European standards under the pressure of administrative convergence (Featherstone, 2022; OECD, 2021). Some of the measures used were:

- Conversion of many public enterprises into private limited companies.

- Partial privatizations and listings of large companies (e.g. Hellenic Telecommunications Organization (OTE), Public Electricity Company (PPC).
- Integration of private financial criteria and performance targets, while their control was assigned to independent regulatory authorities.

These reform efforts aimed to reduce fiscal burdens, enhance competitiveness and align Greece with the rules of the EU single market (Lalousis and Papalexopoulos, 2019). Many of the reforms implemented had positive results in terms of transparency, economic efficiency and social effectiveness, but a large number of reform actions did not bring substantial results, maintained or even intensified governance complexity or led to controversial fiscal benefits due to the significant devaluation of privatized public enterprises (Kalogeropoulou and Karkatsoulis, 2022). The Greek government debt crisis (2009–2018) marked a critical moment for the public company sector. According to the adjustment programs agreed with the European Commission, the European Central Bank and the International Monetary Fund, Greece committed to implementing extensive privatizations, restructurings and fiscal controls in order to cover part of the public debt and at the same time limit fiscal deficits (Spanou and Sotiropoulos, 2021). Significant reform measures were:

- The establishment of the Hellenic Assets and Holdings Fund (HRADF) in 2011 to oversee privatizations
- The creation of the Hellenic Property and Holdings Company (HPEHC) in 2016 as a central holding company for large public utilities
- The transfer of more than 20 strategic businesses to HPEHC with the aim of more technocratic governance, stronger performance monitoring and rationalization of assets (HPEHC, 2023)

These measures contributed to the depoliticization of public enterprise management and improved financial discipline. They also introduced external oversight by European institutions on board appointments, performance targets and corporate governance frameworks (OECD, 2023).

In the post-crisis period and up to now, public enterprises in Greece have shown significant improvements in terms of administrative functioning and digital modernization. Strategies have been launched to redefine the role of public enterprises as instruments of sustainable development and public value creation (Kalogeropoulou and Karkatsoulis, 2022) taking into account emerging challenges such as green infrastructure, digital transformation, high level of competitiveness, promotion of innovation, etc. (OECD, 2023, Belias et al., 2024).

Public enterprises in Greece have historically exhibited the following characteristics: they are established with a focus on carrying out specific missions, they experience gradual expansion (or even oversizing) with strong political interventions, they undergo partial/total privatization or alternatively, an attempt at administrative and financial restructuring is attempted, triggering a process of feedback and modernization. Understanding these historical dynamics is essential for designing sustainable strategies to enhance the performance, legitimacy and public value orientation of public enterprises within the modern administrative state (Rossidis et al., 2020b).

Today, significant improvements have been made in the management of public enterprises in Greece, replacing bureaucratic operation with much more technocratic approaches, emphasizing the promotion of accountability, transparency and meritocracy. However, their administrative autonomy often remains limited, as political power retains significant influence on strategy formulation and executive function, bringing about significant alterations in the final administrative/financial result. This occurs either in the context of the effort to promote the public interest (e.g. promoting public policies or supporting government objectives) or in the context of serving party objectives (e.g. party appointments, setting party-based salaries, targeted pricing policies, etc.), which weakens the decision-making process and creates distortions in the rational management of resources (Spanou & Sotiropoulos, 2021). For example, damaging results may arise because the service of a government policy was prioritized, contradicting the strategic objectives of the public enterprise (such as the promotion of unprofitable low-interest loans to a specific segment of citizens by a public bank in the context of exercising social policy).

Recent reforms within the framework of more managerial approaches have promoted the emphasis on results and the use of performance management tools in order to enhance the competitiveness of public enterprises. The establishment of medium-term strategic planning frameworks has led public enterprises to adopt business plans with specific financial targets, operational indicators and sustainability commitments (OECD, 2023). This orientation creates a more stable basis for administrative operation with a clearer strategic orientation that is directly linked to the promotion of defined public policies (Kalogeropoulou & Karkatsoulis, 2022; Rossidis et al., 2018b). At the same time, through the influence of corporate governance and public governance theories, particular attention is given to the promotion of transparency and accountability through specialized administrative mechanisms and digital transformation tools (Christodoulakis, 2018; Papapolychroniadis et al., 2017; Rossidis et al., 2016). The impact of ethical governance is of particular value, emphasizing the encouragement of diversity and balanced gender representation (OECD, 2023, Belias et al., 2023).

Political interference is still regarded as the most obstinate impediment to effective governance in Greek public enterprises, due to the lack of a coherent long-term strategic management which in turn derives from the strong linkage between their leadership and government terms and pressure for short-term fiscal results as a political advertisement (Spanou & Sotiropoulos, 2021; Kalogeropoulou & Karkatsoulis, 2022; Kriemadis et al., 2023). This short-term political orientation discourages investment, rational risk management and innovation, weakening the ability of public enterprises to contribute to broader development goals (OECD, 2023; Florio & Fecher, 2021). Hence, stronger institutional safeguards are needed to guarantee management autonomy and the implementation of management practices that focus on meeting defined performance targets linked to long-term public value creation.

5. COMPARATIVE ANALYSIS OF GREECE - EUROPE

Public Enterprises in Greece operate in the light of the guidelines and broader strategic orientation of the European Union, where state ownership remains widespread, especially in strategic network sectors such as energy, transport and telecommunications. According to the European Commission (2022), EU Member States collectively control more than 2,000 large public enterprises employing over 5 million people and generating revenues equivalent to 10% of EU GDP. In this context, Greek public enterprises, although representing a relatively small part of the total public sector activity, assume roles of strategic importance in promoting state objectives by operating in important sectors such as transport, infrastructure and utilities. Their average economic size and employment footprint are below the EU average, but their fiscal importance is disproportionately high given their continued reliance on state support and their impact on public debt (OECD, 2023). Comparative indicators compiled by Eurostat (2021) and OECD (2023) suggest that Greek public utilities rank lower than their EU counterparts in terms of profitability, productivity and operational efficiency, while presenting higher risks of political interference and weaker board independence.

European countries have adopted a variety of management models for their public enterprises serving their particular vision and perception towards them. These differentiations can be spotted in the strategic orientation, management structure, organizational structures, organizational culture, ownership, financial efficiency and administrative effectiveness. Overall, these differentiations can be grouped in four broad categories which serve as benchmarks:

- France has adopted a central ownership model with strong state coordination through the Agence des Participations de l'État (APE), emphasizing strategic control and merit-based board appointments (OECD, 2023) far away from political influence. The APE sets clear financial and strategic objectives, ensures a merit-based composition of the board and applies strict reporting standards (OECD, 2023).

- Sweden promotes operational autonomy through a decentralized but performance-oriented model, with strict financial targets (Christiansen and Kim, 2020). Public enterprises operate through performance contracts, independent audits and public disclosure of targets. Ths goal of this approach is the achievement of transparency and public trust (Grossi et al., 2022).
- Finland combines dual boards and transparent reporting, emphasizing long-term value creation and professional management (Grossi et al., 2022). The government appoints professional boards, while setting overall strategic goals through a central coordinating body, promoting stability and professionalism (OECD, 2021).
- Germany uses networked governance structures, with the federal and state governments jointly managing businesses, supported by corporate structures and co-decision arrangements (Bruton et al., 2021).

The evolution of different approaches towards public enterprises' management verifies the fact that different economic, political and societal environments require different approaches in order to achieve the envisaged results.

However, there are certain common characteristics in all the above approaches that contribute to effectiveness and efficiency (OECD, 2021; Grossi et al., 2022). These characteristics are:

- clear separation of responsibilities between political and administrative bodies and development of strong regulatory roles,
- meritocratic appointments of boards of directors based on modern administrative standards,
- activation of clear performance management frameworks aligned with public policy objectives,
- implementation of strong mechanisms for transparency and accountability of administrative action and a focus on substantive audit procedures and the promotion of integrity and ethics.

At a similar level, international organizations such as the Organization for Economic Cooperation and Development (OECD) have issued Guidelines on Corporate Governance of Publicly Owned Enterprises (OECD, 2021), which are widely recognized as the global benchmark for the governance of public utilities. These guidelines emphasize the following:

- clarity and concentration of ownership policy
- transparency and accountability standards modeled after listed companies
- separation of ownership and regulatory functions
- professional and independent boards
- strong performance monitoring systems

The Hellenic Property and Holdings Company has made progress in aligning its portfolio companies with these principles through board professionalization, strategic planning, and transparency and accountability requirements (EESYP, 2023). However, outside the scope of the EESYP, most Greek public companies present several dysfunctions as they lack central ownership supervision, do not have standardized performance frameworks and are absent from systematic board evaluations (OECD, 2023).

In contrast, most countries in Northern and Western Europe have achieved full or advanced compliance, presenting high levels of depoliticization and technocratic operation based on modern administrative practices (Christiansen and Kim, 2020; Grossi et al., 2022). These persisting pathologies limit the prospect of Greek public companies to compete and cooperate in the European and international environment.

The comparative data analyzed highlight a series of conclusions on the necessary reform of Greek public enterprises. In particular, the following should be focused on:

- Creating a single coordinating body that will support the action of all large public enterprises following the model of France and Finland, promoting the strengthening of strategic coherence.
- Implementing transparent, meritocratic board appointment procedures, insulated from political reshuffles based on modern administrative practices, following the Swedish model.
- Developing performance standards and targets that combine economic, social and environmental indicators, linked to incentive structures for management and the organization.
- Strengthening transparency and accountability mechanisms to restore public trust and promote public interests, as observed in the Nordic countries.

Adapting these practices to the Greek administrative and political context could contribute to bridging the gap between Greek public enterprises and their EU counterparts, while enhancing their ability to deliver public value in line with the strategic objectives of the modern administrative state (Rossidis and Belias, 2021).

Table 1. Comparative analysis of public enterprises – Greece and selected European countries

Comparison Dimension	Greece	France	Sweden	Finland	Germany
State ownership model	Fragmented, partially centralized (via HCAP)	Strongly centralized (Agence des Participations de l'État – APE)	Decentralized	Central coordination with professional oversight	Networked, federal structure
Strategic coordination	Limited, uneven implementation of unified strategy	High – clear strategic and financial objectives	High through performance contracts	High, with emphasis on long-term value creation	Medium–high, multi-level coordination
Managerial autonomy	Limited due to political interference	Relatively high, institutionally safeguarded	Very high	High	Moderate
Board appointment process	Frequently politicized	Merit-based and professional	Merit-based, transparent	Professional, stable tenure	Mixed (federal and Länder involvement)
Performance management framework	Partially developed, non-standardized	Strict financial and strategic monitoring	Extensive, with public disclosure	Integrated, long-term oriented	Differentiated by governance level
Economic efficiency	Low–moderate compared to EU average	High	High	High	High
Risk of political interference	High	Low	Very low	Low	Moderate
Transparency & accountability	Insufficient outside HCAP portfolio	High	Very high	Very high	High
Alignment with OECD SOE Guidelines	Partial compliance	Full compliance	Full compliance	Full compliance	Largely compliant

6. CONCLUSIONS AND POLICY RECOMMENDATIONS

The analysis of Public Enterprises in Greece in the light of the contemporary dynamic administrative environment reveals a sector that remains strategically important but institutionally fragile. Historically, Greek public enterprises have evolved through cycles of state expansion, politicization, privatization and administrative restructuring, shaping a multifaceted legacy of hybrid forms, identifying a wide range of ways of organization and governance. (Spanou and Sotiropoulos, 2021; Lalousis and Papalexopoulos, 2019).

The recent reform initiatives introduced during the Greek sovereign debt crisis and afterwards, have significantly improved the operation and overall contribution of public enterprises to state objectives. The improvement actions are summarized in the promotion of transparency, administrative restructuring, financial rationalization and strategic reorientation (OECD, 2023). However, many public enterprises still retain past pathologies, presenting problematic governance systems, low financial returns (even highly loss-making), meritocratic operations, political interventions, etc. (Kalogeropoulou and Karkatsoulis, 2022).

The aforementioned conclusions are also confirmed by comparative analyses of Greek public enterprises with the corresponding public enterprises of European Union member states, presenting significant deficiencies in terms of profitability, productivity and operational efficiency, while at the same time presenting higher risks of political interference and weaker independence of the board of directors (European Commission, 2022; OECD, 2023; Rossidis et al., 2016). This governance gap undermines their ability to deliver public value, attract investment and contribute to national development goals (Kefis and Aspridis, 2014; Rossidis et al., 20218b).

Addressing these challenges requires a comprehensive and sequential reform strategy that addresses structural fragmentation, governance deficiencies and capacity gaps, while integrating public enterprises into a modern ownership framework focused on public values (Rossidis et al., 2020c; Mihiotis et al., 2023). Based on the above, individual reform perspectives are identified that could be translated into strategic priorities. In particular, it is proposed:

1. Concentration of state ownership and reduction of fragmentation. Expansion of the scope of HCAP to include all large public enterprises or the creation of a single central coordinating body along the lines of the Agence des Participations de l'État in France and the State Ownership Steering Unit in Finland (OECD, 2021). This would enhance strategic coherence, reduce overlapping mandates and allow for the development of a single state ownership policy.
2. Professionalise boards and ensure administrative autonomy. Institutionalise board appointments based on merit, stability of tenure and performance assessments based on competency frameworks (HCAP, 2023). Boards and senior management need to be protected from political turnover, while strengthening accountability and efficiency through performance contracts. Such a measure would contribute to the development of administrative expertise, rational management, the formulation of clear strategic directions and a single administrative coherence.
3. Integrate performance-based management and public value measurements. Introduce integrated performance indicators and criteria that combine financial,

operational, social and environmental indicators (Grossi et al., 2022). Link executive incentives to long-term public value outcomes rather than short-term fiscal outcomes, reducing pressures for opportunistic behavior.

4. Invest in digital transformation and knowledge management. Accelerate the adoption of enterprise resource planning systems, data analytics and digital customer interfaces, while creating Knowledge Management systems to support learning, innovation and evidence-based decision-making (OECD, 2023; Belias et al., 2020; Spanou and Sotiropoulos, 2021; Stampelos et al., 2019).
5. Integrate ESG criteria and support the green transition. Require all public companies to integrate environmental, social and governance (ESG) objectives and disclosures into their strategic plans and annual reports, aligning their investments with national and EU climate targets (Florio and Fecher, 2021; OECD, 2023).

Shifting entrenched governance cultures requires broad political consensus and cross-party support, ensuring that reforms survive electoral cycles (Goula et al., 2014; Ntalakos et al., 2023). It also requires building public trust through open disclosure of performance data, stakeholder engagement, and visible improvements in service quality. If implemented, these reforms could transform Greek public enterprises from politically dependent and financially fragile entities into strategic instruments of the modern administrative state — capable of delivering efficient, sustainable, and innovative public services, while contributing to economic resilience and social well-being. This transformation is essential to strengthen the competitiveness of the Greek economy, fulfill political and fiscal commitments to the EU, and restore citizens' trust in public institutions.

REFERENCES

Belias, D., Rossidis, I., Ntalakos, A., Trihas, N., Mantas, C., & Bokogiannis, D. (2023). Ethics in Change Management: Current Issues and Directions for Future Research in the Post-COVID-19 Era. Chapter 12 in “Managing Successful and Ethical Organizational Change”, IGI Global.

Belias, D., Rossidis, I., & Papademetriou, C. (2020). *E-Governance in times of Covid19 - The case of Greece. Problems and prospects.* 16th Hellenic Society for Systemic Studies (HSSS) National & International Conference “Effective Management of Public and Private Organizations through Systemics and Technologies”.

Belias, D., Rossidis, I., & Papademetriou, C. (2024). *Organizational Behavior and Human Resource Management for Complex Work Environments.* IGI Global. DOI: 10.4018/979-8-3693-3466-9

Boycko, M., Shleifer, A., & Vishny, R. W. (1996). *A Theory of Privatisation.* MIT Press. DOI: 10.2307/2235248

Bruton, G. D., Peng, M. W., Ahlstrom, D., & Stan, C. V. (2021). State-owned enterprises around the world as hybrid organizations. *The Academy of Management Perspectives, 35*(2), 219–236.

Christensen, T., & Lægreid, P. (2020). *The Routledge Handbook of Public Sector Reforms.* Routledge.

Christiansen, H., & Kim, H. (2020). State-owned enterprises and the pursuit of public value. *OECD Corporate Governance Working Papers*, No. 15, OECD.

Christodoulakis, N. (2018). Public enterprises in Greece: Governance reforms and fiscal performance’. *South European Society & Politics, 23*(4), 493–512.

Cuervo-Cazurra, A., Inkpen, A., Musacchio, A., & Ramaswamy, K. (2020). Governments as owners: State-owned multinational companies. *Journal of International Business Studies, 51*(9), 1374–1396.

European Commission. (2022). *State-Owned Enterprises in the EU: Overview and Trends.* European Commission.

Eurostat (2021). *Manual on Government Deficit and Debt.* Luxembourg: Eurostat.

Featherstone, K. (2022). *Prime Ministers in Greece: The Paradox of Power.* Oxford University Press.

Featherstone, K., & Papadimitriou, D. (2020). *The Limits of Europeanization: Reform Capacity and Public Policy in Greece* (2nd ed.). Palgrave Macmillan.

Florio, M., & Fecher, F. (2021). The future of public enterprises: Mission-oriented ownership and governance. *Annals of Public and Cooperative Economics*, *92*(2), 187–205.

Goula, A., Kefis, V., Dimakou, S., Pierrakos, G., & Sarris, M. (2014). Organizational change in the public hospital. From bureaucratic participatory management style. *Archives of Hellenic Medicine*, *31*(5), 583–590.

Grossi, G., Papenfuß, U., & Tremblay, M. S. (2022). Corporate governance and accountability of state-owned enterprises: Reforms and challenges. *Public Money & Management*, *42*(6), 397–406.

HCAP. (2023). *Annual Report 2022*. Hellenic Corporation of Assets and Participations.

Kalogeropoulou, E., & Karkatsoulis, P. (2022). State-owned enterprises and administrative reform in Greece: Lessons from the crisis. *International Journal of Public Sector Management*, *35*(4), 452–470.

Katsimardos, P., Bouas, K., Rossidis, I., & Babalioutas, L. (2017). Greek crisis: It's not about growth. It's about governance. *International Journal of Current Research*, *9*(3).

Kefis, V. (1998). *The Management of Public Enterprises and Organizations. Systematic Approach to its Impacts on the Development of the Greek Economy*. Interbooks Publications.

Kefis V. (2010). Public Enterprises and Public Management in Greece, *Administrative News*, 53.

Kefis, V., & Aspridis, G. (2014). Management and development of the human resource of nongovernmental organizations (NGOs) in Greece. Utopia or reality? *International NGO Journal*, *9*(4), 43–52. DOI: 10.5897/INGOJ2014.0289

Kriemadis, A., Rossidis, I., & Belias, D. (2023). *Strategic Human Resources Management as a key element in the implementation of organizational changes. An extensive literature review*. Chapter 1 in "Managing Successful and Ethical Organizational Change", IGI Global.

Ktistaki, S. (1991). Public enterprise and public interest. *Constitution - Foundation for the United States Constitution*, , 297–349.

Lalousis, D., & Papalexopoulos, T. (2019). Public enterprise reform in Greece under the adjustment programmes. *South European Society & Politics*, *24*(3), 321–342.

Mazzucato, M., & Kattel, R. (2020). COVID-19 and public-sector capacity. *Oxford Review of Economic Policy, 36*(S1), S256–S269. DOI: 10.1093/oxrep/graa031 PMID: 40504220

Mihiotis, A., Rossidis, I., & Koutsoukis, N. (2023). The effect of digital transformation in the development of Electronic Governance in Cyprus and Greece. A critical review through the analysis of the Digital Economy and Society Index. *The Cyprus Review, 35*(1).

Moore, M. H. (2019). *Creating Public Value: Strategic Management in Government.* Updated edn. Harvard University Press.

Musacchio, A., & Lazzarini, S. G. (2022). State-owned enterprises in the 21st century: New trends and challenges. *Journal of International Business Studies, 53*(6), 1155–1173.

Ntalakos, A., Belias, D., Rossidis, I., Koustelios, A., Tsigilis, N., & Vasiliadis, L. (2023). *Communicating the Vision of the Change: The Linkage Between Organizational Communication, Organizational Culture, and Organizational Change.* Chapter 4 in "Managing Successful and Ethical Organizational Change", IGI Global. DOI: 10.4018/979-8-3693-0235-4.ch004

OECD. (2021). *OECD Guidelines on Corporate Governance of State-Owned Enterprises.* OECD.

OECD. (2023). *OECD Review of the Corporate Governance of State-Owned Enterprises: Greece.* OECD.

Papapolychroniadis, I., Rossidis I., Aspridis, G., (2017). Comparative analysis of recruitment systems in the public sector in Greece and Europe. Trends and outlook for staff selection systems in the Greek public sector. *Academic Journal of Interdisciplinary Studies.* 6(1).

Pitelis, C. (2018). State-owned enterprises and development in Southern Europe: Historical lessons. *Cambridge Journal of Economics, 42*(3), 525–547.

Rossidis, I. (2014) *Applying Business Management in Greek Public Administration.* Athens: publ. Ath. Stamoulis.

Rossidis, I., Aspridis, G., Katsimardos, P., & Bouas, K. (2018b). *Human Resource Productivity in Greece.* Global Encyclopedia of Public Administration, Public Policy and Governance, Springer Publishing.

Rossidis I., Aspridis, G., Katsimardos, P., Bouas, K., Blanas, N. (2016). Best practices for motivation and their implementation in the Greek public sector for increasing efficiency. *Academic Journal of Interdisciplinary Studies*. 5(3).

Rossidis, I., & Belias, D. (2020). Combining Strategic Management with Knowledge Management. Trends and International perspectives. *International Review of Management and Marketing, 10*(3), 39–45. DOI: 10.32479/irmm.9621

Rossidis, I., & Belias, D. (2021). Evolution of e-Government in the era of the pandemic. May the crisis become an opportunity? The cases of Cyprus and Greece. *The Cyprus Review, 33*(1), 37–66.

Rossidis, I., Belias, D., & Aspridis, G. (2020a). *Change Management and Leadership*. Tziolas Publishing.

Rossidis, I., Belias, D., & Papailias, S. (2020b). *Strategic management and performance in the international environment*. Book of Proceedings International Conference on Cotemporary Marketing Issues.

Rossidis, I., Belias, D., & Papailias, S. (2020c). *Strategic management in the Greek public sector. In search of best practices in the international environment*. Book of Proceedings International Conference on Business & Economics of the Hellenic Open University.

Rossidis, I., Mihiotis, A., & Ntalakos, A. (2023). *The contribution of Change Management to the integration of E-Governance systems*. Chapter 9 in "Managing Successful and Ethical Organizational Change", IGI Global. DOI: 10.4018/979-8-3693-0235-4.ch009

Rossidis, I., Tsiotas, D., Aspridis, G., Belias, D., & Sdrolias, L. (2018a). *Exploring Governance in Higher Education in Europe and Greece*. Global Encyclopedia of Public Administration, Public Policy, and Governance, Springer Publishing.

Spanou, C., & Sotiropoulos, D. A. (2021). Administrative reform and the management of public enterprises in Greece: Between inertia and change'. *Public Administration, 99*(4), 771–789.

Stampelos, X., Nikova, D., Rossidis, I., Aspridis, G., & Pouliana, L. (2019). *Contribution of knowledge management to the function of public administration*. Book of Proceedings, International scientific conference Leadership and Organization Development. Bulgaria, Kiten.

Thynne, I. (2017). The state and public corporations: Governance issues and challenges. *Public Organization Review, 17*(4), 503–517.

Transparency International. (2022). *National Integrity System Assessment*. Transparency International.

Xanthopoulou, P., & Kefis, V. (2019). Public Organizations and Public Management in Greece: The Implementation of Private Management Tools in the Public Sector. *International Journal of Sciences*, *8*(02).

Chapter 9
Judicial Reform, Performance, and Governance:
Evidence From Norway

Anatoliy G. Goncharuk
http://orcid.org/0000-0001-9870-4679
NLA University College, Norway

ABSTRACT

Judicial systems face growing pressure to improve efficiency while preserving fairness, quality, and access to justice. In 2021, Norway implemented a major judicial reform consolidating district courts to address delays and uneven workloads. This chapter evaluates the reform's early performance effects within a public sector governance framework. Using Data Envelopment Analysis (DEA) and the Malmquist Productivity Index, the study compares court efficiency, productivity, and quality before and after the reform, incorporating case timeliness as a quality indicator. The findings show mixed results. While the reform coincided with a positive technological shift linked to digitalization, overall technical efficiency and productivity declined in the short term. Many merged courts exhibited decreasing returns to scale, suggesting consolidation exceeded optimal size in several regions. Quality outcomes, measured by overdue cases, remained largely unchanged. The chapter emphasizes policy learning, benchmarking, and targeted adjustment rather than reform reversal.

DOI: 10.4018/979-8-3373-3526-1.ch009

INTRODUCTION

Access to an efficient and impartial justice system is a fundamental right for citizens in any democracy. While the ideal of impartiality in courts is well understood, the concept of efficiency in the judicial context can be interpreted in multiple ways. From a government's perspective, an efficient judiciary is one that delivers maximum output (case resolutions) with minimum resource input, thereby reducing public expenditures on the courts. Governments often pursue efficiency by streamlining processes, cutting unproductive costs, or even shifting costs to litigants (for example, through court fees). However, for users of the judicial system (individuals and businesses seeking justice) efficiency means obtaining a fair resolution with minimal personal cost, whether in terms of time, money, or stress. Lengthy delays can erode confidence in justice (time is "like money" to litigants), high legal expenses can deter the pursuit of rights, and protracted uncertainty can inflict psychological hardship. In short, judicial performance has two critical dimensions: efficiency (throughput and cost-effectiveness) and quality (fairness and timely justice delivery). Both dimensions are vital for public trust in the legal system.

Many countries have undertaken judicial reforms aiming to improve these facets of performance. Reforms have ranged from increasing court funding (hoping that better pay and resources for judges boost productivity) to reorganizing court structures. Evidence shows, however, that simply infusing more funds or raising judicial salaries does not automatically improve efficiency. For instance, studies found little correlation between higher judicial pay and court output. This raises the question: what truly drives judicial performance, and how can reforms effectively enhance it?

To address this question, researchers have evaluated various performance measures and reform strategies. Early efforts to measure court performance holistically proposed multiple indicators – such as independence, accountability, effectiveness, and access – beyond raw efficiency. Traditional judicial performance evaluations (JPEs) were introduced in the 1970s in the United States, using surveys of court users and staff to rate judges on aspects like demeanor and case management. While JPEs can provide feedback for judges' professional development, they have notable limitations. Survey-based evaluations often carry biases (conscious or unconscious), for example, systematically lower scores for female and minority judges have been observed, even with similar objective performance. Litigants who lose their case might unfairly rate a judge poorly despite an objectively fair process. Moreover, focusing on individual judges in isolation misses the broader institutional context; court efficiency also depends on support staff, case procedures, and infrastructure.

Given these challenges, scholars turned to quantitative, system-wide measures of court efficiency. A landmark study by Lewin et al. (1982) was the first to apply a frontier efficiency analysis to courts. They treated courts as "decision-making units" that use inputs (e.g. number of judges, staff, caseload characteristics) to produce outputs (cases disposed, backlog reduced), using the then-new Data Envelopment Analysis (DEA) method (a linear programming approach introduced by Charnes, Cooper, and Rhodes (1978) to measure relative efficiency of peer units), to evaluate efficiency of 100 U.S. trial courts. Their analysis quantified each court's technical efficiency as a ratio of weighted outputs to inputs, identifying which courts operated on the efficient frontier and which fell behind. This approach allowed performance benchmarking among courts and highlighted how some courts could achieve equal or better caseload outcomes with fewer resources.

Following this pioneering work, the 1990s saw additional applications of DEA in the judicial sector. Notably, Kittelsen and Førsund (1992) evaluated the efficiency of Norwegian district courts for 1983-1988. They not only measured annual efficiency scores for each court but also applied the Malmquist Productivity Index to gauge changes in productivity over time. This index (named after Sten Malmquist's work, later elaborated by Grifell-Tatjé & Lovell (1995)) decomposes productivity change into two components: efficiency change (catching up or falling behind the best practice frontier) and technological change (shifts of the frontier itself). By using DEA and Malmquist, they could assess not only how efficient each Norwegian court was relative to peers, but also whether the overall system's performance was improving – a powerful approach for evaluating reform impact over time.

Subsequent studies in various countries adopted similar methods to examine court performance. For example, Tulkens (1993) used a Free Disposal Hull (FDH, a non-parametric frontier method) to evaluate Belgian courts, identifying how some could increase output with existing resources by emulating best practices. Pedraja-Chaparro & Salinas-Jimenez (1996) assessed Spanish courts' technical, allocative, and overall efficiency. Entering the 21st century, DEA-based analyses of courts proliferated globally: Schneider (2005) examined German labor courts, De Sousa & Schwengber (2005) and later Yeung & Azevedo (2011) assessed Brazilian courts, Guzowska & Strak (2010) and Bełdowski et al. (2020) analyzed Polish courts, Tsai & Tsai (2010) looked at Taiwan, Finocchiaro Castro & Guccio (2014) and Falavigna et al. (2018) focused on Italian courts, Santos & Amado (2014) and Silva (2018) evaluated Portuguese courts, Ferro et al. (2018) studied Argentina, Mattsson & Tidanå (2019) Sweden, Bajrić & Kadrić (2020) Bosnia, Gupta & Bolia (2020) India, among others. This growing body of literature confirms that DEA is a versatile tool to benchmark court efficiency across diverse legal systems.

Importantly, only a subset of these studies explicitly investigated the impact of structural reforms on court performance. One such study by Ferrandino (2010) examined Florida's trial courts before and after a reform known as "Revision 7", which centralized court funding at the state level. Using DEA and Malmquist analysis, Ferrandino found that, with few exceptions, the reform did not make courts more efficient. In contrast, a DEA study of Sweden's court merger reform (2000–2009) by Agrell et al. (2020) found a positive effect: consolidating smaller courts into larger units tended to increase efficiency on average. Similarly, Falavigna et al. (2018) applied a two-stage DEA-Malmquist approach to Italian tax courts and concluded that reorganization (merging or reallocating resources) could improve productivity, primarily by shifting the production frontier upward (technological progress) and by better utilizing judges' work time. Santos & Amado (2014) also argued, based on DEA results for Portuguese courts, that structural reform was needed to boost efficiency. These studies suggest that while court reforms do not guarantee improved performance, data-driven analysis can pinpoint whether a given reform has achieved its intended goals or not. DEA and Malmquist indices are particularly appropriate for such evaluation, as they can detect subtle changes in efficiency and productivity pre- vs. post-reform.

Norway provides an excellent case for studying judicial reform impacts. Ironically, Norway was ahead of the curve in applying efficiency analysis to courts, being the first in Europe to use DEA for evaluating its judiciary back in the early 1990s, yet it was behind its Nordic peers in implementing a sweeping court restructuring. In 2017–2021, Norway embarked on one of the most significant judicial reforms in its history, consolidating many of its first-instance courts. This reform aimed at improving court efficiency, productivity, and quality of service. It came on the heels of mounting evidence that Norwegian courts faced performance challenges: a National Audit Office investigation (Staalesen, 2020) found that, despite some efficiency gains, productivity was declining and case processing times were exceeding statutory targets in the years prior to reform. The Audit report pointed to limited resources and structural issues, effectively justifying the need for systemic reform of the court system. In response, the government and parliament enacted a reorganization to merge district courts. The move was controversial, drawing both criticism (JD, 2022) and praise (Thorsvik, 2021) from different stakeholders in the justice sector. By 2021, the reform was implemented, but as of yet, there had been no rigorous assessment of whether it actually delivered the promised improvements in efficiency, productivity, and quality.

The objective of this chapter is to evaluate how successful Norway's 2021 judicial reform has been in achieving its goals, and to draw lessons for public management and governance of judicial systems. The chapter is organized as follows: The next section recounts the historical evolution of Norway's court system and the reform process. We then review relevant literature on court performance and reforms. The study's research objectives and questions are stated, followed by an overview of the theoretical frameworks and analytical methods (DEA and Malmquist) underpinning our evaluation. Subsequent sections discuss the importance of efficient courts, the governance context of the reform, and an analysis of the reform's advantages and challenges as revealed by the data. We also consider ethical implications of pursuing efficiency in the judiciary and suggest how collaboration and sharing of best practices (domestically and with Nordic neighbors) can foster improvements. We then discuss the implementation and regulatory framework that guided the reform. Finally, we present the conclusion, along with suggestions for policy adjustments and future research directions. By taking a constructive, policy-adaptive tone, we aim to show not just whether the reform "worked," but how its outcomes can inform ongoing efforts to improve judicial performance in Norway and beyond.

HISTORICAL EVOLUTION

The Norwegian court system has evolved over centuries, but the most radical structural change came with the 2021 reform of the district courts (*tingrett*). The district courts are Norway's courts of first instance for civil and criminal cases (historically called city or lord courts before 2002). Each district court serves a geographic judicial district (*rettskrets*), and until recently there were 60 such districts across the country. Norway's Constitution did not even mention district courts explicitly until a 2024 amendment, which enshrined the Supreme Court, Courts of Appeal, and district courts in the Constitution to strengthen judicial independence. The absence of constitutional status for lower courts historically meant that their organization could be altered by statute. Indeed, court structure has been adjusted by legislation in the past, but never at the scale of the 2021 reform.

By the mid-2010s, concerns were growing about uneven workloads and delays in Norway's courts. Smaller courts, especially in rural areas, struggled with low case volumes in some periods and backlogs in others, lacking flexibility to redistribute work. Larger courts in cities faced steadily high caseloads. This imbalance led to calls for a more consolidated court structure to improve efficiency, ensure consistent service quality, and enhance access to justice nationally. Moreover, the auditing authorities (*Riksrevisjonen*) had flagged in 2019 that many courts were breaching target timeframes for case processing, undermining citizens' right to timely justice. In response, the government launched a comprehensive review of the courts' organization.

Key events leading up to and following the 2021 judicial reform in Norway include:

August 11, 2017: The government appointed a new Judicial Commission to examine how the court structure could be improved to boost efficiency, quality, and accessibility of services. The commission was given a three-year mandate to study the issue and make recommendations.

January 1, 2019: A pilot merger was implemented in Vestfold, where the district courts of Nordre Vestfold, Tønsberg, Sandefjord, and Larvik were consolidated into a single Vestfold District Court. This pilot created one of the country's largest courts and was an early test of the merger concept, making Vestfold the fifth-largest court in Norway overnight.

October 1, 2019: The Judicial Commission delivered its report (NOU 2019:17), proposing to reduce the number of district courts from 60 to 22. The recommendation was based on expected efficiency gains from larger courts handling higher volumes, the ability to specialize judges, and better resource allocation. Importantly, the Commission emphasized maintaining geographical access by keeping local courthouses open as satellite offices even if administratively merged.

October 22, 2019: The National Audit Office (Riksrevisjonen) published its investigation into case processing times and efficiency in the courts (covering 2014–2018). It found that while the courts had marginally improved technical efficiency in that period, overall productivity declined due to negative technological change, meaning the system was not innovating or speeding up processes. The report highlighted excessive delays (many cases exceeded the Storting's (parliament's) targets for average processing time) indicating a decline in quality of service. This audit report added urgency to the call for reform and was cited by policymakers as evidence that structural change was needed.

November 15, 2020: The Storting (Parliament) formally approved the judicial reform, voting to merge the existing 60 district courts (and 34 land consolidation courts for property disputes) into significantly fewer units. This legislative decision set in motion the consolidation plan. The approved model settled on reducing the district courts from 60 down to 23 (slightly more than the Commission's proposal of 22, reflecting some political compromises). The number of land consolidation courts (jordskifterett) was reduced from 34 to 19. These changes constituted one of the largest judicial administrative reforms in modern Norwegian history.

April 26, 2021: The court merger reform was implemented on this date. The 60 district courts were reorganized into 23 larger district courts. In practical terms, multiple former courts within a region were now branches of a single new district court. For example, the previous courts of Follo and Nordre Østfold became branch locations of a unified Follo og Nordre Østfold District Court. Each new district court has one chief judge (sorenskriver), with courthouses maintained in multiple towns to preserve local access. Figure 1 illustrates the new court districts on the map. Crucially, reform designers noted that this was not a centralization of justice into cities – all 23 district courts have equal standing, and every locality that previously had a courthouse kept a local court venue (now as part of a larger district). The principle of judicial services "close to the people" was ostensibly preserved by allowing multiple court locations within each new district.

Figure 1. The courts of appeal (6) and district courts (23) in Norway after the reform in 2021

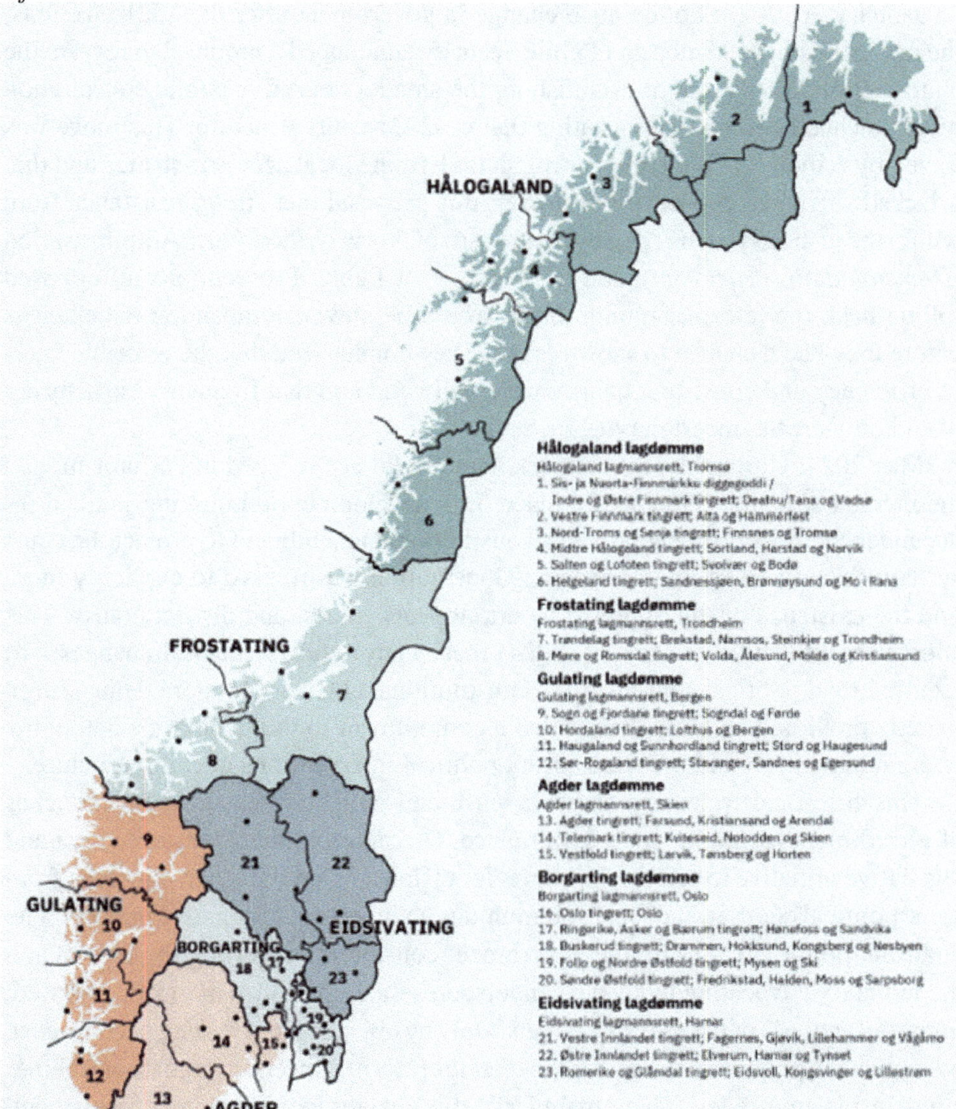

(Domstoladministrasjonen, 2022)

Throughout 2020–2021: In parallel with structural consolidation, the judiciary accelerated the adoption of digital tools (e-filing, digital case management, and even remote hearings) spurred partly by the COVID-19 pandemic. This period saw a rapid modernization of court operations, which would later be reflected in a measured technological improvement in efficiency.

January 26, 2022: Following a change in government after the 2021 elections, the new Minister of Justice and Public Security announced a proposal to reverse the court reform, effectively re-establishing the smaller courts. A public consultation was launched to consider reinstating the pre-2021 court structure. This move was fueled by critiques that the merger might undermine local access to justice and that it lacked sufficient consensus. However, this proposal met strong resistance from within the justice system. The Supreme Court of Norway, the Courts Administration (*Domstoladministrasjonen*), and the Director of Public Prosecutions all opposed rolling back the reform, arguing that it would be unwise to abandon the changes before they had a chance to show results. They emphasized that the reform's goals of efficiency and consistent quality were still valid and that frequent restructuring would only create uncertainty.

May 2024: Ultimately, the rollback attempt did not succeed in Parliament, and the merged structure remained in place. In a development reinforcing judicial independence, the Storting approved a constitutional amendment to protect the court system: Section 88 of the Norwegian Constitution was revised to explicitly mention the existence of the Supreme Court, appeals courts, and district courts. This entrenchment (effective May 21, 2024) means any future structural changes will require broad political consensus (as constitutional changes are more demanding), thereby providing stability. It signaled a commitment to the judiciary's autonomy in organizing itself and prevents abrupt political interventions in court structure.

This historical trajectory shows a push-and-pull between different branches of government regarding court governance. On one side, there was executive and legislative initiative to reform the courts for efficiency; on the other, concerns from some political quarters and local communities about potential negative impacts. The confrontation in 2022 (with the government considering reverting the reform and the judiciary advocating to keep it) underscores the importance of evidence-based, impartial analysis of the reform's effects. Only by objectively assessing performance outcomes can policymakers decide whether the reform is meeting its goals or whether adjustments are needed. The remainder of this chapter focuses on that assessment, examining how the 2021 court reform impacted efficiency, productivity, and quality in Norway's district courts, and what can be learned from this experience in a broader governance context.

It is also instructive to note the regional context: Norway's reform came after similar court consolidations in neighboring Nordic countries. Denmark implemented a major court merger in 2007, reducing its courts from 82 to 24 (Juul-Sandberg, 2016). Sweden reorganized in 2009, cutting district courts from 100 to 48 (Agrell et al., 2020). Finland undertook court consolidations in the 2010s, going from 27 to 20 district courts by 2019 (Nylund, 2023). Thus, Norway was the last among the Scandinavian countries to introduce such a structural reform. These countries reported improvements in efficiency and faster case processing after their reforms. However, Norway's geography, i.e. a long and sparsely populated territory of about 1,750 km length, poses unique challenges. The merger of judicial districts raised concerns about access to justice for remote communities, a theme we will revisit when discussing ethical considerations. With this historical and comparative backdrop in mind, we turn next to the scholarly literature and theoretical foundations relevant to evaluating Norway's court reform.

LITERATURE REVIEW

Judicial performance is a multifaceted concept that has been studied from legal, administrative, and economic perspectives. Early research recognized that courts must balance multiple goals: they should be independent and fair, but also efficient and accessible. Staats et al. (2005), for example, developed a cross-national index of judicial performance with five dimensions: independence, accountability, efficiency, effectiveness, and accessibility. Similarly, Palumbo et al. (2013) highlighted indicators like adjudication fairness and especially trial length as key measures of performance across countries. These works imply that speed and quality of justice go hand in hand in defining performance.

Measuring these concepts in practice, however, is difficult. Traditional qualitative evaluations, such as peer reviews or Judicial Performance Evaluation (JPE) programs, focus on individual judges' behavior and are used for decisions like reappointment or training. As noted, such evaluations can suffer from bias and do not readily translate into an overall assessment of a court's efficiency. Recognizing these issues, Posner & Richard (2005) proposed an economic approach to judge performance, treating judges as rational actors who respond to incentives and constraints much like bureaucrats or elected officials. While conceptually insightful, their approach acknowledged that quantitatively measuring each judge's performance in a real-world setting is nearly impossible – it would require detailed data on individual judges' caseloads, motivations, and behavior, which is seldom available.

Other simple performance metrics (like a judge's conviction rate or number of cases disposed) have proven inadequate or misleading. They often ignore case complexity or the fact that outcomes like convictions depend on factors beyond a judge's control (e.g., evidence strength, prosecution decisions). As Contini et al. (2014) observed, assessing judicial performance is complex and "not capable of easy analysis within a single jurisdiction," let alone across countries. There is no universally agreed yardstick for judicial quality or productivity, given the variety of legal systems and the qualitative values (like justice and fairness) that defy easy quantification.

Because of these challenges in evaluating judge-level performance, research interest shifted toward evaluating courts or court systems as a whole on efficiency criteria. As discussed, the introduction of Data Envelopment Analysis (DEA) by Charnes et al. (1978) provided a new way to measure how well courts convert resources into outputs. Lewin et al. (1982) were pioneers in applying DEA to 100 U.S. courts, effectively treating each court's administration as a production unit. They defined inputs like the number of judges, court staff, population served, etc., and outputs like number of cases disposed and reduction in backlogs. If a court could handle the same caseload with fewer judges or staff than another, DEA would flag the latter as inefficient relative to the former. Lewin's study proved that even within one state, court efficiency varied widely and that there was room to improve many courts by learning from the most efficient ones.

Norway itself contributed early to this line of research: Kittelsen & Førsund (1992) applied DEA to all Norwegian district courts over 1983–1988. Importantly, they introduced intertemporal analysis using the Malmquist Productivity Index, allowing them to measure how efficiency scores evolved over time and whether overall productivity grew or declined. Their work provided recommendations for improvement, illustrating that DEA results could inform policy by identifying which courts were lagging and what scale of improvement was theoretically possible.

In the 1990s and 2000s, DEA and related non-parametric methods became more common in court studies across different jurisdictions. Tulkens (1993), using FDH in Belgium, demonstrated the approach's usefulness for pinpointing inefficiency and testing claims for more resources (e.g., his results suggested Belgian courts could improve output with existing staff, countering arguments that simply hiring more clerks was needed). Pedraja-Chaparro & Salinas-Jimenez (1996) similarly found varying efficiency among Spanish courts, shedding light on resource allocation and best practices.

By the 2000s, a wave of studies applied DEA globally, not just to measure efficiency but sometimes to explore determinants of efficiency and implications for reform. For instance, Schneider (2005) linked German labor courts' efficiency to judges' career incentives. De Sousa & Schwengber (2005) and Yeung & Azevedo (2011) measured efficiency in Brazilian courts, feeding into discussions on judicial resource distribution in Brazil. Guzowska & Strak (2010) and a later study by Bełdowski et al. (2020) evaluated Polish courts. Tsai & Tsai (2010) combined DEA with decision-tree analysis for Taiwan's courts. Finocchiaro Castro & Guccio (2014) examined sources of inefficiency in Italian courts, while Nissi et al. (2019) continued analysis of Italy with two-stage DEA. Santos & Amado (2014) focused on Portugal, where their findings supported arguments for reorganizing the court network. In Sweden, Mattsson & Tidanå (2019) simulated the efficiency effects of merging district courts (just before Sweden actually did so). Studies in developing contexts, e.g. Ferro et al. (2018) in Argentina, Bajrić & Kadrić (2020) in Bosnia, and Gupta & Bolia (2020) in India, extended the use of DEA to highlight systemic issues and potential improvements in those judiciaries.

A key insight from this body of literature is that structural reforms (such as court mergers, jurisdictional changes, or administrative reorganizations) can be rigorously evaluated using DEA and related indices. By comparing efficiency before and after a reform, and tracking productivity changes, researchers can infer whether the reform achieved its intended effect. Several studies explicitly looked at reforms:

Ferrandino (2010) assessed a funding reform in Florida's circuit courts. Using DEA/Malmquist, he found that except for a handful of courts, efficiency did not improve post-reform – a sobering result that more money and state control didn't necessarily yield better performance. This pointed to perhaps flaws in implementation or the limits of funding alone to change outcomes.

Agrell et al. (2020) studied Sweden's consolidation of district courts in the 2000s. They found a positive efficiency impact, suggesting that merging courts and closing very small courts led to scale efficiencies and better resource utilization overall. Their work provides a precedent in the Nordic context that Norway's policymakers certainly noted.

Falavigna et al. (2018), though focused on Italy's tax courts, concluded that reorganization (like redistributing caseloads or resources) can boost productivity, primarily by moving the efficiency frontier (through technology or process innovations) and by enabling judges to handle more cases effectively.

Santos & Amado (2014), regarding Portugal, strongly inferred that without reforming the judicial map (Portugal eventually did a major court merger in 2014), inefficiencies would persist. In a related vein, their findings align with Silva (2018), who analyzed Portuguese courts with output-specific inputs and also suggested opportunities for efficiency gains via restructuring.

These studies collectively indicate that DEA is not only diagnostic but also prescriptive: it can highlight how reforms should be targeted, e.g., which courts to merge, where resources are insufficient or underutilized, etc.

By 2020, Norway found itself at a juncture similar to what some of these studies addressed: a clear need for reform identified by audits and performance metrics, but uncertainty about the reform's likely impact. Notably, Norway had a tradition of using analysis in policymaking, as evidenced by the Audit Office's DEA-based study (Riksrevisjonen, 2019-2020). That study, conducted just before the reform, revealed an unfavorable trend: district courts' efficiency was slipping and productivity was declining, primarily due to a backward slide in technology or processes (perhaps reflecting that the courts hadn't kept up with digitalization or new practices in the mid-2010s). It also underscored an issue with quality: many courts were breaching the recommended timelines, meaning justice delayed for many citizens. The Audit report explicitly recommended structural changes to address these issues. This formed a major impetus for the 2021 consolidation.

By late 2021, once the reform had been put into effect, debate ensued. Some stakeholders lauded the reform for being bold and necessary (Thorsvik, 2021), for instance, op-eds described it as "good district policy" that would strengthen local courts by pooling resources. Others criticized it (JD, 2022), claiming it might diminish local presence or that it was implemented too quickly without full buy-in (the Ministry's 2022 consultation document voiced such criticisms). Amid this debate, one thing was clear: no one had yet verified the outcomes of the reform with data.

Therefore, existing literature provides the tools and comparative cases to evaluate Norway's court reform. To contribute to this body of knowledge, our study will apply DEA and the Malmquist Productivity Index to Norway's district courts, comparing performance before and after the reform. We also incorporate a measure of quality (case timeliness) into the assessment, since efficiency gains must not come at the expense of justice. By doing so, we respond to the literature's call for multidimensional evaluation of judicial reforms and fill the gap of an evidence-based appraisal of Norway's reform. The next section outlines our specific research objectives and questions.

RESEARCH OBJECTIVES

The *primary purpose of this study* is to determine how successful the 2021 judicial reform in Norway has been in improving the performance of the district courts. Success is defined in terms of measurable increases in efficiency, productivity, and quality of service in the post-reform court system. In other words, did the consolidation of courts lead to more cases handled per resource, technological improvements, and timely justice compared to the prior structure? To achieve this, the study focuses on answering *four key research questions*, each targeting a critical aspect of performance:

(1) Productivity Change – How did the reform affect the overall productivity of Norway's courts and the position of the efficiency frontier? This involves examining whether technological progress or regress occurred (e.g. via digitalization or new processes) and if the courts as a whole are handling more (or fewer) cases relative to inputs post-reform.
(2) Efficiency of Courts – How did the reform impact the technical efficiency of individual district courts? We ask whether, after the mergers, courts are oper-

ating closer to optimal efficiency (best practice) or if efficiency scores have declined – essentially, are courts doing more with less, or less with the same, than before?

(3) Improvement Potential – How did the reform alter the capacity for efficiency improvement in the system? This involves identifying slack or unused capacity in the courts (e.g., extra staff or judge time that could be reallocated) and understanding if the gap between efficient and inefficient courts has narrowed or widened. We examine returns to scale for each court to see if courts ended up too large or still too small, indicating where potential efficiency gains or losses lie.

(4) Quality of Justice – How did the reform affect the quality of court services, particularly the timeliness of case processing? We use the share of cases exceeding certain processing time thresholds (overdue cases) as an indicator of quality. The question is whether the consolidated courts managed to reduce delays and backlog (improve quality) or if those metrics stayed the same or even worsened.

By addressing these questions, we aim to present a comprehensive evaluation of the reform. Rather than a single metric, we consider both quantitative efficiency/productivity metrics and a qualitative proxy for quality. This aligns with the balanced approach suggested in literature – acknowledging the trade-offs between efficiency and justice. Additionally, *the objective of this chapter* is to frame the findings in a public management and governance context. That is, beyond the numbers, what do the results imply for managing the judicial sector, for policy adaptation, and for stakeholders (judges, lawyers, citizens)? The reform's success or failure will be discussed not in isolation, but with an eye to governance implications: How should the judiciary and government respond to these findings? What lessons can be drawn for future reforms or for other countries considering similar changes?

Therefore, the study's objectives are both analytical (to measure and compare performance outcomes) and practical (to inform policy on whether course corrections are needed and how to harness any identified improvements). The next section elaborates on the theoretical and methodological framework used to pursue these objectives.

THEORETICAL FRAMEWORKS AND FOUNDATIONS

Evaluating a judicial reform requires a solid grounding in both theory and methodology. This study is built on two key theoretical foundations:

The Efficiency-Justice Trade-off – a conceptual understanding that in public services like courts, efficiency must be balanced with the fundamental purpose of delivering justice.

Production Frontier Analysis – the economic theory underlying tools like Data Envelopment Analysis (DEA) and the Malmquist index, which treat courts as production units transforming inputs into outputs.

As noted by Rubin (1979), there is an inherent tension between efficiency and justice in court systems. Courts are not businesses purely maximizing throughput; their mandate is to deliver fair outcomes. Pushing for faster case processing and higher case clearance rates (efficiency) should not compromise due process, thoroughness of deliberation, or equitable access (quality). This principle guided our framework: we explicitly incorporated a quality metric (cases resolved within acceptable time frames) alongside efficiency metrics, recognizing that a successful reform should improve speed without undermining fairness.

We drew inspiration from management frameworks that examine efficiency vs. effectiveness (or quality) trade-offs in public services. For instance, Lo Storto & Goncharuk (2017) developed an efficiency-effectiveness matrix in healthcare benchmarking. By analogy, we constructed an Efficiency–Quality matrix for the courts, plotting each court's efficiency score against its quality indicator (timeliness) to see how the reform shifted courts in this two-dimensional space. This helps identify if any court managed to improve both efficiency and quality (the ideal scenario), or if gains in one came at the expense of the other.

Ethical considerations also underpin the theoretical framework: any performance evaluation regime must ensure impartiality and equal treatment. For example, if one were to evaluate judges individually, research warns of biases, e.g. Gill et al. 2011 showed JPE scores can be systematically lower for women/minorities. In our system-wide approach, we mitigate such biases by focusing on aggregate court output and delays, rather than subjective opinions of performance. However, we remain cognizant that even aggregate efficiency pursuits have ethical limits, e.g. closing a small courthouse might improve efficiency on paper but hurt community access. Thus, our framework doesn't treat efficiency gains as absolute positives unless accompanied by maintained or improved justice quality.

On the quantitative side, our approach relies on the theory of the production frontier. In economics, a production frontier represents the maximum feasible output that can be produced from a given set of inputs, given current technology. Units operating on the frontier are efficient; those below it are inefficient. DEA is an operational research technique that estimates this frontier from empirical data. It provides each decision-making unit (here, each district court) an efficiency score between 0 and 1, where 1 indicates a court on the frontier (no other court produces more outputs with the same or fewer inputs). For our analysis, we adopted a DEA model with constant returns to scale (CRS) assumptions (the classical CCR model by Charnes et al., 1978) to compute baseline efficiency scores. Constant returns assume that court outputs scale proportionally with inputs – a reasonable first approximation in a short-term analysis where courts sizes did change but the fundamental process is similar. We computed DEA scores for two periods: pre-reform (2019) and post-reform (2022). This allowed a direct comparison of how each court's efficiency changed. An efficiency score of, say, 0.80 means the court could, in theory, achieve the same outputs with 20% fewer inputs if it were operating as efficiently as the best-performing peer. To delve deeper, we used an advanced DEA variant: the Slack-Based Measure (SBM) model introduced by Tone (2001). Unlike basic DEA which gives a single efficiency score, the SBM identifies specific input excesses and output shortfalls (called slacks) for each unit. This is critical for diagnosing where inefficiencies lie, e.g. a court might have too many administrative staff relative to its caseload, or it might clear far fewer cases than another court with the same resources, indicating procedural bottlenecks. By applying the SBM model to each court in both 2019 and 2022, we could quantify the reserves for improvement on each input/output dimension. For example, if a court had a slack indicating 5 extra judges (meaning it could reduce judges by 5 and still handle the same cases if it were efficient), that points to potential overcapacity or misallocation in that court. We also determined the Returns to Scale (RTS) for each court – whether each was operating in a zone of increasing returns (could become more efficient by growing larger), constant returns, or decreasing returns (had become too large and would be more efficient if smaller). RTS was derived via standard DEA methods and tests (e.g. comparing CRS and VRS – variable returns to scale – efficiency scores). This aspect directly informs whether consolidation achieved optimal scales or if it overshot.

The Malmquist Productivity Index is another pillar of our framework. It measures how a unit's productivity changes over time by looking at shifts in the frontier and movement relative to the frontier. Conceptually, Malmquist > 1 means productivity improved, < 1 means it worsened. We broke this down into Efficiency Change (catch-up factor) and Technological Change (frontier shift factor), following the decomposition by Lovell (2003). For the court system, efficiency change indicates whether, on average, courts got closer to best practice or not, while technological change indicates if the best practice itself got better (e.g., due to digitalization or process innovations that let even top courts handle more cases than before). By calculating the Malmquist index from 2019 to 2022, we capture the net effect of reform and other factors (like technology, pandemic recovery) on overall productivity.

METHODOLOGY

Bringing above-mentioned elements together, we designed a nine-stage analytical framework (Figure 2) to evaluate the reform's impact comprehensively.

Figure 2. Research methodology for this study

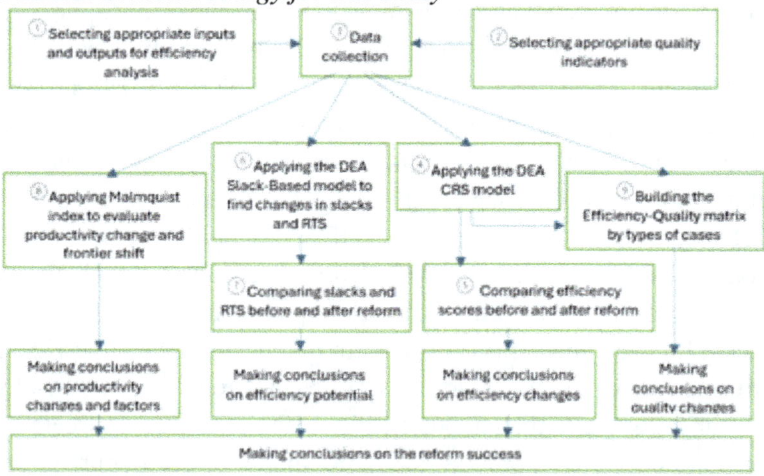

The stages were as follows:

(1) Select Inputs and Outputs: We identified relevant input and output metrics for the efficiency analysis. Inputs chosen were the human resources of the courts: the number of judges (NJ), deputy judges (NDJ), and other court staff (NCS) (clerks, administrative personnel). These capture the primary resource consumption in courts. Outputs chosen were the counts of different case types resolved: settled civil cases (SCC), settled criminal cases with a single judge (SCJ), and settled complex cases (SCM). "Complex cases" here refers to those requiring lay judges or mediation (e.g., cases with mediation panels or extended proceedings). We included multiple output types to reflect the court's multifaceted workload – simple cases vs. complex, civil vs. criminal.

(2) Select Quality Indicators: To evaluate quality, we picked indicators related to case processing times. Specifically, for each of the three case categories (civil, criminal, complex), we collected the average processing time (APT) and the share of overdue cases (SOC) that exceeded stipulated timeframes. While average duration is informative, the overdue share (percent of cases taking longer than a target threshold) was deemed a more actionable quality indicator, as it directly ties to whether courts meet timeliness standards. Ultimately, we used SOC in

our efficiency-quality matrix, as it captures whether delays are systemic. (A high SOC indicates many cases miss the target resolution time.)

(3) Data Collection: We gathered data for these inputs, outputs, and quality metrics from official sources for the relevant years. The sources included annual reports from Norges Domstoler (the Norwegian Courts Administration) and the National Audit Office's report. We focused on 2019 as the pre-reform baseline and 2022 as the first full year of the post-reform system. We intentionally skipped 2020–2021 for baseline comparison because 2020 was heavily disrupted by COVID-19 and 2021 was a transition year with the reform implemented in April and pandemic effects still ongoing. 2019 represents the last "normal" year of the old system, and 2022 represents the new system in stable operation.

(4) Baseline DEA (2019) and Post-reform DEA (2022): Using the inputs and outputs, we ran a constant returns to scale DEA for 2019 (60 district courts as separate units) and for 2022 (23 district courts). Each DEA analysis yielded efficiency scores for that year and identified which courts were on the frontier (score = 1.000) and which were inefficient (score < 1). By comparing the distribution of scores from 2019 to 2022, we could see if efficiency generally improved or declined. Because the number of courts changed (60 down to 23), the analysis for 2022 inherently considers the merged courts as single units – their larger size and combined resources.

(5) Slack Analysis (2019) and (2022): In parallel, we applied the Slack-Based Measure (SBM) DEA to each year's data. This provided the slack values for each input and output for each court. We aggregated these to understand, for example, how many "excess" judges existed system-wide in inefficient courts pre- and post-reform, or how much caseload output could be increased if inefficiencies were eliminated. This addresses the question of efficiency reserves or potential improvements. We also derived each court's Returns to Scale (RTS) status from the slack analysis (and a separate variable-returns DEA): categorizing courts as operating under increasing, constant, or decreasing returns to scale.

(6) Compare Pre- vs. Post-Reform Results: We then compared the efficiency scores, slacks, and RTS patterns from Stage 4 and 5 between 2019 and 2022. This comparison answers questions like: Did the number of efficient courts change? Did the average efficiency score rise or fall? How did the total slack (inefficiency) in the system shift? Notably, we observed if more courts fell into the decreasing returns category after merging – which would indicate they became too large.

(7) Malmquist Productivity Analysis: Next, we conducted an intertemporal DEA analysis combining 2019 and 2022 data to calculate the Malmquist productivity index for each court (or merged court). We effectively treated each district court's 2019 performance and its 2022 performance as points in a combined dataset to compute productivity change. The Malmquist index was decomposed

into Efficiency Change (catch-up) and Technological Change (frontier shift) components. We averaged these indices across all courts to get a sense of the overall system's change. This stage directly addresses whether the efficiency frontier moved (e.g., through tech improvements like e-courts) and whether courts on average moved closer to or farther from the frontier.

(8) Efficiency-Quality Matrix: Using results from Stages 4 and the quality data from Stage 2, we plotted an Efficiency vs. Quality matrix for 2019 and 2022. Specifically, we looked at each case type (civil, criminal, complex) and plotted points for each year representing the average efficiency and the average quality (measured by SOC, share of overdue cases). This visual approach (inspired by Lo Storto & Goncharuk's effectiveness-efficiency matrix) helps visualize if improvements in efficiency coincided with improvements in timeliness or not. For instance, we could see if the average share of overdue civil cases went down when efficiency went up, or if there was no relationship. Additionally, by comparing the 2019 and 2022 positions, we could infer how reform shifted the balance of efficiency and quality.

(9) Synthesis of Findings: Finally, we synthesized all these results to draw conclusions about the reform's success. This involved interpreting sometimes mixed outcomes – e.g., perhaps productivity fell but potential for improvement rose – and judging on balance whether the reform achieved its goals. In doing so, we considered contextual factors (like the pandemic's effect in 2020–2021) and the experience of other countries (benchmarking against Nordic reforms) to temper our conclusions. The synthesis also led to specific recommendations (presented later) on how to adjust the reform to address any shortcomings identified.

This nine-stage framework ensured that our analysis was thorough and structured. It moves from raw data to increasingly nuanced insights: from simple before/after efficiency scores to deep dives into why those efficiency levels changed (slacks and RTS) and what happened to overall productivity and quality.

By following this approach, we adhere to best practices in public-sector performance evaluation: using multiple indicators, comparing across time, and relating results back to policy objectives. The next sections will present the findings in terms of observed advantages and positive outcomes of the reform, followed by the challenges and negative outcomes, always in light of the above theoretical considerations.

This study used the data from official sources, including the Norges Domstoler reports for 2019 and 2022 and Riksrevisjonen (2019-2020). 2019 was chosen for comparison because it is the last year before the COVID pandemic, which can be considered normal without deviations towards online or impossible cases and closed courts. Three categories of Norwegian district court employees were taken as inputs, namely the number of judges, deputy judges and other court staff. The outputs are the number of settled cases of three types, namely civil cases (disputes), ordinary criminal cases (with one judge) and complex cases (with mediators). Descriptive statistics of the collected dataset are presented in the Table 1.

Table 1. Descriptive statistics of the collected dataset for 2022

	Judges (NJ)	**Vice-judges (NDJ)**	**Other court Staff (NCS)**	**Civil cases – settled (SCC)**	**Single-judge criminal cases - settled (SCJ)**	**Complex cases – settled (SCM)**
Mean	16.26	6.83	29.04	531.78	2268.91	607.87
Median	12	5	23	431	1862	490
Stand. dev.	19.19	5.35	24.10	480.47	1955.18	597.55
Min	1	2	4	88	377	150
Max	97	28	123	2337	9673	3108

The smallest district court with only 1 judge is recorded in Vestre Finnmark, and the largest district with 97 judges is in Oslo.

THE RESULTS

In *stages 1* to *3* of this study, relevant indicators were selected from the inputs and outputs of the Norwegian district courts for the years 2019 and 2022, as shown above. At stages 4 and 8, the CRS DEA model was applied to 23 district courts, that is, before and after the reform. The results can be seen in Table 2.

Table 2. Efficiency scores for disrict courts in 2019 and 2022

2019			2022		
No.	DMU Name	Efficiency	No.	DMU Name	Efficiency
1	Agder	1.00000	1	Agder	0.90807
2	Buskerud	0.73603	2	Buskerud	0.60559
3	Follo og Nordre Østfold	0.94216	3	Follo og Nordre Østfold	1.00000
4	Haugaland og Sunnhordland	0.79535	4	Haugaland og Sunnhordland	0.62450
5	Helgeland	1.00000	5	Helgeland	0.92486
6	Hordaland	0.80974	6	Hordaland	0.70465
7	Indre- og Østre Finnmark	0.32652	7	Indre- og Østre Finnmark	0.21574
8	Midtre Hålogaland	0.71604	8	Midtre Hålogaland	0.63884
9	Møre og Romsdal	0.91065	9	Møre og Romsdal	0.72093
10	Nord-Troms og Senja	1.00000	10	Nord-Troms og Senja	0.95205
11	Oslo	1.00000	11	Oslo	0.81799
12	Ringerike, Asker og Bærum	1.00000	12	Ringerike, Asker og Bærum	1.00000
13	Romerike og Glåmdal	1.00000	13	Romerike og Glåmdal	1.00000
14	Salten og Lofoten	0.78995	14	Salten og Lofoten	0.66561
15	Sogn og Fjordane	0.79766	15	Sogn og Fjordane	0.67342
16	Søndre Østfold	1.00000	16	Søndre Østfold	0.92118
17	Sør-Rogaland	0.98372	17	Sør-Rogaland	0.83827
18	Telemark	0.97577	18	Telemark	0.89223
19	Trøndelag	1.00000	19	Trøndelag	1.00000
20	Vestfold	0.77842	20	Vestfold	0.79752
21	Vestre Finnmark	1.00000	21	Vestre Finnmark	1.00000
22	Vestre Innlandet	0.71377	22	Vestre Innlandet	0.64247
23	Østre Innlandet	1.00000	23	Østre Innlandet	1.00000

As can be seen, the number of efficient courts decreased from 10 to 6 over three years. Moreover, the average efficiency score for the sample decreased from 0.88156 to 0.80626. Five of the 10 efficient courts in 2019 ceased to be efficient in 2022. However, one court (Follo og Nordre Østfold) was added to the set of remaining efficient courts in 2022, which was inefficient in 2019. At the same time, 17 out of 23 courts worsened their efficiency score and only 2 courts (Vestfold and Follo og Nordre Østfold) saw a slight improvement in efficiency after the reform.

At stages 5 and 9, the results of applying the DEA slack-based model for the same sample enabled to reveal the reserves of reducing the inputs and increasing the outputs of the district courts of Norway (Figure 3).

Figure 3. Reserves (slacks) for efficiency improvement, per cent

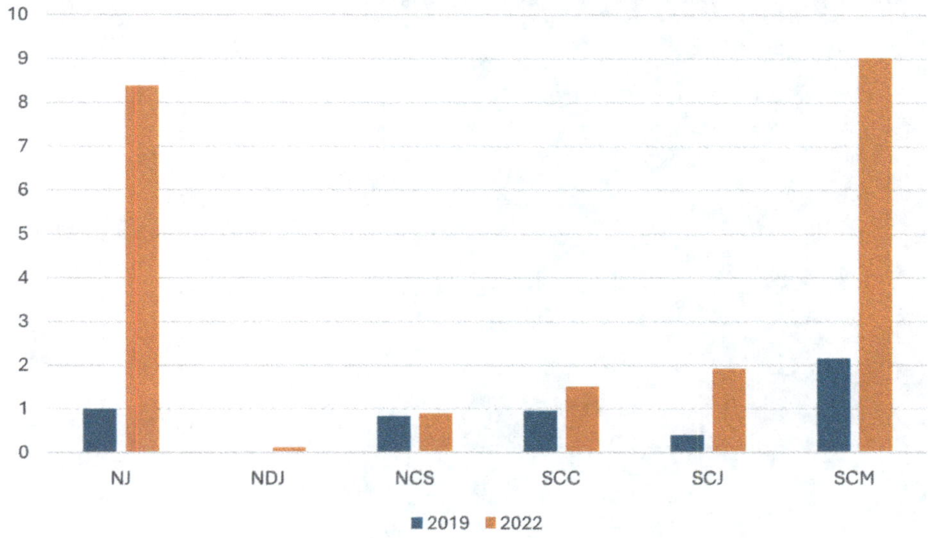

As can be seen, reserves (slacks) for all inputs and outputs have increased, especially for the number of judges and the number of criminal and complex cases. That is, after the reform, the gap between efficient and inefficient courts has grown significantly, especially in terms of judges' productivity and work with criminal and complex cases. In particular, if in 2019 only 4 courts had a small reserve (4) for judges, then in 2022 already 6 courts had a total reserve of 31 judges.

A comparison of the calculated returns to the scale (RTS) revealed a reduction in the number of courts with increasing RTS (from 13 to 9 percent) and a significant increase in courts with decreasing RTS (from 43 to 63 percent). In addition to the reduction in the number of efficient courts, this trend indicates the ineffectiveness of uniting courts that took place during the 2021 reform.

In stage 6, the applying Malmquist productivity index and its decomposition revealed how much the efficiency frontier has shifted and how the productivity and efficiency of the Norwegian district courts have changed over the period 2019-2022 (Table 3).

Table 3. Malmquist productivity index, efficiency change and frontier shift

DMU No.	DMUs in Period 2	Malmquist Index	Efficiency Change	Frontier Shift
1	Agder	1.02320	0.90807	1.12679
2	Buskerud	0.84184	0.82278	1.02316
3	Follo og Nordre Østfold	1.15528	1.06139	1.08846
4	Haugaland og Sunnhordland	0.84117	0.78519	1.07129
5	Helgeland	0.67091	0.92486	0.72542
6	Hordaland	0.95210	0.87022	1.09409
7	Indre- og Østre Finnmark	0.82107	0.66074	1.24266
8	Midtre Hålogaland	0.85737	0.89219	0.96097
9	Møre og Romsdal	0.83797	0.79167	1.05848
10	Nord-Troms og Senja	0.96972	0.95205	1.01856
11	Oslo	0.87345	0.81799	1.06781
12	Ringerike, Asker og Bærum	1.07043	1.00000	1.07043
13	Romerike og Glåmdal	1.03742	1.00000	1.03742
14	Salten og Lofoten	0.87670	0.84260	1.04047
15	Sogn og Fjordane	0.90190	0.84424	1.06830
16	Søndre Østfold	1.00873	0.92118	1.09504
17	Sør-Rogaland	0.96263	0.85214	1.12966
18	Telemark	1.04965	0.91438	1.14793
19	Trøndelag	1.08148	1.00000	1.08148
20	Vestfold	1.09473	1.02454	1.06851
21	Vestre Finnmark	1.27059	1.00000	1.27059
22	Vestre Innlandet	0.91141	0.90010	1.01256
23	Østre Innlandet	1.20557	1.00000	1.20557
	Mean (geom)	*0.96044*	*0.89871*	*1.06868*

The frontier shift turned out to be positive for 21 out of 23 district courts. On average for the country, its increase was almost 7%. However, due to a significant negative efficiency change (by over 10%), this growth didn't ensure a growth in the average productivity. Only 10 of the 23 district courts have an increase in productivity. On average, productivity decreased by almost 4% across the country.

With some understanding of efficiency and productivity and their changes due to the reform, in stage 7, the courts' efficiency scores were compared with their quality indicators (SOC). The results of this comparison by types of cases and years can be seen in Figure 4.

Figure 4. Efficiency-quality matrix by types of cases

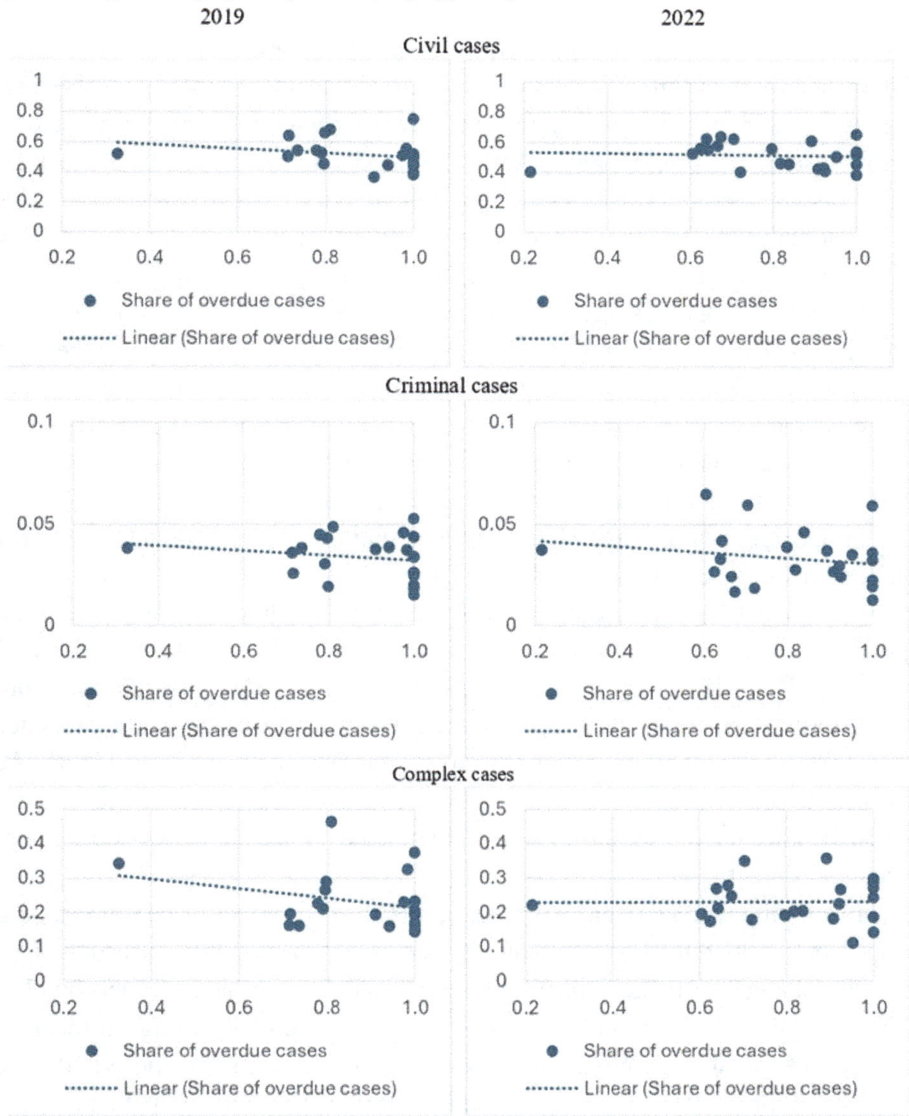

As can seen, changes occurred not only in efficiency, but also in the quality of courts, and both positive and negative. In particular, if on average the share of overdue civil cases remained at the level of 49.4 percent, it increased from 3.2 to 3.3 percent in criminal cases. The average share of overdue complex cases decreased somewhat - from 22.9 to 22.4 percent. That is, the reform did not significantly affect the average share of overdue cases in the district courts of Norway, when their efficiency and productivity decreased.

IMPORTANCE

Why does improving court performance matter? An efficient and high-quality judiciary is a cornerstone of good governance and socio-economic development. Delayed or inefficient justice is effectively denied justice – when courts take too long or waste resources, the public loses confidence in the rule of law. Quick and reliable dispute resolution facilitates economic activity (contracts are enforceable) and social stability (grievances are addressed through law). A World Bank/IMF study by Esposito et al. (2014) went so far as to call judicial reform in Italy "a key to growth," underlining that sluggish courts were a drag on the economy. In Norway's context, while the country consistently ranks high on rule-of-law indices, there was growing alarm that court delays (especially in civil cases) were undermining rights and creating frustration. For example, by 2018-2019, the largest appellate court was warning that statutory time limits were being breached by months or years – an unacceptable situation in a country that values the rule of law.

The importance of this study lies in its contribution to both national and international understanding of judicial reforms. Domestically, as Norway made a controversial change to its court structure, an evidence-based evaluation provides feedback to policymakers: Are the reforms delivering as hoped? If not, where specifically are the gaps? This is critical for accountability (justifying the reform expenditures and disruption) and for making mid-course corrections (tweaking the new system for better results). Our findings can inform the Ministry of Justice, the Courts Administration, and Parliament whether to persist with the new structure, adjust it, or consider alternative measures (such as increasing resources or introducing new management practices).

From a public management perspective, this case is a valuable lesson in change management in the public sector. Court systems, like many public institutions, are resistant to change due to their constitutional role and the many stakeholders involved (judges, lawyers, staff, public). Demonstrating improvement through reform can build support for future innovations. Conversely, if a reform does not yield benefits, understanding why is equally important – it may highlight areas like training, technology, or change management processes that need attention.

Internationally, the Norwegian case adds to the comparative knowledge of judicial reform outcomes. Many countries struggle with backlogs and inefficient courts. Seeing Norway attempt a structural fix (merging courts) provides a reference point. If Norway, a high-capacity and well-funded system, faces difficulties in making consolidation work, that offers a caution or specific insights for others. If it succeeds in some areas (for example, implementing digital courts swiftly), that can serve as a model. The Nordic countries often learn from each other's public sector experiments. Indeed, Norway's reform was motivated in part by the positive reports from

Denmark, Sweden, and Finland's earlier reforms. Thus, our evaluation "closes the loop" by giving back an analysis that can be studied by those countries and beyond.

Finally, efficient courts are important for public trust and legitimacy. In Norway, the judiciary enjoys a high level of trust historically. But that trust could erode if people routinely experience unreasonable delays or perceive inequities in access. By focusing on performance improvement, the judicial branch demonstrates responsiveness to societal needs (faster, accessible justice), which in turn reinforces legitimacy. On the other hand, changes that are seen to distance the courts from the people (like court closures) can harm trust. Our study's importance is thus also to gauge whether the reform struck the right balance to maintain public confidence.

Therefore, improving court performance is not an abstract goal – it has real impacts on economic efficiency, citizens' rights, and the integrity of the justice system. The importance of learning from the 2021 reform cannot be overstated: it ensures that Norway's judiciary continues to serve the public effectively and that any future reforms (in Norway or similar contexts) can be guided by empirical evidence rather than assumptions.

GOVERNANCE

The governance structure of a country's judiciary significantly influences how reforms are implemented and how successful they can be. Norway's court reform sheds light on governance dynamics in at least two ways: judicial independence and administrative autonomy, and inter-branch coordination (or conflict) in reform processes. Norway's judiciary is constitutionally part of the third branch of government, independent of the executive and legislative branches. Judicial governance in Norway features an independent agency – the *Domstoladministrasjonen* (Norwegian Courts Administration) – established in 2002 to handle administrative tasks of courts, somewhat akin to the independent court administrations in Denmark and Sweden. This body took over many functions previously under the Ministry of Justice, to insulate courts from political interference in day-to-day operations. In Denmark, a similar shift (creating an independent Courts Administration and modernizing court management) has been credited with improved efficiency and transparency. Norway followed that model, indicating a governance commitment to judicial self-management. However, major structural reforms, such as altering the number of courts, still require legislation and thus involve the government and parliament. The 2021 reform was initiated by the Ministry of Justice (executive) and approved by the Storting (*legislature*), not by the courts themselves. This raised questions of governance: to what extent should the executive drive changes in the judiciary's structure? The controversy in 2022, when a new government sought to reverse the reform, highlighted potential tensions. Here, the judiciary's top leadership (Supreme Court Chief Justice, heads of prosecution, and the Courts Administration) actively lobbied to maintain the new structure. One could interpret this as the judiciary asserting its perspective on what governance arrangement best serves justice. The situation resembled a tug-of-war between political promises (the new government had campaigned on keeping courts local) and judicial/evidence-based arguments (the courts' leadership argued the reform's logic should be given time).

Good governance in such reforms would entail inclusive decision-making, involving judges, court staff, local communities, and lawyers in planning the changes. It is not fully clear to what extent the 2017–2019 Commission engaged stakeholders, but the pushback in 2020–2021 suggests some felt left out or unconvinced. By contrast, countries like Finland and Sweden, when they did similar consolidations, phased them in gradually and communicated the benefits (like specialization and resources) to mitigate resistance. Governance lessons from Norway's case might be that even when a reform is top-down initiated, it requires bottom-up buy-in to implement smoothly.

The role of regulatory frameworks is also part of governance. The Courts Act (*domstolloven*) governs court structure in Norway. The 2021 reform had to amend these laws to redefine districts. Good governance meant that, despite merging, the "principle of equality" of all district courts was maintained in law – no court was formally superior to others, and each continues to exercise the same jurisdiction. This legal principle was emphasized to alleviate fears of centralization or downgrading local courts. The fact that local courthouses remained open was not just a practical arrangement but a governance choice enshrined in how the reform was executed.

Another governance aspect is oversight and accountability. Post-reform, with fewer, larger courts, how is performance monitored? Each new district court covers a wider area, possibly making it harder for local media or the public to scrutinize performance. The independent Courts Administration will need robust performance tracking to ensure the big units stay responsive. The EU Justice (2024) noted that Norway (though not an EU member) and its Nordic neighbors generally rank high in judicial efficiency and independence. These scores reflect governance that values transparency (publishing court statistics, etc.). In Denmark's reforms, for instance, they reported efficiency gains and increased public trust post-reform, attributing some of that to the independent administration and better management practices put in place. Norway likely will continue to use its governance tools (annual reports, audits) to hold the larger courts accountable.

Finally, the constitutional amendment of 2024 is a significant governance development. By entrenching the structure of the courts in the Constitution, Norway signaled that any future changes must consider the judiciary's constitutional role. It provides an extra safeguard that the judiciary cannot be radically altered without broad consensus (two consecutive parliaments for constitutional changes). This may have been partly in reaction to the turbulence around the 2021 reform essentially to avoid seesawing policies with each election. It strengthens judicial governance by acknowledging the judiciary's co-equal status and protecting it from politicization. As Hoelseth (2024) commented, it creates holistic constitutional protection for the courts.

Therefore, governance played a dual role in Norway's court reform: it enabled the reform (through commissions, legislation, and independent administration involvement) and also tested the resilience of judicial independence (when political winds shifted). The outcome with the reform intact and now constitutionally buttressed suggests a reaffirmation that court governance must be a collaborative enterprise, not just a unilateral government policy. Going forward, strong governance will be needed to implement any recommended adjustments (discussed later) in a way that respects both efficiency goals and judicial independence.

ADVANTAGES AND CHALLENGES

Despite the largely critical tone of initial observations, the 2021 court reform in Norway also yielded several advantages and positive developments. These advantages can be categorized into: technological and process improvements, potential efficiency gains (capacity), specialization and consistency, and maintained access through local presence. Additionally, some courts did experience improved performance, showing that success is possible under the new model.

1. *Technological Modernization and Frontier Shift*: One clear positive outcome was the acceleration of digital transformation in courts. During 2020–2022, Norwegian courts rapidly expanded the use of e-justice tools – including electronic filing of cases, digital document management, and the conduct of remote hearings via video conferencing. These changes were partly driven by necessity during the COVID-19 pandemic, but the reform also underscored the need for modern case handling to manage a larger unified court. The result was measurable technological progress in the judicial production process. Our Malmquist analysis showed that the efficiency frontier shifted upward by about +6.9% from 2019 to 2022. This means that, holding efficiency constant, courts in 2022 could on average handle ~7% more cases with the same resources than in 2019, due to improvements in technology and processes. In fact, 21 out of 23 post-reform courts exhibited a positive frontier shift, indicating that nearly all benefited from system-wide improvements. This is a significant achievement: it suggests the judiciary embraced innovations (like digital caseflow systems and

online dispute mediation) that will serve well in the long run. Even though this frontier shift alone did not immediately translate into productivity gains (because efficiency dropped concurrently), it lays a foundation for future improvements. Once efficiency is re-optimized, the higher frontier means potential output is greater than before, thanks to modernized practices.

2. *Increased Potential Efficiency (Slack Reduction Opportunities)*: Paradoxically, while average efficiency scores fell (a negative we discuss later), the reform created opportunities for greater efficiency gains by revealing where slack exists. The DEA slack analysis found that after the reform, there were larger identifiable reserves of capacity that could be utilized. For example, in 2019 (pre-reform), only a few small courts had excess judge capacity, totaling around 4 judges system-wide that could theoretically be reallocated. By 2022, six courts had slack in judge resources, summing up to 31 judges worth of capacity that could be reaped if inefficiencies are tackled. At first glance, that sounds negative (more slack = more inefficiency). But viewed positively, it means the reform has highlighted where the inefficiencies lie (mostly in larger merged courts now) and thus where management can focus. In other words, the reform's outcome is not a mystery – we can pinpoint that judges' productivity, especially in handling criminal and complex cases, has room for improvement in certain courts. This is a useful diagnostic advantage; it provides a roadmap for internal benchmarking and best-practice sharing. The fact that a few courts remained efficient shows that their practices could be emulated. The Courts Administration can use these findings to encourage under-performing courts to adopt the methods of the efficient courts. This growing slack gives hope for the possibility of improving the efficiency of the Norwegian judicial system through benchmarking. Essentially, the reform created larger courts that can learn internally – inefficiencies within them can potentially be ironed out by redistributing workloads, standardizing procedures, and optimizing staff allocation across courthouses.
3. *Specialization and Expertise*: One of the intended advantages of merging courts was to allow judges to specialize more in particular types of cases. Early signs indicate this benefit is being realized. In the new larger district courts, judges can focus on areas like family law, financial crimes, or labor disputes, rather than each judge handling the entire gamut of cases. According to reform outlines, "judges in the new, larger courts are given the opportunity to specialize in specific areas of law... allowing for more expertise and consistency in legal rulings.". This specialization is expected to improve the quality of decisions and reduce the time needed for complex cases, as specialized judges build experience and handle cases more efficiently. While our quantitative analysis did not directly measure decision quality, specialization is a qualitative advantage that has been noted in similar reforms (e.g., Sweden's reform led to more

consistent rulings as judges focused on their fields). Furthermore, specialized dockets can prevent backlog in areas that previously overwhelmed small courts lacking a dedicated judge for that domain. The reform also aimed to ensure more uniform case processing times across the country. Under the old system, some small courts had much longer delays than larger courts. With consolidation, there's an expectation (still to be fully realized) that cases will be processed with similar efficiency regardless of region, because resources can be pooled and managed more centrally. If one courthouse is overloaded, the chief judge of the new district court has authority to redistribute cases or personnel from a less busy branch to assist, something that was bureaucratically difficult before.

4. *Consistency and Standardization*: A subtle advantage is the move toward more standardized procedures and administration. Instead of 60 independent entities, there are now 23, which means fewer variations in how things are done. Best practices in case management software, scheduling, and administration can be implemented across the merged units. This was observed in Denmark's reform, where merging courts led to the adoption of common best-practice routines, improving overall efficiency. Norway is likely to see a similar effect – indeed the frontier shift we measured partly reflects that new standard procedures (like extensively using digital systems for scheduling) were put in place across courts during the reform.
5. *Maintenance of Local Access*: One often overlooked success of the reform is that it managed to achieve consolidation without shutting citizens out of local courthouses. Despite the political rhetoric about "closing courts," the reform explicitly kept all previous court locations operating as local branches (referred to as "places where judgment can be made"). This means, from a user's perspective, they still go to the same local court building for their hearings in most cases. The difference is administrative – that building is now a part of a larger district court. The Domstoladministrasjonen (2022) emphasized that the reform did not lead to centralization of courts, because the principle of equality of all district courts was maintained. In practical terms, access to justice in small communities was safeguarded by retaining local court venues. This is an important advantage because it mitigates one of the biggest potential drawbacks of consolidation (forcing people in remote areas to travel far for court). It shows the reform was designed with a mind to balance efficiency with accessibility. The local branch model can be a best-practice example for other countries: you can merge administrations without necessarily vacating buildings or abandoning local presence. Moreover, by keeping local offices, the reform ensures that local knowledge (of community context, etc.) is not entirely lost and that trust in the justice system in rural areas is preserved. People still "see" the courthouse in town, even if its name changed.

6. *Positive Examples – Improved Courts*: While the overall trend in efficiency was negative, a couple of district courts showed that improvement is possible under the new system. Notably, Follo og Nordre Østfold District Court (formed by merging two courts) improved its performance and moved from inefficiency to efficiency by 2022. It was the one merged unit that became fully efficient post-reform whereas it had not been before. This suggests that the merger in that region achieved the intended outcome, possibly through better resource pooling or leadership. Another case, Vestfold District Court, which had been a pilot merged in 2019, showed a modest efficiency improvement over the three-year period. While Vestfold was still not 100% efficient, it did manage to slightly reduce its inefficiency, indicating that over a longer adjustment period, improvements can accrue. These examples are important as proof of concept that the reform can work if conditions are right. They provide internal benchmarks: other districts can inquire what Follo og Nordre Østfold did right, e.g. did they implement a new case management system faster? Did they reallocate staff optimally? Was there strong local management?.

In terms of quality, we also saw a small positive change: the share of overdue complex cases (typically lengthy, multi-judge cases) decreased from 22.9% to 22.4% on average. This ~0.5 percentage point reduction suggests the reform did not harm and may have slightly helped the handling of complex cases. Complex cases often benefit from specialization and more judges available, which the larger courts provide. Also, average processing times for some case types might have improved (though we cite overdue percentages, one might infer average times for complex cases shortened slightly since fewer breached deadlines).

Finally, on a higher level, the reform's focus on efficiency has instilled a more performance-oriented culture in the judiciary. The intense scrutiny of outputs and timelines that accompanied the reform (and our evaluation) sends a signal that efficiency is a priority alongside justice. This cultural shift can be advantageous as courts innovate and strive to meet targets, provided it's balanced with judicial independence. In neighboring countries, embracing a culture of continuous improvement in courts has led to sustained efficiency gains long after the initial reform. For example, Sweden's courts continued to improve processing times over a decade, building on the momentum of the 2009 consolidation. Norway's courts now have a similar opportunity to leverage the reform as a catalyst for ongoing improvements.

Therefore, while the immediate quantitative results of Norway's reform were mixed, the advantages provide reasons for optimism. The system is now technologically more advanced, structured in a way that reveals where improvements are needed, capable of offering specialized services, and still accessible to the public. A couple of courts have already demonstrated gains. These positives are building blocks – if the challenges identified are addressed, the advantages put the Norwegian judiciary on a path to eventually realize the reform's goals of an efficient, high-quality court system.

The reform of Norway's district courts, while well-intentioned, encountered several significant challenges and negative outcomes in its early years. These challenges span from empirical performance declines to practical and ethical concerns. Here we detail the main issues: decline in efficiency scores, reduced productivity, uneven performance and scale inefficiencies, persistently high backlogs, transitional disruptions (including the pandemic context), and concerns about access and stakeholder buy-in.

1. *Decline in Efficiency Scores*: Contrary to the reform's primary goal, the technical efficiency of courts worsened overall after the consolidation. In 2019, before the reform, 10 out of 60 district courts were operating efficiently (DEA score = 1) under CRS analysis. By 2022, only 6 out of the 23 new district courts were efficient. Furthermore, the average efficiency score dropped from about 0.882 in 2019 to 0.806 in 2022. To interpret, if 0.882 meant an average court could improve by ~11.8% to reach the frontier, now 0.806 means an average court is about 19.4% away from frontier performance. This is a notable regression. Indeed, 17 of the 23 courts in 2022 had lower efficiency scores than the composite of their predecessor courts in 2019. Only two courts slightly improved (Vestfold and Follo) and one new entrant became efficient (Follo og Nordre Østfold). The rest either remained inefficient or, in many cases, saw efficiency deteriorate. This suggests that the process of merging, instead of eliminating redundancy and fostering best practices as hoped, introduced new inefficiencies or frictions. Possible reasons could include the complexities of merging administrative systems, temporary slowdowns as staff and judges adjusted to new structures, or even morale and communication issues in larger courts. The learning curve of operating at a larger scale might have initially bogged down productivity, for example if judges had to travel more within a larger district or if there were delays in reassigning cases among courthouses.
2. *Decreased Productivity (Malmquist Results)*: When combining efficiency change with technological change, the net effect was a decline in productivity. Our Malmquist index analysis found an average productivity decrease of roughly 4% for Norwegian district courts from 2019 to 2022. The positive technological gain (+7% frontier shift) was outweighed by a negative efficiency change of over -10%. In simpler terms, even though the courts had better tools and potential (technology made it possible to do more), they ended up doing less with what they had. This manifested as fewer cases handled per judge or per staff than before, on average. We also observed that only 10 out of 23 courts achieved

any productivity increase; the majority (13 courts) had productivity stagnation or decline. A particularly stark pattern emerged in 2021, the transition year: analysis of annual data showed 2021 had a severe productivity drop, likely due to the twin impacts of the pandemic's second year and the initial disruption of the reform. Although there was some rebound in 2022 (with the frontier shift turning positive), it was not enough to restore the productivity to pre-reform 2019 levels. This indicates that at least in the short term, the reform did not deliver productivity gains; rather the system slightly regressed.

3. *Scale Inefficiencies – "Too Big" Courts*: One major challenge uncovered is that several of the merged courts appear to suffer from diseconomies of scale. The returns-to-scale analysis showed a worrying trend: the proportion of courts operating under decreasing returns to scale jumped from 43% pre-reform to 63% post-reform. In practical terms, nearly two-thirds of the new courts are too large to be efficient – expanding them (as the reform did) caused them to overshoot the optimal size, meaning they could theoretically be more efficient if they were smaller. Conversely, the share of courts with increasing returns to scale (those that were too small before and would benefit from being larger) fell from 13% to 9%. This indicates the reform possibly over-merged in certain regions. For example, Oslo District Court became an enormous entity (97 judges) and our data suggest it has decreasing returns – hinting that splitting it (or assigning some of its caseload elsewhere) might improve efficiency. Similar issues were found in other large merged courts such as Agder or Helgeland, which had been relatively efficient when smaller but post-merger turned inefficient with noted decreasing returns. This challenge strikes at the logic of the reform: it assumed bigger courts are always more efficient up to a point, but we found many courts have passed that tipping point. Managing a court of, say, 50 judges might introduce administrative overheads, coordination problems, and longer internal wait times for cases than when it was 2 or 3 smaller courts. Essentially, the economies of scale gave way to diseconomies in several instances.
4. *Widened Gap Between Courts (Slack and Inequality)*: Instead of leveling the playing field, the reform seems to have increased performance disparities among courts. The slack analysis showed that inefficient courts became more inefficient relative to the efficient ones. For example, the total slack in judge positions ballooned, indicating some courts now carry a lot of underutilized capacity. We also noted that only a handful of courts remain efficient (or close to efficient), whereas others fell behind further. This widening gap is problematic because one goal of the reform was to ensure uniform service. If some courts (perhaps in urban areas) manage well and others (perhaps covering large rural swathes) lag, the quality of justice becomes uneven regionally. Our efficiency-quality matrix also underscored mixed changes – there wasn't a uniform improvement

in timely case processing, some case types slightly worsened. For instance, the share of overdue criminal cases ticked up from 3.2% to 3.3% – a small rise, but in the wrong direction, considering criminal cases are a priority. Civil cases remained extremely backlogged: about half of civil cases in both 2019 and 2022 were overdue beyond the target time, which is an alarming statistic unchanged by the reform. This implies that the reform did not tackle the structural issues causing civil delays (perhaps related to procedural rules or shortage of judges in busy courts). The "catastrophic" backlog of civil disputes, when every second case overdue, persists, meaning from the citizens' perspective, they haven't felt an improvement in one of the most critical aspects of court service.

5. *Quality Not Significantly Improved*: As just noted, quality of service (timeliness) saw no notable improvement, and in some respects stagnated or worsened. The average overdue case rate remained roughly constant overall (e.g., ~49% for civil, which is very high). The slight improvement in complex cases' timeliness (-0.5%) is positive but marginal, and criminal cases got slightly slower on average. This challenge is key because one of the motivations for reform was to reduce delays (as highlighted by the Audit report's critique of statutory breaches). Two years post-reform, those statistics haven't budged in the right direction. It could be too early, or it could mean the reform didn't address root causes of delay – such as perhaps case management practices, the need for more judges or alternative dispute mechanisms for civil cases, etc. Also, during the transitional period, some delays likely increased due to reorganization uncertainty (for example, a case might have been adjourned to await assignment to a judge in the new merged structure).
6. *Transitional and External Shocks*: It's important to acknowledge the reform unfolded amidst the COVID-19 pandemic, which was an external shock that itself strained court efficiency (courts had to postpone hearings, adopt new routines, etc.). In 2020 and 2021, many courts worldwide saw productivity drops. Our data indeed showed 2021 as a low point, where the productivity dip was sharp. By 2022, the system was recovering, but it's challenging to disentangle how much of the 2019–2022 performance drop was due to the reform versus the pandemic. This is a challenge for interpretation: critics might blame the reform for issues that were partly pandemic-related. Conversely, any slight recovery in 2022 could be credited to "post-pandemic bounce-back" rather than reform. The overlap of these factors is a challenge for clear policy feedback. It suggests that to truly assess the reform, one may need to look at 2023 and 2024 data (once pandemic effects fully subside) – meaning the jury is still out to an extent.
7. *Stakeholder Resistance and Uncertainty*: The attempt to reverse the reform in 2022 illustrates a governance challenge: lack of consensus. Many judges and local officials initially opposed the reform (concerned about local courts closing

or becoming impersonal). While local courthouses stayed, the administrative centralization left some apprehension. Even after implementation, the new government's proposal to undo the reform created uncertainty. For nearly a year, courts operated under a cloud of "will we be split up again?". This uncertainty can be demoralizing and can hamper efficiency as staff wonder about their future. It's possible some courts in 2022 were hesitant to fully streamline operations if they thought the reform might be rolled back. Although that rollback did not happen, the episode highlights that without broad buy-in, reforms face challenge in execution. The Supreme Court's and others' defense of the reform was crucial to keep it, but it also probably means a portion of stakeholders (some politicians, maybe some communities) remain unconvinced. A challenge moving forward is how to communicate the benefits and address the concerns of those who still think the reform was a mistake. If not, any problems (like a high-profile case delay in a merged court) will be seized upon as "proof" the reform failed, making it politically harder to stick to.

8. *Geographic Challenges to Access*: Norway's unique geography with long distances and remote communities poses a challenge for any centralization. Even though local venues remain, there are concerns about whether merged administration might eventually lead to centralizing specialized services in one location. For instance, if all family cases in a region are handled by one judge located in the main city of the district, parties from far towns might have to travel more for certain proceedings. Critics, including some legal professionals, argued that fewer courts could indirectly reduce access, because administrative decisions (like where to hold a hearing) might cluster in the main court. Kjølstad et al. (2023) documented such concerns from smaller communities that merging courts could limit access to justice for people living far from the new court centers. Even if courthouses are open, if staffing is thin there and main expertise is concentrated at the hub, effectively people might feel they lost a local court. It will require vigilance to ensure equal service. Early anecdotal reports (not captured in our data) indicated some remote courthouses had fewer sitting days post-reform. This challenge must be addressed by scheduling and perhaps using technology (like more video hearings in remote locations to avoid travel). Failing to do so could erode the perceived fairness and accessibility of the system, an ethical and practical challenge.
9. *No Immediate Cost Savings*: Although not a focus of our study, it's worth noting that one presumed benefit of mergers is cost efficiency. The reform's short-term challenges likely mean any cost savings (from fewer chief judges or administrative overhead) were eaten up by transition costs (new IT systems, travel, etc.). If efficiency is down, cost per case is up. There isn't evidence yet of reduced spending; indeed, the state had to invest in merging operations. So,

a challenge is also to realize the economic efficiencies. Otherwise, the reform doesn't justify itself fiscally.

In sum, the challenges of Norway's court reform underscore that structural change alone doesn't guarantee better performance. In fact, it can disrupt existing efficiency if not managed extremely well. The initial outcome showed no immediate improvement in efficiency or timeliness – rather the opposite. Many courts became too large to be efficient, and the overall system's output dipped. The persistent backlog in civil justice remains a serious issue, pandemic or not. These challenges provide critical lessons: they highlight where additional measures are needed, e.g. focus on internal efficiency in large courts, perhaps reallocate judges or reconsider optimal sizes. They also show the importance of managing change – ensuring stakeholders are on board and transitional issues (like IT and process integration) are handled to minimize performance hits. In the next sections, we discuss ethical considerations relevant to these challenges and how fostering collaboration and further governance measures can help overcome them.

ETHICAL CONSIDERATIONS

Implementing performance-driven court reforms requires balancing efficiency with core judicial values like fairness, access, and independence. The recent Norway court reform highlights several ethical issues:

(a) *Efficiency vs. Justice*: There is an inherent tension between speed and justice – courts must not sacrifice thoroughness or fairness for the sake of efficiency (Rubin, 1979). Performance metrics should include quality measures (e.g. overdue cases) to ensure due process isn't compromised by a rush to resolve more cases.
(b) *Access in Remote Areas*: Court mergers can unintentionally impede access to justice for people in far regions. If residents of remote villages must travel much farther for court, it creates inequality. Ethically, reforms should ensure rural communities still have equal access, through measures like local court sessions, video hearings, or travel support. Larger courts must be staffed and equipped to serve distant populations so no one is left behind.
(c) *Judicial Independence*: Reforms must preserve judicial impartiality and independence from political influence. The judiciary should not be treated as a "political football." In Norway, for example, judges resisted a 2022 political attempt to undo the reform, leading to a constitutional amendment to shield court structure from partisan changes. Judges also shouldn't feel pressured by

performance evaluations to resolve cases faster at the expense of justice. Any efficiency push must not encroach on judges' freedom to decide cases fairly.

(d) *Fair Evaluation & Bias*: Performance evaluations should be fair and avoid bias. Metrics must be calibrated so they don't encourage focusing on easy cases ("creaming") while neglecting complex or sensitive cases that take more time. All cases, even difficult ones involving vulnerable groups, deserve due attention. The system should not create incentives that indirectly penalize judges or staff for handling harder cases.

(e) *Transparency and Accountability*: A larger, consolidated court system needs strong transparency to maintain public trust. It should openly publish data on case backlogs, wait times, and other performance indicators for each region. This lets the public see whether the new system is working fairly and efficiently, and holds the court administration accountable. (Nordic judiciaries are often praised for transparency, and Norway should continue that tradition.)

(f) *Impact on Personnel and Litigants*: Ethical reform considers its human impact. Court staff and judges should be treated fairly during transitions – with support, training, and clear communication about new roles or locations. Overworking staff to hit efficiency targets is both unethical and counterproductive (leading to burnout and errors). For litigants, every effort must ensure no case is lost or unduly delayed in the administrative shuffle. The rights and experience of court users should remain paramount throughout the reform.

(g) *Respect for Local Legal Culture*: Reforms should respect positive aspects of the existing legal culture and community connection to courts. Tingretten (district courts) have historically been close to the community; that sense of local justice and trust should be preserved. As Kjølstad et al. (2023) note, Norwegian legal culture values local involvement. Thus, even in larger courts, practices like using lay judges from the community or providing services in local languages (e.g. Sami) should continue. This keeps the public engaged and confident in the justice system despite structural changes.

(h) *Monitoring Unintended Consequences*: Authorities have an ethical duty to monitor the reform's impact and address any unintended harms. If, for instance, crime victims start facing longer waits or feel less heard in bigger courts, the system should respond with remedies (like better scheduling or victim support). If lawyers from remote areas are disadvantaged (e.g. more travel or less familiarity with new judges), measures like remote hearings or circuit judges can level the field. Continuous oversight is needed to catch and correct any new inequalities the reform might create.

In summary, efficiency is a means to an end in judiciary, not an end in itself. The success of any court reform must ultimately be judged by how well it upholds fairness, accessibility, and trust in the justice system. No group should be unfairly burdened, and the core mission of the courts – delivering just outcomes – must remain paramount even as processes become more efficient.

CONCLUSION

This study set out to evaluate whether Norway's 2021 court reform succeeded in improving the efficiency, productivity, and quality of the district courts. Using a combination of quantitative analysis (DEA efficiency scores, Malmquist productivity indices) and qualitative assessment (case backlog indicators, comparative context), we have drawn several conclusions:

(a) *Reform Outcomes*: Thus far, the reform has not yet achieved its primary goal of making the courts more efficient or productive. On the contrary, our analysis indicates that in the two years following consolidation, both efficiency and productivity of the district courts declined on average. The average efficiency score fell (from 0.88 to 0.81), and the system's productivity dropped by about 4%. The number of fully efficient courts shrank, and a majority of courts saw their relative efficiency worsen. Quality of service, measured by timely case handling, remained virtually unchanged – meaning the substantial backlog of cases was not significantly reduced by the reform. Every second civil case is still overdue, as was the case before. These findings lead to a sober conclusion: in the short term, the reform has largely been unsuccessful in delivering the promised gains in performance.

(b) *Underlying Issues*: The data suggest that the structural merger led to unintended inefficiencies. Many of the new courts are operating with decreasing returns to scale – they became too large to manage optimally. The consolidation also appears to have widened the gap between the best-performing and worst-performing units, increasing slack (unused capacity) in the system. In essence, combining courts did not magically make the weaker courts catch up; instead, some previously efficient entities were dragged down. The hoped-for synergy effects have yet to materialize. Additionally, external factors like the COVID-19 pandemic in 2020-2021 played a role in dampening performance, but even accounting for that, the trend remains concerning.

(c) *Policy Implications*: Does this mean the reform was a mistake? Not entirely. Our analysis also revealed some silver linings and future potential. The reform has increased the potential for efficiency improvement (reserves of capacity that can be exploited) and spurred a positive technological shift. If these can be harnessed through better management, performance could improve. Moreover, experiences from neighboring Nordic countries indicate that such reforms can yield benefits in the long term. Denmark, Sweden, and Finland all saw eventual improvements in efficiency and service quality after their consolidations, even if transitional issues occurred. It's plausible that Norway's reform, too, may simply need more time and fine-tuning to realize its goals.

(d) *Need for Adjustment*: Based on our findings, it's clear that the 2021 reform requires adjustment and optimization. We do not recommend abandoning the reform (a return to 60 courts would be disruptive and would forfeit the potential long-term gains and investments already made). Instead, we recommend modifying the new system to address the inefficiencies identified. The analysis showed which courts and areas need intervention: for instance, courts operating under decreasing returns likely need to be broken down into smaller or reconfigured units, or have their workflows reorganized to mimic a smaller-court environment. Meanwhile, courts that are still efficient post-reform should be preserved and emulated, not tampered with. The consolidation model itself may be sound, but its implementation should be more flexible – a one-size-fits-all approach (merging everything into large units) may not suit a country with Norway's geography and caseload distribution.

(e) *Recommendations*: In particular, we recommend targeted re-mergers of certain courts (merging an inefficient court with its efficient neighbor where appropriate), splitting some overly large courts back into more manageable divisions, and leaving successful courts untouched. These steps, coupled with management interventions like spreading best practices, could help the system realize efficiency gains without compromising justice. The growing slack we observed can be converted into actual improvements if courts adopt techniques from their more efficient peers – essentially benchmarking and continuous improvement is the way forward.

(f) *Public Management and Governance Context*: In governance terms, this reform underscores that structural change in the public sector must be accompanied by adequate resources, change management, and stakeholder engagement to succeed. The conflict between the government and judiciary in 2022 over possibly reversing the reform highlighted the importance of building consensus and trust. Encouragingly, the judiciary's willingness to identify problems and suggest adjustments shows a constructive approach to making the best of the reform. The emphasis now should be on a policy-adaptive tone – acknowledging the weaknesses uncovered and adapting the policy accordingly, rather than rigidly insisting it has already succeeded or utterly failed. This reflective approach is consistent with good public management: monitor outcomes, feed back into policy adjustments, and implement changes for improvement.

(g) *Long-Term Outlook*: It's important to note that efficiency and quality in the justice system are influenced by many factors beyond structure – including budgets, number of judges, procedural laws, and technology. The reform addressed structure but not these other factors directly. To truly improve performance, Norway might also need to invest in more judges or clerks where needed, streamline certain procedural rules (for example, expanding digital hearings or mediation), and ensure robust training for operating in the new court setup. The reform created a platform (bigger courts, unified administration) that could facilitate such changes. Over time, with these complementary measures, the larger courts could achieve economies of scale and specialization benefits that were intended. We remain cautiously optimistic that learning from this experience, Norway's judicial system can rebound – as happened in Sweden where initial post-merger hiccups were overcome and efficiency ultimately rose.

In conclusion, the 2021 court reform in Norway, in its early results, has not met expectations and is in need of recalibration. However, it is not a lost cause. By identifying its shortcomings through rigorous analysis and comparing with successful Nordic examples, we can chart a path to improve the reform. The focus must shift from whether the reform was "good or bad" to how to make it work better. This includes tweaking court structures on the margins, enhancing governance and collaboration, and keeping the core values of justice in sight. With such an adaptive approach, Norway can transform a currently underperforming reform into a long-term success that delivers a more efficient, accessible, and high-quality justice service for its citizens.

SUGGESTIONS AND FUTURE RESEARCH DIRECTIONS

Based on the findings, several practical steps can help strengthen court performance moving forward. Policy makers should adjust the reform strategy to ensure courts operate at an optimal scale. The data indicate that merging smaller courts did not uniformly improve efficiency. Thus, one recommendation is to re-evaluate court consolidation on a case-by-case basis. Some newly merged courts may need to be partially de-merged or downsized where efficiency has fallen (i.e., where decreasing returns to scale are evident). Conversely, very small courts that remain under-resourced might be merged with a more efficient neighbor to balance workloads. Courts that continue to perform well post-reform can be maintained in their current form. Additionally, continued investment in digital case management and specialized training is advised, building on the positive impact of technological improvements during the pandemic period. These adaptive measures aim to realize the reform's intended goals of greater efficiency and quality across the judiciary.

In addition to these policy adjustments, further research is warranted in several areas. Future evaluations should examine a longer time horizon to determine if efficiency gains emerge over time once courts and staff adapt to the new structure. Monitoring the reform's impact beyond the initial years will help distinguish temporary disruptions from enduring trends. Another important direction is to incorporate qualitative metrics such as user satisfaction and public trust in the judicial system, which were beyond the scope of this analysis. Understanding how court users perceive access to justice and service quality post-reform would complement the quantitative performance indicators. Finally, comparative studies with other countries that have undertaken similar court consolidations (e.g., Sweden or Finland) could yield insights into best practices and contextual factors. Cross-country analyses can help policy makers learn from different experiences to refine Norway's approach to judicial reform.

REFERENCES

Agrell, P. J., Mattsson, P., & Månsson, J. (2020). Impacts on efficiency of merging the Swedish district courts. *Annals of Operations Research, 288*(2), 653–679. DOI: 10.1007/s10479-019-03304-0

Bajrić, H., & Kadrić, E. (2020). Efficiency assessment of municipal courts in federation of Bosnia and Herzegovina using data envelopment analysis. *International Journal of Qualitative Research, 14*(2), 347–368. DOI: 10.24874/IJQR14.02-02

Bełdowski, J., Dąbroś, Ł., & Wojciechowski, W. (2020). Judges and court performance: A case study of district commercial courts in Poland. *European Journal of Law and Economics, 50*(1), 171–201. DOI: 10.1007/s10657-020-09656-4

Charnes, A., Cooper, W. W., & Rhodes, E. (1978). Measuring the efficiency of decision making units. *European Journal of Operational Research, 2*(6), 429–444. DOI: 10.1016/0377-2217(78)90138-8

Contini, F., Anleu, S. R., & Rottman, D. B. (2014). Evaluating Judicial Performance: Editors' Introduction. *Oñati Socio-Legal Series, 4*(5), 836–842.

De Sousa, M., & Schwengber, S. (2005). Efficiency estimates for judicial services in Brazil: Nonparametric FDH (Free Disposal Hull) and the expected order-M efficiency scores for Rio Grande Do Sul courts. *Encontro da anpec, 33th.*

Domstoladministrasjonen (2022). Årsmelding 2021, Domstoladministrasjonen, Trondheim. available at: https://www.regjeringen.no/contentassets/bae078d2e3f44d97bafd4f2af5e07614/arsmelding_2021_domstoladministrasjonen1785613.pdf

Esposito, G., Lanau, M. S., & Pompe, S. (2014). *Judicial system reform in Italy-A key to growth.* International Monetary Fund. DOI: 10.5089/9781475573022.001

Falavigna, G., Ippoliti, R., & Ramello, G. B. (2018). DEA-based Malmquist productivity indexes for understanding courts reform. *Socio-Economic Planning Sciences, 62*, 31–43. DOI: 10.1016/j.seps.2017.07.001

Ferrandino, J. A. (2010). Integrating Theory, Practice and Policy The Technical Efficiency And Productivity Of Florida's Circuit Courts. Doctoral Dissertation. University of Central Florida, *Electronic Theses and Dissertations.* 1610. available at: https://stars.library.ucf.edu/etd/1610

Ferro, G., Romero, C. A., & Romero-Gómez, E. (2018). Efficient courts? A frontier performance assessment. *Benchmarking, 25*(9), 3443–3458. DOI: 10.1108/BIJ-09-2017-0244

Finocchiaro Castro, M., & Guccio, C. (2014). Searching for the source of technical inefficiency in Italian judicial districts: An empirical investigation. *European Journal of Law and Economics*, *38*(3), 369–391. DOI: 10.1007/s10657-012-9329-0

Gill, R. D., Lazos, S. R., & Waters, M. M. (2011). Are judicial performance evaluations fair to women and minorities? A cautionary tale from Clark County, Nevada. *Law & Society Review*, *45*(3), 731–759. DOI: 10.1111/j.1540-5893.2011.00449.x

Grifell-Tatjé, E., & Lovell, C. K. (1995). A note on the Malmquist productivity index. *Economics Letters*, *47*(2), 169–175. DOI: 10.1016/0165-1765(94)00497-P

Gupta, M., & Bolia, N. B. (2020). Efficiency measurement of Indian high courts using DEA: A policy perspective. *Journal of Policy Modeling*, *42*(6), 1372–1393. DOI: 10.1016/j.jpolmod.2020.06.002

Guzowska, M., & Strak, T. (2010). DEA method in examining the efficiency of polish courts. *Transformations in Business & Economics*, *9*(1), 1–12.

Hoelseth, D. T. (2024). Endringer i Grunnloven – et helhetlig grunnlovsvern for domstolene, Lovdata, 22. mai 2024. available at: https://lovdata.no/artikkel/endringer_i_grunnloven__et_helhetlig_grunnlovsvern_for_domstolene/4777

JD. (2022). Forslag om å gjeninnføre strukturen i domstolene sendes på høring, Justis- og beredskapsdepartementet, Pressemelding Nr: 6, 26.01.2022. available at: https://www.regjeringen.no/no/aktuelt/forslag-om-a-gjeninnfore-strukturen-i-domstolene-sendes-pa-horing/id2898552/

Justice, E. U. (2024). *The 2024 EU Justice scoreboard, European Union, COM(2024) 950.* Publications Office of the European Union., https://ec.europa.eu/commission/presscorner/detail/en/ip_24_3164

Juul-Sandberg, J. (2016). Reform and development of preparatory proceedings in the Danish civil justice system: towards (even) more efficient courts. *Current Trends in Preparatory Proceedings: A Comparative Study of Nordic and Former Communist Countries*, 81-107.

Kittelsen, S. A., & Førsund, F. R. (1992). Efficiency analysis of Norwegian district courts. *Journal of Productivity Analysis*, *3*(3), 277–306. DOI: 10.1007/BF00158357

Kjølstad, M. M., Koch, S., & Sunde, J. Ø. (2023). An introduction to Norwegian legal culture. In *Handbook on Legal Cultures: A Selection of the World's Legal Cultures* (pp. 801–848). Springer International Publishing. DOI: 10.1007/978-3-031-27745-0_20

Lewin, A. Y., Morey, R. C., & Cook, T. J. (1982). Evaluating the administrative efficiency of courts. *Omega, 10*(4), 401–411. DOI: 10.1016/0305-0483(82)90019-6

Lo Storto, C., & Goncharuk, A. G. (2017). Efficiency vs Effectiveness: A Benchmarking Study on European Healthcare Systems. *Economics & Sociology (Ternopil), 10*(3), 102–115. DOI: 10.14254/2071-789X.2017/10-3/8

Lovell, C. K. (2003). The decomposition of Malmquist productivity indexes. *Journal of Productivity Analysis, 20*(3), 437–458. DOI: 10.1023/A:1027312102834

Mattsson, P., & Tidanå, C. (2019). Potential efficiency effects of merging the Swedish district courts. *Socio-Economic Planning Sciences, 67*, 58–68. DOI: 10.1016/j.seps.2018.09.002

Nissi, E., Giacalone, M., & Cusatelli, C. (2019). The efficiency of the Italian judicial system: A two stage data envelopment analysis approach. *Social Indicators Research, 146*(1-2), 395–407. DOI: 10.1007/s11205-018-1892-5

Nylund, A. (2023). An introduction to Finnish legal culture. In *Handbook on Legal Cultures: A Selection of the World's Legal Cultures* (pp. 525–556). Springer International Publishing. DOI: 10.1007/978-3-031-27745-0_14

Palumbo, G., Giupponi, G., Nunziata, L., & Mora-Sanguinetti, J. S. (2013). *Judicial Performance and its Determinants: A Cross-Country Perspective* (No. 5). OECD Publishing.

Pedraja-Chaparro, F., & Salinas-Jimenez, J. (1996). An assessment of the efficiency of Spanish Courts using DEA. *Applied Economics, 28*(11), 1391–1403. DOI: 10.1080/000368496327651

Posner, H., & Richard, A. (2005). Judicial Behavior and Performance: An Economic Approach. *Florida State University Law Review. Florida State University. College of Law, 32*(4), 1259–1279.

Riksrevisjonen (2019-2020). Riksrevisjonens undersøkelse av saksbehandlingstid og effektivitet i tingrettene og lagmannsrettene, Dokument 3:3 (2019–2020), Oslo. available at: https://www.riksrevisjonen.no/globalassets/rapporter/no-2019-2020/Domstolene.pdf

Rubin, A. B. (1979). Bureaucratization of the federal courts: The tension between justice and efficiency. *The Notre Dame Lawyer, 55*, 648.

Santos, S. P., & Amado, C. A. (2014). On the need for reform of the Portuguese judicial system–Does Data Envelopment Analysis assessment support it? *Omega, 47*, 1–16. DOI: 10.1016/j.omega.2014.02.007

Schneider, M. R. (2005). Judicial career incentives and court performance: An empirical study of the German labour courts of appeal. *European Journal of Law and Economics*, *20*(2), 127–144. DOI: 10.1007/s10657-005-1733-2

Silva, M. C. A. (2018). Output-specific inputs in DEA: An application to courts of justice in Portugal. *Omega*, *79*, 43–53. DOI: 10.1016/j.omega.2017.07.006

Staalesen, U. E. (2020). Rettsmekling bør tas mer i bruk–både av hensyn til partenes og domstolenes ressursbruk. *Lov og Rett*, *59*(4), 252–257. DOI: 10.18261/issn.1504-3061-2020-04-05

Staats, J. L., Bowler, S., & Hiskey, J. T. (2005). Measuring judicial performance in Latin America. *Latin American Politics and Society*, *47*(4), 77–106. DOI: 10.1111/j.1548-2456.2005.tb00329.x

Thorsvik, I. W. (2021). Domstolsreformen er god distriktspolitikk, Nettavisen, 9.11.2021. https://www.nettavisen.no/norsk-debatt/domstolsreformen-er-god-distriktspolitikk/o/5-95-336576

Tone, K. (2001). A slacks-based measure of efficiency in data envelopment analysis. *European Journal of Operational Research*, *130*(3), 498–509. DOI: 10.1016/S0377-2217(99)00407-5

Tsai, C. F., & Tsai, J. H. (2010, March). Performance evaluation of the judicial system in taiwan using data envelopment analysis and decision trees. In *2010 Second international conference on computer engineering and applications* (Vol. 2, pp. 290-294). IEEE. DOI: 10.1109/ICCEA.2010.208

Tulkens, H. (1993). On FDH efficiency analysis: Some methodological issues and applications to retail banking, courts, and urban transit. *Journal of Productivity Analysis*, *4*(1), 183–210. DOI: 10.1007/BF01073473

Yeung, L. L., & Azevedo, P. F. (2011). Measuring efficiency of Brazilian courts with data envelopment analysis (DEA). *IMA Journal of Management Mathematics*, *22*(4), 343–356. DOI: 10.1093/imaman/dpr002

Chapter 10
New Public Management in Morocco:
Between the Quest for Performance and Challenges of Implementation

Zineb Loukili
http://orcid.org/0009-0008-0889-6602
Ibn Tofaîl University, Morocco

Azzouz Elhamma
Ibn Tofaîl University, Morocco

ABSTRACT

Public sector performance is the central objective of New Public Management (NPM), a model that emerged in the 1980s to modernize public sector organizations, making them more flexible and user-centered through private sector practices. In Morocco, this reform movement has inspired the implementation of major reforms such as program budgeting and Results-Based Management (RBM). These initiatives are based on three fundamental pillars: the definition of clear objectives, the efficient allocation of resources, and the rigorous evaluation of results. Although these principles reflect a desire for a profound transformation of public action, their implementation nevertheless encounters various structural and cultural constraints that can limit their impact.

DOI: 10.4018/979-8-3373-3526-1.ch010

INTRODUCTION

Throughout the world, the performance of public organizations has become an imperative and a necessity. As a result, we see that the management of public organizations is beginning to abandon traditional management methods in favor of new management methods inspired by private management. Thus, since the 1980s, New Public Management (NPM) has become a predominant model of public administration reform, particularly in Anglo-Saxon countries, before gradually spreading to Europe and around the world.

New Public Management is the set of processes for finalizing, organizing, leading, and controlling public organizations aimed at developing their overall performance and steering their evolution in accordance with their vocation. This new management approach assumes that managerial methods from the private sector are more effective than those implemented in the public sector. Thus, we are transitioning to a management style that prioritizes the pursuit of performance, as opposed to the traditional management style. In this context, government action must prioritize the conditions for success in terms of effectiveness and efficiency by using tools and techniques specific to this field.

Like other countries in the world, Morocco has not been an exception and has decided to integrate this new mode of management into its public organizations, through several public sector reform projects aimed at achieving performance and while abandoning traditional methods suffering from several handicaps (bureaucracy, excessive centralization, etc.) (Elhamma & El-Moumane, 2025; Elhamma & Loukili, 2025; El-Moumane, 2026)).

In light of these reforms, our research is structured around two questions: What is the contribution of New Public Management to the performance of Moroccan public organizations? And what are the main obstacles encountered in the implementation of NPM that prevent the achievement of the expected results?

The objective of this chapter is to highlight the role of New Public Management in improving the performance of Moroccan public organizations and to present the difficulties related to the objectives, means and results encountered in the implementation of NPM reforms. For this, this work in the form of a bibliographic review allowed us to present the general framework of the implementation of this new trend in Morocco and to note that New Public Management can only achieve its ultimate objective, which is performance, through radical changes at the level of public organizations.

1. LITERATURE REVIEW: REFERENCE FRAMEWORK FOR THE NEW PUBLIC MANAGEMENT (NPM) AND THE PERFORMANCE OF PUBLIC ORGANIZATIONS.

1.1 Performance

1.1.1. Origin and Evolution of the Concept

The term performance comes from the Latin "performare", it was borrowed from English in the 15th century "performance" derived from "to perform" which means to accomplish a task with regularity, method and application, to execute and complete it in an appropriate manner (Khemakhem, 1976).

According to Bourguignon (1995), the term performance is widely used without there being unanimity on its definition. There are multitudes of definitions relating to the concept of performance.

Chandler and Behar (1992) define performance as a combination of functional and strategic effectiveness. Functional effectiveness involves improving products, purchasing, production processes, marketing, and human relations within the firm. Strategic effectiveness involves staying ahead of the competition by entering a growing market or exiting a declining market.

For Marchesnay (1991), "Company performance can be defined as the degree to which the desired goal is achieved." Goal analysis reveals three performance measures:

- Effectiveness: the result obtained in relation to the desired goal.
- Efficiency: the result obtained in relation to the resources implemented.
- Effectiveness: the level of satisfaction obtained in relation to the result obtained.

According to Lorino (1997), Performance in the company is everything that contributes to the achievement of strategic objectives. Which amounts to saying that "performance in the company is everything that contributes to improving the value-cost ratio."

1.1.2. The Principal Models of Performance Measurement

The central issue for contemporary public and private organizations is the search for performance (Gauzente, 2000). Despite the multiplicity of possible methods for understanding performance, its absorption by management control leads to the identification of three main models.

a. The EEE model

According to Demeestère (2002), "every organization seeks efficiency and strives to fulfill its mission by managing its resources as effectively as possible. Performance can be represented by the triptych Objectives–Resources–Results. It is within the relationship among these three elements that the economy, efficiency, and effectiveness of an organization are shaped."

The term "economy" refers to the relationship between objectives and the means used to achieve them. Effectiveness describes the relationship between objectives and results, while efficiency describes the relationship between means and results.

Figure 1. The Performance Triangle

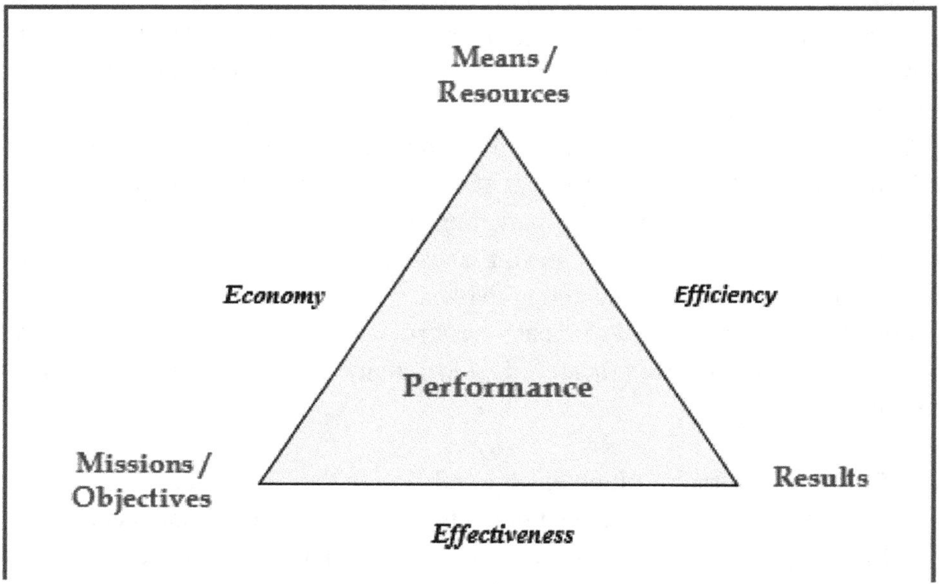

Source: Demeestère (2002)

Economics or budgeting: it consists of monitoring the cost of the production factors of a particular service without taking into account the result. It involves defining the resources necessary to achieve the set objectives. Its axes of analysis are "budgeting", "definition of action plans" and "identification of management levers". It also measures a posteriori the gap between the announced objectives and the resources mobilized.

Effectiveness: Management control analyzes the results achieved in relation to the objectives that the organization had set for itself. The axes of analysis aim to identify and explain the gaps between what was planned and what was actually achieved.

After analyzing the results, management control can help define corrective actions to better achieve the objectives by setting alert thresholds or rescheduling activities.

Efficiency: relates results to resources. The objective is to determine whether results have been achieved optimally, i.e., without waste. Economists in two ways (Jackson, 1982) define efficiency:

- Technical efficiency, which refers to the cost per unit produced (collecting a ton of waste, an hour of teaching in secondary schools, etc.).
- Allocative efficiency, which refers to the degree to which services are aligned with user preferences. The first definition is the most commonly accepted.

b. The Inputs-Outputs-Outcomes Model

The Input-Output-Results model offers a broader range of criteria for evaluating organizational performance. The main difference with the previous model lies in the distinction between outputs (products, deliverables) and outcomes (impacts, effects). Indeed, this model breaks down the result of the action into two "sub-results". "Results" are measured by non-financial indicators representing the social benefits provided by the action, while outputs designate levels of activity without it being possible to assert that these productions will lead to results.

This model integrates the three elements of the previous model: economy is integrated with inputs, efficiency is the ratio of outputs to inputs, and outcomes include effectiveness. According to Boyne et al. (2002), this model makes explicit the dimensions of performance that are at best implicit in the EEE model.

Figure 2. The Inputs-Outputs-Outcomes Model

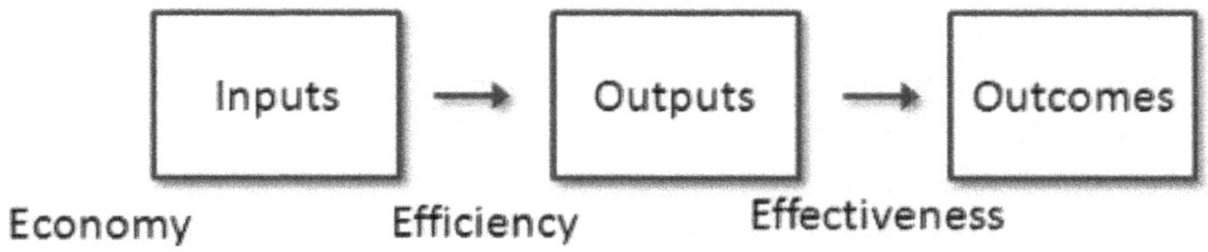

Source: Jones, P. (2012)

c. The Balanced Scorecard

The Balanced Scorecard (BSC) is a method developed in 1992 by Kaplan and Norton (2005). It aims to measure a company's activities along four axes: customer, process, learning, and finance (Elhamma, 2023, 2025; Elhamma & Snoussi, 2026).

The BSC advocates a new management philosophy, going beyond financial indicators alone to truly align management control with strategy on the one hand and operations on the other. A good management system must highlight strategic priorities and select the most relevant areas and indicators, paying particular attention to quality, deadlines, customer value, and the improvement of internal processes.

The method for creating a balanced scorecard differs from that of a traditional dashboard. Whereas a traditional dashboard places a premium on adaptation to the company's specific conditions, a balanced scorecard prescribes four major axes of analysis.

Figure 3. The Balanced Scorecard

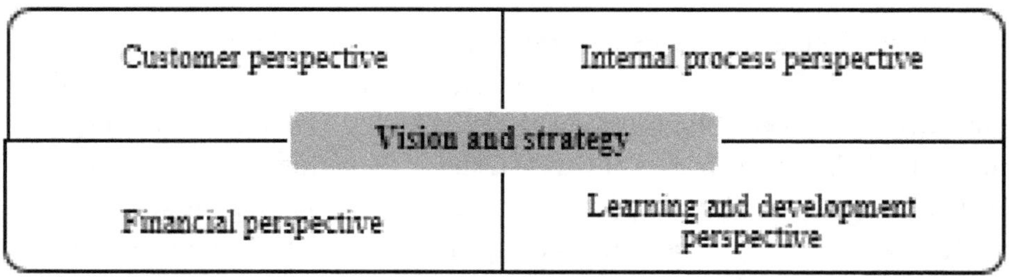

Source: Kaplan, R. S., and D. P. Norton. (1992)

Kaplan and Norton's concern is therefore to rebalance the traditional approach to performance by adding, to the axis of financial performance, three other axes which take into account the other dimensions of performance:

A "customer" axis: with five generic measures:

- Market share
- Customer retention
- New customer acquisition
- Customer satisfaction
- Profitability by segment

An "internal processes" axis: whose objective is to take into account all internal processes, with particular attention to innovation, after-sales service, and production. Regarding the innovation process, a first step consists of defining the market by identifying new or latent customer needs.

An "organizational learning" axis: considered as the axis of the means that enable the objectives of the three previous axes to be achieved, this is the axis for which management systems are the most basic. Kaplan and Norton propose—without being exhaustive—measuring employee satisfaction and motivation, labor productivity by measuring the share of revenue per employee, employee loyalty by measuring turnover, and the capacity of information systems.

1.2 New Public Management

1.2.1 Origin and Expansion of NPM

New Public Management (NPM) emerged in the United Kingdom in the 1980s, initiating a wave of privatizations and public management reforms aimed at improving the quality of public services and optimizing the use of public funds. Following this approach, executive agencies were created in 1988, whose mission is to provide public services while adopting a mode of operation similar to that of private companies and ensuring the quality of public service at the lowest cost. This reform was followed by the development of a regulatory framework adapted to the new context, promoting the effectiveness, efficiency and equity of public service. Moreover, many states have successively adhered to the principles of NPM: the United States in 1993, Canada in 1994, Belgium in 1994, Japan in 1996 and Germany in 1999. However, adherence to this paradigm only emerged in the 2000s in France, in certain OECD countries and in many developing countries.

According to Charbonneau (2012), "New Public Management is a model of public administration management set up in opposition to the bureaucratic management model." For him, NPM is based on the principles of results-based management, with the main objectives being the establishment of an efficient cost management system and the production of services that satisfy citizens. Another advantage offered by NPM is management flexibility, allowing for a better decision-making process.

Batley and Larbi (2004) grouped the characteristics of New Public Management into two ideological branches.

- The first focuses on the restructuring of the public management system, notably by introducing decentralization, disaggregation, and downsizing. NPM is thus a "results-oriented managerial approach" (Holmes and Shand, 2005), whose objectives are to reduce government spending, improve the quality of public services, and optimize the process of implementing public reforms.
- The second ideological branch emphasizes the principles of market forces, competitiveness, privatization of procedures, and outsourcing of government services. It thus defines NPM as a set of managerial tools and techniques primarily inspired by private sector practices and adapted to the public sector.

1.2.2 The Principles of NPM

The main idea of NPM is that the public sector organized according to the principles of Weberian bureaucracy is inefficient, and that it is preferable to transfer management methods from the private sector to the public sector. In the face of the rigidity of centralized bureaucratic administration focused on its own development, NPM embodies a performance-based vision of the public sector that can meet the needs of a constantly changing environment.

Christopher Hood (1991), who analyzed in detail the general principles of this new way of managing public organizations, refers to seven principles that underlie NPM:

- Breakdown of the public sector into strategic "entrepreneurial" units organized by "manageable" product.
- Introduction of competition between public organizations and between public and private organizations.
- Use of management techniques from the private sector.
- Movement toward control of public organizations by visible managers exercising discretionary power.
- More rational use of resources with an active search for alternative, lower-cost means of production.
- Emphasis on results measurement and movement toward the adoption of more explicit, measurable, or more controllable performance standards.
- Decentralization of power.

Paulo URIO (1999), also developed 10 principles of NPM, namely:

- The principle of economic efficiency.
- The separation between strategic and operational decisions.
- The principle of decentralization.
- Orienting activity based on results and therefore customer satisfaction, rather than on compliance with procedures.
- A systematic cost-cutting policy.
- The primacy of financial control.
- The widespread use of audits and performance evaluation.
- A transfer of power in favor of managers.
- Deregulation of the labor market.
- The marginalization of unions.

1.2.3 Literature Review on the Implementation of New Public Management in Countries

Although the principles of New Public Management are widely discussed in the literature, their actual and concrete implementation and integration prove to be a complex process, highly sensitive to institutional and organizational contexts. This section therefore reviews the main insights from the literature regarding the implementation of New Public Management.

The literature on New Public Management has long highlighted a gap between the theoretical principles on which the model is based and their concrete implementation by countries. Primarily recognized as a coherent set of reforms aimed at enhancing the performance of public action, NPM relies on instruments such as results-based management, performance evaluation, and the accountability of public managers (Hood, 1991; Urio, 1999).

In this context, Pollitt and Bouckaert (2017) propose an analytical framework that helps explain the emergence of New Public Management (NPM) in several countries through a classification based on the 4M model, ordered according to a decreasing degree of radical reform in the field of New Public Management. This model reflects four ideal types of public management reform trajectories and serves to capture the diversity of national experiences: Marketizers, Modernizers, Minimizers, and Maintainers. Countries classified as Marketizers, such as the United Kingdom, rely on radical reforms that incorporate market mechanisms, contractualization, competition, and increased reliance on outsourcing and the private sector, notably through public–private partnerships (PPPs). Modernizers pursue a managerial modernization of public administration primarily based on results-oriented management and performance evaluation, while preserving the central role of the state. Minimizers seek above all to reduce the scope of public action through expenditure control, privatization, and the withdrawal of the state from certain activities. Finally, Maintainers are characterized by more gradual reforms that prioritize administrative continuity and incremental adjustments rather than a radical transformation inspired by New Public Management. This classification highlights that New Public Management (NPM) cannot be regarded as a unified approach or a uniform model, but rather as the outcome of a variable combination of reform mechanisms shaped by national administrative traditions and institutional contexts (Pollitt & Bouckaert, 2017).

The literature on New Public Management (NPM) generally agrees that this management approach is primarily a normative and conceptual framework for public policy reform, aimed at improving the efficiency, performance, and accountability of public administrations. However, since Christopher Hood's seminal work (1991), several authors have emphasized that the practical implementation of this vision has proven more complex than its theoretical formulation. Accordingly, a substantial body of research highlights the existence of a gap between the objectives pursued by New Public Management and the outcomes observed during its implementation. Ewan Ferlie (1996) show that the introduction of managerial tools has frequently encountered existing legal frameworks, organizational rigidities, and resistance to change within public administrations. These constraints have limited the effective appropriation of New Public Management instruments and have often resulted in a partial or largely formal implementation of the reforms within the public sector.

In the same vein, Christopher Hood (1991) shows that, despite their conceptual coherence, the principles of New Public Management are difficult to translate into administrative practices due to institutional constraints inherent to the public sector. B. Guy Peters (2001) likewise highlights that the incorporation of performance mechanisms and contractual arrangements may lead to a fragmentation of public action and a weakening of the state's coordination capacities. Finally, Laurence Lynn Jr. (2006) emphasizes the context-dependent nature of NPM implementation, noting that the observed differences between objectives and outcomes largely stem from national administrative traditions and institutional capacities.

2. THE IMPACT OF NEW PUBLIC MANAGEMENT ON THE PERFORMANCE OF THE MOROCCAN PUBLIC SECTOR

2.1. The Major Projects of Moroccan Administrative Reform

The reform of Moroccan public administration is not a recent concern. Indeed, during the 1990s, the urgent need for administrative reform gradually became apparent. This awareness led to the implementation of a series of reforms aimed at improving the efficiency and effectiveness of public administration. In 1998, the Moroccan government developed the "Good Management Pact" which established a new management approach. This awareness culminated in an economic and social development plan for the period 2000–2004. This plan aimed to modernize public administration and improve its governance, thus responding to the growing need for efficiency and responsiveness to the challenges facing the country.

Since 2003, some of the measures promised during previous initiatives have been implemented under the Public Administration Reform Support Program (PARAP), developed in partnership with the African Development Bank, the World Bank, and the European Union. In addition to budget reform, this program included a component aimed at improving the efficiency of human resource management. Its implementation took place in four phases. In 2011, a new Constitution was adopted and several articles were devoted to good governance and public service.

2.1.1. Good Management Pact 1998

The "Good Management Pact" is a document aimed at improving the morality of the civil service, rationalize public expenditure, strengthening communication within the administration, and improving its external relations. This is a first in developing countries. More widespread in Australia, Canada, and England, this practice is also known in France as the General Civil Service Code (CGFP). The Good Management Pact embodies the government's desire to translate a policy of change into concrete, daily actions and constitutes a common frame of reference that defines the values and principles on which administrations must implement concrete actions of change.

The good management pact is based on three axes:

- **The moralization of public service:** The objective is to offer citizens equal access to services and to strengthen relationships of trust between the administration and its environment. The administration must act with transparency and in strict compliance with ethical rules.
- **Rationalization of public property management:** Faced with the continued decline in resources and the scale of needs, public authorities must be imaginative in combating all forms of abuse and waste. Officials must therefore be accountable for their management, both in terms of regularity and punctuality.
- **Communication with public service users:** This commitment aims to develop a culture of dialogue and consultation within the administration and with its environment. In short, to adapt the service to the real needs of citizens.

2.1.2. Economic and Social Development Plan 2000-2004

The 2000-2004 Economic and Social Development Plan set the objective of achieving strong and sustainable growth, capable of curbing the rise in unemployment and maintaining the fundamental balances of the economy at controlled levels, while defining the conditions for its achievement. These objectives were set on the basis of a macroeconomic framework guaranteeing overall coherence and based on the achievement of an adequate level of investment, on the one hand, and on the implementation of a set of measures and reforms aimed at improving the business environment and investment performance, on the other.

This Plan aims to set Morocco on a new path, characterized, on the one hand, by optimal use of human and material resources, and, on the other hand, by improving the performance of all development actors, led by the State. The objective is to accelerate the pace of growth and gradually address the social deficits that have widened inequalities between urban and rural areas, as well as between men and women.

2.1.3. Public Administration Reform Support Program (PARAP)

In 2003, the government implemented the Public Administration Reform Support Program (PARAP). This program, developed in partnership with the World Bank and the European Union, is based on a common matrix comprising a series of specific measures structured around successive operations aimed at gradually implementing the structural elements of a complex reform.

The Public Administration Reform Support Program (PARAP) has a budget of 9.6 billion dirhams, financed in four tranches by the World Bank, the EU and the AfDB.

The "Public Administration Reform Support Program" aims to pursue four main objectives:

- Improve the administration's efficiency in budget management;
- Improve the administration's efficiency in human resources management;
- Control the growth of the public sector payroll;
- Simplify and optimize administrative procedures and formalities;

To achieve its objectives, PARAP was structured around four (4) components, namely:

- **Strengthening public finance management:** through the establishment of a rolling multi-annual budgetary framework, the introduction of credit globalization mechanisms, contractualization and partnership, the strengthening of internal auditing and the introduction of performance evaluation and control, and the modernization of the information system.
- **Strengthening the effectiveness of human resources management:** through the development and implementation of the job and skills framework, the introduction of new recruitment methods and encouraging mobility, the establishment of a system for promoting and evaluating the performance of civil servants, and the implementation of continuing training plans.
- **Control of the wage bill in the public sector:** through forecasting the evolution of the wage bill in the public sector, the qualitative re-profiling of the public sector, and the stabilization of the number of public sector employees.
- **Simplification of administrative procedures and formalities:** through the inventory of procedures, publishing the listed procedures online and optimizing them.

2.1.4. The New Constitution 2011

The Moroccan Constitution of 2011 constitutes the current supreme legal standard of the Kingdom of Morocco. It is the sixth Moroccan constitution. The new Moroccan Constitution of 2011 established new principles governing public management, namely transparency, managerial accountability, and reporting. In accordance with the Constitution, numerous reforms have been implemented. In the budgetary sphere, the Organic Law on the Finance Law (LOF) was adopted in 2015 to provide the Kingdom with a more efficient and transparent financial management framework.

This new text establishes the foundations for results-based budget management in order to modernize public finances. The main measures introduced by this law are as follows (Boumkhaled & al, 2018):

- **Improving the performance of public management:** The new Organic Finance Law introduces measures to strengthen coherence between sectoral strategies and provide greater visibility for public managers. These measures include the development of the Finance Law according to the rolling three-year programming and the adoption of a budget nomenclature based on an objectives/results logic, presenting expenditures by programs/projects and actions. In addition, the new law has just strengthened accountability through the conduct of performance audits by the General Inspectorate of Finance and the submission of reports to Parliament.
- **Strengthening budgetary principles and rules:** This new legal framework aims to strengthen the transparency of public finances through the introduction of the principle of budgetary sincerity in the development of assumptions prior to the preparation of the finance law. In addition, accrual accounting and cost accounting are introduced to better monitor budgetary expenditures.
- **Strengthening parliamentary control:** The power of control granted to parliament will be strengthened by its integration from the first phases of preparation of the finance law and by enriching the information communicated to it by the government.

2.2. Le New Public Management et Performance Public au Maroc

2.2.1. Towards Results-Oriented Management (RBM)

Results-based management (RBM) is a new management approach that involves shifting from a means-based management logic to a results-based logic. The old conventional management adopted for several years in Morocco had no visibility on the effectiveness and efficiency of public action, so results-based management (RBM) directs financial and human resources towards achieving clearly defined results. When adopting a results-based management approach, all actors contributing directly or indirectly to the achievement of a set of results ensure that their processes, products and services contribute to the achievement of the desired results.

Some definitions from the literature concerning Results-Based Management:

- Meier (1998), defines RBM as "an approach that aims to bring about significant changes in the way organizations operate, with an emphasis on improving performance as expressed through results. RBM includes a management framework and tools that facilitate strategic planning, risk management, performance monitoring, and evaluation. Its primary objective is to improve the organization's learning capabilities and enable it to fulfill its accountability obligations through performance reporting."
- The OECD5 (2000), defines results-based management as "a management style focused on the results to be achieved, a management strategy aimed at changing the way institutions operate, focusing on the means and improving their effectiveness, i.e., achieving results."
- According to UNDP6, results-based management means "a management strategy or method applied by an organization to ensure that its procedures, products and services contribute to the achievement of clearly defined results."

As part of a series of structural and institutional reforms, Morocco adopted a results-based management that began in the 2000s. It mainly concerns the reform of the budgetary system, multi-year programming and the reform of the organic finance law. This reform aims to improve the efficiency of public spending as well as the public services provided to users of the public administration.

a. Globalization of Credits

The globalization of appropriations consists of giving authorizing officers greater flexibility in the use and management of the appropriations made available to them, while making them accountable for achieving predefined objectives, measured by quantified indicators.

Authorizing officers and their sub-authorizing officers can thus make transfers between the lines of a paragraph within the chapters of the general budget, the budgets of autonomous administrations relating to capital expenditure and miscellaneous expenditure, as well as investment expenditure, and the special Treasury accounts, without prior intervention from the Ministry of Finance. In return, authorizing officers are responsible for achieving the objectives assigned to them through performance indicators and are required to report on these results.

b. Multi-Year Programming

Multi-year programming is part of Article 5 of Organic Finance Law No. 130-13: "The finance law for the year is drawn up with reference to a three-year budget program updated annually to adapt it to changes in the country's financial, economic, and social situation."[1]

Multi-year programming provides greater visibility to strategic choices by encouraging ministerial departments to adopt indicative programming instruments, "medium-term expenditure frameworks" (MTEFs), which go beyond the framework of an annual state budget and are spread over three years. This programming will be updated annually to adapt it to changes in the economic situation.

c. The Implementation of Modulated Expenditure Control (CMD)

Modulated expenditure control (CMD) is a simplified expenditure control system aimed at improving its effectiveness and efficiency. Authorizing officers are therefore required to establish an internal control system to manage and streamline the expenditure cycle. Modulated expenditure control involves replacing ex ante control, which is sometimes cumbersome and ineffective, at the stage of commitment and payment of expenditure, with strengthening the management capacities of authorizing officers through the creation of internal control bodies and strengthening ex post control through the evaluation of results and performance, with increased accountability of authorizing officers.

d. Budgetary Decentralization

The main objective of decentralization is to involve all stakeholders, at the central and decentralized levels, in a management and decision-making process that allows the administration to be closer to citizens and more open to its environment.

Fiscal decentralization, on the other hand, consists of ensuring greater budgetary rationality; it aims to bring decision-making closer to its point of application by delegating powers from the central government to its local representatives through the implementation of objectives/means contracts (contractualization). This strengthens the autonomy of local managers and makes them accountable for achieving objectives. These contracts set the resources necessary to achieve objectives based on the Medium-Term Expenditure Framework.

2.2.2. The Emergence of the Internal Audit Function Within Public Bodies

The organizational world is constantly evolving due to globalization and economic liberalization. This context forces public organizations to improve their governance and adopt new management methods. They must therefore adapt to the demands of a diverse environment. New Public Management believes that the best way to govern is to introduce new management methods within public institutions. Therefore, integrating the internal audit function can help organizations improve their procedures and results. Internal audit will therefore be the tool for evaluating the achievements of public institutions in order to improve the effectiveness of their management, comply with good governance practices, and achieve the desired economic and social development objectives.

According to the ISO 9000 standard, "auditing is a methodical, independent, and documented process designed to gather audit evidence and objectively evaluate it to determine the extent to which audit criteria are met."

According to the IIA, internal auditing is "an independent and objective activity that provides an organization with assurance on the degree of control over its operations, provides advice for improvement, and contributes to the creation of added value."

In Morocco, internal auditing of public bodies was established following a royal letter addressed by His Majesty King Hassan II to Prime Minister Mohammed Karim Lamrani in July 1993. Thanks to the creation of internal audit units within ministries, administrations, and public institutions, managers now have a powerful tool enabling them to comply with policies, directives, and instructions. This allows them to prevent and detect malfunctions and provide appropriate solutions.

In September 1993, the Prime Minister reiterated the royal instructions in a circular containing the following elements:

- The creation of internal audit departments within industrial and commercial public institutions;
- The creation of general inspectorates within administrative public institutions;
- The requirement for all aspects of the management of these institutions to be subject to internal and external audits.

2.2.3. The Implementation of a Management Control System

Long considered a strategic asset due to its importance, management control has become the cornerstone of progress and continuous improvement for all types of organizations. It is a function whose goal is to motivate managers and encourage them to carry out activities that contribute to the achievement of specific objectives.

Management control is a constantly evolving field; its definitions vary according to authors and eras, reflecting advances in knowledge, techniques, and practices. As a function, management control fulfills its missions by relying on several management systems, instruments, and mechanisms, such as cost accounting and budgeting.

Some definitions of management control presented by authors:

- Alfred Chandler defines management control as a tool for coordination, evaluation, and planning.
- Henri Bouquin defines management control as "the systems and processes that ensure consistency between strategy and concrete day-to-day actions."
- Robert Newton Anthony defines management control as a process by which managers obtain assurance that resources are obtained and used effectively and efficiently to achieve the organization's objectives.

The mission of management control is to define, on the one hand, long-term objectives and general objectives, and on the other hand, the strategy to be adopted to guide management towards achieving the objectives set as quickly as possible and at the lowest cost and with maximum quality in accordance with forecasts.

Management control must perform several tasks: forecasting, consulting, monitoring, and developing procedures.

- **At the forecasting level:** management control must develop objectives, define the means to achieve them, and, above all, prepare contingency plans in case the plans established in advance fail. Similarly, management control must ensure the compatibility of budgets from different departments.
- **At the consulting level:** management control must provide the different responsibility centers with the information necessary to implement a set of means to improve their management.
- **At the control level:** management control must determine responsibilities and ensure ongoing monitoring of the company's activity, maintaining compatibility between them through dashboards.
- **At the procedure development level**: the mission of management control consists of developing indicators and standardizing them so that the comparison of the company with its environment is consistent.

Management control is a performance tool in private organizations, and has begun to be adopted by public sector organizations in recent years. In Morocco, public administrations are being called upon to equip themselves with modern management control systems to support a new governance approach that focuses on the organization's overall performance.

Implementing a SCG in a public organization requires a real organizational change where administrative procedures should respond to greater transparency to provide a superior quality public service. However, its public nature, the multiplicity of its missions and functions, and its broad scope of intervention require adaptation and careful selection of management control tools to be used, providing assistance in terms of support and management dialogue, which is now a mandatory dimension of management. Performance management relies on a good understanding and use of management mechanisms such as: budgets, cost accounting, and dashboards.

2.3. The Main Difficulties and Obstacles Related to the Implementation of New Public Management (NPM) in Morocco

Over recent years, Morocco has undertaken major reforms inspired by the principles of New Public Management. These reforms have led to notable advances in terms of the modernization and improvement of public action. However, from the very outset of their implementation, these reforms have encountered a range of constraints and difficulties that have limited the scope of their effects. The analysis of the constraints associated with the integration of New Public Management principles in Morocco is based on the performance triangle, which articulates three interdependent dimensions, namely effectiveness, efficiency, and results.

2.3.1. Difficulties Related to Objectives

New Public Management (NPM), by introducing a performance-oriented logic, presupposes planning based on clear, measurable, and shared strategic objectives across all levels of public administration. In Morocco, however, results-based management (RBM) within public administrations remains largely approached in a normative manner. Objectives set within performance frameworks are often vague, repetitive, or disconnected from operational realities. Stakeholder involvement is further constrained by insufficient managerial training, the absence of a strong planning culture, and limited consultation during the objective-setting process. Moreover, the scope of RBM in Morocco remains limited, as the approach has focused primarily on its budgetary dimension, thereby overlooking the broader and multidimensional nature of results-based management. As a result, the objectives pursued do not fully incorporate all of its components, which considerably restricts the scope and potential impact of the approach.

Furthermore, the objectives of reforms are often poorly understood; they are commonly perceived as instruments of authority, discipline, and sanction rather than as essential tools for management and improvement. This misunderstanding leads reforms to be viewed as "weapons" or political instruments, which undermines stakeholder engagement and cooperation.

Similarly, the management control function struggles to rely on coherent objectives effectively deployed at the operational level, as links between national strategies and concrete operations are frequently weak. As for internal audit, its ability to inform decision-makers about the relevance of objectives is limited by its insufficient integration into a forward-looking or strategic approach. Internal audit therefore remains too often confined to formal compliance-based practices.

2.3.2. Difficulties Related to Resources

The success of managerial reforms depends on the availability of adequate human, technical, and financial resources. In this respect, the Moroccan public sector faces significant constraints. Results-based management (RBM) relies on rigorous tools, such as performance indicators, dashboards, and information systems, that require robust data engineering capabilities, which remain insufficient across several administrative services. The shortage of statisticians, evaluators, and skilled managers constitutes a major obstacle. Many public entities have not yet implemented the management tools required under the Organic Finance Law (LOF), including performance indicators, dashboards, and variance analysis, thereby creating a substantial implementation gap.

With regard to the internal audit function, Morocco, on the one hand, lacks a unified and binding legal framework governing internal audit across all public entities, resulting in heterogeneous practices. On the other hand, internal audit units are often hierarchically attached to the general management or to the entities they are supposed to audit, which creates risks of conflicts of interest and undermines the objectivity of the audit process. Internal audit thus faces a dual challenge: a shortage of auditors trained in modern approaches (risks, performance, governance) and limited autonomy in conducting audit missions, particularly when assessing the management of sensitive public programs.

Management control, although essential for monitoring and optimizing the use of resources, remains poorly structured and is often undervalued within institutional hierarchies. It suffers from a lack of legitimacy and weak organizational commitment to this analytical function. The absence of a centralized information system further complicates the collection, processing, and analysis of data required for effective management control, constituting a major operational constraint (Lkhoyaali & Maailif, 2023).

In practice, performance indicators frequently prove inadequate, as they are often poorly defined, difficult to quantify, or lack a clear linkage to strategic objectives.

Management controllers also face limited access to information and encounter difficulties in collecting timely, reliable, and centralized data, which further constrains the effective implementation of performance-based management.

2.3.3. Difficulties Related to Results

One of the major contributions of New Public Management (NPM) lies in the establishment of a results-oriented culture intended to guide public decision-making. However, in Morocco, results-based management (RBM) often focuses on the production of quantitative, activity-based indicators, with limited emphasis on impact evaluation. Outputs and tangible results struggle to align effectively with predefined strategic objectives and orientations, particularly as the information collected is sometimes partial or unreliable. Moreover, the implementation of RBM faces both technical and social challenges, generating discrepancies between public policies and public management practices (Boumkhaled et al., 2018).

The use of management control within public administrations remains limited and its application is often constrained. Where it exists, it is generally confined to administrative reporting, without in-depth variance analysis or the implementation of improvement plans. In many institutions, the absence of a centralized performance culture means that the prevailing approach remains focused on resource management rather than on the achievement of results, thereby hindering the integration of management control tools. Internal evaluation instruments have largely been marginalized, with greater emphasis placed on external evaluations conducted by the Court of Accounts, the General Inspectorate of Finance, and Parliament, as well as on monitoring and evaluation mechanisms. Consequently, management control and internal audit have received comparatively less attention.

Internal audit missions also remain limited in scope, being primarily oriented toward compliance and regularity, with a near absence of audits focused on effectiveness, despite the formal attachment of audit units to higher hierarchical levels. Audit recommendations are frequently underestimated, ignored, or only weakly implemented, owing to the absence of systematic follow-up and evaluation mechanisms or to insufficient managerial commitment.

CONCLUSION

For several years now, we have seen that the management of public organizations is beginning to move away from traditional management methods and be replaced by new management methods inspired by the private sector and aimed at achieving performance. In this context, most countries in the world, including Morocco, have embarked on public sector reform projects. Influenced by several factors, it was in the 1990s that Morocco embarked on a series of reforms and projects based on the principles of New Public Management (the good management pact, the economic and social development plan, the PARAP and the new constitution of 2011).

However, the implementation of these principles faces numerous structural and cultural constraints that limit their real impact on the ground. Regarding objectives, we observe that those defined in performance frameworks can sometimes seem vague, repetitive, or lack a direct link to operational realities. The approach to RBM in Morocco focuses primarily on the budgetary aspect, without covering all its facets. Moreover, reform objectives are sometimes perceived in a limited way, as instruments of authority rather than as means of improvement. There is also the absence of a clearly defined general strategy, broken down into concrete actions and explicit priority objectives.

Regarding resources, the success of these reforms requires appropriate human, technical, and financial resources, an area where the Moroccan public sector faces significant needs. RBM requires solid data engineering and specialized skills (statisticians, evaluators), which are still insufficient in many departments. For internal audit, the lack of a unified legal framework leads to a diversity of practices, and challenges remain regarding its autonomy and training in modern approaches. Management control, while essential, is sometimes underestimated and is hampered by the lack of a centralized information system for data collection and analysis.

Finally, regarding results, a performance-oriented culture is struggling to establish itself, with RBM focused on activity indicators rather than impact assessment, the application of management control remains limited to simple reporting, and internal audit missions remain focused on compliance, with recommendations overlooked or barely implemented.

Furthermore, despite the ambition of the reforms undertaken by Morocco, the ultimate goal of a high-performance public organization is not yet achievable. The effective implementation of New Public Management in Morocco remains severely limited by a set of structural, cultural, and institutional factors. Thus, although NPM represents a significant effort to streamline and modernize public action in Morocco, its impact is mixed; it oscillates between formal adoption and incomplete implementation, highlighting the confrontations between an aspiration for modernity and the realities of an administration still influenced by its bureaucratic heritage. A detailed study of these dynamics underlines the importance of a contextual, progressive, and participatory strategy, good support, and a system for evaluating and monitoring achievements capable of measuring short-term performance without neglecting the cultural aspect. This aims to sustainably anchor the principles of New Public Management in the public sphere in Morocco.

REFERENCES

Batley, R., & Larbi, G. (2004). Changing approaches to public sector management. In *The Changing Role of Government: The Reform of Public Services in Developing Countries* (pp. 31–53). Palgrave Macmillan UK. DOI: 10.1057/9780230001053_2

Bourguignon, A. (1995). *Peut-on définir la performance.* Revenue Francaise de Comptabilite. Revenue Francaise de Comptabilite.

Boumkhaled, M., Lkhoyaali, B., & El Halaissi, M. (2018). La gestion axée sur les résultats (GAR) au Maroc: une lecture critique. Revue du contrôle, de la comptabilité et de l'audit, 2(4).

Boyne, G., Gould-Williams, J., Law, J., & Walker, R. (2002). Plans, performance information and accountability: The case of best value. *Public Administration, 80*(4), 691–710. DOI: 10.1111/1467-9299.00324

Chandler, A. D., & Behar, J. M. (1992). *Organisation et performance des entreprises.* Les Éditions d'Organisation.

Charbonneau, M. (2012). Nouveau management public. Le Dictionnaire encyclopédique de l'administration publique, www.dictionnaire.enap.ca

Demeestère, R. (2002). *Le contrôle de gestion dans le secteur public.* LGDJ.

Elhamma, A. (2023). The relationship between organisational decentralisation, balanced scorecard, and its perceived benefits in Moroccan SMEs. International Journal of Accounting. *Auditing and Performance Evaluation, 19*(2), 185–202. DOI: 10.1504/IJAAPE.2023.132384

Ferlie, E. (1996). *The new public management in action.* Oxford university press.

Gauzente, C. (2000). Mesurer la performance des entreprises en l'absence d'indicateurs objectifs: Quelle validité? Analyse de la pertinence de certains indicateurs. *Finance Contrôle Stratégie, 3*(2), 145–165.

Elhamma, A. (2025), "Exploring the main determinants of the balanced scorecard as a managerial innovation: Evidence from Moroccan companies", Martínez-Falcó, J., Sánchez-García, E., & Marco-Lajara, B. (Eds.), Research and development practices in innovation, IGI Global, Hershey, PA, pp. 83-102. https://doi.org/DOI: 10.4018/979-8-3373-0812-8.ch004

Elhamma, A., & El-Moumane, R. (2025), "The role of strategic planning in resilience and crisis management: A case study of a public organization in Morocco", Rouco, J.C. & Figueiredo, P.C. (Eds.), Enhancing resilience in business continuity management, IGI Global, Hershey, PA, pp. 433-460. https://doi.org/DOI: 10.4018/979-8-3693-8809-9.ch015

Elhamma, A., & Loukili, Z. (2025), "Emergence of public-private partnership policies: A comparative study of Morocco and France", Baporikar, N. (Ed.), Public private partnerships for social development and impact, IGI Global, Hershey, PA, pp. 155-178. https://doi.org/DOI: 10.4018/979-8-3373-3471-4.ch007

Elhamma, A., & Snoussi, N. (2026), "Challenges to the adoption of the balanced scorecard as a managerial innovation in Moroccan SMEs", Jamil, G.L., Jamil, L.C., Paletta, F.C., Geada, N., & Vieira, A.A.P. (Eds.), Innovation management for disruptive maturity in competitive scenarios, IGI Global, Hershey, PA, pp. 249-272. https://doi.org/DOI: 10.4018/979-8-3693-4030-1.ch011

El-Moumane, R. (2026), "The impact of IPSAS on the quality of financial reporting in public sector organizations: An empirical study", Elhamma, A. (Ed.), Adoption, impact, and challenges of international financial reporting standards, IGI Global, Hershey, PA, pp. 247-276. https://doi.org/DOI: 10.4018/979-8-3373-1902-5.ch009

Hassani. K. & EL Moussali N. (2020) «Le New Public Management: quels enjeux pour le système de santé publique au Maroc ? », Revue Internationale des Sciences de Gestion « Numéro 6 / Volume 3: numéro 1 » pp: 454 – 474.

Hood, C. (1991). A public management for all seasons? *Public Administration*, *69*(1), 3–19. DOI: 10.1111/j.1467-9299.1991.tb00779.x

Jackson, G. A. (1982). Public efficiency and private choice in higher education. *Educational Evaluation and Policy Analysis*, *4*(2), 237–247. DOI: 10.3102/01623737004002237

Jones, P. (2012). Inputs, Outputs, Outcomes: Using a misunderstood approach, successfully.

Kaplan, R. S., & Norton, D. P. (2005). *The balanced scorecard: measures that drive performance* (Vol. 70). Harvard Business Review.

Khemakhem, A. (1976). *La dynamique du contrôle de gestion*. Dunod.

Lahjouji, K., & El Menzhi, K. (2018). Le Nouveau Management Public au Maroc, quels apports?

Lkhoyaali, B., & Maailif, S. (2023) « Le contrôle de gestion dans le secteur public: quelles spécificités? », Revue du contrôle, de la comptabilité et de l'audit « Volume 7: numéro 4 » pp: 129-150. Loi organique n° 130-30, WWW.lof.finances.gov.ma

Lorino, P. (1997). Méthodes et pratiques de la performance: Le guide du pilotage 1re édition. Paris: Editions d'organisation.

Lynn Jr, L. E. (2006). Public management: Old and new. Routledge. Maroc diplomatique « L'audit dans le secteur public, une garantie de l'efficacité et de la reddition de comptes » www. maroc-diplomatique.net

Marchesnay, M. (1991). La PME: Une gestion spécifique. *Économie Rurale (Paris), 206*(1), 11–17. DOI: 10.3406/ecoru.1991.4231

Moumene, J., & Benhrimida, M. (2016). La performance de l'Administration Publique Marocaine: Contribution du contrôle de gestion. *Moroccan Journal of Business Studies, 1*(1).

Najim, I. (2019). Management Public: Du contrôle des dépenses au contrôle de gestion: Processus d'implantation d'un système de contrôle de gestion applicable aux administrations publiques marocaines (Doctoral dissertation, faculté des sciences juridiques économiques et sociales de casablanca-UH2 de casablanca).

Peters, B. G. (2001). *The future of governing*. Studies in Government and Public Policy.

Pollitt, C., & Bouckaert, G. (2017). *Public management reform: A comparative analysis* (4th ed.). Oxford University Press.

Urio, P. (1999). La gestion publique au service du marché. In Hufty, M. (Ed.), *La pensée comptable: État, néolibéralisme, nouvelle gestion publique* (pp. 91–124).

ENDNOTE

1 http://lof.finances.gov.ma/sites/default/files/loi_organique_130-30_fr18.pdf

Chapter 11
Unlocking Hospital Performance:
NPM Tool Appropriation as a Key Mediator in the Moroccan Context

Cherkaoui Dekkaki Achraf
http://orcid.org/0009-0005-4797-4237
Ibn Tofaîl University, Morocco

Azzouz Elhamma
http://orcid.org/0000-0003-3382-0278
Ibn Tofaîl University, Morocco

ABSTRACT

In response to two decades of New Public Management (NPM) inspired reforms, the Moroccan public hospital sector is undergoing a profound transformation. This study analyzes the impact of NPM tool adoption on hospital performance, with a specific focus on the appropriation of these tools by local actors. Drawing on a quantitative survey of 240 hospital managers, our findings reveal that tool appropriation plays a crucial mediating role. This process, resulting in an organizational hybridization that merges managerial logics with public service values, is a critical determinant of effective performance improvement. Furthermore, the results confirm the influence of contingency factors, including hospital size, autonomy, and organizational culture. The study concludes that the simple transposition of NPM tools is insufficient. Instead, their effectiveness is contingent upon a contextual appropriation that promotes dynamics of hybridization.

DOI: 10.4018/979-8-3373-3526-1.ch011

INTRODUCTION

Since the late 20th century, New Public Management (NPM) has emerged as the dominant paradigm for state reforms worldwide. By importing private-sector logics, NPM seeks to enhance the efficiency, quality, and responsiveness of public services using tools such as management by objectives, contractual agreements, and performance indicators (Hood, 1991; Pollitt & Bouckaert, 2017). The hospital sector, with its organizational complexity and significant societal stakes, has been a prime yet contested field for these principles (Belorgey, 2010).

In line with this global trend, Morocco has been pursuing ambitious hospital reforms since the early 2000s, driven by national policies and international recommendations (Ministry of Health, 2012, 2019, 2023). This modernization effort has recently entered an unprecedented phase with the "refounding" of the national health system under Framework Law No. 06.22. The expansion of social protection and the creation of Territorial Health Groups (Groupements Sanitaires Territoriaux, GST) have further intensified the pressure on public hospitals to improve their performance and governance.

However, more than two decades after their inception, a persistent gap remains between the formal adoption of NPM tools and their effective appropriation by frontline actors. This gap, fueled by specific contextual, institutional, and cultural factors, threatens to render reforms superficial and ineffective, calling into question their ability to generate tangible performance improvements (Chabih, 2018; El Aoufi & Bensaïd, 2015).

To understand this challenge, this study moves beyond a simple evaluation of reform outcomes to investigate the underlying mechanisms. It addresses the central research question: To what extent does the adoption of NPM tools by Moroccan public hospitals lead to effective appropriation and improved hospital performance? The research posits that the appropriation of these tools is not merely a consequence of reform but the critical mediating factor determining its success. The primary contribution of this research is therefore to model and empirically test this mediating role. By quantifying this mechanism, the study aims to explain how managerial reforms translate—or fail to translate—into tangible performance.

The central objective is to test a model of organizational appropriation as a mediator between NPM tool adoption and institutional performance, using a quantitative methodology grounded in an integrated theoretical framework. The study draws upon the Diffusion of Innovation theory (Rogers, 2003), neo-institutionalism (DiMaggio & Powell, 1983), and contingency theory (Lawrence & Lorsch, 1967) to inform the model. The model was tested using survey data from a sample of 240 Moroccan hospital managers.

This article is structured as follows: the next section reviews the literature and develops the theoretical framework. Then, the methodology is presented, followed by the empirical results. The paper concludes with a discussion of the findings and their implications for hospital modernization in Morocco.

LITERATURE REVIEW

New Public Management in the Hospital Sector: A Reform Under Tension

Emerging in the 1980s from the Anglo-Saxon world amidst a crisis of the welfare state and the rise of neoliberalism, New Public Management (NPM) quickly became the dominant paradigm for public sector reform globally (Hood, 1991). NPM advocates for importing private-sector management techniques into public organizations to enhance performance. Its core principles include: a shift from a resource-based logic to a focus on measurable results; the use of contractual agreements to define responsibilities; increased autonomy and accountability for managers; and the deployment of performance indicators to steer efficiency and foster competition (Hood, 1991; Bezes et al., 2012; Pollitt & Bouckaert, 2017).

The hospital sector, with its inherent complexity and societal importance, has been a primary target for NPM-inspired reforms. Managerial tools like strategic dashboards, quality indicators, and performance contracts have been widely introduced to improve efficiency, resource allocation, and transparency (Belorgey, 2010; Bezes et al., 2012). This transforms the hospital into an autonomous, performance-driven organization, managed with mechanisms akin to those in the private sector.

However, implanting this model into healthcare settings creates significant tensions. A primary criticism is the structural conflict between managerial logic—focused on measurement, standardization, and efficiency and the professional logic of care, which is rooted in ethics, clinical autonomy, and personalized patient treatment (Waring & Currie, 2009; Kirkpatrick, et al., 2011). This clash can lead to negative outcomes such as professional disengagement, a deteriorating organizational climate, and the use of indicators for mere compliance rather than genuine quality improvement.

Crucially, the success of such reforms is highly contingent on the institutional, cultural, and political contexts in which they are deployed (Akinwale & Kuye, 2023). The uncritical adoption of NPM tools without local adaptation often leads to disjointed practices, bureaucratic bloat, and a loss of meaning for frontline staff (Ferlie et al., 1996; Pierre, 2000). Effective implementation, therefore, is not a technocratic exercise but requires inclusive governance and careful adaptation to local realities to truly enhance healthcare quality and system performance.

This challenge of contextual adaptation is especially relevant to Morocco's current health system overhaul, initiated in 2021 by Framework Law No. 06.22. This reform introduces Territorial Health Groups (GSTs) to promote decentralized governance and integrated care, drawing heavily on NPM principles of contractualization and accountability. Yet, without sufficient investment in training, managerial autonomy, and cultural alignment, these new structures risk repeating past failures. This situation underscores the need for a managed hybridization of imported tools and local practices, making contextual adaptation a critical prerequisite for improving care quality and overall hospital performance in Morocco.

The Moroccan Context: A Fertile Ground for Hybridization

Aligning with the global trend, Morocco began implementing NPM-inspired hospital reforms in the 2000s, a push driven by both international donors and a domestic agenda for administrative modernization (Ministry of Health, 2012, 2019, 2023). These reforms introduced tools such as contractual agreements, performance indicators, and management control systems designed to enhance accountability, efficiency, and quality of care.

Despite these efforts, implementation has been severely hampered by the unique structural, institutional, and socioeconomic features of the Moroccan context (Harfaoui et al., 2024). The health system is characterized by a stark duality: a high-performing private sector serves the affluent, while the public sector, often seen as under-resourced and overburdened, struggles to meet demand. This creates profound inequalities in access to care and an imbalanced competition for resources (Chabih, 2018). These challenges are compounded by deep territorial disparities between urban and rural areas, which prevent the uniform application of managerial reforms (El Aoufi & Bensaïd, 2015).

Organizational constraints present further barriers. A chronic shortage of qualified staff, particularly those with hospital management training, and inadequate IT and logistical infrastructures cripple the effective use of NPM tools, which depend on robust data systems and a results-oriented culture (Ministry of Health, 2012, 2019, 2023). Moreover, a persistent administrative culture of hierarchy, centralized authority, and bureaucratic inertia fosters resistance to change, exacerbated by the limited autonomy granted to local managers and minimal team involvement in decision-making (Dekkaki & Elhamma, 2024).

Given these constraints, a mechanical or "copy-paste" adoption of NPM tools is not merely ineffective; it is counterproductive. Yet, this high-tension environment is more than just an obstacle it is a fertile ground for hybridization. It forces local actors to move beyond passive implementation and become what can be described as organizational "tinkerers" (bricoleurs). These actors actively select, adapt, and blend imported managerial tools with pre-existing local practices and logics. Therefore, to truly assess the impact of these reforms, it is analytically essential to look beyond formal adoption and understand these deep dynamics of appropriation.

From Adoption to Performance: The Mediating Role of Appropriation and Hybridization

The introduction of NPM tools into hospitals is often driven by more than just a rational pursuit of efficiency. Neo-institutional theory explains that public organizations frequent adopt new practices due to isomorphic pressures—be they coercive (from regulators), mimetic (imitating successful peers), or normative (from professional standards) (DiMaggio & Powell, 1983). This can lead to "ceremonial conformity," where organizations adopt prescribed tools without fundamentally altering their core routines, a phenomenon known as decoupling (Bobkova, 2018). While this initial adoption may be superficial, it is a necessary first step that exposes the organization to new ideas and triggers a local process of adaptation. In turn, contingency theory posits that the effectiveness of these adaptations depends on their alignment with contextual factors like organizational size, resources, and culture (Lawrence & Lorsch, 1967; Otley, 1980).

This adaptation process is best understood through the concept of appropriation, defined as the active process by which actors seize, shape, and integrate management tools into their professional work (Denis et al., 2015). Appropriation materializes as organizational hybridization—the blending of managerial logics (e.g., performance, control) with professional logics (e.g., care, ethics) (Brunsson & Sahlin-Andersson, 2000; Nafzaoui & Ferdoussi, 2024). This supports the long-standing argument that without genuine appropriation, NPM tools remain "empty shells" incapable of driving meaningful change in practice (Hood, 1995; Pollitt & Bouckaert, 2011). As shown in Table 1, hybridization takes several forms within the organization.

Table 1. Forms of organizational hybridization

Form of Hybridization	Description	Key References
Indicator Adaptation	Modifying metrics to fit local realities and culture	Denis & al. (2015)
Requirement Negotiation	Modifying metrics to fit local realities and culture	Nafzaoui & Ferdoussi (2024)
Practice Selection	Choosing tools compatible with the public service mission	Brunsson & Sahlin-Andersson (2000)

Through such hybridization, tools become compatible with local needs and values (Rogers, 2003), turning them into effective levers for improvement. This process is enabled by factors like committed leadership and change management support (Chabih, 2018; Kotter, 1996), but hindered by obstacles such as limited autonomy, resource shortages, and professional resistance (Bouabdellah et al., 2024; Dent, 2003). The impact of these enablers and barriers is further shaped by contingency factors.

Table 2. Key contingency factors influencing appropriation

Factor	Potential Effect on Appropriation
Institution Size	Affects the capacity to integrate new tools
Managerial Autonomy	Enables or constrains local adaptation
Available Resources	Determines the feasibility of reforms
Organizational Culture	Fosters or impedes innovation
Institutional Environment	Creates external incentives or constraints

Note. Adapted from Lawrence & Lorsch (1967), Otley (1980)

Synthesizing these theories, a more nuanced model emerges. If formal adoption is merely the starting point, then its effect on performance is unlikely to be direct. Instead, we posit that adoption improves performance only when it is followed by genuine appropriation. In this model, appropriation and hybridization play a mediating role; they are the transmission mechanism that converts the input (tool adoption) into the output (performance improvement). As Hassen Teufel (2022) notes, successful transformation depends less on formal compliance and more on an organization's ability to intelligently bridge performance goals with its unique human and organizational realities.

Figure 1. The process of adoption and appropriation of NPM tools

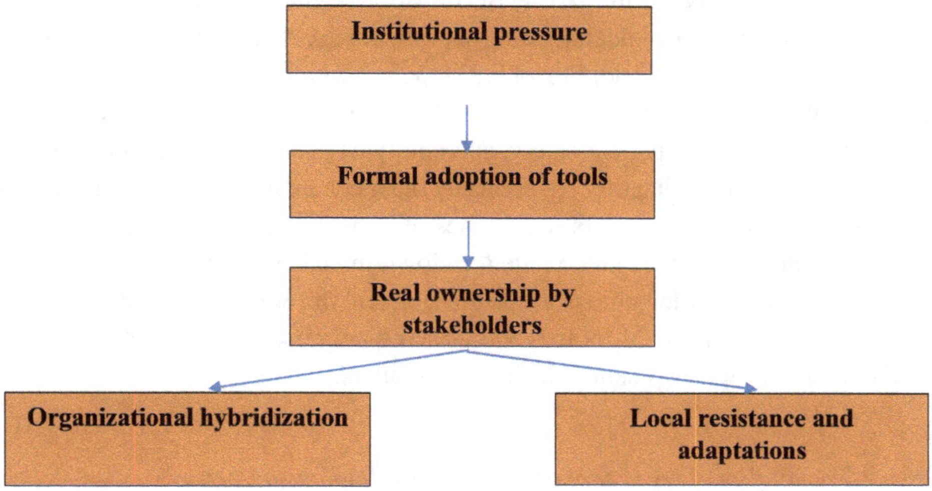

(Based on Rogers (2003), DiMaggio & Powell (1983), Denis et al. (2015), Brunsson & Sahlin-Andersson (2000))

This theoretical framework establishes appropriation and hybridization as the central mechanisms that transform NPM tools into effective levers of performance, a relationship we explore empirically in this study.

Hospital Performance: A Multidimensional Concept

Hospital performance is a complex, multidimensional concept that extends far beyond simple productivity or financial metrics. A holistic approach is essential, integrating dimensions such as efficiency, quality of care, equity of access, economic viability, and stakeholder satisfaction (Akhnif et al., 2024; Sicotte, et al., 1999).

Efficiency, a core tenet of NPM, measures the optimal use of resources to produce health services and outcomes (Berman & Hijal-Moghrabi, 2022). Quality encompasses both technical excellence (adherence to medical standards) and the patient's perceived experience (Arah et al., 2006). Equity of access is a fundamental pillar for public hospitals, gauging their ability to serve all populations without discrimination —a critical issue in contexts with significant territorial disparities, such as Morocco (Arah et al., 2006). Finally, financial viability ensures the institution's long-term sustainability, while stakeholder satisfaction is crucial for securing buy-in and maintaining a high-quality public service (Arah et al., 2006; Sicotte et al., 1999).

More recently, the concept of public value has enriched this framework, focusing on a hospital's broader societal contributions, such as strengthening social cohesion and fulfilling its public service mission beyond purely economic indicators (Moore, 1995; Nuti, Vainieri, & Bonini, 2021; Berrada & Marghich, 2023).

This multidimensional understanding of performance is central to our research. It explains why a mechanical adoption of NPM tools—which often prioritize financial efficiency alone—inevitably clashes with the values of healthcare professionals, who see quality of care, patient safety, and equity as paramount. The processes of appropriation and hybridization are precisely the mechanisms through which front-line actors navigate the trade-offs among these competing performance dimensions. They represent an attempt to reconcile top-down managerial imperatives with the bottom-up realities of the public service mission and the ethic of care. Without this successful integration, NPM tools risk producing perverse effects, such as professional demotivation or worsening health inequalities.

Table 3. The duality of NPM tool appropriation: Impacts and risks

Positive Impacts	Associated Limitations and Risks	Key References
Increased Efficiency	Professional Demotivation	Pollitt & Bouckaert (2017), Bezes & al. (2012)
Improved Quality	Superficial Compliance ("Ceremonial Conformity")	Propper et al. (2008), Denis & al. (2015)
Enhanced Accountability	Exacerbation of Territorial Inequalities	Chabih (2018), El Aoufi & Bensaïd (2015)
Stakeholder Satisfaction	Negative Effects on Internal Dynamics	Nuti & al. (2021), Brunsson & Sahlin-Andersson (2000)

Note. Author's own elaboration

In summary, this review establishes that appropriation and hybridization are the critical mechanisms that translate the formal adoption of NPM tools into tangible improvements in hospital performance. These processes, shaped by powerful contextual factors, form the theoretical bedrock for the empirical analysis that follows.

RESEARCH METHODOLOGY AND EMPIRICAL ANALYSIS

This section outlines the quantitative methodology used to test the relationships between New Public Management (NPM) tool adoption, organizational appropriation, and performance in Moroccan public hospitals. We present our research hypotheses, conceptual model, and the procedures for data collection and analysis.

Hypotheses and Conceptual Model

Based on our theoretical review, we formulated the following hypotheses:

- H1: The adoption of NPM tools is positively associated with organizational appropriation/hybridization.
- H2: Organizational appropriation/hybridization is positively associated with hospital performance.
- H3: Organizational appropriation/hybridization mediates the relationship between NPM tool adoption and hospital performance.

These relationships are illustrated in the conceptual model shown in Figure 2.

Figure 2. Conceptual research model

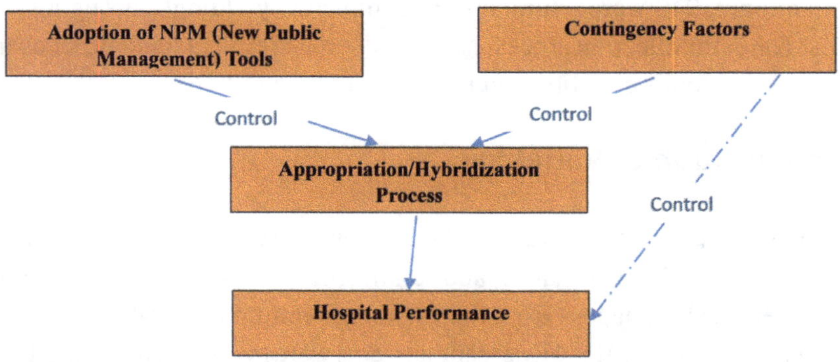

Note. The model represents the hypothesized mediating role of hybridization

Research Design and Methods

Epistemological Stance and Approach

This study employs a quantitative, positivist approach to empirically test our hypotheses. Following a hypothetico-deductive logic, we aim to identify and measure the causal relationships between our core constructs: adoption, appropriation, and performance. This approach, common in public management and organizational studies (e.g., Denis et al., 2015; Pollitt & Bouckaert, 2017), allows for the objectification of organizational phenomena and the generation of generalizable findings. By modeling these relationships based on structured survey data, our goal is to move beyond descriptive accounts and build a robust explanatory model that controls for contextual factors.

Sampling and Data Collection

Data were collected between April 2024 and February 2025 through a survey of managers and senior staff in Moroccan public hospitals. We used a purposive (non-probability) sampling strategy to ensure the relevance and quality of the data. Respondents were selected based on three criteria: (1) they were a member of a management, coordination, or steering team; (2) they had at least two years of experience at their institution; and (3) they were directly involved in using or implementing NPM tools (e.g., dashboards, performance indicators). This strategy was chosen to guarantee that participants had the requisite knowledge and direct experience to provide valid perceptual data on the reform processes.

The sample includes 25 public hospitals of various types (university, regional, and provincial) across Morocco. Of the 300 questionnaires administered (both in-person and online), 240 were returned fully completed, yielding a strong response rate of 80%. The data collection process strictly adhered to ethical standards, ensuring informed consent, confidentiality, and participant anonymity.

Operationalization of Variables

The study's core constructs (NPM Tool Adoption, Organizational Appropriation/Hybridization, Hospital Performance) and contingency factors were operationalized using multi-item scales adapted from the existing literature (e.g., Morgan & Hunt, 1994; Meier & O'Toole, 2001). All perceptual items were measured on a Likert scale.

Table 5. Measurement scale for NPM tool adoption

Code	Item
NPM1	Our institution regularly uses dashboards to manage its activities.
NPM2	Performance indicators are systematically tracked in our departments.
NPM3	Objective-setting contracts between management and departments are standard practice.
NPM4	Budgetary control is rigorously enforced.
NPM5	Management tools inspired by the private sector are integrated into our practices.
NPM6	Management meetings rely on quantitative data and indicators.
NPM7	Our institution has undergone or initiated accreditation/certification processes.

Table 6. Measurement scale for organizational appropriation/hybridization

Code	Item
HYB1	The NPM tools we use have been adapted to our institution's specific context.
HYB2	Our staff have genuinely appropriated these new management tools.
HYB3	A hybrid of traditional practices and new NPM tools has emerged.
HYB4	The introduction of NPM tools was accompanied by significant local adaptation.
HYB5	NPM tools are used effectively in our daily decision-making.
HYB6	Consultation between managers and clinicians has facilitated the integration of these tools.
HYB7	Healthcare professionals actively participate in adapting management tools.
HYB8	NPM-inspired practices coexist with established public-sector approaches.

Note. Author's own elaboration

Table 7. Measurement scale for hospital performance

Code	Item
PF1	The quality of care has improved over the past two years.
PF2	Patient satisfaction has been increasing.
PF3	Our managerial efficiency (cost-to-outcome ratio) has improved.
PF4	Patient wait times have been reduced.
PF5	Resources are now used and allocated more effectively.
PF6	The transparency of our management processes has increased.
PF7	Our key performance indicators show a positive trend.
PF8	Equity of access to care has improved.
PF9	Our teams are more engaged in achieving collective goals.
PF10	The hospital's public reputation has improved.

Note. tems adapted from Morgan and Hunt (1994).

Contextual variables were included as control variables. They were operationalized as follows:

Table 8. Operationalization of control variables (contingency factors)

Code	Item	Références
CTG1	Institution Size (Number of beds)	Meier & O'Toole (2001)
CTG2	Location (Urban / Rural / Mixed)	Boyne (2003)
CTG3	Institution Type (University, Regional, Provincial Hospital, etc.)	Ferlie et al. (1996)
CTG4	Institution Age (Years since establishment)	Christensen & Lægreid (2007)
CTG5	Managerial Autonomy	Moynihan & Pandey (2010)
CTG6	Respondent Profile (Role, seniority, management training)	Rainey & Steinbauer (1999)
CTG7	Institutional Pressures (Perceived level)	DiMaggio & Powell (1983)
CTG8	External Support (Perceived level from ministry, partners)	Brunsson & Sahlin-Andersson (2000)

Note. Compiled by the researchers based on Meier & O'Toole (2001), Moynihan & Pandey (2010).

Measurement Scale Validation

To ensure the reliability and validity of the measurement scales, a series of validation tests were performed using SPSS (v. 28). We conducted Principal Component Analysis (PCA) to assess the unidimensionality of each construct, calculated Cronbach's alpha to measure internal consistency, and performed the Kaiser-Meyer-Olkin (KMO) measure and Bartlett's Test of Sphericity to confirm the suitability of the data for factor analysis. The standard acceptance thresholds used are detailed in Table 9.

Table 9. Statistical thresholds for scale validation

Indicator	Recommended Threshold	Purpose
KMO Measure (Kaiser-Meyer-Olkin)	> 0.80	Confirms sampling adequacy for factor analysis
Bartlett's Test	p < 0.05	Confirms significant correlations between items
Variance Explained (PCA)	> 50%	Indicates strong explanatory power of the primary component
Cronbach's Alpha	> 0.70 (satisfaisant) ; > 0.80 (très bon) ; > 0.90 (excellent)	Indicates acceptable internal consistency reliability

These preliminary tests confirm that the measurement instruments are robust and suitable for the subsequent statistical analyses.

RESULTS AND DISCUSSION

This section presents the results of our empirical analysis. We first report on the validation of the measurement scales, followed by descriptive statistics, a correlation analysis, and the results of the mediation model testing our hypotheses.

Measurement Model Validation

Table 10. Total variance explained and eigenvalues

Variable	Nb of Items	Eigenvalue	% Variance Explained
Adoption of NPM Tools	7	5.23	74.71%
Appropriation/Hybridization	8	4.89	61.13%
Hospital Performance	10	5.17	51.70%

Note. Results derived from primary survey data (N = 240).

Prior to hypothesis testing, we assessed the reliability and validity of our measurement scales. Principal Component Analysis (PCA) confirmed the unidimensionality of each construct, with the first component explaining 74.71% of the variance for Adoption, 61.13% for Appropriation, and 51.70% for Performance.

Table 11. KMO index and Bartlett's test

Variable	KMO	Bartlett (χ^2)	ddl	Sig.
Adoption of NPM Tools	0.86	1021.45	21	< 0.001
Appropriation/Hybridization	0.90	1455.32	28	< 0.001
Hospital Performance	0.85	1234.67	45	< 0.001

Note. Results derived from primary survey data (N = 240).

The Kaiser-Meyer-Olkin measures were excellent (0.85 to 0.90), and Bartlett's tests of sphericity were highly significant ($p < 0.001$), confirming the factorability of the data. Finally, all scales demonstrated high internal consistency, with Cronbach's alpha coefficients of 0.91 for Adoption, 0.90 for Appropriation, and 0.86 for Performance. These results confirm the robustness of our measurement model.

Table 12. Scale reliability test

Variable	Cronbach's Alpha	Number of Items
Adoption of NPM Tools	0.912	7
Appropriation/Hybridization	0.895	8
Hospital Performance	0.855	10

Note. Results derived from primary survey data (N = 240).

Descriptive Statistics and Correlations

Table 13. Descriptive statistics of composite variables

Variable	Mean	Std. Dev	Min	Max
Adoption of NPM Tools	3.45	0.72	1.5	5.0
Appropriation/Hybridization	3.05	0.80	1.0	5.0
Hospital Performance	3.15	0.70	1.5	4.5

Note. Results derived from primary survey data (N = 240).

Descriptive statistics (on a 5-point scale) revealed that respondents perceived the Adoption of NPM tools most positively (M = 3.45, SD = 0.72), followed by Hospital Performance (M = 3.15, SD = 0.70). The lowest mean was for Appropriation/Hybridization (M = 3.05, SD = 0.80), suggesting a gap between the formal implementation of reforms and their substantive integration into practice.

Table 14. Pearson correlation matrix ($p < 0.01$)

	Adoption of NPM Tools	Appropriation/ Hybridization	Hospital Performance
Adoption of NPM Tools	1	0.57**	0.45**
Appropriation/ Hybridization	0.57**	1	0.62**
Hospital Performance	0.45**	0.62**	1

Note. Results derived from primary survey data (N = 240).

The Pearson correlation matrix indicated significant positive relationships among all constructs ($p < 0.01$). Notably, the strongest correlation was between Appropriation and Performance ($r = 0.62$), while the correlation between Adoption and Performance was weaker ($r = 0.45$). This preliminary result suggests that appropriation may play a critical mediating role.

Hypothesis Testing: Mediation Analysis

To test our hypotheses, we conducted a mediation analysis using Hayes' PROCESS macro (Model 4) with 5000 bootstrap samples. The results are summarized below and support all three hypotheses.

Table 15. Appropriation predicted by NPM adoption

Independent variable	Beta	t	p-value	R^2
Adoption of NPM Tools	0.58	11.3	< 0.001	0.33

Note. Results derived from primary survey data (N = 240).

H1 Supported: The adoption of NPM tools had a significant positive effect on appropriation ($\beta = 0.58$, $p < 0.001$), explaining 33% of its variance ($R^2 = 0.33$).

Table 16. Performance predicted by NPM adoption

Independent variable	Beta	t	p-value	R^2
Adoption of NPM Tools	0.32	5.2	< 0.001	0.20

Note. Results derived from primary survey data (N = 240).

H2 Supported: In the final model, appropriation had a strong, significant positive effect on hospital performance ($\beta = 0.55$, $p < 0.001$).

Table 17. Performance predicted by adoption and appropriation

Independent Variable	Beta	t	p-value
Adoption of NPM Tools	0.12	1.8	0.073
Appropriation/Hybridization	0.55	9.8	< 0.001
Total R^2	**0.46**		

Note. Results of the final regression model. Total R^2 = .46.

H3 Supported: The bootstrap analysis revealed a significant indirect effect of adoption on performance through appropriation (Effect = 0.32, 95% CI [0.22, 0.42]). Crucially, the direct effect of adoption on performance became non-significant ($\beta = 0.12$, $p = 0.073$) when the mediator was included.

This pattern of a significant indirect effect and a non-significant direct effect confirms full mediation. The findings demonstrate that the positive effect of adopting NPM tools on hospital performance is transmitted entirely through the process of organizational appropriation. The full model explained 46% of the variance in hospital performance ($R^2 = 0.46$).

Robustness Check with Control Variables

Table 18. Direct and indirect effects (bootstrap mediation model)

Effect	Estimate	95% CI	p-valeur	Interpretation
Indirect (a×b)	0.32	[0.22 ; 0.42]	< 0.001	Appropriation significantly mediates the relationship.
Direct (c')	0.12	[−0.01 ; 0.25]	0.073	The direct effect is not significant.
Total (c)	0.44	[0.34 ; 0.54]	< 0.001	The total effect is significant.

Note. Indirect and direct effects estimated using Hayes' (2022) PROCESS macro (Model 4) with 5,000 bootstrap samples

The significant indirect effect ($p < 0.001$) and the non-significant direct effect ($p = 0.073$) confirm a full mediation: the impact of NPM adoption on performance passes entirely through appropriation. The central result of our analysis lies in the confirmation of a full mediation. The effect of NPM tool adoption on performance ($c' = 0.12$, $p = 0.073$) becomes statistically non-significant when appropriation is taken into account, whereas the indirect effect ($a*b = 0.32$) is significant and robust. This demonstrates that adoption alone is not enough; its impact on performance passes almost exclusively through the process of appropriation and hybridization by actors.

Table 19. Performance predicted by adoption, appropriation, and control variables

Variable	Beta	t-value	p-value
Adoption of NPM Tools	0.10	1.6	0.113
Appropriation/Hybridization	0.53	9.5	< 0.001
Institution Size	0.15	2.2	0.028
perceived managerial autonomy	0.22	3.1	0.002
Ressources	0.08	1.3	0.198
Organizational culture	0.18	2.5	0.012

Note. Robustness check including control variables.

A final multiple regression analysis was conducted to assess the robustness of the model. The results indicate that the effect of appropriation on performance remains highly significant ($\beta = 0.53$, $p < 0.001$), while the effect of adoption is non-significant ($p = 0.113$), confirming mediation. Additionally, the analysis of control variables offers valuable insights. The size of the institution ($p = 0.028$), perceived managerial autonomy ($p = 0.002$), and organizational culture ($p = 0.012$) all significantly and positively influence performance. This suggests that reforms are more likely to succeed in larger, potentially better-structured hospitals, especially those with a culture conducive to change and where managers have genuine autonomy. Notably, the level of available resources does not appear to be a direct predictor of performance in this model ($p = 0.198$). This does not imply that resources are unimportant; rather, it may indicate that how they are managed and utilized is a more critical factor than their overall quantity.

Discussion

The empirical analysis provides strong support for the central argument of this research: the appropriation of NPM tools is the critical mechanism through which their adoption translates into improved hospital performance. The finding of full mediation (H3) represents the study's most significant theoretical contribution, demonstrating that simply implementing managerial tools is insufficient for organizational change. Their effectiveness is strictly contingent on being actively adapted, integrated, and hybridized by frontline actors.

This result helps explain the gap observed in the descriptive data between relatively high levels of formal adoption and more moderate levels of perceived performance. While a majority of hospitals in the sample use tools such as dashboards (86%) and performance indicators (79%), a significantly smaller proportion of managers perceive these tools as well-adapted to their specific local context (54%). This "appropriation deficit" appears to be a major bottleneck for the success of health reforms in Morocco.

The survey data suggest that this deficit is driven by key contextual challenges, consistent with the literature on public sector reform in Morocco (Chabih, 2018; Dekkaki & Elhamma, 2024). Specifically, a lack of qualified staff (reported by 72%), a dominant bureaucratic culture (68%), and limited managerial autonomy (74%) were identified as significant barriers to effective tool integration. These findings have critical implications for the ongoing health system overhaul. Without a deliberate strategy to build capacity, foster a collaborative culture, and empower local managers, the new Territorial Health Groups (GSTs) may fail to move beyond superficial, formal changes.

Conversely, the analysis of control variables highlights the enabling role of organizational factors. The positive impact of managerial autonomy and a supportive culture on performance underscores that where local actors are granted the freedom to innovate, reforms are more likely to succeed. This aligns with international research showing that NPM reforms are most effective when they are adapted locally rather than implemented through uniform, top-down mandates (Pollitt & Bouckaert, 2017). Furthermore, the non-significant effect of resources suggests that how resources are managed—a function of autonomy and culture—may be more determinant than their absolute quantity.

CONCLUSION AND FUTURE PERSPECTIVES

This research demonstrates that the adoption of New Public Management (NPM) tools has a positive but highly conditional impact on performance in Moroccan public hospitals. The empirical findings establish that organizational appropriation and hybridization serve as the cornerstone of successful reform. When managerial tools are actively adapted to local realities and integrated by hospital staff, they become powerful levers for improving care quality, efficiency, and patient satisfaction. Without this deep integration, however, formal adoption risks generating resistance or superficial compliance, yielding minimal impact.

Managerial and Policy Implications

The findings offer clear guidance for Moroccan policymakers and hospital leaders. To unlock the full potential of NPM reforms, the focus must shift from mandating tool adoption to enabling genuine appropriation. This requires a multifaceted strategy centered on:

- **Capacity Building:** Implement continuous training programs for both managers and clinicians on how to use and adapt NPM tools to their specific environments.
- **Empowerment:** Grant institutions greater managerial autonomy to experiment and customize reforms, fostering a sense of local ownership.
- **Collaboration:** Create structured platforms for dialogue between managers and clinicians to co-construct hybrid practices that bridge the gap between managerial and clinical priorities.
- **Transparency:** Ensure open communication about resource allocation and performance results to build trust and legitimize change among all stakeholders.
- **Resource Allocation:** Provide the necessary human and material resources to support implementation, especially in underserved areas.
- **Adaptive Governance:** Establish robust monitoring and evaluation systems to learn from implementation and continuously refine strategies.

LIMITATIONS AND FUTURE RESEARCH

While this study confirms the central role of appropriation, other variables undoubtedly shape reform outcomes. Building on the work of contingency theorists (Lawrence & Lorsch, 1967; Otley, 1980), several avenues for future research are suggested to build a more comprehensive understanding:

- Contextual Analysis: Comparative studies could explore how the urban-rural divide and other regional variations in Morocco affect reform implementation.
- Longitudinal Studies: Tracking the appropriation of new governance tools over time within the recently established Territorial Health Groups (GSTs).
- Micro-level Factors: Investigating individual-level variables, such as the motivation and leadership styles of managers or the professional engagement of clinicians.
- Health System Dynamics: Assessing the impact of the nationwide expansion of Compulsory Health Insurance (Assurance Maladie Obligatoire, AMO) on the performance culture in public hospitals.
- Qualitative Inquiry: Utilizing qualitative methods to gain a deeper, more nuanced understanding of how frontline actors perceive and navigate NPM-inspired reforms.

In summary, organizational appropriation and hybridization are not by-products of reform, but the core engines of meaningful change. Fostering these dynamics is essential for improving hospital performance and enhancing the capacity of the Moroccan public health system to meet the evolving needs of its citizens.

REFERENCES

Akhnif, E. H., Belmadani, A., Mataria, A., & Bigdeli, M. (2024). UHC in Morocco: A bottom-up estimation of public hospitals' financing size based on a costing database. *Health Economics Review*, *14*(1), 25. DOI: 10.1186/s13561-024-00501-x PMID: 38557700

Akinwale, O. E., & Kuye, O. L. (2023). Ouchi's management model relevance to healthcare management efficiency among government tertiary hospitals during the COVID-19 pandemic season in Lagos state, Nigeria. *Technological Sustainability*, *2*(1), 20–43. DOI: 10.1108/TECHS-01-2022-0005

Arah, O. A., Klazinga, N. S., Delnoij, D. M., Ten Asbroek, A. H., & Custers, T. (2006). Conceptual frameworks for health systems performance: A quest for effectiveness, quality, and improvement. *International Journal for Quality in Health Care : Journal of the International Society for Quality in Health Care*, *18*(4), 377–398. PMID: 14527982

Belorgey, N. (2010). *L'hôpital sous pression. Enquête sur le nouveau management public*. La Découverte. DOI: 10.3917/dec.belor.2010.01

Berman, E. M., & Hijal-Moghrabi, I. (2022). *Performance and Innovation in the Public Sector : Managing for results*. Routledge. DOI: 10.4324/9781003304753

Berrada, H., & Marghich, A. (2023). Performance hospitalière : État de l'art. Revue du contrôle, de la comptabilité et de l'audit, 7(1).

Bezes, P., Demazière, D., Le Bianic, T., Paradeise, C., & Normand, R. (2012). New public management et professions dans les organisations publiques. Sociologies pratiques, 25(2), 9–22.

Bobkova, E. (2018). The Use of New Public Management in Healthcare. Lessons for Transition Economies. *Journal of Management and Strategy*, *9*(1), 78–87.

Bouabdellah, M., & Ferdoussi, M. (2024). Management hospitalier au Maroc: Défis et perspectives. *Revue Marocaine de Gestion Publique*, *29*(1), 45–62.

Brunsson, N., & Sahlin-Andersson, K. (2000). Constructing organizations: The example of public sector reform. *Organization Studies*, *21*(4), 721–746. DOI: 10.1177/0170840600214003

Chabih, Y. (2018). L'hôpital public au Maroc: Entre transition institutionnelle et recomposition des pratiques professionnelles. *Revue Francophone Internationale de Recherche Infirmière*, *4*(3), 134–145.

Christensen, T., & Lægreid, P. (2007). The whole-of-government approach to public sector reform. *Public Administration Review, 67*(6), 1059–1066. DOI: 10.1111/j.1540-6210.2007.00797.x

Dekkaki, A. C., & Elhamma, A. (2024). The contribution and impact of management control on the performance of public hospitals in Morocco: Moving beyond the" New Public Management. *Revue Internationale du Chercheur, 5*(2).

Denis, J. L., Ferlie, E., & Van Gestel, N. (2015). Understanding hybridity in public organizations. *Public Administration, 93*(2), 273–289. DOI: 10.1111/padm.12175

Dent, M. (2003). *Remodelling hospitals and health professions in Europe: Medicine, nursing and the state*. Palgrave Macmillan. DOI: 10.1057/9781403938411

DiMaggio, P. J., & Powell, W. W. (1983). The iron cage revisited: Institutional isomorphism and collective rationality in organizational fields. *American Sociological Review, 48*(2), 147–160. DOI: 10.2307/2095101

El Aoufi, N., & Bensaïd, M. (2015). Modernisation des services publics au Maroc: entre injonction managériale et inertie institutionnelle.

Ferlie, E., Ashburner, L., Fitzgerald, L., & Pettigrew, A. (1996). *The New Public Management in Action*. Oxford University Press. DOI: 10.1093/acprof:oso/9780198289029.001.0001

Harfaoui, W., Belyamani, L., Zentar, A., Lekehal, B., & Obtel, M. (2024). The New Reform of the National Health System in Morocco: An Opportunity to Meet the Challenges and Improve the Practice of Anesthesiology.

Hassen Teufel, P. (2022). Comment les politiques publiques changent-elles? Une perspective pragmatique sur la réforme de l'hôpital. *Revue Française de Science Politique, 72*(2), 267–290.

Hood, C. (1991). A public management for all seasons? *Public Administration, 69*(1), 3–19. DOI: 10.1111/j.1467-9299.1991.tb00779.x

Hood, C. (1995). The "new public management" in the 1980s: Variations on a theme. *Accounting, Organizations and Society, 20*(2–3), 93–109. DOI: 10.1016/0361-3682(93)E0001-W

Kirkpatrick, I., Dent, M., & Jespersen, P. K. (2011). The contested terrain of hospital management: Professional projects and healthcare reforms in Denmark. *Current Sociology, 59*(4), 489–506. DOI: 10.1177/0011392111402718

Kotter, J. P. (1996). *Leading change*. Harvard Business Press.

Lawrence, P. R., & Lorsch, J. W. (1967). *Organization and environment: Managing differentiation and integration*. Harvard Business School Press.

Meier, K. J., & O'Toole, L. J.Jr. (2001). Managerial strategies and behavior in networks: A model with evidence from US public education. *Journal of Public Administration: Research and Theory*, *11*(3), 271–294. DOI: 10.1093/oxfordjournals.jpart.a003503

Moore, M. H. (1995). *Creating Public Value: Strategic Management in Government*. Harvard University Press.

Morgan, R. M., & Hunt, S. D. (1994). The commitment-trust theory of relationship marketing. *Journal of Marketing*, *58*(3), 20–38. DOI: 10.1177/002224299405800302

Nafzaoui, H., & Ferdoussi, M. (2024). Hybridation et performance: Étude des réformes hospitalières au Maghreb. *Revue Nord-Africaine de Gestion Publique*, *3*(1), 55–74.

Nuti, S., Vainieri, M., & Bonini, A. (2021). Public value in health care: A new approach to performance measurement. *Health Policy (Amsterdam)*, *125*(2), 167–172.

Otley, D. T. (1980). The contingency theory of management accounting: Achievement and prognosis. *Accounting, Organizations and Society*, *5*(4), 413–428. DOI: 10.1016/0361-3682(80)90040-9

Pierre, J. (2000). *Debating governance: Authority, steering, and democracy*. Oxford University Press. DOI: 10.1093/oso/9780198295143.001.0001

Pollitt, C., & Bouckaert, G. (2011). *Public management reform: A comparative analysis—New public management, governance, and the neo-Weberian state*. Oxford University Press.

Pollitt, C., & Bouckaert, G. (2017). *Public Management Reform: A Comparative Analysis—Into the Age of Austerity* (4th ed.). Oxford University Press.

Propper, C., Sutton, M., Whitnall, C., & Windmeijer, F. (2008). Did 'targets and terror' reduce waiting times in the English NHS? *The B.E. Journal of Economic Analysis & Policy*, *8*(2), 5. Advance online publication. DOI: 10.2202/1935-1682.1863

Rainey, H. G., & Steinbauer, P. (1999). Galloping elephants: Developing elements of a theory of effective government organizations. *Journal of Public Administration: Research and Theory*, *9*(1), 1–32. DOI: 10.1093/oxfordjournals.jpart.a024401

Rogers, E. M. (2003). *Diffusion of Innovations* (5th ed.).

Sicotte, C., Champagne, F., & Contandriopoulos, A. P. (1999). A conceptual framework for the analysis of performance in health care organizations. *Health Services Management Research, 12*(4), 253–268. PMID: 10178368

Waring, J., & Currie, G. (2009). Managing expert knowledge: Organizational challenges and managerial futures for the UK medical profession. *Organization Studies, 30*(7), 755–778. DOI: 10.1177/0170840609104819

Chapter 12
Between National Discretion and Collective Norms:
The Challenge of Revising the EU's Common Position on Arms Exports

Theofania Antoniou
http://orcid.org/0009-0001-8469-9714
Hellenic Open University, Greece

ABSTRACT

The Common Position 2008/944/CFSP constitutes the principal legal instrument governing the European Union's regime for the control of military technology and arms exports. The escalation of hostilities in Gaza (2023–2025) has revealed significant structural deficiencies and implementation gaps within this framework, primarily stemming from the decentralised nature of enforcement and the divergent administrative and judicial practices of the Member States. These developments have raised criticism concerning the absence of a centralised supervisory authority, the limited enforceability of the Common Position's criteria, and the need for enhanced harmonisation and transparency. The Gaza crisis illustrates the enduring challenge of reconciling national discretion with collective EU norms, highlighting the necessity of further strengthening the legal coherence and practical effectiveness of the EU's export control regime in safeguarding compliance with international humanitarian law.

DOI: 10.4018/979-8-3373-3526-1.ch012

1. INTRODUCTION

The European Union's (EU) Common Position 2008/944/CFSP on arms exports remains the central normative framework for regulating the transfer of military technology and equipment from EU Member States. Adopted in December 2008 as the continuation of the 1998 EU Code of Conduct on Arms Exports, it codifies eight criteria that national authorities must assess when granting or denying export licenses. These criteria reflect a blend of international commitments, such as respect for human rights, international humanitarian law (IHL), regional security, and non-proliferation obligations, with the EU's own Common Foreign and Security Policy (CFSP) objectives (Council of the European Union, 2008; Antoniou, 2014).

Since its adoption, the Common Position has been regarded as the main instrument attempting to unify arms export controls within the EU (Bromley, 2020; Bauer & Cops, 2014). Yet, practice has consistently revealed a substantial implementation gap, since arms export licensing remains a national competence, embedded in domestic administrative procedures, subject to national parliaments, and protected under Article 346 of the Treaty on the Functioning of the European Union (TFEU), under the umbrella of common principles (Eeckhout, 2021).

The Gaza war that began in October 2023 has exposed these structural weaknesses. Israel's military operations following the Hamas attacks of 7 October 2023, led to unprecedented civilian casualties and large-scale destruction in the Gaza Strip (United Nations Office for the Coordination of Humanitarian Affairs [UNOCHA], 2024). These events provoked widespread public mobilisation, litigation by non-governmental organisations (NGOs), and renewed calls for an EU-wide arms embargo on Israel. Within the EU, however, Member States responded divergently. Spain and the Netherlands suspended licences to Israel, sometimes under judicial pressure, while Germany initially continued approvals before reconsidering them. Belgium's courts forced regional governments to block transit permits, while Austria, the Czech Republic, and Hungary maintained permissive policies. This fragmentation reflects the constant balance in EU export control policy between national discretion and collective norms.

Every five years the Council of the EU reviews the operation of the Common Position. The first review (2014) focused on procedural adjustments, while the second (2019) aligned EU rules with the 2013 Arms Trade Treaty (ATT) and enhanced transparency requirements. The third review, launched in 2023 and concluded in April 2025, was the most politically charged yet. It was shaped by two parallel crises: the urgent need to authorise large volumes of military transfers to Ukraine after Russia's full-scale invasion in 2022, and the mounting controversy over arms exports to Israel during the Gaza war (Besch, 2023).

The Council's April 2025 Conclusions reaffirmed commitments to "responsible and transparent trade in arms," expanded work on post-shipment controls and end-use monitoring, and addressed long-standing challenges of jointly developed European equipment (Council of the European Union, 2025). Yet, despite significant NGO lobbying, the reforms stopped short of establishing supranational enforcement or harmonised denial criteria (Saferworld, 2023). The review thus underlines the ever ending dichotomy between the EU's normative international role and the preservation of Member States' sovereignty (Antoniou, 2011; Antoniou, 2012; Antoniou, 2013).

The 2023–2025 Gaza conflict provides a particularly revealing case study for analysing the Common Position. Unlike other conflicts (such as the Saudi-led intervention in Yemen or the Libyan civil war), Israel represents both a key Western ally and a major arms importer from several EU states, namely Germany, Italy, Netherlands, and Czech Republic (SIPRI, 2024). The humanitarian consequences of Israeli military operations, combined with the visibility of European-supplied weapons, generated intense pressure for compliance with Common Position Criterion Two: prohibiting exports where there is a clear risk of serious violations of IHL. Courts in the Netherlands and Belgium directly applied this criterion, treating it as justiciable and enforceable, while German courts remained cautious, framing arms export licensing as an executive prerogative.

This divergence illustrates the fragmentation at the heart of the EU's system, leading to the production of radically different outcomes when applying the same Common Position depending on domestic legal frameworks and political cultures. Therefore, this chapter aims to address the question of how m/s interpreted and applied the Common Position during the Gaza conflict (2023–2025) and how has the third review of the Common Position responded to the political and legal challenges. Further on, it examines the reforms that have been proposed to reconcile national discretion with collective norms, and discusses their prospects.

By analysing these questions, the chapter contributes to the discussion on the EU's external action and the problem of consistency (Antoniou, 2019; Antoniou, 2016; Antoniou, 2014) by examining the interaction between CFSP instruments and national implementation (Balfour & Raube, 2015) and it adds to comparative research on arms export governance, situating the EU's experience alongside global trends in the ATT and national export control regimes (Casey-Maslen et al., 2016). The chapter argues that while the EU has developed a sophisticated normative framework, its effectiveness ultimately depends on Member States' willingness and capacity to implement it faithfully. The Gaza conflict apart from highlighting the above mentioned internal tension, it may also generate momentum for reform.

2. THE EU COMMON POSITION: LEGAL AND POLITICAL FRAMEWORK

The EU's arms-export regime evolved from a non-binding, peer-pressure instrument into a legally binding CFSP act. The 1998 EU Code of Conduct on Arms Exports relied on voluntary "denial notifications," annual reports, and political commitment to eight criteria (Bromley, 2020). While innovative in transparency and mutual learning, the Code lacked legal effect and uniformity, allowing wide divergence among Member States. In 2008, the Council approved a Common Position that binds Member States as a matter of EU law while leaving licensing decisions at national level (Council of the European Union, 2008). This "soft-to-hard" shift formalised convergence tools and articulated eight criteria that must be applied case-by-case to all proposed exports of military technology and equipment on the EU Common Military List.

The renewed 2008 Common Position included a duty to assess risk ex ante against criteria derived from international law (e.g., IHL and human rights) and EU security policy without centralizing decision-making (Bauer & Cops, 2014; Besch, 2023). Moreover, it embedded structured peer coordination through the COARM working group (notifications, information-sharing, User's Guide updates). It also preserved national discretion, since Member States remain the competent licensing authorities and the CJEU's jurisdiction over CFSP acts is limited (Eeckhout, 2021). As a result, the regime is binding but decentralized. It should be noted that the Common Position is adopted under Article 24(1) TEU and Article 275 TFEU, which foresee an exceptional—permitted primarily for restrictive measures and to police delimitation with non-CFSP competences (Eeckhout, 2021; Larik, 2017) review of CFSP. In other words, breach of a criterion does not generate a direct EU-law cause of action at Union level, rather accountability is channeled through national law, politics, and peer pressure in COARM. Arms-export licensing remains under national competence (article 346 TFEU). While all eight criteria apply, Criteria 1–4 & 7 tend to carry mandatory-denial implications when thresholds are met (Council of the European Union, 2008). The User's Guide encourages a documented balancing where criteria point in different directions, but it stresses that Criterion 2 and Criterion 7 often prevail industrial or diplomatic benefits when credible risk is established (Saferworld, 2020).

Considering that EU and all Member States are parties to the Arms Trade Treaty (ATT), the 2019 review of the Common Position clarified alignment with the ATT, and the User's Guide has moved practice toward shared risk indicators (Casey-Maslen et al., 2016; Saferworld, 2020). More precisely, many licensing authorities and scholars now treat the Common Position's "clear risk" as functionally equivalent to the ATT's "overriding risk", once credible evidence shows a realistic, non-speculative likelihood of misuse (Casey-Maslen et al., 2016). The Dutch Court of Appeal explicitly read the two standards together in 2024, reinforcing this equivalence in adjudication. Furthermore, authorities must weigh type of equipment, operational context, end-use assurances, and mitigation measures (e.g., training, restrictive clauses).

The denial-notification system is designed to prevent national licence differentiation through consultation and peer pressure. Empirical research and civil-society monitoring, however, suggest that it persists, especially in politically salient destinations (Besch, 2023; European Parliament, 2020). The Gaza and Yemen case studies show that even where several Member States apply strict interpretations of Criterion 2, others may authorise deliveries under different appraisals of risk, evidentiary weight, or mitigation.

The 2025 review responded with process-oriented improvements (more structured information-sharing; attention to jointly developed systems; end-use monitoring) rather than alignment of denial criteria, consistent with CFSP's constitutional design. The 2023–2025 review cycle acknowledged these realities, opting for incremental improvements, particularly around post-shipment controls and joint development rather than a redesign of competences.

3. NATIONAL DIVERGENCE AMID THE GAZA CRISIS (2023–2025)

The two year Gaza crisis became the sharpest stress test yet for the European Union's Common Position 2008/944/CFSP. Since October 2023, Member States' responses to Israeli operations in Gaza have varied widely, reflecting divergent national policies on arms exports. Some European governments have publicly reined in exports to Israel, while others continue substantial deliveries. The result is a number of unilateral measures that underscore the tension between national prerogatives and EU common commitments.

Spain, for instance, announced that it had "suspended all military exports to Israel" immediately after October 2023, even cancelling contracts for Israeli ammunition, and has been among the most vocal European critics of Israel's conduct in Gaza. Italy likewise disclosed in mid-2024 that it had effectively "frozen all new arms export licenses to Tel Aviv" since the war began, a decision referenced during a parliamentary session on Gaza. France initially fully supportive of Israel's actions, by spring 2025 warned that Europe might "toughen" its collective stance and even impose sanctions if Israel did not change course. In private, Paris signaled that new French licences would not be granted for weapons likely to be used in IHL violations (Antoniou et al, 2025).

By contrast, other Member States have maintained or even accelerated arms sales to Israel. Germany in 2023 licensed over €326 million in military exports to Israel (roughly one third of Israel's arms imports) (European Parliament, 2024) — though it reduce approvals markedly in early 2024 (ECCHR, 2025). Austria, the Czech Republic and Hungary have remained firmly pro-Israel, continuing to approve exports and abstaining from EU votes critical of Israel (European Parliament, 2024). Other EU countries have taken intermediate positions. In some cases (such as the UK — though no longer an EU member, or Greece and Cyprus in NATO) domestic criticism has led to partial suspensions or stricter review of deals with Israel (European Parliament, 2024). But generally, there is no common EU embargo on Israel (unlike the EU arms embargoes the Union imposes on certain other conflict zones) (Council of the EU, 2024).

These divergent policies affected the review process, leading to some member states (often Northern and Western EU members) promoting stricter controls to "build convergence" of policies, whereas others insist on preserving national decision-making autonomy (Council of the EU, 2024; European Parliament, 2024). Several judicial rulings in national courts have underscored the political stakes of arms exports to conflict zones. Two emblematic cases in the Netherlands and Germany have tested how courts interpret EU criteria and the extent to which citizens can compel governments to halt arms shipments on legal grounds. These cases have already had political repercussions and are contributing to the EU-level debate on the Common Position's implementation.

Overall, three patterns emerge regarding national practice and the implementation of the Common Position's criteria:

a. Criterion 2 (IHL/IHRL) became the hinge of restrictive decisions after a number of national courts' rulings. The Netherlands' appellate ruling operationalised "clear risk" as a justiciable threshold, while Belgium's transit order linked Criterion 2 with Criterion 7 to police flows through Antwerp and Spain invoked Criterion 2 to justify suspensions and contract cancellations (ECCHR, 2025).
b. Criterion 7 (diversion) gained salience through debates on post-shipment control and supply-chain opacity. The Dutch and Belgian cases demonstrated that transit and global maintenance chains can engage EU criteria, highlighting the value, as stressed in the 2025 review, of end-use verification and tracing (Council of the EU, 2025; European Parliament, 2024).
c. Criteria 3–5 (internal/regional security, allies' security) underpinned permissive policies. Germany's emphasis on Israel's security and alliance commitments mapped onto Criterion 5, while Czechia/Hungary anchored permissive stances in security and geopolitical solidarity. The result was genuine balancing across criteria, but with asymmetric evidentiary burdens. States favouring restriction

invoked documented IHL risks, states favouring permission emphasised strategic and alliance factors, or questioned the predictive certainty of IHL risk assessments (European Parliament, 2024).

Another interesting observation is that as the Gaza crisis evolved through time and national pressure (whether judiciary, political or civil society driven) accelerated, m/s presented a rhetorical convergence alongside policy divergence. In Council and Parliament debates, most governments refer to IHL—proportionality, humanitarian access, accountability. Yet, as demonstrated above licensing outcomes remain uneven because different national interpretations of evidence and thus criteria are used.

4. ISSUES RAISED DURING THE 3RD COMMON POSITION'S REVIEW

In the context of the third review of the EU Common Position on conventional arms export controls, enhancing transparency and the quality of data reporting emerged as a central demand from both academia and civil society. Researchers and non-governmental organisations have pointed out that the current EU system of annual, aggregated reporting does not allow for meaningful monitoring or comparison of Member States' practices (Cops, 2019; Saferworld, 2023). In this context, a move from summary reporting to a system of license-level transparency, with detailed data by category of equipment, end-user and country of destination, was proposed.

The European Parliament has repeatedly argued that public access to detailed delivery data by end-user would enhance democratic scrutiny and make it easier to identify deviations by national authorities from the criteria of the Common Position (European Parliament, 2024). The lack of such data limits the ability of the Parliament, but also of civil society, to assess whether licensing decisions are consistent with the Union's commitments.

At the same time, civil society organisations have proposed linking eligibility for EU funding or participation in defence procurement programmes to Member States' performance in the field of arms exports. This approach would act as an incentive mechanism, encouraging greater transparency, consistent application of the criteria and compliance with the EU framework (Saferworld, 2023).

At the theoretical and practical level, significant emphasis has also been placed on the need to strengthen enforcement mechanisms. Scholars have pointed out that the Common Position suffers less at the level of rules and more at the level of implementation (Bromley, 2012; SIPRI, 2024). In this context, it has been suggested that clearer guidelines for post-shipment verification, the expansion of on-site end-use controls and a more systematic exchange of best practices between national licensing authorities should be developed (SIPRI, 2024). Post-shipment verification, modelled on the American Blue Lantern programme, has been recognised as an effective tool for reducing the risk of diversion and for giving substance to Criterion 7 of the Common Position, which concerns the risk of diversion of arms to unauthorised users (Bonaiuti, 2022). Despite its importance, this practice remains limited and unevenly implemented across Member States.

Another key issue that has emerged concerns the divergences in national risk assessments in relation to human rights and international humanitarian law. Scholars have highlighted that different interpretations of the same factual data by Member States undermine the objective of convergence pursued by the Common Position (Wisotzki, 2022; Maletta, 2021). In this context, the European Parliament has proposed strengthening COARM's mandate, requiring Member States to justify in writing deviations from the common criteria and to communicate more systematically decisions to refuse authorisations (European Parliament, 2024).

Some legal scholars have gone further, arguing that enforcement could be strengthened if arms exports were reclassified, at least in part, as a field of trade policy. Such a development would bring arms exports under the jurisdiction of the European Commission and the Court of Justice of the European Union, enhancing legal accountability (Bonaiuti, 2022; CER, 2023). However, this proposal has met with strong resistance from Member States, who invoke reasons of national sovereignty and Article 346 TFEU, making any treaty change politically extremely difficult (CER, 2023).

At the same time, the alignment of the Common Position with the Arms Trade Treaty (ATT) has been another persistent demand for reform. All EU Member States are parties to the Treaty, whose Article 6 prohibits arms transfers when there is a predominant risk of serious violations of international humanitarian law (UN Office for Disarmament Affairs, 2013). Although Criterion 2 of the Common Position reflects the same obligation, it remains open to interpretation. Comparative analyses show that clearer legal alignment could contribute to standardizing the evidentiary thresholds used in export denial decisions (Maletta, 2021). Notably, the Dutch Court of Appeal treated the ATT Treaty and the Common Position as equivalent obligations when assessing arms exports to conflict zones (Wisotzki, 2022), which strengthens the case for legal clarification.

Equally important was the involvement of non-state actors in the screening process. NGOs such as Saferworld, Transparency International and the European Network Against Arms Trade have long argued that meaningful civil society participation can enhance accountability and public trust in the arms export control system (Saferworld, 2023). Although the European External Action Service has experimented with NGO forums within COARM and stakeholder consultations, these practices have remained partially institutionalised (European Parliament, 2024). It has therefore been suggested that a formal civil society advisory mechanism or oversight group be established to permanently institutionalise consultation and public reporting (Cops, 2019; Saferworld, 2023).

The third review process, launched in 2023 under the Austrian Presidency of the Council, was characterised by intensive negotiations within COARM and other relevant Council working groups. The process included the establishment of three thematic 'focus groups' on: (a) the review of criteria and policy, (b) transparency and data reporting, and (c) enforcement mechanisms (Saferworld, 2023; Forum on the Arms Trade, 2024). Although the initial aim was to complete the process in early 2024, the consultations were extended until late 2024 and early 2025. Finally, on 14 April 2025, the Council adopted both a Decision amending the Common Position and Conclusions on arms export control, marking the completion of the third review (Council of the European Union, 2025a).

5. OUTCOME OF THE 3RD REVIEW

The amending Decision (CFSP) 2025/779 introduced the most significant textual updates since 2019, marking a step-change in normative specificity and procedural obligations (Council of the EU, 2025a), addressing a number of the above mentioned concerns and suggestions.

Criterion One expands the list of binding obligations and commitments. The insertion of the Global Framework for Through-life Conventional Ammunition Management (GFTAM) and Criterion Two elaborations on gender-based violence and protected groups raise the salience of human-security concerns. For administrations and courts, these textual anchors make it more difficult to characterise IHL-risk objections as merely political. By explicitly adding GFTAM to Criterion One, the amendments codify the EU's ammunition-safety agenda and align conventional-ammunition governance with export licensing (Council of the EU, 2025a; UNODA, 2025). Criterion Two retains the "clear risk" standard but specifies that denials are required where transfers may be used to commit or facilitate serious IHL violations against protected groups, naming gender-based violence and serious acts against women and children as illustrative triggers. This change reflects recent court decisions (e.g., Dutch F-35 case) and aligns EU law more closely with contemporary IHL/IHRL risk assessments (Council of the EU, 2025a).

A number of modifications were agreed regarding the evaluation of end-uses. Article 5 now provides the clearest legal basis to post-shipment verification to date, requiring licences to be granted only on the basis of reliable prior knowledge of end-use, typically through a thoroughly checked end-user certificate, and encourages monitoring tools such as on-site verification. By pairing this with Council

Conclusions, which promote pilot verification and best practices, the instrument drives m/s toward post-shipment controls, albeit without mandating a uniform SOP. This reflects persistent diversion concerns (especially in SALW) and advocacy from research institutions and NGOs (Council of the EU, 2025a; Council of the EU, 2025b; Forum on the Arms Trade, 2024).

Efforts were also made to link the Common Decision the EU Dual-Use Regulation with \ view to tight controls at the defence- security interface. Article 6 now extends the Common Position's criteria to certain dual-use exports under Regulation 2021/821 where there are serious grounds to believe the end-user is military or internal security forces (Council of the EU, 2025a). In the same direction, article 7 strengthens cooperation on risk assessment and end-use monitoring. Notably, Article 7(2) introduces "facilitating mechanisms" for joint defence projects, addressing chronic bottlenecks where one partner's denial paralyses co-produced systems. This legitimises ex ante consultation frameworks and is expected to reduce deliverability risks without undermining Criterion Two denials (Council of the EU, 2025a; Council of the EU, 2025b).

Finally, article 15 provides for a five-year implementation period, foreseeing the next review for April 2030, (Council of the EU, 2025a). Overall, the amendments raise normative specificity in Criteria 1–2, tighten procedural baselines on end-use knowledge and monitoring, and formalise cooperation for joint projects, without creating centralised EU enforcement.

6. WHAT CHANGED IN POLICY: THE APRIL 2025 COUNCIL CONCLUSIONS

The Council Conclusions of April 2025 complement the recent amendments to the regulatory framework by providing clearer political guidance and assigning specific tasks to the Working Party on Conventional Arms Exports (COARM). In doing so, the Council seeks to translate legislative changes and political commitments into more tangible and operational practices (Council of the EU, 2025b).

First, the Conclusions respond to long-standing criticisms from both the European Parliament and the academic literature that European arms export data reporting was characterised by a high level of aggregation and significant time delays (European Parliament, 2020). In this context, Member States commit to adhere to stricter timelines, to follow more detailed guidelines and to report, where possible, the actual values of exports rather than simply authorised amounts. This reporting, even with the clause "where available", signals a gradual shift towards greater transparency and enhanced accountability at Union level (Council of the EU, 2025b).

Secondly, the Conclusions explicitly strengthen the dimension of prevention of diversion, which has long been one of the weakest aspects of the European arms export control system. The Council calls on Member States to strengthen tracing measures, promote the marking and identification of ammunition and continue to support the iTrace Global Reporting Mechanism. At the same time, pilot projects for end-user monitoring are encouraged, which have so far been implemented piecemeal and mainly at bilateral level (Council of the EU, 2025b; Forum on the Arms Trade, 2024). This emphasis reflects the growing concern about the re-emergence of European military equipment in conflict zones or to unauthorised users.

Third, it is particularly important to explicitly recognise the industrial dimension of arms exports. The Conclusions underline that cooperation between Member States in the field of jointly developed defence capabilities requires more coordinated and predictable licensing procedures. In this context, COARM is called upon to facilitate exports of jointly developed products, in line with the European Defence Industrial Strategy. This approach signals a clearer coupling between EU export control policy and industrial policy, which raises questions about the balance between economic, strategic and humanitarian criteria (Council of the EU, 2025b).

Finally, the Conclusions embrace the new revised 2025 Firearms Framework and place particular emphasis on protecting vulnerable and protected groups from armed violence. They also call for stricter stockpile management standards, enhanced control of intangible technology transfers, a more systematic approach to industry and a strengthening of end-user certificates for small arms and light weapons (SALW) (Council of the EU, 2025b). These points suggest an attempt to fill gaps that have been repeatedly highlighted by international organisations and NGOs.

In parallel with the Conclusions, the Council adopted an updated User's Guide (document ST-6881/25), which, although not legally binding, has established itself as an authentic reference tool for national licensing authorities. The Guide interprets the criteria of the Common Position, clarifies the sources of evidence and details the procedures for notifications, consultations and due diligence for end-use. The hosting of the 2025 edition by the European External Action Service (EEAS) and the provision for regular updates indicate a clear intention to further institutionalise and deepen convergence of practices between Member States (Council of the EU, 2025c).

7. A CRITICAL EVALUATION OF THE CURRENT STATE OF PLAY

While modest on paper, the combined amendments and Conclusions, particularly commitments to report actual exports and adopt monitoring tools, could significantly improve comparability, timeliness, and peer review, mitigating undercutting opacity.

The Council's 2025 conclusions reaffirm the EU's core principles, since they express commitment to "responsible and transparent trade in arms" and to "preventing diversion of arms to unauthorized users," as well as to "building convergence of national arms export policies" under the CFSP (Council of the European Union, 2025a). The conclusions also set a forward-looking agenda, listing topics for future work, including tracing of equipment, end-user verification and monitoring, exports of jointly-developed equipment, controls on intangible transfers, and joint capacity-building for exports (Council of the European Union, 2025a). Notably, the Council specifically mentions "facilitating exports of equipment jointly developed in the EU," addressing long-standing obstacles where export licenses by one partner can hold up deliveries by others (Council of the European Union, 2025a). The updated User's Guide for licensing officers was also endorsed as part of this review (Council of the European Union, 2025a). The Council set the next review timeline, concluding by 2030, at the end of the document.

It should be noted that the final text makes only modest substantive changes: the focus is on implementation tools rather than new criteria. For example, on-site post-shipment controls were raised as a key issue during negotiations. SIPRI and NGO experts urged the review to include guidance on how Member States can conduct such checks to enforce Criterion 7 on diversion risk (Bromley, 2012; SIPRI, 2024). The adopted conclusions do call for work on tracing and end-use monitoring (Council of the European Union, 2025a), which may encompass post-shipment visits. In practice, the review seems to have broadened the toolkit (guidance, focus groups, user's guide, EU projects) rather than tightening rules.

The broader political context influenced these outcomes. EU arms deliveries to Ukraine were explicitly cited by Council officials as one trigger for the review (Council of the European Union, 2025a). Several Member States (especially in Western Europe) have pushed for greater convergence on IHL-related licenses after Gaza, while others (in the East and South) have urged the EU to support European defence industries by easing licensing for co-development projects. According to Saferworld analysts, the 2024 review was seen by many capitals as an "opportunity for significant improvements" in transparency and enforcement, but the result was largely a compromise "package" of soft measures (Saferworld, 2024).

The divergent national reactions and mixed EU-level reforms highlight the core tension on the question of who decides where EU-origin arms go. On one hand, Member States insist on their sovereign right to license weapons exports in line with national interests and policies. National parliaments typically demand oversight and accountability at national level. On the other hand, arms exports by any Member State can implicate all EU countries. EU law and policy rest on the idea of shared responsibility under the Common Foreign and Security Policy: all Member States "have agreed to high common standards" for arms exports (Centre for

European Reform [CER], 2023). A key purpose of EU-level controls is to prevent undercutting—one country fulfilling an order that another refused, negating the effect of the refusal (European Parliament, 2024).

National legal systems reinforce national control. The German court explicitly affirmed that "arms export licensing is a political act" mainly for the executive, not the judiciary (Armstrade Litigation Monitor, 2024). This echoes CER research warning that, despite the EU Common Position, "arms exports ultimately remain a matter of national competence" (CER, 2023). Even so, the Common Position aims to "drive convergence," largely through information-sharing and peer pressure (European Parliament, 2024; Wisotzki, 2022). However, until today transparency reports aggregate data only on broad categories, and much detail remains confidential (Cops, 2019). Civil society and the European Parliament have long argued that EU reporting is insufficient; the Parliament has demanded more detail over 8,000 times, stating that the current transparency "is insufficient to provide adequate scrutiny" (European Parliament, 2024).

The 2025 Council conclusions emphasize "transparency" and mutual commitment, yet reaffirm that licensing remains national, "encouraging" the Commission to support capacity-building and continue data-sharing (Council of the European Union, 2025a). retaining that the Common Position is binding in CFSP but not directly enforceable in EU law (CER, 2023). Thus, if a Member State were found to misapply the criteria, there is no EU court remedy, only political pressure (Bonaiuti, 2022).

The review process demonstrates that genuine harmonization depends less on legal compulsion and more on sustained political will, transparency, and peer accountability (Bonaiuti, 2022; Council of the European Union, 2025a). Ultimately, the EU's challenge is to reconcile its dual identity as both a normative power committed to human-rights standards and a strategic actor promoting a competitive defence industry (Maletta, 2021). Whether future reviews—particularly the one scheduled for 2030—can deliver stronger convergence and enforcement will depend on whether the Union is prepared to move from voluntary coordination toward genuine collective responsibility (CER, 2023; European Parliament, 2024).

8. CONCLUDING REMARKS: THIRD REVIEW OF THE COMMON POSITION AND THE GAZA CRISIS

Reflecting on the above, we could conclude that the Gaza crisis did have an impact on the Common Position's review. The elaboration of Criterion Two on protected groups and gender-based violence mirrors the evidentiary pattern of civilian harm in urban warfare and the way courts and NGOs documented risk, such as in the Dutch appellate reasoning on F-35 parts. Provisions on end-use verification and actual-exports reporting respond to concerns about supply-chain and transit pathways highlighted in Belgian and Netherlands litigation, as well as the difficulty of tracking deliveries versus approvals. Meanwhile, joint-project facilitation acknowledges intra-EU frictions that surfaced when partners' IHL assessments diverged between 2023 and 2025. Normatively, the review tightens the framework where consensus existed such as IHL, protection of groups, ammunition governance, and dual-use with military end-users. It also operationalises convergence through requirements for end-use knowledge and monitoring, facilitation of joint projects, and incremental moves toward actual-exports reporting. Institutionally, the reforms respect the intergovernmental character of CFSP and invest in COARM-centric governance tools like user guidance, peer exchange, outreach, and transparency.

Overall, the EU arms-export regime reaffirms intergovernmental governance under a binding but decentralised legal framework. The Common Position translates a shared set of substantive criteria (1–8) into nationally executed licensing decisions. Institutionally, this generates a dual structure of accountability. On one hand, vertically to EU norms, but without centralised adjudication given the CJEU's limited CFSP jurisdiction, and on the other hand, horizontally through peer-review processes such as COARM denial notifications, annual reports, and the *User's Guide*. The Gaza war highlighted both the strengths of this model, especially towards the IHL and its weaknesses, namely policy divergence where domestic legal pathways, evidentiary cultures, and political incentives differ.

The April 2025 package raised the normative floor by specifying IHL obligations (Criterion 2 elaborations on protected groups and gender-based violence), reinforcing ammunition governance, and linking more explicitly to the Dual-Use Regulation (Council of the EU, 2025a). It also opened new pathways for convergence through end-use monitoring, post-shipment verification, and mechanisms for facilitating joint projects (Council of the EU, 2025b). The credibility of the next review cycle, in 2030, will hinge on concrete implementation, demonstrable post-shipment checks, more comparable delivery-level reporting, and reduced undercutting in high-risk destinations.

The Gaza conflict made the tension between national sovereignty and EU collective norms more visible. It provoked domestic friction, litigation, and public debate on the values underpinning arms-export controls. National courts in the Netherlands and Belgium demonstrated how judicialisation can translate Criteria 2 and 7 into enforceable duties, shaping both administrative practice and EU-level rhetoric (Antoniou et al, 2025). Germany, by contrast, illustrates the limits of judicialisation where incorporation is soft and courts defer to executive discretion, producing rhetorical convergence on IHL but only incremental policy adjustments (ECCHR, 2025).

The third review (2023–2025) did not centralise licensing or create new enforcement mechanisms. Instead, it promoted convergence through practice, guidance, and peer processes rather than centralised enforcement. Approaching 2030, three priorities emerge: (1) institutionalising post-shipment verification, with reporting to COARM and corrective measures when diversion is detected, (2) moving from opaque licence-value data to more transparent delivery-value reporting, even in partial or aggregated form and (3) stabilising co-production exports by operationalising Article 7(2) through pre-agreed export principles and justification templates (Forum on the Arms Trade, 2024; Saferworld, 2023).

The EU's credibility in external action rests not only on what it proclaims but also on what it licenses. The Common Position has evolved from a soft code to a binding framework. At this stage, further gains will come not from constitutional redesign but from administrative craft, evidence-driven practice, and enhanced transparency. If Member States use the 2025 reforms to standardise documentation, verify end-use, and report deliveries, the EU can narrow the gap between collective norms and national discretion and better align arms-export governance with the international humanitarian law that the EU identifies as a cornerstone of its external identity.

REFERENCES

Antoniou, A., Béraud-Sudreau, L., & Dorsey, J. (2025). European arms exports and international humanitarian law: Judicial and political challenges. *Journal of European Security Studies*, *14*(2), 115–137.

Antoniou, T. (2011). The Stockholm Programme and the Treaty of Lisbon: A space of Freedom, Sewcurity and Justice or just Security? Challenges for human rights respect in the years to come, in International cooperation in global and regional level (ed. St. Perrakis), I. Sideris, Athens, December.

Antoniou, T. (2012). *The responsibility to protect and EU's international role after the treaty of Lisbon: from theory to practice, December*. I. Sideris.

Antoniou, T. (2013). Overseeing the EU's external borders: Legislative / political developments and the Greek Presidency, Annual Conference of the Hellenic Society of International Law and International Relations, "Greece and Europe in the face of the major crises of the pre- Greek Presidency of the EU", Livani, Athens.

Antoniou, T. (2014). The new European Maritime Border Surveillance Regulation: A Critical Approach, Rhodes-Kastelorizo Symposium "Implementation of International Law and Politics 20 Years after the Enactment of the Maritime Law Convention: Detecting the Aegean Sea and the Mediterranean Sea 2014", Livani, Athens.

Antoniou, T. (2016). Demystifying the concept of solidarity in the EU Area of Freedom, Security and Justice in the aftermath of the refugee crisis, Annual Conference of the Hellenic Society of International Law and International Relations, "Global Challenges – Common Responsibilities, An Evaluation of the UN 70 years" December 19, 2015, Panteion University, Livani, Athens.

Antoniou, T. (2019). Solidarity in the EU: a moral imperative or a legal reality? Concept, aspects and implementation during the Refugee Crisis, Conference on Solidarity Developments in the field of refugee protection in the European Union and challenges in the EU and in Greece, Nomiki Bibliothiki, Athens.

Armstrade Litigation Monitor. (2024). *German court rulings on arms export licensing*. https://armstradelitigationmonitor.org

Balfour, R., & Raube, K. (2015). European external action and the question of consistency. *Journal of European Integration*, *37*(3), 349–367.

Bauer, S., & Cops, D. (2014). Enforcing the EU's arms export regime: Brokering and diversion. *European Foreign Affairs Review*, *19*(4), 525–552.

Besch, S. (2023). *Up in arms: Europe's contentious arms export regime*. Centre for European Reform.

Bonaiuti, C. (2022). Arms transfers and human rights: Assessing the impact and enforcement of the EU Common Position in a multilevel analysis. *European Foreign Affairs Review, 27*(4), 463–484. DOI: 10.54648/EERR2022035

Bromley, M. (2012). *The review of the EU Common Position on arms exports: Prospects for strengthened controls* (EU Non-Proliferation Paper No. 7). SIPRI.

Bromley, M. (2020). *The European Union Common Position on arms exports: Prospects for reform*. SIPRI.

Casey-Maslen, S., Clapham, A., Giacca, G., & Parker, S. (2016). *The Arms Trade Treaty: A Commentary*. Oxford University Press.

Centre for European Reform. (2023). *EU arms export controls: Balancing sovereignty and responsibility*. https://cer.eu

Cops, D. (2019). *Strengthening EU transparency on arms exports: Ways forward.* Vlaams Vredesinstituut.

Council of the European Union. (2008). *Council Common Position 2008/944/CFSP defining common rules governing control of exports of military technology and equipment*. Official Journal of the European Union.

Council of the European Union. (2024). *Council conclusions on the review of the Common Position on arms exports (2008/944/CFSP).*

Council of the European Union. (2025a). *Council Decision (CFSP) 2025/779 of 14 April 2025 amending Common Position 2008/944/CFSP.*

Council of the European Union. (2025b). *Council Conclusions on arms export control (7534/25).*

Council of the European Union. (2025c). *User's Guide to the Common Position on arms exports.*

Court of Appeal of The Hague. (2024, February 12). ECLI *[Oxfam Novib et al. v. The State of the Netherlands]. NL:GHDHA, 2024,* 191.

ECCHR. (2025). *Legal actions on German arms exports to Israel*. ECCHR.

Eeckhout, P. (2021). *EU external relations law* (3rd ed.). Oxford University Press.

European Parliament. (2020). *Recommendations for a transparent and detailed reporting system on arms exports within the EU and to third countries.*

European Parliament. (2024). *Implementation of the Common Position on arms exports.*

European Parliament. (2024). *Report on arms export control in the European Union.*

Forum on the Arms Trade. (2024). *Post-shipment verification and end-use monitoring in arms transfer control.*

Forum on the Arms Trade. (2024, January 17). *The 2024 review of the EU Common Position on arms exports: An opportunity for stronger cooperation on post-shipment controls?* Herrmann, L., & Mirbach, A. (2024, July 23). Berlin Administrative Court rejects pre-emptive interim relief against German weapons exports to Israel. *German Practice in International Law.*

Verwaltungsgericht Frankfurt am Main. (2024, December 16). *Rüstungsgüter für Israel.*

International Court of Justice. (2024a, April). [*Nicaragua v. Germany.*]. *Order,* •••, 30.

International Court of Justice. (2024b). [*Nicaragua v. Germany] [Docket]. CASE (Philadelphia, Pa.),* •••, 193.

Kassoti, E. (2017). The Council v Front Polisario case: The Court of Justice and international law. *European Papers, 2*(1), 339–356.

Larik, J. (2017). Rosneft: Establishing jurisdiction in the field of CFSP. *Common Market Law Review, 54*, 925–951.

LTO. (2024a, June 11). *VG Berlin: Anträge gegen Waffenexporte nach Israel unzulässig.*

LTO. (2024b, December 19). *OVG Berlin-Brandenburg: Kein Auskunftsanspruch über Waffenlieferungen an Israel.*

Maletta, G. (2021). Seeking a responsible arms trade to reduce human rights violations: The case of the EU. *European Review of International Studies, 8*(1), 77–95.

RTBF. (2025, July 17). *La justice ordonne à la Flandre de stopper tout transit d'équipement militaire vers Israël.*

Saferworld. (2020). *EU arms export controls: Achievements, challenges and opportunities.*

Saferworld. (2023). *The EU Common Position review: Fixing or fiddling?* SIPRI. (2024). *Trends in international arms transfers 2023.* Stockholm International Peace Research Institute.

United Nations Office for Disarmament Affairs. (2013). *The Arms Trade Treaty*. ATT.

United Nations Office for Disarmament Affairs. (2025, May 28). *EU statement to the UN First Committee*.

United Nations Office for the Coordination of Humanitarian Affairs. (2023). *Reporting on civilian casualties and damage in the Gaza Strip*.

United Nations Office for the Coordination of Humanitarian Affairs. (2024). *Gaza crisis: Situation reports*.

Verellen, J. (2021). In the name of the rule of law? *H v Council*. *European Papers*, *6*(2), 1013–1040.

Wisotzki, S. (2022). No common position! European arms export control in crisis. *Global Constitutionalism*, *11*(3), 453–472.

Chapter 13
Normative Gatekeepers: The Role of National Courts in Shaping EU Responses to the Gaza Crisis

Theofania Antoniou
http://orcid.org/0009-0001-8469-9714
Hellenic Open University, Greece

Maria-Daniella Marouda
Panteion University, Greece

ABSTRACT

EU's capacity to enforce International Humanitarian Law is constrained by national divergences. Increased political polarization, the prioritization of the humanitarian dimension, and the reinforcement of legal discourse on the unlawful nature of settlements have shaped the Union's external action. National judicial bodies have increasingly acted as normative gatekeepers by scrutinizing arms export authorizations for compliance with IHL. Recent landmark judgments in the Netherlands and Germany have annulled or suspended export licenses for military equipment destined for Israel, citing substantial risks of contributing to grave breaches of international law in Gaza.. By asserting the primacy of legal obligations over political choices, national courts thus function as a constraining and legitimizing force, shaping or even modifying the political discourse of a number of EU member states influencing indirectly EU's external affairs policies. This paper analyses the pivotal role of national courts in influencing the European Union's legal and policy responses to the Gaza crisis.

DOI: 10.4018/979-8-3373-3526-1.ch013

1. INTRODUCTION

Over the last decade, there is a growing debate among scholars regarding the distinction of powers in democracies, namely the length of judicial interference, especially in the area of external relations. When national courts engage in the review of foreign relations decisions, they often adopt what has been described as an "administrative" approach, focusing on process, reasoning, and compliance with legal constraints in a manner analogous to administrative law review (Golia, 2021). Yet this function is bounded by doctrines of deference and the political question doctrine, which limit the judiciary's ability to second-guess executive judgments in matters of diplomacy or national security (Sitaraman, 2019; Chachko, 2020). Lack of access to information is another factor which limits judiciary control, as established by a recent report (Asser Institute, 2025). Scholars have noted a broader trend toward the "normalization" of foreign relations law, whereby external affairs are increasingly treated as ordinary legal questions rather than as exceptional domains immune from judicial scrutiny (Harvard Law Review Forum, 2015). At the same time, some argue that courts must not overstep institutional limits, particularly given their informational disadvantages and the potential geopolitical consequences of intrusive review (Williams, 2020). The integration of global administrative law principles—such as accountability, transparency, and proportionality—into judicial review of foreign relations thus promises to enhance legality and legitimacy, while simultaneously raises questions about judicial overreach and the proper separation of powers in a globalized legal order (Golia, 2021). This paper aims to contribute to this discussion by reflecting on the role of the national judge in influencing the EU's external policy, especially regarding the ongoing Gaza crisis (2023-2025).

The Gaza crisis has posed a fundamental test to the European Union's foreign policy coherence, revealing internal fractures and normative contradictions. All during the ongoing negotiations of the EU's common position on arms exports. While the EU officially upholds the two-state solution based on the 1967 borders and consistently condemns acts of terrorism (Council Conclusions on the Middle East Peace Process, 18 January 2021), the intensification of hostilities has complicated its ability to maintain a unified external stance. Member States have expressed divergent interpretations of IHL obligations, particularly regarding the legality of Israeli military actions, settlement expansion, and the collective punishment of civilian populations (European Parliament Resolution 2023/2739(RSP), 6 July 2023).

The EU's position has evolved from rhetorical support for peace negotiations to an increased use of concerns regarding human rights and violations of IHL. The European External Action Service (EEAS), along with the European Parliament, has increasingly invoked international legal standards to frame its condemnations of indiscriminate violence, civilian casualties, and the humanitarian blockade of

Gaza (EEAS Statement, 31 October 2023). However, this shift has been tempered by political realpolitik, arms trade interests, and the divergent historical alliances of individual Member States.

Recent EU declarations have explicitly referenced the illegality of Israeli settlements under international law, aligning with the 2004 Advisory Opinion of the International Court of Justice and United Nations Security Council Resolution 2334 (2016). Despite these pronouncements, enforcement remains weak. The lack of an autonomous EU defense and sanctions mechanism leads to inconsistency and perceptions of double standards, since it all comes down to the various national discretions (Anghel S. et al, 2020).

In this setting, the 2023–2024 armed conflict between Israel and Hamas in the Gaza Strip triggered intense diplomatic debate within European Union (EU) member states. The Netherlands, Belgium and Germany, geographically close but traditionally taking somewhat different approaches to the Middle East, each underwent notable rhetorical and policy shifts throughout the conflict. This paper analyses how their positions evolved and how these shifts affected their roles within EU institutions, especially before and after domestic judicial interventions concerning arms exports.

2. NORMATIVE TRENDS IN THE CONTEXT OF EU EXTERNAL POLICIES

Over the last 15 years the EU has tied foreign policy ever more tightly to law-anchored values (fundamental rights, self-determination, IHL). That shift isn't just rhetorical, it's embedded in hard law and reviewed by courts.

The 2019 update of the EU's arms-export rules (Common Position 2008/944/CFSP, as amended by Decision 2019/1560) sharpened criteria and reporting, the 2020 EU Global Human Rights Sanctions Regime created Magnitsky-style listings and the 2021 Dual-Use recast added a human-rights "catch-all" for cyber-surveillance exports. All this in the context of the international obligation for respect of international humanitarian law which prohoibits states from assting of aiding violations of the Geneva Conventions (William Thomas Worster, 2025).

Notably, the European Parliament has incorporated references to national judicial decisions in several resolutions, advocating for stricter controls in arms exports. The EP Resolution 2023/2739(RSP) of 6 July 2023 welcomed judicial scrutiny as a mechanism for ensuring compliance with the EU's Common Position 2008/944/CFSP and called for harmonized enforcement standards across Member States. It explicitly encouraged the Commission and the EEAS (EEAS) to support national authorities in applying legal obligations under IHL more rigorously.

The EEAS, in its communications on the Gaza crisis (Statement of 31 October 2023), has increasingly invoked the findings of international bodies such as the International Criminal Court (ICC) and the International Court of Justice (ICJ). The Statement referred to the ICJ's provisional measures in South Africa v. Israel (2024), framing the EU's humanitarian calls within the context of international law. This rhetorical shift suggests a greater integration of judicial discourse into the Union's diplomatic positions.

The CJEU, although formally restricted in CFSP matters under Article 275 TFEU, has echoed principles of judicial review in adjacent domains. In the H v. Council and Commission (C-455/14 P, 2017), the Court reaffirmed that fundamental rights and procedural guarantees apply to restrictive measures within the EU's external action, thereby indirectly validating judicial oversight over foreign policy instruments. This jurisprudence has bolstered the normative authority of national courts, creating indirect channels through which EU-level practices are increasingly subject to legal accountability.

3. THE LEGAL FRAMEWORK: THE EU COMMON POSITION AND DOMESTIC INCORPORATION

The European Union's external policy framework, particularly under the Common Foreign and Security Policy (CFSP), is fundamentally constrained by institutional and legal limitations that hamper a coherent response to international crises such as the Gaza conflict. Probably the most obvious constraint is the principle of unanimity enshrined in Article 24(1) of the Treaty on European Union (TEU), which requires that all 27 Member States agree before common foreign policy decisions can be adopted. This procedural requirement often leads to the lowest common denominator outcomes or outright paralysis in the face of divergent national interests (Cremona, 2017).

Power asymmetries among Member States further complicate decision-making. Larger states with substantial arms industries and historical alliances in the Middle East, such as France and Germany, frequently prioritize economic and geopolitical interests over a uniform application of IHL. Smaller or more normatively inclined Member States, like Ireland or Luxembourg, often advocate for a rights-based approach grounded in international law, resulting in persistent divergences in the Council (Blockmans & Koutrakos, 2018).

Moreover, the CFSP lacks judicial enforceability comparable to other EU policy areas. The European Court of Justice (CJEU) exercises limited jurisdiction over CFSP matters under Article 275 TFEU, which explicitly excludes CFSP acts from standard judicial review mechanisms, except in narrow circumstances (Lazowski &

Wessel, 2020). This further diminishes accountability and allows political discretion to dominate over legal consistency.

As a result, the EU often struggles to uphold its normative agenda when political consensus is lacking. The fragmentation is further evidenced by Member States' unilateral approaches to arms exports, where divergent risk assessments and licensing criteria lead to legal incoherence. Such fragmentation underscores the need for enhanced judicial engagement and harmonisation mechanisms to ensure that legal commitments to IHL are not overridden by political expediency.

In this context, the EU's Common Position 2008/944/CFSP on arms exports establishes binding rules governing the assessment of military technology and equipment exports. This Common Position constitutes the central legal framework guiding arms exports from Member States, setting out eight legally binding criteria for the assessment of export license applications. These include respect for human rights and IHL in the country of final destination (Criterion Two), and the preservation of regional peace, security and stability (Criterion Three). Although the Common Position lacks direct enforceability at the EU level, it obliges national authorities to assess risks rigorously and to deny exports if there is a clear risk that the items might be used for serious violations of IHL and to take into account the recipient state's past and present behaviour (Criteria Two and Six) (Holtom & Bromley, 2010).

Despite its CFSP legal basis, the Common Position has been incorporated into domestic law to varying degrees. In the Netherlands, it is directly referenced in the Strategic Goods Decree, which states that export permits will not be granted "to the extent that this follows from international obligations." Dutch courts have treated the Common Position as binding through this clause (Gerechtshof Den Haag, 2024). In Belgium, the Common Position has been embedded in the regional arms-trade decrees of Wallonia and Flanders, which explicitly require authorities to apply its criteria when issuing or suspending export permits. German law, by contrast, reflects the Common Position primarily through the Politische Grundsätze (Political Principles on Arms Exports) and the Foreign Trade and Payments Act/Ordinance (AWG/AWV), while the War Weapons Control Act (KrWaffKontrG) provides a more stringent framework for "war weapons." Unlike the Netherlands and Belgium, Germany lacks an explicit statutory provision tying licensing to "international obligations" enforceable in court (see below relevant court decisions).

In recent years, national courts across the European Union have begun to play a more assertive role in scrutinising foreign policy decisions, particularly in the sensitive field of arms exports. Traditionally, export licensing was regarded as an area of high executive discretion, closely tied to foreign and security policy, and therefore "protected" from intensive judicial review (Balfour & Raik, 2015). However, the increasing incorporation of IHL and human rights standards into EU and national export regimes—such as the EU's Common Position 2008/944/CFSP on arms exports and the Arms Trade Treaty (ATT)—has opened legal avenues for claimants to challenge governmental discretion before domestic courts (Casey-Maslen, 2016).

Domestic courts have taken an increasingly active role in interpreting these criteria in the context of international law, particularly where arms transfers may contribute to violations of the Geneva Conventions. Courts in the Netherlands and Germany have held that a "serious risk" does not require evidence of past misuse, but may be established through a credible risk assessment based on reports by international bodies, including the UN, NGOs, and journalistic investigations (Court of Appeal, The Hague, 2024; VG Berlin, 2024). Moreover, the burden of proof has shifted from civil society actors to the state. It is no longer sufficient for governments to assume good faith by the end-user state. Rather, they must demonstrate due diligence and incorporate ongoing conflict assessments into licensing decisions (Droege & Casey-Maslen, 2012).

This jurisprudential shift signifies a deepening convergence between national administrative law and IHL, reinforcing the interpretive authority of domestic courts within the EU's external policies legal framework. It also highlights the judiciary's potential to institutionalize legal accountability in a field traditionally dominated by executive discretion.

This judicialisation has been most visible in high-risk conflict scenarios where exports to states engaged in active hostilities pose a "clear risk" of contributing to serious IHL violations. In such cases, civil society groups and NGOs have addressed national courts, arguing that government decisions to authorise exports are inconsistent with international and EU obligations. The rise of arms-export jurisprudence reflects a broader trend of "rights-based foreign policy," where domestic courts discuss and decide on cases of foreign policy conformity to constitutional rights, EU law, or international humanitarian standards. Scholars have traced this trend in other domains, such as migration control, counter-terrorism, and climate policy, where courts increasingly subject foreign policy decisions to legality and proportionality review (Ferreira, 2022; Milanovic, 2011). In the arms-export context, this has meant that values traditionally associated with EU external relations—human rights, rule of law, and consistency with international law—are now enforced through national jurisprudence, with direct implications for diplomacy and defence-industrial policy.

Far from being isolated incidents, these cases illustrate the growing judicialisation of foreign policy within Member States while indirectly turning national judges to enforcement agents of european and international norms at the operational level. By interpreting treaty-based obligations as justiciable, courts ensure that national governments cannot evade accountability for external action by invoking broad foreign policy prerogatives. In doing so, they contribute to the multi-level system of judicial guardianship in the EU, complementing the role of the CJEU and embedding rights-based scrutiny deeper into the Union's foreign policy architecture. Furthermore, they contribute in shaping the political discourse within the EU institutions, ultimately influencing the decision-making process.

4. LANDMARK JUDGMENTS: CASES FROM THE NETHERLANDS, BELGIUM AND GERMANY

In 2024, as mentioned above, courts in Germany, Belgium and the Netherlands issued very important rulings regarding arm exports, providing legal precedents in the realm of arms export controls and their alignment with IHL.

The Dutch Case

In February 2024, The Hague Court of Appeal delivered a landmark judgment ordering the Dutch State to halt the export of U.S.-owned F-35 fighter jet parts stored in Woensdrecht and destined for Israel, annulling the relative export licenses. The case was brought by Dutch NGOs—Oxfam Novib, PAX, and The Rights Forum—arguing that the continued shipment of F-35 parts created a clear risk of IHL violations in Gaza (Court of Appeal, The Hague, Case No. 200.327.006/01, 2024).

The District Court had previously dismissed the claim, emphasizing executive discretion in foreign policy. The Court of Appeal reversed, grounding its reasoning in the Strategic Goods Decree, which incorporates international obligations including the Arms Trade Treaty (ATT) and the aforementioned Common Position. More specifically, the Court found that the "clear risk" threshold under Criterion Two of the Common Position and Article 7 of the ATT applied. The judgment emphasized that the existence of a serious risk—rather than definitive proof of misuse—was sufficient to impose a legal duty on the state to suspend arms transfers, aligning with Criterion Two and Six of the EU Common Position 2008/944/CFSP. It relied heavily on credible open-source evidence—UN reports, NGO documentation, and media reports—showing a consistent pattern of high civilian casualties and attacks on civilian infrastructure by the Israeli Air Force. The Court also applied Common Article 1 of the Geneva Conventions, emphasising the duty of states not only to respect but also to "ensure respect" for IHL. Once the clear risk was established, the Court held that balancing against industrial, diplomatic, or security interests was impermissible, thus rendering it mandatory under Dutch law.

The Dutch ruling operationalises the Common Position as enforceable domestic law. It shows that national courts can treat Criterion Two as a justiciable factual standard, capable of being satisfied by NGO and UN evidence. The case also illustrates how incorporation clauses in national law ("international obligations") can transform CFSP instruments into binding standards. In November 2024, the Advocate General at the Supreme Court advised affirming the judgment, reinforcing the appellate court's interpretation (Advocate General Vlas, 2024). The final Supreme Court ruling is pending at the time of writing.

Belgian Case

Belgium's regionalised arms-control system has made Wallonia and Flanders the key actors in export licensing. Between 2018 and 2021, Belgian NGOs repeatedly challenged Walloon licenses for arms exports to Saudi Arabia, citing risks of misuse in the Yemen conflict. The Council of State, Belgium's highest administrative court, suspended and annulled multiple licenses, ruling that the Walloon authorities had failed to apply Criteria Two, Four, and Six of the Common Position properly (Bromley & Maletta, 2024). The Council insisted that licensing authorities must evaluate the recipient's past behavior (Criterion Six) and cannot ignore the "clear risk" test. It criticised inadequate reasoning and failure to engage with credible evidence of IHL violations (Maletta, 2021).

On 17 July 2025, the Brussels Court of First Instance issued an interim order against the Flemish Government, halting the transit of armoured vehicle components through Antwerp destined for Israel. The Court imposed a coercive fine of €50,000 per container in case of breach. It found that Flemish authorities had failed to enforce their obligations under the Wapenhandeldecreet (Arms Trade Decree), which incorporates the Common Position's criteria and mandates denial in high-risk cases (Rechtbank Brussel, 2025).

Although formally about transit rather than export, the judgment stressed that the same normative logic applied. The Common Position's risk-based obligations extend to any authorisation that facilitates the movement of arms through EU territory. Belgian courts have been consistent in treating the Common Position as binding domestic law, directly enforceable in judicial review. The Council of State's rulings reinforced that failure to reason adequately in light of Common Position criteria constitutes grounds for annulment. The Brussels Court expanded this logic to transit, demonstrating that arms-control obligations cannot be circumvented by labelling flows as "transit."

The German Case

German courts have been the latest to join other national courts in "interfering" with sensitive foreign policy areas. Until 2024, German courts have largely avoided merits-based application of the Common Position's criteria. Instead, they emphasized separation of powers and the executive's foreign-policy prerogative. The absence of a clear statutory incorporation of "international obligations" has left the Common Position less judicially actionable. German litigation has therefore focused on justiciability and procedure rather than substantive risk assessment. That was the case in the recent judgments of the Berlin Administrative Court (June 2024) and the Frankfurt Administrative Court (December 2024), followed the position of the Federal Constitutional Court as had been proclaimed in 2014. In 2014, the Federal Constitutional Court held that the Bundestag had a right to information on arms exports, enhancing parliamentary accountability but without creating enforceable individual rights (BVerfG, 2014). This transparency ruling strengthened democratic oversight but fell short of turning the Common Position into a judicially enforceable standard (Klafki 2025).

In June 2024, the Berlin Administrative Court rejected preventive interim measures sought by Palestinian applicants and NGOs to block possible future arms exports to Israel. The Court emphasised that preventive interim relief (*vorbeugender Rechtsschutz*) is exceptional, and absent a concrete administrative act, it would not presume illegality by the government (Verwaltungsgericht Berlin, 2024). Similarly, the Frankfurt Administrative Court denied interim relief against exports classified as "other military equipment," ruling that broad foreign-policy discretion limited the court's ability to intervene pre-emptively. It distinguished between war weapons (subject to the KrWaffKontrG) and other equipment, where judicial review is even narrower (Verwaltungsgericht Frankfurt, 2024).

Nevertheless, the Gaza crisis coincided with increasing litigation over arms exports in several other EU states, influencing Germany. In 2024, the Higher Administrative Court of North Rhine-Westphalia (OVG Münster) signalled that arms-export approvals to Israel required stricter scrutiny under both the EU Common Position 2008/944/CFSP and the Arms Trade Treaty (OVG NRW, 2024). While German administrative courts in Berlin and Frankfurt dismissed preventive injunctions against pending export decisions (VG Berlin, 2024; VG Frankfurt, 2024), the Münster decision underscored that executive discretion is not unlimited. Furthermore, the Berlin Administrative Court, in a highly publicized interim measure, suspended a permit for the export of surveillance technology on the basis that the federal government had failed to sufficiently assess whether its use could facilitate disproportionate targeting of civilian infrastructure (VG Berlin, Case No. 1 L 271/24, 2024). The court reinforced the requirement of proactive due diligence and imposed an obligation of transparency on licensing authorities (ECCHR, 2024).

Geopolitically, these judgments have placed pressure on national governments to realign their foreign policies with their legal commitments under EU and international law. They have also fueled diplomatic tensions, with affected arms manufacturers lobbying for indemnification and foreign ministries facing backlash from both pro-Israel and pro-Palestinian constituencies. At the EU level, the rulings have catalyzed discourse on the harmonization of export criteria and have reignited debates within the European Parliament on establishing a centralized oversight mechanism (Bromley & Maletta, 2024).

5. THE INFLUENCE OF NATIONAL COURTS IN THE NORMATIVE DIRECTION OF EU'S EXTERNAL ACTION

Germany's Rhetorical Shift on the Gaza Crisis (2023–2024), Following the National Court's Decisions: From Unconditional Solidarity to Rights-Based Language

Germany has historically been one of Israel's most steadfast supporters within the European Union (EU). Rooted in the legacy of the Holocaust, the principle that Israel's security is part of Germany's *raison d'état* has been a consistent refrain in Berlin's foreign policy (Brockmeier, 2022). This long-standing orientation has shaped Germany's interventions in the EU's Foreign Affairs Council, in the European Council, and within the European Parliament (Kaim, 2021). Until recently, Germany consistently adopted a pro-Israel stance in EU foreign policy. This position was visible in the blocking or watering-down of EU statements critical of Israeli military operations, particularly during the 2014 Gaza war (Malmvig, 2015). German representatives in the Foreign Affairs Council routinely stressed Israel's right to self-defence while resisting language that framed Israel's actions in terms of disproportionate force or humanitarian violations (European Council, 2014).

Within the European Parliament, German Members of the European Parliament (MEPs) from the major parties—the CDU/CSU (EPP), SPD (S&D), and FDP (Renew)—traditionally supported pro-Israel amendments and resisted calls for arms embargoes or ceasefire demands (VoteWatch Europe, 2018). Although the Greens occasionally diverged, the overarching pattern was one of caution toward EU initiatives that might undermine the bilateral "special relationship."

More precisely, immediately after the October 7 Hamas attacks, Chancellor Olaf Scholz and Foreign Minister Annalena Baerbock declared that "*Israel's security is Germany's Staatsräson,*" strongly supporting Israel's right to self-defence (Auswärtiges Amt, 2023a). Germany resisted early European Union (EU) proposals for a ceasefire or arms-embargo discussions, insisting on Israel's right to eliminate Hamas' military capacities (EEAS. (2023). Overall, Germany's early diplomatic focus was on condemning Hamas and preventing escalation to the northern front (Auswärtiges Amt, 2023b). Humanitarian references were limited and framed as compatible with military objectives. This first phase was followed by the entry of humanitarian concerns in the Discourse (January–June 2024). As civilian casualties in the Gaza Strip rose and international criticism intensified, Germany's rhetoric began including stronger references to IHL (IHL) and humanitarian pauses. Foreign Affairs Minister, Baerbock repeatedly stressed that "the protection of civilians is not optional" and called for "humanitarian windows" (Auswärtiges Amt, 2023b).

Yet, the judicial pressure produced a rhetorical shift in Germany's stance. Among others, it strengthened public debate about Germany's obligations under international law, particularly Article 7 of the Arms Trade Treaty (Casey-Maslen, 2016). It strengthened voices within the coalition, especially the Greens, who argued that continued arms exports to Israel risked contravening the Common Position's Criterion Two (clear risk of IHL violations). Although these judicial decisions did not immediately halt exports, they created a new legal risk context that influenced German policy discourse. Following the OVG Münster signal, senior officials, notably Foreign Affairs Minister Baerbock, began coupling reaffirmations of Israel's security with explicit references to Germany's obligations under IHL and to the need to protect civilians (Auswärtiges Amt, 2023b). This marked a rhetorical recalibration: Germany maintained its long-standing framing of Israel's security as part of its Staatsräson while incorporating legal language that acknowledged humanitarian imperatives. The effect was to recast humanitarian considerations not solely as moral concerns, but as legal duties arising from both national and EU law.

While the fundamental line of solidarity with Israel remains intact, official statements and parliamentary debates increasingly emphasise compliance with IHL (IHL), civilian protection, and support for international investigative mechanisms such as the International Court of Justice (ICJ) and the International Criminal Court (ICC). At the Foreign Affairs Council (FAC) meetings in early 2024, Germany stopped blocking compromise language calling for "sustained humanitarian pauses" and allowed Council conclusions to reference potential accountability mechanisms—something Berlin had resisted in late 2023 (Council of the European Union, 2023–2025). By late 2024, Germany increasingly accepted humanitarian and legal framing, while still defending Israel's security needs. The government began conditioning export approvals more strictly. In mid-2025, Germany suspended some categories of arms exports to Israel, particularly spare parts for offensive systems (Federal Government statements, 2025).

This shift in framing also affected Germany's conduct inside EU institutions. Prior to these judicial signals, in late 2023, Germany actively blocked references to "ceasefire" and opposed any linkage of EU–Israel relations to human rights clauses in the conclusions of the FAC (Council of the European Union, 2023–2025). By mid-2024, after the judicial interventions, Germany stopped vetoing humanitarian language, allowing the inclusion of "sustained humanitarian pauses" and "respect for IHL" in FAC conclusions (Council of the European Union, 2023–2025). It also allowed discussions in the EU Council Working Party on Conventional Arms Exports (COARM) to open discussions on strengthening risk assessments under the Common Position 2008/944/CFSP, a marked change from its earlier defensive posture. In mid-2025, the government went further by suspending certain export licences for offensive components destined for Israel, explicitly citing IHL risk concerns (Federal Government statements, 2025). In the European Parliament, German MEPs from the Greens and SPD increasingly pushed for references to the ICJ and ICC in resolutions, signalling support for international accountability mechanisms (VoteWatch Europe, 2024). Abstentions and defections on ceasefire amendments rose compared to earlier periods, indicating a loosening of the traditional cross-party consensus.

Germany's rhetorical evolution is significant for EU foreign policy. It increases the likelihood of EU consensus around stricter application of Common Position 2008/944/CFSP criteria and may stimulate debate about revising the instrument to strengthen enforcement. While Germany continued opposing EU-level sanctions or suspension of the EU–Israel Association Agreement, which some member states such as Ireland and Spain advocated (European Council, 2023), its acceptance of stronger humanitarian language shifts the EU's overall balance toward a rights-based approach.

The judicial interventions therefore did not compel an immediate halt to arms exports, rather they functioned as a catalyst for policy recalibration. They provided a legal rationale that enabled Germany to soften its stance in EU deliberations, moving from an obstructive position to a more accommodating one on humanitarian conditionality and risk assessment, while still resisting broader EU-level sanctions or suspension of the EU–Israel Association Agreement. In this way, domestic judicial pressure indirectly contributed to Germany's gradual shift from a security-dominant position to a more legally conditioned and humanitarian-sensitive role within EU institutions.

The Case of the Netherlands

In the immediate aftermath of the October 7 Hamas attacks, the Dutch government under Prime Minister Mark Rutte expressed unequivocal solidarity with Israel, emphasizing its right to self-defense under international law. The Netherlands aligned with a group of EU states—such as Germany, Austria, and Czech Republic—that resisted calls for a ceasefire or criticism of Israeli military operations (EEAS, 2023). At this stage, Dutch rhetoric framed Palestinian civilian casualties largely as indirect consequences of Hamas' tactics rather than of Israeli actions. Humanitarian concerns were present but subordinate to the prioritization of Israel's security (Meijer & Zaslove, 2024). In the European Council statement of 26 October 2023, Dutch diplomats—together with Germany, Czech Republic, and Austria—pressed for strong language on Israel's right to self-defense while resisting references to disproportionate use of force (Council of the European Union, 2023–2025). In the Foreign Affairs

Council (FAC) meeting of 13 November 2023, Dutch representatives joined Germany in requesting the removal of the term "ceasefire" from the draft conclusions, which was replaced by "humanitarian corridors" (EEAS, 2023). In United Nations voting coordinated at the EU level, the Netherlands abstained from the UN General Assembly resolution of 27 October 2023 (A/ES-10/L.25) calling for an immediate humanitarian truce, joining a minority of EU states (United Nations, 2023).

However, as the humanitarian toll in Gaza mounted, Dutch rhetoric began to shift. Statements from the Ministry of Foreign Affairs increasingly stressed the need to respect IHL (IHL) and called for safe humanitarian access to Gaza (Rijksoverheid, 2023b). While continuing to affirm Israel's right to self-defense, the Netherlands began emphasizing proportionality and the protection of civilians.

This recalibration moved the Netherlands somewhat closer to the EU mainstream, which by late 2023 was gravitating toward calls for "humanitarian pauses" in the fighting (Council of the European Union, 2023–2025).

After the Court Ruling (Feb–late 2024) in the FAC meeting of 18 March 2024, Foreign Minister Hanke Bruins Slot supported including references to potential "individual accountability for violations of IHL" (EEAS, 2024). Further on, in May 2024, the Netherlands voted in favor of the UN General Assembly resolution granting enhanced observer status to the State of Palestine (United Nations, 2024) and stopped blocking proposals in the EU Council Working Party on Human Rights (COHOM) to mandate monitoring of possible war crimes in Gaza and supported joint EU backing for the International Criminal Court (ICC) investigation into alleged violations by all parties (EEAS, 2024).

Finally, by mid-2024, the Dutch position had shifted further, with official statements endorsing humanitarian ceasefires and the need for accountability for war crimes by all parties, while reaffirming support for a two-state solution. This positioned the Netherlands as a more centrist actor within the EU, capable of bridging pro-Israel states and more critical member states such as Ireland, Spain, and Belgium (Balfour & Radeljic, 2024).

The Case of Belgium

Belgium adopted an early and sustained emphasis on humanitarian protection and ceasefire. By early March 2024, Foreign Minister Hadja Lahbib publicly called for an "immediate cease-fire," linking this to humanitarian imperatives and support for a two-state framework (Lahbib, 2024). Belgium also chose not to suspend funding to UNRWA in January 2024 when some donors paused contributions, and it subsequently signed a new multi-year funding agreement in April 2024 (UNRWA, 2024). Belgium voted in favor of UN General Assembly resolutions in December

2024 calling for a ceasefire in Gaza and the preservation of UNRWA's mandate, signalling its humanitarian and multilateral approach (Belgian MFA, 2024).

Before judicial pressure (Oct 2023–Jan 2024), Belgium supported language emphasizing humanitarian access and pauses, helping secure references to IHL and civilian protection in the text (Council of the European Union, 2023–2025). As incoming Council of the European Union Presidency, Belgium signaled it would prioritise humanitarian access and IHL compliance in Council agendas and parliamentary debates (Wilson Center, 2024; EP, 2024). Within EU budget debates, Belgium argued against freezing UNRWA funding and coordinated with like-minded states to keep UNRWA operational (UNRWA, 2024).

However, after judicial interventions in the Foreign Affairs Council of 18 March 2024, Belgium backed references to individual accountability for IHL violations, aligning with the EU mainstream (EEAS, 2024). Belgium supported pro-humanitarian UN votes, including the December 2024 ceasefire/UNRWA mandate resolution (Belgian MFA, 2024).

These judicial and executive actions strengthened Belgium's ability to argue for stricter IHL-based risk assessments in EU working parties (e.g., COARM/COHOM), support for International Criminal Court (ICC) accountability processes, and stronger humanitarian conditionality in EU texts (Council of the European Union, 2023–2025).

Table 1. Judicial triggers, rhetorical adjustments, EU-level impacts

Country	Judicial Trigger	Rhetorical Adjustment	EU-Level Impact
Netherlands	Hague Court of Appeal (12 Feb 2024) orders suspension of F-35 parts exports to Israel (Gerechtshof Den Haag, 2024), AG Paul Vlas supports ruling at Supreme Court of the Netherlands (Nov 2024).	Shifted official discourse to stress compliance with IHL (IHL), proportionality, and accountability mechanisms, reduced resistance to humanitarian pause language.	At Foreign Affairs Council (FAC), supported stronger humanitarian references and coordination with Spain/ Ireland, increased openness to linking EU–Israel agreements to human rights clauses (European Council, 2023).
Belgium	Council of State (2018–2021) suspends Walloon licences to Saudi Arabia, Brussels Court of First Instance (17 Jul 2025) halts transit of military goods via Antwerp to Israel (Rechtbank Brussel, 2025).	Prime Minister Alexander De Croo and regional governments adopt stronger humanitarian and accountability rhetoric, emphasis on ICC/ICJ investigations and arms-control obligations.	Became one of the most vocal advocates for humanitarian ceasefires in Council debates, strengthened pressure for stricter interpretation of Common Position 2008/944/CFSP (Antwerp transit ruling — interim order with coercive fine, 2025).
Germany	Administrative Court of Berlin & Administrative Court of Frankfurt (2024) deny preventive injunctions, Higher Administrative Court of Münster (OVG NRW) signals stricter review (2024) but limited effect (VG Berlin, 2024; VG Frankfurt, 2024; OVG NRW, 2024).	Federal rhetoric more cautious: Baerbock & Scholz reaffirm Israel's Staatsräson but increasingly stress IHL compliance, civilian protection, and humanitarian pauses (Auswärtiges Amt, 2023a, 2023b).	Stopped blocking humanitarian ceasefire language in Council conclusions, in mid-2025 suspended some arms exports to Israel (Federal Government statements, 2025), but resisted broader EU sanctions or treaty suspensions.

6. CONCLUSION

The above analysis has demonstrated that there is a linkage between national judicial decisions and political positions adopted by governments of EU member states, influencing ultimately EU foreign policy. While Germany's shift remains cautious, the Netherlands and Belgium illustrate how courts can act as "accountability multipliers," embedding Common Position criteria into both domestic licensing and EU discourse. Germany remains a central supporter of Israel but now speaks in a language more attuned to the EU's values discourse. This may pave the way for greater consistency in the EU's collective arms-export policy and a more integrated rights-based approach to external action. The Netherlands and Belgium illustrate two distinct but converging cases. The Netherlands shifted from staunch pro-Israel alignment to a centrist role, especially after judicial pressure in 2024, while Belgium started with humanitarian and ceasefire rhetoric and, following judicial interventions in 2024–2025, reinforced its focus on IHL, accountability, and humanitarian conditionality. Overall, Belgium and the Netherlands are more willing to push for restrictive measures (license suspensions, transit blocks, potential linkage to EU-Israel agreements), whereas Germany emphasizes humanitarian law rhetorically but avoids endorsing embargoes or treaty suspensions.

These cases show how domestic legal pressures and humanitarian considerations can reshape member states' stances within EU foreign policymaking structures, ending up influencing EU policies. All three governments now use rights-based language—emphasizing IHL, accountability, and civilian protection—in EU debates. The convergence in rights-based language marks an important evolution in EU foreign policy, signaling the growing judicialisation of external action.

This adapted rhetoric contributes to gradual adaptation of the EU's collective stance on arms exports and may accelerate discussions on revising Common Position 2008/944/CFSP, currently pending. EU and national courts have evolved into crucial guardians of consistency in EU external relations. Already the ECJ, through landmark judgments, has bound CFSP to internal constitutional standards, extended preliminary ruling jurisdiction, recognised damages liability, and enforced international law obligations. National courts have reinforced these standards in export and transit cases, operationalising EU values on the ground.

The result is a more coherent and legally accountable EU foreign policy. While risks of politicization and diplomatic tension remain, the above mentioned judicialisation ensures that the Union's external action lives up to the constitutional values it proclaims. Far from weakening the EU, this role strengthens its normative credibility in a contested international order.

REFERENCES

Advocate General Vlas. (2024, November 29). *Advocate General's recommendation to Supreme Court: Court of Appeal's decision that Dutch State must cease exports of F-35 parts to Israel can be upheld.* Supreme Court of the Netherlands. https://www.hogeraad.nl

Amt, A. (2023a). *Statement by Foreign Minister Annalena Baerbock on the situation in Gaza, October 2023.* https://www.auswaertiges-amt.de

Amt, A. (2023b). *Federal Government statements on humanitarian law in the Middle East conflict, 2023–2024.* https://www.auswaertiges-amt.de

Anghel, S., Immenkamp, B., Lazarou, E., Saulnier, J. L., & Wilson, A. B. (2020). *On the path to "strategic autonomy".* European Parliamentary Research Service. https://www.europarl.europa.eu/RegData/etudes/STUD/2020/652096/EPRS_STU%282020%29652096_EN.pdf

Asser Institute. (2025). Transparency in European Arms Exports: Access to Information and National Jurisprudence (June 30, 2025)_https://www.asser.nl/media/798021/transparency_in_european_arms_exports_law_clinic_report_30_june_2025_asser_institute.pdf?utm_source=chatgpt.com

Balfour, R., & Radeljic, B. (2024). *EU foreign policy and the Gaza conflict: Diverging member state responses.* European Policy Centre.

Balfour, R., & Raik, K. (2015). European external action and the question of consistency. *Journal of European Integration, 37*(3), 349–367.

Berlin, V. (2024, June 11). *VG 4 L 44/24, 119/24, 148/24 – Waffen an Israel: Kein vorbeugender vorläufiger Rechtsschutz.* https://www.berlin.de

Berlin, V. (2024). *Press Release No. 16/2024 – Weapons to Israel: Preventive relief denied.* Verwaltungsgericht Berlin.

Blockmans, S., & Koutrakos, P. (2018). *Research handbook on the EU's Common Foreign and Security Policy.* Edward Elgar. DOI: 10.4337/9781785364082

BMWK (Bundesministerium für Wirtschaft und Klimaschutz). (2023). *Rüstungsexportbericht 2023.* BMWK.

Brockmeier, S. (2022). Germany and Israel: Continuity and change in a special relationship. *German Politics, 31*(4), 567–584.

Bromley, M., & Maletta, G. (2024). *European arms export controls and the Middle East: Trends and challenges.* SIPRI Report.

Brussel, R. (2025). *Beschikking AR 25/69/C (Antwerp transit ruling).* https://www.rechtbanken-tribunaux.be

Bundesministerium für Wirtschaft und Klimaschutz. (2019, June 26). *Politische Grundsätze der Bundesregierung für den Export von Kriegswaffen und sonstigen Rüstungsgütern.* https://www.bmwk.de

Bundesverfassungsgericht. (2014, October 21). *2 BvE 5/11 – Informationsrecht der Bundestagsabgeordneten über Rüstungsexporte.* https://www.bundesverfassungsgericht.de

Casey-Maslen, S. (2016). *The Arms Trade Treaty: A commentary.* Oxford University Press.

Chachko, E. (2020). Revisiting judicial review in foreign affairs. *Harvard Law School Program on International Law and Armed Conflict Research Paper.* https://doi.org/DOI: 10.2139/ssrn.3607463

CJEU. (2017). *Case C-455/14 P, H v. Council and Commission, Judgment of 30 May 2017.*

Council Common Position 2008/944/CFSP of 8 December 2008.

Council of the European Union. (2023–2025). *EU position on the situation in the Middle East.* https://www.consilium.europa.eu/

Court of Appeal, The Hague. (2024, February 12). *Case No. 200.327.006/01, Judgment.*

Cremona, M. (2017). Structural principles and their role in EU external relations law. *Common Market Law Review, 54*(1).

Droege, C., & Casey-Maslen, S. (2012). Arms transfers and IHL. *International Review of the Red Cross, 94*(885).

ECCHR. (2024). *Preliminary injunction against surveillance technology exports to Israel.*

EEAS. (2023). *Foreign Affairs Council conclusions on the Middle East (November 2023).*

EEAS. (2024). *EU statement at the UN Security Council – Situation in the Middle East, including the Palestinian question (March 2024).*

EJIL. Talk! (Zwanenburg, M., & Voetelink, J.). (2024, February 16). *Appeals judgment in case concerning shipment from the Netherlands of parts for F-35 fighter aircraft to Israel.* https://www.ejiltalk.org

European Council. (2014). *Council conclusions on the Middle East Peace Process, 22 July 2014.* General Secretariat.

European Council. (2023). *Council conclusions on the Middle East, October 2023.* General Secretariat.

European Parliament. (2023, July 6). *Resolution 2023/2739(RSP).*

Ferreira, N. (2022). Rights-based litigation and the external dimension of EU law. *European Constitutional Law Review, 18*(4), 665–692.

Frankfurt am Main, V. (2024, December 16). *5 L 2333/24.F – Rüstungsgüter für Israel.* https://verwaltungsgerichtsbarkeit.hessen.de

Frankfurt am Main, V. (2024). *Press Release No. 20/2024 – Military goods for Israel.*

Gerechtshof Den Haag. (2024). *ECLI:NL:GHDHA:2024:191 (Oxfam Novib et al. v. The State of the Netherlands).* Rechtspraak. https://uitspraken.rechtspraak.nl

Golia, A. J. (2021). Judicial review, foreign relations and global administrative law: The administrative function of courts in foreign relations. In Aust, H. P., & Kleinlein, T. (Eds.), *Encounters between foreign relations law and international law: Bridges and boundaries* (pp. 130–158). Cambridge University Press., DOI: 10.1017/9781108942713.008

Harvard Law Review Forum. (2015). Foreign relations law and the purported shift away from exceptionalism. *Harvard Law Review Forum, 128*(105), 105–121. https://harvardlawreview.org/forum/vol-128/foreign-relations-law-and-the-purported-shift-away-from-exceptionalism/

Holtom, P., & Bromley, M. (2010). *Implementing the EU Common Position on arms exports: Improvements, but more needed.* SIPRI Background Paper.

ICJ. (2024, January 26). *South Africa v. Israel, Provisional Measures Order.*

Kaim, M. (2021). Germany's Middle East policy: Between historical responsibility and current interests. *SWP Research Paper.* Stiftung Wissenschaft und Politik, Berlin.

Klafki, A. (2025). Judicial review of foreign administrative action in Germany. *European Public Law, 31*(1), 35–52. https://kluwerlawonline.com/journalarticle/European%2BPublic%2BLaw/31.1/EURO2025002. DOI: 10.54648/EURO2025002

Lahbib, H. (2024, March 5). *Belgium calls for immediate cease-fire in Gaza [press remarks]*. Anadolu Agency. https://www.aa.com.tr/

Lazowski, A., & Wessel, R. A. (2020). The juridification of EU foreign policy: Implications for the CJEU's jurisdiction. *European Constitutional Law Review, 16*(3).

Maletta, G. (2021). Seeking a responsible arms trade to reduce human suffering in Yemen. *The International Spectator, 56*(1), 73–91. DOI: 10.1080/03932729.2021.1876862

Malmvig, H. (2015). The European Union and the Israeli–Palestinian conflict: A story of a gap between words and deeds. *European Security, 24*(3), 422–440.

Meijer, H., & Zaslove, A. (2024). Dutch foreign policy after October 7: Balancing values and interests. *Clingendael Spectator, 78*(1), 12–18.

Milanovic, M. (2011). *Extraterritorial application of human rights treaties: Law, principles, and policy*. Oxford University Press. DOI: 10.1093/acprof:oso/9780199696208.001.0001

OVG NRW (Oberverwaltungsgericht Nordrhein-Westfalen). (2024). *Judgment 4 A 1234/23 – Arms export to Israel*. Münster.

Parliament, F. (2012). *Wapenhandeldecreet*. Codex Vlaanderen. https://codex.vlaanderen.be

Raad van State (Belgium). (2019). *Suspension of Walloon arms export licences to Saudi Arabia*. Arms Trade Litigation Monitor. https://armstradelitigationmonitor.org

Raad van State (Belgium). (2018–2021). *Suspension and annulment of Walloon arms export licences to Saudi Arabia*. Arms Trade Litigation Monitor. https://armstradelitigationmonitor.org

Rechtbank Den Haag. (2024). *ECLI:NL:RBDHA:2024:1234 — Judgment on F-35 parts export to Israel.*

Rechtbank van eerste aanleg Brussel. (2025, July 17). *Beschikking AR 25/69/C (Antwerp transit ruling)*. https://www.rechtbanken-tribunaux.be

Rijksoverheid. (2023a). *Minister-President Rutte expresses solidarity with Israel following attacks*. https://www.rijksoverheid.nl

Rijksoverheid. (2023b). *The Netherlands calls for humanitarian access to Gaza*. https://www.rijksoverheid.nl

Rijksoverheid. (2024). *Minister Bruins Slot calls for accountability and two-state solution in Middle East*. https://www.rijksoverheid.nl

Ryngaert, C. (2022). Risk assessment in arms export controls: Between precaution and evidence. *Journal of International Humanitarian Legal Studies, 13*(1).

Sitaraman, G. (2019). Foreign hard look review. *Administrative Law Review, 66*(3), 489–541. https://administrativelawreview.org/wp-content/uploads/sites/2/2019/01/Sitaraman_66.3.pdf

United Nations. (2023). *General Assembly resolution A/ES-10/L.25.*

United Nations. (2024). *General Assembly resolution ES-10/23 on the status of the State of Palestine.*

UNRWA. (2024, April 19). *Belgium signs new EUR 27.5m agreement with UNRWA (2024–2026).* https://www.unrwa.org/

Verwaltungsgericht Berlin. (2024, March 8). *Case No. 1 L 271/24, Ruling.*

Vlas, A.-G. (2024). Conclusion recommending to uphold Hague Court of Appeal ruling on F-35 parts to Israel (ECLI [). Rechtspraak.]. *NL:PHR, 2024*, 1424.

VoteWatch Europe. (2018). *European Parliament votes on Israel and Palestine, 2014–2018.* https://www.votewatch.eu

VoteWatch Europe. (2024). *Debates and plenary votes on Gaza, 2023–2024.* https://www.votewatch.eu

Williams, R. C. (2020). "Judicial role" and judicial duty in foreign affairs. *Fordham International Law Journal, 43*(5), 1259–1312. https://ir.lawnet.fordham.edu/ilj/vol43/iss5/3

Wisotzki, S., & Mutschler, M. (2021). No common position! European arms export control in crisis. *Zeitschrift für Friedens- und Konfliktforschung, 10*(2), 273–293. https://doi.org/DOI: 10.1007/s42597-022-00071-x

Worster, W. T. (2025). — "Assurances on the Use of Exported Arms in the Gaza Conflict. *Israel Law Review, 2025*(58), 306–342. DOI: 10.1017/S0021223725100095

Compilation of References

Abernethy, A., Adams, L., Barrett, M., Bechtel, C., Bhatia, A., Brawley, O., Conway, P., & Gorman, P. (2022). The promise of digital health: Then, now, and the future. *NAM Perspectives*, *2022*(22), 1–25. DOI: 10.31478/202206e PMID: 36177208

Acemoglu, D. (2024). The simple macroeconomics of AI*. *Economic Policy*, *40*(121), 13–58. DOI: 10.1093/epolic/eiae042

Acemoglu, D., & Robinson, J. (2019). *The Narrow Corridor: States, Societies, and the Fate of Liberty*. Penguin Press.

Advocate General Vlas. (2024, November 29). *Advocate General's recommendation to Supreme Court: Court of Appeal's decision that Dutch State must cease exports of F-35 parts to Israel can be upheld.* Supreme Court of the Netherlands. https://www.hogeraad.nl

Agranoff, R., & McGuire, M. (2001). Big questions in public network management. *Journal of Public Administration: Research and Theory*, *11*(3), 295–326. DOI: 10.1093/oxfordjournals.jpart.a003504

Agrell, P. J., Mattsson, P., & Månsson, J. (2020). Impacts on efficiency of merging the Swedish district courts. *Annals of Operations Research*, *288*(2), 653–679. DOI: 10.1007/s10479-019-03304-0

Ahmad, A., Faisal, F., Akhtar, R., & Abdul Wahab, S. (2020). Change management capability: The contribution of organizational structure and leadership. *Journal of Organizational Change Management*, *33*(7), 1503–1519.

Ahmed, P. K. (1998). Culture and climate for innovation. *European Journal of Innovation Management*, *1*(1), 30–43. DOI: 10.1108/14601069810199131

Ajzen, I. (1991). The theory of planned behavior. *Organizational Behavior and Human Decision Processes*, *50*(2), 179–211. DOI: 10.1016/0749-5978(91)90020-T

Akhnif, E. H., Belmadani, A., Mataria, A., & Bigdeli, M. (2024). UHC in Morocco: A bottom-up estimation of public hospitals' financing size based on a costing database. *Health Economics Review, 14*(1), 25. DOI: 10.1186/s13561-024-00501-x PMID: 38557700

Akinwale, O. E., & Kuye, O. L. (2023). Ouchi's management model relevance to healthcare management efficiency among government tertiary hospitals during the COVID-19 pandemic season in Lagos state, Nigeria. *Technological Sustainability, 2*(1), 20–43. DOI: 10.1108/TECHS-01-2022-0005

Akrivos, D., Reklitis, P., & Prifti, E. (2013). Greek public administration reform: How to improve the effectiveness of strategic changes. *Procedia: Social and Behavioral Sciences, 73*, 710–717. DOI: 10.1016/j.sbspro.2013.02.109

Allen, J., Jimmieson, N. L., Bordia, P., & Irmer, B. E. (2007). Uncertainty during organizational change: Managing perceptions through communication. *Journal of Change Management, 7*(2), 187–210. DOI: 10.1080/14697010701563379

Alvina, L., Venky, S., & Ouh Eng, L. (2024). Enhancing citizen service management through AI-enabled systems – a proposed AI readiness framework for the public sector. In Charalabidis, Y., Medaglia, R., & van Noordt, C. (Eds.), *Research Handbook on Public Management and Artificial Intelligence* (pp. 79–96). Edward Elgar Publishing.

Amelicheva, L., Martyniuk, O., Pyroha, I., Qaracayev, C., & Myroshnychenko, V. (2021). Implementation of constitutional human rights and social guarantees of security in the context of digitalization. *Amazonia Investiga, 10*(43), 375–385. DOI: 10.34069/AI/2021.45.09.26

Amt, A. (2023a). *Statement by Foreign Minister Annalena Baerbock on the situation in Gaza, October 2023*. https://www.auswaertiges-amt.de

Amt, A. (2023b). *Federal Government statements on humanitarian law in the Middle East conflict, 2023–2024*. https://www.auswaertiges-amt.de

Andrews, M., Pritchett, L., & Woolcock, M. (2017). *Building state capability: Evidence, analysis, action*. Oxford University Press. DOI: 10.1093/acprof:oso/9780198747482.001.0001

Andrews, R., Beynon, M. J., & McDermott, A. M. (2017). Organizational capability in the public sector: A configurational approach. *Journal of Public Administration: Research and Theory, 26*(2), 239–258. DOI: 10.1093/jopart/muv005

Andrews, R., Boyne, G. A., Law, J., & Walker, R. M. (2012). Strategic management and public service performance: The way forward. *Public Administration Review, 72*(3), 405–413.

Anghel, S., Immenkamp, B., Lazarou, E., Saulnier, J. L., & Wilson, A. B. (2020). *On the path to "strategic autonomy"*. European Parliamentary Research Service. https://www.europarl.europa.eu/RegData/etudes/STUD/2020/652096/EPRS_STU%282020%29652096_EN.pdf

Ansell, C., & Trondal, J. (2022). Governing turbulence: Leadership and adaptation in public administration. *Public Administration Review, 82*(5), 849–862.

Antoniou, T. (2011). The Stockholm Programme and the Treaty of Lisbon: A space of Freedom, Sewcurity and Justice or just Security? Challenges for human rights respect in the years to come, in International cooperation in global and regional level (ed. St. Perrakis), I. Sideris, Athens, December.

Antoniou, T. (2013). Overseeing the EU's external borders: Legislative / political developments and the Greek Presidency, Annual Conference of the Hellenic Society of International Law and International Relations, "Greece and Europe in the face of the major crises of the pre- Greek Presidency of the EU", Livani, Athens.

Antoniou, T. (2014). The new European Maritime Border Surveillance Regulation: A Critical Approach, Rhodes-Kastelorizo Symposium "Implementation of International Law and Politics 20 Years after the Enactment of the Maritime Law Convention: Detecting the Aegean Sea and the Mediterranean Sea 2014", Livani, Athens.

Antoniou, T. (2016). Demystifying the concept of solidarity in the EU Area of Freedom, Security and Justice in the aftermath of the refugee crisis, Annual Conference of the Hellenic Society of International Law and International Relations, "Global Challenges – Common Responsibilities, An Evaluation of the UN 70 years" December 19, 2015, Panteion University, Livani, Athens.

Antoniou, T. (2019). Solidarity in the EU: a moral imperative or a legal reality? Concept, aspects and implementation during the Refugee Crisis, Conference on Solidarity Developments in the field of refugee protection in the European Union and challenges in the EU and in Greece, Nomiki Bibliothiki, Athens.

Antoniou, A., Béraud-Sudreau, L., & Dorsey, J. (2025). European arms exports and international humanitarian law: Judicial and political challenges. *Journal of European Security Studies, 14*(2), 115–137.

Antoniou, T. (2012). *The responsibility to protect and EU's international role after the treaty of Lisbon: from theory to practice, December*. I. Sideris.

Aphecetche, T., Canton, E., Garrone, M., & Hobza, A. (2022). Understanding the Political Economy of Reforms: Lessons from the EU (Economic Brief 070). Luxembourg: European Commission, Directorate-General for Economic and Financial Affairs. Ανάκτηση 6 20, 2025, από https://economy-finance.ec.europa.eu/system/files/2022-01/eb070_en_political_economy_reforms_0.pdf

Arah, O. A., Klazinga, N. S., Delnoij, D. M., Ten Asbroek, A. H., & Custers, T. (2006). Conceptual frameworks for health systems performance: A quest for effectiveness, quality, and improvement. *International Journal for Quality in Health Care : Journal of the International Society for Quality in Health Care, 18*(4), 377–398. PMID: 14527982

Argyris, C., & Schön, D. A. (1978). *Organizational learning: A theory of action perspective*. Addison-Wesley.

Argyris, C., & Schön, D. A. (1996). *Organizational learning II: Theory, method, and practice*. Addison-Wesley.

Armenakis, A. A., & Bedeian, A. G. (1999). Organizational change: A review of theory and research in the 1990s. *Journal of Management, 25*(3), 293–315. DOI: 10.1177/014920639902500303

Armenakis, A. A., Bernerth, J. B., Pitts, J. P., & Walker, H. J. (2007). Organizational change recipients' beliefs scale: Development of an assessment instrument. *The Journal of Applied Behavioral Science, 43*(4), 481–505. DOI: 10.1177/0021886307303654

Armenakis, A. A., & Harris, S. G. (2002). Crafting a change message to create transformational readiness. *Journal of Organizational Change Management, 15*(2), 169–183. DOI: 10.1108/09534810210423080

Armenakis, A. A., & Harris, S. G. (2009). Reflections: Our journey in organizational change research and practice. *Journal of Change Management, 9*(2), 127–142. DOI: 10.1080/14697010902879079

Armenakis, A. A., Harris, S. G., & Mossholder, K. W. (1993). Creating readiness for organizational change. *Human Relations, 46*(6), 681–703. DOI: 10.1177/001872679304600601

Armstrade Litigation Monitor. (2024). *German court rulings on arms export licensing*. https://armstradelitigationmonitor.org

Asatryan, Z., Heinemann, F., & Pitlik, H. (2017). 6). Reforming the public administration: The role of crisis and the power of bureaucracy. *European Journal of Political Economy, 48*, 128–143. DOI: 10.1016/j.ejpoleco.2016.08.004

Ashby, W. R. (1968). Variety, constraint and the law of requisite variety. In Buckley, W. (Ed.), *Modern systems research for the behavioural scientist*. Aldine Publishing Co.

Aspridis, G., & Pouliana, E. (2021). Organizational culture in public administration: The case of Greece. *Academicus International Scientific Journal*, *12*(23), 133–148.

Asser Institute. (2025). Transparency in European Arms Exports: Access to Information and National Jurisprudence (June 30, 2025) https://www.asser.nl/media/798021/transparency_in_european_arms_exports_law_clinic_report_30_june_2025_asser_institute.pdf?utm_source=chatgpt.com

Avalekar, U. A., Mehta, V., Mishra, B. R., Prasanna, L., Rajlakshmi, P. V., & Manjunath, T. C. (2025). The current advances in AI-driven education. In Babulak, E. (Ed.), *Educational AI humanoid computing devices for cyber nomads* (pp. 173–196). IGI Global Scientific Publishing., DOI: 10.4018/979-8-3693-8985-0.ch008

Avolio, B. J., Bass, B. M., & Jung, D. I. (1999). Re-examining the components of transformational and transactional leadership using the Multifactor Leadership Questionnaire. *Journal of Occupational and Organizational Psychology*, *72*(4), 441–462. DOI: 10.1348/096317999166789

Bacong, A. M., & Menjívar, C. (2021). Recasting the immigrant health paradox through intersections of legal status and race. *Journal of Immigrant and Minority Health*, *23*(5), 1092–1104. DOI: 10.1007/s10903-021-01162-2 PMID: 33656653

Bajrić, H., & Kadrić, E. (2020). Efficiency assessment of municipal courts in federation of Bosnia and Herzegovina using data envelopment analysis. *International Journal of Qualitative Research*, *14*(2), 347–368. DOI: 10.24874/IJQR14.02-02

Baker, D. (2007). *Strategic change management in public sector organizations*. Chandos Publishing.

Balfour, R., & Radeljic, B. (2024). *EU foreign policy and the Gaza conflict: Diverging member state responses*. European Policy Centre.

Balfour, R., & Raube, K. (2015). European external action and the question of consistency. *Journal of European Integration*, *37*(3), 349–367.

Balogun, J. (2003). From blaming the middle to harnessing its potential: Creating change intermediaries. *British Journal of Management*, *14*(1), 69–83. DOI: 10.1111/1467-8551.00266

Bamford, D. R., & Forrester, P. L. (2003). Managing planned and emergent change within an operations management environment. *International Journal of Operations & Production Management*, *23*(5), 546–564. DOI: 10.1108/01443570310471857

Bandura, A. (1997). *Self-efficacy: The exercise of control.* W.H. Freeman.

Bartunek, J. M., & Moch, M. K. (1987). First-order, second-order, and third-order change and organization development interventions: A cognitive approach. *The Journal of Applied Behavioral Science, 23*(4), 483–500. DOI: 10.1177/002188638702300404

Bass, B. M. (1985). *Leadership and performance beyond expectations.* Free Press.

Bass, B. M., & Avolio, B. J. (1997). *Full range leadership development: Manual for the Multifactor Leadership Questionnaire.* Mind Garden.

Batley, R., & Larbi, G. (2004). Changing approaches to public sector management. In *The Changing Role of Government: The Reform of Public Services in Developing Countries* (pp. 31–53). Palgrave Macmillan UK. DOI: 10.1057/9780230001053_2

Battaglio, R. P. (2021). *Public human resource management: Strategies and practices in the 21st century* (2nd ed.). SAGE Publications., DOI: 10.4135/9781071809273

Battilana, J., Gilmartin, M., Sengul, M., Pache, A. C., & Alexander, J. A. (2010). Leadership competencies for implementing planned organizational change. *The Leadership Quarterly, 21*(3), 422–438. DOI: 10.1016/j.leaqua.2010.03.007

Baudet, C., & Medina, M. J. (2023). The paradoxes of trust and transparency of blockchain technologies. *Journal of Global Information Management, 31*(12), 1–22. DOI: 10.4018/JGIM.321111

Bauer, S., & Cops, D. (2014). Enforcing the EU's arms export regime: Brokering and diversion. *European Foreign Affairs Review, 19*(4), 525–552.

Beck, U. (1992). *Risk Society Towards a New Modernity.* SAGE Publications.

Bełdowski, J., Dąbroś, Ł., & Wojciechowski, W. (2020). Judges and court performance: A case study of district commercial courts in Poland. *European Journal of Law and Economics, 50*(1), 171–201. DOI: 10.1007/s10657-020-09656-4

Bel, G., & Casula, M. (2024). *Re-organizing the service-delivery machine in a "post-NPM" era: a shopping-basket approach?* DOI: 10.1080/14719037.2024.2315569

Belias, D., Rossidis, I., & Papademetriou, C. (2020). *E-Governance in times of Covid19 - The case of Greece. Problems and prospects.* 16th Hellenic Society for Systemic Studies (HSSS) National & International Conference "Effective Management of Public and Private Organizations through Systemics and Technologies".

Belias, D., Rossidis, I., Ntalakos, A., Trihas, N., Mantas, C., & Bokogiannis, D. (2023). Ethics in Change Management: Current Issues and Directions for Future Research in the Post-COVID-19 Era. Chapter 12 in "Managing Successful and Ethical Organizational Change", IGI Global.

Belias, D., Velissariou, S., Papailias, S., Manta, F., Rossidis, I. (2019). Change Management – Obstacles and Perspectives for the Integration of Changes in Greek Public Hospitals. *Advances in Management & Applied Economics.* 9(2).

Belias, D., Ntalakos, A., Rossidis, I., Giannakos, K., & Koustelios, A. (2025). Can Leadership Styles Affect the Integration to Change and the Commitment to Change? A Case Study on Employees of Greek Four and Five-Star Hotels. In Pivac, T., Castanho, R. A. M. D., Martinelli, E., & Gonçalves, E. C. C. (Eds.), *The Innovative Pathway on Sustainable Culture Tourism. CST 2024. Advances in Science, Technology & Innovation.* Springer., DOI: 10.1007/978-3-031-86745-3_20

Belias, D., & Rossidis, I. (2025). *Change Management. Organizational Change and elements of Organizational Behaviour.* Tziolas publications.

Belias, D., & Rossidis, I. (2025). *Change Management: Organizational Change and Organizational Behavior* [in Greek]. Tziolas Publications.

Belias, D., Rossidis, I., Mantas, C., & Ntalakos, A. (2024). Change Management and Emotional Intelligence Leadership: Strategies That the Emotional Intelligence Leadership Can Adopt During a Change Industry. In *Belias, D., Rossidis, I, Papademetriou, C. Organizational Behavior and Human Resource Management for Complex Work Environments* (pp. 186–203). IGI Global., DOI: 10.4018/979-8-3693-3466-9.ch010

Belias, D., Rossidis, I., & Papademetriou, C. (2024). *Organizational Behavior and Human Resource Management for Complex Work Environments.* IGI Global. DOI: 10.4018/979-8-3693-3466-9

Belias, D., Rossidis, I., Papademetriou, C., Masouras, A., & Anastasiadou, S. (2023). *Managing Successful and Ethical Organizational Change.* IGI Global. DOI: 10.4018/979-8-3693-0235-4

Belias, D., & Trihas, N. (2023). How can we predict the integration and the success of organizational change in the hospitality sector? *Journal of Quality Assurance in Hospitality & Tourism, 25*(6), 2011–2045. DOI: 10.1080/1528008X.2023.2216952

Belias, D., Trihas, N., Dimou, I., & Kourgiantakis, M. (2023d). The effect of goal motivation on the integration and the success of an organizational change in the hospitality sector. *In Proceedings on the 6th International Conference on Tourism Research*, 34-42. DOI: 10.34190/ictr.6.1.1083

Belias, D., Trihas, N., & Ntalakos, A. (2024b). Crisis Leadership, Group Dynamics, and Change Management: A Literature Review and Future Perspectives. In Katsoni, V., & Cassar, G. (Eds.), *Recent Advancements in Tourism Business, Technology and Social Sciences. IACuDiT 2023. Springer Proceedings in Business and Economics*. Springer., DOI: 10.1007/978-3-031-54342-5_13

Belias, D., Trihas, N., Ntalakos, A., Dimou, I., Rossidis, I., & Kourgiantakis, M. (2025b). Strategic Leadership and Its Effect on the Integration and the Success of Organizational Change on Four and Five Star Hotels. In Castanho, R. A., Pivac, T., & Mandić, A. (Eds.), *Legacy and Innovation. CST 2023. Advances in Science, Technology & Innovation*. Springer., DOI: 10.1007/978-3-031-59325-3_21

Belias, D., Velissariou, S., Papailias, S., Manta, F., & Rossidis, I. (2019). Change Management – Obstacles and Perspectives for the Integration of Changes in Greek Public Hospitals. *Advances in Management & Applied Economics.*, *9*(2), 37–50.

Belorgey, N. (2010). *L'hôpital sous pression. Enquête sur le nouveau management public*. La Découverte. DOI: 10.3917/dec.belor.2010.01

Berlin, V. (2024). *Press Release No. 16/2024 – Weapons to Israel: Preventive relief denied*. Verwaltungsgericht Berlin.

Berlin, V. (2024, June 11). *VG 4 L 44/24, 119/24, 148/24 – Waffen an Israel: Kein vorbeugender vorläufiger Rechtsschutz*. https://www.berlin.de

Berman, A., de Fine Licht, K., & Carlsson, V. (2024). Trustworthy AI in the public sector: An empirical analysis of a Swedish labor market decision-support system. *Technology in Society*, *76*, 102471. Advance online publication. DOI: 10.1016/j.techsoc.2024.102471

Berman, E. M., Bowman, J. S., West, J. P., & Van Wart, M. R. (2021). *Human resource management in public service: Paradoxes, processes, and problems* (7th ed.). CQ Press., DOI: 10.4135/9781071809266

Berman, E. M., & Hijal-Moghrabi, I. (2022). *Performance and Innovation in the Public Sector : Managing for results*. Routledge. DOI: 10.4324/9781003304753

Bernerth, J. B., Walker, H. J., & Harris, S. G. (2011). Change fatigue: Development and initial validation of a new measure. *Work and Stress*, *25*(4), 321–337. DOI: 10.1080/02678373.2011.634280

Berrada, H., & Marghich, A. (2023). Performance hospitalière : État de l'art. Revue du contrôle, de la comptabilité et de l'audit, 7(1).

Berry, F. S., & Wechsler, B. (1995). State agencies' experience with strategic planning: Findings from a national survey. *Public Administration Review, 55*(2), 159–168. DOI: 10.2307/977181

Besch, S. (2023). *Up in arms: Europe's contentious arms export regime.* Centre for European Reform.

Bezes, P., Demazière, D., Le Bianic, T., Paradeise, C., & Normand, R. (2012). New public management et professions dans les organisations publiques. Sociologies pratiques, 25(2), 9–22.

Blockmans, S., & Koutrakos, P. (2018). *Research handbook on the EU's Common Foreign and Security Policy.* Edward Elgar. DOI: 10.4337/9781785364082

BMWK (Bundesministerium für Wirtschaft und Klimaschutz). (2023). *Rüstungs-exportbericht 2023.* BMWK.

Bobkova, E. (2018). The Use of New Public Management in Healthcare. Lessons for Transition Economies. *Journal of Management and Strategy, 9*(1), 78–87.

Bonaiuti, C. (2022). Arms transfers and human rights: Assessing the impact and enforcement of the EU Common Position in a multilevel analysis. *European Foreign Affairs Review, 27*(4), 463–484. DOI: 10.54648/EERR2022035

Bordia, P., Hunt, E., Paulsen, N., Tourish, D., & DiFonzo, N. (2004). Uncertainty during organizational change: Is it all about control? *European Journal of Work and Organizational Psychology, 13*(3), 345–365. DOI: 10.1080/13594320444000128

Bordia, P., Restubog, S. L. D., Jimmieson, N. L., & Irmer, B. E. (2011). Haunted by the past: Effects of poor change management history on employee attitudes and turnover. *Group & Organization Management, 36*(2), 191–222. DOI: 10.1177/1059601110392990

Bouabdellah, M., & Ferdoussi, M. (2024). Management hospitalier au Maroc: Défis et perspectives. *Revue Marocaine de Gestion Publique, 29*(1), 45–62.

Bouckenooghe, D. (2010). Positioning change recipients' attitudes toward change in the organizational change literature. *The Journal of Applied Behavioral Science, 46*(4), 500–531. DOI: 10.1177/0021886310367944

Bouckenooghe, D., Devos, G., & Van den Broeck, H. (2009). Organizational change questionnaire–climate of change, processes, and readiness: Development of a new instrument. *The Journal of Psychology, 143*(6), 559–599. DOI: 10.1080/00223980903218216 PMID: 19957876

Boumkhaled, M., Lkhoyaali, B., & El Halaissi, M. (2018). La gestion axée sur les résultats (GAR) au Maroc: une lecture critique. Revue du contrôle, de la comptabilité et de l'audit, 2(4).

Bourdieu, P. (2007). *Science of Science and Reflexivity*. Patakis.

Bourguignon, A. (1995). *Peut-on définir la performance*. Revenue Francaise de Comptabilite. Revenue Francaise de Comptabilite.

Bovaird, T. (2008). Emergent strategic management and planning mechanisms in complex adaptive systems. *Public Management Review, 10*(3), 319–340. DOI: 10.1080/14719030802002741

Boycko, M., Shleifer, A., & Vishny, R. W. (1996). *A Theory of Privatisation*. MIT Press. DOI: 10.2307/2235248

Boyne, G. A. (2002). Public and private management: What's the difference? *Journal of Management Studies, 39*(1), 97–122. DOI: 10.1111/1467-6486.00284

Boyne, G. A., & Walker, R. M. (2010). Strategic management and public service performance: Moving beyond the rhetoric. *Public Administration Review, 70*(3), 415–423.

Boyne, G., Gould-Williams, J., Law, J., & Walker, R. (2002). Plans, performance information and accountability: The case of best value. *Public Administration, 80*(4), 691–710. DOI: 10.1111/1467-9299.00324

Bozeman, B. (1987). *All organizations are public: Bridging public and private organizational theories*. Jossey-Bass.

Brockmeier, S. (2022). Germany and Israel: Continuity and change in a special relationship. *German Politics, 31*(4), 567–584.

Bromley, M. (2012). *The review of the EU Common Position on arms exports: Prospects for strengthened controls* (EU Non-Proliferation Paper No. 7). SIPRI.

Bromley, M., & Maletta, G. (2024). *European arms export controls and the Middle East: Trends and challenges*. SIPRI Report.

Bromley, M. (2020). *The European Union Common Position on arms exports: Prospects for reform*. SIPRI.

Brummel, L. (2021). Social accountability between consensus and confrontation: Developing a theoretical framework for societal accountability relationships of public sector organizations. *Administration & Society*, *53*(9), 1437–1463. DOI: 10.1177/0095399720988529

Brunsson, N. (2006). 9). Administrative reforms as routines. *Scandinavian Journal of Management*, *22*(3), 243–252. DOI: 10.1016/j.scaman.2006.10.007

Brunsson, N., & Sahlin-Andersson, K. (2000). Constructing organizations: The example of public sector reform. *Organization Studies*, *21*(4), 721–746. DOI: 10.1177/0170840600214003

Brussel, R. (2025). *Beschikking AR 25/69/C (Antwerp transit ruling)*. https://www.rechtbanken-tribunaux.be

Bruton, G. D., Peng, M. W., Ahlstrom, D., & Stan, C. V. (2021). State-owned enterprises around the world as hybrid organizations. *The Academy of Management Perspectives*, *35*(2), 219–236.

Bryson, J., & George, B. 2020. Strategic management in public administration. In Oxford research encyclopedia: politics (pp. 1–26). DOI: DOI: 10.1093/acrefore/9780190228637.013.139

Bryson, J. M. (2004). *Strategic planning for public and nonprofit organizations: A guide to strengthening and sustaining organizational achievement* (3rd ed.). Jossey-Bass.

Bryson, J. M., Crosby, B. C., & Bloomberg, L. (2014). *Public value and public administration*. Georgetown University Press.

Bryson, J. M., Crosby, B. C., & Bryson, J. K. (2009). Understanding strategic planning and the formulation and implementation of strategic plans as a way of knowing: The contributions of actor-network theory. *International Public Management Journal*, *12*(2), 172–207. DOI: 10.1080/10967490902873473

Bryson, J. M., Cunningham, G. L., & Lokkesmoe, K. J. (2002). What to do when stakeholders matter: The case of problem formulation for the African American Men Project of Hennepin County, Minnesota. *Public Administration Review*, *62*(5), 568–584. DOI: 10.1111/1540-6210.00238

Buchanan, D., Fitzgerald, L., Ketley, D., Gollop, R., Jones, J. L., Lamont, S. S., Neath, A., & Whitby, E. (2005). No going back: A review of the literature on sustaining organizational change. *International Journal of Management Reviews*, *7*(3), 189–205. DOI: 10.1111/j.1468-2370.2005.00111.x

Bundesministerium für Wirtschaft und Klimaschutz. (2019, June 26). *Politische Grundsätze der Bundesregierung für den Export von Kriegswaffen und sonstigen Rüstungsgütern.* https://www.bmwk.de

Bundesverfassungsgericht. (2014, October 21). *2 BvE 5/11 – Informationsrecht der Bundestagsabgeordneten über Rüstungsexporte.* https://www.bundesverfassungsgericht.de

Burke, W. W. (2018). *Organization change: Theory and practice* (5th ed.). Sage Publications.

Burnes, B. (2004). Emergent change and planned change–competitors or allies? The case of XYZ construction. *International Journal of Operations & Production Management, 24*(9), 886–902. DOI: 10.1108/01443570410552108

Burnes, B., Hughes, M., & By, R. T. (2018). Reimagining organisational change leadership. *Leadership, 14*(2), 141–158.

By, R. T. (2005). Organisational change management: A critical review. *Journal of Change Management, 5*(4), 369–380. DOI: 10.1080/14697010500359250

By, R. T., Burnes, B., & Oswick, C. (2016). Change management: Leadership, values and ethics. *Journal of Change Management, 12*(1), 1–5. DOI: 10.1080/14697017.2011.652371

By, R. T., Kuipers, B. S., & Proctor, S. (2023). Understanding change in public organizations: The role of leadership and culture. *Journal of Organizational Change Management, 36*(2), 213–229.

Caiden, G. (1976). Implementation - the Achilles Heel of Administrative Reform. In *The management of change in goverment* (pp. 142–164). MARTINUS NIJHOFF. DOI: 10.1007/978-94-010-1383-3_6

Cameron, E., & Green, M. (2019). *Making sense of change management: A complete guide to the models, tools and techniques of organizational change* (5th ed.). Kogan Page.

Cameron, K. S., & Quinn, R. E. (2011). *Diagnosing and changing organizational culture: Based on the competing values framework* (3rd ed.). Jossey-Bass.

Casey-Maslen, S. (2016). *The Arms Trade Treaty: A commentary.* Oxford University Press.

Casey-Maslen, S., Clapham, A., Giacca, G., & Parker, S. (2016). *The Arms Trade Treaty: A Commentary.* Oxford University Press.

Cavatorto, S., & La Spina, A. (2020). The Politics of Public Administration Reform in Italy. Cham: The Politics of Public Administration Reform in Italy.

Centre for European Reform. (2023). *EU arms export controls: Balancing sovereignty and responsibility.* https://cer.eu

Cepiku, D., Giordano, F., Boviatsou, A., & Tcherning, K. (2016). The second wave of performance management reforms in Southern Europe: Weberian bureaucracy and the Greek case. *Public Organization Review, 16*(1), 81–97.

Chabih, Y. (2018). L'hôpital public au Maroc: Entre transition institutionnelle et recomposition des pratiques professionnelles. *Revue Francophone Internationale de Recherche Infirmière, 4*(3), 134–145.

Chachko, E. (2020). Revisiting judicial review in foreign affairs. *Harvard Law School Program on International Law and Armed Conflict Research Paper.* https://doi.org/DOI: 10.2139/ssrn.3607463

Chandler, A. D., & Behar, J. M. (1992). *Organisation et performance des entreprises.* Les Éditions d'Organisation.

Charalabidis, Y., Lampathaki, F., & Askounis, D. (2015). A comparative analysis of national interoperability frameworks. In Janssen, M., Scholl, H. J., Wimmer, M. A., & Tan, Y. (Eds.), *Electronic Government and Electronic Participation: Joint Proceedings of Ongoing Research and Projects of IFIP EGOV and EPart 2015* (pp. 91–98). IOS Press.

Charbonneau, M. (2012). Nouveau management public. Le Dictionnaire encyclopédique de l'administration publique, www.dictionnaire.enap.ca

Charnes, A., Cooper, W. W., & Rhodes, E. (1978). Measuring the efficiency of decision making units. *European Journal of Operational Research, 2*(6), 429–444. DOI: 10.1016/0377-2217(78)90138-8

Cheung, A. B., & Low, D. (2023). Crisis management and administrative reforms: lessons from Hong Kong and Singapore. In S. F. Goldfinch (Ed.), Handbook of Public Administration Reform (pp. 182-206). Cheltenham·Northampton: Edward Elgar. DOI: 10.4337/9781800376748.00015

Chib, S., Mehta, A. K., Saravanan, A., Mishra, B. R., & Manjunath, T. C. (2025). Mental health challenges and solutions in high-pressure work environments. In Harriott, S. (Ed.), *Innovative approaches to managing conflict and change in diverse work environments* (pp. 247–272). IGI Global Scientific Publishing., DOI: 10.4018/979-8-3693-9556-1.ch011

Chiu, M., & Salerno, H. (2019). *Change Change Management. An open-source approach*. Gartner.

Choi, M., & Ruona, W. E. (2011). Individual readiness for organizational change and its implications for human resource and organization development. *Human Resource Development Review, 10*(1), 46–73. DOI: 10.1177/1534484310384957

Chowdhary, S., Selvakumar, P., Sangeetha, B., Sarvaani, V. V., Anute, N., & Sharma, M. (2025). The role of social capital in entrepreneurial development. In Martínez-Falcó, J., Sánchez-García, E., & Marco-Lajara, B. (Eds.), *Support networks for entrepreneurs: Social capital and strategic collaborations* (pp. 311–338). IGI Global Scientific Publishing., DOI: 10.4018/979-8-3693-9836-4.ch013

Christensen, T., & Lægreid, P. (2007). The Whole-of-Government Approach to Public Sector Reform. *Public Administration Review, 67*(6), 1059–1066. DOI: 10.1111/j.1540-6210.2007.00797.x

Christensen, T., & Lægreid, P. (2020). The rise of the post-NPM regime. *Administration & Society, 52*(2), 247–271.

Christensen, T., & Lægreid, P. (2020). The rise of the post-NPM regime: Lessons from international public sector reform. *Administration & Society, 52*(2), 247–271.

Christensen, T., & Lægreid, P. (2020). *The Routledge Handbook of Public Sector Reforms*. Routledge.

Christiansen, H., & Kim, H. (2020). State-owned enterprises and the pursuit of public value. *OECD Corporate Governance Working Papers*, No. 15, OECD.

Christodoulakis, N. (2018). Public enterprises in Greece: Governance reforms and fiscal performance'. *South European Society & Politics, 23*(4), 493–512.

Christofoletti, R. (2021). Transparency, innovation, and journalism. In Stahl, B. C., & Coeckelbergh, M. (Eds.), *Innovation reconsidered: Ethics and values in a digital world* (pp. 125–138). Wiley., DOI: 10.1002/9781119730767.ch6

Cinite, I., Duxbury, L. E., & Higgins, C. (2009). Measurement of perceived organizational readiness for change in the public sector. *British Journal of Management, 20*(2), 265–277. DOI: 10.1111/j.1467-8551.2008.00582.x

CJEU. (2017). *Case C-455/14 P, H v. Council and Commission, Judgment of 30 May 2017.*

CMI (Change Management Institute). (2019). *The Organizational Change Maturity Model*. Change Management Institute.

Coates, J. M., Santhanalakshmi, K., Dinesh, N., Gandhimathi, S., Chandel, P. S., & Mohit. (2025). Assessment and evaluation in transnational staff development. In G. Morris & J. Ye (Eds.), *Training and development in transnational higher education* (pp. 387–406). IGI Global Scientific Publishing. DOI: 10.4018/979-8-3373-1897-4.ch019

Coch, L., & French, J. R. P.Jr. (1948). Overcoming resistance to change. *Human Relations*, *1*(4), 512–532. DOI: 10.1177/001872674800100408

Cohen, N. (2023). Public administration reform and political will in cases of political instability: Insights from the Israeli experience. *Public Policy and Administration*, *38*(4), 405–423. DOI: 10.1177/09520767221076059

Cohen, W. M., & Levinthal, D. A. (1990). Absorptive capacity: A new perspective on learning and innovation. *Administrative Science Quarterly*, *35*(1), 128–152. DOI: 10.2307/2393553

Cole, A., & Eymeri-Douzans, J.-M. (2010). Introduction: Administrative reforms and mergers in Europe - research questions and empirical challenges. International Review of Administrative Sciences, 76(3), σσ. 395-406. DOI: 10.1177/0020852310373881

Conklin, J. (2006). *Wicked problems and social complexity*. CogNexus Institute.

Contini, F., Anleu, S. R., & Rottman, D. B. (2014). Evaluating Judicial Performance: Editors' Introduction. *Oñati Socio-Legal Series*, *4*(5), 836–842.

Cops, D. (2019). *Strengthening EU transparency on arms exports: Ways forward.* Vlaams Vredesinstituut.

Council Common Position 2008/944/CFSP of 8 December 2008.

Council of the European Union. (2008). *Council Common Position 2008/944/CFSP defining common rules governing control of exports of military technology and equipment*. Official Journal of the European Union.

Council of the European Union. (2023–2025). *EU position on the situation in the Middle East*. https://www.consilium.europa.eu/

Council of the European Union. (2024). *Council conclusions on the review of the Common Position on arms exports (2008/944/CFSP).*

Council of the European Union. (2025a). *Council Decision (CFSP) 2025/779 of 14 April 2025 amending Common Position 2008/944/CFSP.*

Council of the European Union. (2025b). *Council Conclusions on arms export control (7534/25).*

Council of the European Union. (2025c). *User's Guide to the Common Position on arms exports.*

Court of Appeal of The Hague. (2024, February 12). ECLI *[Oxfam Novib et al. v. The State of the Netherlands]. NL:GHDHA, 2024*, 191.

Court of Appeal, The Hague. (2024, February 12). *Case No. 200.327.006/01, Judgment.*

Cremona, M. (2017). Structural principles and their role in EU external relations law. *Common Market Law Review*, *54*(1).

Crosby, B. C., & Bryson, J. M. (2010). Integrative leadership and the creation and focus of governing for networks. *The Leadership Quarterly*, *21*(2), 231–245.

Cuervo-Cazurra, A., Inkpen, A., Musacchio, A., & Ramaswamy, K. (2020). Governments as owners: State-owned multinational companies. *Journal of International Business Studies*, *51*(9), 1374–1396.

Cunha, M. P., & Tsoukas, H. (2015). Reforming the state: Understanding the vicious circles of reform. European Management Journal, 33(4), σσ. 225-229. DOI: 10.1016/j.emj.2015.05.001

Dalakou, V. (2022). Digital Transparency and Openness in the Contemporary Regulatory Framework for Digital Governance: Challenges and Opportunities for the Greek Public Administration. Public Administration and Digital Governance, 1, pp. 39-54. Athens: Association of Students of PA-EAP. Retrieved October 2, 2024, from https://heyzine.com/flip-book/ddfb84e80b.html

Dalakou, V. (2022). Modern Legislation and Administrative Control Institutions: Complementarity with Respect to Ethics and Deontology Rules. In Proceedings of Two-Day Conference: Ethics and Deontology in Public Administration. Necessity and Prospects, 1-2 October, Association of Students PA-EAP (pp. 157-164). Athens: Association of Students PA-EAP.

Dan, S., & Pollitt, C. (2015). NPM Can Work: An optimistic review. *Public Management Review*, *17*(9), 1305–1332. DOI: 10.1080/14719037.2014.908662

Dator, J., Pratt, D., & Seo, Y. (2006). *Fairness, Globalization, and Public Institutions. East Asia and Beyond.* University of Hawai'i Press. DOI: 10.2307/j.ctv3zp081

Daviotis, F., Belias, D., & Ntalakos, A. (2025). Organizational Commitment, Organizational Culture and Readiness for Change: Case study – Prevention Centers for Addiction and Promotion [in Greek]. *Epitheorisi Dimosias Dioikisis*, *5*(1), 1–24.

De Sousa, M., & Schwengber, S. (2005). Efficiency estimates for judicial services in Brazil: Nonparametric FDH (Free Disposal Hull) and the expected order-M efficiency scores for Rio Grande Do Sul courts. *Encontro da anpec, 33th.*

Dekkaki, A. C., & Elhamma, A. (2024). The contribution and impact of management control on the performance of public hospitals in Morocco: Moving beyond the" New Public Management. *Revue Internationale du Chercheur, 5*(2).

Demeestère, R. (2002). *Le contrôle de gestion dans le secteur public.* LGDJ.

Denhardt, J., & Denhardt, R. (2015). *The new public service: Serving, not steering* (4th ed.). Routledge.

Denis, J. L., Ferlie, E., & Van Gestel, N. (2015). Understanding hybridity in public organizations. *Public Administration, 93*(2), 273–289. DOI: 10.1111/padm.12175

Dent, M. (2003). *Remodelling hospitals and health professions in Europe: Medicine, nursing and the state.* Palgrave Macmillan. DOI: 10.1057/9781403938411

Diefenbach, T. (2009). New public management in public sector organizations: The dark sides of managerialistic enlightenment. *Public Administration, 87*(4), 892–909. DOI: 10.1111/j.1467-9299.2009.01766.x

DiFonzo, N., & Bordia, P. (1998). A tale of two corporations: Managing uncertainty during organizational change. *Human Resource Management, 37*(3-4), 295–303. DOI: 10.1002/(SICI)1099-050X(199823/24)37:3/4<295::AID-HRM10>3.0.CO;2-3

DiMaggio, P. J., & Powell, W. W. (1983). The iron cage revisited: Institutional isomorphism and collective rationality in organizational fields. *American Sociological Review, 48*(2), 147–160. DOI: 10.2307/2095101

Dolowitz, D., & Marsh, D. (2000). Learning from Abroad: The Role of Policy Transfer in Contemporary Policy-Making. Governance, 13, σσ. 5-23. DOI: 10.1111/0952-1895.00121

Domstoladministrasjonen (2022). Årsmelding 2021, Domstoladministrasjonen, Trondheim. available at: https://www.regjeringen.no/contentassets/bae078d2e3f44d97bafd4f2af5e07614/arsmelding_2021_domstoladministrasjonen1785613.pdf

Droege, C., & Casey-Maslen, S. (2012). Arms transfers and IHL. *International Review of the Red Cross, 94*(885).

Dunleavy, P., & Carrera, L. (2020). *Growing the productivity of government services.* Edward Elgar.

Dunleavy, P., Margetts, H., Bastow, S., & Tinkler, J. (2006). *Digital-era governance: IT corporations, the state, and e-government.* Oxford University Press. DOI: 10.1093/acprof:oso/9780199296194.001.0001

Dunleavy, P., Margetts, H., Bastow, S., & Tinkler, J. (2006). New Public Management Is Dead—Long Live Digital-Era Governance. *Journal of Public Administration: Research and Theory, 16*(3), 467–494. DOI: 10.1093/jopart/mui057

ECCHR. (2024). *Preliminary injunction against surveillance technology exports to Israel.*

ECCHR. (2025). *Legal actions on German arms exports to Israel.* ECCHR.

EEAS. (2023). *Foreign Affairs Council conclusions on the Middle East (November 2023).*

EEAS. (2024). *EU statement at the UN Security Council – Situation in the Middle East, including the Palestinian question (March 2024).*

Eeckhout, P. (2021). *EU external relations law* (3rd ed.). Oxford University Press.

EJIL. Talk! (Zwanenburg, M., & Voetelink, J.). (2024, February 16). *Appeals judgment in case concerning shipment from the Netherlands of parts for F-35 fighter aircraft to Israel.* https://www.ejiltalk.org

El Aoufi, N., & Bensaïd, M. (2015). Modernisation des services publics au Maroc: entre injonction managériale et inertie institutionnelle.

Elhamma, A. (2025), "Exploring the main determinants of the balanced scorecard as a managerial innovation: Evidence from Moroccan companies", Martínez-Falcó, J., Sánchez-García, E., & Marco-Lajara, B. (Eds.), Research and development practices in innovation, IGI Global, Hershey, PA, pp. 83-102. https://doi.org/DOI: 10.4018/979-8-3373-0812-8.ch004

Elhamma, A., & El-Moumane, R. (2025), "The role of strategic planning in resilience and crisis management: A case study of a public organization in Morocco", Rouco, J.C. & Figueiredo, P.C. (Eds.), Enhancing resilience in business continuity management, IGI Global, Hershey, PA, pp. 433-460. https://doi.org/DOI: 10.4018/979-8-3693-8809-9.ch015

Elhamma, A., & Loukili, Z. (2025), "Emergence of public-private partnership policies: A comparative study of Morocco and France", Baporikar, N. (Ed.), Public private partnerships for social development and impact, IGI Global, Hershey, PA, pp. 155-178. https://doi.org/DOI: 10.4018/979-8-3373-3471-4.ch007

Elhamma, A., & Snoussi, N. (2026), "Challenges to the adoption of the balanced scorecard as a managerial innovation in Moroccan SMEs", Jamil, G.L., Jamil, L.C., Paletta, F.C., Geada, N., & Vieira, A.A.P. (Eds.), Innovation management for disruptive maturity in competitive scenarios, IGI Global, Hershey, PA, pp. 249-272. https://doi.org/DOI: 10.4018/979-8-3693-4030-1.ch011

Elhamma, A. (2023). The relationship between organisational decentralisation, balanced scorecard, and its perceived benefits in Moroccan SMEs. International Journal of Accounting. *Auditing and Performance Evaluation*, *19*(2), 185–202. DOI: 10.1504/IJAAPE.2023.132384

El-Moumane, R. (2026), "The impact of IPSAS on the quality of financial reporting in public sector organizations: An empirical study", Elhamma, A. (Ed.), Adoption, impact, and challenges of international financial reporting standards, IGI Global, Hershey, PA, pp. 247-276. https://doi.org/DOI: 10.4018/979-8-3373-1902-5.ch009

Elving, W. J. (2005). The role of communication in organisational change. *Corporate Communications*, *10*(2), 129–138. DOI: 10.1108/13563280510596943

Esposito, G., Lanau, M. S., & Pompe, S. (2014). *Judicial system reform in Italy-A key to growth*. International Monetary Fund. DOI: 10.5089/9781475573022.001

European Commission. (2019). The Quality of Public Administration: A Toolbox for Public Administration Professionals (2nd ed.). (F. Hauser, Ed., & A. Karvounis, Trans.) Athens: Ministry of Interior. Retrieved November 26, 2024, from https://www.ypes.gr/wp-content/uploads/2019/12/Q_P_A_Final.pdf

European Commission. (2021). *Public administration reforms in Greece during the economic adjustment programmes: 2010-2018. Discussion Paper 167*. Publications Office of the European Union.

European Commission. (2022). *State-Owned Enterprises in the EU: Overview and Trends*. European Commission.

European Commission. (2023c). *Report on Migration and Asylum 2022*. European Commision.

European Commission. (2024). The Digital Decade of Europe: Digital. *Targets, 2030*, •••. Retrieved October 23, 2024, from https://commission.europa.eu/strategy-and-policy/priorities-2019-2024/europe-fit-digital-age/europes-digital-decade-digital-targets-2030_el

European Council. (2014). *Council conclusions on the Middle East Peace Process, 22 July 2014*. General Secretariat.

European Council. (2023). *Council conclusions on the Middle East, October 2023.* General Secretariat.

European Parliament. (2020). *Recommendations for a transparent and detailed reporting system on arms exports within the EU and to third countries.*

European Parliament. (2023, July 6). *Resolution 2023/2739(RSP).*

European Parliament. (2024). *Implementation of the Common Position on arms exports.*

European Parliament. (2024). *Report on arms export control in the European Union.*

European Parliament. (2024). Shaping Digital Transformation: Explaining the EU Strategy. Retrieved October 23, 2024, from https://www.europarl.europa.eu/topics/el/article/20210414STO02010/diamorfosi-psifiakou-metaschimatismou-epexigisi-tis-stratigikis-tis-ee

Eurostat (2021). *Manual on Government Deficit and Debt.* Luxembourg: Eurostat.

Evans, P. B., Rueschemeyer, D., & Skocpol, T. (Eds.). (1985). *Bringing the state back in.* Cambridge: Cambridge University Press.

Falavigna, G., Ippoliti, R., & Ramello, G. B. (2018). DEA-based Malmquist productivity indexes for understanding courts reform. *Socio-Economic Planning Sciences, 62*, 31–43. DOI: 10.1016/j.seps.2017.07.001

Farazmand, A. (1999). Administrative reform in global perspectives: A symposium. *International Journal of Public Administration, 22*(6), 805–816. DOI: 10.1080/01900699908525405

Farazmand, A. (2001). *Administrative Reform in Developing Nations.* Bloomsbury Publishing.

Featherstone, K. (2015). External conditionality and the debt crisis: The 'Troika' and public administration reform in Greece. *Journal of European Public Policy, 22*(3), 295–314. DOI: 10.1080/13501763.2014.955123

Featherstone, K. (2022). *Prime Ministers in Greece: The Paradox of Power.* Oxford University Press.

Featherstone, K., & Papadimitriou, D. (2020). *The Limits of Europeanization: Reform Capacity and Public Policy in Greece* (2nd ed.). Palgrave Macmillan.

Ferlie, E. (1996). *The new public management in action.* Oxford university press.

Ferlie, E., Ashburner, L., Fitzgerald, L., & Pettigrew, A. (1996). *The New Public Management in Action.* Oxford University Press. DOI: 10.1093/acprof:oso/9780198289029.001.0001

Fernandez, C. B., & Hui, P. (2022). Life, the metaverse and everything: An overview of privacy, ethics, and governance in metaverse. In *2022 IEEE 42nd International Conference on Distributed Computing Systems (ICDCS)* (pp. 1515–1524). IEEE. https://doi.org/DOI: 10.1109/ICDCS54860.2022.00192

Fernandez, S., & Rainey, H. G. (2017). Managing successful organizational change in the public sector. *Public Administration Review, 77*(6), 789–803.

Ferrandino, J. A. (2010). Integrating Theory, Practice and Policy The Technical Efficiency And Productivity Of Florida's Circuit Courts. Doctoral Dissertation. University of Central Florida, *Electronic Theses and Dissertations.* 1610. available at: https://stars.library.ucf.edu/etd/1610

Ferreira, N. (2022). Rights-based litigation and the external dimension of EU law. *European Constitutional Law Review, 18*(4), 665–692.

Ferro, G., Romero, C. A., & Romero-Gómez, E. (2018). Efficient courts? A frontier performance assessment. *Benchmarking, 25*(9), 3443–3458. DOI: 10.1108/BIJ-09-2017-0244

Finocchiaro Castro, M., & Guccio, C. (2014). Searching for the source of technical inefficiency in Italian judicial districts: An empirical investigation. *European Journal of Law and Economics, 38*(3), 369–391. DOI: 10.1007/s10657-012-9329-0

Flick, U. (2014). *An Introduction to Qualitive Research* (5th ed.). SAGE Publications Ltd.

Florio, M., & Fecher, F. (2021). The future of public enterprises: Mission-oriented ownership and governance. *Annals of Public and Cooperative Economics, 92*(2), 187–205.

Flynn, N., & Talbot, C. (1996). Strategy and strategists in UK local government. *Journal of Management Development, 15*(2), 24–37. DOI: 10.1108/02621719610109186

Flyvbjerg, B. (2006). Five misunderstandings about case-study research. Qualitative Inquiry, 12(2), σσ. 219-245. DOI: 10.1177/1077800405284363

Ford, J. D., Ford, L. W., & D'Amelio, A. (2008). Resistance to change: The rest of the story. *Academy of Management Review, 33*(2), 362–377. DOI: 10.5465/amr.2008.31193235

Forum on the Arms Trade. (2024). *Post-shipment verification and end-use monitoring in arms transfer control.*

Forum on the Arms Trade. (2024, January 17). *The 2024 review of the EU Common Position on arms exports: An opportunity for stronger cooperation on post-shipment controls?* Herrmann, L., & Mirbach, A. (2024, July 23). Berlin Administrative Court rejects pre-emptive interim relief against German weapons exports to Israel. *German Practice in International Law.*

Fountain, J. E. (2001). *Building the virtual state: Information technology and institutional change.* Brookings Institution Press.

Frankfurt am Main, V. (2024). *Press Release No. 20/2024 – Military goods for Israel.*

Frankfurt am Main, V. (2024, December 16). *5 L 2333/24.F – Rüstungsgüter für Israel.* https://verwaltungsgerichtsbarkeit.hessen.de

Fung, A. (2015). Putting the public back into governance: The challenges of citizen participation and its future. *Public Administration Review, 75*(4), 513–522. DOI: 10.1111/puar.12361

Gagnon, M. P., Attieh, R., Ghandour, E. K., Légaré, F., Ouimet, M., Estabrooks, C. A., & Roch, G. (2014). A systematic review of instruments to assess organizational readiness for knowledge translation in health care. *PLoS One, 9*(12), e114338. DOI: 10.1371/journal.pone.0114338 PMID: 25474622

Gauzente, C. (2000). Mesurer la performance des entreprises en l'absence d'indicateurs objectifs: Quelle validité? Analyse de la pertinence de certains indicateurs. *Finance Contrôle Stratégie, 3*(2), 145–165.

Gekas, R., Goupios, G., & Koutsouri, D. (2022). The Reform Technique through the Historical Evolution of Administrative Reforms 1975-2020. Athens: ELIAMEP - E.E.T.A.A.

General Secretariat for Coordination. (2024). Greece 2.0 | National Recovery and Resilience Plan. Retrieved October 23, 2024, from https://gsco.gov.gr/rrp-reforms/

General Secretariat for Coordination. (2024a). National Reform Program. Retrieved October 23, 2024, from https://gsco.gov.gr/nrp/

George, B., Walker, R. M., & Monster, J. (2019). Does strategic planning improve organizational performance? A meta-analysis. *Public Administration Review, 79*(6), 810–819. DOI: 10.1111/puar.13104

Gerechtshof Den Haag. (2024). *ECLI:NL:GHDHA:2024:191 (Oxfam Novib et al. v. The State of the Netherlands).* Rechtspraak. https://uitspraken.rechtspraak.nl

Gianluca, L., & Giovanni, C. (2025). The Process of 'Capacity Building' in the Public Administration: Artificial Intelligence, Transparency and New Models of the Administrative Decision. *Frontiers in Political Science, 7,* 1605729. Advance online publication. DOI: 10.3389/fpos.2025.1605729

Giannakos, K., Belias, D., Ntalakos, A., & Rossidis, I. (2024). Change Management and Communication Satisfaction: Adopting Effective Change Management Strategies for Enhancing Communication Satisfaction, Chapter 12 in "*Organizational Behavior and Human Resource Management for Complex Work Environments*". Publisher: IGI Global, pp. 221-241.

Giannakos, K., Belias, D., Ntalakos, A., Rossidis, I., & Koustelios, A. (2024c). Are leadership styles related to change integration and commitment? The case of general hospitals in the area of Thessaly (Greece). *Archives of Hellenic Medicine/ Arheia Ellenikes Iatrikes*, 41(3).

Giannakos, K., Belias, D., Ntalakos, A., Rossidis, I., & Koustelios, A. (2024). Are Leadership Styles related to Change Integration and Commitment? The case of General Hospitals. *Archives of Hellenic Medicine, 41*(3).

Gilley, A., Dixon, P., & Gilley, J. W. (2008). Characteristics of leadership effectiveness: Implementing change and driving innovation in organizations. *Human Resource Development Quarterly, 19*(2), 153–169. DOI: 10.1002/hrdq.1232

Gill, R. (2003). Change management—Or change leadership? *Journal of Change Management, 3*(4), 307–318. DOI: 10.1080/714023845

Gill, R. D., Lazos, S. R., & Waters, M. M. (2011). Are judicial performance evaluations fair to women and minorities? A cautionary tale from Clark County, Nevada. *Law & Society Review, 45*(3), 731–759. DOI: 10.1111/j.1540-5893.2011.00449.x

Goldfinch, S. (2007). Pessimism, computer failure, and information systems development in the public sector. *Public Administration Review, 67*(5), 917–929. DOI: 10.1111/j.1540-6210.2007.00778.x

Golia, A. J. (2021). Judicial review, foreign relations and global administrative law: The administrative function of courts in foreign relations. In Aust, H. P., & Kleinlein, T. (Eds.), *Encounters between foreign relations law and international law: Bridges and boundaries* (pp. 130–158). Cambridge University Press., DOI: 10.1017/9781108942713.008

Goula, A., Kefis, V., Dimakou, S., Pierrakos, G., & Sarris, M. (2014). Organizational change in the public hospital. From bureaucratic participatory management style. *Archives of Hellenic Medicine, 31*(5), 583–590.

Gow, J. I. (2012). “Administrative Reform”. In L. Côté, & J.-F. Savard (Eds.), Encyclopedic Dictionary of Public Administration. Quebec City: École nationale d'administration publique. Retrieved 9 26, 2024, from https://dictionnaire.enap.ca/Dictionnaire/en/home.aspx

Graaf, G., Hengeveld-Bidmon, E., Carnochan, S., Salomone, M., & Austin, M. J. (2019). Change communication in public sector cutback management. *Public Organization Review, 19*(4), 453–472. DOI: 10.1007/s11115-018-0408-8

Graziano, P. R., & Vink, M. P. (2013). Europeanization: Concept, Theory, and Methods. In Bulmer, S., & Lequesne, C. (Eds.), *States of the European Union* (2nd ed., pp. 31–56). Oxford University Press.

Greenwood, R., & Hinings, C. R. (1996). Understanding radical organizational change: Bringing together the old and the new institutionalism. *Academy of Management Review, 21*(4), 1022–1054. DOI: 10.2307/259163

Grifell-Tatjé, E., & Lovell, C. K. (1995). A note on the Malmquist productivity index. *Economics Letters, 47*(2), 169–175. DOI: 10.1016/0165-1765(94)00497-P

Grossi, G., Papenfuß, U., & Tremblay, M. S. (2022). Corporate governance and accountability of state-owned enterprises: Reforms and challenges. *Public Money & Management, 42*(6), 397–406.

Gupta, M., & Bolia, N. B. (2020). Efficiency measurement of Indian high courts using DEA: A policy perspective. *Journal of Policy Modeling, 42*(6), 1372–1393. DOI: 10.1016/j.jpolmod.2020.06.002

Guzowska, M., & Strak, T. (2010). DEA method in examining the efficiency of polish courts. *Transformations in Business & Economics, 9*(1), 1–12.

Haenraets, R., & van Berkel, R. (2021). Sustainable employability in public sector HRM: A comparative study. *Journal of Public Administration: Research and Theory, 29*(2), 112–130. DOI: 10.1093/jopart/muaa032

Hameed, I., Waris, I., & Amin ul Haq, M. (2019). Predicting eco-conscious consumer behavior using theory of planned behavior in Pakistan. *Environmental Science and Pollution Research International, 26*(15), 15535–15547. DOI: 10.1007/s11356-019-04967-9 PMID: 30945077

Hansen, J. R., & Ferlie, E. (2016). Applying strategic management theories in public sector organizations: The importance of context-specificity, ambiguity, and power relations. *Public Management Review, 18*(1), 17–40.

Harfaoui, W., Belyamani, L., Zentar, A., Lekehal, B., & Obtel, M. (2024). The New Reform of the National Health System in Morocco: An Opportunity to Meet the Challenges and Improve the Practice of Anesthesiology.

Harvard Law Review Forum. (2015). Foreign relations law and the purported shift away from exceptionalism. *Harvard Law Review Forum, 128*(105), 105–121. https://harvardlawreview.org/forum/vol-128/foreign-relations-law-and-the-purported-shift-away-from-exceptionalism/

Hassani. K. & EL Moussali N. (2020) «Le New Public Management: quels enjeux pour le système de santé publique au Maroc ? », Revue Internationale des Sciences de Gestion « Numéro 6 / Volume 3: numéro 1 » pp: 454 – 474.

Hassan, S., & Wright, B. E. (2020). The public service motivation causal chain: Personality, socialization, public service motivation, and work outcomes. *International Public Management Journal, 23*(3), 356–379.

Hassen Teufel, P. (2022). Comment les politiques publiques changent-elles? Une perspective pragmatique sur la réforme de l'hôpital. *Revue Française de Science Politique, 72*(2), 267–290.

Hayes, J. (2018). *The theory and practice of change management* (5th ed.). Palgrave Macmillan. DOI: 10.1057/978-1-352-00132-7

HCAP. (2023). *Annual Report 2022*. Hellenic Corporation of Assets and Participations.

Heckman, R., Nimon, K., Chuang, A., & Kinney, T. B. (2021). The relationship between HR capability and business strategy, competitive strategy, and macro-environmental factors. *Personnel Review, 50*(2), 589–603.

Heifetz, R. A., & Linsky, M. (2002). *Leadership on the line: Staying alive through the dangers of leading*. Harvard Business School Press.

Helfrich, C. D., Li, Y. F., Sharp, N. D., & Sales, A. E. (2009). Organizational readiness to change assessment (ORCA): Development of an instrument based on the Promoting Action on Research in Health Services (PARIHS) framework. *Implementation Science : IS, 4*(1), 38. DOI: 10.1186/1748-5908-4-38 PMID: 19594942

Herold, D. M., Fedor, D. B., Caldwell, S., & Liu, Y. (2008). The effects of transformational and change leadership on employees' commitment to a change: A multilevel study. *The Journal of Applied Psychology, 93*(2), 346–357. DOI: 10.1037/0021-9010.93.2.346 PMID: 18361637

Herscovitch, L., & Meyer, J. P. (2002). Commitment to organizational change: Extension of a three-component model. *The Journal of Applied Psychology, 87*(3), 474–487. DOI: 10.1037/0021-9010.87.3.474 PMID: 12090605

Hiatt, J. M. (2006). *ADKAR: A model for change in business, government, and our community*. Prosci Learning Center Publications.

Hiatt, J., & Creasey, T. J. (2012). *Change management: The people side of change* (2nd ed.). Prosci.

Higgs, M., & Rowland, D. (2005). All changes great and small: Exploring approaches to change and its leadership. *Journal of Change Management, 5*(2), 121–151. DOI: 10.1080/14697010500082902

Higgs, M., & Rowland, D. (2011). What does it take to implement change successfully? A study of the behaviors of successful change leaders. *The Journal of Applied Behavioral Science, 47*(3), 309–335. DOI: 10.1177/0021886311404556

Hill, C. W. L., & Jones, G. R. (2013). *Strategic management: An integrated approach* (10th ed.). Cengage Learning.

Hoelseth, D. T. (2024). Endringer i Grunnloven – et helhetlig grunnlovsvern for domstolene, Lovdata, 22. mai 2024. available at: https://lovdata.no/artikkel/endringer_i_grunnloven__et_helhetlig_grunnlovsvern_for_domstolene/4777

Höglund, L., Holmgren Caicedo, M., Mårtensson, M., & Svärdsten, F. (2021). Strategic management accounting in the public sector context: The case of the Swedish Transport Administration. *Journal of Public Budgeting, Accounting & Financial Management, 33*(4), 468–486. DOI: 10.1108/JPBAFM-12-2019-0180

Hoglund, L., Martensson, M., & Thomson, K. (2021). Strategic triangle and public value in Swedish public sector: A longitudinal case study on management control practices. *Accounting, Auditing & Accountability Journal, 34*(7), 1608–1634. DOI: 10.1108/AAAJ-11-2019-4284

Holt, D. T., Armenakis, A. A., Feild, H. S., & Harris, S. G. (2007). Readiness for organizational change: The systematic development of a scale. *The Journal of Applied Behavioral Science, 43*(2), 232–255. DOI: 10.1177/0021886306295295

Holtom, P., & Bromley, M. (2010). *Implementing the EU Common Position on arms exports: Improvements, but more needed.* SIPRI Background Paper.

Hood, C. (1991). A public management for all seasons? *Public Administration, 69*(1), 3–19. DOI: 10.1111/j.1467-9299.1991.tb00779.x

Hood, C. (1995). The "new public management" in the 1980s: Variations on a theme. *Accounting, Organizations and Society*, *20*(2–3), 93–109. DOI: 10.1016/0361-3682(93)E0001-W

Hood, C. (2004). Controlling public services and government: towards a cross-national perspective. In Hood, C., James, O., Peters, B. G., & Scott, C. (Eds.), *Controlling Modern Government. Variety, Commonality and Change* (pp. 3–24). Edward Elgar. DOI: 10.4337/9781845423599.00009

Hooghe, L., & Marks, G. (2016). *Community, scale, and regional governance: A postfunctionalist theory of governance*. Oxford University Press. DOI: 10.1093/acprof:oso/9780198766971.001.0001

Huber, T., Swart, J., & Hecker, A. (2015). Initial impacts of organizational change: Emotions in a technology company. *Team Performance Management*, *21*(5/6), 303–318.

Hughes, M. (2018). *Managing and leading organizational change*. Routledge. DOI: 10.4324/9781351265966

Hupe, P., & Hill, M. (2007). Street-level bureaucracy and public accountability. *Public Administration*, *85*(2), 279–299. DOI: 10.1111/j.1467-9299.2007.00650.x

Hussain, S. T., Lei, S., Akram, T., Haider, M. J., Hussain, S. H., & Ali, M. (2018). Kurt Lewin's change model: A critical review of the role of leadership and employee involvement in organizational change. *Journal of Innovation & Knowledge*, *3*(3), 123–127. DOI: 10.1016/j.jik.2016.07.002

Huy, Q. N. (2001). In praise of middle managers. *Harvard Business Review*, *79*(8), 72–79. PMID: 11550632

IBM. (2024). *What is artificial intelligence (AI)?* Retrieved 8 20, 2025, from https://www.ibm.com/think/topics/artificial-intelligence

ICJ. (2024, January 26). *South Africa v. Israel, Provisional Measures Order*.

Inkina, S. (2022). Comparative Administrative Reforms. In Farazman, A. (Ed.), *Global Encyclopedia of Public Administration, Public Policy, and Governance* (pp. 1942–1949). Springer., DOI: 10.1007/978-3-030-66252-3_1276

International Court of Justice. (2024a, April). [*Nicaragua v. Germany.*]. *Order*, •••, 30.

International Court of Justice. (2024b). [*Nicaragua v. Germany] [Docket]. CASE (Philadelphia, Pa.)*, •••, 193.

Jackson, G. A. (1982). Public efficiency and private choice in higher education. *Educational Evaluation and Policy Analysis, 4*(2), 237–247. DOI: 10.3102/01623737004002237

Jacobs, G., van Witteloostuijn, A., & Christe-Zeyse, J. (2013). A theoretical framework of organizational change. *Journal of Organizational Change Management, 26*(5), 772–792. DOI: 10.1108/JOCM-09-2012-0137

Jacobs, S. R., Weiner, B. J., Reeve, B. B., Hofmann, D. A., Christian, M., & Weinberger, M. (2015). Determining the predictors of innovation implementation in healthcare: A quantitative analysis of implementation effectiveness. *BMC Health Services Research, 15*(1), 6. DOI: 10.1186/s12913-014-0657-3 PMID: 25608564

JD. (2022). Forslag om å gjeninnføre strukturen i domstolene sendes på høring, Justis- og beredskapsdepartementet, Pressemelding Nr: 6, 26.01.2022. available at: https://www.regjeringen.no/no/aktuelt/forslag-om-a-gjeninnfore-strukturen-i-domstolene-sendes-pa-horing/id2898552/

Jensen, U. T., Andersen, L. B., & Holten, A. L. (2019). Explaining a dark side: Public service motivation, presenteeism, and absenteeism. *Review of Public Personnel Administration, 39*(4), 487–510. DOI: 10.1177/0734371X17744865

Johnsen, Å. (2016). Strategic management in a complex world: Perspectives on knowledge creation and strategy process in Norwegian municipalities. *International Review of Administrative Sciences, 82*(3), 517–534.

Johnson, D. (2015). Technology with No Human Responsibility? *Journal of Business Ethics, 127*(4), 707–715. DOI: 10.1007/s10551-014-2180-1

Jones, P. (2012). Inputs, Outputs, Outcomes: Using a misunderstood approach, successfully.

Jones, R. A., Jimmieson, N. L., & Griffiths, A. (2005). The impact of organizational culture and reshaping capabilities on change implementation success: The mediating role of readiness for change. *Journal of Management Studies, 42*(2), 361–386. DOI: 10.1111/j.1467-6486.2005.00500.x

Joyce, P. (2015). *Strategic management in the public sector* (2nd ed.). Routledge. DOI: 10.4324/9781315740355

Judge, T. A., & Piccolo, R. F. (2004). Transformational and transactional leadership: A meta-analytic test of their relative validity. *The Journal of Applied Psychology, 89*(5), 755–768. DOI: 10.1037/0021-9010.89.5.755 PMID: 15506858

Judge, W. Q., & Douglas, T. (2009). Organizational change capacity: The systematic development of a scale. *Journal of Organizational Change Management*, *22*(6), 635–649. DOI: 10.1108/09534810910997041

Justice, E. U. (2024). *The 2024 EU Justice scoreboard, European Union, COM(2024) 950*. Publications Office of the European Union., https://ec.europa.eu/commission/presscorner/detail/en/ip_24_3164

Juul-Sandberg, J. (2016). Reform and development of preparatory proceedings in the Danish civil justice system: towards (even) more efficient courts. *Current Trends in Preparatory Proceedings: A Comparative Study of Nordic and Former Communist Countries*, 81-107.

Kaim, M. (2021). Germany's Middle East policy: Between historical responsibility and current interests. *SWP Research Paper*. Stiftung Wissenschaft und Politik, Berlin.

Kalampokis, E., Tambouris, E., & Tarabanis, K. (2013). Linked open government data analytics. In Wimmer, M., Janssen, M., & Scholl, H. J. (Eds.), *Electronic Government* (pp. 99–110). Springer. DOI: 10.1007/978-3-642-40358-3_9

Kalema, N. L. (2025). *What DOGE Could Mean for the Future of Democracy. Notes from the New Frontier of Power [Blog Series]*. Retrieved 10 10, 2025, from Carr Center for Human Rights Policy, Harvard Kennedy School: https://www.hks.harvard.edu/centers/carr-ryan/our-work/carr-ryan-commentary/what-doge-could-mean-future-democracy#:~:text=divesting%20critical%20capabilities%20and%20skills,%E2%80%9Cmanaged%20services%E2%80%9D%20of%20cloud%20empires

Kalogeropoulou, E., & Karkatsoulis, P. (2022). State-owned enterprises and administrative reform in Greece: Lessons from the crisis. *International Journal of Public Sector Management*, *35*(4), 452–470.

Kalyvas, S., Pagoulatos, G., & Tsoukas, H. (2012). Introduction. In Kalyvas, S., Pagoulatos, G., & Tsoukas, H. (Eds.), *From Stagnation to Forced Adjustment* (pp. 1–8). Columbia University Press.

Kaplan, R. S., & Norton, D. P. (1996). *The balanced scorecard: Translating strategy into action*. Harvard Business School Press.

Kaplan, R. S., & Norton, D. P. (2005). *The balanced scorecard: measures that drive performance* (Vol. 70). Harvard Business Review.

Karamanou, A. (2021). Civil Protection and Risk Management: "The Greek Civil Protection System." Athens: EKDDA. Retrieved October 22, 2024, from https://eclass.ekdd.gr/esdda/modules/document/file.php/KZ_AEID_APP107/%CE%95%CE%9D%CE%9F%CE%A4%CE%97%CE%A4%CE%91%206%20%CF%83%CE%B7%CE%BC%CE%B5%CE%B9%CF%8E%CF%83%CE%B5%CE%B9%CF%82.pdf

Karamouzis, N., & Anastasatos, T. (2024, 3). Lessons from the Greek Crisis. Eurobank research. Economy and Markets, 14(1), pp. 1-38. Retrieved 10 25, 2024, from https://www.eurobank.gr/-/media/eurobank/omilos/oikonomikes-analuseis/oikonomiki-epitheorisi/2019/lessons-from-the-greek-crisis.pdf

Karkatsoulis, P. (2001). Governance as Content and as the Decision-Making Process for Public Affairs. Science and Society. *Review of Political and Ethical Theory*, (7), 205–224. DOI: 10.12681/sas.633

Karkatsoulis, P. (2004). *The State in Transition. From "administrative reform" and "New Public Management" to "Governance."*. I. Sideris.

Karkatsoulis, P. (2004). *The State in Transition: From "Administrative Reform" and "New Public Management" to "Governance."*. I. Sideris.

Karkatsoulis, P. (2010). The crisis effect on performance based budgeting. *Public Administration Quarterly*, *34*(4), 449–469.

Karkatsoulis, P. (2016). Administrative Reform in Greece: Public administration evolves through self-reflection – not borrowed identities. In Dimitropoulos, G., Gromitsaris, A., & Schulte, M. (Eds.), *State Reform for a Better Europe* (pp. 113–160). Duncker & Humblot.

Karkatsoulis, P. (2020). The impact of Covid-19 on Better Regulation agenda. *HAPSc Policy Briefs Series*, *1*(1), 100–106. DOI: 10.12681/hapscpbs.24954

Karkatsoulis, P. (2023). *Crisis and disaster management in the example of Civil Protection*. Ellinoekdotiki.

Karkatsoulis, P. (2023a). *Crisis and Disaster Management in the Example of Civil Protection*. Ellinobooks.

Kassoti, E. (2017). The Council v Front Polisario case: The Court of Justice and international law. *European Papers, 2*(1), 339–356.

Katsimardos, P., & Bouas, K. (2013). Strategic Analysis and Evaluation of Large-Scale Reform Programs: "The Memorandum as a Policy Tool." Athens: Institute for Regulatory Policy Research.

Katsimardos, P., Bouas, K., Rossidis, I., & Babalioutas, L. (2017). Greek crisis: It's not about growth. It's about governance. *International Journal of Current Research, 9*(3).

Kefis V. (2010). Public Enterprises and Public Management in Greece, *Administrative News*, 53.

Kefis, V. (1998). *The Management of Public Enterprises and Organizations. Systematic Approach to its Impacts on the Development of the Greek Economy.* Interbooks Publications.

Kefis, V., & Aspridis, G. (2014). Management and development of the human resource of nongovernmental organizations (NGOs) in Greece. Utopia or reality? *International NGO Journal, 9*(4), 43–52. DOI: 10.5897/INGOJ2014.0289

Kelly, P., & Hofbauer, S. (2023). Methodological Pluralism and the Pursuit. In Parker, L. (Ed.), *Education in the Age of Misnformation. Philosophical and Pedagogical Explorations* (pp. 33–54). Palgrave Macmillan. DOI: 10.1007/978-3-031-25871-8_3

Khemakhem, A. (1976). *La dynamique du contrôle de gestion.* Dunod.

Kickert, W. (2014). Specificity of change management in public organizations: Conditions for successful organizational change in Dutch ministerial departments. *American Review of Public Administration, 44*(6), 693–717. DOI: 10.1177/0275074013483871

Kickert, W., & Randma-Liiv, T. (2017). *Europe Managing the Crisis: The Politics of Fiscal Consolidation.* Routledge.

Kiel, L. D. (1995). *Managing chaos and complexity in government: A new paradigm for managing change, innovation, and organizational renewal.* Jossey-Bass.

Killian, J., & Eklund, N. (2008). Handbook of administrative reform. An international perspective. Boca Rayton: CRC Press-Taylor & Francis Group. DOI: 10.1201/9780849380662

Kirkpatrick, I., Dent, M., & Jespersen, P. K. (2011). The contested terrain of hospital management: Professional projects and healthcare reforms in Denmark. *Current Sociology, 59*(4), 489–506. DOI: 10.1177/0011392111402718

Kittelsen, S. A., & Førsund, F. R. (1992). Efficiency analysis of Norwegian district courts. *Journal of Productivity Analysis, 3*(3), 277–306. DOI: 10.1007/BF00158357

Kjølstad, M. M., Koch, S., & Sunde, J. Ø. (2023). An introduction to Norwegian legal culture. In *Handbook on Legal Cultures: A Selection of the World's Legal Cultures* (pp. 801–848). Springer International Publishing. DOI: 10.1007/978-3-031-27745-0_20

Klafki, A. (2025). Judicial review of foreign administrative action in Germany. *European Public Law*, *31*(1), 35–52. https://kluwerlawonline.com/journalarticle/European%2BPublic%2BLaw/31.1/EURO2025002. DOI: 10.54648/EURO2025002

Klarner, P., Probst, G., & Soparnot, R. (2008). Organizational change capacity in public services: The case of the World Health Organization. *Journal of Change Management*, *8*(1), 57–72. DOI: 10.1080/14697010801937523

Klein, S. M. (1996). A management communication strategy for change. *Journal of Organizational Change Management*, *9*(2), 32–46. DOI: 10.1108/09534819610113720

Klijn, E.-H., & Koppenjan, J. (2016). *Governance networks in the public sector.* Routledge.

Knies, E., Boselie, P., Gould-Williams, J., & Vandenabeele, W. (2021). Strategic human resource management and public sector performance: Context matters. *International Journal of Human Resource Management*, *32*(14), 2432–2444. DOI: 10.1080/09585192.2017.1407088

Knowles, B., Greatbanks, R., & Manville, G. (2013) Scorecards and strategy maps: top ten factors in performance management. In: Third Sector Performance: Management and Finance in Not-for-Profit and Social Enterprises. Gower, Farnham, GB, pp. 189-198.

Kohler, K., & Scharte, B. (2020). Integrating AI into Civil Protection. *CSS Analyses in Security Policy*(260). DOI: 10.3929/ethz-b-000408269

Konstantinidou, A. (2020). The Role of E-Governance and ICT in the Service of the Reform Framework of the Greek Public Administration. Public Administration. Athens: Panteion University of Social and Political Sciences. Retrieved September 26, 2024, from https://www.didaktorika.gr/eadd/bitstream/10442/48868/1/48868.pdf

Kooiman, J., & van Vliet, M. (1993). Governance and public management. In Eliassen, K. A., & Peters, B. G. (Eds.), *Modern governance: New government-society interactions* (pp. 58–72). SAGE Publications.

Kotanidis, S. (2024). *Rules on 'revolving doors' in the EU: Post-mandate restrictions on members of EU institutions and parliamentarians in Member States. In-depth analysis.* European Parliamentary Research Service. Brussels: European Union. Retrieved 9 20, 2025, from https://www.europarl.europa.eu/RegData/etudes/IDAN/2024/762290/EPRS_IDA(2024)762290_EN.pdf

Kotarski, K. (2023, 4 10). The New Era of Polycrisis and How to Tackle it. DOI: 10.53121/ELFFEUJ3

Kotter, J. P. (1996). *Leading change*. Harvard Business School Press.

Kriemadis, A., Rossidis, I., & Belias, D. (2023). *Strategic Human Resources Management as a key element in the implementation of organizational changes. An extensive literature review*. Chapter 1 in "Managing Successful and Ethical Organizational Change", IGI Global.

Kriemadis, A., Rossidis, I., & Belias, D. (2023). Strategic Human Resources Management as a key element in the implementation of organizational changes. An extensive literature review. Chapter 1 in "*Managing Successful and Ethical Organizational Change*", IGI Global. DOI: 10.4018/979-8-3693-0235-4.ch001

Krogh, A. H., & Triantafillou, P. (2024). Developing New Public Governance as a public management reform model. *Public Management Review*, *26*(10), 3040–3056. DOI: 10.1080/14719037.2024.2313539

Ktistaki, S. (1991). Public enterprise and public interest. *Constitution - Foundation for the United States Constitution*, , 297–349.

Kuenzi, M., & Schminke, M. (2009). Assembling fragments into a lens: A review, critique, and proposed research agenda for the organizational work climate literature. *Journal of Management*, *35*(3), 634–717. DOI: 10.1177/0149206308330559

Kuhlmann, S., & Wollmann, H. (2019). *Introduction to comparative public administration: Administrative systems and reforms in Europe* (2nd ed.). Edward Elgar.

Kuipers, B. S., Higgs, M., Kickert, W., Tummers, L., Grandia, J., & Van der Voet, J. (2018). The management of change in public organizations: A literature review. *Public Administration*, *96*(1), 144–171.

Kuipers, B. S., & Van der Voet, J. (2020). Change management in government: Balancing continuity and innovation. *Public Management Review*, *22*(6), 838–856.

Ladner, A., Keuffer, N., & Baldersheim, H. (2019). *Self-rule index for local authorities (1990–2014)*. Routledge.

Lahbib, H. (2024, March 5). *Belgium calls for immediate cease-fire in Gaza [press remarks]*. Anadolu Agency. https://www.aa.com.tr/

Lahjouji, K., & El Menzhi, K. (2018). Le Nouveau Management Public au Maroc, quels apports?

Lalousis, D., & Papalexopoulos, T. (2019). Public enterprise reform in Greece under the adjustment programmes. *South European Society & Politics*, *24*(3), 321–342.

Lambropoulou, E. (2013). Illegal markets in a collapsing economy. In P. Saitta, J. Shapland, & A. Verhage (Eds.), *Getting by or Getting Rich? The Formal, Informal and Criminal Economy in a* (pp. 61-94). Haag: Eleven International Publishing. Retrieved from https://ierp.gr/ergo/erevnes/illegal-markets-in-a-collapsing-economy-el

Lampropoulou, M., & Oikonomou, G. (2018). Theoretical models of public administration and patterns of state reform in Greece. International Review of Administrative Sciences, 84(1), σσ. 101-121. DOI: 10.1177/0020852315611219

Lapsley, I. (2009). New Public Management: The Cruellest Invention of the Human Spirit? *Abacus*, *45*(1), 1–21. DOI: 10.1111/j.1467-6281.2009.00275.x

Lapsley, I., & Miller, P. (Eds.). (2024). *The Resilience of New Public Management.* Oxford University Press. DOI: 10.1093/oso/9780198883814.001.0001

Lapuente, V., & Van de Walle, S. (2020). The effects of new public management on the quality of public services. *Governance: An International Journal of Policy, Administration and Institutions*, *33*(3), 461–475. DOI: 10.1111/gove.12502

Larik, J. (2017). Rosneft: Establishing jurisdiction in the field of CFSP. *Common Market Law Review*, *54*, 925–951.

Lawrence, P. R., & Lorsch, J. W. (1967). *Organization and environment: Managing differentiation and integration.* Harvard Business School Press.

Layne, K., & Lee, J. (2001). Developing fully functional e-government: A four stage model. *Government Information Quarterly*, *18*(2), 122–136. DOI: 10.1016/S0740-624X(01)00066-1

Lazowski, A., & Wessel, R. A. (2020). The juridification of EU foreign policy: Implications for the CJEU's jurisdiction. *European Constitutional Law Review*, *16*(3).

Levin, A. T., Owusu-Boaitey, N., Pugh, S., Fosdick, B. K., Zwi, A. B., Malani, A., Soman, S., Besançon, S., Kashnitsky, I., & Inddy, F. (2022). Assessing the burden of COVID-19 in developing countries: Systematic review, meta-analysis and public policy implications. *BMJ Global Health*, *7*(5), e008477. DOI: 10.1136/bmjgh-2022-008477 PMID: 35618305

Levy, A., & Merry, U. (1986). *Organizational transformation: Approaches, strategies, theories.* Praeger Publishers. DOI: 10.5040/9798400693960

Lewin, A. Y., Morey, R. C., & Cook, T. J. (1982). Evaluating the administrative efficiency of courts. *Omega*, *10*(4), 401–411. DOI: 10.1016/0305-0483(82)90019-6

Lewis, L. K. (2000). Communicating change: Four cases of quality programs. *Journal of Business Communication*, *37*(2), 128–155. DOI: 10.1177/002194360003700201

Lindgren, I., & Van Veenstra, A. F. (2018). Digital government transformation: A case illustrating public e-service development as part of public sector transformation. *In Proceedings of the 19th Annual International Conference on Digital Government Research: Governance in the Data Age* (pp. 1-6). DOI: 10.1145/3209281.3209302

Lindquist, E. A. (2022, 8 29). The digital era and public sector reforms: Transformation or new tools for competing values? Canadian Public Administration, 65(3), σσ. 547-568. DOI: 10.1111/capa.12493

Lines, R. (2004). Influence of participation in strategic change: Resistance, organizational commitment and change goal achievement. *Journal of Change Management, 4*(3), 193–215. DOI: 10.1080/1469701042000221696

Liu, S. (2024). *Research on the Characteristics, Limitations, and Future Directions of Artificial Intelligence.* Applied and Computational Engineering., DOI: 10.54254/2755-2721/97/20241398

Lkhoyaali, B., & Maailif, S. (2023) « Le contrôle de gestion dans le secteur public: quelles spécificités? », Revue du contrôle, de la comptabilité et de l'audit « Volume 7: numéro 4 » pp: 129-150. Loi organique n° 130-30, WWW.lof.finances.gov.ma

Lo Storto, C., & Goncharuk, A. G. (2017). Efficiency vs Effectiveness: A Benchmarking Study on European Healthcare Systems. *Economics & Sociology (Ternopil), 10*(3), 102–115. DOI: 10.14254/2071-789X.2017/10-3/8

Lodge, M., & Wegrich, K. (2020). *Executive politics in times of crisis.* Palgrave Macmillan.

Loi, M., & Spielkamp, M. (2021). Towards accountability in the use of artificial intelligence for public administrations. In *Proceedings of the 2021 AAAI/ACM Conference on AI, Ethics, and Society* (pp. 760–768). DOI: 10.1145/3461702.3462631

Lok, P., & Crawford, J. (2004). The effect of organisational culture and leadership style on job satisfaction and organisational commitment: A cross-national comparison. *Journal of Management Development, 23*(4), 321–338. DOI: 10.1108/02621710410529785

Lorino, P. (1997). Méthodes et pratiques de la performance: Le guide du pilotage 1re édition. Paris: Editions d'organisation.

Lovell, C. K. (2003). The decomposition of Malmquist productivity indexes. *Journal of Productivity Analysis, 20*(3), 437–458. DOI: 10.1023/A:1027312102834

LTO. (2024a, June 11). *VG Berlin: Anträge gegen Waffenexporte nach Israel unzulässig.*

LTO. (2024b, December 19). *OVG Berlin-Brandenburg: Kein Auskunftsanspruch über Waffenlieferungen an Israel.*

Luhmann, N. (1984). *Soziale Systeme: Grundriß einer allgemeinen Theorie.* Suhrkamp.

Lynn Jr, L. E. (2006). Public management: Old and new. Routledge. Maroc diplomatique « L'audit dans le secteur public, une garantie de l'efficacité et de la reddition de comptes » www. maroc-diplomatique.net

Lynn, L. E. (2001). Globalization and Administrative Reform: What is Happening in Theory? Public Management Review, 3(2), σσ. 191-208. DOI: 10.1080/14616670010029584

Maggeti, M., & Trein, P. (2021). 3). More is less: Partisan ideology, changes of government, and policy integration reforms in the UK. *Policy and Society*, *40*(1), 79–98. DOI: 10.1080/14494035.2021.1908673

Maistros, P. G. (2009). *The Three Waves of Public Administration Reforms in Greece* [1975-2015+]. Papazisis Editions.

Makrydemetres, A., Zervopoulos, P. D., & Pravita, M. E. (2016). Reform of public administration in Greece: Evaluating structural reform of central government departments in Greece. *GreeSE Paper* No. 97. Hellenic Observatory, London School of Economics.

Makrydimitris, A. (2004). *Approaches to Organization Theory* (2nd ed.). Kastaniotis Editions.

Maksimentseva, N. O. (2023). The principles of administrative law vs. the principles of public administration. *Formy Mediatsii ta Yikh Znachennia u Yurydychnii Praktytsi, 6*, 311–321. DOI: 10.32782/chern.v6.2023.18

Maletta, G. (2021). Seeking a responsible arms trade to reduce human rights violations: The case of the EU. *European Review of International Studies*, *8*(1), 77–95.

Maletta, G. (2021). Seeking a responsible arms trade to reduce human suffering in Yemen. *The International Spectator*, *56*(1), 73–91. DOI: 10.1080/03932729.2021.1876862

Malmvig, H. (2015). The European Union and the Israeli–Palestinian conflict: A story of a gap between words and deeds. *European Security*, *24*(3), 422–440.

Manoharan, A. P., Melitski, J., Holzer, M., Kim, S., & Song, M. (2022). E-governance and public trust: A global perspective. *Government Information Quarterly*, *39*(1), 101663.

Manoharan, A. P., Melitski, J., Holzer, M., Kim, S., & Song, M. (2022). E-government and public trust: A global perspective. *Government Information Quarterly*, *39*(1), 101663.

Marchesnay, M. (1991). La PME: Une gestion spécifique. *Économie Rurale (Paris)*, *206*(1), 11–17. DOI: 10.3406/ecoru.1991.4231

Marr, B., & Creelman, J. (2011). *More than a pretty face: A holistic review of the balanced scorecard*. Cranfield School of Management.

Mattsson, P., & Tidanå, C. (2019). Potential efficiency effects of merging the Swedish district courts. *Socio-Economic Planning Sciences*, *67*, 58–68. DOI: 10.1016/j.seps.2018.09.002

Mazzucato, M., & Kattel, R. (2020). COVID-19 and public-sector capacity. *Oxford Review of Economic Policy*, *36*(S1), S256–S269. DOI: 10.1093/oxrep/graa031 PMID: 40504220

McCabe, L. (2015). *Understanding and managing organizational change in the public sector*. Routledge.

McMillan, K., & Perron, A. (2013). Nurses amidst change: The concept of change fatigue offers an alternative perspective on organizational change. *Policy, Politics & Nursing Practice*, *14*(1), 26–32. DOI: 10.1177/1527154413481811 PMID: 23549748

Mehra, J., Madaan, S., & Balu, N. Mohit, & Manjunath, T. C. (2025). The ubiquitous internet and smart computation available 24/7 for anyone and anywhere. In E. Babulak (Ed.), *Educational AI humanoid computing devices for cyber nomads* (pp. 247–270). IGI Global Scientific Publishing. DOI: 10.4018/979-8-3693-8985-0.ch010

Meier, K. J., & O'Toole, L. J.Jr. (2001). Managerial strategies and behavior in networks: A model with evidence from US public education. *Journal of Public Administration: Research and Theory*, *11*(3), 271–294. DOI: 10.1093/oxfordjournals.jpart.a003503

Meijer, H., & Zaslove, A. (2024). Dutch foreign policy after October 7: Balancing values and interests. *Clingendael Spectator*, *78*(1), 12–18.

Men, L. R. (2014). Why leadership matters to internal communication: Linking transformational leadership, symmetrical communication, and employee outcomes. *Journal of Public Relations Research*, *26*(3), 256–279. DOI: 10.1080/1062726X.2014.908719

Mergel, I., Edelmann, N., & Haug, N. (2019). Defining digital transformation: Results from expert interviews. *Government Information Quarterly*, *36*(4), 101385. DOI: 10.1016/j.giq.2019.06.002

Meyer, A. D., Brooks, G. R., & Goes, J. B. (1990). Environmental jolts and industry revolutions: Organizational responses to discontinuous change. *Strategic Management Journal, 11*, 93–110.

Miake-Lye, I. M., Delevan, D. M., Ganz, D. A., Mittman, B. S., & Finley, E. P. (2020). Unpacking organizational readiness for change: An updated systematic review and content analysis of assessments. *BMC Health Services Research, 20*(1), 106. DOI: 10.1186/s12913-020-4926-z PMID: 32046708

Michalopoulos, N. (2003). *From Public Bureaucracy to Public Management.* Papazisis Editions.

Mihiotis, A., Rossidis, I., & Koutsoukis, N. (2023). The effect of digital transformation in the development of Electronic Governance in Cyprus and Greece. A critical review through the analysis of the Digital Economy and Society Index. *The Cyprus Review, 35*(1).

Milanovic, M. (2011). *Extraterritorial application of human rights treaties: Law, principles, and policy.* Oxford University Press. DOI: 10.1093/acprof:oso/9780199696208.001.0001

Mintzberg, H. (1994). *The rise and fall of strategic planning: Reconceiving roles for planning, plans, planners.* The Free Press.

Mintzberg, H. (2004). *Managers Not MBAs: A Hard Look at the Soft Practice of Managing and Management Development.* Berrett-Koehler Publishers.

Mintzberg, H., Ahlstrand, B., & Lampel, J. (2009). *Strategy safari: A guided tour through the wilds of strategic management* (2nd ed.). Prentice Hall.

Moore, M. H. (2019). *Creating Public Value: Strategic Management in Government.* Updated edn. Harvard University Press.

Moore, M. (2014). *Public value: Theory and practice.* Palgrave Macmillan.

Moore, M. H. (1995). *Creating public value: Strategic management in government.* Harvard University Press.

Moore, M. H. (1995). *Creating Public Value: Strategic Management in Government.* Harvard University Press.

Morgan, R. M., & Hunt, S. D. (1994). The commitment-trust theory of relationship marketing. *Journal of Marketing, 58*(3), 20–38. DOI: 10.1177/002224299405800302

Morris, B., & Hodges, J. (2020). Public sector resilience during crises: A comparative analysis. *International Review of Administrative Sciences, 86*(2), 234–251.

Moumene, J., & Benhrimida, M. (2016). La performance de l'Administration Publique Marocaine: Contribution du contrôle de gestion. *Moroccan Journal of Business Studies, 1*(1).

Moynihan, D. P., & Pandey, S. K. (2007). The role of organizations in fostering public service motivation. *Public Administration Review, 67*(1), 40–53. DOI: 10.1111/j.1540-6210.2006.00695.x

Musacchio, A., & Lazzarini, S. G. (2022). State-owned enterprises in the 21st century: New trends and challenges. *Journal of International Business Studies, 53*(6), 1155–1173.

Nafzaoui, H., & Ferdoussi, M. (2024). Hybridation et performance: Étude des réformes hospitalières au Maghreb. *Revue Nord-Africaine de Gestion Publique, 3*(1), 55–74.

Naimi-Sadigh, A., Asgari, T., & Rabiei, M. (2022). Digital transformation in the value chain disruption of banking services. *Journal of the Knowledge Economy, 13*(2), 2915–2934. DOI: 10.1007/s13132-021-00759-0

Najim, I. (2019). Management Public: Du contrôle des dépenses au contrôle de gestion: Processus d'implantation d'un système de contrôle de gestion applicable aux administrations publiques marocaines (Doctoral dissertation, faculté des sciences juridiques économiques et sociales de casablanca-UH2 de casablanca).

Neumann, O., Guirguis, K., & Steiner, R. (2024). Exploring artificial intelligence adoption in public organizations: A comparative case study. *Public Management Review, 26*(8), 1234–1257. DOI: 10.1080/14719037.2022.2048685

Niiranen, V., & Joensuu, S. (2014). Managerial decision-making in public administration: An empirical examination of administrative reform. *International Review of Administrative Sciences, 80*(1), 97–118.

Nikitas, V., & Vasilopoulou, V. (2022). Public Administration Reforms in Greece during the Economic Adjustment Programmes. Brussels: European Commission. Ανάκτηση 10 25, 2024, από https://economy-finance.ec.europa.eu/document/download/97fb3144-72fb-4ec6-aeef-f35edfdf4292_en?filename=dp167_en.pdf

Nisha Angeline, M., Selvakumar, P., Gupta, M. K., Nazar, N., Elumalai, D., & Bhattacharya, S. (2025). Emerging materials for energy storage and environmental applications. In K. Muduli, B. Moharana, S. Ales, & D. Biswal (Eds.), *Using computational intelligence for sustainable manufacturing of advanced materials* (pp. 53–72). IGI Global Scientific Publishing. DOI: 10.4018/979-8-3693-7974-5.ch003

Niskanen, W. (1971). *Bureaucracy and representative government*. Aldine-Atherton.

Nissi, E., Giacalone, M., & Cusatelli, C. (2019). The efficiency of the Italian judicial system: A two stage data envelopment analysis approach. *Social Indicators Research, 146*(1-2), 395–407. DOI: 10.1007/s11205-018-1892-5

Noordegraaf, M. (2007). From "pure" to "hybrid" professionalism: Present-day professionalism in ambiguous public domains. *Administration & Society, 39*(6), 761–785. DOI: 10.1177/0095399707304434

Norman, L. (2007). Controlling financial management: The use of management control systems to manage agency costs. *Journal of Management Control, 18*(2), 125–149.

North, D. (1990). *Institutions, institutional change and economic performance.* Cambridge University Press. DOI: 10.1017/CBO9780511808678

Ntalakos, A., Belias, D., Koustelios, A., & Tsigilis, N. (2022). Organizational culture and group dynamics in the tourism industry. *In Silva, C., Oliveira, M., Silva, S., ICTR 2022 5th International Conference on Tourism Research, Porto, Portugal,* 19-20 May, 2022, 286-293.

Ntalakos, A., Belias, D., Rossidis, I., Koustelios, A., Tsigilis, N., & Vasiliadis, L. (2023). Communicating the Vision of the Change: The Linkage Between Organizational Communication, Organizational Culture, and Organizational Change. Chapter 4 in "*Managing Successful and Ethical Organizational Change*", IGI Global.

Ntalakos, A., Belias, D., Rossidis, I., Koustelios, A., Tsigilis, N., & Vasiliadis, L. (2023). *Communicating the Vision of the Change: The Linkage Between Organizational Communication, Organizational Culture, and Organizational Change.* Chapter 4 in "Managing Successful and Ethical Organizational Change", IGI Global. DOI: 10.4018/979-8-3693-0235-4.ch004

Nuti, S., Vainieri, M., & Bonini, A. (2021). Public value in health care: A new approach to performance measurement. *Health Policy (Amsterdam), 125*(2), 167–172.

O'Flynn, J. (2021). From New Public Management to public value: Paradigmatic change and managerial implications. *Australian Journal of Public Administration, 80*(4), 741–755.

OECD. (2006). *OECD Journal on Budgeting.* Public Governance and Territorial Development Directorate, OECD. Paris: OECD Publishing. Retrieved 9 20, 2025, from https://www.oecd.org/content/dam/oecd/en/publications/reports/2007/05/oecd-journal-on-budgeting-volume-2006-issue-4_g1gh7bf9/budget-v6-4-en.pdf

OECD. (2009). *Contracting Out Government Functions and Services: Emerging Lessons from Post-Conflict and Fragile Situations.* Partnership for Democratic Governance Series. Paris: OECD Publishing. Retrieved 9 20, 2025, from https://www.oecd.org/content/dam/oecd/en/publications/reports/2009/12/contracting-out-government-functions-and-services_g1ghb7b6/9789264066212-en.pdf

OECD. (2010). *Making reform happen: Lessons from OECD countries.* OECD Publishing.

OECD. (2015). *Government at a glance 2015.* OECD Publishing.

OECD. (2017). Systems Approaches to Public Sector Challenges-Working with Change. Observatory of Public Sector Innovation in the Public Sector Reform Division. Paris: OECD. Ανάκτηση 07 29, 2024, από https://oecd-opsi.org/wp-content/uploads/2018/07/Systems-Approaches-to-Public-Sector-Challenges_Working-with-Change.pdf

OECD. (2019). *Government at a glance 2019.* OECD Publishing.

OECD. (2021). *Government at a Glance 2021.* OECD Publishing.

OECD. (2021). *OECD Guidelines on Corporate Governance of State-Owned Enterprises.* OECD.

OECD. (2023). *Governance at a glance 2023.* OECD Publishing.

OECD. (2023). *OECD Review of the Corporate Governance of State-Owned Enterprises: Greece.* OECD.

OECD. (2024). *2023 OECD Digital Government Index: Results and key findings.* OECD Publishing., DOI: 10.1787/1a89ed5e-

OECD. (2024a). OECD Survey on Drivers of Trust in Public Institutions 2024 Results - Country Notes: Greece. Paris: OECD. Retrieved 9 9, 2024, from https://www.oecd.org/en/publications/oecd-survey-on-drivers-of-trust-in-public-institutions-2024-results-country-notes_a8004759-en/greece_56edc018-en.html

OECD. (2024b). Public governance and administration reforms. Retrieved 10 5, 2024, from https://www.oecd.org/en/topics/sub-issues/public-governance-and-administration-modernisation.html

OECD. (2025). *Governing with Artificial Intelligence: The State of Play and Way Forward in Core Government Functions.* OECD Publishing., DOI: 10.1787/795de142-

OGP. (2024). Joining OGP. Ανάκτηση 10 29, 2024, από https://www.opengovpartnership.org/process/joining-ogp/

Ongardo, E. (2014). The relationship between the new European governance emerging from the fiscal crisis and administrative reforms: Qualitatively different, quantitatively different, or nothing new? A plea for a research agenda. Administrative Culture, 15(1), σσ. 10-20. Ανάκτηση 10 6, 2024, από https://www.researchgate.net/publication/286111934_The_relationship_between_the_new_European_governance_emerging_from_the_fiscal_crisis_and_administrative_reforms_Qualitatively_different_quantitatively_different_or_nothing_new_A_plea_for_a_research_ag

Ongaro. (2010). The Napoleonic Administrative Tradition and Public Management Reform in France, Greece, Italy, Portugal and Spain. Στο M. Painter, & G. B. Peters (Επιμ.), Tradition and Public Administration (σσ. 174-190). London: Palgrave Macmillan. DOI: 10.1057/9780230289635_13

Oreg, S. (2006). Personality, context, and resistance to organizational change. *European Journal of Work and Organizational Psychology*, *15*(1), 73–101. DOI: 10.1080/13594320500451247

Oreg, S., Vakola, M., & Armenakis, A. (2011). Change recipients' reactions to organizational change: A 60-year review of quantitative studies. *The Journal of Applied Behavioral Science*, *47*(4), 461–524. DOI: 10.1177/0021886310396550

Osborne, D., & Gaebler, T. (1992). *Reinventing Government: How the Entrepreneurial Spirit is Transforming the Public Sector*. Addison-Wesley Publishing Inc., DOI: 10.2307/3381012

Osborne, S. P. (2006). The new public governance? *Public Management Review*, *8*(3), 377–387. DOI: 10.1080/14719030600853022

Osborne, S. P. (2010). *The new public governance? Emerging perspectives on the theory and practice of public governance*. Routledge. DOI: 10.4324/9780203861684

Osborne, S. P. (2020). *Public Service Logic: Creating Value for Public Service Users, Citizens, and Society Through Public Service Delivery*. Routledge. DOI: 10.4324/9781003009153

Osborne, S. P., Nasi, G., & Powell, M. (2021). Beyond co-production: Value creation and public services. *Public Administration*, *99*(4), 877–891. DOI: 10.1111/padm.12718

Otley, D. T. (1980). The contingency theory of management accounting: Achievement and prognosis. *Accounting, Organizations and Society*, *5*(4), 413–428. DOI: 10.1016/0361-3682(80)90040-9

Overman, S., & Schillemans, T. (2022). Toward a public administration theory of felt accountability. *Public Administration Review, 82*(4), 763–776. DOI: 10.1111/puar.13417

Overmans, T., & Noordegraaf, M. (2014). Managing austerity: Rhetorical and real responses to fiscal stress in local government. *Public Money & Management, 34*(2), 99–106. DOI: 10.1080/09540962.2014.887517

OVG NRW (Oberverwaltungsgericht Nordrhein-Westfalen). (2024). *Judgment 4 A 1234/23 – Arms export to Israel.* Münster.

Palumbo, G., Giupponi, G., Nunziata, L., & Mora-Sanguinetti, J. S. (2013). *Judicial Performance and its Determinants: A Cross-Country Perspective* (No. 5). OECD Publishing.

Papadopoulos, I., Ozbilgin, M., & Ozbilgin, N. F. (2013). Understanding changing patterns of migration behaviour during the Greek crisis. *International Migration (Geneva, Switzerland), 52*(3), 61–80.

Papapolychroniadis, I., Rossidis I., Aspridis, G., (2017). Comparative analysis of recruitment systems in the public sector in Greece and Europe. Trends and outlook for staff selection systems in the Greek public sector. *Academic Journal of Interdisciplinary Studies*. 6(1).

Papoulias, D. B. (2007). Gold Is the Public Sector: Rhetoric and Reality of Reforms. Athens: Bookstore "ESTIAS".

Papoulias, D. B. (2019). *How Reforms Are Accomplished.* Alexandria Editions.

Paré, G., Trudel, M. C., Jaana, M., & Kitsiou, S. (2015). Synthesizing information systems knowledge: A typology of literature reviews. *Information & Management, 52*(2), 183–199. DOI: 10.1016/j.im.2014.08.008

Parliament, F. (2012). *Wapenhandeldecreet.* Codex Vlaanderen. https://codex.vlaanderen.be

Pawson, R. (2002). Evidence and policy and the realist perspective. In Tilley, N. (Ed.), *Analysis for policy: Evidence and every day practice* (pp. 14–32). Policy Press.

Pedraja-Chaparro, F., & Salinas-Jimenez, J. (1996). An assessment of the efficiency of Spanish Courts using DEA. *Applied Economics, 28*(11), 1391–1403. DOI: 10.1080/000368496327651

Perry, J. L., & Wise, L. R. (1990). The motivational bases of public service. *Public Administration Review, 50*(3), 367–373. DOI: 10.2307/976618

Peters, B. G. (2001). *The future of governing*. Studies in Government and Public Policy.

Peters, B. G. (2021). *The politics of bureaucracy* (8th ed.). Routledge.

Peters, B. G. (2021). *The politics of bureaucracy: An introduction to comparative public administration* (8th ed.). Routledge.

Peters, B. G. (2022). Institutional theory and public sector reform: Change, stability, and adaptation. *International Review of Administrative Sciences, 88*(3), 469–487.

Peters, B. G., & Savoie, D. J. (Eds.). (2000). *Governance in the twenty-first century: Revitalizing the public service*. Canadian Centre for Management DevelopmentDOI: 10.1515/9780773568884

Pettigrew, A. M., Woodman, R. W., & Cameron, K. S. (2001). Studying organizational change and development: Challenges for future research. *Academy of Management Journal, 44*(4), 697–713. DOI: 10.2307/3069411

Piderit, S. K. (2000). Rethinking resistance and recognizing ambivalence: A multidimensional view of attitudes toward an organizational change. *Academy of Management Review, 25*(4), 783–794. DOI: 10.2307/259206

Pierre, J. (2000). *Debating governance: Authority, steering, and democracy*. Oxford University Press. DOI: 10.1093/oso/9780198295143.001.0001

Pinheiro, R., Geschwind, L., Hansen, H. F., & Pulkkinen, K. (2019). *Reforms, Organizational Change and Performance in Higher Education. A Comparative Account from the Nordic Countries*. Palgrave Macmillan. DOI: 10.1007/978-3-030-11738-2

Pitelis, C. (2018). State-owned enterprises and development in Southern Europe: Historical lessons. *Cambridge Journal of Economics, 42*(3), 525–547.

Poister, T. H., Pitts, D. W., & Edwards, L. H. (2010). Strategic management research in the public sector: A review and synthesis. *American Review of Public Administration, 40*(5), 522–545. DOI: 10.1177/0275074010370617

Pollitt, C., & Bouckaert, G. (2011). *Public management reform: A comparative analysis* (3rd ed.). Oxford University Press.

Pollitt, C., & Bouckaert, G. (2011). *Public management reform: A comparative analysis—New public management, governance, and the neo-Weberian state*. Oxford University Press.

Pollitt, C., & Bouckaert, G. (2017). *Public management reform: A comparative analysis – Into the age of austerity* (4th ed.). Oxford University Press.

Pollitt, C., & Bouckaert, G. (2017). *Public Management Reform: A Comparative Analysis – Into the Age of Austerity*. Oxford University Press.

Pollitt, C., & Bouckaert, G. (2017). *Public management reform: A comparative analysis—Into the age of austerity* (4th ed.). Oxford University Press.

Pollitt, C., & Bouckaert, G. (2017). *Public Management Reform: A Comparative Analysis—Into the Age of Austerity* (4th ed.). Oxford University Press.

Popay, J., Roberts, H., Sowden, A., Petticrew, M., Britten, N., Arai, L., & Duffy, S. (2006). *Narrative synthesis in systematic reviews: A product from the ESRC methods programme*. University of Southampton.

Porter, M. E. (1980). *Competitive strategy: Techniques for analyzing industries and competitors*. The Free Press.

Posner, H., & Richard, A. (2005). Judicial Behavior and Performance: An Economic Approach. *Florida State University Law Review. Florida State University. College of Law*, *32*(4), 1259–1279.

Propper, C., Sutton, M., Whitnall, C., & Windmeijer, F. (2008). Did 'targets and terror' reduce waiting times in the English NHS? *The B.E. Journal of Economic Analysis & Policy*, *8*(2), 5. Advance online publication. DOI: 10.2202/1935-1682.1863

Prosci. (2018). *Best practices in change management (10th ed.)*. Prosci.

Raad van State (Belgium). (2018–2021). *Suspension and annulment of Walloon arms export licences to Saudi Arabia*. Arms Trade Litigation Monitor. https://armstradelitigationmonitor.org

Raad van State (Belgium). (2019). *Suspension of Walloon arms export licences to Saudi Arabia*. Arms Trade Litigation Monitor. https://armstradelitigationmonitor.org

Rafferty, A. E., & Griffin, M. A. (2006). Perceptions of organizational change: A stress and coping perspective. *The Journal of Applied Psychology*, *91*(5), 1154–1162. DOI: 10.1037/0021-9010.91.5.1154 PMID: 16953776

Rafferty, A. E., Jimmieson, N. L., & Armenakis, A. A. (2013). Change readiness: A multilevel review. *Journal of Management*, *39*(1), 110–135. DOI: 10.1177/0149206312457417

Rafferty, A. E., & Restubog, S. L. D. (2010). The impact of change process and context on change reactions and turnover during a merger. *Journal of Management*, *36*(5), 1309–1338. DOI: 10.1177/0149206309341480

Rainey, H. G. (2009). *Understanding and managing public organizations* (4th ed.). Jossey-Bass.

Rainey, H. G., & Steinbauer, P. (1999). Galloping elephants: Developing elements of a theory of effective government organizations. *Journal of Public Administration: Research and Theory, 9*(1), 1–32. DOI: 10.1093/oxfordjournals.jpart.a024401

Rammata, M. (2018). Reform Attempts in the Greek Public Administration. Theory and Practice of Administrative Law(8-9), pp. 708-721. Retrieved October 8, 2024, from https://www.academia.edu/37631851

Rammata, M. (2011). *Modern Greek Public Administration: Between Bureaucracy and Management*. Kritiki.

Rammata, M. (2021). *Public Policies: Citizens and Deliberation in Greece and Abroad*. Nomiki Bibliothiki.

Randma-Liiv, T., & Kickert, W. (2017, 3 15). The Impact of Fiscal Crisis on Public Administration Reforms in Europe. Journal of Comparative Policy Analysis: Research and Practice, 19(2), σσ. 1387-6988. DOI: 10.1080/13876988.2017.1286781

Rechtbank Den Haag. (2024). *ECLI:NL:RBDHA:2024:1234 — Judgment on F-35 parts export to Israel.*

Rechtbank van eerste aanleg Brussel. (2025, July 17). *Beschikking AR 25/69/C (Antwerp transit ruling)*. https://www.rechtbanken-tribunaux.be

Rhodes. (2017). The Hollowing Out of the State. In *Network Governance and the Differentiated Polity: Selected Essays* (Vol. I). Oxford: Oxford University Press. DOI: 10.1093/oso/9780198786108.003.0008

Rhodes, R. A. W. (2017). Understanding governance: Ten years on. *Organization Studies, 38*(10), 1243–1264.

Riccucci, N. M. (2021). *Public personnel management: Current concerns, future challenges* (6th ed.). Routledge., DOI: 10.4324/9781003124567

Rijksoverheid. (2023a). *Minister-President Rutte expresses solidarity with Israel following attacks*. https://www.rijksoverheid.nl

Rijksoverheid. (2023b). *The Netherlands calls for humanitarian access to Gaza*. https://www.rijksoverheid.nl

Rijksoverheid. (2024). *Minister Bruins Slot calls for accountability and two-state solution in Middle East*. https://www.rijksoverheid.nl

Riksrevisjonen (2019-2020). Riksrevisjonens undersøkelse av saksbehandlingstid og effektivitet i tingrettene og lagmannsrettene, Dokument 3:3 (2019–2020), Oslo. available at: https://www.riksrevisjonen.no/globalassets/rapporter/no-2019-2020/Domstolene.pdf

Rittel, H. W. J., & Webber, M. M. (1973). Dilemmas in a general theory of planning. *Policy Sciences*, *4*(2), 155–169. DOI: 10.1007/BF01405730

Robinson, M. (2015). From Old Public Administration to the New Public Service: Implications for Public Sector Reform in Developing Countries. Heng Mui Keng Terrace: UNDP.

Robson, C. (2010). Η έρευνα του πραγματικού κόσμου. Ένα μέσο για κοινωνικούς επιστήμονες και επαγγελματίες ερευνητές (2η εκδ.). Αθήνα: Gutemberg.

Roehl, U. B., & Hansen, M. B. (2024). 3 26). Automated, administrative decision-making and good governance: Synergies, trade-offs, and limits. *Public Administration Review*, *84*(6), 1–16. DOI: 10.1111/puar.13799

Rogers, E. M. (2003). *Diffusion of Innovations* (5th ed.).

Rossidis I., Aspridis, G., Katsimardos, P., Bouas, K., Blanas, N. (2016). Best practices for motivation and their implementation in the Greek public sector for increasing efficiency. *Academic Journal of Interdisciplinary Studies*. 5(3).

Rossidis, I. (2014*) Applying Business Management in Greek Public Administration.* Athens: publ. Ath. Stamoulis.

Rossidis, I. (2014). *Applying Business Management in Greek Public Administration.* Athens: publ. Ath. Stamoulis.

Rossidis, I., & Belias, D. (2020). Combining Strategic Management with Knowledge Management: Trends and International Perspectives. International Review of Management and Marketing, 10(3), σσ. 39-45. DOI: 10.32479/irmm.9621

Rossidis, I., & Belias, D. (2021). Evolution of e-Governance in the Era of the Pandemic. Will the Crisis Become an Opportunity? The Cases of Cyprus and Greece. The Cyprus Review, 33(1), σσ. 37-66. Ανάκτηση 10 26, 2024, από https://cyprusreview.org/index.php/cr/article/view/775/627

Rossidis, I., Aspridis, G., Katsimardos, P., & Bouas, K. (2018b). *Human Resource Productivity in Greece*. Global Encyclopedia of Public Administration, Public Policy and Governance, Springer Publishing.

Rossidis, I., Belias, D., & Papailias, S. (2020). *Strategic management in the Greek public sector. In search of best practices in the international environment.* Book of Proceedings International Conference on Business & Economics of the Hellenic Open University.

Rossidis, I., Belias, D., & Papailias, S. (2020b). Strategic management and performance in the international environment. Book of Proceedings International Conference on Cotemporary Marketing Issues.

Rossidis, I., Belias, D., & Papailias, S. (2020c). Strategic management in the Greek public sector. In search of best practices in the international environment. Book of Proceedings International Conference on Business & Economics of the Hellenic Open University.

Rossidis, I., Mihiotis, A., & Ntalakos, A. (2023). The contribution of Change Management to the integration of E-Governance systems. Chapter 9 in "*Managing Successful and Ethical Organizational Change*", IGI Global.

Rossidis, I., Mihiotis, A., & Ntalakos, A. (2023). *The contribution of Change Management to the integration of E-Governance systems.* Chapter 9 in "Managing Successful and Ethical Organizational Change", IGI Global. DOI: 10.4018/979-8-3693-0235-4.ch009

Rossidis, I., Tsiotas, D., Aspridis, G., Belias, D., & Sdrolias, L. (2018a). *Exploring Governance in Higher Education in Europe and Greece.* Global Encyclopedia of Public Administration, Public Policy, and Governance, Springer Publishing.

Rossidis, I. (2014). *Applications of Business Management in the Greek Public Administration* (1st ed.). A. Stamoulis.

Rossidis, I., & Belias, D. (2021). Evolution of e-governance in the era of the pandemic. May the crisis become an opportunity? The cases of Cyprus and Greece. *The Cyprus Review*, *33*(1), 37–66.

Rossidis, I., & Belias, D. (2021). Evolution of e-Government in the era of the pandemic. May the crisis become an opportunity? The cases of Cyprus and Greece. *The Cyprus Review*, *33*(1), 37–66.

Rossidis, I., & Belias, D. (2025). *Change Management. Organizational Change and Elements of Organizational Behavior.* Tziolas.

Rossidis, I., Belias, D., & Aspridis, G. (2020). *Change management and leadership.* Tziolas Publications. (Original work published 2020). [in Greek]

Rossidis, I., Belias, D., & Aspridis, G. (2023). *Change Management and Leadership*. Tziola Publications.

RTBF. (2025, July 17). *La justice ordonne à la Flandre de stopper tout transit d'équipement militaire vers Israël.*

Rubin, A. B. (1979). Bureaucratization of the federal courts: The tension between justice and efficiency. *The Notre Dame Lawyer, 55*, 648.

Rucker, P., & Costa, R. (2017). *The Washington Post.* Retrieved 10 5, 2025, from https://www.washingtonpost.com/politics/top-wh-strategist-vows-a-daily-fight-for-deconstruction-of-the-administrative-state/2017/02/23/03f6b8da-f9ea-11e6-bf01-d47f8cf9b643_story.html

Rumelt, R. P. (2011). *Good strategy, bad strategy: The difference and why it matters.* Crown Business.

Ryngaert, C. (2022). Risk assessment in arms export controls: Between precaution and evidence. *Journal of International Humanitarian Legal Studies, 13*(1).

Saferworld. (2020). *EU arms export controls: Achievements, challenges and opportunities.*

Saferworld. (2023). *The EU Common Position review: Fixing or fiddling?* SIPRI. (2024). *Trends in international arms transfers 2023.* Stockholm International Peace Research Institute.

Sagie, A., & Koslowsky, M. (2000). *Participation and empowerment in organizations: Modeling, effectiveness, and applications.* Sage Publications. DOI: 10.4135/9781452231341

Santos, S. P., & Amado, C. A. (2014). On the need for reform of the Portuguese judicial system–Does Data Envelopment Analysis assessment support it? *Omega, 47*, 1–16. DOI: 10.1016/j.omega.2014.02.007

Schein, E. H. (2010). *Organizational culture and leadership* (4th ed.). Jossey-Bass.

Schneider, B., Ehrhart, M. G., & Macey, W. H. (2013). Organizational climate and culture. *Annual Review of Psychology, 64*(1), 361–388. DOI: 10.1146/annurev-psych-113011-143809 PMID: 22856467

Schneider, M. R. (2005). Judicial career incentives and court performance: An empirical study of the German labour courts of appeal. *European Journal of Law and Economics, 20*(2), 127–144. DOI: 10.1007/s10657-005-1733-2

Schnitzer, P., & Betcherman, G. (2025). *World Bank Blogs – Digital Development.* Retrieved 10 5, 2025, from https://blogs.worldbank.org/en/digital-development/ai-in-public-employment-services--unlocking-potential--avoiding-

Schomaker, R. M., & Bauer, M. W. (2020). What Drives Successful Administrative Performance during Crises? Lessons from Refugee Migration and the Covid-19 Pandemic. Public Administration Review, 80(5), σσ. 845-850. DOI: 10.1111/puar.13280

Scott, R. J., & Boyd, R. (2020). Determined to succeed: Can goal commitment sustain interagency collaboration? *Public Policy and Administration, 38*(1), 3–33. Advance online publication. DOI: 10.1177/0952076720905002

Scott, W. R. (2014). *Institutions and organizations: Ideas, interests, and identities* (4th ed.). Sage Publications.

Scott, W. R., & Davis, G. F. (2015). *Organizations and organizing: Rational, natural and open systems perspectives.* Routledge. DOI: 10.4324/9781315663371

Scupola, A., & Mergel, I. (2022). Co-production in digital transformation of public administration and public value creation: The case of Denmark. *Government Information Quarterly, 39*(2), 101685. DOI: 10.1016/j.giq.2021.101650

Senge, P. M. (1990). *The fifth discipline: The art and practice of the learning organization.* Doubleday.

Shadish, W. R., Cook, T. D., & Campbell, D. T. (2002). *Experimental and quasi-experimental designs for generalized causal inference.* Houghton Mifflin.

Shava, E., & Mazenda, A. (2021). Ethics in South African public administration: A critical review. *International Journal of Management Practice, 14*(4), 526–544. DOI: 10.1504/IJMP.2021.115107

Shea, C. M., Jacobs, S. R., Esserman, D. A., Bruce, K., & Weiner, B. J. (2014). Organizational readiness for implementing change: A psychometric assessment of a new measure. *Implementation Science : IS, 9*(1), 7. DOI: 10.1186/1748-5908-9-7 PMID: 24410955

Sheikh, H., Prins, C., & Schrijvers, E. (2023). *Mission AI: The New System Technology.* The Netherlands Scientific Council for Government Policy (WRR). Cham: Springer. Retrieved 8 25, 2025, from https://link.springer.com/content/pdf/10.1007/978-3-031-21448-6.pdf

Sicotte, C., Champagne, F., & Contandriopoulos, A. P. (1999). A conceptual framework for the analysis of performance in health care organizations. *Health Services Management Research, 12*(4), 253–268. PMID: 10178368

Silva, M. C. A. (2018). Output-specific inputs in DEA: An application to courts of justice in Portugal. *Omega, 79*, 43–53. DOI: 10.1016/j.omega.2017.07.006

Simmons, A., & Chappell, S. (1988). Artificial intelligence-definition and practice. *IEEE Journal of Oceanic Engineering, 13*(2), 14–42. DOI: 10.1109/48.551

Sitaraman, G. (2019). Foreign hard look review. *Administrative Law Review*, *66*(3), 489–541. https://administrativelawreview.org/wp-content/uploads/sites/2/2019/01/Sitaraman_66.3.pdf

Sotirakou, T., & Zeppou, M. (2004). The "MATE" model: a strategic knowledge management technique on the chessboard of public-sector modernization. *Management Decision*, *42*(1), 69–88. DOI: 10.1108/00251740410504430

Sotiropoulos, D. A. (2021). Public Administration in the Post-Covid Era. Athens: diaNEOsis.

Sotiropoulos, D. A., & Christopoulos, L. (2017, November). Multiplicity, Maladministration and Bureaucracy in Greece: Analysis of Past Failures and Proposals for Remedial Interventions. Athens: diaNEOsis.

Sotiropoulos, D. A. (2004). Southern European public bureaucracies in comparative perspective. *West European Politics, 27*(3), 405–422. DOI: 10.1080/0140238042000228077

Sotiropoulos, D. A. (2007). *State and Reform in Contemporary Southern Europe: Greece-Spain-Italy-Portugal*. Potamos.

Spano, A. (2009). Public Value Creation and Management Control Systems. *International Journal of Public Administration*, *32*(3–4), 328–348. https://doi-org.proxy.eap.gr/10.1080/01900690902732848

Spanou, C. (1996). 1). Penelope's suitors: Administrative modernisation and party competition in Greece. *West European Politics, 19*(1), 97–124. DOI: 10.1080/01402389608425123

Spanou, C. (2008). State reform in Greece: Responding to old and new challenges. *International Journal of Public Sector Management, 21*(2), 150–173. DOI: 10.1108/09513550810855645

Spanou, C. (2018). *Public administration and policy in Greece*. Routledge.

Spanou, C. (2020). External influence on structural reform: Did policy conditionality strengthen reform capacity in Greece? *Public Policy and Administration*, *35*(2), 135–157. DOI: 10.1177/0952076718772008

Spanou, C., & Sotiropoulos, D. A. (2011). The Odyssey of Administrative Reforms in Greece, 1981–2009: A Tale of Two Reform Paths. *Public Administration*, *89*(3), 723–737. DOI: 10.1111/j.1467-9299.2011.01914.x

Spanou, C., & Sotiropoulos, D. A. (2021). Administrative reform and the management of public enterprises in Greece: Between inertia and change'. *Public Administration*, *99*(4), 771–789.

Spar, D. L. (2024). *Has the 'battle over big government' era ended?* Retrieved 10 5, 2024, from Institute for Business in Global Society: https://www.hbs.edu/bigs/has-the-battle-over-government-ended

Staalesen, U. E. (2020). Rettsmekling bør tas mer i bruk–både av hensyn til partenes og domstolenes ressursbruk. *Lov og Rett*, *59*(4), 252–257. DOI: 10.18261/issn.1504-3061-2020-04-05

Staats, J. L., Bowler, S., & Hiskey, J. T. (2005). Measuring judicial performance in Latin America. *Latin American Politics and Society*, *47*(4), 77–106. DOI: 10.1111/j.1548-2456.2005.tb00329.x

Stacey, R. D., & Griffin, D. (Eds.). (2005). *A complexity perspective on researching organizations: Taking experience seriously*. Routledge.

Stacey, R. D., & Mowles, C. (2016). *Strategic management and organizational dynamics: The challenge of complexity* (7th ed.). Pearson Education.

Stampelos, X., Nikova, D., Rossidis, I., Aspridis, G., & Pouliana, L. (2019). *Contribution of knowledge management to the function of public administration*. Book of Proceedings, International scientific conference Leadership and Organization Development. Bulgaria, Kiten.

Stirman, S. W., Kimberly, J., Cook, N., Calloway, A., Castro, F., & Charns, M. (2012). The sustainability of new programs and innovations: A review of the empirical literature and recommendations for future research. *Implementation Science : IS*, *7*(1), 17. DOI: 10.1186/1748-5908-7-17 PMID: 22417162

Stoker, G. (2006). Public value management: A new narrative for networked governance? *American Review of Public Administration*, *36*(1), 41–57. DOI: 10.1177/0275074005282583

Sukhera, J. (2022). Narrative reviews: Flexible, rigorous, and practical. *Journal of Graduate Medical Education*, *14*(4), 414–417. DOI: 10.4300/JGME-D-22-00480.1 PMID: 35991099

Sun, T. Q., & Medaglia, R. (2019). Mapping the challenges of artificial intelligence in the public sector: Evidence from public health. *Government Information Quarterly, 36*(2), 368–383. DOI: 10.1016/j.giq.2018.09.008

Tasiopoulos, S. (2021). General Presentation and Public's Sector Reforms in Greece. Ανάκτηση από https://site.imodev.org/nos-activites/europe/grece/general-presentation-and-publics-sector-reforms-in-greece

Teece, D. J. (2007). Explicating dynamic capabilities: The nature and microfoundations of (sustainable) enterprise performance. *Strategic Management Journal, 28*(13), 1319–1350. DOI: 10.1002/smj.640

tenCouncil of Europe. (2025). *Common ethical challenges in AI.* Retrieved 10 10, 2025, from https://www.coe.int/el/web/human-rights-and-biomedicine/common-ethical-challenges-in-ai#%22123745781%22:[7]

The Conversation. (2022). *Permacrisis: what it means and why it's word of the year for 2022.* Retrieved 10 5, 2025, from https://theconversation.com/permacrisis-what-it-means-and-why-its-word-of-the-year-for-2022-194306

Thomann, E., & Lieberherr, E. (2024). Public policy implementation and accountability. In *Handbook of Public Policy Implementation* (pp. 53–66). Edward Elgar Publishing., DOI: 10.4337/9781800885905.00011

Thomas, R., & Davies, A. (2005). Theorizing the micro-politics of resistance: New public management and managerial identities in the UK public services. *Organization Studies, 26*(5), 683–706. DOI: 10.1177/0170840605051821

Thorsvik, I. W. (2021). Domstolsreformen er god distriktspolitikk, Nettavisen, 9.11.2021. https://www.nettavisen.no/norsk-debatt/domstolsreformen-er-god-distriktspolitikk/o/5-95-336576

Thynne, I. (2017). The state and public corporations: Governance issues and challenges. *Public Organization Review, 17*(4), 503–517.

Tone, K. (2001). A slacks-based measure of efficiency in data envelopment analysis. *European Journal of Operational Research, 130*(3), 498–509. DOI: 10.1016/S0377-2217(99)00407-5

Transparency International. (2022). *National Integrity System Assessment.* Transparency International.

Trivellas, P., Reklitis, P., & Platis, C. (2013). The effect of job related stress on employees' satisfaction: A survey in health care. *Procedia: Social and Behavioral Sciences, 73*, 718–726. DOI: 10.1016/j.sbspro.2013.02.110

Tsagdi, G. (2024). Public Value: A New Governance perspective within the Parent Ministry-Agency context. Athens: Athens University of Economics and Business. Retrieved 10 7, 2024, from https://www.didaktorika.gr/eadd/bitstream/10442/56629/1/56629.pdf

Tsai, C. F., & Tsai, J. H. (2010, March). Performance evaluation of the judicial system in taiwan using data envelopment analysis and decision trees. In *2010 Second international conference on computer engineering and applications* (Vol. 2, pp. 290-294). IEEE. DOI: 10.1109/ICCEA.2010.208

Tsekos, Th. (2021). Introduction: From One Crisis to the Next. In Barouxis, Ch., Kakepaki, M., Saris, N., Tramontanis, A., & Tsekeris, K. (Eds.), *The Political Portrait of Greece II: Stakes and Challenges* (pp. 11–36). National Centre for Social Research., DOI: 10.17902/9789606834462

Tulkens, H. (1993). On FDH efficiency analysis: Some methodological issues and applications to retail banking, courts, and urban transit. *Journal of Productivity Analysis*, *4*(1), 183–210. DOI: 10.1007/BF01073473

Tummers, L., & van Berkel, R. (2021). Employer engagement and inclusive HRM in public organizations. *Human Resource Management Journal*, *31*(3), 456–472. DOI: 10.1111/1748-8583.12245

Twizeyimana, J. D., & Andersson, A. (2019). The public value of e-governance – A literature review. *Government Information Quarterly*, *36*(2), 167–178. DOI: 10.1016/j.giq.2019.01.001

Ubaldi, B.-C., Van Ooijen, C., & Welby, B. (2019). *A data-driven public sector. Enabling the strategic use of data for productive, inclusive and trustworthy governance*. OECD Publishing., Retrieved from https://www.researchgate.net/publication/364119468_A_data-driven_public_sector_Enabling_the_strategic_use_of_data_for_productive_inclusive_and_trustworthy_governance

UNDP. (2015). *Public Administration Reform Practice Note*. UNDP.

UNDP. (2019). *Human Development Report 2019: Beyond income, beyond averages, beyond today*. UNDP.

UNDP/BDP/CDG. (2006). *Institutional Reform and Change Management*. UNDP.

United Nations Office for Disarmament Affairs. (2013). *The Arms Trade Treaty*. ATT.

United Nations Office for Disarmament Affairs. (2025, May 28). *EU statement to the UN First Committee*.

United Nations Office for the Coordination of Humanitarian Affairs. (2023). *Reporting on civilian casualties and damage in the Gaza Strip.*

United Nations Office for the Coordination of Humanitarian Affairs. (2024). *Gaza crisis: Situation reports.*

United Nations. (2023). *General Assembly resolution A/ES-10/L.25.*

United Nations. (2024). *General Assembly resolution ES-10/23 on the status of the State of Palestine.*

UNRWA. (2024, April 19). *Belgium signs new EUR 27.5m agreement with UNRWA (2024–2026).* https://www.unrwa.org/

Upadhyaya, A. N., Debnath, P., Rani, P., Manjunath, T. C., & Bhattacharya, S. (2025). AI-based disaster prediction and early warning systems. In Mobo, F. (Ed.), *AI and emerging technologies for emergency response and smart cities* (pp. 55–74). IGI Global Scientific Publishing., DOI: 10.4018/979-8-3693-9770-1.ch003

Urio, P. (1999). La gestion publique au service du marché. In Hufty, M. (Ed.), *La pensée comptable: État, néolibéralisme, nouvelle gestion publique* (pp. 91–124).

Valle-Cruz, D., Gil-Garcia, J. R., & Sandoval-Almazan, R. (2024). Artificial intelligence algorithms and applications in the public sector: a systematic literature review based on the PRISMA approach. In Charalabidis, Y., Medaglia, R., & van Noordt, C. (Eds.), *Research handbook on public management and artificial intelligence* (pp. 8–26). Edward Elgar Publishing., DOI: 10.4337/9781802207347.00010

Valle-Cruz, D., Ruvalcaba-Gomez, E. A., Sandoval-Almazan, R., & Criado, J. I. (2019). A review of artificial intelligence in government and its potential from a public policy perspective. In Chen, Y.-C., Salem, F., & Zuiderwijk, A. (Eds.), *A review of artificial intelligence in government and its potential from a public policy perspective-Dubai* (pp. 91–99). Association for Computing Machinery., DOI: 10.1145/3325112.3325242

Van de Ven, A. H., & Poole, M. S. (2005). Alternative approaches for studying organizational change. *Organization Studies, 26*(9), 1377–1404. DOI: 10.1177/0170840605056907

Van der Voet, J. (2014). The effectiveness and specificity of change management in a public organization: Transformational leadership and a bureaucratic organizational structure. *European Management Journal, 32*(3), 373–382. DOI: 10.1016/j.emj.2013.10.001

Van der Voet, J., Groeneveld, S., & Kuipers, B. S. (2014). Talking the talk or walking the walk? The leadership of planned and emergent change in a public organization. *Journal of Change Management, 14*(2), 171–191. DOI: 10.1080/14697017.2013.805160

Van der Voet, J., Kuipers, B. S., & Groeneveld, S. (2015). Held back and pushed forward: Leading change in a complex public sector environment. *Journal of Organizational Change Management, 28*(2), 290–300. DOI: 10.1108/JOCM-09-2013-0182

Van der Voet, J., Kuipers, B. S., & Groeneveld, S. (2016). Implementing change in public organizations: The relationship between leadership and affective commitment to change in a public sector context. *Public Management Review, 18*(6), 842–865. DOI: 10.1080/14719037.2015.1045020

Van der Voet, J., & Steijn, B. (2021). Organizational change and public employees: The role of leadership and participation. *Review of Public Personnel Administration, 41*(4), 589–608.

Van der Voet, J., & Vermeeren, B. (2017). Change management in hard times: Can change management mitigate the negative relationship between cutbacks and the organizational commitment and work engagement of public sector employees? *American Review of Public Administration, 47*(2), 230–252. DOI: 10.1177/0275074015625828

van Klink, B. (2016). Symbolic Legislation: An Essentially Political Concept. In van Klink, B., van Beers, B., & Poort, L. (Eds.), *Symbolic Legislation Theory and New Developments in Biolaw* (pp. 19–36). Springer., DOI: 10.1007/978-3-319-33365-6_2

Vandy, J. F. (2023). Bridging the gap for effective public sector management: Reviewing the critical role of strategic human resource management. *International Journal of Research Publication and Reviews, 4*(4), 347–360. DOI: 10.55248/gengpi.2023.4.4.34741

Verellen, J. (2021). In the name of the rule of law? *H v Council. European Papers, 6*(2), 1013–1040.

Vermeeren, B. (2021). HRM and performance in public sector organizations: A review of the evidence. *Public Management Review, 23*(5), 678–695. DOI: 10.1080/14719037.2020.1722213

Verwaltungsgericht Berlin. (2024, March 8). *Case No. 1 L 271/24, Ruling.*

Verwaltungsgericht Frankfurt am Main. (2024, December 16). *Rüstungsgüter für Israel.*

Vial, G. (2019). Understanding digital transformation: A review and a research agenda. *The Journal of Strategic Information Systems*, *28*(2), 118–144. DOI: 10.1016/j.jsis.2019.01.003

Vittou, F. (2023, October 18). Ways of Strengthening and Reforming National Public Administrations by the European Union. Retrieved October 28, 2024, from https://odeth.eu/

Vittou, P. (2024). The contribution of change management during the implementation process of administrative reforms [Master's thesis]. Panteion University of Social and Political Sciences.

Vlas, A.-G. (2024). Conclusion recommending to uphold Hague Court of Appeal ruling on F-35 parts to Israel (ECLI []). Rechtspraak.]. *NL:PHR*, *2024*, 1424.

Vogel, R., & Masal, D. (2023). Leadership and change in public organizations: A systematic review. *Public Management Review*, *25*(1), 1–22.

VoteWatch Europe. (2018). *European Parliament votes on Israel and Palestine, 2014–2018.* https://www.votewatch.eu

VoteWatch Europe. (2024). *Debates and plenary votes on Gaza, 2023–2024.* https://www.votewatch.eu

Waldo, D. (1948). *The administrative state; A Study of the Political Theory of American Public Administration.* Ronald Press Company.

Walker, R. M., Brewer, G. A., Boyne, G. A., & Avellaneda, C. N. (2011). Market orientation and public service performance: New public management gone mad? *Public Administration Review*, *71*(5), 707–717. DOI: 10.1111/j.1540-6210.2011.02410.x

Wanberg, C. R., & Banas, J. T. (2000). Predictors and outcomes of openness to changes in a reorganizing workplace. *The Journal of Applied Psychology*, *85*(1), 132–142. DOI: 10.1037/0021-9010.85.1.132 PMID: 10740964

Wang, Q., & Guan, Z. (2023). Can sunlight disperse mistrust? A meta-analysis of the effect of transparency on citizens' trust in government. *Journal of Public Administration: Research and Theory*, *33*(1), 11–31. DOI: 10.1093/jopart/muac040

Waring, J., & Currie, G. (2009). Managing expert knowledge: Organizational challenges and managerial futures for the UK medical profession. *Organization Studies*, *30*(7), 755–778. DOI: 10.1177/0170840609104819

Weber, M. (1978). *Economy and society: An outline of interpretive sociology.* University of California Press.

Weick, K. E., & Quinn, R. E. (1999). Organizational change and development. *Annual Review of Psychology, 50*(1), 361–386. DOI: 10.1146/annurev.psych.50.1.361 PMID: 15012461

Weinberg, D. B., & Lewis, D. (2009). Strategic management: Combining human resources and information technology. *International Journal of Strategic Human Resource Management, 9*(1), 21–37.

Weiner, B. J. (2009). A theory of organizational readiness for change. *Implementation Science : IS, 4*(1), 67. DOI: 10.1186/1748-5908-4-67 PMID: 19840381

Weiner, B. J., Amick, H., & Lee, S. Y. D. (2008). Conceptualization and measurement of organizational readiness for change: A review of the literature in health services research and other fields. *Medical Care Research and Review : MCRR, 65*(4), 379–436. DOI: 10.1177/1077558708317802 PMID: 18511812

Weiner, B. J., Lewis, C. C., Stanick, C., Powell, B. J., Dorsey, C. N., Clary, A. S., Boynton, M. H., & Halko, H. (2017). Psychometric assessment of three newly developed implementation outcome measures. *Implementation Science : IS, 12*(1), 108. DOI: 10.1186/s13012-017-0635-3 PMID: 28851459

Williams, M. R., & Lewis, D. (2008). Strategic management tools and public sector management: The challenge of context specificity. *Public Management Review, 10*(5), 653–671. DOI: 10.1080/14719030802264382

Williams, R. C. (2020). "Judicial role" and judicial duty in foreign affairs. *Fordham International Law Journal, 43*(5), 1259–1312. https://ir.lawnet.fordham.edu/ilj/vol43/iss5/3

Wilson, J. Q. (1989). *Bureaucracy: What government agencies do and why they do it.* Basic Books.

Wilson, W. (1989). The study of administration. *Political Science Quarterly, 104*(3), 481–506.

Wiltsey Stirman, S., Calloway, A., Toder, K., Miller, C. J., DeVito, A. K., Meisel, S. N., & Crits-Christoph, P. (2013). Community mental health provider modifications to an evidence-based psychosocial treatment and implications for sustained implementation. *Psychiatric Services (Washington, D.C.), 64*(10), 1056–1059. DOI: 10.1176/appi.ps.201200456 PMID: 24081406

Wirtz, B. W., Weyerer, J. C., & Geyer, C. (2019). Artificial Intelligence and the Public Sector—Applications and Challenges. *International Journal of Public Administration, 42*(7), 596–615. DOI: 10.1080/01900692.2018.1498103

Wisotzki, S., & Mutschler, M. (2021). No common position! European arms export control in crisis. *Zeitschrift für Friedens- und Konfliktforschung, 10*(2), 273–293. https://doi.org/DOI: 10.1007/s42597-022-00071-x

Wisotzki, S. (2022). No common position! European arms export control in crisis. *Global Constitutionalism, 11*(3), 453–472.

Worster, W. T. (2025). — "Assurances on the Use of Exported Arms in the Gaza Conflict. *Israel Law Review, 2025*(58), 306–342. DOI: 10.1017/S0021223725100095

Wright, B. E., & Pandey, S. K. (2010). Transformational leadership in the public sector: Does structure matter? *Journal of Public Administration: Research and Theory, 20*(1), 75–89. DOI: 10.1093/jopart/mup003

Xanthopoulou, P., & Kefis, V. (2019). Public Organizations and Public Management in Greece: The Implementation of Private Management Tools in the Public Sector. *International Journal of Sciences, 8*(02).

Yallop, A. C., Gică, O. A., Moisescu, O. I., & Coro , M. M. (2021). The digital traveller: Implications for data ethics and data governance in tourism and hospitality. *International Journal of Contemporary Hospitality Management, 33*(10), 293–308. DOI: 10.1108/IJCHM-10-2020-1207

Yamamoto, H. (2003). New Public Management - Japan's Practice. Tokyo: Institute for International Policy Studies. Retrieved 7 2, 2025, from https://npi.or.jp/en/research/data/bp293e.pdf

Yankelovich, D. (2015). *Wicked problems, workable solutions: lessons from a public life*. Rowman & Littlefield.

Yeung, L. L., & Azevedo, P. F. (2011). Measuring efficiency of Brazilian courts with data envelopment analysis (DEA). *IMA Journal of Management Mathematics, 22*(4), 343–356. DOI: 10.1093/imaman/dpr002

Yin, R. K. (2014). *Case Study Research: Design and Methods* (5th ed.). SAGE Publications, Inc.

Yolles, M. (2006). Organizations as complex systems. *Journal of Applied Systems and Cybernetics, 35*(2), 183–202.

Zahra, S. A., & George, G. (2002). Absorptive capacity: A review, reconceptualization, and extension. *Academy of Management Review, 27*(2), 185–203. DOI: 10.2307/4134351

Zeraatkar, S., & Rajabi Farjad, H. (2021). Exploration of the challenges of human resource management in the public sector and their effects on productivity. *Human Resource Management Journal*, *15*(1), 35–54. DOI: 10.52547/hrmj.15.1.3

About the Contributors

Vassilis Kefis was born in Athens. He is Professor of Business Organization and Public Management at Public Administration Department and the Dean of School of Economy and Public Administration, Panteion University of Social and Political Sciences. He teaches courses on Public Management, Human Resource Management, Strategic Business Development, Management of Natural Resources and Energy, Total Quality Management and Business Administration. Regarding the postgraduate level, is involved in teaching courses related to TQM, Business Planning and Research Methods. Moreover, he serves as a member of staff of the Graduate Studies Program "Management Science and Public Management". He has also strong presence in academic institutions such as the University of Aegean, the Technological Educational Institute of Piraeus and the Technological Educational Institute of Athens where he has served as a visit lecturer. Furthermore, he is supervising five doctoral theses and is a member of plenty of academic committees and Electoral Boards. He is the author of five books on the subject of Business Administration and the editor of four. A large number of articles have been published in recognized scientific journals both in Greece and abroad. He has participated in scientific conferences, within and outside Greece.

Rossidis Ioannis is Assistant Professor of Public Management at the Department of Public Administration of Panteion University. Dr. Rossidis studied Business Administration at the University of Piraeus, holds a Master's degree in Business Administration (MBA) from the University of the Aegean, a Master's Degree in Health Services Management from the National School of Public Health and a PhD in Public Management from Panteion University. Over the last decade, he has taught in a number of undergraduate and postgraduate programs in Universities. At the same time, he was employed at Hellenic Authority for Higher Education as Director of the Administrative Support Department, at the Ministry of Finance as Head of Department, at ATEBank as Head of the Operations Department and in other private sector companies as a senior executive. His academic and research interests focus among others on public management, business administration, strategic management, change management. Dr. Rossidis has participated as a speaker in numerous scientific conferences and is also the author of numerous scientific articles, books and monographs.

Dimitris Belias is an Assistant Professor in the Department of Business Administration, School of Management and Economics, at the University of Thessaly, Greece, with the subject " Organization and Services Management in the Tourist Market ". His research interests are in the areas of Management, Human Resource Management, Organizational Behavior, Tourism Business Administration, Educational Management, Service Quality and Tourism and Hospitality Management. He has published 1 book and 52 chapters in books on Service Management, Organizational Behavior and Tourism and Hospitality Management, 90 articles in national and international peer-reviewed journals, and has more than 90 conference presentations in the areas of organization behavior, human resource management, Organization and Services Management and Tourism and Hospitality Management. His work is internationally recognized as it has more than 5.800 references and i10-index 34 (PorP). Currently he is member in many scientific and professional bodies.

***

Anatoliy G. Goncharuk is a Full Professor, Dr.habil. in Business Economics and Management, PhD in Organizing Management, Planning and Regulation of Economy. His research interests are in performance measurement and management, efficiency and productivity analysis, motivation studies, benchmarking, and their application in food&beverage industry, energetics, higher education, and healthcare. He wrote 15 monographs, 20 textbooks and has published over 120 articles in refereed journals.

Giorgos Kentas (PhD) is Associate Professor (tenured) of International Politics and Governance at the University of Nicosia and Director of the Graduate Program in Public Administration. His research interests focus on international politics and governance, strategic management, and conflict management. He published in peer-reviewed journals and written and/or co-authored books and book chapters.

P. Selvakumar is currently an Associate Professor in the Department of Science and Humanities at Nehru Institute of Technology, Coimbatore, Tamil Nadu, India. Prior to joining Nehru Institute of Technology, he held positions as an Assistant Professor in the Department of Science and Humanities various engineering colleges in Coimbatore, Tamil Nadu, India, spanning from 2011 to 2023. Dr.P. Selvakumar's academic and research interests lie primarily in the field of phytochemistry. He has made significant contributions to his field, with an impressive record that includes 30 journal publications, 12 patents, and 20 conference papers. Additionally, he has organized 5 seminars and conferences, further demonstrating his commitment to academic and scientific exchange. Throughout his career, Dr. P.Selvakumar has been recognized for his dedication and excellence in teaching, having been honored with several awards, including the Best Teacher Awards. He holds a prominent position in the academic community, contributing actively to research.

Pamarthi Satyanarayana, specialize in Constitutional Law and Legal Order, focusing my research on the interface between individual rights and public policy, with a strong emphasis on civil liberties, social justice, and the right to privacy. Over the past 36 months, I have served as an Assistant Professor of Law at Vel Tech Rangarajan Dr. Sagunthala R&D Institute of Science and Technology in Chennai, Tamil Nadu. Here, I teach courses such as Constitutional Law, Legal Research and Writing, and both Civil and Criminal Law. My passion for teaching and in-depth subject knowledge have earned me recognition as a dedicated educator. In addition to my academic role, I actively engage with the community, partnering with legal clinics to provide pro bono services to underprivileged individuals. Looking forward, I aim to expand my research into emerging legal issues in the digital age, especially in privacy rights, while guiding aspiring law students and future legal scholars. Dr Pamarthi Satyanarayana, Vel Tech Rangarajan Dr.Sagunthala R&D Institute of Science and Technology, VEL TECH University, School of Law, Tamil Nadu, India, e-mail id: satishgoudpamarthi@gmail.com

S. Udayakumar, M.Com., M.L., Ph.D. (Law), is an accomplished academician and legal scholar currently serving as an Assistant Professor in the School of Law at Vel Tech Rangarajan Dr. Sagunthala R&D Institute of Science and Technology, Chennai, Tamil Nadu. With a strong interdisciplinary academic foundation, Dr. Udayakumar holds postgraduate qualifications in Commerce and Law, complemented by a Doctorate in Law, reflecting his deep engagement with both legal theory and its practical intersections with commerce and governance. His academic journey demonstrates a sustained commitment to legal education, research, and scholarly excellence. At Vel Tech, Dr. Udayakumar is actively involved in teaching, mentoring, and academic development, contributing to the intellectual growth of law students through a learner-centric and research-oriented approach. His teaching emphasizes conceptual clarity, analytical reasoning, and the application of legal principles to contemporary social and institutional challenges. Dr. Udayakumar's academic interests lie in the broader domains of legal studies and interdisciplinary legal research, and he remains engaged in scholarly activities that support institutional research goals and legal education standards. He contributes to the academic environment through participation in curriculum development, academic discussions, and other scholarly initiatives within the School of Law. Known for his dedication to students and commitment to academic integrity, Dr. Udayakumar continues to contribute meaningfully to the field of legal education, striving to cultivate ethical awareness, critical thinking, and professional competence among aspiring legal professionals.

Labros Vasiliadis is an Assistant Professor at the Department of Port and Shipping Management, School of Economics and Political Sciences of the National and Kapodistrian University of Athens in the field of "Management", having over fifteen years of teaching experience in the subjects of Management, Marketing, Business Strategy, and Entrepreneurship and Innovation Management. He has been a member of the Collaborating Educational Staff (CED) of the Hellenic Open University (E.A.P.) in the undergraduate Program "Marketing I" (DEO23) and in the graduate program "Banking Administration" (TPA61) as well as Head of the Adult Education Center (AEC) of Evia prefecture (Institute of Continuing Adult Education, General Secretariat of Lifelong Learning, Ministry of Education, Lifelong Learning and Religious Affairs). During the period in question, he participated as a Manager and Member of the Stakeholder Group for the internal evaluation of Educational Structures and Programs of the Institute of Continuing Education for Adults for the Prefecture of Evia. He is a member of international research centers and editorial teams of international scientific journals

Foteini Vittou is currently a PHD student in the dpt of Public Administration at Panteion University of Social and Political Studies. She graduated with honours from the Department of Public Administration of the Hellenic Open University and holds a Master's degree in Administrative Science and Public Management from the Department of Public Administration of Panteion University. At the same time, she is a postgraduate student in the Democracy, Citizenship and Change programme at Dalarna University in Sweden, enhancing her knowledge on democracy and political participation. She works a public servant since 2009.

Index

A

Administrative Models 47, 49, 55, 57, 58, 61, 97, 170, 189, 253
Administrative reform 1, 2, 3, 4, 5, 6, 8, 13, 14, 21, 23, 25, 28, 30, 31, 32, 33, 34, 35, 36, 37, 38, 41, 48, 59, 60, 63, 95, 96, 98, 108, 120, 165, 218, 219, 224, 271, 273, 328
Appropriation 328, 343, 344, 347, 348, 349, 350, 351, 352, 353, 355, 356, 357, 358, 359, 360, 361
Arm Exports 393
Arms Exports 367, 368, 370, 371, 372, 373, 374, 376, 377, 378, 379, 382, 383, 384, 388, 389, 391, 394, 395, 397, 398, 401, 402, 403, 405
Artificial Intelligence 13, 18, 62, 68, 76, 80, 82, 83, 85, 90, 91, 93, 113, 115, 116, 117, 118, 119, 120, 122, 123, 124, 125, 126, 176, 189, 196, 234

B

Bureaucracy 5, 9, 13, 16, 20, 28, 31, 34, 38, 40, 41, 44, 47, 48, 49, 51, 52, 53, 55, 57, 58, 60, 61, 63, 65, 77, 94, 99, 107, 108, 126, 138, 145, 151, 175, 191, 195, 241, 245, 252, 261, 320, 326

C

Change Management 2, 27, 28, 29, 30, 33, 34, 40, 41, 64, 66, 131, 139, 151, 152, 163, 166, 167, 169, 170, 171, 172, 173, 174, 180, 181, 182, 184, 185, 186, 187, 188, 189, 190, 191, 192, 193, 194, 196, 197, 198, 199, 200, 203, 204, 208, 209, 211, 213, 214, 215, 216, 217, 218, 219, 220, 221, 222, 223, 224, 225, 227, 229, 231, 232, 233, 234, 235, 236, 237, 238, 239, 240, 241, 242, 243, 244, 245, 246, 247, 249, 251, 270, 273, 298, 312, 348
Complex Adaptive Systems 129, 130, 132, 146, 147, 163

D

Data Envelopment Analysis 275, 277, 284, 288, 315, 317, 318
Democratic Accountability 113, 120, 159
digital transformation 1, 2, 13, 16, 17, 18, 32, 35, 57, 61, 62, 63, 65, 79, 82, 85, 91, 132, 170, 171, 175, 181, 183, 184, 187, 189, 195, 198, 214, 219, 221, 222, 231, 234, 247, 251, 253, 255, 258, 260, 261, 262, 263, 269, 272, 301
District Courts 275, 277, 278, 279, 280, 282, 283, 284, 285, 286, 291, 293, 294, 295, 296, 297, 300, 302, 303, 304, 305, 310, 311, 315, 316, 317
Dynamic Capabilities 133, 137, 148, 167

E

Efficiency 3, 4, 5, 12, 13, 16, 17, 21, 24, 44, 47, 48, 49, 50, 51, 52, 53, 54, 55, 56, 57, 58, 59, 62, 63, 66, 77, 80, 83, 85, 86, 88, 102, 103, 106, 113, 114, 115, 117, 120, 140, 154, 156, 159, 169, 170, 171, 172, 173, 174, 175, 176, 178, 179, 181, 183, 185, 186, 187, 188, 189, 191, 196, 199, 209, 220, 248, 253, 254, 256, 258, 260, 261, 262, 264, 265, 267, 268, 273, 275, 276, 277, 278, 279, 280, 282, 283, 284, 285, 286, 287, 288, 289, 290, 291, 292, 294, 295, 296, 297, 299, 300, 301, 302, 303, 304, 305, 306, 307, 308, 309, 310, 311, 312, 313, 314, 315, 316, 317, 318, 320, 321, 322, 323, 325, 326, 327, 328, 330, 332, 333, 336, 341, 344, 345, 346, 347, 349, 350, 353, 360, 362
EU Foreign Policy 396, 398, 401, 402, 403, 406

F

Frontier Shift 289, 292, 296, 301, 302, 303, 305, 306

G

Gaza Crisis 367, 371, 373, 379, 385, 387, 388, 390, 395, 396
governance 1, 2, 8, 9, 12, 13, 16, 17, 18, 19, 21, 33, 35, 36, 37, 38, 39, 40, 41, 43, 44, 47, 48, 50, 51, 53, 54, 55, 56, 57, 58, 59, 61, 62, 63, 64, 65, 66, 68, 69, 70, 71, 73, 74, 76, 77, 78, 79, 80, 82, 83, 84, 85, 86, 87, 88, 90, 92, 95, 96, 98, 99, 103, 106, 107, 109, 110, 111, 112, 113, 114, 115, 116, 119, 120, 122, 124, 125, 126, 132, 138, 144, 145, 148, 153, 156, 157, 159, 162, 165, 166, 167, 170, 171, 172, 173, 175, 176, 177, 179, 181, 184, 190, 191, 193, 194, 195, 196, 229, 234, 242, 247, 249, 253, 254, 255, 258, 259, 260, 261, 262, 263, 264, 265, 267, 268, 269, 270, 271, 272, 273, 275, 278, 282, 287, 298, 299, 300, 301, 307, 309, 312, 313, 328, 334, 336, 337, 344, 346, 360, 361, 364, 369, 375, 380, 381
Greece 1, 2, 3, 6, 8, 9, 14, 15, 16, 17, 18, 19, 20, 22, 23, 25, 27, 32, 36, 37, 38, 39, 40, 41, 43, 47, 49, 50, 61, 64, 65, 66, 93, 100, 110, 111, 117, 120, 129, 169, 194, 195, 196, 197, 219, 225, 227, 242, 243, 246, 247, 250, 253, 254, 255, 261, 262, 263, 264, 267, 270, 271, 272, 273, 274, 367, 372, 382, 387

H

Hollowing Out of the State 125
Hospital Management 346, 363
Hospital Performance 343, 344, 346, 349, 350, 351, 352, 353, 355, 356, 357, 358, 359, 361
Humanitarian Law 367, 368, 374, 381, 382, 387, 389, 402, 403

I

institutional change 31, 65, 243

J

Judicial System 276, 302, 313, 314, 315, 317, 318

L

Law and Public Administration 67, 83, 88

M

Malmquist Productivity Index 275, 277, 284, 286, 289, 291, 295, 296, 316
Morocco 319, 320, 329, 331, 332, 334, 335, 336, 337, 338, 339, 341, 343, 344, 345, 346, 349, 352, 359, 361, 362, 363

N

New Public Management 3, 37, 41, 47, 48, 50, 51, 52, 53, 57, 58, 60, 61, 65, 93, 94, 96, 97, 113, 122, 124, 126, 127, 145, 156, 164, 165, 170, 173, 175, 195, 198, 220, 242, 250, 251, 253, 257, 258, 259, 261, 319, 320, 321, 325, 327, 328, 331, 334, 336, 338, 339, 340, 341, 343, 344, 345, 350, 360, 362, 363, 364
NPM 2.0 93, 95, 96, 109, 112, 113, 114, 115, 119, 120

O

Organizational Change 4, 29, 39, 64, 66, 139, 150, 151, 165, 166, 173, 174, 181, 185, 193, 194, 195, 196, 198, 199, 200, 207, 208, 209, 210, 212, 222, 224, 237, 238, 239, 240, 241, 242, 244, 245, 246, 247, 248, 249, 251, 270, 271, 272, 273, 336, 359
Organizational Hybridization 343, 347
Organizational Restructuring 169, 170, 171, 172, 174, 180, 183, 184, 185,

191, 213

P

Performance 8, 15, 19, 20, 39, 40, 41, 50, 52, 53, 58, 65, 72, 77, 84, 90, 92, 97, 99, 101, 102, 113, 123, 126, 131, 133, 136, 138, 140, 141, 142, 143, 146, 154, 155, 156, 159, 163, 164, 165, 166, 167, 169, 179, 182, 184, 186, 188, 189, 199, 202, 209, 214, 217, 218, 219, 220, 221, 223, 231, 236, 238, 241, 245, 251, 254, 255, 258, 260, 262, 263, 264, 265, 266, 267, 268, 269, 270, 273, 275, 276, 277, 278, 279, 282, 283, 284, 285, 286, 287, 288, 291, 292, 298, 299, 300, 301, 304, 305, 306, 307, 309, 310, 311, 313, 314, 315, 316, 317, 318, 319, 320, 321, 322, 323, 324, 326, 327, 328, 329, 330, 331, 332, 333, 335, 336, 337, 338, 339, 340, 341, 342, 343, 344, 345, 346, 347, 348, 349, 350, 351, 352, 353, 355, 356, 357, 358, 359, 360, 361, 362, 363, 364, 365, 373

Productivity 20, 27, 92, 99, 102, 193, 209, 256, 264, 268, 272, 275, 276, 277, 278, 280, 282, 283, 284, 285, 286, 287, 289, 291, 292, 295, 296, 297, 302, 305, 306, 307, 311, 315, 316, 317, 318, 325, 349

Public Administration 1, 2, 4, 5, 8, 9, 11, 12, 13, 14, 15, 16, 17, 18, 19, 20, 21, 23, 24, 25, 26, 28, 29, 30, 31, 32, 33, 34, 35, 36, 37, 38, 39, 40, 41, 42, 44, 47, 48, 49, 50, 51, 55, 57, 58, 59, 60, 61, 63, 64, 65, 66, 67, 68, 69, 71, 73, 75, 76, 77, 78, 79, 80, 81, 82, 83, 84, 85, 87, 88, 90, 91, 92, 96, 97, 98, 99, 112, 113, 114, 115, 118, 121, 122, 123, 125, 126, 127, 129, 132, 160, 163, 164, 165, 166, 167, 168, 170, 171, 172, 173, 175, 180, 181, 182, 190, 193, 194, 195, 197, 198, 217, 218, 219, 220, 221, 222, 223, 224, 225, 227, 231, 232, 233, 234, 235, 237, 240, 242, 243, 245, 246, 247, 248, 249, 251, 252, 255, 257, 272, 273, 320, 325, 327, 328, 330, 332, 336, 340, 341, 363, 364

Public Enterprises 64, 253, 254, 255, 256, 257, 258, 259, 260, 261, 262, 263, 264, 265, 266, 267, 268, 269, 270, 271, 273

Public Governance 12, 39, 47, 48, 50, 51, 53, 54, 55, 56, 57, 58, 59, 61, 63, 65, 95, 99, 112, 124, 170, 173, 249, 253, 254, 263

public management 1, 3, 9, 20, 28, 37, 38, 39, 41, 47, 48, 50, 51, 52, 53, 55, 57, 58, 60, 61, 64, 65, 91, 92, 93, 94, 96, 97, 98, 99, 105, 113, 122, 123, 124, 125, 126, 127, 137, 138, 145, 156, 163, 164, 165, 166, 168, 170, 173, 175, 194, 195, 196, 198, 220, 240, 242, 244, 245, 249, 250, 251, 253, 257, 258, 259, 261, 271, 274, 278, 287, 298, 312, 319, 320, 321, 325, 327, 328, 331, 334, 336, 338, 339, 340, 341, 342, 343, 344, 345, 350, 351, 360, 362, 363, 364

Public Sector 2, 4, 9, 10, 13, 15, 16, 17, 23, 29, 31, 33, 37, 38, 39, 40, 43, 47, 48, 49, 50, 55, 56, 62, 64, 66, 83, 89, 90, 92, 96, 98, 99, 104, 105, 106, 113, 119, 122, 124, 126, 127, 129, 130, 131, 132, 134, 135, 136, 137, 138, 140, 143, 147, 150, 151, 152, 154, 155, 159, 160, 161, 163, 164, 165, 166, 167, 168, 169, 170, 171, 172, 173, 174, 175, 178, 180, 181, 182, 183, 185, 189, 190, 191, 192, 193, 194, 195, 196, 197, 198, 199, 200, 201, 202, 203, 204, 205, 206, 207, 208, 209, 210, 211, 212, 213, 214, 215, 216, 217, 218, 219, 221, 222, 223, 225, 226, 228, 229, 231, 232, 233, 234, 235, 236, 237, 242, 243, 247, 250, 251, 252, 254, 255, 264, 270, 271, 272, 273, 274, 275, 298, 312, 319, 320, 325, 326, 328, 330, 335, 337, 339, 340, 341, 345, 346, 359, 362, 363

Public Sector Reform 38, 40, 104, 122,

169, 170, 171, 172, 174, 175, 183, 185, 189, 191, 192, 193, 195, 217, 232, 320, 339, 345, 359, 362, 363
Public Value 5, 12, 41, 47, 48, 51, 53, 56, 57, 58, 59, 61, 62, 63, 65, 66, 91, 129, 130, 133, 134, 135, 136, 138, 142, 143, 144, 148, 154, 155, 156, 157, 159, 161, 163, 164, 165, 167, 173, 175, 186, 189, 191, 195, 236, 253, 254, 258, 262, 263, 264, 266, 268, 269, 270, 272, 349, 364

R

Readiness for Change 197, 200, 204, 206, 212, 242, 246, 248, 251, 252
Reform 1, 2, 3, 4, 5, 6, 8, 9, 13, 14, 15, 17, 19, 20, 21, 23, 24, 25, 26, 27, 28, 29, 30, 31, 32, 33, 34, 35, 36, 37, 38, 39, 40, 41, 44, 48, 50, 51, 52, 59, 60, 63, 64, 65, 78, 83, 87, 94, 95, 96, 97, 98, 101, 102, 104, 107, 108, 113, 114, 115, 120, 122, 124, 125, 134, 141, 145, 147, 151, 156, 165, 166, 169, 170, 171, 172, 174, 175, 176, 177, 178, 179, 180, 181, 182, 183, 185, 186, 188, 189, 190, 191, 192, 193, 194, 195, 197, 203, 217, 218, 219, 220, 221, 223, 224, 225, 226, 227, 231, 232, 233, 234, 235, 236, 237, 242, 246, 247, 249, 250, 255, 261, 262, 266, 268, 271, 273, 275, 276, 277, 278, 279, 280, 282, 283, 284, 285, 286, 287, 288, 289, 290, 291, 292, 293, 294, 295, 296, 297, 298, 299, 300, 301, 302, 303, 304, 305, 306, 307, 308, 309, 310, 311, 312, 313, 314, 315, 316, 317, 319, 320, 325, 327, 328, 330, 332, 339, 340, 342, 344, 345, 346, 352, 359, 360, 361, 362, 363, 364, 369, 374, 379, 383
Results-Based Management 5, 77, 97, 113, 319, 325, 327, 331, 332, 336, 337, 338

S

State Capacity 93, 114, 115
Strategic Management 40, 56, 58, 59, 66, 129, 131, 132, 133, 134, 135, 136, 137, 138, 140, 141, 142, 143, 145, 147, 148, 150, 154, 155, 156, 157, 158, 159, 160, 161, 162, 163, 164, 165, 166, 167, 168, 247, 264, 272, 273, 364
Strategic Planning 2, 55, 60, 61, 131, 133, 134, 139, 140, 155, 156, 161, 163, 164, 165, 240, 255, 263, 266, 332, 341

W

Wicked Problems 5, 42, 130, 132, 141, 147, 148, 149, 153, 160, 161, 164, 168

www.ingramcontent.com/pod-product-compliance
Lightning Source LLC
LaVergne TN
LVHW062334300926
849161LV00007B/1683